When Readers Struggle

Teaching that Works

K-3

Gay Su Pinnell

Irene C. Fountas

Heinemann
Portsmouth, NH

Heinemann
361 Hanover Street
Portsmouth, NH 03801-3912
www.heinemann.com

Offices and agents throughout the world

Library of Congress Cataloging-in-Publication Data
Pinnell, Gay Su.
    When readers struggle : teaching that works / Gay Su Pinnell, Irene C. Fountas.
      p. cm.
    Includes bibliographical references and index.
    ISBN 978-0-325-01826-3
    1. Reading--Remedial teaching.   2. Reading (Early childhood) I. Fountas, Irene C
II. Title.
    LB1050.5.P533 2009   2008044997
    372.43—dc22

ISBN-13: 978-0-325-01826-3
ISBN-10: 0-325-01826-X

Printed in Shenzhen, China
0514/14003578
16 15 14 RRD 10 11 12 13

We dedicate this book to all teachers who care about and work hard to teach readers who struggle.

Table of Contents

Acknowledgments

This book is rooted in many years of learning from teachers and children. It builds on our work in classroom literacy, assessment, and on our book *The Continuum of Literacy Learning: A Guide to Teaching, K-8*. It has been informed by our work with struggling readers as we learned from our experiences in Reading Recovery and other small group interventions. In each of these ventures, we were fortunate to work with a remarkable group of colleagues. We have learned from them. By their work and by example, they have all contributed to this book.

The Continuum of Literacy Learning (2007), Benchmark Assessment System (2008), and Leveled Literacy Intervention (2009), all three of which support the material in this book, represent a monumental body of our work. Each required our collaboration with a wonderful Heinemann team. So many Heinemann team members worked "behind the scenes" to bring these works to press that it would be impossible to acknowledge each of them by name. Producing both Benchmark and LLI represented some new challenges for Heinemann, and the company undertook the projects because of its confidence in their benefit to teachers and children. We are grateful to Wayne Smith for believing in the work from the start. We thank Lesa Scott for her visionary leadership, her enthusiastic support, and her adherence to the highest standards for materials for teachers and children. We thank Alan Huisman for his expert editing, and express special appreciation for Lisa Fowler's gifted artistic design touch that makes our books and materials so accessible and attractive. We wish also to acknowledge the unending patience, skill, creativity, and good humor of Mike Conlon, who so well understands the packaging and delivery complexities of our books. We are especially grateful to Margaret Broucek and her team, including Larry Mondi, for the marvelous work they did in the production of the *Professional Development and Tutorial DVDs* for LLI, which set the standard for excellence in professional development DVDs.

We would like to acknowledge the tremendous contribution of Tina Miller. Her brilliant thinking brought to fruition *The Continuum of Literacy Learning*, a comprehensive and practical tool that forms the foundation for the products that came after. Throughout the process of creating the continuum, as well as the Benchmark Assessment System, and Leveled Literacy Intervention, Tina has been both a generous partner and an excellent source of advice

As always, we are in awe of the artistic brilliance that Michael Cirone, our extraordinary production manager, brings to all of the work we do together. As we often say, we would not undertake a new publication without Michael on the team. His standard of excellence is the highest; and we thank him also for his endless patience and countless hours of work. And, to our new editor, Marie Spano, we extend our sincerest appreciation for joining the team and dedicating herself to the creation of these complex and comprehensive resources. Her expertise has added significantly to the quality of our work.

This book would not have been possible without the leadership, quick thinking, problem-solving, and downright savvy of Mary Lou Mackin, who managed a process so complex that it would be impossible to describe it. She has been our partner throughout this process, and it has been a pleasure to work with her over the last three years. We are also grateful to Bert Crossland for his early encouragement and creative input, and to Carmen Clark for providing assistance whenever and wherever needed. We also welcome with much enthusiasm an outstanding marketing professional, Olive McRae, to the expert team; we value her forward-thinking suggestions for making our books accessible to the widest possible audience. The professional development team, including Director Vicki Boyd, Cherie Bartlett, and Karen Belanger, have helped us maintain the ultimate goal of supporting the highest caliber of teacher learning. We appreciate their energy and vision.

Marie Brown, of Brown Publishing Network, led the creative team that wrote and illustrated the children's books for LLI, many of which are featured in this volume. We are especially grateful to Marie and to Kathy Reynolds, Elinor Chamas, and Mary Ann Dobeck for their roles in creating these wonderful books that children will enjoy so much. The role of series books is much highlighted in this book; the high quality of the series books and many other texts featured here can be attributed to our friend and talented colleague Deb Eaton. Deb's extraordinary writing and editorial ability brought artistry to every text she touched.

We also wish to recognize the team who reviewed Benchmark and LLI books, including Kris Haveles-Pelletier, Linda Garbus, Chris Chase, Carol Woodworth, Maureen Monahan, Diane Powell, Diane Wesselhoft, Joanna Pincus, Leslie Ryan, Pat Martin, Susan Sullivan, Jill Eurich, Toni Czekanski, Mechelle Abney, Carly Bannish, Sue Baylies, Cyndi Joensu, Sheila Burke, LuAnn Mussari, Candace Chick, and Barbara Fisher.

Much detailed organizational work on the wonderful CD for LLI was accomplished with impressive competence by Alison Buraczenski, Tara DeLeo, and Anna DeLeo. We also thank Susan Sullivan, Shannon Campbell, Kathy Ha, and Kris Pelletier and their students for their assistance with artwork. We also wish to express appreciation to Jan Rossi who has provided so much efficient help in the complex editing process. And, as always we are very grateful to Sharon Freeman, whose superb organization has provided so much support for the work.

As always, we are grateful to our colleague Carol Lyons, not only for her own work, from which we have learned much, but for reading and providing feedback on chapters of this volume. This manuscript has also benefited from many significant contributions by Diane Powell, who created the tutorials for Benchmark and LLI, did incredibly precise work on the *Prompting Guide*, read and provided critical feedback on many sections of the text, and spent countless hours perfecting a good number of the technical art pieces. We also thank Linda Garbus, Diane Powell, and Christine Chase for their detailed work on the *Prompting Guide*, the examples in these chapters, and their valuable chapter feedback. We appreciate the dedication and attention to accuracy that characterize the thoughtful work of these wonderful educators. Thank you for your flexibility and hard work.

We also are very grateful to Cindy Downend for providing valuable content and assistance, and to Kathy Ha, whose expertise in working with English language learners has contributed so much to this work. We also thank Emily Dexter for her superb research skills and her insights.

This book is based on the work of many generous teachers. Over 1,000 LLI teachers have contributed to this work by their service to children and their invaluable feedback on lessons. Their work is reflected in the examples in this book, and we also thank the children who provided examples of talking, reading, writing, and drawing. We especially thank Kris

Haveles-Pelletier, Michael Buonaiuto, Moira Owens, and Chris Chase, who were willing to share their teaching on the LLI DVDs.

Many of our colleagues have been providing professional development to help teachers learn to use assessment effectively. Their work is basic to identifying and working with struggling readers, and it has contributed to the work discussed in this book. We thank Carol Beatrice, Joyce Cecil, Elizabeth Conner, Charlotte Doyle, Ann Fontaine, Linda Garbus, Janice Hilt, Judith Neal, Leslie Ryan, Lee Skandalaris, Dianne Stuart, Julie Teal, Sandy Tilton, Diane Walworth, and Dianne Wesselhoft. We are especially grateful to Joyce Gordon and Diane Wesselhoft who have made many valuable suggestions for describing Benchmark and LLI.

We treasure the memory of Cecelia Osborn and her contributions to our Benchmark Assessment System, as well as her dedication to Reading Recovery and all of the work she did on behalf of at-risk children. This work is only a small part of her legacy to education; we are proud to have been her colleagues.

We have the good fortune to work with wonderful colleagues at our universities. They encourage us and contribute through their own scholarship and research. We acknowledge the leadership and scholarship of Pat Scharer, Emily Rodgers, Lea McGee, Mary Fried, Andrea McCarrier, Joan Wiley, Lynda Mudre, and Sonny Whitehead at Ohio State University and Mechelle Abney, Margaret Crosby, Toni Czekanski, Jill Eurich, Kathy Ha, Cindy Downend, Helen Sisk, Eva Konstantellou, and Diane Powell at Lesley University. We are extremely grateful to Carol Woodworth whose expertise in analyzing texts informs us constantly.

No effort like this can be accomplished without the encouragement and belief of our friends and families. We constantly recognize the contributions of Mike Gibbons and Lois Bridges, who have been generous colleagues and dear friends for years. The love and support, along with good humor, of Ron Melhado and Ron Heath has been constant and sustaining across the years. We can not thank them enough. Finally, we must acknowledge the contributions of a new family member, Meli Fountas Melhado, whose picture and stories you will find and enjoy in this volume.

Introduction

In every classroom, school, and district, teachers are working with children who find literacy learning difficult. The search for ways to prevent and ameliorate reading difficulties has occupied much of the educational literature for the last fifty years. In recent years, educators have faced the twin challenges of meeting the needs of every child and raising test scores. These two goals may seem compatible, but often they are not. There are many ways to raise test scores, and focusing resources on the very lowest achievers is not necessarily one of them. Yet we must meet our responsibility to raise all readers to the level of achievement they need to function and succeed in the world. Literacy does not automatically guarantee a high quality of life, but low levels of literacy can seriously undermine it. Children who have difficulty in reading often face the struggle throughout their lives.

For many years, there have been flurries of interest around slight upturns in test scores, but those upturns are almost always misleading. Scores fluctuate for a complex variety of reasons, which are often unrelated to any particular bandwagon a school may have jumped on prior to testing.

Decades of school reform have yielded only slight, and we suspect transient, results. On the 2007 reading assessment conducted by the National Assessment of Educational Progress, 4th graders scored 2 points higher in 2007 than they did in previous years—up 4 points compared to 15 years ago. Higher percentages of students were performing at or above the *Basic* and *Proficient* achievement levels than in previous years. The average reading score for 8th graders was up 1 point since 2005 and 3 points since 1992; however, the trend of increasing scores has not been consistent over all assessment years. If we compare 1992 and 2005, the percentage of students performing at or above the *Basic* level increased, but there was no significant change in the percentage of students at or above the *Proficient* level. Furthermore, while white, black, and Hispanic students tended to score slightly higher in 2007 than they did 15 years ago, these improvements did not always result in the narrowing of the achievement gaps between minority and white children (Lee, Grigg, Donahue 2007).

While we greet these point gains with cautious optimism, we also know that a gain of a few points (which will not necessarily hold in the assessment of the next cohort) does not tell us much about the overall state of literacy education. Many millions of dollars have been poured into materials and programs designed exclusively to raise test scores rather than to produce effective readers and writers. We need to see more profound results from these expenditures.

Moreover, in the rush to raise test scores, schools have tended to adopt program after program until teachers are confused. Many programs provide for highly scripted arrangements in which every teacher and child do exactly the same thing; yet, providing the same instruction for every child (if that is even possible) does not assure the same achievement, as scores have shown since testing began. Critics of NCLB can point to the lack of change and say that this initiative has not fulfilled its promise; but we must remember that no initiative since we started having initiatives has made much difference. We still have the same average scores; we still have children who have a hard time learning to read and write.

Just about every teacher in the United States teaches children who find literacy learning difficult. These children exist in every classroom, at all educational and economic levels. They represent a constant concern and challenge. Children want to learn; and teachers want to help them. We are all generally opposed to leaving children behind. But there is no simple solution to helping all children learn. There are many reasons why a child might find learning difficult—some particular to the child but most particular to the inability of the school system to provide the type and level of support our diverse students might need.

Vulnerable children require year after year of excellent instruction and many will need particular kinds of carefully designed interventions and extra instruction as well. The sequence, intensity, quality, focus, and consistency of support are key.

If we are serious about teaching every child, then we need to take the position that no one program or set of policies will result in proficient reading for all children. In the past thirty years, we have seen many promising approaches come and go in school districts, but three factors have stood in the way of real success:

❑ *Few have been applied with integrity and quality.* Almost always, funding, policies, and lack of resolve result in fatal modifications so that the program or approach no longer does what it was designed to do. Emphasis may shift from outcomes to numbers "served," whether results are there or not.

❑ *Few have been sustained long enough to fulfill the promise.* Changing administration, funding sources, and politics constantly force attention in a new direction, regardless of results. We know many school districts with documented results that drop everything when a new superintendent comes in.

❑ *Attempts have been isolated efforts rather than coordinated and comprehensive systems.*

Over the last thirty years, we have learned much about what it is going to take to truly leave no child behind. The task is daunting, but the consequences of not applying what we know are devastating to individuals and society. "Longitudinal studies reveal that there is a 90% chance that a child who is a poor reader at the end of grade one will remain a poor reader at the end of grade four" (Juel 1998). Low achieving fourth grade readers tend to experience this placement as a life sentence. "Assignment to a group predicts future educational outcomes with alarming accuracy. Most children placed in high-ability groups remain in those groups and go on to college. Most children placed in the low-achievement group remain there and are far more likely (1) to leave school before graduating; (2) to fail a grade; (3) to be placed in special education; 4) to become a teenage parent; (5) to commit a juvenile criminal offense; and, (6) to remain less than fully literate. "It is distressing to think that our schools are so ineffectual with children who begin school with few literacy experiences that we can predict with horrifying accuracy what lifestyles different six-year-olds will attain when they reach adulthood" (Allington 1998). We need to ask ourselves, "How many children are we willing to throw away?" Some authors have rightly referred to the task as "racing against catastrophe" (Natriello, McDill, Pallas 1990).

We need a many-layered and coordinated approach that offers high-quality instruction in the variety of forms necessary to serve each child at the level needed. The goal is achievable for most children. Research indicates that "90-95% of children with reading problems can overcome their difficulties if they receive appropriate treatment at an early age." (*The Special Edge* 2000, 6—cited in ERS Spectrum.)

In this volume, we offer suggestions for helping readers who find literacy learning difficult. We stress the value of prevention in the form of excellent classroom teaching. Good classroom teachers do make a difference. They deliver instruction all day every day of the school year. The more they can bring low achieving students into active engagement in the classroom, the fewer low achievers there will be.

We also offer suggestions for intervention. If children are not thriving in spite of excellent classroom instruction, then they need extra help. "Without systematic, focused and intensive intervention, the majority of children with reading difficulties rarely catch up and that failure to develop reading skills by age 9 may result in a lifetime of illiteracy." (Lyon 2001) Intervention must be effective and focused on outcomes rather than simply on numbers of children served. "Service" is not enough. That rather hopeless view suggests to us that no one really expects children to catch up. We have to ask: "Are they served if they do not become readers?" We would also say that "progress," as currently defined, is not enough. Children are served in small remedial reading groups year after year. Each year some progress is reported, but these children continue to lag behind the rest; few become truly proficient readers; and almost none become voluntary readers.

The most effective intervention is implemented early in a child's school career—before the cycle of failure is established. We have seen what individual tutoring, the most intensive level of early intervention, can do, particularly when it is offered at a precise moment in time. For many children who have reading difficulties, well-designed individual intervention at a particular point in time can make all the difference. According to Slavin (1994), "preventive tutoring deserves an important place in discussions of reform in compensatory, remedial and special education. If we know how to ensure that students will learn to read in the early grades, we have an ethical and perhaps legal responsibility to see that they do so."

We have also seen what can be done in supplementary small group instruction that is intensive and well designed. Currently, most supplementary small group instruction is ineffective because:

- ❏ Groups are too large.
- ❏ Instruction is not well planned and sequenced.
- ❏ Participants in the group are not truly well matched; there is great diversity among members, which makes it difficult for the teacher to plan for instruction.
- ❏ Too often, supplementary teachers have the job of dragging children through the assigned classroom materials rather than providing the appropriate reading materials and skilled teaching that will help them make progress.
- ❏ Insufficient professional development is provided for intervention teachers.

We believe that supplementary small group instruction has a place in a well-coordinated literacy program. It is the responsibility of educators to fine-tune instructional services so that classroom, small group, and individual teaching occur when and for whom they are needed in a timely way and with high quality. There are three keys to success: (1) expert teaching; (2) good books; and (3) good instructional design. The most important of these is achieved through professional development for teachers.

In all of this, we should not forget the true goal of schooling, which is to support learning that will lead to a higher quality of life for our citizens. We want readers who make literacy an integral part of their lives and find it both useful and enjoyable. We want readers who pick up books and other materials voluntarily and grow from them. A literate life is the right of every child—even (or especially) those who initially find it difficult. We recognize that accountability is important; a well-coordinated program will have the result of raising test scores and other measures of achievement. But the real measure of a school's effectiveness is the care taken to meet the needs of every child—not just with service but with real results.

In this volume, we present a variety of ways to help readers, specifically those who need extra help. We will target those approaches toward classroom, small group, and individual instruction, knowing that a coordinated combination of all three will have the greatest chance for success.

Section 1, *When Readers Struggle,* explores the contexts for learning as well as issues related to effective and ineffective processing. In Chapter 1, A Comprehensive Approach to Literacy Success, we describe in broad strokes the instructional contexts for teaching within a comprehensive literacy program. An important point in this chapter is that struggling readers require effective classroom instruction. We make the case for *coherent* instruction that helps readers learn across contexts. You can use the suggestions in this book as you work in whole group, small group, or individual contexts with your students. In Chapter 2 (Effective Readers: What Do They Do?) and Chapter 3 (Going Off Track: Why and How?), we look at the processing systems for reading. In working with struggling readers, it is important to know what effective processing is like, because that gives us a vision for what we want to help struggling readers do. If we intervene to help struggling readers, we want to do so in a way that will prevent further difficulties. The ability to observe and interpret reading behavior is foundational to effective teaching of struggling readers, and we address this in Chapter 4, Reading Behavior: What Does It Tell Us? We also need to recognize how the processing system changes over time as readers develop. In Chapter 5, Change Over Time: Processing Systems in the Making, you will find specific descriptions of readers at several points in time. Here, we will also show that readers arrive at the common outcome of a self-extending system for reading, but they may take different paths to get there. Finally in Chapter 6, Text Matters: A Ladder to Success, we examine in detail the role that a gradient of text can play in supporting readers as they change over time.

Section 2, *Language Systems and Literacy Learning,* goes deeper into the systems of information that readers must acquire and orchestrate to effectively process print. Chapter 7, Language Matters: Talking, Reading, and Writing, describes the oral language foundation that is essential for learning to read and write. Chapter 8, Words Matter: Building Power in Vocabulary, is also related to oral language. Here, we explore the important area of vocabulary development, the way texts make increasing demands on the reader's vocabulary knowledge. We also suggest ways to increase word learning. In Chapter 9, The Phonological Base for Learning to Read and Write, we discuss the sound system of the language along with ways to help learners become more aware of and learn how to use sounds in words.

Section 3, *Learning Written Language Systems,* focuses on the challenges of learning how written language "works." In Chapter 10, Learning About Print: Early Reading Behaviors, we look at the basic understandings about the conventions of print that young readers must develop early. Chapter 11, Learning to Solve Words: Effective and Efficient Phonics, examines nine areas of learning related to word-solving strategies. We provide many examples of ways to help readers learn how to use letter-sound relationships, as well as word patterns and word structure, to read and write words. In Chapter 12, Building and Using a Repertoire of Words, we discuss the benefit to learners of acquiring the ability to recognize a large body of words rapidly and without effort. Rapid recognition of words fuels fluency and frees attention for thinking about the meaning of texts.

Section 4, *Teaching that Works*, is the largest section of the book. Here you will find detailed descriptions and examples of ways to work with struggling readers. We begin with descriptions of how to use writing to support readers' development of strategic actions for word solving and to extend their comprehension of texts. You will find this information in Chapter 13, Extending Reading Power Through Writing. Chapter 14 (Teaching for Problem Solving While Processing Texts: Early Reading Behaviors and Searching for Information) and Chapter 15 (Teaching for Independence in Processing Texts: Solving Words, Self-Monitoring and Self-Correcting Behaviors) focus directly on ways you can teach for, prompt for, and reinforce effective reading behaviors. These chapters present specific examples on how teachers can work with struggling readers from Levels A to N. Chapter 16, Teaching for Fluency in Processing Texts: Six Dimensions, presents a discussion of the important role of fluency in processing texts with comprehension. Here you will find examples of how you can teach for, prompt for, and reinforce several dimensions of fluency. In Chapter 17, Teaching for Comprehending: Thinking Before, During, and After Reading, we discuss the active process of comprehending texts and provide suggestions for helping children deeply comprehend texts. Our goal is to help them think actively while reading: making predictions, inferring and connecting, synthesizing new information, and analyzing and critiquing the texts that they read. Chapter 18, Working Successfully with English Language Learners, brings together many different ways to adjust instruction to accommodate the needs of English language learners. These suggestions can be used while working with whole classes or individuals, but they will be especially effective when working with small groups. The next two chapters, 19 (Engaging Readers' Attention and Memory in Successful Learning) and 20 (Engaging Readers' Emotion and Motivation in Successful Learning) focus on factors in the brain that affect literacy learning. A theme that runs through both chapters is deep engagement with texts. We end this volume with Chapter 21, Keys to Effective Intervention: Success for All Children. In this final chapter, we describe multi-layered intervention systems to help readers and give some practical suggestions for allocating teacher time. We also present a framework for intervention lessons, Levels A though N.

Writing this book has allowed us to bring together a great deal of our thinking. We drew from our own experience in teaching children who have difficulty learning to read and write, as well as from the large body of research that is available to us as educators. As with all professional materials, you will want to take from this volume those ideas that will best fit the students you teach and adjust them as learners change over time. We hope that the entire volume communicates the deep respect we have for all of you who work with readers/writers in difficulty. For those children, you provide the gateway to a literate future.

Gay Su Pinnell
Irene C. Fountas

When Readers Struggle

IN THIS SECTION, *we look at how processing systems are built and how readers develop over time. We first present the instructional contexts that are essential for learning. Struggling readers need high-quality instruction across all of these contexts. We also focus on what effective readers do, what happens when readers go off track, and the power of systematic observation. This is essential information for teachers working with any reader, but it is critical for working with readers who struggle. We end the section with a look at the key role the text gradient plays in all of our work with struggling readers.*

A Comprehensive Approach to Literacy Success

THE EARLY YEARS OF SCHOOL ARE IMPORTANT for every child, but for those who find literacy learning difficult, every one of these years is critical. We do need a coordinated group of services to provide effective intervention if readers are struggling, but we should not forget that they must have excellent classroom instruction. In this chapter, we describe a comprehensive approach to provide strong teaching across classroom instructional contexts and supplementary intervention services. School districts seeking to close the achievement gap must consider good classroom teaching, multiple layers of intervention, the role of short-term intensive tutoring, and the ongoing development of highly qualified teachers.

Almost all the conventional ways of referring to children who find literacy learning difficult imply a weakness in the children. We take the position that teaching must be designed to meet the needs of each child and that educators must constantly search for effective ways to serve the children they teach. Because this book is about teaching children who find literacy learning difficult, whenever we use the word *children*, those are the children we mean, unless otherwise indicated.

For thirteen years, children spend six hours every day in the classroom. During the academic year, most children spend almost as much of their waking time with their teachers as they do with their parents. We need to provide the opportunity to every child to lead a literate life, recognizing that there will be great diversity in the skills and knowledge children bring to the classroom.

With rare exception, by the time they start school all children have developed the ability to use language and have learned a great deal about how to do so. Many have:

- ❏ Listened to stories being read and followed along with the words and illustrations.
- ❏ Experimented with writing.
- ❏ Used oral and perhaps written language to communicate with others.
- ❏ Observed print in the community.
- ❏ Told stories about their experiences.

However, not every culture or every home is focused on literacy. Families deal with different problems and have different values. Economic circumstances vary. After food and shelter have been provided, there may be no money left for purchasing children's books. Economic or other issues may mean that both parents work at one or several jobs to support the family, and their "quality time" may be spent in activities other than reading or writing. Even affluent families often have schedules that are hectic, and the child care these children receive may not include one-on-one literacy experiences.

Whatever their situation, all children have a natural tendency toward inquiry. They bring to school their intelligence, curiosity, and ability to use language to communicate. In general, children respond to what their environment offers. As important as it is to respect and communicate with parents and other caregivers, and no matter how much the family can help, literacy instruction is the job of the school.

Children's early educational experiences often make the difference between being actively engaged in learning or being turned off by learning. High-quality preschool programs that build a strong base of language and story-telling are extremely beneficial. Preschoolers are incredibly fast language learners. Listening to stories, telling stories, talking with their peers, and playing oral games and games that include contact with print add a rich foundation of language and literacy to what children already know. Preschool can also be seen as the first level of prevention. These positive experiences provide the information children need to access as they encounter the world of print. They have high expectations of print and are able to bring meaning to it and avoid confusion.

Even when children have had limited literacy experiences prior to kindergarten, school can make the difference. Our Literacy Collaborative experience (literacycollaborative.org) indicates that skilled teaching and rich literacy experiences in kindergarten help most children develop early reading and writing strategies before they enter first grade. And building on the same elements in first grade turns them into readers who have the beginning of a self-extending system, one that enables them to learn more about literacy through reading and writing (Clay 2001). We do not mean that they need no further instruction. In fact, most children need good teaching of reading and writing from kindergarten through high school. Instruction changes with the type and complexity of the texts they are expected to read and write.

We have also learned that some children require more than good classroom instruction; therefore, a range of interventions has been designed to meet the different needs of students. Excellent classroom instruction, accompanied by a powerful intervention (or even several) can make it possible for all students to become successful users of literacy. As a literacy intervention, Reading Recovery is particularly effective (see Gomez-Bellenge 2006). Reading Recovery has provided us with a wake-up call. We cannot give up on children just because they enter school with a weak foundation of knowledge or are confused about the basics. We know from the research related to this one-to-one-tutorial approach that almost all children have enormous potential for success in literacy. We also have had excellent success with small-group interventions such as Leveled Literacy Intervention.[1] In this book, we describe ways to work effectively with struggling readers. These techniques may be used in the classroom, in small-group intervention, or when working with individual readers.

---

[1] Leveled Literacy Intervention, developed and written by Irene Fountas and Gay Su Pinnell and published by Heinemann (2009), is a short-term, small-group intervention designed to bring children to grade level performance (Levels A–N). Three systems (Orange, Green, and Blue) are specially developed for children in the primary grades.

Figure 1-1	**Essential Experiences for Children Who Find Literacy Difficult**
Talk	*Children need the opportunity to:* • Engage in conversation that helps them expand their use of language. • Engage in conversation about their experiences with texts. • Tell stories from their experiences. • Listen and respond to language.
Texts	*Children need to **read** and talk about:* • A large number of texts every day. • A large number of texts they can read independently. • Texts they can read with fluency and comprehension. • Texts that interest and engage them. • Texts that contain language they recognize and find meaningful. • Texts in many different genres—fiction and nonfiction. • Texts that, with teacher support, help them expand their reading powers. • Texts that provide a strong basis for discussion and writing. *Children need to **hear** and talk about:* • Texts that interest and engage them. • Age-appropriate and grade-appropriate texts. • Texts in many different genres—fiction and nonfiction. • Texts that offer opportunities to expand their vocabulary, language, and content knowledge. • Texts that provide a strong basis for discussion and writing. • Texts that help them learn more about writing. *Children need to **respond** to texts in meaningful ways:* • Talk about reading with their teacher and their peers. • Write about reading in a variety of genres and forms. • Draw about reading.
Teaching	*Children need explicit, clear, effective instruction so that they:* • Understand letter-sound relationships (phonics). • Understand how words "work" (use visual analysis, word structure, spelling patterns, word-solving actions). • Understand how to use their knowledge of letters, sounds, and words while reading texts. • Understand how to use their knowledge of letters, sounds, and words while writing texts.

► Essential Literacy Experiences

Essential experiences for supporting children who find literacy difficult are summarized in Figure 1-1.

Talk

Every day, evaluate whether your students have enough time to talk with others and share their stories. The more effectively they can use oral language, the more knowledge they can bring to becoming literate. And there is only one way to develop oral language—through meaningful interactions with others. Nothing is as important for children as the interactions you have with them. Your conversations with children are authentic in that you listen and talk with them about something that really matters. You intentionally structure your conversations to increase student learning. The interactions may take place during whole-class and small-group instruction as well as individual conferences, but the key is the give-and-take of the interchange and your genuine interest in their stories, their questions, and their feedback. Simply talking *to* students is not as effective as having genuine interactions *with* them.

Texts

Rich texts are necessary to give children the foundation they need to become proficient readers and writers. They need to hear many age- and grade-appropriate texts read aloud; and when that experience is accompanied by discussion, children's understanding of the language and meaning of texts increases. Reading aloud and discussing texts with children helps them become interested in print, notice characteristics of genres, and expand their vocabulary and content knowledge; it gives them something of substance to think about and talk about. Text-based conversation supports them as they take on new language structures.

Even more than children who learn easily, children who have reading difficulties need to process continuous text (meaningful books). They need to read texts that are interesting and engaging. They need to expand their reading abilities by reading "just-right" texts with your support; they also need to read many easy texts on their own. Fill your classroom library with many texts your students can read independently. Quantity matters. The higher the quality of the texts they read and comprehend, the stronger their foundation for talking and writing.

Teaching

Finally, whatever your classroom curriculum, children who find literacy learning difficult need strong teaching in many contexts. Children need to hear numerous texts read aloud and have the opportunity to engage with the language. It helps young children to hear the same texts (their favorites) read several times so that they can internalize the structure of written language.

Making adjustments to help readers who are having difficulty may occasionally seem inconsistent with the essential experiences just described. In small-group instruction, you may need to limit text choice; create a very precise sequence of texts; slow down to work closely on a text; or provide some very explicit and systematic work with letters, sounds, and words in isolation. All of these adjustments, however, are temporary and are made with the goal of reading continuous text with ease and understanding. The bottom line is that children who find literacy learning difficult need to spend most of their time reading and writing continuous text, and they need carefully designed instruction as they do so.

► Designing Programs with Coherence: Getting on the Same Page

It has long been said that classroom teachers, reading teachers, and special education teachers must work together so that children experience coherent instruction, but opportunities for this level of cooperation are rare. Far more commonly, supplemental instruction is very different from classroom instruction, and children receive mixed messages. Alternatively, children are dragged passively through a classroom curriculum they don't learn, nor do they *learn how to learn.*

Thus the challenge is still there: we need comprehensive literacy approaches in which the efforts of every teacher a child works with are complementary and enable students to make faster progress. The test of any kind of supplemental instruction is whether children have learned how to do something as readers that they can do independently in the classroom literacy program.

We consider the importance of effective teaching in three contexts: the classroom; supplemental early intervention programs; and education for students with special needs (supplemental or self-contained). An example of the flow or layers of services in a coordinated, cohesive design is shown in Figure 1-2.

The classroom is the first venue for providing expert help for readers. Good first teaching is essential at every grade level. Children who enter school with a rich knowledge of literacy can survive almost any kind of instruction because they fit new information into already understood constructs of reading and writing. Children who do not start with a rich literacy foundation are vulnerable as they try, with greater or lesser success, to make sense of the instruction that is offered. So adjusting classroom instruction to individual differences is very important.

Children who show early signs of confusion may need early intervention, either as a member of a small group or individually. This intervention should be short term and intensive, in order to enable children to make accelerated progress so that they can fully benefit from classroom instruction. For many children, high-quality early intervention works so well in closing the gap that they can continue to learn after the supplemental help is no longer provided, given competent classroom instruction. For a few children, specialized teaching is needed, sometimes for several years. Here, again, the goal is to enable children to read and write independently in the classroom.

▶ Classroom Literacy: Good First Teaching

Most of the essential experiences that low-achieving children need can be provided only in a classroom in which there is time to engage deeply with texts. Only in classroom instruction will children have the opportunity to hear a wide variety of texts read aloud, to discuss these texts with peers, and to read and write for long periods of time. Only in the classroom is there time for daily, specific lessons to help children learn the building blocks of print—letters, sounds, and words.

An elementary education curriculum must comprise an articulated, cohesive system of language and literacy experiences. The classroom is the foundation, and differentiated instruction needs to be provided to meet diverse needs. The high-quality language and literacy teaching in the classroom needs to bring most of the children to at least grade-level expectations. A small number of children may also require supplemental instruction. If classrooms produce too many children who seem to need extra help, then a central focus should be on improving the effectiveness of classroom instruction.

FIGURE 1-2 Coordinated Services to Children

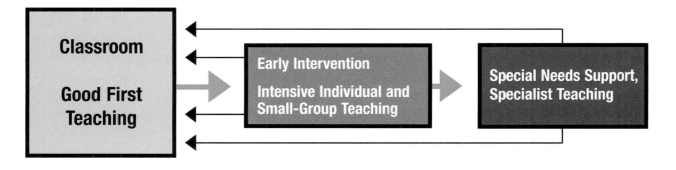

Classroom literacy instruction is implemented in many ways, and at-risk children need to experience them all. There are numerous opportunities throughout the school day to provide essential classroom experiences through whole-group, small-group, and individual instruction (Figure 1-3). All of these contexts are directly beneficial to children who find literacy learning difficult.[2]

Whole-class instruction in the classroom encompasses the following contexts:

❏ *Interactive read-aloud.* The teacher reads a story aloud and invites thinking before, during, and after the reading to help children deepen their understanding and develop the ability to talk with one another about texts.

❏ *Shared/interactive writing.* The teacher acts as scribe as she guides children in composing and then reading a text. As the teacher writes, she may draw children's attention to specific aspects of print, including letters and sounds. Shared writing becomes interactive writing when the teacher invites children to "share the pen" in writing the text.

❏ *Shared reading.* The teacher and children read a text in unison, talk about the meaning, and attend to aspects of text such as directionality, voice-print match, punctuation, letter-sound relationships, or parts within words. Children have the opportunity to behave like readers with the teacher's support.

❏ *Reading minilesson/individual work/group share.* The teacher provides a brief, explicit lesson on a

particular aspect of reading. Often texts that have previously been read aloud are used as examples. The minilesson is usually followed by small-group work (such as guided reading, literature discussion, or literacy centers) and independent reading. Children then share what they have learned.

❏ *Writing minilesson/individual work/group share.* The teacher provides a brief, explicit lesson on a particular aspect of writing. Often texts that have previously been read aloud are used as mentor texts. After the lesson, children work on their own pieces and then share their writing.

❏ *Phonics/spelling minilesson/individual work/ group share.* The teacher provides a concise, explicit lesson on a principle related to letters, sounds, and words: phonemic awareness, letters, letter-sound relationships, high-frequency words, vocabulary, spelling patterns, word structure, or ways of solving words. The minilesson is followed by an application activity in which children individually apply what they have learned and then by a group share.

Small-group instruction in the classroom encompasses the following contexts:

❏ *Guided reading.* The teacher works with a small group of children who have similar enough needs that they can be taught together. From a series of texts organized by level of difficulty, the teacher selects a book that the children can read with support. The teacher provides explicit instruction to help the children read the text proficiently and at the same time learn more about the reading process. Guided reading usually includes several minutes of explicit word work at the end of the lesson.

❏ *Book clubs.* Children read or listen to a book being read and meet in small heterogeneous groups to discuss the book with one another. The teacher demonstrates how to think and talk about books and supports the children's discussion.

❏ *Guided writing.* The teacher brings together a small group of children, all of whom need to attend to a particular aspect of writing, and provides a specific lesson that they can use to

---

[2] For detailed information on each of these instructional contexts see the following:

- Pinnell, G. S., and I. C. Fountas. 2006. *Leveled Books, K–8: Matching Texts to Readers for Effective Teaching.* Portsmouth, NH: Heinemann.
- Fountas, I. C., and G. S. Pinnell. 2006. *Teaching for Comprehending and Fluency: Thinking, Talking, and Writing About Reading.* Portsmouth, NH: Heinemann.
- Pinnell, G. S., and I. C. Fountas. 2003. *Phonics Lessons: Grades K, Grade 1, Grade 2, and Grade 3 (Word Study).* Portsmouth, NH: Heinemann.
- Fountas, I. C., and G. S. Pinnell. 2001. *Guiding Readers and Writers: Teaching Comprehension, Genre, and Content Literacy.* Portsmouth, NH: Heinemann.
- McCarrier, A. M., G. S.Pinnell , and I.C. Fountas. 2000. *Interactive Writing: How Language and Literacy Come Together, K–2.* Portsmouth, NH: Heinemann.
- Pinnell, G. S., and I. C. Fountas. 1998. *Word Matters: Teaching Phonics and Spelling in the Reading-Writing Classroom.* Portsmouth, NH: Heinemann
- Fountas, I. C., and G. S. Pinnell. 1996. *Guided Reading: Good First Teaching for All Children.* Portsmouth, NH: Heinemann.

Figure 1-3 The Structure of Classroom Literacy Instruction

Context	Specific Instructional Approach	Benefits
Whole-Class Teaching	• Interactive read-aloud • Shared/interactive writing • Shared reading • Reading minilesson/individual or small group work/group share • Writing minilesson/individual or small group work/group share • Phonics/spelling minilesson/group share	• Children learn what it is like to be part of a community of learners. • Children experience explicit teaching of reading, writing, and phonics competencies. • Meaning is socially constructed. • Children expand the repertoire of texts they know. • Children compose their own texts and engage with print as they write them. • Children learn principles for how letters, sounds, and words work and have an opportunity to apply them in hands-on activities.
Small-Group Teaching	• Guided reading • Book clubs • Guided writing	• Children have the opportunity to read a text selected to help them expand their reading abilities. • Children have the opportunity to focus on particular writing needs. • Children receive explicit instruction in a particular aspect of reading or writing. • Children have an opportunity to apply their knowledge of phonics to the reading of continuous text. • Children have an opportunity to discuss specific texts with their peers. • Instruction is targeted to the specific skills that the small group of children need.
Individual Teaching	• Individual interactions during guided reading and writing • Reading conferences during reading workshop • Writing conferences during writing workshop • Individual teaching during word study application	• Teachers have an opportunity to assess what a child knows and tailor interactions to his specific needs. • A child participates in one-on-one conversation with an adult. • A child receives the specific help he needs.

improve their writing. The goal is to have children apply the learning to their own writing.

Individual instruction in the classroom encompasses the following contexts:

❑ *Individual interactions during guided reading.* After introducing the book, the teacher listens to individuals in the group as they read the text for themselves softly or silently. On-the-spot assessment may prompt a powerful teaching interaction; alternatively, the teacher may have in mind specific instruction to help the student in a previously identified area.

❑ *Reading conferences during the reading workshop.* As children are reading self-selected books independently (from browsing boxes of books the teacher has prepared or from author, series, genre, or content collections in the classroom library), the teacher engages them in brief interactions that support the student's comprehension, word solving, and other reading strategies.

❏ *Writing conferences during the writing workshop.* As children work on their writing, the teacher conducts conferences with individuals. The conference may focus on any aspect of writing that is relevant to the student's work.

❏ *Word study applications.* An independent hands-on activity (such as sorting words or letters, matching letters and sounds, playing a word game) takes place after a word study mini-lesson and helps the children apply what they are learning. They may work as individuals, with a partner, or in small groups. The teacher may conduct brief individual interactions during this time to reinforce and extend learning.

Teachers organize their day by moving between whole-class, small-group, and individual work as appropriate. Many teachers of young children also have them engage in meaningful, productive work at literacy centers. These centers can greatly enhance young children's literacy opportunities by providing:

❏ Experiences with reading or responding to poetry.

❏ Opportunities to listen to audio recordings of texts.

❏ Further work with letters, sounds, and words.

❏ More independent reading (and rereading) of texts.

❏ More opportunities to write about reading or content-area learning.

❏ Chances to respond to or interpret texts through art and drama.

Adjusting instruction to help the lowest achievers and trying to take advantage of every learning opportunity can be challenging, especially when you have the varying needs of twenty-five to thirty students to consider. A school day of six hours sounds long; in reality, however, it is hard to find enough time to teach. When planning for the literacy support of low-achieving children, administrators, leadership teams, and teachers first need to examine teaching in classrooms. More time can be found to help low-achieving readers by:

❏ Minimizing time spent on logistical announcements and school assemblies.

❏ Creating large blocks of time in which to provide concentrated instruction.

❏ Scheduling special subjects, such as art and music, so that they do not fragment the day.

❏ Avoiding unnecessary testing.

❏ Providing rich and varied text resources so that all readers have appropriate selections for independent reading.

❏ Managing transitions so as not to lose time.

▶ Early Intervention

When we think about what readers need, the first consideration is what can be done in classrooms. Without rich classroom opportunities, no intervention will work. But what about children who have difficulty learning to read and write even in classrooms where the literacy opportunities are many and of high quality? Children who are confused about aspects of literacy often do not fully profit from classroom instruction. A child who has trouble identifying letters that are embedded in continuous print, for example, may not know where to look when you ask the class to find the first letter of a word. Children who have trouble hearing individual sounds in words will have difficulty connecting them to letters when you help them try to solve words. Children who have trouble remembering how specific words look will not be able to locate those words in a text. Children who are focusing only on the print may not understand what you mean when you try to help them anticipate the next word or understand dialogue. Children who are attending to aspects of print may "mumble along" during shared reading without looking anywhere near the right place in the print. Classroom instruction, even though excellent, may help the majority of children but miss the mark entirely with a few.

You will have no trouble identifying these children, and there are many ways of adjusting instruction to help them, including making whole-group instruction multilevel, providing small-group instruction, and tailoring individual interactions to support learners. This book offers suggestions for adjusting instruction to maximize opportunities for children who find literacy learning difficult. All of them can be used with whole-group, small-group, and individual instruction.

But there are always children who need supplemental help, some for a very short time, a very small percentage for their entire school careers. For these children, a layer of early intervention is imperative. We cannot wait until failure takes its emotional toll and the gap is too great to bridge. It must take place *early* in the child's school career. There are critical times in learning when it is easy to get back on track. The longer we wait, the harder it is to move children into the mainstream of instruction—where they must be able to take advantage of good classroom teaching. The intermediate and middle school grades benefit from the combination of good primary classroom teaching and early intervention: special needs services are then provided for the few children who need help for a longer period of time.

Early intervention is supplemental teaching—extra help above and beyond good classroom instruction. This extra teaching *should not take the place of opportunities to learn in the classroom*. A great deal of coordination and communication is necessary to accomplish this goal with coherence and efficiency.

Small-Group Supplemental Instruction

Since the late sixties, it has been common to take children out of the classroom (pull-out) or bring a reading teacher into a classroom (push-in) for compensatory small-group instruction in reading. Yet the number of children who have difficulty learning to read remains about the same and in some cases has even increased. Critics of pull-out programs claim that too much time is lost when children are separated from their classmates for thirty to forty-five minutes a day, that the instruction children receive is often inadequate and disorganized, that much instructional time is lost in

transitions, that the instruction is not coordinated with the classroom, and that the children might be better off participating fully in classroom instruction (Allington 1983, 1994; Allington & McGill-Franzen 1989). Analysis also shows that during supplementary group instruction, children get very little opportunity to read and write and spend most of their time on "activities" and drill (Pinnell et al. 1993). Yet teachers continue to demand extra small-group help for more and more of their students. Too often the help is not "extra" help, as it takes the place of classroom instruction.

Supplemental small-group instruction has not worked in the past because:

- ❏ It is inefficient (going down the hall and returning, moving to another area of the classroom, getting out materials and putting them away, etc.).

- ❏ It is not usually coordinated or cohesive with the classroom program; children are often confused by two very different approaches.

- ❏ It does not include large chunks of time spent reading continuous text with expert teacher support. Some are essentially phonics programs, not reading programs that include phonics.

- ❏ It often involves dragging children through texts or assignments that are too difficult for them.

- ❏ It often makes children dependent on adults to help them complete work.

- ❏ It is not true intervention but rather long-term remediation; children tend to stay in the groups year after year, losing hope and motivation.

- ❏ A stigma is attached to participation.

- ❏ Characteristics vary widely. Some teachers use highly prescriptive programs that do not fit children's individual learning paths; others provide too little structure to help readers know how to move forward.

Supplemental small-group instruction can enable children to make faster progress in reading and thus profit from good classroom teaching as long as you recognize three facts:

1. To make a real contribution to students' learning, small-group instruction must be organized, coherent, highly effective, and more uniquely

tailored to students' needs than the instruction they would be getting in the same amount of time in the classroom.

2. The small-group instruction *must be supplemental* to good classroom instruction.

3. Some children will require individual tutoring; small-group help will not be sufficient.

Small-group supplemental instruction has many advantages, especially if children are well-matched and the groups are small. It makes no sense, for example, to offer extra instruction to eight or more children who are inevitably too different from one another to profit from the same instruction. All the suggestions in this book will be appropriate as you work with children in groups and interact with them individually. Review the general suggestions for making supplemental small-group instruction work in Figure 1-4. These suggestions range from efficient transitions and management to the precise kind of teaching you will be doing with small groups. While we know that the urge is to serve as many children as possible, supplemental group work must be kept within a reasonable range to be effective. Special instruction without results is a misuse of public money. It is better to work intensively and effectively with a small group for thirty minutes than to double the group and provide ineffectual instruction for an hour. It is better to work with a smaller group (three or four) for half a year, than a larger group (five to eight) for a whole year. Keep the group size to five or fewer; three or four is best. Remember that many of the young children who receive supplemental instruction are confused or find the learning difficult. They need your continuous attention to help them focus and learn. The smaller the group, the better the results.

It is essential to create a strong structure for supplemental small-group instruction—a lesson framework that reflects both your readers and your curricular goals. A predictable sequence of activities offers children security, and they learn and use essential learning routines more quickly. A predictable lesson framework also helps you pace your instruction to include reading, writing, and word study, all of

Figure 1-4 Making Supplemental Small-Group Instruction Work

- Keep the group size small.
- Group and regroup children over the year to be sure they are well matched.
- Minimize the time it takes to switch from the classroom to the small group and back.
- Schedule the group at the same time each day if possible to create a routine.
- Design lessons that emphasize reading and writing continuous text.
- Create and use a strong, predictable lesson framework that includes reading; writing; and explicit, systematized phonics.
- Provide very clear, explicit demonstrations of what you want children to learn and do.
- Match texts to readers and sequence them so that a ladder of progress is created.
- Base instruction on sound assessment so that it responds precisely to what children need to learn how to do next and builds on their strengths.
- Coordinate classroom and supplemental teaching to provide coherent teaching.

which are necessary for helping at-risk readers. Within the framework, you can adjust your instruction to your learners' precise needs.

Individual Instruction

Some children have so much difficulty that they require one-to-one tutoring. The U.S. Department of Education's Institute of Education Sciences identified "one-on-one tutoring by qualified tutors for at-risk readers in grades 1–3" (Institute of Education Sciences 2003) as meeting the gold standard for what works. For children who have extreme difficulty in their first year of classroom instruction, Clay (2003) recommends a short series of individually designed lessons. When well-designed individual lessons are applied at the right time, the long-term effect on initially struggling readers can be profound.

The most dynamic and highly regarded example of individual tutoring is Reading Recovery, which has demonstrated the ability to help well over a million low-achieving first graders make accelerated progress and get "back on track." (See Schmidt et al. 2005 for detailed information about Reading Recovery and its results.) Researchers have examined Reading Recovery and found the following benefits (Schmidt et. al., 78):

- ❏ Instruction is at an appropriate level and is built on the child's current strengths.

- ❏ Expectations and challenges are appropriate.

- ❏ The pace of instruction is appropriate.

- ❏ The child's attention is focused on literacy tasks.

- ❏ The child is an active and constructive learner.

- ❏ Time is designated daily for reading and writing continuous text with skilled guidance.

- ❏ Language and communication skills are enhanced.

- ❏ The child receives immediate feedback and explicit guidance.

- ❏ There is an opportunity for accelerated learning and a quicker, successful return to mainstream literacy instruction.

- ❏ Children receive emotional support that fosters learning—support that enhances attitudes, motivation, confidence, and trust.

Simply providing one-to-one instruction will not do the job. The instruction must have the advantages listed above and be delivered by a teacher who has been trained to work with learners who have the most difficulty learning to read. Pinnell, Lyons, and Deford (1993) identified three factors required for successful intervention: (a) one-to-one teaching, (b) a structured lesson framework with procedures designed to provide very specific help to learners, and (c) long-term professional development for teachers so that they can make the most of the individual time. Clay (2003, 303) insists:

> There is a categorical difference between the kinds of teaching and learning interactions that can occur in individual instruction and the kinds of teaching that can occur in group and class settings. We will have to differentiate our theories rather than treat the two categories as if they were one. It is acceptable to believe that in learning to play golf and learning to play the cello, individual tuition will be more productive than group tuition, and I believe that following surgery, individual intensive care suited to my critical condition will be the treatment of choice for a short period of time even when the level of care provided in the general wards of hospitals is superb!

Many school districts in the United States provide short periods (twelve to twenty weeks) of daily one-to-one instruction for children in grade 1 who are in the lowest achieving twenty to twenty-five per cent of the class. The payoff is great because tutoring at this critical time helps the great majority of children accelerate to the point that they can progress with their peers. Applying one-to-one intensive help early on greatly reduces the number of children who need continuing service of any kind (see Schmidt et al. 2005).

▶ The Role of Professional Development

Simply providing a variety of contexts for learning and early intervention in classroom instruction—supplementary, small group, and individual—will not guarantee success for low-achieving children. The key is teacher knowledge and skill. Effective teachers of children who need extra support:

- ❏ Have a deep understanding of the reading and writing processes.

- ❏ Know how to observe and analyze children's precise reading and writing behaviors.

- ❏ Are able to use the information from their observations to make effective moment-to-moment teaching decisions while working with children as a whole class, in small groups, and individually.

❏ Differentiate instruction, making decisions that are tailored to individuals, even in group settings.

❏ Know how to listen carefully to children and respond to their ideas.

❏ Use clear, precise language to help children understand concepts and principles.

❏ Know how to interact with children effectively, having conversations that will help children expand their use of language.

❏ Create and use strong frameworks for instruction.

❏ Know how to analyze texts and understand their role in supporting children.

❏ Know how to select high-quality texts that engage children and help them expand their language and content knowledge.

❏ Use instructional time effectively.

❏ Understand the role of language in literacy, particularly when working with English language learners or other children whose home/community language is not English.

❏ Understand language and cultural differences and their implications for teaching and learning.

❏ Learn from teaching as they engage in it and have experiences with different children over time.

❏ Examine their own teaching effectiveness, always taking responsibility for children's learning and continually seeking greater skill.

The most vulnerable children need the best teaching, and the key to providing it is ongoing professional development. Teachers need support to become more expert with every year of teaching. School districts seeking to close the achievement gap must consider good classroom teaching, multiple layers of intervention, the role of short-term intensive tutoring, and the ongoing development of highly qualified teachers.

▶ Suggestions for Professional Development

EVALUATING THE DESIGN AND OUTCOMES OF SUPPLEMENTARY APPROACHES

1. Work with your colleagues to make a list of the current approaches you use to help children who are having difficulty learning to read and write.
2. Discuss the potential of each approach and its current level of effectiveness.
3. After examining "Essential Experiences for Children Who Find Literacy Difficult" (Figure 1-1), ask yourselves these questions:

   ❑ How are we considering the effectiveness of classroom programs as part of the prevention of reading difficulties?

   ❑ What are the results of our classroom programs?

   ❑ What aspects of classroom instruction particularly support these readers? What needs to be developed?

   ❑ What kind of supplemental literacy services are provided in the school? Are they efficient, structured, coherent, and coordinated?

   ❑ Do we need to reduce the *number* of different programs offered to at-risk readers in order to increase their effectiveness?

   ❑ What kinds of changes can be made to provide a more coordinated and cohesive program—classroom instruction, supplemental small-group instruction, and tutoring?

   ❑ What kind of professional development will be needed to make these changes?

4. Think and talk about the effectiveness of your current supplemental small-group instruction. Use "Making Supplemental Small-Group Instruction Work" (Figure 1-4) to ground your discussion. Discuss any changes you might want to make.
5. Develop an action plan for revising or improving your program for helping children who have difficulty in learning to read and write.

Effective Readers: What Do They Do?

IT IS IMPORTANT TO KNOW WHAT EFFECTIVE PROCESSING is like because that gives us a vision for what we want to help struggling readers learn how to do. In this chapter, we look at the networks of strategic actions that make up an effective reading processing systems. That is our vision for every reader, but we also recognize that each child has a different path of progress as they build their systems for processing increasingly challenging texts, and we present some examples here.

Let's begin with a close look at readers who develop proficient processing systems to help us understand how readers who struggle go off track. Reading proficiency is defined in relation to the experience of the reader. Clay (1998) described children's journeys to literacy as "different paths to common outcomes." This prompts us as teachers to look closely at the unique journeys of individuals and the way they become literate over time. Young children differ from one another in what they notice about print, the personal connections they make with print, the stories that engage them, the language they remember, the way they interpret stories, the words they notice and learn, and many other ways. The common thread is that most children acquire a fully developed literacy processing system that grows and expands over the years. If we had

descriptions of many proficient readers and writers of every age beginning at three, we could then chart the continuous development of literacy proficiency. It is helpful to have in mind a clear picture of what effective readers do as they build their systems so we can think about what all readers need to be able to do.

▶ Systems of Strategic Actions

Throughout your life, your tastes and the competence with which you process different genres of texts vary. Interest, curiosity, and job requirements make you more familiar with some genres than others. But there is a core process incorporating *systems of strategic actions* that enables you to construct meaning from text rapidly and efficiently.

Thinking Within the Text

As a proficient reader, you:

❏ Process print rapidly, automatically, and unconsciously, effortlessly recognizing almost all words and solving a very few new ones without being aware of it.

❏ Monitor your understanding of texts and search for and use more information when needed to correct errors.

❏ Search for and use different kinds of information found in the text.

❏ Remember information and carry it forward in summary form, often long after reading a text.

❏ Sustain fluency and phrasing by unconsciously grouping words and using punctuation in silent reading and reflecting the meaning of the text through stress, intonation, and phrasing when reading out loud.

❏ Adjust reading by changing pace or approach for different texts and purposes or by slowing down to problem solve and then speeding up again.

Most of the time, these actions are unconscious. You don't mentally tell yourself, "Now, I have to search for information." You just do it when prompted by internal questions. When studying a text for a test, for example, you might consciously remember details or a summary (often writing notes to help you), but most of the time, you simply understand the text and recall the important information automatically. We call this *thinking within the text* (see Fountas and Pinnell 2000, 2006). Since you do not need to pay attention to the processing, your mind can be working on something else.

Thinking Beyond the Text

As a proficient reader, you also:

❏ Predict what will happen next—what a character will do, how a character will feel, what will happen next, what kind of information will be provided next.

❏ Make connections—apply background knowledge, think about your own experiences in light of what is going on in a text, think how charac-

ters remind you of people you know, consider how a text is like another you have read.

❏ Synthesize new information—change your own understanding based on new information or ideas encountered in a text.

❏ Infer what the writer is implying but not saying—motives and feelings of characters, underlying causes for problems.

These strategic actions are related to *thinking beyond the text*. Again, you do not consciously undertake these actions; they happen while you are reading. Much of your comprehension of a text comes not from the print itself but from what you bring to the reading. Anyone who has been a member of a book club knows that every person in the group has a slightly different interpretation of the text. These variations in interpretation are quite valuable when they are shared—everyone's thinking is enriched.

Thinking About the Text

Finally, as a proficient reader, you are *thinking about the text*—you notice, appreciate, or criticize something about the writing. When you say, "Amy Tan is one of my favorite writers," you are indicating that you like her style, the subjects she writes about, the way she organizes and tells a story, her choice of language, and so on. You are holding up the text as an object to be admired. Talking with others, you might offer examples or go into greater detail. Similarly, you might question the accuracy or authenticity of a text or be critical of the author's motives or qualifications. As a proficient reader you are able to:

❏ Analyze the text while reading it and when reflecting on what you've read.

❏ Critique the text while reading it and when reflecting on what you've read.

Sometimes analyzing and critiquing are conscious efforts, especially if you plan to talk about the text with others; but just as often, they are unconscious. Proficient readers think analytically and critically all the time while they are reading.

These twelve *systems of strategic actions* (see Figure 2-1) are well established in most readers by about the

Figure 2-1 **Systems of Strategic Actions: Ways of Thinking Within, Beyond, About Texts**		
Ways of Thinking	**Systems of Strategic Actions for Processing Written Texts**	
Thinking Within the Text	Solving Words	Using a range of strategies to take words apart and understand what words mean while reading continuous text.
	Monitoring and Correcting	Checking on whether reading sounds right, looks right, and makes sense.
	Searching For and Using Information	Searching for and using all kinds of information in a text.
	Summarizing	Putting together, remembering, and carrying forward important information while reading, and disregarding irrelevant information.
	Maintaining Fluency	Integrating sources of information in a smoothly operating process that results in expressive, phrased reading.
	Adjusting	Reading in different ways as appropriate to the purpose for reading and the type of text.
Thinking Beyond the Text	Predicting	Thinking about what will follow while reading continuous text.
	Making Connections • Personal • World • Text	Searching for and using connections to knowledge gained through personal experiences, learning about the world, and reading other texts.
	Synthesizing	Putting together information from the text and from background knowledge in order to create new understandings.
	Inferring	Going beyond the literal meaning of a text to think about what is not there but is implied by the writer.
Thinking About the Text	Analyzing	Examining elements of a text to know more about how it is constructed.
	Critiquing	Evaluating a text based on personal, world, or text knowledge.

middle of second grade. From then on, readers continue to grow in their ability to process and understand increasingly complex texts into adulthood, but the process is basically the same. A key factor is the reader's ability to initiate the strategic activities to gain independent inner control of these complex behaviors.

▶ Children on the Way to Being Proficient Readers

Let's look at two readers who are in different places on their way to becoming literate.

Chad as a Reader

We tend to think of learning to read as a simple process of using letter/sound information to decode words and then perhaps thinking a little about the meaning. In fact, a complex processing system is in place from the beginning. Chad is a young boy just learning to read.

Chad was reading *Friends* (Level A), a very simple story about a big dog and a little dog who live together (see Figure 2-2). On every two-page spread, the little dog, Taco, and the big dog, Orson, are contrasted in repetitive sentences: everything belonging to Taco is little and everything belonging to Orson is big. Each line begins with one or the other dog's name—a challenge, since Chad must use the visual information or print (at least the first letter) to identify the word. Chad also noticed that the text switches back and forth between Orson and Taco and was assisted in reading the words by using the pictures.

As you introduce this text to a small group of children, you would have them notice the two dogs in the pictures, say the dogs' names, and locate these names on several pages. You would invite them to think about how the size of the objects matches the size of the dogs. Children might draw on their own knowledge of dogs to identify the objects belonging to each dog. You would help them understand that on pages 10 and 11 the writer switches from real objects to the way the dogs sound. On page 16, you

would invite them to talk about the dogs as friends (going back to the title of the story) and ask them to think about what kind of friend Orson has, big or little. A sample introduction is provided in Figure 2-3. Notice that Ms. F not only helped children use letter-sound information to locate a new and important word used many times in the text but also helped them understand how the story "works."

During this introduction Chad received a high level of support from his teacher. His comments ("And Taco has a little bone." "It's loud and big?") show he is beginning to understand the way the story is structured. He is also bringing background knowledge to understanding the text and making some inferences about the feelings of the two characters. An excerpt from his first reading of the text is presented in Figure 2-4.

Chad learned more about how to read by reading. As he processed the text, he grew increasingly competent in using the language structure and the organization of the text. His substitution, *Orson is barking,* makes sense, especially since he was looking at the picture with the speech bubble. But once Ms. F called his attention to the mismatch, Chad used his knowledge of letter-sound relationships to monitor his reading of that word in the rest of the text. Recognizing the difference between *is* and *has* is a key distinction, and Chad is in the process of acquiring *has* as a known high-frequency word.

In the discussion after reading, Chad pointed out that it sounds "funny" to say "Orson had a big bark," but that it really is big. He said he liked the way Orson's bark looks bigger to show that it sounds bigger. He also said again that it is nice for them to be friends so that they won't be lonesome and can play together.

Review the running record Ms. F took the next day (Figure 2-5). Chad made three substitutions (*dog* for *big, tag* for *collar,* and *dish* for *bowl*). We can hypothesize that he used both visual information and voice-print match to monitor his reading and self-correct *big* on page 2. His other two substitutions indicate that he was using meaning but not cross-checking the meaning with the visual information. When he read the book for the first time the day before, he substi-

FIGURE 2-2 Page Layout of *Friends* from Leveled Literacy Intervention, Green System (Heinemann 2009)

Figure 2-3 Introduction to *Friends* (Level A)

Speaker	Interaction	What the Teacher Is Attending to
Ms. F	Our new book today is called *Friends*. Look at the cover. These two dogs are friends. What do you notice?	*Introduces title and the concept of dogs being friends. Invites observation of details in the pictures.*
Chad	One dog is really big and one is just a little dog.	
Ms. F	That's right. Put your finger on the big dog. His name is Orson. Listen. *(Says Orson's name and claps it.)* Say Orson and clap it with me.	*Reinforces thinking. Draws attention to pictures of a character and has children rehearse the name, practicing phonological awareness.*
Children	Or *(clap)* son *(clap)*!	
Ms. F	The little dog's name is Taco. Listen. *(Says Taco and claps it.)* Say Taco and clap it with me.	*Introduces the other character and sets the scene for the contrast.*
Children	Ta *(clap)* co *(clap)*.	
Ms. F	In this story you are going to see some things that belong to Orson and some things that belong to Taco. Turn the page. Do you see Orson? On this page it says "Orson is a big dog." Say *is*. *Is* starts with *i* and ends with *s*. Find *is* and put your finger under it.	*Reveals content of the story, provides some of the language, and has children locate a known word.*
Children	*(Locate and say* is.*)*	
Ms. F	Look at the next page. Who is the writer telling about now?	*Invites attention to the pictures.*
Children	Taco!	
Ms. F	Yes, Taco, is the little dog, isn't he? So you are going to read something about Taco. Turn the page and you will see Orson again. This time, the writer is showing something Orson has. What kind of collar would you expect Orson to have?	*Reinforces thinking, foreshadows story structure, and invites prediction.*
Laquita	He needs a big collar.	
Sherry	My dog has a big collar.	
Ms. F	Yes, he has a big collar. Say the word *has*. *(Children say it.)* What letter would you expect to see at the beginning of *has*?	*Helps children hear sounds in words (phonemic awareness) and locate words.*
Children	h	
Ms. F	Find the word *has* and run your finger under it. *(Children locate the word.)* That word will help you read this book because it is on many of the pages. Now what kind of collar do you think Taco has?	*Draws attention to a word, points out a feature of the text that will help in reading it, and invites prediction.*
Chad	A little collar.	
Ms. F	Yes, you are going to see that in this book when you look at this page *(shows it)* you will always see something that Orson has, and it will always be . . .	

continues

Figure 2-3 **Introduction to** *Friends, continued*		
Speaker	**Interaction**	**What the Teacher Is Attending to**
Sherry	Big!	
Ms. F	Yes. So you look at the left page and you can see Orson and something big in the picture and you will read about it. Look over to the right page and you will see Taco and something little that he has. Look at page 6. What does it say Orson has?	*Explicitly shows children the structure of the text.*
Laquita	A bone.	
Chad	And Taco has a little bone.	
Ms. F	Look at page 10. Orson is doing something interesting there. He is barking, and you can see that in the speech bubble. What kind of bark do you think Orson has?	*Helps children understand a change in concept and points out a text feature.*
Chad	A loud bark because it's big there *(pointing to speech bubble).*	
Sherry	And Taco isn't very loud.	
Ms. F	I'll bet it's loud, and they are showing that because the letters in Orson's speech bubble are much bigger than in Taco's. It is saying that Orson has a big bark.	
Chad	It's loud and big?	
Ms. F	Yes, and at the end you are going to see that they are friends—a big friend and a little friend. Do you think Taco likes it that he has a big friend?	*Foreshadows change of concept at the end and invites inference.*
Chad	He likes it because they live in the same house. I have a big dog and he is friends with my uncle's dog. They like to play chase. It's a funny idea to think of having two dogs that are so different.	
Ms. F	So Orson and Taco are friends. Go back to page 1 and point and read softly to yourself.	*Confirms concept.*

tuted *is* for *has* but was able to use letter-sound information in connection with language structure to solve the word. Chad knew many letter-sound relationships, and he needed encouragement and teaching to notice consistently how words look. At the word *friend,* he appealed to his teacher, who first said, "You try" (Y), and then told him the word. Chad did not make an attempt but he read the word accurately on the next line. Overall, Chad was making good progress and had demonstrated competent reading on this Level A text. He pointed under the words carefully and crisply, suggesting that he has voice-print match under control on one line of text. He also used appropriate stress on

words to convey meaning. His comments indicate that he understood the story.

After taking the running record, Ms. F made a quick teaching point designed to help Chad learn more about reading (see Figure 2-6). She opened with a brief comment related to the meaning, to which Chad responded with a summary statement of the story. She then took him back to page 4, where Chad read *tag* for *collar.* Ms. F had told Chad the word *collar* when he was reading.

We would not expect every child to provide evidence of every type of strategic thinking in every lesson. Doing so would formulize the conversation and

Signs of strategic actions (meaning) monitors

Figure 2-4 Excerpt from Chad's First Reading of *Friends* (Level A)

Speaker	Interaction
Chad	*(Reading)* Orson is a dog dog—no, big—big dog.
	Taco is a l-little dog.
	Orson is, is . . . *(appeals to Ms. F, who tells him the word.)*
	Orson has a big tag.
	Is that a tag?
Ms. F	It's called a collar.
Chad	*(Reading)* Orson has a big collar.
	Taco *(pause)* has a big— no, little—little collar.
	Orson has a big bone.
	Everything he has is big. It's really big
Ms. F	So what does Taco have?
Chad	*(Reading)* Taco has a little bone.
	Orson has a big b-ball. *(Checks picture.)*
	Taco has a little ball.
	Orson is barking *(looks at the picture and speech bubble and stops).*
Ms. F	Were you right?
Chad	No. *(Reading.)*
Ms. F	*(Points to the word has.)* That says *has.* Try that again and make it match. *(Reading)* Orson has a big bark. Did that match?
Chad	Yes. *(Reads the rest of the story without support.)*

perhaps turn it into an interrogation. Ms. F and Chad had natural discussions after the first and second readings, although it is clear she was doing some very intentional teaching. When we evaluate evidence of Chad's beginning control of the twelve systems of strategies (see Figure 2-7), we see significant evidence that he can engage in complex behaviors even on this Level A text. His responses are not sophisticated, and

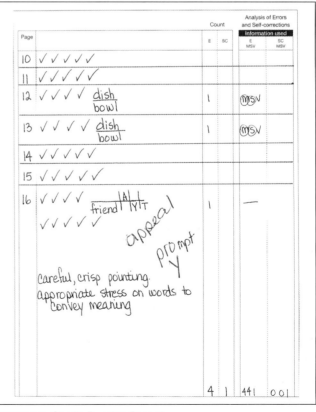

FIGURE 2-5 Chad's Running Record

Figure 2-6 Teaching After the Running Record

Speaker	Interaction
Ms. F	They each have a friend. Orson has a little friend.
Chad	That's Taco. He's a little friend. And Taco has a big friend and that's Orson.
Ms. F	Looks like they really like each other. Let's go back to page 4. Read that again. Where was the tricky part here?
Chad	*(Points to collar)*
Ms. F	You were thinking about the story when you said *tag*, but what letter did you see first?
Chad	c
Ms. F	Yes, so tag wouldn't fit here. You have to think about the story and decide what word would look right here.
Chad	*(Reads sentence accurately)*
Ms. F	Yes, you thought about what would look right in the story.

he is not labeling his thinking (he does not say, *I am making a prediction or a connection*, for example). However, that is not the goal. In fact, asking children to label strategies can interfere with efficient processing. What is important is that readers like Chad use everything they know to process and comprehend an engaging story.

Brian as a Reader

Now let's look at a child at the beginning of second grade, but one still building an early reading process. In this example, you see Brian's second reading of *The Ladybug and the Cricket*, which the teacher has coded. (See Figure 2-9.) This text is a simple story reminiscent of a folk tale. The two characters have parallel problems; although they are friends, each admires the other for different reasons.

The reader would need to infer characters' motivations and to see the end of the story as a true sign of friendship. Some vocabulary (for example *beauti-*

ful, chirpy, sighed) will be challenging for many readers, both for decoding and comprehension. Most of these words, however, are repeated several times in the text, so the reader should be able to gain momentum across the text. The use of comparison places additional demands on young readers. The text also has some literary language that is demanding, for example, "Then she smiled a ladybug smile."

Brian had read the text once before in small group reading. For the second reading of the text, the teacher observed and coded Brian's reading behavior. He processed the text with 96% accuracy. He consistently monitored his reading, slowing down to problem solve and resuming a good rate. He showed the ability to take words apart (for example, *won-der, wonderful*), and he was consistently looking beyond the first letter and using word parts. His word-solving techniques did not work well on *sighed* or *chirpy*, perhaps words that were not likely to be in Brian's oral vocabulary. He did work actively, however, to make attempts at the words before appealing. His comments after reading indicated good understanding of the theme of the story. He connected the text to another story he knew and to the genre. Although he did not use the label "genre," his comments serve as evidence that he had noticed something about the text structure, the significant characteristics. He also made inferences about the feelings of the characters. The record of reading 234 words of the story offers significant evidence that Brian was solving words and searching for, using, and remembering important information as he read the text. He gained momentum across the text as he learned about the vocabulary and writing style. He was thinking beyond the text when he connected the story to another and inferred characters' feelings. For example, he commented:

> This story was kind of like *The Lion and the Mouse* because they really helped each other to do what they wanted. And they didn't mind that they weren't really as pretty or sing as good as each other. They were just happy that they were good friends and they thought enough of each other to try to make each other happy, but I think it was kind of dumb to paint the beetle like that. They should just be happy the way they are and like each other because not everybody had to be alike.

Figure 2-7 **Ways of Thinking: Observing for Evidence**			
Thinking	**Systems of Strategic Actions**		**Evidence From Observation: Introduction, First Reading, Discussion, Running Record**
Within the Text	Solving Words		Used visual information to SC *dog* to *big*.
	Monitoring and Self-Correction	✓	Showed stretches of accurate reading with 95% accuracy overall. Had self-correction ratio of 1:5. Appealed on *friend* and *collar*. Used careful, crisp pointing.
	Searching For and Using Information	✓	Noticed details in the pictures during introduction. Searched pictures to check meaning while reading. Used meaning and structure on errors: *tag* for *collar* and *dish* for *bowl*. Noticed layout and features of print (size and boldface type).
	Summarizing	✓	Made brief summary statement—essence of the story.
	Maintaining Fluency	N/A	Stressed words appropriately to convey meaning. Still pointed word by word (not fluent).
	Adjusting	✓	Slowed down to problem solve. Gained momentum through the text.
Beyond the Text	Predicting	✓	Predicted Taco would have a little collar and a little bone. Predicted Orson would have a loud bark.
	Making Connections • Personal • World • Text	✓	Connected *loud* and *big*. Connected to personal experience. Knew that dogs have tags. Commented that sometimes little dogs chase big dogs.
	Synthesizing		—
	Inferring	✓	Inferred that Taco likes having a friend. Speculated on who might be "boss."
About the Text	Analyzing	✓	Commented on story structure (contrast of big and little).
	Critiquing	✓	Said illustrations were funny.

FIGURE 2-8 Page Layout of *The Ladybug and the Cricket* from Leveled Literacy Intervention, Blue System (Heinemann 2009)

He even offered a bit of criticism of the characters (which could be interpreted as critiquing the text itself). As indicated in the analysis in Figure 2-10, even this very brief excerpt from Brian's reading provides evidence that he is simultaneously applying a complex set of strategic actions.

Like Chad, Brian is a developing reader, although he is much farther along. He will continue to learn over the next few years, but he is off to a very good start. He will continue to apply these strategic actions to more and more challenging texts.

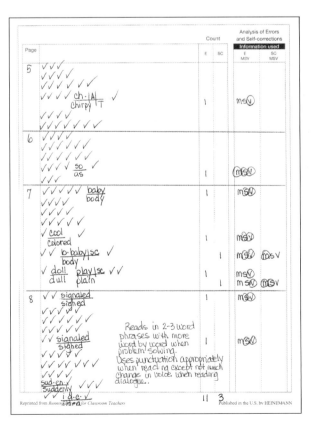

FIGURE 2-8 Page Layout of *The Ladybug and the Cricket, continued*

▶ Paths of Progress

Both Chad and Brian are on a successful journey toward literacy. They are taking individual paths toward a fully developed and complex reading process. If we showed twenty other effective readers in

FIGURE 2-9 Excerpt from Brian's Second Reading

Figure 2-10 **Ways of Thinking: Observing for Behavioral Evidence**			
Thinking	**Systems of Strategic Actions**		**Evidence From Reading and Comments**
Within the Text	Solving Words	✓	Taking words apart while focusing on the meaning. Using word parts in attempts at words. Actively working to solve difficult words that are unfamiliar.
	Monitoring and Self Correction	✓	Accurate reading on most of the text (94%). Two self corrections. Appealed on challenging words after trying.
	Searching for and Using Information	✓	Remembered important details from the text.
	Summarizing	✓	Stated the main theme after reading.
	Maintaining Fluency	✓	Read fluently with phrasing.
	Adjusting	✓	Slowed down to problem solve and speeded up again.
Beyond the Text	Predicting	✓	—
	Making Connections • Personal • World • Text	✓	Connected to a familiar fable.
	Synthesizing		—
	Inferring	✓	Inferred characters' feelings and motivations.
About the Text	Analyzing	✓	—
	Critiquing	✓	Stated opinions about the way the story went.

this chapter, each would build her processing systems differently. Each would process print using different strengths and different information. Each would solve problems in different ways. Certainly, each would make different connections and bring different interpretations to the reading. But these readers would also share much. They would initiate problem-solving actions; they would all search for and use different kinds of information; they would always be thinking beyond the particular text.

In the competency of Chad and Brian, we see the roots of the highly sophisticated reader who will be required to read complex texts in middle school, high school, and beyond. Notable in these two examples is

the complexity and strategic combination of ways of thinking about the text that are evident from the beginning. Most important is that each is working actively on text, learning more about problem-solving actions by using them.

But many things can go wrong in a reader's path of progress. Our job as teachers is not only to identify the children who find learning to read and write difficult but also to create the circumstances that help them have the same daily opportunities to build effective processing systems as Chad and Brian are having. This requires matching texts to readers and strong teaching that allows children to apply reading strategies to increasingly challenging texts.

▶ Suggestions for Professional Development

ANALYZING EVIDENCE OF SYSTEMS OF STRATEGIC ACTIONS

1. With your grade-level colleagues, study the two examples presented in this chapter. What are each boy's strengths? What does each boy need to learn how to do next?

2. Select two texts at an appropriate level for several children in your classroom.

   ❏ Take a running record or a Reading Record of a student reading an instructional level text. (Each should have an accuracy rating of at least 90% through Level K or at least 95% at Level L and beyond.)

   ❏ Bring the records to your next grade-level meeting and, as a group, make comparisons, noting and discussing similarities and differences in the readers' strategic actions. Refer to Figure 2-1. Look for strengths and needs.

   ❏ Working in pairs or small groups, search for evidence that children are using each system of strategies. Make a chart like the ones in Figures 2-7 and 2-10 for each child (a blank form for Observing for Evidence is included in Appendix A).

Going Off Track: Why and How?

MOST LEARNING PROBLEMS EXIST NOT WITHIN THE CHILD but in the inadequacy of the system to find a way to teach him. In this chapter, we explore when, how, and why children seem to go "off track" in the early years of becoming literate. Without intervention, they can perpetuate confusions and fall into behaviors that we then diagnose as reading disabilities. What was an early weakness that would respond to instruction becomes a long-term deficit. We need to remember that a difficulty is not necessarily a disability. By intervening early and using a repertoire of different instructional techniques, we can put most children back on track.

We have known for several decades that no single approach to teaching will meet the needs of all children. We have also recognized that what makes the difference in children's learning is not primarily the particular methods or materials but the quality of the *teaching* (Bond and Dykstra 1967). The responsibility for solving most learning problems of children who go "off track" in the early years of becoming literate rests with the schools.

Our literacy work over the last thirty years tells us that many intelligent young children have difficulty learning to read. Problems may include:

❑ Giving little or no attention to print.

❑ Having trouble learning and remembering words.

❑ Being unable to write one's name even after practice.

❑ Having difficulty understanding that the print rather than the pictures carries the message.

❑ Having difficulty learning how to distinguish one letter from other.

❑ Making drawings that are random lines or that lack details.

❑ Having difficulty remembering stories.

❑ Not being able to recount details from stories.

❑ Not writing voluntarily.

❑ Having difficulty forming letters.

❑ Holding the pen or pencil very awkwardly, writing laboriously.

❑ Knowing the names of very few letters.

❑ Producing letter-like forms that are not related to sounds.

❑ Having difficulty hearing the sounds in words.

❑ Being confused about left-to-right directionality, often moving around print haphazardly.

❑ Not using information from pictures, or depending solely on the pictures.

❑ Remembering predictable text rather than associating the words with the symbols on the page.

❑ Inventing stories in response to print rather than using visual information to monitor accuracy.

❑ Not noticing mismatches when reading simple, familiar texts.

❑ Mumbling along during shared reading, or not participating at all.

❑ Having trouble locating letters and words that are embedded in print.

Of course, no one student will exhibit all these signs; learners who have difficulty are highly diverse. They may know one aspect of reading but be unable to connect it with others. For example, many children can recite the alphabet and identify many letters but do not use this information consistently to monitor their reading of continuous text. Some children are very good at remembering stories and "talking like a book" but resist following along word by word and do not notice mismatches with visual information. Others are able to match letters and sounds but utter nonsense syllables when trying to read words.

All reading difficulties have explanations, but it is more productive to think about instruction that will help children overcome them (or at least not get in the way; Marie Clay [1987] has articulated the startling concept that poor instruction can *induce* reading difficulties). Many children come to school with a sound foundation for literacy. They recognize print and understand that it represents a particular kind of language. They understand something about letters and related sounds. This broad understanding of literacy makes them less vulnerable to poor instruction.

Whatever the school program offers them, they can fit it into an already well-organized schema. Others, like David, may not get off to a good start.

David was a lively five-year-old who had always been considered bright by his family. He loved sports and television. When he entered kindergarten, he could write his name but little else. He listened avidly to stories that were read aloud to him by his teacher. During shared reading, he tended to join in only on very predictable phrases, and his attention was everywhere but on the print. He knew few letters and had difficulty sorting words by their first or last sound.

During the year, he was able to recognize a few letters by name, but when he picked up simple beginning texts, he would make up the story from what he remembered from shared reading. He avoided pointing along word by word. During writing sessions, he spent most of his time drawing. He could write his name and one or two words, but he made few attempts to spell words; when he did, the letters only occasionally matched the sounds. When his teacher asked children to predict the first letter of a word or locate words within four or five lines of text, David didn't know where to look. He wasn't considered "ready" for small-group reading instruction. He continued to pretend to read and grew more and more confused.

And so David's class moved beyond him in their ability to attend to and use print. His "masking" techniques kept him from getting the help he needed, either in small-group instruction or through individual tutoring, to understand how print works, learn about letters and sounds, and notice mismatches so he could monitor his own reading. Left to flounder on his own, it took many more months for him to discover how print works. Meanwhile, he was given increasingly challenging material to read that he could not process. Each day he pretended to read, tried to "remember" texts, struggled with words, and perpetuated errors.

Children like David fall into behavior that is often diagnosed as a reading disability. Confusions that could have been untangled through early intervention instead become long-term deficits. A difficulty is not necessarily a disability. By intervening early and using a repertoire of instructional techniques, we can put most children back on track. Some will continue to need extra support, but with information from early intervention, we can do a better job of it.

▶ Why Do Some Children Have Reading Difficulties?

Literacy deficiencies have already been the subject of a great deal of research. The first consideration when children are having learning difficulties is whether or not they have a physical impairment. Certainly, every child should have regular medical checkups, including vision and hearing tests. But many reasons for reading difficulties do not reside within the child:

❑ Child care that includes little exposure to print, stories, or language beyond what is offered on television.

❑ Inattention to language or print when the opportunity is offered, perhaps because other things are more interesting.

❑ Inadequate literacy opportunities or instruction in preschool and kindergarten.

❑ A mismatch between the child's developmental path and the literacy opportunities available at home and in school.

Reading difficulties can be instructionally induced; that is, the classroom curriculum may emphasize one aspect of the reading process over another to an extreme and detrimental degree. In fact, most programs are slightly unbalanced, because it is impossible to teach every single thing children should know about this complex process within the allotted time. Children are expected to "fill in" the missing information, whatever it is, and the amazing thing is that most of them do. Very vulnerable children, however, may not be able to bridge the gap.

▶ What Are Some Areas of Reading Difficulty?

Reading difficulties are revealed when the instruction children receive is not appropriate to their experience. That is, the instruction assumes knowledge that is not there, is very limited, or is confused. Several categories of literacy instruction (Figure 3–1) may or may not be met in a particular classroom program. Children may have difficulty in more than one area, which means a range of instructional approaches will be necessary.

Language Processing

Reading consists of processing written *language*. The most important resource children bring to the task is the language that they have learned in a natural way through interactions with people in their homes and communities. Every language comprises:

❑ A *semantic or meaning system.* Over thousands of years, language was invented, has grown, and has changed so that people can communicate meaningful information. The semantic system of a language contains the cultural concepts, ideas, emotions, and labels that bring meaning to a text.

❑ A *syntactic or language system.* Meaning is conveyed through syntax, which is governed by rules. These rules are a language's *grammar* (as opposed to the "proper" grammar we learned in elementary school)—in other words, the predictable ways speakers of a language string words together, for example, "I have a red coat" instead of "coat I red have a." Knowledge of language syntax helps young readers predict how a sentence will go and monitor whether what they are reading "sounds right." They use their knowledge of how language sounds to anticipate what will come next as they read.

❑ A *phonological or sound system.* Learning a language is learning how to interpret a system of sounds. This is an unconscious process in which children gradually become more aware of the sounds of language. It is enhanced by using rhymes, poetry, and songs. Eventually, children need to be able to recognize the individual sounds of phonemes that make up words in order to learn the alphabetic principle that sounds and letters are related. They need to match the unit of sound they hear with the printed symbols they see in order to be able to read.

❑ A *lexicon.* The words we know make up our vocabularies. The word *vocabulary* really refers to all the words an individual uses in oral language.

Figure 3-1 **Areas of Reading Difficulty**

Area	Definition
1. Language Processing	*The ability to use the systems of language while reading.* • Language has a meaning system, a syntactic system, and a phonological system. • All these systems are governed by rules.
2. Phonological Processing	*The understanding that speech is made up of sounds.* • Phonological awareness is a broad sensitivity to the sounds of the language. • Phonemic awareness is the ability to identify, isolate, and manipulate the individual sounds or phonemes in spoken words.
3. Visual Processing	*The ability to notice and use visual features of letters and words.* • Basic to visual processing is knowledge of how print works—the layout and sequence of letters within words and words within text, as well as the motor behavior required to process these words and letters. • Visual discrimination of letters (noticing distinctive features) is necessary so that letters and sounds can be connected. • Visual discrimination of letters in a left-to-right sequence within words is essential for learning words.
4. Use of Background Knowledge to Construct Meaning	*The ability to bring information that exists in the reader's head to the processing of print.* • Personal knowledge is built through experiences. • Content knowledge is built through learning about the world. • Literary knowledge is built through engagement with texts.
5. Connecting Reading and Writing	*The ability to acquire information in one area and use it to support learning in the other area.* • Reading expands children's knowledge of print and language that they can later use in writing. • Writing helps children use language and attend closely to print, which will help them solve words in reading.
6. Reading Fluency	*The ability to use print and language to convey the meaning of the text in oral reading.* • Fast, automatic processing is required for reading fluency, but it is not enough. • Fluency includes appropriate pausing, phrasing, word stress, and intonation.
7. Attention	*The ability to sustain one's attention while reading and direct that attention to the most helpful and useful information.* • Readers divide their attention so that they can decode print while understanding what it means. • Readers are selective in directing their attention—they are efficient.
8. Memory	*The ability to remember and access information while reading.* • Readers remember information that they need to bring to reading (phonology and its relationship to letters and words and background information). • Readers remember what has been previously read and use it to fuel subsequent reading.
9. Processing Actions/ Cognitive Actions	*The ability to initiate in-the-head activities while reading.* • Readers acquire a large body of information about print—how letters and sounds work together, word structure, print layout. • Readers acquire background experience and knowledge that they can use while reading. • Readers need to use these sources of information as they problem-solve. • The system expands as readers use effective processing actions on increasingly difficult texts.
10. Emotion and Motivation	*The affective factors that have an impact on all areas of reading.* • Readers develop healthy self-esteem through successful problem solving. • Reading successfully motivates children to continue reading.

(The "shades of knowing" a word is discussed later in this book.)

Facility with oral language is very helpful to young children learning to read:

❏ Knowledge of language syntax reduces alternatives and helps children anticipate words in a line of print (which they can check with the visual information).

❏ Knowledge of language syntax gives children a way to check to be sure their reading "sounds right."

❏ Knowledge of meaning gives children a way to check whether their reading "makes sense."

❏ Knowledge of phonology helps children identify sounds and connect them with letters.

❏ A large vocabulary is a big advantage in learning to read; if you know a word, it is easier to decode it.

Children's texts should reflect natural oral language as much as possible, but it must be said that written language is different from oral language in important ways. The grammatical structures, and even the frequently used words, are different. (No one would say that the sentence *"Come on, Jake," said Mom, "it is time to go"* sounds exactly like spoken language.) Also, it is important for early texts to contain many easy high-frequency words along with those that have a predictable enough structure that children can learn decoding skills.

Children who have a limited knowledge of the English language have not internalized the syntactic rules. Those children need many opportunities to hear and *repeat* some of the complex examples of English language that they will be expected to read. As adult speakers of English, we may think sentences such as *I went to the store with my mom* are simple. To someone who is just learning the language, however, it may not be so easy.

Children who have had stories read to them have an advantage. They have internalized many of the structures of oral language and can sometimes "talk like a book" when they pretend to read storybooks (Clay 1997, 78). They not only have a more fully elaborated oral language system but also know something about how reading is supposed to sound.

Many children have not fully developed their oral language systems by the time they are presented with the task of learning to read. A limited vocabulary makes it more difficult to solve words, because the new words they encounter are either unknown or seldom used. Little exposure to elaborated sentences makes reading texts with adjectives, adverbs, and embedded clauses a challenge. They may be very articulate users of oral language but be unfamiliar with the characteristics of book language, making it harder for them to see reading as language.

Many children in our schools may speak a language other than English in their homes. They may have all the advantages described above: every language has semantic, syntactic, and phonological systems. But that knowledge doesn't automatically translate when they are trying to learn to read in English.

All children who experience difficulties in language processing need rich, interactive experiences in preschool and kindergarten. Children are exceptionally fast language learners; their brains are "hard wired" to internalize vocabulary and syntax. At the same time, these learners may need extra support in reading their first texts.

Phonological Processing

Several concepts are related to the ability to develop and use the sound system of language.

PHONOLOGICAL AWARENESS

Phonological awareness is the understanding that speech is made up of sounds. As they learn to talk, speakers of a language internalize meaningful sound patterns and begin to use them. To connect oral with written language, speakers must not only *hear* the sounds but sort them and connect them to patterns they recognize. Encountering and responding to rhymes, songs, and poems, they implicitly recognize and appreciate the sounds of language, and their understanding grows. Knowing when words rhyme helps children make connections and notice word parts. Knowing how to hear syllable breaks will help them take words apart and notice endings and prefixes.

Phonological awareness includes a wide range of units of sounds—words (*cat*), syllables (*el-e-phant*), onsets (the opening consonant in a syllable, like *b, ch, pl*), rimes (the vowel-bearing part of a syllable, like *ar, ain, o, en*), and individual sounds (phonemes, like *c-a-t*). When considering words in isolation, children can hear beginning, middle, and ending sounds and, ultimately, connect them to beginning, middle, and ending sounds of other words.

We may not "hear" all word breaks as we talk, but we know they are there because we understand the language; we have acquired a *lexicon,* or collection of words, and we can isolate and analyze them. Children may be somewhat confused by words that are closely fused in meaning, such as *macaroni and cheese* or *hot dog.* (Many words in our language have been made by combining such word groups—*goodnight, peanut,* and *lighthouse,* for example.)

PHONEMIC AWARENESS

Phonemic awareness is a specific aspect of phonological awareness. The term refers to the ability to identify, isolate, and manipulate *individual* sounds, or phonemes, in spoken words. At some point, children need to know that oral language is made up of discrete sounds (Liberman, Shankweiler, and Liberman 1989). Becoming aware of phonemes is essential for good word recognition (Clay 2006). Children who have difficulty hearing the individual sounds in words are likely to find it hard to connect the sound to a letter— that is, to grasp the *alphabetic principle* (the sounds of oral language can be represented by letters and clusters of letters). Children also need to be able to hear the sounds in a word in order. The child who can identify and isolate the sound of /t/ at the beginning or end of a word and who has some idea of the sequence of sounds within a word will be ready to connect the sound to the letter and then to use that information to solve words and monitor reading of text.

FLUENT PHONOLOGICAL PROCESSING

Children must not only be able to connect words by hearing, identifying, and manipulating sounds in words, but they must also be able to do it rapidly and uncon-

sciously. Most children are aware of the sounds in words and very quickly learn to separate individual sounds from the patterns they hear in spoken words. There may be a brief period during which they give it conscious attention. For some children, however, separating the sounds of the language is very difficult and they need to give it a great deal of attention—to hear and think about it—which can detract from other aspects of reading. For example, to hear sounds they may need to say them again and again, consciously requiring the brain to identify the sounds. Early language experiences can help them become fluent in working with sounds, freeing their attention for other aspects of reading, such as processing the print and the meaning.

Visual Processing

Print is a visual display that the reader must connect to language. The eyes take in images that the brain interprets as words with particular meanings. An individual may *see* lines of print, words, or letters but not know how to connect them with patterns of oral language. Looking at print requires particular kinds of visual processing that are quite different from looking at everything else in the environment (see Figure 3-2).

LETTERS

The ability to recognize and name letters has long been recognized as an important predictor of reading success (Adams 1990; Walsh, Price, and Gillingham 1988). Recognizing letters requires understanding how to look for the very small features that distinguish one letter from another. Many letters are exactly alike except for features such as orientation (*u, n*); size of components like sticks (*d, g*); presence or absence of features such as sticks (*a, o*); presences of crosses (*t, f*) or dots (*i, j*); placement of the letter above or below the line (*q, d*); and left or right orientation (*d, b*). Children who do not know how to look for these small differences may not benefit from instruction on the letters of the alphabet. They may parrot along with the rest of a group when a letter is shown but be at a loss when asked to identify it within a group of letters or within continuous print.

Figure 3-2 **Visual Processing of Print**	
Letters	Children need to know *how to look at print*—that is, distinguish letters by their distinctive features. This is basic to learning the *alphabetic principle* (sounds and letters are related).
Words	Children need to learn *how to learn words,* which requires understanding the alphabetic principle. After learning a core group of high-frequency words, they have ways to learn many more.
Concepts About Print	Children need to learn *how print works,* including the use of space to define words, left-to-right directionality and return sweep, and the use of punctuation and capitalization.
Motor Behavior	Children need to learn ways of *moving left-to-right across print* in order to process it efficiently.

As proficient readers, we instantly process the print all around us without thinking about it. Only when we try to read someone's handwriting or a very difficult font do we even think about the letters. This instant and unconscious processing doesn't take place in young children just learning about letters. Children look first at whatever is meaningful to them and captures their attention. They don't need to master the names of all the letters before they begin to use what they know about print. For example, four-year-old Sam cannot read and can write only his name, but he notices the *S* wherever he sees it. With help, he can find the number for his floor on the elevator control panel. On the computer, he can use the mouse to go to sites and click on different links. He can see the letters (for example, *PBS*) and type them. Print is meaningful to him, and very soon he will be noticing and using letters that are embedded in continuous text.

WORDS

Children learn their first words by remembering how they look, which requires that they recognize let-

ter features. A child who does not know how to distinguish letters and does not understand the alphabetic principle cannot learn more than a few dozen words (Moats 2005). However, as children begin to connect letters and sounds, they can use known words to learn more words. For example, if you know *an*, it is easier to learn *and, can,* and *candy.* Children who can recognize letters easily and identify the sounds they represent are on their way to developing a system for learning words.

Children who find it hard to learn words are probably trying to memorize them rather than integrate cues (sounds, letters, sequence, and meaning) in order to solve them. Each new word is laboriously acquired and takes too much attention. Having only a small repertoire of known words impedes fluent reading and writing, and the meaning of the text is lost because so much attention is being paid to solving words.

CONCEPTS ABOUT PRINT

Children may study the alphabet and learn to hear sounds but still be confused about the way print works. There are rules about the way words are displayed in a text—left to right, top to bottom, left page before right. (These rules are not the same in all languages. They are *arbitrary* conventions.) *First* means at the top and on the left. Words are defined by white spaces. Capital letters are used in particular ways. Punctuation signals meaning. The rules for any language are arbitrary and must be learned through many experiences with text. Effective readers internalize these rules very quickly. They are "at home" with print and apply the rules without effort.

Children who do not understand how print works may be lost in instructional situations. For example, in shared reading the teacher might say, "Let's start with the first word. It begins with *b*." Not knowing where to look, a child may focus on a random area of print and may not benefit from instruction. Some children scan a page of print exactly as if they were looking at a landscape or picture, letting their eyes roam around to anything interesting in no particular order. Having to consciously apply the rules of print can lead the reader to ineffective strategies such as trying to remember the language of a text.

MOTOR BEHAVIOR

Readers and writers engage the eyes and the body in coordinated movements that unconsciously apply the directional rules associated with language. At first, young readers point with a finger to help their eyes move left to right and to read word by word (using the spaces), attending to left-to-right sequence—words in a line and letters within each word. Following the finger slows reading down in order to achieve coordination, much as you might slow down the steps of a dance in order to learn them. Very soon, however, the eyes and brain take over the process, and the motor behavior becomes automatic, freeing the reader to pay more attention to meaning. One of the main reasons the first texts for reading must include very simple and familiar concepts and vocabulary is that children are initially concentrating on the coordination of motor behavior with knowledge of letters, sounds, and words.

If motor behavior is not automatic and readers remain confused about voice-print match, they will try to depend on memorization—either of words or of the language of the text. Persistence in applying these compensatory strategies beyond the first easy texts can interfere with the development of an effective reading process.

FLUENT PROCESSING OF VISUAL INFORMATION

All aspects of visual processing—noticing visual features of letters and words and connecting them to sounds, knowing how to locate information in print, and using left to right directional movement across a line of print and across words—must work together smoothly and automatically so that readers can give their full attention to constructing meaning. Confusion in any area can cause a persistent problem and hold a reader's development back.

Using Background Knowledge to Construct Meaning

Although print must be decoded in order to prompt thought, the most important factors in constructing meaning are not in the text but in the reader's head. The print is *visible*, but readers also use *invisible* information such as their knowledge of phonology, syntax, vocabulary, and meaning. Underlying these invisible systems is the reader's background knowledge (see Figure 3-3):

- ❑ *Knowledge obtained from everyday experiences.* Children come to understand family members, everyday objects and events, pets and other animals, the neighborhood, family problems and crises, feelings and emotions.

- ❑ *Knowledge about the world.* Many children have traveled extensively and seen many environments first hand; others have spent time going to places like petting farms, zoos, and museums that enrich their knowledge. Still others have heard books read to them, gone to movies, or browsed the Internet. In all those circumstances, children learn about places, things, and people beyond their immediate environment.

- ❑ *Knowledge gained from print.* Children who have heard many stories read aloud, listened to storytellers, told stories themselves, or pretended to read texts they have heard someone read have learned more than facts or vocabulary. They learn how texts are organized—how they begin,

Figure 3-3 Using Background Knowledge to Construct Meaning While Reading

Personal Knowledge	Understanding built through everyday experiences.
Content Knowledge	Understanding about the world gleaned through direct experiences as well as reading and listening.
Literary Knowledge	Understanding, including the general characteristics of particular kinds of texts, built by reading texts.

how a series of events unfolds, and how they end. They internalize the syntax of written language and expand their vocabulary. They can connect one text with another. All of this information serves as a foundation for reading.

Every child comes to school with background knowledge acquired in the home and the community. Sometimes those cultural experiences don't correspond with the predominant culture of the school, and learners, unable to use what they know with any success, become confused. Skillful teachers try to make sure a child's home culture is visible at school and at the same time expand the knowledge and experiential base of all learners.

Of course, a rich preschool experience is no guarantee that children will learn to read. Many children with strong language foundations have difficulty using the visual information of print. Children with a strong sense of language syntax can "override" the words printed on the page. But in general, children who haven't attended preschool and have little knowledge of stories or story reading may find it more difficult to learn to read because they:

- ❑ Find it hard to predict while reading.
- ❑ Tend to approach texts in isolation, almost as a list of words.
- ❑ Lack the concepts or the labels for concepts (vocabulary).
- ❑ Find it hard to relate their own lives to what they see and read in books.
- ❑ Are unfamiliar with the syntax of written language.
- ❑ Find it hard to use information from pictures because they cannot interpret them or do not recognize the objects or actions depicted.

Connecting Reading and Writing

Reading and writing are different but complementary systems. Through reading, children have many opportunities to process words visually and learn the syntax of written language. Reading helps them understand the constraints of written language as opposed to oral language—you must compose a sentence that you can write and you need to remember it as you write it.

Writing supports reading by slowing down the process so that children can closely attend to the visual details. Practicing efficient movements to make letters helps children learn their distinctive features. Saying words slowly to separate the sounds they contain helps them connect sounds to letters. Writing high-frequency words quickly helps them overlearn them so they can read faster. Using punctuation in writing makes it easier to notice and use it when reading print.

Readers who see these two activities as completely separate, with no connection, will have fewer resources in both. Active teaching can remind children to use what they know about one to assist them in the other.

Fluent Processing

There is a distinction between the broader category of *fast processing* and what we usually refer to as *fluent, phrased reading.*

FAST PROCESSING

Fast processing refers to just about everything children do in reading and the related area of writing. It means quick, efficient, coordinated, integrated "brainwork." It involves language, motor behavior, and visual and phonological processing. Proficient, efficient, and fluent reading and writing depend on fast, fluent, and automatic processing on many levels, including the ability to:

- ❑ Easily recognize the distinctive features of letters.
- ❑ Quickly recognize letters within words.
- ❑ Recognize and locate words with the eyes.
- ❑ Recognize groups of words that go together.
- ❑ Move left to right across a line of print and across words, matching voice to print without the support of a pointing finger.
- ❑ Notice and use punctuation to guide meaning.
- ❑ Write letters and words efficiently.

A child may read or write (or copy) accurately but do so very slowly and laboriously. In that case, meaning will inevitably be lost and slow reading may become habitual. Daily reading of too-hard texts and a struggle for accuracy will compound the problem.

FLUENT, PHRASED READING

Fast processing is required in order to read fluently, but much more is involved (see Figure 3-4). Children must realize that reading involves *language*, with its deeper meaning, grammatical structure (or syntax), and predictable rules. In fluent, phrased oral reading, children reflect the meaning of the text by:

- ❑ Pausing appropriately as cued by punctuation.
- ❑ Phrasing groups of words to reflect the meaning of the text.
- ❑ Appropriately varying the stress on words within sentences.
- ❑ Varying their intonation to reflect meaning.
- ❑ Proceeding at a rate appropriate for communicating the meaning of the text (not too fast or too slow).

Figure 3-4 **Characteristics of Fluent Reading**	
Pausing	Pausing appropriately as cued by the punctuation.
Phrases	Grouping words to reflect the meaning of the text, marking phrases with very brief pauses.
Stress	Stressing the appropriate words within sentences to convey meaning.
Intonation	Using rising and falling tones, as well as louder and quieter tones, to reflect the meaning of the text.
Rate	Reading in a way that helps the listener understand the text—not too fast and not too slow.
Integration	Orchestrating all aspects of processing in a smoothly operating system.

All of these elements work together when a reader is processing a text fluently. We can observe evidence of their use when children read aloud to us, and we can assume that they are monitoring their reading and achieving some level of fluency when reading silently. The first years of school are paramount in establishing reading fluency.

Attention

Proficient readers pay attention to sources of information that are helpful in processing a text: the visual information in print and its connection to phonological elements, the language systems they access as they process print, and the concepts and ideas evoked by the text. The tricky part is that readers must divide their attention among all these information sources simultaneously. Moreover, they must selectively attend to just the right information and often do so in a particular order (Clay 2001).

Many children find it hard to know what to pay attention to. They may overattend to one aspect of reading (the letters, for example) and neglect others. Other children may expend so much energy and attention retrieving information that they have little left for comprehending, making the processing highly inefficient.

One reason children may find it hard to pay attention is that the task is too hard: their processing systems are overloaded. Working constantly on hard texts gives readers very little experience in learning to direct their attention strategically.

Memory

Proficient readers use memory in strategic ways. For example, they remember:

- ❑ Specific words and word parts.
- ❑ Letter/sound relationships and how they work in words.
- ❑ The meaning of words.
- ❑ The meaning of certain objects, events, and concepts.
- ❑ What has been read before in order to predict what might come next.

Children who don't know how to look at print may also find it hard to remember letters and words—how they look or what they mean. They haven't yet learned what is important to attend to. New learning builds on what is already known. The ability to retrieve known information depends on how the learner has organized it and how well it was learned in the first place. For example, a group of low-achieving first- and second-grade readers were drilled weekly on five new words. Each Friday, they could read those words perfectly from the word cards. However, the words were not conceptualized, and there was no opportunity to read or write them within continuous text. Consequently, when the children encountered those words within texts, they could read very few of them.

Memory, too, is affected when readers attempt to process texts that are too difficult. Again, the system is overloaded. Think how often you have to consult, read, and reread directions to complete a complex task as opposed to how you perform everyday tasks! Children who find it hard to remember may need special and specific help, perhaps even overlearning some techniques so that they become automatic.

Processing Actions/Cognitive Actions

Proficient readers are efficient. They are able to access and apply all the information they need in a smoothly orchestrated way. If they encounter problems in a text, they use information in the most efficient way possible. They:

- ❑ Search for and use multiple sources of information while maintaining a sense of the meaning of the text.
- ❑ Monitor their reading using many different kinds of information to check on accuracy or understanding.
- ❑ Work on and correct errors to assure that the meaning, language, and print fit together.

Proficient reading changes over time as readers engage with more and more challenging texts. In order to expand their processing systems, children need to engage with texts that are slightly more challenging than those they can read accurately on their own. When a text offers just the right amount of problem-solving opportunity, the reader can learn how to problem-solve better. Problem solving new texts with teacher support strengthens literacy and helps readers use all aspects of their processing systems smoothly, at the same time.

Clay (2001) uses the term *working systems* to describe the in-the-head strategic actions that readers assemble and mobilize to solve problems while they are processing texts. Holmes (1960, cited by Clay 2001) defines *working systems* as a dynamic set of sub-abilities mobilized in order to solve a particular problem. Using these sub-abilities we simultaneously:

- ❑ Scan and recognize features of letters.
- ❑ Look for letter sequences that form words or parts of words.
- ❑ Use our knowledge of syntax to determine meaning.
- ❑ Use our knowledge of text structure to search for and use information.
- ❑ Combine our background knowledge with information from the text.
- ❑ Bring out emotions and responses that make characters, events, or information meaningful.

All readers need the opportunity to process appropriate-level texts with the expert help of a teacher who works alongside, encouraging and prompting. Often, low-achieving readers have the *least* number of opportunities to read real books. Their time is spent being drilled in isolated actions. There is no doubt that they do need much practice, but they also must have time to read. We can take a lesson from Reading Recovery (Clay 2006); in those tutoring sessions, young readers spend most of their time reading and writing continuous text and becoming highly proficient readers.

Emotion and Motivation

We have never met a kindergartner who doesn't want to learn to read and write. Even those who may not have thought much about it soon get the "bug." They come to school with the expectation that they will learn to read and write as easily as they have learned how to do other things. If they find learning hard, emotional responses are set up and motivation is seriously undermined.

Children's home experiences are beyond our control; some are the victims of neglect or tragedy. These emotional factors may interfere with learning, but most young children respond to a predictable, safe school environment, even perceiving it as a haven. That sense of safety has to encompass the critical task of the first three grades—learning how to read at about the same rate as most of their peers. Daily struggles will quickly result in avoidance behavior. Our job is to assure daily success at school, the only aspect of the child's environment we control.

▶ A Literacy Processing System

In proficient reading, all systems of strategic actions (see Figure 2-1) work together in a smoothly orchestrated process. Let's review those strategic activities, along with ways some readers may run into trouble:

❑ *Solving words.* Phonological information, visual perception, language syntax, vocabulary, memory, and background experience all affect the process of solving words. Children who have weaknesses in these areas may have to expend too much of their attention trying to solve words, use inefficient techniques, or develop rigid and limited ways of solving words. Often they have difficulty linking sound to letter and letter to sound in a coordinated process.

❑ *Monitoring and correcting.* Readers use their knowledge of sounds and letters, language syntax, and meaning (related to background experience and language) to check on and monitor their reading, making sure that it makes sense, sounds right, and looks right. Proficient readers listen to themselves so they can notice mismatches and are aware when they do not understand what they are reading. When their reading does not sound like language, or when the letters don't look right, they notice the dissonance and work to self-correct. Younger readers self-correct overtly. We can see them stop; reread a sentence, phrase, or word; and try again. This behavior changes over time so

that more proficient readers do it mentally. Some readers either do not have enough knowledge to self-monitor and self-correct, or they do not know how to apply their knowledge in this way. They may simply "read on," not knowing they do not understand or that it doesn't sound right or look right; they are just reading words.

❑ *Searching for and using information.* Readers need quick and ready access to the visual information in print; the related phonological information; the language structures; and the labels, concepts, and ideas that the print conveys. Readers also need to search the illustrations and graphics for information that will help them solve words or comprehend the overall meaning. Readers who do not have easy access to information; have gaps in their knowledge base; or do not know how to search the print, language, or meaning may flounder. Further, they need to be able to use meaning, language, and print together as they read. Readers who struggle often focus on one source of information at a time.

❑ *Summarizing.* Readers use organized ways to store and remember information so that they can access it during and after reading. To be able to mentally construct a summary, readers must remember what has been read. This is affected by the attention paid while reading and their understanding of the text in the first place. If readers cannot select and attend to the most important information, and carry it forward, they will have difficulty understanding the text.

❑ *Maintaining fluency.* Strong readers not only use many sources of information but also engage in all processes rapidly, without much effort. They maintain fluency by solving words rapidly (recognizing most immediately) and using their knowledge of language syntax to "feed forward," thinking all the time about meaning. They read in phrase units, stress the appropriate words, and use intonation and punctuation to interpret the meaning of the text. When readers are slow to access any kind of information, fluency is undermined.

❑ *Adjusting.* Proficient readers are flexible; they have many ways of working on text and are ready to vary their problem-solving actions as they monitor their reading. Readers who have difficulty often become very rigid in their approach. They try the same action over and over, losing hope that they will achieve results, and finally become dependent on the teacher.

❑ *Predicting.* Proficient readers can adjust their reading to the type of text they are processing. Proficient readers use their background, text, and language knowledge to predict what will happen in sentences, paragraphs, and the complete text. They are always thinking in advance of the print they are reading. Some readers may have difficulty mustering the resources they need to make predictions while reading. They focus on the immediate meaning (the word or sentence) without anticipating what will follow.

❑ *Making connections.* Readers are always making connections between what they read and their personal experiences, their content knowledge, and the other texts they have read or heard. The more gaps there are in background knowledge and experiences, or the greater the mismatch between those and the texts they read in school, the harder it will be to use their funds of knowledge in new texts they read.

❑ *Synthesizing.* Readers acquire new information as they read and change their understanding in response. When readers have to give too much attention to word solving or have difficulty using language or content experiences, all their efforts must be directed simply toward reading the text accurately. It will be very difficult, if not impossible, for these readers to learn new concepts and ideas at the same time. Readers may not even identify new information, let alone think about how to use it.

❑ *Inferring.* Inferring requires thinking beyond the text while reading it, a process that is possible when most of the actions are performed with ease and automaticity. Then the reader is able to speculate on how characters feel or what motivates them. Readers who must struggle simply to read the text accurately have difficulty thinking beyond the text. Not knowing how to pick out the important information, they cannot put it together as a basis for inference.

❑ *Analyzing.* Looking analytically at a text requires processing it in the fullest possible way—reading

with accuracy and fluency and understanding what is being said. The analytic reader is able to notice the way the text is crafted. A reader who cannot process a text will find it very hard to notice wonderful language that the writer has used or get "above the text" to understand the way it is organized.

❑ *Critiquing.* Critical thinking implies not only effective processing and deep understanding but also simultaneously forming one's own opinions about the text. As with analytic thinking, full and fluent processing is essential. Readers who struggle are often not able to attend to personal critique.

It may seem that the last six systems of strategic actions (predicting, making connections, synthesizing, inferring, analyzing, and critiquing) are so far beyond beginning readers, especially children who find literacy difficult, that we shouldn't be concerned with them; but nothing could be farther from the truth. It is essential that even beginning readers process texts smoothly enough to be able to think about the ideas. A beginning reader can predict, at a very simple level, what is going to happen and make connections to their own lives and to other books they know. When they are working proficiently, beginning readers can be surprised by something new in pictures or text, empathize with characters, notice what the writer or illustrator has done to make a text funny or interesting, and form opinions about what they read.

Unless all those opportunities to think beyond and about the text are always available, readers develop a misleading perception of reading. Reading disability and incomprehension may be instructionally induced. If any strategic action is emphasized to the detriment of others, you will not be helping readers develop full proficiency.

▶ Prevention and Intervention

Children who have strong control of the ten areas of learning that contribute to reading proficiency (Figure 3-1) are not likely to have difficulty learning to read. Shouldn't our first approach, then, be to design classroom programs that provide rich and effective instruction in each of these ten areas?

Let's think about our goals for all children. We want to engage them in using oral language to build their background knowledge of content and texts so that they have more to bring to reading. We want to help them connect reading and writing, so that they develop competence in both and so that one area of learning can inform the other. Certainly we want to teach children, as a specific part of reading instruction, to hear sounds in words, distinguish letters, and learn words. Then we want to take learning further by helping them apply their knowledge to the reading of continuous texts so that they develop systems of strategic actions that will become more sophisticated over time. Finally, we want to do everything we can to ensure that children are successful learners by introducing them to interesting texts that they can read with our support. This kind of success will support memory, motivate them to read more, and help them avoid emotional blocks.

A good classroom literacy curriculum will go a long way toward preventing reading difficulties. When supplementary instruction is needed, it should take place in the classroom whenever possible and be directed toward the specific needs of small groups and individuals. The goal of intervention is to help children use their strengths to learn what they need to know next to benefit fully from classroom instruction. A symbiotic relationship between each layer of instruction ensures the success of our most vulnerable children.

▶ Suggestions for Professional Development

ANALYZING READING DIFFICULTIES

1. With a group of colleagues, look at recent running records or Reading Records in conjunction with the accompanying book from a benchmark assessment.
2. Select five instructional-level examples from proficient, high-level readers and five from readers who struggle.
3. Make a chart of what you notice about each proficient reader's actions.
    - ❑ What do you notice about the accurate reading?
    - ❑ What do you notice about the phrasing and fluency?
    - ❑ What do you notice about the kinds of information used?
    - ❑ What does the reader do when she encounters difficulty? After an incorrect attempt?
    - ❑ What to you notice about the reader's ability to self-correct?
4. Repeat the process for the five readers who struggle.
5. Summarize what you have learned by creating a list of insights into what readers who struggle need to learn how to do.
6. Compare your list with the areas of reading difficulty listed in Figure 3-1. Most will fit into one of the ten categories.

Reading Behavior: What Does it Tell Us?

THE ABILITY TO OBSERVE, ANALYZE, AND INTERPRET reading behavior is foundational to effective teaching. It is the first step in helping struggling readers. In this chapter we describe several different kinds of assessment that, used in combination, will inform instructional decisions. We begin with finding out what level students can read with support to determine a starting place for reading instruction. We then move to how students read—the behaviors and understandings that provide evidence of strategic activities. This information is essential to inform daily planning for instruction that begins with the child's strengths and needs.

It is a mistake to talk about *the* struggling reader, because students who experience difficulty in learning are an even more diverse group than those who do not. Struggling readers require either individual or small-group intervention and instruction that is tailored to them. Educators often try to solve the problem by grouping students into whole classes of "good" and "poor" readers. On the surface, this seems logical—it makes it easier for teachers to pitch their instruction to as many students as possible. But anyone who has ever been in such classrooms quickly finds a range of reading abilities in these seemingly homogeneous environments. In many classrooms,

students are still being asked to read texts that are too hard for them and therefore cannot develop and extend their reading powers.

A few instructional contexts *are* appropriate for an entire class (interactive read-aloud and reading mini-lessons, for example), and they can contribute to overall reading competence; but intensive teaching for systems of strategic actions in small groups is essential for most readers. Furthermore, readers who struggle often need additional intensive small-group teaching; some need individual teaching. To make the most of teaching small groups and individuals, observe each student carefully and analyze what this behavior tells you.

Gathering data on which to base your instruction requires systematic benchmark assessment, targeted diagnostic assessments, and ongoing systematic observation of reading behavior over time. These kinds of assessments, in combination, will help you make sound instructional decisions.

To determine a starting place for daily reading instruction, first identify the level of text students can read with appropriate accuracy, understanding, and fluency. You can then move on to analyze behaviors that provide evidence of whether and how well they are able to use strategic actions.

▶ Using Systematic Benchmark Assessment

A *benchmark* is a standard against which to measure something. The benchmark is the level of text a reader can process effectively—that is, with high accuracy *and* comprehension.

We have developed a valid and reliable text gradient, moving from the easiest text level, A, through the most challenging level, Z (Figure 4-1). As you move up the gradient, the texts make increasing demands on readers. As students stretch their abilities to meet those demands, they expand their processing systems. A reader who is processing effectively at Level G, for example, demonstrates the ability to process sentences containing nouns, verbs, adjectives, adverbs, and prepositions; read phrases and dialogue; and understand simple, straightforward plots and characters.

You can use systematic benchmark assessment of your class to identify the readers who need intervention. The levels in the *Fountas and Pinnell Benchmark Assessment System* (Heinemann, 2011 2008) correlate directly with the text levels in our text gradient. If you do not have access to our Benchmark Assessment System, see the chart provided in Figure 4-2, that shows the reading levels of a class of children at the beginning of a school year. Each X on the scatter graph represents one student and the instructional level (from A to K) of text that she can read—that is, with 90–94% (95–97% at Level L and beyond) accuracy

and satisfactory comprehension. The horizontal shaded area represents the district's reading-level expectations; ideally, all readers should be within or above that range. Those who fall below the range are in jeopardy. They will need intervention to raise their

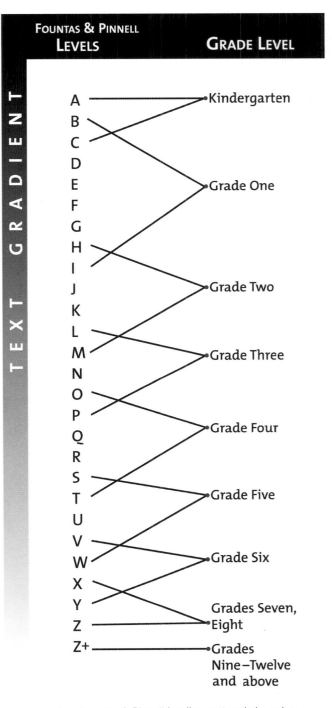

FIGURE 4-1 The Fountas & Pinnell leveling system is based on a gradient of text difficulty.

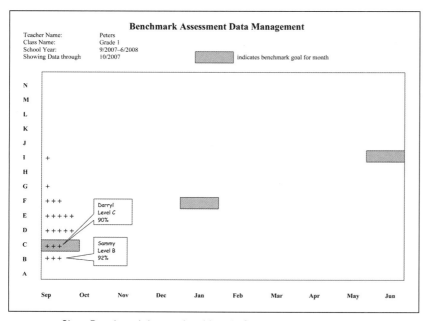

Figure 4-2 Class Benchmark Instructional Levels Scatter Plot *(Fountas and Pinnell Benchmark Assessment System I)*

competence to a level that will allow them to fully benefit from classroom instruction.

For practical reasons, most classroom instruction is pitched toward the average readers in a class—to what most of the readers need. Effective teachers then make adjustments to challenge advanced readers and help readers who struggle. Small-group reading instruction is an essential part of the classroom program, and often teachers also find a little time to work individually with some.

A child like Sammy (Level B), however, probably needs more help. His reading ability is well below that of the others in the class. Even if he makes progress, he will still be behind. Sammy needs intervention that will help him make *greater* progress than the rest of the students. Because his teacher recognizes this, he is selected to receive intervention at the beginning of the year.

Another student to keep an eye on is Darrell (Level C). Because he is reading close to average level, he doesn't qualify for intervention at the beginning of the

year. However, his teacher will need to watch his behavior as a reader for evidence that he has the ability to actively search for and use information, use what he knows to get to what he does not know, notice the parts of words in order to solve them, and keep meaning in mind while processing print. These behaviors (among others) will help Darrell learn more every time he reads texts (provided the texts are well matched to his present ability).

Now let's look at Sammy's spring assessment (see Figure 4-3). His reading scores show that his learning has accelerated. With a combination of good classroom teaching and strong intervention beginning the third week of school, Sammy has been able to catch up with his peers. Even after he stopped receiving the extra support, he continued to make steady progress and finished the year well within average performance range.

On the other hand, Darrell was not able to keep up with the class (see Figure 4-4). Classroom instruction alone was not providing enough support to keep him

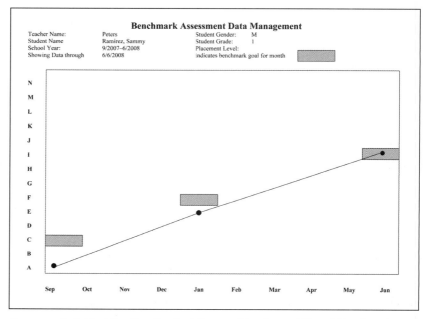

Figure 4-3 Individual Reading Graph of Sammy *(Fountas and Pinnell Benchmark Assessment System I Data Management Tool)*

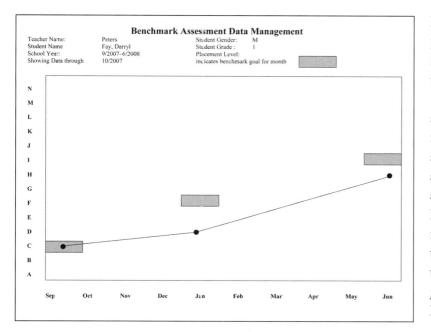

Figure 4-4 Individual Progress Graph for Darrell *(Fountas and Pinnell Benchmark Assessment System I)*

from falling further behind. In February, his teacher placed him in a small group receiving extra instruction in developing independent reading strategies. With the extra help, Darrell scored within the average range at the end of the year.

In spite of their excellent progress in grade 1, both Sammy and Darrell remain vulnerable. They should continue to grow as readers without additional support, but if they miss school for significant amounts of time, encounter uneven instruction, experience life changes, or change schools, their progress could slow. They will need to be closely monitored using both benchmark assessment and ongoing systematic observation.

Systematic assessment tells you not only what children can read with understanding and fluency without teacher support (their independent reading level) but also their instructional level and hard

levels (see Figure 4-5). Accuracy and comprehension are the two important variables in determining the independent, instructional, and hard reading levels.

High accuracy and good comprehension are essential criteria for *independent* reading, because readers receive very little support from you. The *instructional* level is a little more challenging, which is appropriate because readers will have your support. By providing strong instruction, you help readers effectively process more challenging texts and enable them to expand their systems of strategies. (See *www.fountasand pinnellbenchmarkassessmentsystem.com* for Level Expectations Charts.)

▶ Analyzing Reading Behaviors

The accuracy rate is a good (but not the only) indicator of the reader's ability to process text effectively. In general, children reading at Levels A–K

Figure 4-5 Fountas & Pinnell Benchmark Criteria

Fountas & Pinnell Benchmark Assessment Criteria for Levels A–K

Accuracy	Comprehension			
	Excellent 6–7	Satisfactory 5	Limited 4	Unsatisfactory 0–3
95 – 100%	Independent	Independent	Instructional	Hard
90 – 94%	Instructional	Instructional	Instructional	Hard
Below 90%	Hard	Hard	Hard	Hard

Fountas & Pinnell Benchmark Assessment Criteria for Levels L–Z

Accuracy	Comprehension			
	Excellent 9–10	Satisfactory 7–8	Limited 5–6	Unsatisfactory 0–4
98 – 100%	Independent	Independent	Instructional	Hard
95 – 97%	Instructional	Instructional	Hard	Hard
Below 95%	Hard	Hard	Hard	Hard

should have an accuracy rate of 90 percent or higher so that they can solve problems against a backdrop of accurate reading.

But further analysis is needed to inform your teaching. You can gather a great deal of qualitative information by looking carefully at the error and self-correction behavior of your readers to see what sources of information they are attending to and neglecting as well as the strategic activities they control. Self-corrections indicate that:

❑ The reader notices mismatches (the error doesn't look right, sound right, or make sense).

❑ The reader is able to use different kinds of information (letter-sound correspondence and meaning, for example).

❑ The reader is checking one source of information against another.

❑ The reader is able to persevere in making the reading look right, sound right, and make sense.

Self-corrections aren't either good or bad. Your evaluation of them depends on the context and what your analysis tells you about the reader. But in general, a high self-correction rate is a good sign in the early reader.

▶ Analyzing Ben's Reading Behaviors

Figure 4-6 is a record of Ben's reading of *Playing* in the spring of kindergarten. Here we see the beginning of an effective reading process. He read across the print from left to right and returned to the left margin to read the next line. He showed that he already knew a few high-frequency words, and he pointed carefully under each word and read one spoken word for each printed word. He checked himself and corrected some of his errors. He reread to search for more information.

Ben's accuracy rate on this reading was high—96 percent; he had only a few problems to solve and he could pay attention to meaning. His self-correction rate was 1 to 2: he made a total of six errors but corrected four of them.

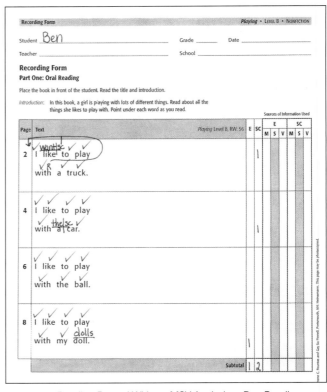

Figure 4-6 Reading Record Without MSV Analysis—Ben Reading *Playing (Fountas and Pinnell Benchmark Assessment System 1),* p. 1

Figure 4-6 Ben's Reading Record, p. 2

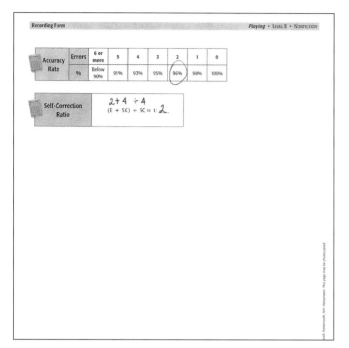

Figure 4-6 Ben's Reading Record, p. 3

He was not yet fluent, because he was just gaining control of early reading behaviors, but he had no trouble comprehending this simple nonfiction text. When his teacher talked with him about the reading afterward, he was able to remember several important facts from the text, had insights into the probable attitudes of the girl, and predicted that her very favorite toys might be dolls (which tells us something about his cultural understanding).

What Do Errors Tell About Readers' Use of Sources of Information?

Reading is more than saying a series of words. It involves reading words in phrases, phrases in sentences, and sentences that communicate a bigger message. As they mature, readers use various sources of information in a text to work their way through its challenges. Good readers decide which sources of information to attend to, and they work to integrate all this data. Sources of information include:

- ❑ *Meaning information*—the main idea or message of the story. Meaning is also conveyed through the pictures.

- ❑ *Structural information*—syntax of the language used in the text, whether familiar, natural, literary, or some combination.

- ❑ *Visual/phonological information*—the print representing the sounds of the language; that is, the letters, clusters, words, spaces, and punctuation used.

Let's analyze Ben's errors using the three columns—M (meaning), S (structural), or V (visual) information—following the E (error) column in Figure 4-7:

- ❑ Ask: does the error make sense in terms of the meaning or the message of the story? (Remember that meaning is also conveyed through the pictures.) If it does, circle the *M* (or just put a check mark in the column).

- ❑ Ask: is the error influenced by the structure (syntax) of the sentence *up to and including* the error? (Another way to ask this question is: "Does the error sound right in English?") If so, circle the *S*.

- ❑ Ask: does the error resemble the word in the text? (Look not only at the beginning of the word but also at the middle and end.) If so, circle the *V*.

The goal is to hypothesize what led Ben to substitute one word for another. On page 2 he read *I want* for *I like*, which made sense and fit the structure of the sentence. Possibly he already read a book that used the *I want* pattern; maybe he just assumed the girl in the picture was saying *I want*. In any case, Ben produced an acceptable English phrase. So his teacher circled both *M* and *S*. On page 4, Ben read *the* for *a*, again an acceptable English sentence that did not change the meaning. The teacher circled *M* and *S*. On page 8, Ben read *dolls* for *doll*, an error that fit the language structure and the visual information, so the teacher circled *S* and *V*. It's evident that Ben is using meaning, because he read the word *dolls*; however, there is clearly only one doll in the picture, so the teacher did not circle *M*.

Ben's other errors (*truck* for *train*, *airplane* for *plane*, and *big* for *boat*) all showed that he was attending to language structure and visual information. In

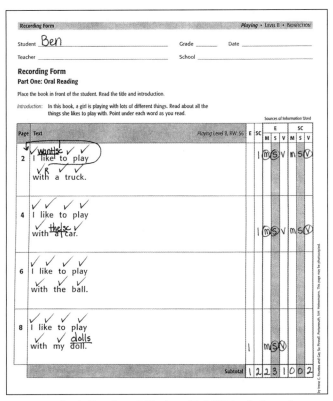

Figure 4–7 Ben's Reading of *Playing* with MSV Analysis, p. 1

Figure 4–7 Ben's Reading Record, p. 3

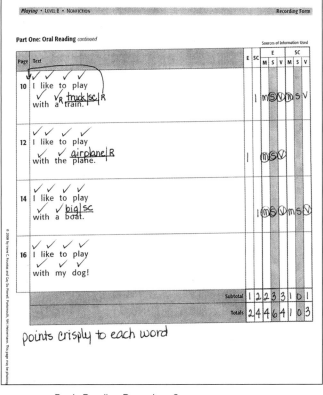

Figure 4–7 Ben's Reading Record, p. 2

the case of *airplane* for *plane*, he was also attending to meaning, and his repetition of this word may indicate that he noticed something was wrong but didn't try to work it out. We see a pattern in Ben's reading: he was using all sources of information, always more than one at a time. And ultimately four of his initial errors were not errors.

What Do Self-Corrections Tell About Readers' Use of Information?

As readers learn more about reading, they become aware that they need to match their ideas with the printed information in the book, and they begin to notice mismatches and fix them—correct their reading.

Let's analyze Ben's self-correction behavior. What made him go back and fix an error? Did he use additional M, S, or V information? Choose the *one* thing that probably sent him back to investigate further and circle the appropriate letter. (Here you are not concerned with whether the error "fits" with meaning, language structure, or visual information. Rather, you are hypothesizing about the precise information that sends readers back to correct themselves.)

In his reading of *Playing,* Ben made six errors and corrected four of them. He read *want* for *like* on page 2, but after reading the word *with* he went back to the beginning of the sentence and reread it, this time correctly. His teacher hypothesized that Ben processed the visual information, noticed the mismatch, and went back to correct it. Therefore she circled the *V.* You can see the completed analyses in Figure 4-7.

Now let's look at Ben's Reading Record for *The Loose Tooth,* Level E (see Figure 4-8). Ben read the text without pointing, so his eyes have taken over the process: early behaviors such as left-to-right directionality and voice-print match have been internalized and are largely automatic. Ben also demonstrated the ability to read in phrases, although he still needed more work on fluency.

He read the text with 94 percent accuracy, indicating that E is probably a good instructional level for him. There are still problems to solve, but he can read with enough accuracy that he does not become frustrated. The self-correction ratio of 1:2 indicates that he was also closely monitoring or checking on his reading: for every two errors, he corrected one. His errors indicate he can use all sources of information. For example, on page 1, he read *has* for *had,* using the present tense; this tense error was repeated in his substitution of *play* for *played,* which he corrected. Ben was using several sources of information at the same time. Several times he substituted two words for a contraction (*do not* for *didn't*), but he corrected this error on page 9. As you look at Ben's errors and his teacher's analysis of sources of information used, you can see a pattern of competence. This young reader is well on his way to developing an efficient processing system, and the change in just a few weeks is enormous.

As you code Reading Records, look for patterns in readers' ways of responding. Their attempts at words are partially correct, not simply wrong. As patterns emerge, you will begin to see possible next teaching steps. You will also learn when it is appropriate to intervene to help readers who struggle.

▶ Looking for Indicators of Confusion

You cannot see into children's minds, but their behaviors can guide your teaching decisions. This is especially true for beginning readers and that's a good thing, because it can inform your intervention efforts. Intervention is appropriate when analysis indicates that the process is going wrong.

Look at Sammy's Reading Record for *Playing* (Level B) at the beginning of grade 1 (Figure 4-9). Use the Guide for Observing and Noting Reading Behaviors (Appendix B) to analyze his strategic activity on the left side of the record. Sammy previously read a Level A text at almost 100 percent accuracy, but this text appears to be too hard for him. Nevertheless, he caught the gist of the text: he named some of the things in the book that the girl likes to play with.

Sammy did well at matching voice to print and moved from left to right across the page, although occasionally his finger slid along the words. On page 8, Sammy omitted the word *doll* and, running out of words, went back and reread the page correctly, evidence that he was using voice-print match to monitor his reading. However, he didn't do this consistently (for example, he read *I look at a boat* for *I like to play with a boat* on page 14 and went on). His strength is his grasp of language structure. This sentence made sense and sounded right to him. It also matched the picture. But he was not effectively using visual information along with the meaning and structure.

▶ Analyzing Reading Records: Examples

To help you get a feel for using Reading Records, brief analyses of six reading samples are presented starting on page 55. The first five are based on readings of a simple Level B text, *My Little Dog* (see the sample spread in Figure 4-10).

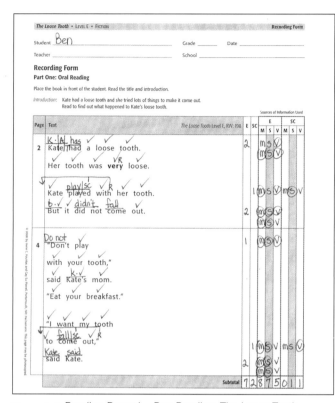

Figure 4–8 Reading Record—Ben Reading *The Loose Tooth,* *(Fountas and Pinnell Benchmark Assessment System 1),* p. 1

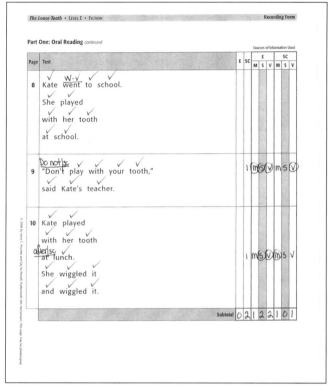

Figure 4–8 Ben's Reading Record, p. 3

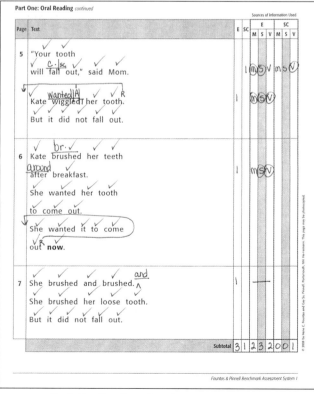

Figure 4–8 Ben's Reading Record, p. 2

Figure 4–8 Ben's Reading Record, p. 4

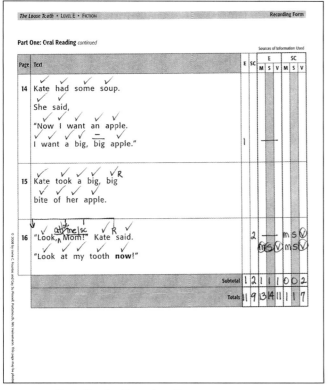

Figure 4–8 Ben's Reading Record, p. 5

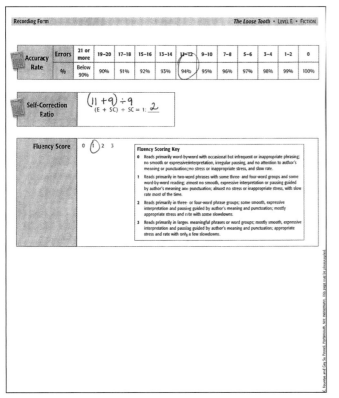

Figure 4–8 Ben's Reading Record, p. 6

Figure 4–9 Sammy's Reading of *Playing*, p. 1

Figure 4–9 Sammy's Reading Record, p. 2

He likes
to jump with me.

My little dog likes me!

My little dog likes
to read with me.

Figure 4-10 Page Spreads from *My Little Dog* from *Fountas and Pinnell Benchmark Assessment System 1* (Heinemann 2008)

Kara

As Kara read, she slid her finger under the words but did not point precisely, so she was not able to use voice-print match to monitor her reading. She constructed meaning by looking at the pictures and produced grammatically meaningful sentences but didn't attend to the print. She mostly didn't use visual information to notice mismatches. Because she didn't notice features of letters and words, she was not able to use letter/sound relationships to solve words. She understood the gist of this simple story, but she will not be able to move to more advanced levels of text using such primitive strategies. Without careful teaching to help her notice print, use letters and sounds, and monitor her reading, Kara will become more and more confused.

Clive

Clive pointed to the text when reading and matched voice to print. He read *He, likes, to, dog, me* accurately. When he substituted his own words for words in the story, he showed little awareness of the visual features of the words but more understanding of the language structure and meaning of the story. Although meaning and language structure are important understandings in learning to read, without careful attention to the visual detail of print, he will not be able to assemble an effective reading processing system.

Rachel

Rachel matched voice to print and attempted every word except *likes,* which she skipped. She noticed the first letter of each word but was not able to use letter-sound information in combination with language and meaning. She didn't repeat lines in order to check other sources of information. Four times, she appealed to her teacher and was told the word. Her behavior resulted in highly dependent reading. Her perception may have been that if she didn't know the word, she should not even try to solve it by herself.

Steven

Steven exhibited an interesting technique often seen in young children who are having difficulty learning to read (and almost always taught to them by a well-meaning adult): he skipped every word he didn't immediately recognize. As a result, his reading didn't make sense or sound like language; even so, he didn't look for other sources of information. If he persists in this kind of behavior, he will not develop the word-solving or monitoring strategies he needs.

Howard

Howard matched voice to print and attempted to solve every word after the first word, *He,* which he appealed. (The first word in a sentence is always quite difficult for struggling readers, because there is often no context, the reader must rely solely on letter-sound information.) His substitutions (*jog/jump, loves/likes,* and *rest/read*) indicate that he was using meaning and syntax. He probably understood this simple text, even though he didn't monitor his reading using *precise* visual information. Three of his substitutions made sense and also started with the same letter as the word in the text, so meaning was not lost. However, it's also apparent that Howard didn't look beyond the first letter. *Two errors,* substituting *behind/with* and *near/with,* indicates that Howard ignored visual information altogether. He made *seven errors* in *nineteen* words of text. If he continues to approach text in this way, he will not be able to construct an accurate meaning of the text.

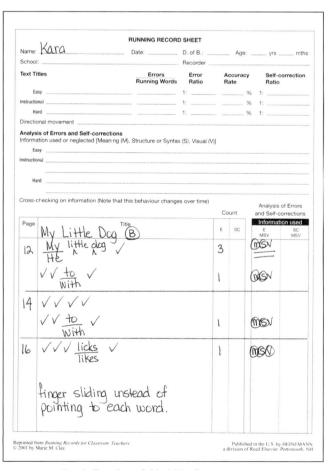

Figure 4–11 Kara's Reading of *My Little Dog*

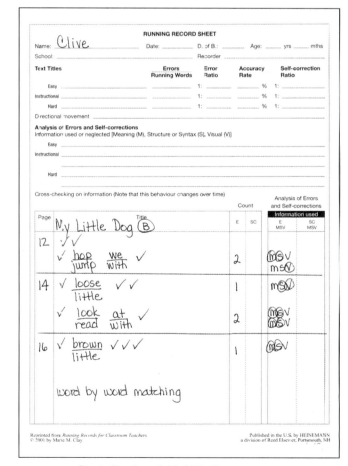

Figure 4–12 Clive's Reading of *My Little Dog*

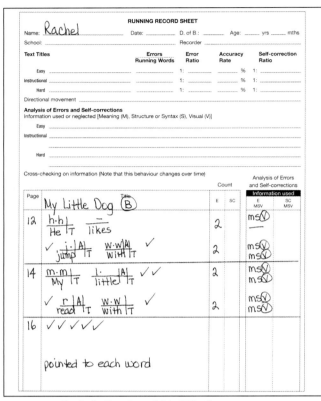

Figure 4–13 Rachel's Reading of *My Little Dog*

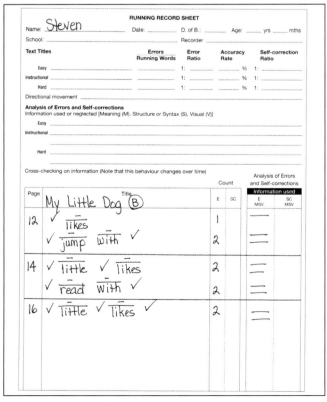

Figure 4–14 Steven's Reading of *My Little Dog*

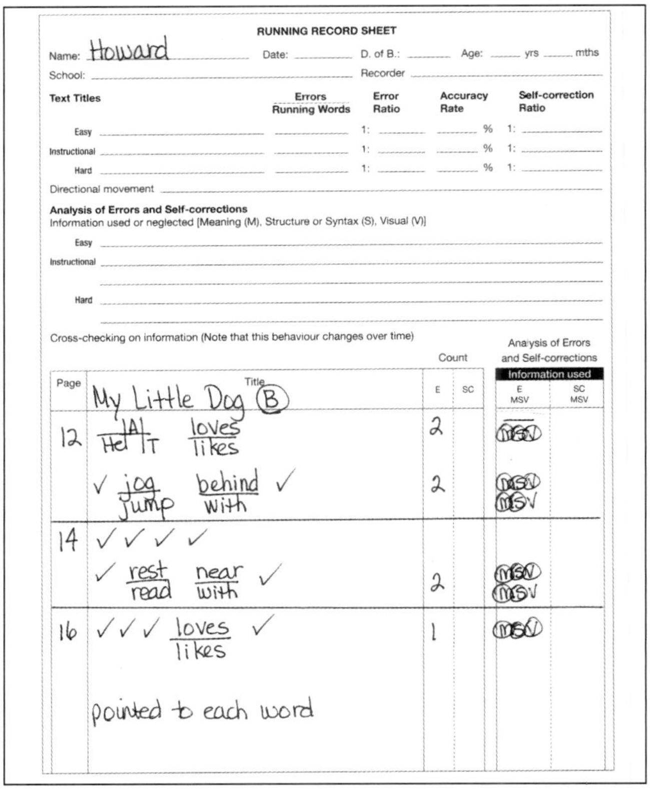

Figure 4–15 Howard's Reading of *My Little Dog*

Alisha

Alisha has learned more about print and how it works; nevertheless, she struggled through *Jack and the Beanstalk*. (Figure 4-16 shows a spread from the book; Figure 4-17 shows her reading of the first eighty-nine words.)

Alisha made twelve errors; her 86 percent accuracy rate indicates the text was too difficult for her. However, you can still analyze her problem-solving behavior. When stuck on a word, Alisha tended to sound out the word as her first and only action. She consistently used the first letter and proceeded left to right but was seldom able to go beyond the first syllable. This action sometimes resulted in her saying the word accurately (*c-l-c-l-o-clouds* in paragraph 1, for example). When sounding out the first syllable wasn't successful, Alisha appealed to her teacher rather than using other strategies. In all, the "appeal and told" pattern applied to four of her errors on the first page of the book. Alisha almost always tried to solve the word, which indicates her perseverance, but she had only one way of solving the problem and reacted passively when it didn't work. Constantly stopping to appeal interfered with the flow of the text and undermined her understanding (her comments on the story were very broad and included few details).

Alisha's strengths include her:

❑ Ability to recognize some easy high-frequency words.

❑ Ability to use letter-sound relationships to start the word and sound out the first part.

❑ Awareness of when she didn't know a word (she self-monitored and appealed to the teacher).

What was in Alisha's way that prevented effective processing? She relied almost completely on sounding out words. While sound analysis (sounding out) is one important way to work on words, she also needed to use larger word parts, notice word endings, make predictions using language structure, and be sure that her reading made sense and sounded right. Her use of visual information was too limited— she was not using it in relation to language structure and meaning. This use of visual information is typical of children working on much easier levels of text, but at this level we should see a wider range. Alisha was inflexible in the way she worked on a text, applying the same strategy over and over. While she knew some high-frequency words, her repertoire was small (she missed *out* and *because*, for example). She was unable to use known words to solve new ones (as might have happened with *upon* and *there*; language structure should also have informed *here/there*). There was very little evidence of self-monitoring and no self-correction behavior. Her reading wasn't fluent, because she had to devote so much of her attention to solving words.

Figure 4–16 Page Spreads from *Jack and the Beanstalk* from Leveled Literacy Intervention, Blue System (Heinemann 2009)

▶ Building on Strengths

Obviously Sammy and Darrell need intervention to help them make more rapid progress. Kara, Clive, Rachel, Steven, Howard, and Alisha may also need intervention; certainly they need to work on books at levels they can process effectively. Also, each of them probably needs *different* teaching; that's the challenge of working with readers struggling to build a network of strategic actions.

Looking for evidence of strengths, weaknesses, and confusions in children's early reading behavior reveals where the reading process breaks down. With strong teaching, all of the young readers we just examined can develop and extend their reading strategies and build more effective processing systems. Use a level of text that, with your support, readers will be able to process successfully and efficiently. That is how a processing system is built over time.

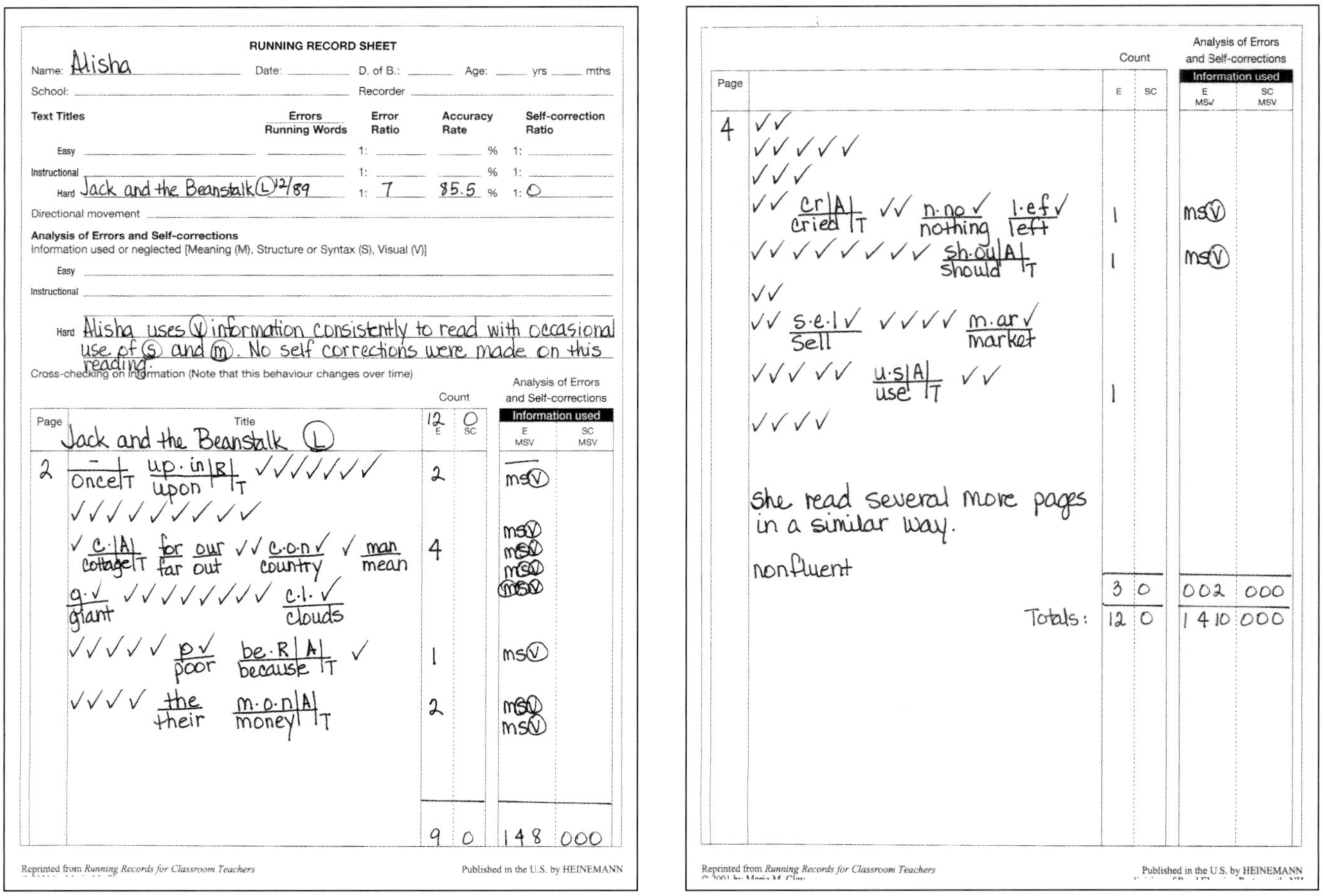

Figure 4–17 Excerpt from Alisha's Reading of *Jack and the Beanstalk*

▶ Suggestions for Professional Development

OBSERVING AND NOTING READING BEHAVIORS

1. Examine and discuss the partial Reading Records shown for Kara, Clive, Rachel, Steven, Howard, and Alisha.

2. Take some running records (on blank forms) or Reading Records (with typed text) on readers in your classroom who are having difficulty.

   ❑ Find a text that is sufficiently readable (at least a 90 percent accuracy rate, Levels A–K) so that the reader can demonstrate his or her best processing. (If a text is extremely difficult, the strategies of even a good beginning reader will break down.)

   ❑ List the reader's strengths and areas of difficulty. Be sure to think about the way the reader uses sources of information in combination, as well as the flexibility with which he works. Look for active problem solving rather than passive behavior. List the actions the reader takes at points of difficulty or after an error.

   ❑ Now, using the Guide for Observing and Noting Reading Behaviors (Appendix B), make notes on each reader on a separate form. The guide will help you think about behaviors in each system that can be observed in oral reading.

3. Bring your records and forms and discuss these readers at a meeting with your grade-level colleagues. Talk about the implications of your observations for your teaching. Be sure to talk about the language you would use to foster independent control of problem-solving actions.

Change Over Time: Processing Systems in the Making

EVEN THOUGH WE ALL PROCESS AND THINK ABOUT TEXTS in different ways, the strategies we use to set up reading systems have many characteristics in common, and that helps us as teachers to create a vision of the reading process. We are always observing to learn about the child's processing system at the present time, remembering that for the young reader, the system is constantly adjusting and changing as learning occurs. In this chapter, we take a close look at three readers, Jerome, Rosa, and Tia, and their progress over a critical period of time from early levels to the beginning of a self-extending system for reading (one that continues to grow in sophistication and competency through wide reading).

The precise observation of reading behaviors is at the heart of effective teaching. Readers who have difficulty with literacy learning are different from one another. Each reader builds a unique processing system over time. Our goal as teachers is to observe what readers can do, can almost do, and can not yet do so that we can help them build systems that resemble the systems of effective, flexible proficient readers.

Too often, teachers base their instruction solely on their students' ability to name letters or identify letter-sound relationships. Such assessments do provide valuable information, and we support their appropriate use. But to offer the best instruction, observe what students do while reading orally and note in detail what you see and hear. We have listed, defined, and provided coding and scoring information (to use when taking running or reading records) for a range of important behaviors to help you understand the records in this book (see Figure 5-1). Close observation of reading behaviors gives you the evidence from which to infer a child's in-the-head-actions, those strategic actions that cannot be directly observed (see Figure 5-2).

Over time, readers "assemble working systems" to meet the demands of increasingly difficult texts (Clay 2001). Teachers support the process through teaching

Coding and Scoring Errors At-A-Glance

Behavior	What Reader Does	How to Code	Example		How to Score	
Accurate Reading	Reads words correctly	Do not mark or place check (✓) above word	no mark _or_ ✓✓✓ Get the ball			No error
Substitution	Gives an incorrect response	Write the substituted word above the word	can could		Substitution, not corrected	1 error
Multiple Substitutions	Makes several attempts at a word	Write each substitution in sequence above the word	will | want was		Multiple substitutions, not corrected	1 error for each incorrect word in text
			will | want | sc was		Multiple substitutions; self-corrected (SC)	No error; 1 SC
			will want was was		Multiple misreadings of the same word, not corrected	1 error for each incorrect word in text
			Jay Jasey Jesse Jesse		Multiple misreadings of names and proper nouns	1 error first time missed; no errors after that
			did not didn't didn't did not		Misreading contractions (reads contraction as two words or two words as contraction)	1 error each time
Self-correction	Corrects a previous error	Write the error over the word, followed by SC	can | sc could			No error, 1 SC
Insertion	Adds a word that is not in the text	Write in the inserted word using a caret	only ∧			1 error per word inserted
Omission	Gives no response to a word	Place a dash (-) above the word	— and		Skipping a word	1 error per word
					Skipping a line	1 error per line
Repetition	Reads same word again	Write R after the word	✓ R play			No error
Repeated Repetitions	Reads the same word more than once	Write R for first repetition, then write a number for additional repetitions	✓ R2 each			No error
Rereading	Returns to the beginning of sentence or phrase to read again	Write an R with an arrow back to the place where rereading began	↙ ✓ ✓ ✓ R			No error
	Rereads and self-corrects	Write an R with an arrow back to the place where rereading began and a SC at point of self-correction	↙ ✓ ✓ ✓ ants | sc ✓ R bugs			No error, 1 SC
Appeal	Verbally asks for help	Write A above the word	each | A		Follow up with "You try it"	No error
"You Try It"	The child appeals, the teacher responds with "You try it"	Write Y after the word	each | A | Y		"You try it" followed by correct word	No error
					"You try it" followed by omission, incorrect word, or Told	1 error
Told	Child doesn't attempt a word even after "You try it"	Write T after the word or the ✓	each | A | Y | T			1 error
Spelling Aloud	Child spells word by saying names of letters	Write the letters in all capital letters	N·E·T net		Spelling followed by correct word	No error, no SC
					Spelling followed by incorrect word	1 error
Sounding Out	The child makes the sounds associated with the letters in the word	Write the letters in lower case with hyphens between them	p·a·st·✓ past		"Sounding out" followed by correct word	No error, no SC
			p·a·st past		"Sounding out" followed by incorrect word or no word	1 error
			a·|sc bugs		Sounding the first letter incorrectly, and then saying the word correctly	No error, 1 SC

Coding system developed by Marie Clay as part of the running record system in *An Observation Survey of Early Literacy Achievement, Revised Second Edition.* 2006, Heinemann.

Figure 5-1 Coding and Scoring Errors At-A-Glance from Leveled Literacy Intervention (also see Appendix C)

(demonstrating or showing), prompting (calling the reader to action), and reinforcing effective reading behaviors. By thinking deeply about a reader's behaviors, you can arrive at a tentative theory about how the child's "in the head" processing system is working at the present time, always remembering that the system is constantly changing, or "reassembling," as learning occurs.

In this chapter you'll follow Jerome, Rosa, and Tia as they progress from reading at Level B to Level K, each along a different path, as they develop a self-extending system for reading that continues to grow in complexity.

▶ Jerome

Level B

Jerome's reading of *The Hat* (Level B; see Figure 5-3) is captured in Figure 5-4. Jerome read *The Hat* with 90 percent accuracy and satisfactory comprehension (rating fluency is not encouraged at this level). His errors indicate that he used meaning

Observing Reading Behaviors

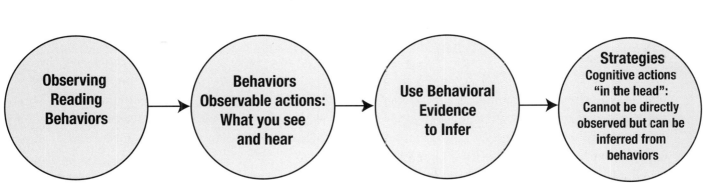

Figure 5-2 Observing Reading Behaviors

Figure 5-3 Page Layout of *The Hat* from Leveled Literacy Intervention, Orange System (Heinemann 2009)

and structure as primary sources of information. It is evident that he used language structure to monitor his reading (that is, the text probably *sounded right* to him as he read). He may have relied heavily on the language pattern of this repetitive text, and he used information conveyed by the pictures ("meaning"

information). We can also conclude from his pointing behavior that he controls left-to-right directionality.

This young reader made no self-corrections. He needed to begin using visual information or known words to monitor his reading. Although he sometimes recognized high-frequency words, he needed to learn

Figure 5-3 *The Hat, continued*

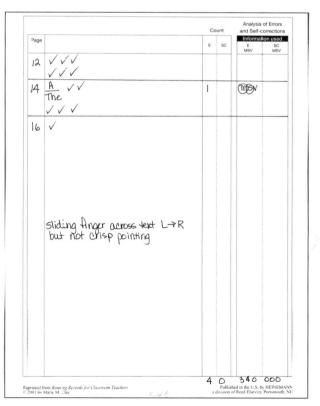

Figure 5-4 Running Record—Jerome's Reading of *The Hat*, p. 1

Figure 5-4 Jerome's Running Record, p. 2

more of them and be able to locate and recognize them while reading continuous print. After Level B, he would no longer be able to rely so heavily on repetitive text; he would need to use more than one source of information to notice mismatches, such as the substitution of *a* for *the*. Just as important, Jerome needed to gain firm control of voice-print match. Sliding his finger under the words did not help him use the precise visual information—groups of blank marks and the white spaces in between.

Jerome would be challenged by higher-level texts that have fewer language patterns, longer and more complex sentences, several lines of print, and more high-frequency words. Jerome's teacher needed to help him learn to monitor his reading. Essential teaching included working with Jerome on:

- ❏ Matching voice to print.
- ❏ Cross-checking—checking one source of information against another to monitor and correct reading.
- ❏ Using first-letter cues to self-monitor.
- ❏ Recognizing easy phonograms or spelling patterns.
- ❏ Constructing simple words easily and fluently.
- ❏ Adding endings (*s*, for example) to root words to make additional words.
- ❏ Hearing the individual sounds in words.
- ❏ Representing sounds with letters.
- ❏ Recognizing high-frequency word patterns.

(See Chapter 10 for specific examples.)

Level D

Two months later, Jerome read *Time for Lunch* (Level D; see Figure 5-5). His reading behavior is captured in Figure 5-6. He found the text difficult; the accuracy rate was 83 percent, his comprehension was unsatisfactory, the fluency score was 0. He had learned quite a few more high-frequency words and had greater knowledge of letters and sounds as well. He noticed and used first-letter cues to attempt to solve words. He continued to use information conveyed by the pictures, and voice-print match was firmly established. Although he had learned some things about print, Jerome showed signs of ineffective processing and was falling behind his classmates.

Overall, there was a pattern of dependency. Eight times, when Jerome came to a word he didn't know, he

sounded the first letter and then appealed to his teacher. This behavior suggested he was self-monitoring, but he needed to know more ways to use sounds to take words apart. He did not self-correct, nor did he use his knowledge of high-frequency words (for example, he failed to notice substitutions like *gets* for *got* and *runs* for *ran* even though he had seen the words in several texts). Sometimes his sense of language structure superseded the visual information (for example, *Mother Bear said* for *said Mother Bear*).

His errors revealed a heavy reliance on visual information, mostly employed in unsuccessful attempts to solve a word using the first letter. His reading was mostly word by word, and he largely ignored punctuation. The first thing Jerome's teacher needed to do was give Jerome lower-level text he could process more effectively. Essential teaching included:

- ❏ Helping Jerome notice and use last-letter cues.
- ❏ Supporting strategic actions for taking words apart using sounds and letters.
- ❏ Using known high-frequency words to monitor reading.
- ❏ Demonstrating and supporting rereading as a way to search for and use information, particularly more than one source of information.
- ❏ Drawing attention to punctuation and demonstrating what it means to use it.
- ❏ Encouraging reading in phrases.

(See Chapters 14, 15, and 16 for specific examples.)

Level H

A few months later Jerome read the Level H text *All About Chimps* (see Figure 5-7). His reading behavior is captured in Figure 5-8. Jerome read the text with 97 percent accuracy and satisfactory comprehension; his self-correction ratio was 1:4. On a scale of 0 to 3, his fluency also improved (the 1 rating indicates he had begun to read in two- and three-word phrases).

He used known words and word parts to solve problems while reading. Rereading had become part of his process—for example, on page 2, he read the first syllable of *forest* and then repeated the phrase *in the forest*, using

Figure 5-5 Page Layout of *Time for Lunch* from Leveled Literacy Intervention, Green System (Heinemann 2009)

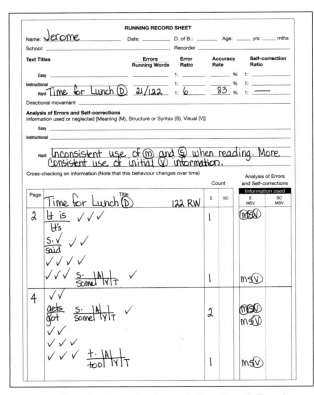

Figure 5-6 Running Record—Jerome's Reading of *Time for Lunch*, p. 1

language structure in combination with visual information to solve the word. On page 4, he showed that he knew how to separate words into onsets and rimes.

Jerome could probably read at an instructional level of I, but his teacher did not move him to a higher level without first seeing smoother problem solving and greater fluency. Although Jerome consistently used the first syllable or letter cluster of a word, and sometimes used the second syllable as well, he needed to demonstrate that flexible word solving (using meaning, structure, and visual information in an integrated way) was beginning to happen in his head. Reading higher-level texts at that point required too much work at the word level and undermined Jerome's fluency and comprehension.

Jerome's comprehension of this Level H informational text was satisfactory. However, to be able to understand the denser content at higher levels, he needed to develop faster and smoother processing, so that his mind was free to notice, search for, and remember (and later discuss) important information.

Figure 5-6 Jerome's Running Record, p. 2

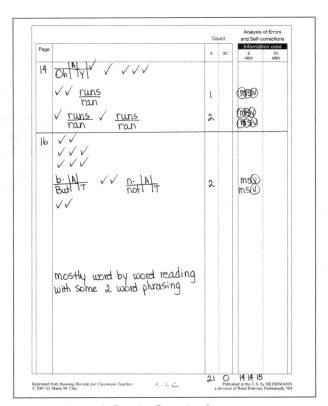

Figure 5-6 Jerome's Running Record, p.3

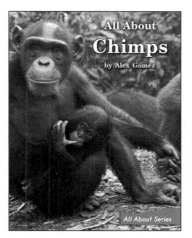

All About
Chimps
by Alex Gomez

All About Series

What Chimps Do

Chimps live in groups.
They make sounds to talk
to each other.
Chimps help each other
find food.

Chimps clean each other's
hair with their fingers.
This chimp looks for bugs
and dirt.
If he finds a bug,
he eats it!

7

Chimps

This is a chimp.
Chimps have dark hair.
They have big ears
and big hands.

Most chimps live
in the forest.
They spend a lot of time
in trees.

2

3

What Chimps Eat

Chimps eat fruit,
leaves, flowers,
and seeds.
They also
eat eggs
and bugs.

Some chimps work as
a team to find their food.
They share the food
they find.

8

9

Chimps have long arms.
Their arms are very strong.
Chimps can swing
from tree to tree.

This is a chimp's foot.
Look at the big toe!
It helps the chimp
climb trees.

4

5

Chimps use tools.
This chimp uses a stick
to catch bugs.
The chimp pokes the stick
into a hole.

Bugs crawl up the stick.
The chimp pulls the stick
out and eats the bugs.

10

11

Figure 5-7 Page Layout of *All About Chimps* from Leveled Literacy Intervention, Green System (Heinemann 2009)

continues

How Chimps Live

Chimps sleep in the trees.
They make nests from
branches and leaves.
Some chimps make
a new nest every night.

This is a baby chimp.
She is with her mother.

The baby chimp rides on
her mother's back.

Most chimp mothers have
one baby at a time.
But this chimp mother
had twins!

Figure 5-7 *All About Chimps, continued*

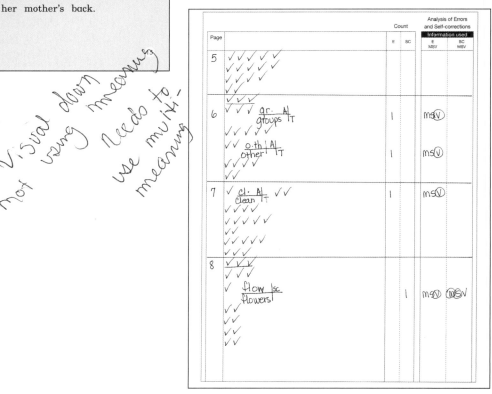

Figure 5-8 Running Record—Jerome's Reading of *All About Chimps*, p. 1

Figure 5-8 Jerome's Running Record, p. 2

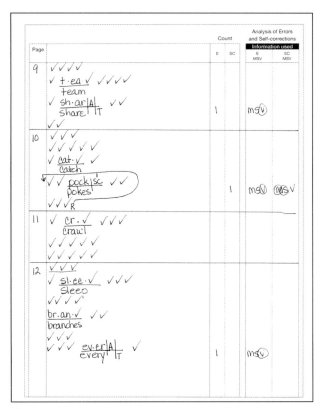

Figure 5-8 Running Record—Jerome's Reading of *All About Chimps*, p. 3

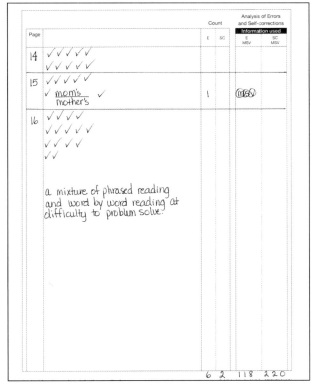

Figure 5-8 Jerome's Running Record, p. 4

Essential teaching included:

- ❑ Teaching for and prompting for a range of word-solving strategies (for example, using word parts, letters, letter clusters, sounds, and known words as analogies).

- ❑ Supporting Jerome in integrating several sources of information as he monitored and corrected his reading.

- ❑ Helping him read with fluency—pause, use intonation suggested by punctuation, stress words appropriately, use proper phrasing.)

(See Chapters 14, 15, and 16 for specific examples.)

Level K

A few more months later, Jerome read *Puddle Play*, Level K (see Figure 5-9). A sample of his reading behavior is captured in Figure 5-10. His accuracy rate was 99.5 percent; he had a 1:1 self-correction ratio, satisfactory comprehension, and a fluency score of 3. He was actively solving words in flexible ways. On page 3, his correction of *splished* for *splashed* and *washed* for *watched* indicated he was paying close attention to the sounds and letters as well as thinking about the meaning. These errors and corrections didn't slow down his reading or interrupt the processing. His reading was largely accurate and showed that he could use several sources of information in a smoothly integrated way. He read fluently, paused at punctuation, and was able to understand dialogue.

Jerome could now read at an instructional level of L, possibly even M. He was already reading beginning chapter books, and he was reading silently most of the time. As the demands of texts increased, he would need to sustain processing and remember meaning over longer and longer stretches of text. He would also need to process texts that had denser content and required more concentrated attention. Essential teaching included:

- ❑ Explicitly teaching genre and text structure to help Jerome use the organization of the book to sustain his reading of longer texts.

❏ Demonstrating how to take apart longer words by syllables, and supporting Jerome as he applied this understanding when reading longer texts.

❏ Supporting on-the-run word solving using known words and word parts.

❏ Prompting Jerome to pause, use intonation suggested by punctuation, stress words appropriately, and phrase word groupings appropriately.

(see Chapters 14, 15, and 16 for specific examples.)

Figure 5-9 Page Layout of *Puddle Play* from Leveled Literacy Intervention, Blue System (Heinemann 2009)

Jerome's progress over time is summarized in Figure 5-11. His reading had developed from ineffective processing at Level B to a smoothly operating system of integrated strategic actions at Level K.

Mother sat down in the grass. Roxy and Andy sat beside her.

"Oh, my, it **is** hot out here," said Mother. She looked at the puddle. "You know, when I was a little fox, I liked puddles, too," she said.

"You did?" asked Roxy.

"Yes, I did. And I loved putting my toes in the mud," said Mother.

"Really?" asked Andy.

"What other things did you like?" asked Roxy.

12   13

"I liked playing in puddles," said Mother with a wink.

"I knew you were going to say that!" said Andy.

He flicked a bit of mud at his mother. Then he looked a little worried. But Mother smiled and flicked the mud back at Andy.

14

Roxy ran to the puddle. "You can't catch me!" she called.

"Yes, I can!" said Mother.

Mother and Andy ran to catch Roxy.

15

And they all played in the mud until the sun went down.

16

Figure 5-9 *Puddle Play, continued*

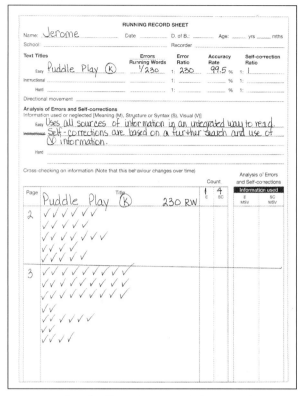

Figure 5-10 Running Record—Jerome's Reading of *Puddle Play*, p. 1

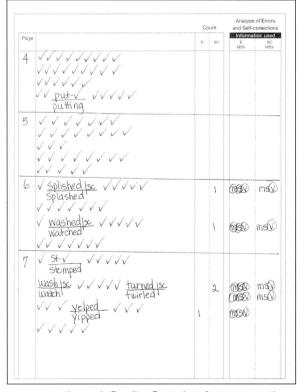

Figure 5-10 Jerome's Reading Record, p. 2   *continues*

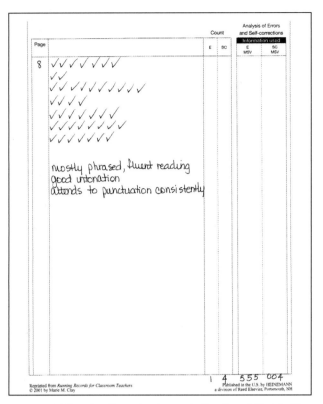

Figure 5-10 Running Record—Jerome's Reading of *Puddle Play*, p. 3

▶ Rosa

Rosa read the same books as did Jerome, so we can compare her progress with his. The two children had different strengths and weaknesses, but both were working toward developing an effective reading process.

Level B

Rosa's reading of *The Hat* (Level B) is captured in Figure 5-12. Her accuracy rate was 80 percent, and she made no self-corrections. Her comprehension was satisfactory. (Again, rating fluency is not encouraged at this level.) Rosa demonstrated that she could use some letter-sound knowledge and recognize high-frequency words. She tended to start a word and then either appeal or wait to be told rather than use the first letter in connection with meaning and language structure. She did not reread to gather more information about language structure.

Rosa neglected meaning and structure when she had difficulty. For example, Rosa knew most of the names of the animals in the story, yet she didn't appear to connect the animals in the pictures with the first letters of their names. If she had, she would have been able to solve words like *duck*. Her word-solving strategy depended too much on first letters and not enough on language processing. She did, however, pick up on the language pattern, showing that she could learn from the text. Rosa had full control of voice-print match (she pointed crisply under each word) and left-to-right directionality. This behavior helped her monitor her reading, although she needed to use other sources of information.

To be able to read higher-level texts, Rosa needed to use more information than the first letters of words. She would encounter embedded phrases and clauses and would need a good sense of the language structure to understand the text. Also, it would be very detrimental if she continued to neglect meaning and structure. She did not even take advantage of looking at the pictures for help. Of course, she needed more work on letters and sounds but not at the expense of meaningful reading. Rosa's teacher needed to make it a priority to help her use meaning and language structure.

Essential teaching for Rosa using texts at Level A included:

❑ Supporting searching for and using many sources of information, like looking for information in the pictures and thinking about letter-sound relationships.

❑ Demonstrating and supporting rereading up to the point of error or difficulty and thinking what would make sense and sound right in the sentence.

❑ Increasing the number of high-frequency words she knew so she would be able to pay more attention to the meaning of the text. She could also use high-frequency words to monitor her reading.

(See Chapters 8, 12, and 14 for specific examples.)

Figure 5-11 **Changes in Jerome's Reading Behavior Over Time**			
Systems	*The Hat* **Level B** **Acc. 90%** **Comp. S** **SC nil** **Fluency n/a**	*Time for Lunch* **Level D** **Acc. 83%** **Comp. U** **SC nil** **Fluency 0**	*All About Chimps* **Level H** **Acc. 97%** **Comp. S** **SC 1:4** **Fluency 1**	*Puddle Play* **Level K** **Acc. 99.5%** **Comp. S** **SC 1:1** **Fluency 3**
SOLVING WORDS Strength (S) Need (N)	(S) Sometimes recognized high-frequency words in text (N) Needed to learn more high-frequency words *(the, a)* and read them in text consistently	(S) Noticed and used first-letter cues to attempt to solve words (N) Needed to notice/use last-letter cues and take words apart using sounds of individual letters	(S) Used known words and word parts (onsets and rimes) to solve unknown words (N) Needed to demonstrate flexible solving of new words in the head and use M, S, and V information	(S) Demonstrated active word solving at a good pace and used flexible ways to solve new words
MONITORING AND CORRECTING Strength (S) Need (N)	(S) Used language structure to monitor reading (N) Needed to match oral reading with print in order to monitor and correct reading	(N) Needed to cross-check many sources of information (N) Needed to use high-frequency words *(got, said, ran)* to monitor reading	(S) Corrected errors immediately and reread to problem-solve and confirm (N) Needed to use all sources of information to monitor and correct reading	(S) Used all sources of information to correct errors immediately and to monitor reading
SEARCHING FOR AND USING INFORMATION Strength (S) Need (N)	(S) Used pictures and language patterns to read texts (N) Needed to use visual information in connection with meaning and structure	(S) Used some information conveyed by pictures to process text (N) Needed to reread, search for, and use information	(S) Used information conveyed by pictures to process text (N) Needed to notice, search for, remember, and discuss information that was important	(S) Searched for and used many sources of information, including dialogue, to understand text
MAINTAINING FLUENCY Strength (S) Need (N)	(S) Controlled left-to-right directionality (N) Needed to point to the appropriate words as he said them	(N) Read mostly word by word; needed to read words in groups (phrasing) (N) Needed to pay attention to punctuation	(S) Used a mixture of word-by-word and phrased reading (N) Needed to read with fluency, using appropriate phrasing and many sources of information	(S) Demonstrated fluent, phrased reading (S) Demonstrated an awareness of the function of punctuation

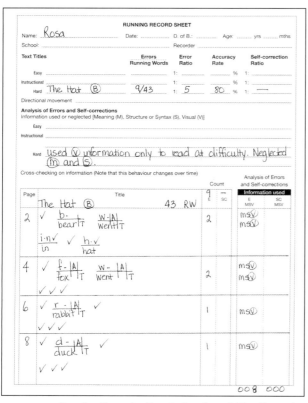

Figure 5-12 Running Record—Rosa's Reading of *The Hat*, p. 1

Figure 5-12 Rosa's Running Record, p. 2

Level D

Rosa's reading of *Time for Lunch* (Level D) is captured in Figure 5-13. She read this story with 83 percent accuracy; the text was difficult. However, her fluency rating was 2. She made no self-corrections. By now she had increased the number of high-frequency words she knew and recognized; she read them in continuous text. She consistently used language structure and meaning in combination with the first letters of words. Her repeated errors—*bugs* for *berries* and *says* for *said*—were consistent with her understanding of language structure.

Rosa needed to recognize more high-frequency words and use them to monitor her reading (*said, got,* and *like* should be familiar now). She needed to reread up to an unfamiliar word and coordinate using visual information with meaning and structure to solve it. Her word-solving strategies needed to expand beyond using first letters.

Her reading was phrased and smooth, and she proceeded at a good pace. Her teacher monitored her reading fluency closely, continued to select texts Rosa could read smoothly, and reinforced phrasing and intonation. As Rosa learned to monitor her reading more closely, overt problem solving became evident.

Essential teaching for Rosa using texts at Level C included:

- ❑ Expanding Rosa's knowledge of high-frequency words: looking closely at words, building them with magnetic letters, and writing them.

- ❑ Locating high-frequency words in continuous text.

- ❑ Looking at word parts and making connections among words that have the same parts.

- ❑ Demonstrating rereading, saying the first sound of a word, and thinking what would sound right, make sense, and look right.

- ❑ Helping her look beyond the first letter to solve words.

- ❑ Drawing her attention to the pictures, helping her use them to process and understand the text.

- ❑ Continuing to reinforce phrased reading that included placing the appropriate stress on

RUNNING RECORD SHEET

Name: Rosa   Date: _____ D. of B.: _____ Age: _____ yrs _____ mths

School: _____   Recorder _____

Text Titles	Errors Running Words	Error Ratio	Accuracy Rate	Self-correction Ratio
Easy		1:	%	1:
Instructional		1:	%	1:
Hard Time for Lunch (D)	20/122	1: 6	83 %	1: —

Directional movement _____

Analysis of Errors and Self-corrections
Information used or neglected [Meaning (M), Structure or Syntax (S), Visual (V)]

Easy _____

Instructional _____

Hard Uses (m) and (S) consistently. At error (V) information is used at the beginning of the word. No self-corrections.

Cross-checking on information (Note that this behaviour changes over time)

Page	Title		Count 20 0	E / SC	Analysis of Errors and Self-corrections Information used E MSV / SC MSV
	Time For Lunch (D) 122 RW				
2	It is ✓✓✓ / It's			1	(MSV)
	says ✓✓ / said			1	(MSV)
	✓✓✓ bugs / berries			1	(MSV)
	✓✓✓✓ bugs / berries			1	(MSV)
4	✓✓				
	gets ✓ bugs / got berries			2	msv msv
	✓✓ / ✓✓✓				
	✓✓ bugs. ✓ / berries			1	msv

Figure 5-13 Running Record—Rosa's Reading of *Time for Lunch*, p. 1

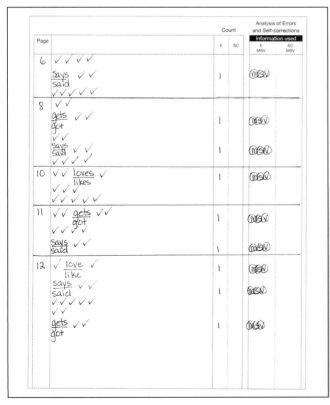

Page			Count E / SC	Analysis of Errors and Self-corrections Information used E MSV / SC MSV
6	✓✓✓✓			
	says ✓ ✓ / said ✓✓✓✓		1	(MSV)
8	✓✓			
	gets ✓✓ / got		1	(MSV)
	✓✓ / says ✓ ✓ / said ✓✓✓		1	(MSV)
10	✓✓ loves ✓ / likes ✓✓✓ / ✓✓✓✓		1	(MSV)
11	✓✓ gets ✓✓ / got ✓✓✓		1	(MSV)
	says ✓✓ / said		1	(MSV)
12	✓ love ✓ / like		1	(MSV)
	says ✓✓ / said ✓✓✓✓ / ✓✓		1	(MSV)
	gets ✓✓ / got		1	(MSV)

Figure 5-13 Rosa's Running Record, p. 2

Page			Count E / SC	Analysis of Errors and Self-corrections Information used E MSV / SC MSV
14	✓✓ says ✓ ✓ / said ✓✓✓		1	(MSV)
	S- |A| ✓ ✓✓✓ / She |Y|		
16	✓✓			
	says ✓✓ / said		1	(MSV)
	✓ love ✓ / like		1	(MSV)
	and ✓✓✓ / But ✓✓		1	(MSV)
	phrased, smooth reading at a good pace.			

Figure 5-13 Rosa's Running Record, p. 3

words (but allowing her to slow down when she was monitoring her reading and searching for information to help her solve words and apprehend meaning).

(See Chapters 14, 15, and 16 for specific examples.)

Level H

Rosa's reading of *All About Chimps* (Level H) is captured in Figure 5-14. Rosa read at a 92 percent accuracy rate and handled two- and three-word phrases fluently. Her comprehension was satisfactory, and her fluency rating was 2. These numeric scores indicate that Level H was the right instructional level for Rosa.

However, when her teacher examined her processing, there was cause for concern. Although Rosa knew many more high-frequency words and used sequential letter sounds and word parts to solve new words, she was still not actively searching for and using information from other sources, like the pictures. Her word solving was still superficial. She continued to rely on known words and appeal when

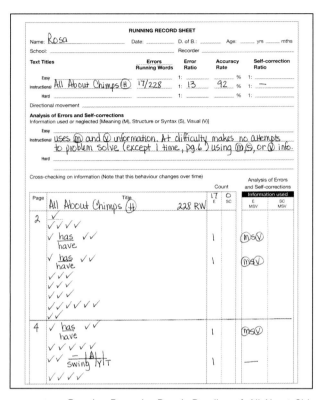

Figure 5-14 Running Record—Rosa's Reading of *All About Chimps,* p. 1

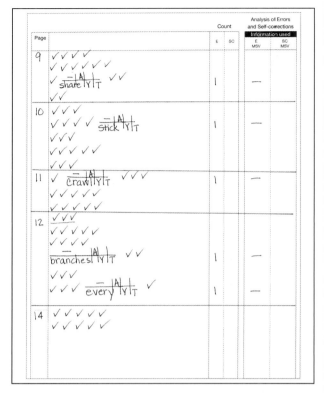

Figure 5-14 Rosa's Running Record, p. 3

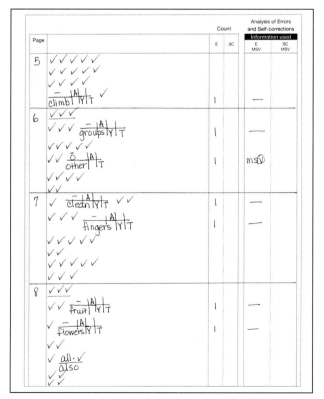

Figure 5-14 Rosa's Running Record, p. 2

Figure 5-14 Rosa's Running Record, p. 4

stuck (she appealed thirteen times in this 228-word text). She was unable to read with understanding without her teacher's help. This would become debilitating as she tried to read longer and more complex texts.

Moving to an easier level would not in itself change Rosa's reading behavior. She needed some strong intervention to help her become a more active reader. She needed to practice phrased, fluent reading and learn how to use many sources of information. Essential teaching included:

❑ Prompting Rosa to notice and detect errors (asking her to go back and fix something that was not quite right, for example).

❑ Introducing a text by drawing attention to the information conveyed by the pictures and explicitly demonstrating how to notice details and use them to read and understand the text.

❑ Prompting her to search for and use information conveyed by the pictures in combination with the visual features of words.

❑ Demonstrating a range of flexible ways to take apart words (letter clusters, word parts, analogy to known words) and prompting Rosa to use these word-solving activities.

(See Chapter 15 for specific examples.)

Level K

Rosa's reading of *Puddle Play* (Level K, the grade-level expectation) is captured in Figure 5-15. It provides a very different picture of Rosa as a reader, although she still needed some specific teaching. Her accuracy was 100 percent; her comprehension was excellent; her fluency score was 2; and her self-correction ratio is 1:1.

We would need to look at more records of Rosa reading a higher-level text in order to examine her reading behavior, but this record shows that Rosa had developed a reading process. She used letter-sound relationships to solve some difficult words, always reading smoothly and accurately. However, she didn't attend to punctuation consistently and read with little intonation. On pages 5, 6, and 7, she corrected her errors close to the point of making them. She noticed

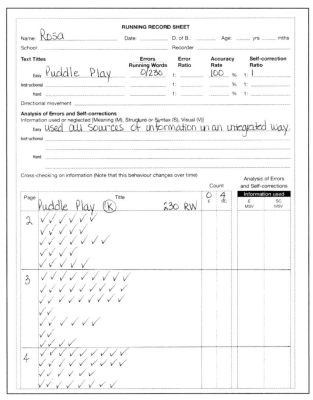

Figure 5-15 Running Record—Rosa's Reading of *Puddle Play*, p. 1

Figure 5-15 Rosa's Running Record, p. 2

and remembered information that was important to understanding the text.

Essential teaching for Rosa at Level L or M included:

❑ Reinforcing flexible word-solving strategies.

❑ Supporting the solving of three- and four-syllable words.

❑ Extending understanding through discussion.

❑ Explicitly teaching for, prompting for, and reinforcing that readers must pay attention to punctuation.

(See Chapters 15 and 16 for specific examples.)

Rosa's progress over time is summarized in Figure 5-16. She demonstrated a smoothly operating processing system when reading texts at Level K, although she could improve her reading by paying closer attention to punctuation.

▶ Tia

Again, Tia read the same texts as Jerome and Rosa. When you examine her Reading Records, think about the varied ways in which the individuals in any group of readers develop over time.

Level B

Tia's reading of *The Hat* (Level B) is captured in Figure 5-17. Her accuracy rate was only 66 percent. She recognized the high-frequency word *the* and used some information conveyed by the pictures to solve words. She controlled voice-print match and left-to-right directionality.

What you will notice immediately about Tia's reading was the number of appeals—eleven in this short text! There was a pattern of making the sound of the first letter, then asking to be told the word. When a word began with a vowel (*in*, for example), Tia didn't even make the sound of the first letter but appealed immediately. She was told the word *went* seven times but didn't remember and use it in the context of a sentence on another page. Tia (1) didn't use visual information beyond the first letter, (2) didn't recognize high-frequency words, (3) didn't remember

words, and (4) didn't know how to use meaning or language structure to help her.

Tia's teacher needed to help her use what she knew about print to solve her own problems as a reader. Tia also needed to learn many more high-frequency words (*in* and *went*, for example). It was possible that she could recognize high-frequency words in isolation but not in context. She also needed to learn to monitor her reading using known high-frequency words. Even more important, she needed to notice and use the first letter of words to monitor reading and cross-check using more than one kind of information (for example, noticing *bunny* and *rabbit* have the same meaning but different first letters).

Tia did use some information conveyed by pictures, but she showed very little knowledge of language structure, even in this text with a strong, simple pattern. She appeared to be looking at each word individually, without considering language structure or meaning. And she didn't use most of the visual information successfully.

Essential teaching for Tia included:

❑ Increasing Tia's ability to recognize high-frequency words and introducing ways of looking at and learning words (magnetic letters, letter-by-letter checking).

❑ Teaching for, prompting for, and reinforcing cross-checking one source of information with another to monitor and solve problems while reading.

❑ Prompting Tia to use known high-frequency words to monitor her reading.

❑ Showing her that her reading has to "sound right" and "look right."

(See Chapter 14 for specific examples.)

Level D

Tia's reading of *Time for Lunch* (Level D) is captured in Figure 5-18. She had made quite a bit of progress. She read the text with 100 percent accuracy, but her error behavior gives us insights into the development of her processing system. She consistently used meaning, language structure, and visual information to monitor and correct her reading. She also reread (on page 10, for example) and used the first letters of words

Figure 5-16 Changes in Rosa's Reading Behavior Over Time

Systems	*The Hat* Level B Acc. 80% Comp. S SC nil Fluency n/a	*Time for Lunch* Level D Acc. 83% Comp. U SC nil Fluency 2	*All About Chimps* Level H Acc. 92% Comp. S SC nil Fluency 1	*Puddle Play* Level K Acc. 100% Comp. E SC 1:1 Fluency 2
SOLVING WORDS Strength (S) Need (N)	(S) Used some letter-sound knowledge: identified first letter and connected it to a sound (S) Recognized high-frequency words *(the, in)* (N) Needed to use the first letter of a word in connection w/meaning and language structure	(S) Recognized and read many high-frequency words (S) Errors were consistent *(says* for *said)* (N) Needed to recognize and read more high-frequency words *(said, got, like)*	(S) Used syntax to read high-frequency words (S) Used letter sounds and word parts in sequence (consonant clusters) to problem-solve (S) Needed to attempt unfamiliar words and demonstrate flexible ways of solving them (take them apart, use meaning and syntax)	(S) Used letter-sound relationships to solve more complex words (S) Demonstrated competent, active, flexible word solving
MONITORING AND CORRECTING Strength (S) Need (N)	(S) Used voice-print match to monitor reading (S) Used first letter of word to monitor reading (N) Needed to cross-check many sources of information (N) Needed to correct errors using meaning conveyed by text and pictures	(S) Used language structure and meaning consistently (N) Needed to reread to search for information (notice errors/mismatches) (N) Needed to cross-check visual information with meaning and syntax (N) Needed to use multiple sources of information	(N) Needed to notice and correct errors (N) Needed to monitor reading using all sources of information and attempt corrections	(S) Corrected errors immediately (S) Used visual information to monitor and correct reading
SEARCHING FOR AND USING INFORMATION Strength (S) Need (N)	(S) Used some letter-sound understanding and language structure (N) Needed to use information conveyed by pictures and language structure to help read text	(S) Used language structure and meaning in connection with first letters or words (N) Needed to reread and use letters beyond the first (N) Needed to notice details in pictures and use them to process and understand text	(S) Used meaning and visual information consistently (N) Needed to use pictures to help process/understand text	(S) Noticed and remembered important information
MAINTAINING FLUENCY Strength (S) Need (N)	(S) Pointed crisply and controlled voice-print matching and directionality	(S) Demonstrated phrased, smooth reading at a good pace	(S) Demonstrated some two- and three-word phrasing and emerging fluency (N) Needed to practice phrased, fluent reading and use many sources of information	(S) Demonstrated phrased, fluent reading (N) Needed to pay closer attention to punctuation

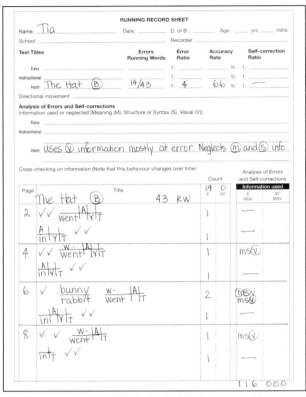

Figure 5-17 Running Record—Tia's Reading of *The Hat*, p. 1

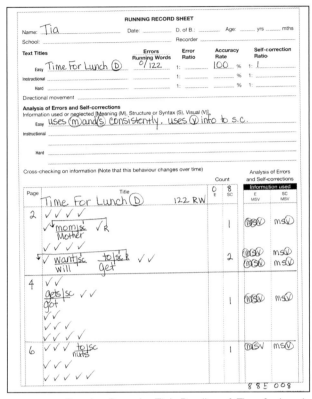

Figure 5-18 Running Record—Tia's Reading of *Time for Lunch*, p. 1

Figure 5-17 Tia's Running Record, *The Hat*, p. 2

Figure 5-18 Tia's Running Record, *Time for Lunch*, p. 2

(*b-but* on page 16) to solve words. She paid close attention to print (indicated by her correction of *don't* for *do not*). Her reading, though primarily word by word, showed she was aware of the role of phrasing.

Essential teaching for Tia included:

❑ Helping her use the structure of words to solve them.

❑ Showing her how to use word parts to solve longer words.

❑ Helping her learn more high-frequency words.

❑ Demonstrating how to use phrasing while reading and prompting her to read this way herself.

(See Chapter 15 for specific examples.)

Level H

Tia's reading of *All About Chimps* (Level H) is captured in Figure 5-19. Tia had learned more about taking words apart while reading. She read this text with 98 percent accuracy and a 1:2 self-correction ratio. She was now an active reader who always tried something

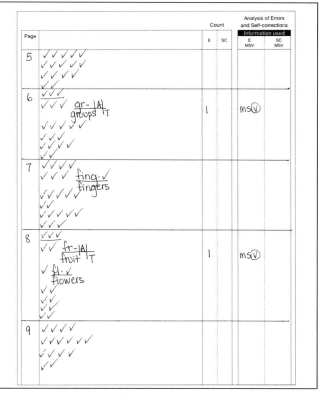

Figure 5-19 Tia's Running Record, p. 2

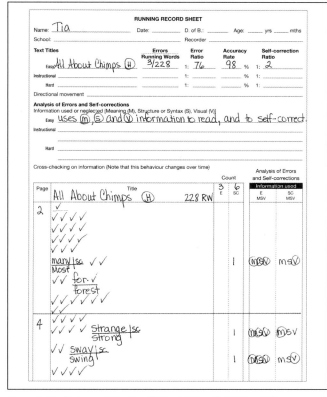

Figure 5-19 Running Record—Tia's reading of *All About Chimps*, p. 1

Figure 5-19 Tia's Running Record, p. 3

before asking to be told the word. Her attempts indicate that she used visual information in combination with meaning and language structure and that she looked at all parts of the word (she corrected her miscue of *very* for *every,* for example, and said the first syllable of *fingers* before reading it accurately). On the other hand, her reading was still mostly word by word with very little two-word phrasing, and she didn't notice and use punctuation consistently.

Level H was probably a good instructional level for Tia. Essential teaching included:

❑ Reinforcing word-solving strategies and extending their application to three- and four-syllable words.

❑ Prompting Tia to pay specific and consistent attention to phrasing.

❑ Emphasizing fluency.

❑ Demonstrating how to notice punctuation and prompting Tia to use it in her reading.

(See Chapters 14, 15, and 16 for specific examples.)

Level K

Tia's reading of *Puddle Play* (Level K) is captured in Figure 5-20. She was now reading with very high accuracy. She corrected most errors immediately, and used good intonation when she reread. She now had a smoothly operating processing system. She could take words apart skillfully, and there is evidence that she was noticing middle vowels, base words, and endings (on page 8, she read *big* for *biggest*—noticing a word part—read on, then went back and corrected herself). Her reading was now fluent and phrased and included good intonation, indicating that she was using punctuation as a cue.

Essential teaching for Tia included:

❑ Reinforcing word-solving strategies and extending their application to three- and four-syllable words.

❑ Reinforcing fluent, phrased reading and prompting Tia to pay attention to punctuation.

❑ Teaching for, prompting for, and reinforcing how punctuation is used to cue fluent reading.

(See Chapters 15 and 16 for specific examples.)

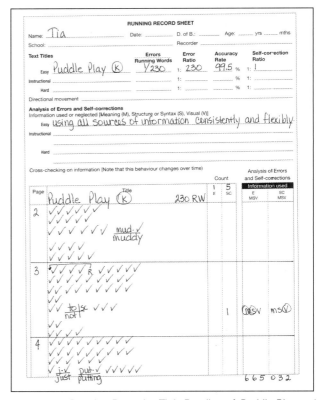

Figure 5-20 Running Record—Tia's Reading of *Puddle Play,* p. 1

Figure 5-20 Tia's Running Record, p. 2

Tia's progress over time is summarized in Figure 5-21. At the time of her first assessment, Tia had trouble reading even very simple Level B texts. However, she had the advantage of being able to control voice-print match and use it to monitor her reading. Tia had since learned to use many sources of information and known words to monitor and correct her reading. She had developed a flexible range of strategies for solving words and became very efficient in the process. She now demonstrated smooth, fluent, expressive reading of Level K texts.

▶ Summary

To understand how each reader built unique processing systems, review the comparative analysis of all three readers, at four levels of text, in four categories of strategic actions (Figure 5-22).

All three readers moved from Level B to Level K, but they did not exhibit the same reading behaviors at each level, and they did not progress at the same rate. Each reader took a different path, building a processing system in a unique way. Even at the early Level B stage, we see variations:

❑ Jerome used pictures and language structure but slid his finger over the words. He was unable to monitor using visual information or voice-print match. He could locate only a few high-frequency words. He needed strong teaching to help him monitor his reading using more than one source of information.

❑ Rosa used some letter-sound knowledge and had good control of voice-print match. She could monitor her reading using voice-print match and visual information. She needed to learn to use more than one source of information.

❑ Tia knew some high-frequency words but didn't use them consistently to monitor or correct herself. She controlled voice-print match and searched for and used information conveyed by the pictures.

At this point, Tia, Rosa, and Jerome could be taught in the same group using Level A texts. Jerome's reading of *The Hat* was the most accurate of the three, but his reading behaviors were in many ways not as strong as those of Rosa and Tia.

Jerome and Rosa both found reading at Level D difficult, but Tia read *Time for Lunch* with 100 percent accuracy. Again, differences are apparent:

❑ Jerome used first letters and related sounds to solve words, and he read more high-frequency words. *Time for Lunch* was hard for him (his accuracy rate was only 83 percent), and he made a few of the same errors repeatedly. He controlled voice-print match but didn't consistently use several sources of information to monitor his reading. His reading was not fluent, and he asked to be told words regularly. Jerome needed support to help him develop strategic actions for taking words apart; he also needed to be prompted to search for and use more than one source of information.

❑ Rosa also found *Time for Lunch* a hard text. She too had increased the number of high-frequency words she knew, but she didn't consistently use them to monitor and correct her reading. Nor did she solve words by rereading and using language structure or the first letter of the word. Her reading was fluent and phrased, but she needed to be prompted to monitor her reading using several sources of information.

❑ Tia found *Time for Lunch* easy. She had learned more high-frequency words by this time but needed support to increase her repertoire and recognize them quickly. She needed to be prompted to pay attention to letter-sound information in connection with meaning and language structure; she also needed to pay attention to punctuation and consistently put words together in phrases.

At this point in their development, the three children had different needs. Jerome and Rosa might be grouped together, after first determining a true instructional level for each of them. However, their teacher would need to interact with them in different ways to achieve different goals. For example, Jerome needed a great deal of prompting for phrased reading, while the priority for Rosa was monitoring her reading. Tia, on her own, would need to read a book

Figure 5-21 **Changes in Tia's Reading Behavior Over Time**				
Systems	*The Hat* Level B Acc. 66% Comp. S SC nil Fluency n/a	*Time for Lunch* Level D Acc. 100% Comp. S SC 1:1 Fluency 1	*All About Chimps* Level H Acc. 98% Comp. S SC 1:2 Fluency 0	*Puddle Play* Level K Acc. 99.5% Comp. S SC 1:1 Fluency 3
SOLVING WORDS Strength (S) Need (N)	(S) Recognized *the* (N) Needed to learn/recognize high-frequency words *(in/went)* and use when reading text	(S) Recognized many high-frequency words (S) Made connections between letters/sounds and spelling patterns (N) Needed to use word parts	(S) Demonstrated knowledge of flexible ways to solve new words (S) Took words apart in clusters and by parts (N) Needed to apply word solving to multisyllable words	(S) Demonstrated flexible, efficient use of multiple sources of information to solve new words (N) Needed to apply word solving to multisyllable words
MONITORING AND CORRECTING Strength (S) Need (N)	(N) Needed to cross check using different sources of information (N) Needed to monitor with known high-frequency words *(the, a)* (N) Needed to use first letter of ways to monitor *bunny rabbit*	(S) Cross checked multiple sources of information (S) Used known words to self monitor	(S) Self corrected many errors immediately (S) Used multiple sources of information to cross check	(S) Self corrected using precise information. Used meaning, language, visual sources consistently (N) Needed to monitor punctuation
SEARCHING FOR AND USING INFORMATION Strength (S) Need (N)	(S) Used some information from pictures (N) Needed to use language patterns to help read text	(S) Reread to search for information S) Used text meaning and language to help read text	(S) Used information from the pictures to process text	(S) Searched for information in illustration to support text interpretation
MAINTAINING FLUENCY Strength (S) Need (N)	(S)Controlled voice-print match	(N) Mixture of word by word reading, some two-word phrasing (N) Needed to read in word groups	(N) Mostly word by word reading (N) Needed to practice phrased, fluent reading and use multiple sources of information to support meaning (N) Needed to notice punctuation	(S) Demonstrated phrased, fluent reading with good intonation (N) Needed to notice and use punctuation

Figure 5-22 Comparative Analysis of Jerome's, Rosa's, and Tia's Changes in Reading Behavior Over Time

Systems	*The Hat* Level B Jerome 90% Rosa 80% Tia 66%	*Time for Lunch* Level D Jerome 83% Rosa 83% Tia 100%	*All About Chimps* Level H Jerome 97% Rosa 92% Tia 98%	*Puddle Play* Level K Jerome 99.5% Rosa 100% Tia 99.5%
Solving Words				
Jerome	Located and used some high-frequency words in text	Used first letter sounds to problem-solve	Used known words and word parts (onsets and rimes) to solve unknown words	Used many sources of information and efficient, active word solving
Rosa	Used some known letter-sounds and recognized some high-frequency words	Read more high-frequency words; made repeated errors	Used language structure and visual information (consonant clusters) to problem-solve	Used many sources of information to solve words competently, actively, and flexibly
Tia	Recognized *the* but did not consistently monitor reading using high-frequency words	Recognized more high-frequency words; made corrections between letters and sounds	Solved new words flexibly and took words apart	Used many sources of information to solve words efficiently
Monitoring and Correcting				
Jerome	Used language structure to monitor reading	Did not consistently use many sources of information to monitor reading	Corrected errors immediately and reread to confirm	Actively solved words using multiple sources of information. Self-corrected using visual information
Rosa	Monitored reading using word-by-word matching and the first letter of words	Used language structure and meaning consistently	Did not notice/detect errors; made no self-corrections	Corrected errors at the point they were made using many sources of information
Tia	Did not monitor or self-correct	Cross-checked many sources of information	Cross-checked many sources of information; corrected errors immediately	Corrected using precise meaning, syntax, and visual information

continued

Figure 5-22 Comparative Analysis of Jerome's, Rosa's, and Tia's Changes in Reading Behavior Over Time, *continued*

Systems	*The Hat* Level B Jerome 90% Rosa 80% Tia 66%	*Time for Lunch* Level D Jerome 83% Rosa 83% Tia 100%	*All About Chimps* Level H Jerome 97% Rosa 92% Tia 98%	*Puddle Play* Level K Jerome 99.5% Rosa 100% Tia 99.5%
Searching For and Using Information				
Jerome	Used information conveyed by pictures and language patterns (meaning and syntax)	Used meaning and information conveyed by pictures	Used information conveyed by pictures to support understanding	Used many sources of information to process texts
Rosa	Used some letter-sound relationships and language structure	Used meaning and syntax to solve new words	Used meaning consistently	Noticed and remembered important information
Tia	Used some information conveyed by pictures to read text	Reread to search for information; used meaning and syntax to solve words	Used many sources of information, including pictures, to process text	Searched for information conveyed in pictures to support meaning
Maintaining Fluency				
Jerome	Slid finger across from left to right (didn't point word by word)	Mostly read word by word	Used some phrasing; still occasionally read word by word	Demonstrated phrased, fluent reading and paid attention to punctuation
Rosa	Pointed crisply and controlled voice-print match	Read smoothly at a good pace; incorporated phrasing	Read fluently; included some two- and three-word phrasing	Demonstrated phrased, fluent reading but did not pay careful attention to punctuation
Tia	Controlled voice-print match	Mixed word-by-word reading with some phrasing	Mostly read word by word	Demonstrated fluent reading

that was at least at Level E in order to expand her reading abilities.

Looking at the Reading Records of the children at Level H, you see that all three made significant progress. Rosa read *All About Chimps* with an accuracy rate of 92 percent, which indicated that this was her instructional level. Jerome and Tia both read the text with very high accuracy. Yet all three were developing a processing system in different ways:

❑ Jerome used known words and word parts (onsets and rimes) to solve unknown words. He corrected errors close to the point they were made and reread to confirm accuracy (checking whether it "looks right, sounds right, and makes sense"). He used information conveyed by the pictures to support understanding. He phrased some word groups, read others word by word. Jerome needed support that reinforced his effective behaviors, expanded his repertoire of word-solving strategies, and improved his fluency.

❑ Rosa used language structure in combination with visual information to solve words. She knew about consonant clusters but did not notice and correct errors (she made no self-corrections). She read fluently, including two- and three-word phrases. Rosa needed teaching that would reinforce her ability to use meaning consistently; she also needed to be prompted to monitor her reading using various sources of information.

❑ Tia used many sources of information to solve words efficiently. She had an impressive repertoire of word-solving strategies, but she needed to increase the automaticity of her word solving as well as her knowledge of high-frequency words. This learning would contribute to fluency, but she also needed specific prompting related to phrased, fluent reading.

If these assessments had taken place at the same time in the school year, Jerome and Tia could have worked in the same instructional group using texts at Level I or J. Rosa was reading well at Level H, but moving her to a higher level immediately might have interfered with her progress. Her instructional level should be H.

The Level K text was easy for all three children. All three made significant progress and exhibited many similar characteristics. Although still different from one another, they showed common competencies in all four categories shown in Figure 5-22:

❑ *Solving words.* Jerome, Rosa, and Tia made efficient use of many sources of information to solve words. They were flexible and proactive.

❑ *Monitoring and correcting.* All three children corrected miscues using many sources of information.

❑ *Searching for and using information.* All three readers actively searched for information conveyed by the pictures, text content, language structure, and print.

❑ *Maintaining fluency.* All three readers exhibited phrased and fluent reading, although Rosa needed more help paying attending to punctuation.

By the time they were reading at Level K, these three readers demonstrated aspects of a complex reading process. They were able to build their reading systems daily by effective processing of instructional level texts. Subsequent teaching needed to be directed toward:

❑ Increasing their repertoire of known words.

❑ Expanding their vocabulary.

❑ Expanding their strategic actions for solving multisyllable words.

❑ Expanding their ability to monitor their reading using many sources of information.

❑ Expanding their thinking beyond the text (inferring and predicting).

❑ Bringing background information to reading.

❑ Reading longer and more complex sentences fluently.

❑ Noticing aspects of the writer's craft.

❑ Thinking analytically about texts.

Jerome, Rosa, and Tia brought individual understanding with them when they read. Each of them built a unique processing system over time, taking different paths to common outcomes. Of course, they developed effective strategic actions in different ways, at different times, with differentiated teaching. Remember too that Jerome, Rosa, and Tia read these four texts at different times in the school year. The readers in any one class demonstrate a range of instructional levels. Your challenge is to differentiate your instruction so that all your students become accomplished readers.

▶ Suggestions for Professional Development

AN IN-DEPTH LOOK AT READING BEHAVIORS OVER TIME

It is highly instructive to study readers over time—to analyze the rich behavioral data gained from detailed observations—not simply to look at test scores. Finding time for this kind of analysis can be challenging. If you are able to form a study group or arrange a series of professional development sessions, conducting case studies of individual readers over time is a powerful learning experience. From close study of a few readers, you will gain critical understanding that will guide your decision-making regarding all the children you teach. If you can extend this over a year or more, the learning will be even more significant. Here are some suggestions:

1. Working in cross-grade-level groups, each teacher selects three students to study. (You need to begin with enough students that if some move, your work can continue.) You can choose students that are "typical," "lower progress," or "higher progress" readers. (It's best to avoid subjects who are at opposite ends of the continuum.)

2. Using the same text (one considered average for the time of year at your grade level), assess these students at the beginning of the year, at two midpoints, and again at the end of the year. (This assessment is different from benchmark assessment, which is designed to determine instructional and independent reading levels at two or three points in the year on instructional and independent level text.)

3. Each time you administer an assessment, use the Guide for Observing and Noting Reading Behaviors to help you think about the readers' strategic activities (see Appendix B).

4. Meet with your colleagues to discuss the readers' characteristics and progress:

   ❏ What are the strengths and teaching needs of each reader?

   ❏ What strategic activities do you observe?

   ❏ What kinds of teaching, prompting, and reinforcing are needed by each reader? (See *Fountas and Pinnell Prompting Guide 1*.)

   ❏ If your group is able to study the same students over several years, different teachers will assess and report on them, each time analyzing reading strengths and teaching needs.

   ❏ When you have finished, save the documentation in your students' records.

Text Matters: A Ladder to Success

THE TERM STRUGGLING IS ALWAYS UNDERSTOOD in relation to the difficulty of the text and to school expectations. The first thing we must do is put an end to the struggle. A gradient of text is a powerful tool to help us find books that will support and, at the same time, extend readers' abilities. Finding the right books alone will not be sufficient to help struggling readers; however, once we achieve this goal, we need to create a setting within which we can do powerful teaching. In this chapter, we examine in detail the role that the gradient, along with high-quality texts, plays in supporting readers as they change over time.

The first step in teaching struggling readers is to match the text to their ability to read it. You cannot provide intensive and powerful instruction unless the text is appropriate to support learning. To help you match books to your readers, first observe their oral reading, as described in Chapter 4. Then use the Fountas and Pinnell text gradient to choose books that will both support readers and help them extend their skills. Of course, the "right" books will not, in and of themselves, help children with reading difficulties. However, once you have the appropriate texts to use as tools, you are on your way to creating a setting for successful teaching and learning.

▶ Identifying Struggling Readers

Struggling readers are defined relative to the difficulty of the text and to your school's expectations for achievement. Let's examine this process in detail.

Look at Kulsum's Reading Record for *Anna's New Glasses* (Figure 6-1). She read accurately (indicated by the check marks above words) for the most part and was able to solve problems. On page 9, she said the first part of the word *purple,* then the entire word, indicating that she could take words apart "on the run." (She did the same with *gla–glasses* on page 11 and *for–forgot* on

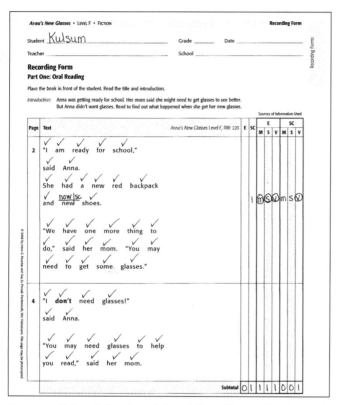

Figure 6-1 Kulsum's Reading of *Anna's New Glasses (Fountas and Pinnell Benchmark Assessment System 1)*, p. 1

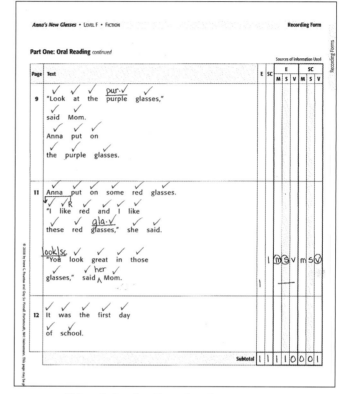

Figure 6-1 Kulsum's Reading Record, p. 3

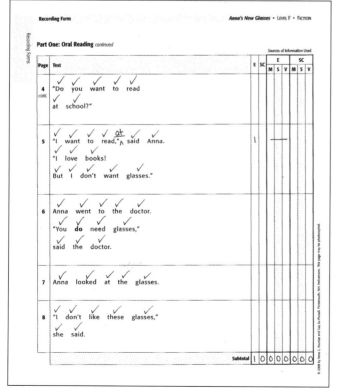

Figure 6-1 Kulsum's Reading Record, p. 2

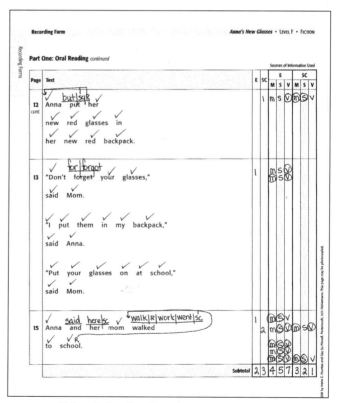

Figure 6-1 Kulsum's Reading Record, p. 4

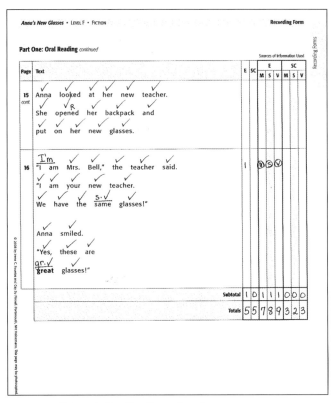

Figure 6-1 Kulsum's Reading Record, p. 5

page 13.) She reread to confirm or self-correct on pages 11 and 15, indicating that she was able to use sentence structure and meaning to process continuous text. She could attend to the visual information in print, particularly the first letter; on page 11, for example, she substituted *look* for *you*, which made sense at that point, but immediately noticed the first letter and corrected herself. She was flexible about using different kinds of information to monitor her reading. On page 12, she read *but* for *put* (two words that are very close visually); however, she knew something was not right. Meaning and language structure probably alerted her to the error, and she went back to the beginning of the sentence to read *Anna put*.

Kulsum did some interesting problem solving on page 15. First she read *Anna said here* for *Anna and her*. These errors make sense and are in line with the visual information. But by searching for additional visual information and attending to meaning, Kulsum immediately corrected *her*. Then notice how hard she worked at the word *walked*, getting the first part of the word, sensing something was wrong, trying *work* and *went*,

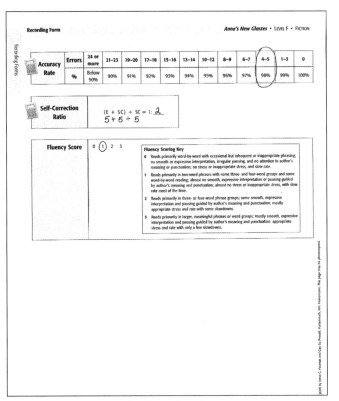

Figure 6-1 Kulsum's Reading Record, p. 6

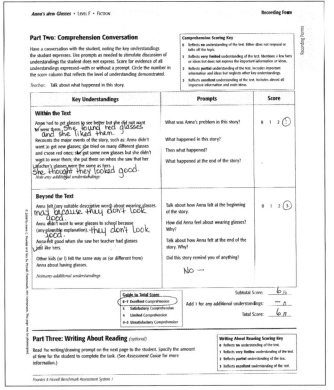

Figure 6-1 Kulsum's Reading Record, p. 7

and then reading on to the end of the sentence. At this point, meaning and language structure probably connected with her initial correct reading of the first syllable, and she went back and read *walked* correctly.

Kulsum exhibited many strengths during this reading—she knew many high-frequency words, she monitored her reading using several sources of information, and she solved a number of problems. Her comprehension, when assessed, was excellent.

Kulsum's reading of *Bubbles* (see the Reading Record in Figure 6-2) was also predominantly accurate, and she solved some problems using several sources of information. Substitutions like *bubbles* for *balloons* and *bubbling* for *blowing* make sense in context and sound right grammatically. Although inaccurate, they indicate Kulsum was able to recognize beginning and ending letters. Although she read *stray* for *straw*, she recognized the letter cluster at the beginning of the word, and she probably used meaning and language structure to correct the error. She missed the last letter of *girl's*. This seeming non-recognition of the possessive may be related to her

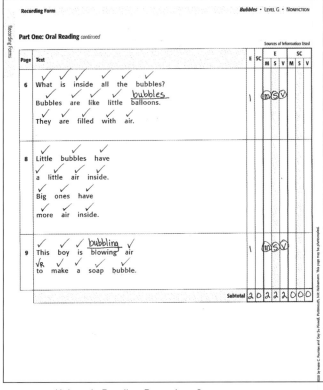

Figure 6-2 Kulsum's Reading Record, p. 2

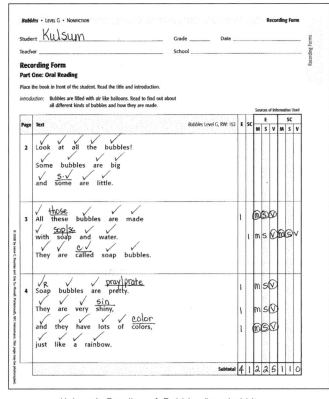

Figure 6-2 Kulsum's Reading of *Bubbles* (Leveled Literacy Intervention, Orange System), p. 1

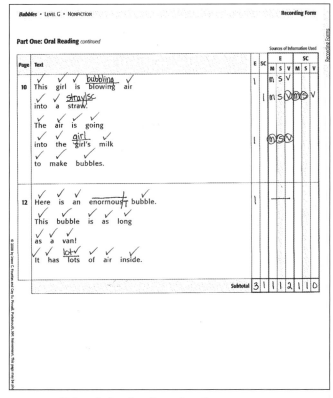

Figure 6-2 Kulsum's Reading Record, p. 3

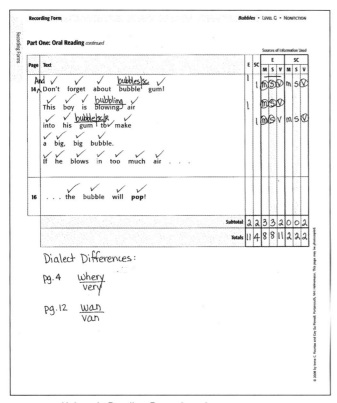

Figure 6-2 Kulsum's Reading Record, p. 4

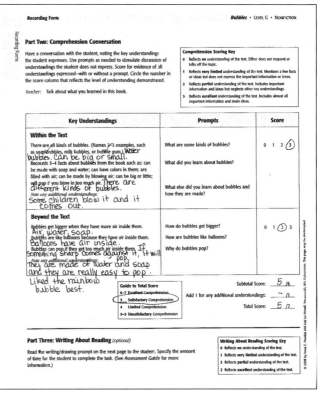

Figure 6-2 Kulsum's Reading Record, p. 6

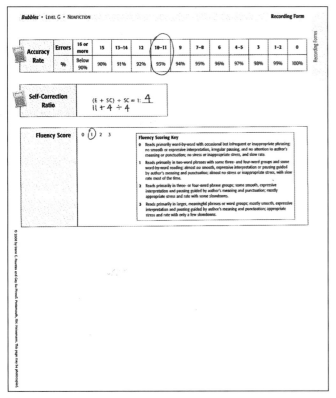

Figure 6-2 Kulsum's Reading Record, p. 5

Figure 6-2 Kulsum's Reading Record, p. 7

understanding of the convention. Kulsum is an English language learner. *Lot–lots* on page 12 shows she took words apart and noticed details of visual information. She did not attempt the word *enormous*.

Overall, Kulsum actively worked to solve problems. There is evidence of "fast brainwork," or a range of effective strategic activities. Kulsum's comprehension, assessed at the end of the reading, was satisfactory. And, notice her reflection of meaning in writing.

Kulsum's reading of *The Sleepover Party* (see the Reading Record in Figure 6-3) also reveals some strengths, particularly her perseverance. She almost always tried something when she came to an unknown word. There is ample evidence that she attended to visual information: for example, the substitution of *homes* and *home* for *house; sum, sun,* and *sunk* for *snacks;* and *p–put* for *pulled.* Several times she worked hard but unsuccessfully at a word—*p–poke, pick, pick, poch* for *pajamas,* which is interesting because the entire story is about going to a sleepover party and meaning might be expected to play a bigger role.

However, this Reading Record indicates that although Kulsum was working hard, the process was breaking down. She no longer had the forward momentum of long stretches of accurate reading to help her make sense of her reading. Thus, she made attempt after attempt using only the first letter, degenerated into wild guessing, and then moved on. It is easy to imagine how this reading might sound and what the reader's comprehension might be. Indeed, Kulsum's assessed comprehension was unsatisfactory.

If you did not know that all three examples were by the same reader, you would of course identify reader 3 as the struggling reader. But it is Kulsum each time. The first text was easy for her (Level F); the second was just a little harder (Level G); the third was clearly too hard (Level H). In two settings, she looked competent; in the third, she looked like a struggling reader. A struggling reader is one who cannot effectively process the text he or she is expected to read. *Any reader can look like a struggling reader when the text is too hard.*

Readers who demonstrate the kind of reading seen in Figure 6-3 daily are practicing ineffective strategic actions over and over, using the same problem-solving

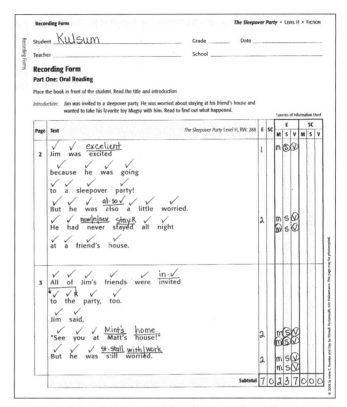

Figure 6-3 Kulsum's Reading of *The Sleepover Party (Fountas and Pinnell Benchmark Assessment System 1),* p. 1

Figure 6-3 Kulsum's Reading Record, p. 2

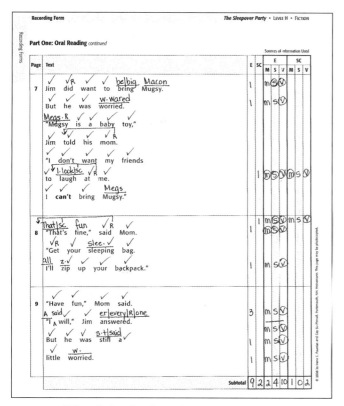

Figure 6-3 Kulsum's Reading Record, p. 3

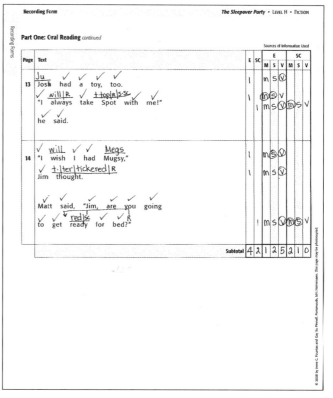

Figure 6-3 Kulsum's Reading Record, p. 5

Figure 6-3 Kulsum's Reading Record, p. 4

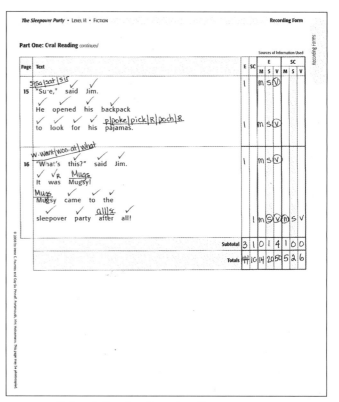

Figure 6-3 Kulsum's Reading Record, p. 6

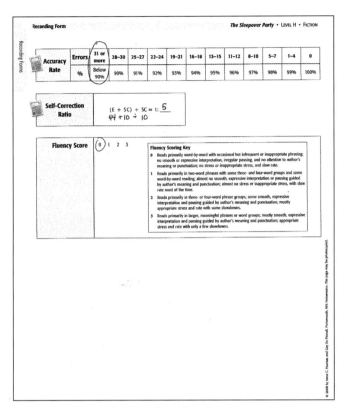

Figure 6-3 Kulsum's Reading Record, p. 7

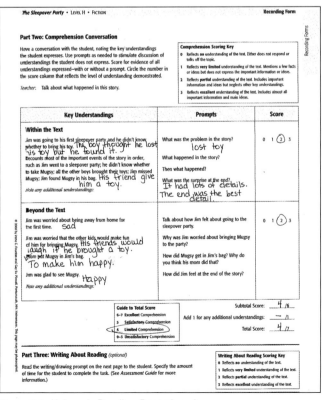

Figure 6-3 Kulsum's Reading Record, p. 8

approach time after time and habituating poor processing. At some point, they will no longer expect reading to make sense or sound like language. Most often, the readers resort to word by word solving that sounds painful. But when they read an instructional level text, the "struggle" is removed, and they can learn.

The roots of reading problems go very deep. There are many areas of potential difficulty. Problems related to hearing sounds or recognizing letters can cause lasting confusion. Given all these complexities, *it is important to consider carefully the texts that children are expected to read.* The accessibility of the text matters. It is the first step in helping readers who struggle behave like effective readers.

▶ The Demands of Texts

All texts make demands on readers in terms of how they are written, illustrated, or designed. Text demands encompass all aspects of language as well as the unique demands of print. The proficient reader deals competently with all these demands. As you think about the demands of any text, ask, "What must the reader be able to do to process this text with accuracy, fluency, and understanding?" (Figure 6-4 lists some general suggestions for helping struggling readers learn about texts.) Interactive read-aloud provides ideal opportunities for building children's understandings of all of these text factors. You can then build on their knowledge in small group instruction or independent reading conferences.

Genre and Form

Every genre has particular characteristics. The degree to which the reader understands these characteristics impacts comprehension. Understanding the genre helps readers:

❑ *Predict text structure.* The genre of a text clues the sophisticated reader in to how it will be organized. Informational text will likely be organized into categories. A narrative will probably be a series of sequential problems and resolutions.

❑ *Predict the reading behavior that will be needed.* Readers call on specific resources when reading

Figure 6-4 Suggestions for Helping Struggling Readers Learn about Text Factors

Text Characteristics	For Whole Group Interactive Read-Aloud, Small Group Reading Instruction, and Independent Reading
1. Genre/Form	• Select a variety of text genres. • Be sure that the classroom library has good examples of an appropriate range of genres. • Discuss how books that are the same genre are like each other (for example, with talking animals or true information.)
2. Text Structure	• Draw children's attention to the way the text is organized (for example, time passing). • Use drawing and writing to represent aspects of structure, for example sequence, a circular story, or how items are related to each other.
3. Content	• Select texts that provide some new content but be sure that it is accessible to students with their current knowledge. • Provide background knowledge before reading the text. • Remind readers to think about what they already know before reading an informational text and/or have them briefly talk about understandings. • Using shared or interactive writing, list what students know before reading; then list some new information they learned after reading.
4. Themes and Ideas	• Select texts with themes and ideas that are age appropriate and accessible to students. • Involve students in deep discussion of the text to enrich their understanding of themes and ideas. • Model stating the themes or talking about the big ideas in a text. • Use shared or interactive writing to quickly list the important ideas in a text.
5. Language and Literary Features	• Make a judgment about the amount of literary language children can understand. • Explain literary language such as figures of speech. • Draw students' attention to literary features such as where the story takes place (using pictures and print), the characters and what they are like, the problem in the story, and the ending.
6. Sentence Complexity	• Read aloud selections that will expand students' ability to listen to and understand more complex sentences. • Invite students to join in on refrains to give them experience in saying more complex language. • When introducing texts in small group reading, demonstrate one or two of the more complex sentences. • Have students say some of the more difficult sentences or phrases prior to reading a text.
7. Vocabulary	• Read aloud selections that will expand students' vocabulary. • Explain words that students do not know. • Have students say some of the vocabulary that might be new to them prior to reading a text. • Use new vocabulary in conversation. • Reread texts and discuss the meaning of new words again.

continues

Figure 6-4 Suggestions for Helping Struggling Readers Learn about Text Factors, *continued*

Text Characteristics	For Whole Group Interactive Read-Aloud, Small Group Reading Instruction, and Independent Reading
8. Words	• Uses new words in conversation before reading. • Have students predict the first sound and then locate a few new words before reading a new text. • After reading, have students locate one or two words that were new to them. • Have students build words with magnetic letters and check them by running a finger under the word left to right. • Build students' knowledge of high-frequency words to free attention for solving longer content words. • Demonstrate and prompt students to take apart multisyllable words by looking at base words, endings, and syllables.
9. Illustrations	• Draw attention to the illustrations before, during, and after reading. • Invite students to talk about what they have learned from the illustrations in a fiction or nonfiction text. • Explicitly demonstrate how to "read" and understand the various kinds of graphics that are found in informational texts. • Invite students to appreciate the beauty, humor, or other quality of illustrations in fiction.
10. Book and Print Features	• For small group instruction and independent reading, select texts that are of appropriate length for students and with supportive font and print layout. • Draw students' attention to and demonstrate the use of punctuation. • Draw students' attention to and demonstrate the use of words in bold, italics, or enlarged print. • Draw students' attention to and demonstrate the use of text features such as table of contents, index, glossary, headings and subheadings, chapter titles, etc. • Remind students to use text features to help them understand the text and how information is presented.

a particular genre. For example, when reading a mystery (a special form of narrative), readers expect to look for "clues" or important details. When reading all texts, particularly informational texts, readers draw on what they already know about a topic. When reading a narrative, readers expect to understand how the characters behave or change.

❑ *Adjust expectations.* Being familiar with a genre allows readers to form expectations that are appropriate to the text's purpose, pace, and action. Readers expect information in a factual text—in both the illustrations and the words. Readers of realistic fiction expect to respond to the mood or the characters' feelings and may appreciate how the illustrations help them visualize the action. Readers of fantasy expect to suspend disbelief and accept unusual circumstances, settings, and characters.

❑ *Make connections to other texts.* Readers familiar with a genre can make connections to other examples of the genre. These connections can enrich their comprehension and their appreciation of the writer's craft.

The only way to become familiar with the characteristics of different genres is to read hundreds of examples. By reading lots of examples, even young children learn what to expect from traditional tales as opposed to stories about everyday life.

Some readers have had very little exposure to genres. Their experience in hearing and discussing books at home may be limited. Some schools limit the amount of time teachers are allowed to read aloud to children. This severely deprives students who have few out-of-school experiences with text. Also, readers who struggle often do not read many texts, and often those texts they do read—"decodable" texts or very simple picture books, for example—may not be true representatives of a genre.

Text Structure

Structure refers to the way the writer "builds" and organizes a text. A complex narrative may have an attention-getting opening, a description of the setting, an exposition of the problem, a recounting of a series of events, and a resolution. An informational text may be arranged into categories and subcategories that are then described, sequenced, compared and contrasted, or developed through problem/solution or cause/effect.

The experienced reader intuitively detects these structures and uses them as tools for comprehension. The structure helps readers follow the events being described or search for information. The structure also helps readers remember what they've already read. When readers cannot identify the underlying structure of a text, these important supports are unavailable. Struggling readers often work so hard reading individual words that they miss the "big picture" or how the book works.

Rereading a text will help struggling readers see the structure, but it may not be enough. Many readers

need very explicit instruction. For example, notice how the comic strip helps readers understand a story entitled "A Surprise for Roxy" (Figure 6-5). It calls attention to the temporal sequence and the parts-to-whole relationship that create the surprising and humorous ending—like many children, Roxy always says she won't like an unfamiliar ingredient but when they are combined to make a pizza, she likes it!

Content

It is ironic that a major factor in readers' comprehension is not their reading skill but what they already know! The more you already know about a topic, place, or type of problem, the easier it is to understand what someone has written about it. Readers build their knowledge of the world through direct experiences and by reading about other people's direct experiences. Some readers have had little or no opportunity to build this knowledge, and the knowledge they have may not be represented in the books they are trying to read. This makes comprehension difficult, but you can provide critical information when introducing a text, and the children can immediately apply this information

Figure 6-5 Child's Map of *A Surprise for Roxy*

when they begin reading. This way, they learn the cognitive operation of activating and using background knowledge. They also come to understand that they are supposed to bring what they already know to the experience of reading.

Themes and Ideas

Fiction always has a theme (often more than one), which is the overarching or larger meaning. Informational texts have ideas that range from simple to complex. True comprehension encompasses understanding the important themes and ideas of a text. Texts for young readers usually have very simple themes—making friends, helping, playing tricks, caring for pets, family relationships. The themes are centered on familiar experiences. As they become more sophisticated, readers can understand more complex themes, such as learning a lesson or growing and changing.

Identifying the overarching theme and understanding the important ideas of a text require complex thinking. Students need to follow the story and understand what is happening. They need to gather the important information as they read. And then they need to infer what the text is really about. This process requires that readers are able to pay attention to this kind of thinking and understand that there is something to think about! It takes many reading experiences for readers to be able to do this kind of thinking.

Children who have listened to, read, and talked about many texts already know how to recognize the important ideas. As they begin to read for themselves, this skill develops automatically. It is enough just to ask them what they learned from the story or what it was about. But some readers need explicit modeling of this process.

Look at the page layout of *Bear's Birthday* and the conversation children had after reading it (Figure 6-6). In this conversation, the teacher noticed that the children were stating some details from the text but were not coming to a deeper understanding. She therefore modeled searching for and using key information, thinking about what theme these events related to, and inferring what the theme implied.

Language and Literary Features

Language and literary features make texts appealing. We delight in interesting or poetic language. We notice aspects of the writer's craft. We feel satisfaction when the ending reflects the events in the text.

Frog Songs is a story from a series that features a well-loved frog character and his friends. (See the sample page layout in Figure 6-7.) Froggy wants to sing, but his croaking is rejected by the birds. Froggy is very sad until his friends join him. Notice the sentence on pages 10 and 11. Using *late that day* as an introductory phrase is more literary than simply saying, "They came to see him later in the day." Given the problem of the story, conveying the happy ending in the phrase "very, very LOUD songs" is charming and satisfying. Young children notice this kind of language and begin to emulate it in their own writing.

Baby Bird (see Figure 6-8) is an even simpler story, but notice how the writer keeps repeating information about the baby bird's beak, legs, and wings throughout. This repetition, as the baby bird grows bigger and stronger over the pages, brings coherence to the text and gives page 15 deeper meaning. The story has mystery and drama.

An important literary feature is the way a character changes. Notice Lily's behavior and attitude (shown in both text and pictures) in the three scenes from *Old Jacket, New Jacket* (Figure 6-9). She moves from rejecting the old jacket to teaching her sister a lesson about turning a situation around to make it positive. Character change is a literary understanding that skilled readers look for and understand.

Young children may first hear literary language in traditional literature read aloud. Even before they can read, many children are at home with such phrases as "once upon a time," "down came the giant," or "lived happily ever after." Look at page 3 of *The Fox and the Gulls* (see Figure 6-10). The story starts with "long ago" and a statement about the setting. The tone is literary. Also notice the vocabulary: *startled, rumbled,* and *tasty feast.* These words communicate precise meaning that makes the story more vivid.

FIGURE 6-6 Page Layout of *Bear's Birthday* from Leveled Literacy Intervention, Green System (Heinemann 2009)

Figure 6-6 Discussion of *Bear's Birthday*—Demonstration of Deriving the Theme

Speaker	Interaction	What the Teacher Is Attending to
Mr. D	Bear had a great birthday, didn't he? But he almost didn't.	*Invites children to talk about the story.*
Sarah	Yeah, because nobody came until the end.	*Notices that children are not showing that they understand the theme.*
Mark	He got stuff from everybody but they didn't come.	
David	Yes, they did come!	
Mr. D	You know, when I'm thinking about a story, I go back and think what happened at the beginning. Let me show you. Look at page 4. You know Bear had the idea of having a party and he decided to bake a cake, but he didn't have any eggs. What is happening now?	*Demonstrates looking back in the story to understand it.*
David	He is asking Rabbit for some eggs.	
Sarah	The rabbit is giving him some eggs in a basket.	
Mr. D	That's really nice of Rabbit isn't it? And what is happening on page 5?	*Directs children's attention to important information.*
Sarah	She is crying.	
Mr. D	Oh, yes, look at that tear. And so I have to think, "Why is Rabbit so sad?" We can't tell from the picture, can we? Read this page again softly to yourself and see why Rabbit was sad.	*Models thinking and searching for information.*
	Children read.	
Mr. D	Kelly, read the last part of page 5 to us.	*Focuses the group on important information.*
Kelly	Kelly reads, "Why didn't Bear ask me to his party? Rabbit asked sadly.	
David	She's sad because Bear didn't invite her to the party.	
Mr. D	That's right. So I am thinking that Bear told Rabbit about the party. He asked her for the eggs and she gave them to him. Then, he just went away. "Why didn't Bear ask me to his party?" Rabbit asked sadly.	*Models thinking and searching for information.*
Kelly	He should have invited her.	
Mr. D	I wonder why he didn't? So now I am thinking that Bear did the same thing to other friends. He went to Beaver and got paper, but he didn't invite him. Look at page 11.	*Models questioning. Directs attention to more examples.*
Mark	He got some balloons from Fox, but he didn't invite him.	

continues

Speaker	Interaction	What the Teacher Is Attending to
Mr. D	You are right. They were all sad. Look at page 12 and 13. It looks like Bear is sad here.	*Models interpreting the picture and searching for reasons.*
Kelly	He is all ready for the party.	
Mark	But nobody is there.	
Mr. D	So, let's turn the page and all think hard. What lesson did Bear learn?	*Asks children to think about the theme.*
Sarah	He should invite his friends to the party.	
Mr. D	It's important when you have a party to invite your friends. He just forgot about it. And they were all sad and Bear was nearly sad. I would be thinking: "I wonder what Bear should do next time he wants to give a party?"	*Restates what happened in the story.* *Asks children to infer implications of the theme.*
Mark	He'll remember to invite his friends at the beginning.	
Mr. D	I hope he will do that. You really wouldn't tell someone about a party, and then borrow something from them. And then, not invite them! A good friend needs to think about his friends and invite them to the party. How would you feel if Bear did not invite you?	*Restates the theme.* *Asks children to infer feelings of characters.*
Kelly	I would be sad.	
Sarah	They might think Bear didn't like them or want them to come.	
David	It would hurt their feelings.	

Figure 6-6 Discussion of *Bear's Birthday*—Demonstration of Deriving the Theme, *continued*

FIGURE 6-7 Pages from *Frog Songs,* from Leveled Literacy Intervention, Blue System (Heinemann 2009)

Once there was a baby bird.
The baby bird had
a small beak.
She had small legs.
She had small wings.
She was very small,
but she was warm and happy.

Then something happened.

2   3

"Ouch!" said the baby bird.
"I am too big for this space.
My legs are too long.
My wings are too big.
What can I do?"

10   11

The baby bird began to grow.

"Oh, my," said the baby bird.
"My beak is getting stronger.
My legs are getting longer.
My wings are getting
bigger, too."

4   5

"I know what I can do!"
said the baby bird.
"I can peck with my beak.
My strong, sharp beak
will get me out of here."

The baby bird pecked
and pecked.
She did not stop.

Then something happened.

12   13

The baby bird grew and grew.

"Oh, my!" said the baby bird.
"Look at me!
I am getting bigger
and bigger.
If I grow much more,
I will run out of room here."

6   7

Crack! Crack! Crack!

The baby bird got out
of the egg.
The baby bird was free!

The baby bird said,
"Now my long legs can hop.
Now my big wings can flap.
Now I have **lots** of space!"

14   15

The baby bird grew
more and more.

The baby bird said,
"Look at me!
My beak is getting stronger—
a lot stronger!
My legs are getting longer—
a lot longer!
My wings are getting bigger—
a lot bigger!
This space is just too small
for me."

8   9

"Have a bug!"
said the mother bird.

16

FIGURE 6-8 Page Layout of *Baby Bird* from Leveled Literacy Intervention, Green System (Heinemann 2009)

Iris shook her head.
"I don't want that old thing,"
said Iris.
"I want a *new* jacket
to wear with my jeans."

"But this is a good jacket,"
said Mom.
"It will look good on you, Iris."

4

5

At first, Iris felt sad.
Then she felt mad.
Dana's old jacket was
not the same as a new one.
Iris wanted a jacket
that was just for her.

6

Iris stared at the jacket.
She wanted to make it special.
What could she do?
She put a heart pin on it.
That didn't look right.
But the pin gave Iris an idea.

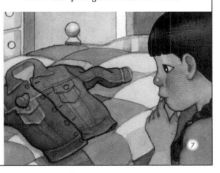

7

Just then Dana came in.
"Nice jacket!" said Dana.
"Can I have one, too?"
she asked Mom.

"It's easy," said Iris.
"Just get an old jacket
and make it brand new!"

16

FIGURE 6-9 Page Spreads from *Old Jacket, New Jacket* from Leveled Literacy Intervention, Blue System (Heinemann 2009)

Dialogue is another literary feature of texts. Notice the progression of complexity in the story excerpts shown in Figure 6-11. In *The Little Red Hen,* there is one speaker per page. In *The Trip,* there are two speakers per page. In *Bear's Birthday,* dialogue is separated by narrative. *The Fox and the Gulls* contains much longer and more literary dialogue in which Fox is really talking to himself rather than to another person.

While literary features make a text enjoyable for readers, they also often present a challenge in terms of language structure and vocabulary. Literary texts frequently include similes and metaphors, which may be very difficult to grasp, especially for English language learners. The only way to become familiar with the literary features of texts is to experience them again and again. You can contribute a great deal to these understandings by reading stories aloud every day and pointing out and discussing examples of literary features and things that are well said.

Many struggling readers have had little exposure to literary features and need the extra support of read-alouds, thorough introductions to texts, and discussions of plots and characters. An activity very beneficial in helping struggling readers understand and appreciate dialogue is readers' theater. Children love it. They have the experience of reading aloud for an authentic reason,

FIGURE 6-10 Page Spread from *The Fox and the Gulls* from Leveled Literacy Intervention, Blue System (Heinemann 2009)

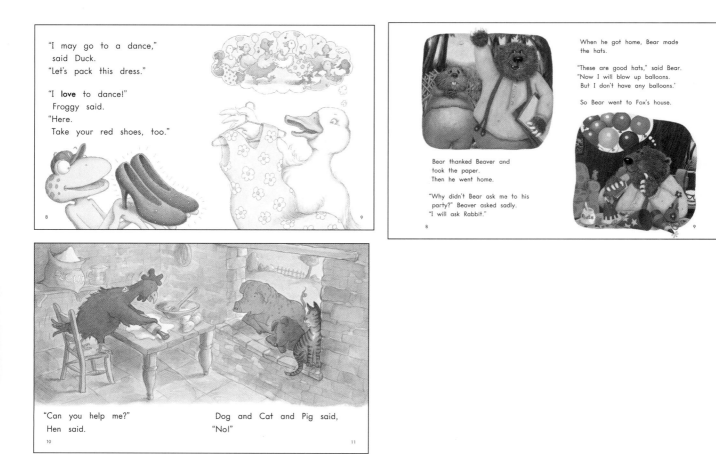

FIGURE 6-11 Page Spreads from *The Trip, The Little Red Hen, and Bear's Birthday* from Leveled Literacy Intervention, Blue and Green Systems (Heinemann 2009)

and they have the opportunity to process dialogue while thinking about meaning. (Figure 6-12 is a readers' theater script created for *The Fox and the Gulls*. The words are taken from the text verbatim, but it has been reformatted as a play.) Readers' theater does not require memorization; with just a little practice, children can confidently perform a play like this for themselves or others. (Resist the temptation to create costumes and use props. Your purpose is to help students with comprehension and fluency.)

Sentence Complexity

Language complexity is an important factor in reading difficulty. (Look at the sentences in Figure 6-13, and notice their increasing complexity.) The more complex the language structure, the more challenging it will be to the reader. Children need to be immersed in texts in order to process the complex sentences that make these texts enjoyable. They need to hear texts read to them, they need rich introductions to the texts they are reading, and they need many opportunities to reread texts.

Vocabulary

Vocabulary is a major challenge for struggling readers. (Look at the increasingly demanding words in Figure 6-14.) Learning new words means much more than knowing the sounds and letters and being able to decode them. Children need to know the meaning of the words they encounter in texts. Many words they meet in texts will not be in their oral vocabularies; therefore, children need to know how to learn new words from reading.

Some children have had so few learning-related interactions with adults that they do not even know the familiar names of objects and animals. They may never have visited a zoo, noticed and talked about features of the environment, or heard books read aloud. Some vocabulary comes only from reading (or perhaps from hearing stories being read on television)—a phrase like *long ago*, for example. Just as in other areas, experience counts. When children's experiences are limited, their vocabulary will also be limited. While struggling readers are building simple concepts and learning labels like *lion* and *camel*, texts are making ever increasing demands that assume this vocabulary is already in

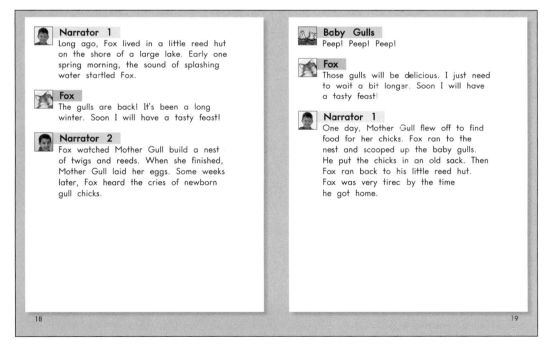

Narrator 1
Long ago, Fox lived in a little reed hut on the shore of a large lake. Early one spring morning, the sound of splashing water startled Fox.

Fox
The gulls are back! It's been a long winter. Soon I will have a tasty feast!

Narrator 2
Fox watched Mother Gull build a nest of twigs and reeds. When she finished, Mother Gull laid her eggs. Some weeks later, Fox heard the cries of newborn gull chicks.

Baby Gulls
Peep! Peep! Peep!

Fox
Those gulls will be delicious. I just need to wait a bit longer. Soon I will have a tasty feast!

Narrator 1
One day, Mother Gull flew off to find food for her chicks. Fox ran to the nest and scooped up the baby gulls. He put the chicks in an old sack. Then Fox ran back to his little reed hut. Fox was very tired by the time he got home.

18   19

FIGURE 6-12 Page Spread from *The Fox and the Gulls* from Leveled Literacy Intervention, Blue System (Heinemann 2009)

Figure 6-13 **Increasing Sentence Complexity**

Title	Level	Page Spread	Analysis
*Baby**	A	 Baby is crawling.	Subject, verb (present participle).
Hiding	B	 Puff likes to hide behind the chair.	Subject, verb, two prepositional phrases.
Flap, Flap, Fly	C	 Mother Duck can eat. She eats and eats. She eats by the pond.	Subject, compound verb. Subject, prepositional phrase.
A Surprise for Roxy	D	 Father got some mushrooms. "I do not want mushrooms," said Roxy.	Embedded clause with subject, verb, and verb object.
All About Sharks	F	 A great white shark has 5,000 teeth. Its teeth are long and sharp. This shark can eat and eat and eat!	Possessive pronoun, passive verb, adjectives. Article, subject, compound verb.

* A variety of texts from Leveled Literacy Intervention (Heinemann 2009)

Figure 6-13 Increasing Sentence Complexity, *continued*

<table>
<tr><th>Title</th><th>Level</th><th>Page Spread</th><th>Analysis</th></tr>
<tr><td>Plants That Eat Bugs*</td><td>H</td><td>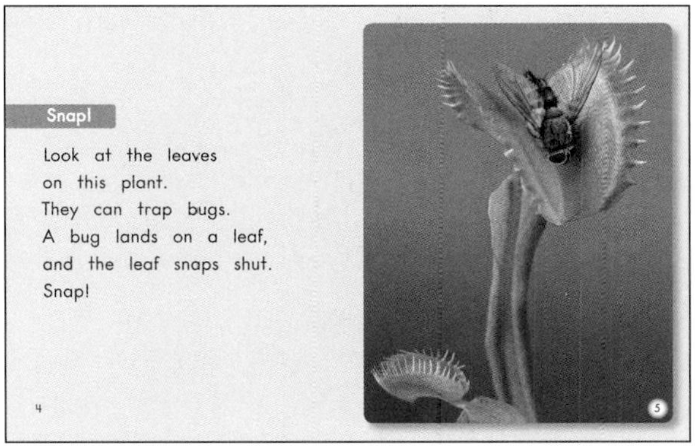
Snap!
Look at the leaves
on this plant.
They can trap bugs.
A bug lands on a leaf,
and the leaf snaps shut.
Snap!
4
5</td><td>Present tense, compound sentence.</td></tr>
<tr><td>Elephant and Tiger</td><td>I</td><td>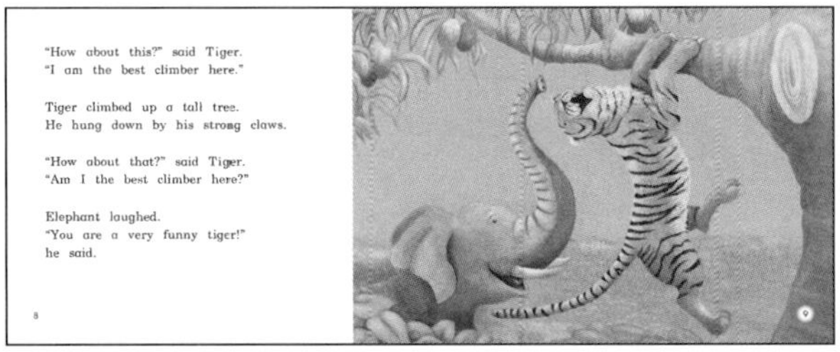
"How about this?" said Tiger.
"I am the best climber here."
Tiger climbed up a tall tree.
He hung down by his strong claws.
"How about that?" said Tiger.
"Am I the best climber here?"
Elephant laughed.
"You are a very funny tiger!"
he said.
8
9</td><td>Question and embedded clause.
Question in dialogue, adjective.</td></tr>
<tr><td>The Fox and the Gulls</td><td>M</td><td>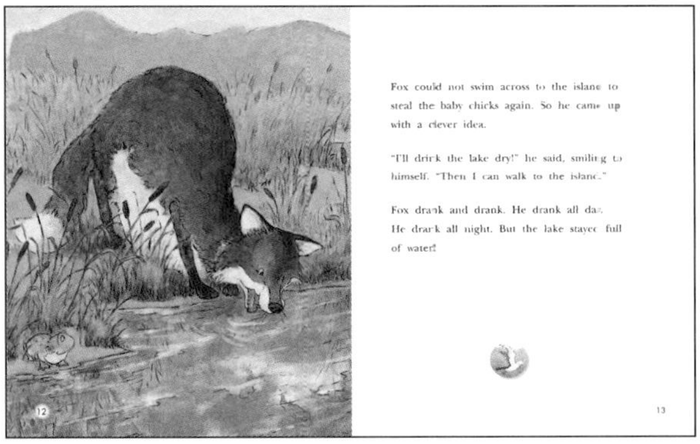
Fox could not swim across to the island to steal the baby chicks again. So he came up with a clever idea.
"I'll drink the lake dry!" he said, smiling to himself. "Then I can walk to the island."
Fox drank and drank. He drank all day. He drank all night. But the lake stayed full of water!
12
13</td><td>Embedded clause with adjective, adverbial phrase, second embedded clause with prepositional phrase.</td></tr>
<tr><td>Chester Greenwood's Big Idea</td><td>N</td><td>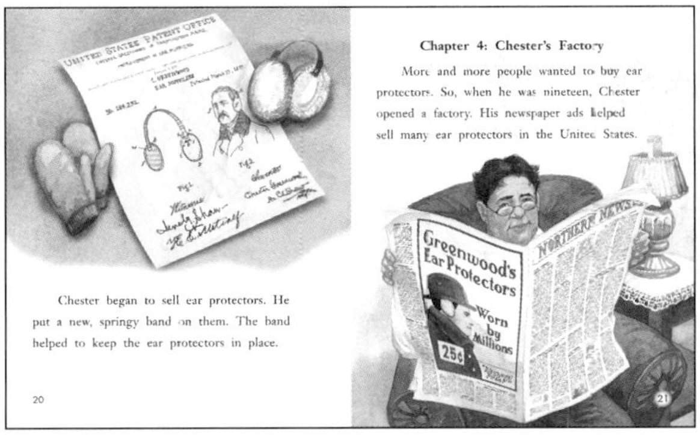
Chester began to sell ear protectors. He put a new, springy band on them. The band helped to keep the ear protectors in place.
20
Chapter 4: Chester's Factory
More and more people wanted to buy ear protectors. So, when he was nineteen, Chester opened a factory. His newspaper ads helped sell many ear protectors in the United States.
Greenwood's Ear Protectors
Worn by Millions
25¢
NORTHERN NEWS
21</td><td>Introductory independent clause.
Introductory prepositional phrase, subject verb, adjective, noun, and difficult prepositional phrase.</td></tr>
</table>

* A variety of texts from Leveled Literacy Intervention (Heinemann 2009)

place. Instead of thinking actively about the meaning of the text, the struggling reader is distracted by decoding individual words and has little attention left to devote to the big picture.

For younger readers, vocabulary is built through hearing books read aloud and by *talking* about them. Text-based talk is the best way to expand vocabulary.

Figure 6-14 **Increasing Vocabulary in Texts**			
Title	**Level**	**Examples of Vocabulary**	
Baby	A	sleeping crying eating sitting	crawling playing smiling laughing
Hiding	B	in under behind box	bag basket bed
Flap, Flap, Fly	C	walks swims eat	fly pond
A Surprise for Roxy	D	peppers mushrooms	surprise
All About Sharks	F	shark great	bigger fin
Plants That Eat Bugs	H	leaves sticky traps	smooth inside
Elephant and Tiger	I	scariest roared heard	knocked climber
The Fox and the Gulls	M	rumbled island floated tasty	safely thorny middle
Chester Greenwood's Big Idea	N	thought invention through	remembers ads protectors

Instructional reading often contains either words that are unfamiliar to children or familiar words used in new ways. You'll want to be sure that you "unpack" all the unfamiliar words during your introductory conversations. You can also revisit words after reading and extend children's understanding by asking them to write about their reading.

Words

To read, children must solve the words of a text "on the run" while reading continuous print. Word-reading strategies include:

❑ *Recognizing words quickly and automatically.* Readers are constantly expanding the repertoire of words that they can recognize instantly. This includes not only high-frequency words but also words they have read several times and now know.

❑ *Using letter and sound relationships.* Readers connect the sounds in words with the letters and letter clusters that represent them. They look at the letters and come up with the associated sounds. Effective decoders are flexible in recognizing these relationships.

❑ *Using spelling patterns.* Readers notice the spelling patterns that appear frequently in words and connect them to sound patterns to solve words. Using the larger parts of words makes decoding more efficient.

❑ *Using word parts.* Readers learn to take words apart quickly by recognizing base and root words, prefixes and suffixes, and all kinds of endings.

❑ *Using syllables.* Readers take longer words apart by noticing the syllables and then using letters or spelling patterns to solve each one.

❑ *Connecting words.* Readers connect new words to words they already know. They make these connections using letters, letter clusters, word parts, or spelling patterns. The connection makes word solving faster.

❑ *Using meaning and language structure in combination with many kinds of visual information.* Strategic readers use a full range of visual information to solve words, but they check that the word makes sense and sounds right in the sentence. They also use language structure and meaning in a predictive way that narrows the alternatives and makes it easier to use visual features of words. In short, the whole system works together.

Struggling readers may have difficulty with just about all these strategic activities. They do not know enough words and so must work on many of them. They are slow at using visual information; often, the whole process breaks down. They lose the sense of meaning as they work on one word after another and are unable to use language structure and meaning.

Matching books to readers' current abilities is the first step in smoothing out the process. There are also specific techniques for helping students learn more high-frequency words and look at word parts and patterns. Ultimately, they need many opportunities to use these skills while reading continuous print. You will notice the increase in decoding challenges from books at Level A to Level Z.

Illustrations

Illustrations are the first thing young children see when they open a book. They pore over and touch the pictures in books that are read to them, connecting what they see to the language they hear. Illustrations take various forms as we grow as readers. Although most of us read longer fictional books with no illustrations, we often read illustrated nonfiction and enjoy the art and photographs. Illustrations do not lose their appeal or usefulness no matter how old we get.

As children build a reading process, illustrations play different roles at different levels (see Figure 6-15). In very simple books, much of the meaning is conveyed in the pictures. If you read only the text for very easy Level A or B texts, you'll find that many are "flat" unless you are looking at the humorous pictures. Since we want children to appreciate characters and eventually create their own stories, pictures are a good way to engage them with text and enrich their comprehension.

Figure 6-15 **Role of Illustrations in Texts**		
	Fiction	**Nonfiction**
Early Texts	• Provide critical information • Carry the meaning of the story • Engage the reader	• Provide critical information • Illustrate concepts, some of which are not familiar • Closely match information in the print • Very simple, often photographs
Middle Level Texts	• Add humor • Add meaning to use for inference and interpretation	• Add information through simple labels • Closely match information in print • Provide more details
Higher Level Texts	• Add artistry to the text • Create a mood • Communicate emotion • Provide aesthetic experiences • Teach about the illustrator's role	• Add important information to be interpreted and integrated with the print • Utilize a variety of graphics (maps, charts, graphs, cutaways) • Complex information • Different information from the body of the text

It is important that readers actively search for meaning in the illustrations of fictional texts. Some struggling readers focus so much on sounding out words that they overlook information that is readily available in the illustrations. As readers become more sophisticated, they draw most of the meaning of a text from print, but illustrations still add meaning. The illustrations in more complex texts still help readers interpret the theme or mood of a story.

It is also important for readers of nonfiction texts to use the information provided in graphics to help clarify the text. Graphics play an increasingly important role in complex text, especially in the content areas. Readers need to notice and use the information in graphics early on, and many students will need very explicit teaching to be able to do so. It is a complex process to integrate the information in illustrations and in print. As they work to read the words, some struggling readers ignore or neglect the meaning and information in pictures.

Book and Print Features

Print features include type size and layout, the design of illustrations and print, and text elements such as headings and subheadings. Punctuation is related to sentence complexity and helps the reader parse sentences. Noticing punctuation helps readers pause appropriately and use correct intonation. Other helpful features, such as the table of contents, glossary, and index, enable readers to navigate texts.

Print size and layout are especially important for beginning readers (see Chapter 10, Learning About Print: Early Reading Behaviors). Notice the strong reader support provided at Levels A and B and how that level of support is gradually withdrawn by Levels J and N in these excerpts (Figure 6-16). When readers are struggling, it is important to select texts for them that have a straightforward and friendly layout. Readers who have difficulty processing visual information need print to be as clear as possible.

▶ Using Texts to Support Reading Progress Over Time

Looking at texts organized by degree of difficulty, we see that the demands increase across all ten text factors. A text gradient is a very helpful tool in choosing texts that increase these demands gradually so that children can learn to process effectively at each level. It will not help struggling readers to constantly try to process texts that are too hard. Children need both an appropriate text and intensive teaching at that text level to be able to move to the next level.

It is also important for texts to be varied and appealing. Use a good mix of fiction and nonfiction texts with your students. By reading texts they can process effectively and moving from one genre to another, children become more flexible. Below are some additional suggestions that will help you provide extra support for struggling readers.

Books in a Series

Series books can play a special role in supporting all readers, but struggling readers in particular respond to them in very positive ways. Some values of series books include:

- ❑ Children become interested in the topics, characters, or plots so that they are motivated to read more.

- ❑ As children move through a series, they experience the satisfaction of bringing a great deal of background knowledge to their reading.

- ❑ They become very familiar with the characters; they are better able to talk about their traits and infer their feelings and motivations.

- ❑ Children have the experience of reading connected text over time.

- ❑ Readers learn to make connections between texts—typical situations, problems, settings, character traits, style of writing, and illustrations.

When readers find a series they like, they get "hooked" and gobble up book after book. Of course,

Figure 6-16 **Print Layout Across Four Levels**

Title	Level	Page Spreads	Characteristics of Layout
*Funny Things**	A	Look at the funny socks.	• 1 line of print • Print on left, illustration on right • Large print • Clear space between each word • Period and exclamation point
Hop, Hop, Hop	B	I can hop, hop, hop on the bed.	• 2 lines of print • Print on left, illustration on right • Sentences starting on the left margin • Large print • Clear space between each word and each line • Print layout helps readers put together words in the preposition phrase • Period, exclamation point, comma
How Bear Lost His Tail	J	This made Fox unhappy. He thought his own long, bushy tail was the most beautiful tail of all. So Fox made a plan. Fox knew that Bear loved fish more than anything else. So Fox cut out a hole in the ice. He fished all day long until he had a great big pile of fish. When he heard Bear coming, Fox hid the fishing pole and dipped his tail into the cold, icy water.	• Some words in all capital letters • Sentences starting in the middle of a line • Clear spaces between lines • Spaces to indicate paragraphing • Smaller but still clear font • Period, exclamation point, comma, quotation mark • Speech bubbles
Chester Greenwood's Big Idea	N	**Chapter 3: A New Idea** Chester thought and thought. He needed to put something warm over his ears. A scarf was too itchy. What could he use? Then he had an idea. Socks! He found two socks. Next, he got some wire and put it through the socks. Then he tried on his invention. His ears felt warm.	• Chapter numbers and titles • Indentation to indicate paragraphs • Clear spaces between lines • Spaces to indicate paragraphing • Smaller but still clear font • Period, exclamation point, comma, quotation mark

* A variety of texts from Leveled Literacy Intervention (Heinemann 2009)

you don't want them to read *only* series books, but reading a large quantity of meaningful print quickly helps children control language structures, expand their vocabulary, and read more fluently.

After children have read one book in a series, they know what to expect from the others. They can predict the structure; they know the genre. They know the names of important characters and almost feel they are real people. It is easy to make connections to other texts, to understand the problem of a story, and to infer characters' motivations and feelings. *Readers feel competent* when they read a series book that they like.

Series books can be fiction or nonfiction, and there are some fundamental qualitative differences between the two. Series books are not all narratives about the same characters. Some books in a series have other kinds of similarities. Let's look at a few examples.

FICTION SERIES/ANIMAL FANTASY

The Moosling series includes texts from Levels D through M (see Figure 6-17). Over time, readers come to know that Moosling is young and curious, which sometimes gets him into trouble. He is also very friendly and helpful and loves baby animals. After reading several Moosling books, readers know that there will probably be a problem and a humorous situation. They also know that Moosling is a good character; everyone likes him and helps him learn.

Figure 6-17 **Moosling Series: Animal Fantasy**

Moosling is a young moose who is just learning about life. His playful nature and helpfulness endear him to all of his friends in the forest.

Title	Level	Page Spreads	Synopsis
*A Picnic in the Rain**	D	 But the umbrella was too small. Mouse wanted to have a picnic with Rabbit. But it was raining.	The forest friends plan a picnic but it rains. Moosling enjoys the rain and helps everyone out by keeping them out of the rain.
The Hug	E	 "I wish I could get a hug!" said Pins. "Will you hug me, Skunk?" "I can't!" said Skunk. "Do you want to shake hands?"	A little porcupine wants a hug, but no one will do it because of her spines. Moosling solves the problem!
Moosling the Babysitter	G	 One day, Skunk asked Moosling to watch the little skunks. Moosling said yes. He liked the baby skunks. They never ran away or climbed too high or fell in the pond. They just followed Moosling in a line, like good little skunks.	All the baby animals love Moosling and he loves to babysit. Moosling takes care of the baby skunks with disastrous results!
Footprints	H	 Soon Moosling saw more footprints. "I think Skunk made those," he said. "I will follow them and see." He followed them . . . And there was Rabbit! "Rabbit!" said Moosling. "I found you!" "You did?" asked Rabbit.	Moosling discovers that he can follow his friends by looking at their footprints. He finds a set of footprints that he does not know—his own!

* A variety of texts from Leveled Literacy Intervention (Heinemann 2009)

continues

Figure 6-17 Moosling Series: Animal Fantasy, *continued*

Title	Level	Page Spreads	Synopsis
*Hide and Seek**	J	Moosling ran here and there. He didn't know where to hide. Could he hide behind a rock? . . . or behind a tree? . . . or in the pond? Could he hide in the tall grass? . . . or behind the hill? He sat down to think.	Moosling is so big that he finds it difficult to hide–until he finds the perfect disguise to win the game.
Moosling in Winter	K	The birds were gone. It was quiet in the woods. It was **too** quiet. Moosling went to look for his friends. "Hello, Frog!" said Moosling. "Hello, Moosling," said Frog. "And good-bye." "What?" said Moosling. "Are you flying away, like the birds?" "I can't fly. I dig down into the mud," said Frog. "I'll sleep there all winter long." Then Frog dug down deep into the mud, and she was gone. First the birds went away, and now Frog was gone. Moosling was beginning to feel sad.	Moosling sees that many of his friends are leaving or sleeping for the winter, so he tries hard to do the same. In the process, he learns something about what to do for his first winter.
Moosling the Hero	L	Then they tried to get the bird's nest off Moosling's head. First, Beaver tugged at it. Then Rabbit tugged even harder. That didn't work, so Beaver, Rabbit, and Skunk all tugged at it together. But the nest was stuck! "My babies are too little to leave the nest," their mother said. "They will have to stay there on Moosling's head until they can fly."	Moosling rescues some birds' eggs and finds himself faced with a lot of responsibility.
The Costume Party	M	All the animals came to the party. They danced and played games. "Is that you, Pins?" said a dentist. "Yes!" said the clown. "Is that you, Beaver?" "Yes, it's me!" said the dentist. "All the costumes are great! It will be hard for Mouse to choose the best one." Rabbit was dressed up as a cowboy. He hopped here and there, saying "Howdy!" to everyone. Frog was dressed as a prince, and Turtle's shell was painted to look like a race car. Mouse looked pretty dressed up as a sunflower. Hoot looked very pretty, too. The owl was sitting in a tree, watching the fun.	Moosling wants to attend the costume party and he is so big that none of the costumes fit him.

* A variety of texts from Leveled Literacy Intervention (Heinemann 2009)

FICTION SERIES/
REALISTIC FICTION

Orson and Taco are two dogs who are good friends but who also are very different from each other. Taco is a feisty terrier, and Orson is a sometimes clumsy sheepdog. In the first book, which is Level A, we learn that they are friends, and even this very easy text sets up the contrast. There are quite a few books in the series; layouts from six of them are shown in Figure 6-18.

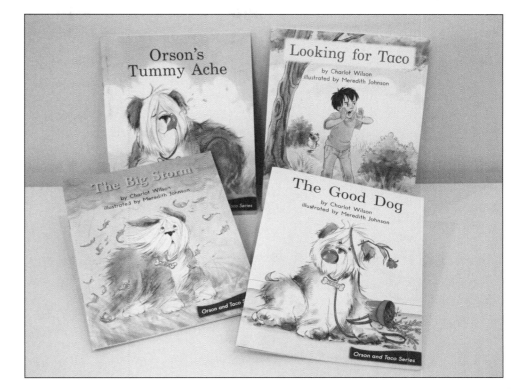

Figure 6-18 Orson and Taco Series: Realistic Fiction

Orson and Taco are two dogs who live together. Orson is a big sheepdog and Taco is a feisty little terrier.

Title	Level	Page Spreads	Synopsis
*Friends**	A	Orson has a big bed. Taco has a little bed. 14 15	This simple text describes the relationship between the big dog and little dog and sets up the contrast.
Orson's Tummy Ache	B	The big dog ate a little bug. 14 15	Big Orson eats just about everything and ends up with a tummy ache.

* A variety of texts from Leveled Literacy Intervention (Heinemann 2009)

continues

Figure 6-18 Orson and Taco Series: Realistic Fiction, *continued*

Title	Level	Page Spreads	Synopsis
*Looking for Taco**	C	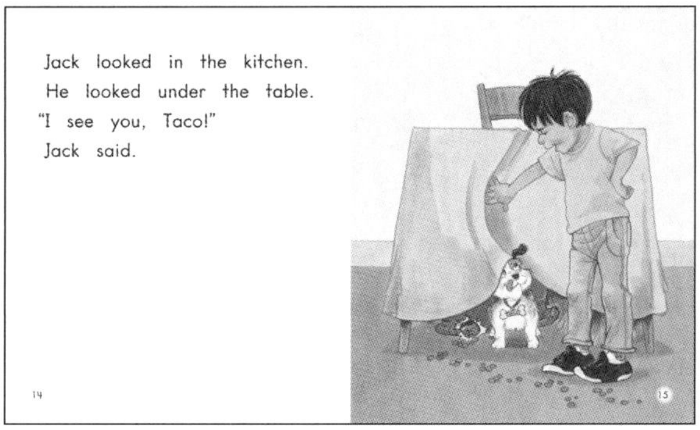 Jack looked in the kitchen. He looked under the table. "I see you, Taco!" Jack said.	Big Orson leads the way to find his lost friend.
Brave Taco	E	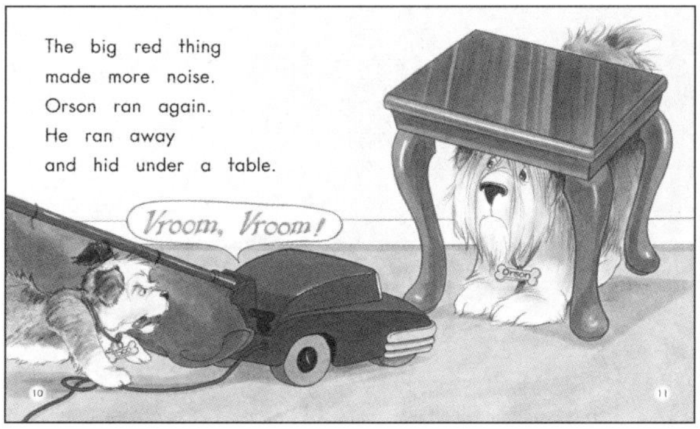 The big red thing made more noise. Orson ran again. He ran away and hid under a table. *Vroom, Vroom!*	Little Taco barks and barks at the vacuum cleaner and feels very proud when he finally "makes it stop."
The Big Storm	F	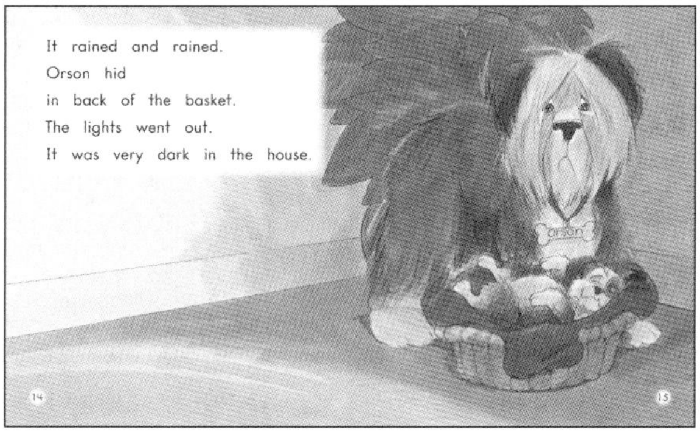 It rained and rained. Orson hid in back of the basket. The lights went out. It was very dark in the house.	Little Taco helps Orson when he is terrified because of a storm.
A Trip to the Laundromutt	H	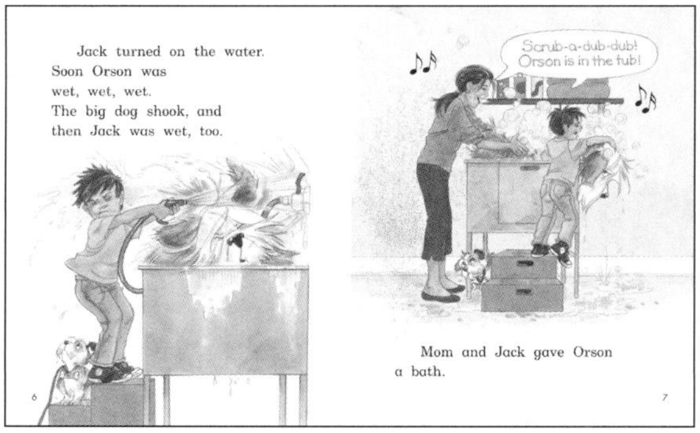 Jack turned on the water. Soon Orson was wet, wet, wet. The big dog shook, and then Jack was wet, too. Scrub-a-dub-dub! Orson is in the tub! Mom and Jack gave Orson a bath.	Both dogs go to the Laundromutt to be bathed and groomed, but they react to the procedure very differently.

* A variety of texts from *Leveled Literacy Intervention* (Heinemann 2009)

INFORMATIONAL SERIES

The figure below shows layouts from several of the books in an informational series about a real dog, Meli (see Figure 6-19). As readers encounter various stories about Meli's life, they build background information about dogs and how to take care of them.

Figure 6-19 Meli Series: Informational Text

This series is about a real life dog and how her owner takes care of her.

Title	Level	Page Spreads	Synopsis
The New Puppy*	A	I got a little bed. [image of dog bed labeled "Meli"]	Ron goes to the pet store and gets things for a new puppy. Finally, he gets the new puppy.
Meli on the Stairs	C	She likes to take her ball up the stairs. Up, up, up. [image of dog on stairs]	Playful Meli likes to take toys up and down the stairs. Children will enjoy predicting what happens after the end.

* A variety of texts from Leveled Literacy Intervention (Heinemann 2009)

continues

Figure 6-19 Meli Series: Informational Text, *continued*

Title	Level	Page Spreads	Synopsis
*A Walk with Meli**	E	 She sniffs and she sniffs and she sniffs. Meli can smell so much with her little black nose! She knows that another dog walked on the grass. She can smell it! 6 7	Ron and Meli take a walk and Meli sniffs at everything.
Meli at the Pet Shop	E	 Jan picks up the new puppy. He is so little! Meli kisses his nose. 8 9	Ron and Meli visit the pet shop to buy things for Meli and meet a new puppy.
Meli at the Vet	E	 The vet gives Meli a shot. Meli sits very still. "Good girl, Meli," the vet says. Some pets do not like to go to the vet, but Meli likes it! She gives the vet a big, wet kiss. 14 15	Ron takes Meli to the vet for a check-up.

* A variety of texts from Leveled Literacy Intervention (Heinemann 2009)

continues

Figure 6-19 Meli Series: Informational Text, *continued*

Title	Level	Page Spreads	Synopsis
*Taking Care of Meli**	F	Ron takes Meli for a walk every day. Dogs need to walk and play. Meli likes to go to the dog park. She loves to play with all the big dogs and little dogs at the park.	Ron shows all of the things he does to take care of Meli. Children will enjoy learning about pet care—even brushing the dog's teeth!
Meli at School	G	Meli is learning not to jump on Karen, too! Karen wants Meli to have fun. She makes up games to help Meli learn.	This book shows Meli learning all of the things dogs learn at dog school.
The Problem with Meli	J	That day, Ron takes Meli for a long walk. When they get home, Meli lies down on her red blanket. She doesn't bark that night. The next day, Ron plays with Meli for a long time in the afternoon. Later, Meli doesn't bark at all. Karen was right! After that, Ron gives Meli more exercise. Meli doesn't bark at dinnertime again, until . . .	This book shows Ron solving a problem with Meli by asking advice from the dog trainer.

* A variety of texts from Leveled Literacy Intervention (Heinemann 2009)

TOPICAL SERIES

Another series contains factual books on many different topics (see Figure 6-20). Many are about animals; others are about topics that would be of special interest to children. When students see the signal words "All About" on the front covers of the books in the series, they form immediate expectations about the genre and the way the content will be presented. All of the books in the All About series are on different topics, but by reading them, students internalize the characteristics of nonfiction.

Figure 6-20 **All About Series: Informational Text on Different Topics**

Nonfiction texts are presented with a similar format. When readers notice the "All About" logo on the book, they will expect to read a series of interesting facts about a topic. They will also expect to interpret photographs, diagrams, and other nonfiction text features.

Title	Level	Page Spreads	Synopsis
*All About Snakes**	C	A snake can hide. This snake is hiding under a rock.	Readers learn about a variety of snakes and their characteristics.
All About Animal Babies	F	This mother lion cleans her baby. She licks her baby lion to keep it clean.	Readers learn how animals take care of their young.

* A variety of texts from Leveled Literacy Intervention (Heinemann 2009)

continues

Figure 6-20 All About Series: Informational Text on Different Topics, *continued*

Title	Level	Page Spreads	Synopsis
*All About Chimps**	H		Readers learn interesting facts about chimps and the way they take care of their families.
All About Dinosaurs	I		Readers learn how the bones of dinosaurs give us clues to what they were like.
All About African Elephants	K		Readers learn about how elephants live and take care of their babies.
All About Volcanoes	N	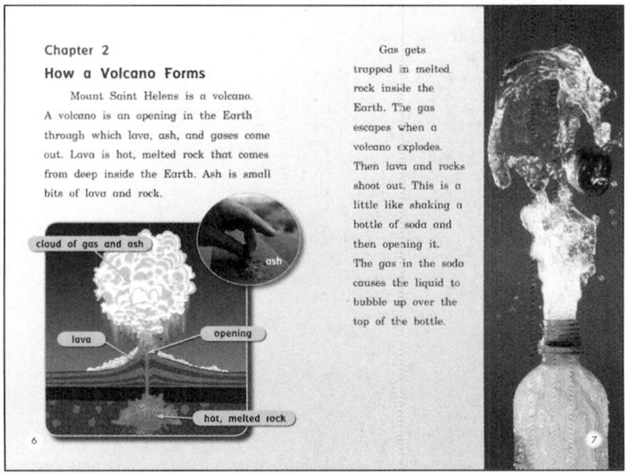	Readers learn the causes of volcanoes.

* A variety of texts from Leveled Literacy Intervention (Heinemann 2009)

GENRE SERIES

Below you can see page spreads from several books in a series of traditional tales (see Figure 6-21).

Traditional tales have very similar structures and characteristics, including:

- ❏ Animals that talk.
- ❏ A lesson learned.
- ❏ Magic.
- ❏ Literary language *(long ago)*.

As children notice the familiar format, they begin to internalize these characteristics and expect to find them in other traditional tales.

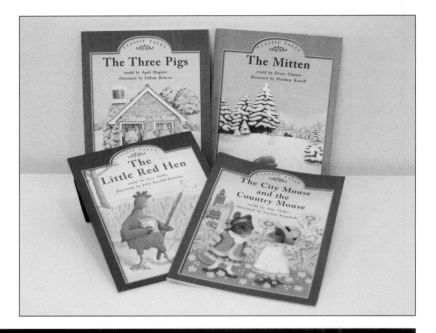

Figure 6-21 Genre Series: Traditional Tales

Traditional tales are presented in a similar format (size, title, look of the title page.) The stories are different but have some similarity in that they are fantasy, have talking animals, and characters play tricks and sometimes learn a lesson.

Title	Level	Page Spreads	Synopsis
*The Hat**	B	A duck went in the hat.	This version of the tale of cold animals squeezing into one item is told in very simple language, with the traditional surprise ending.
The Little Red Hen	C	"Can you help me?" Hen said. "No," said Dog and Cat and Pig.	Students can bring their own background knowledge to this version of the little red hen, which is told through dialogue.

---

* A variety of texts from Leveled Literacy Intervention (Heinemann 2009)

continues

Figure 6-21 Genre Series: Traditional Tales, *continued*

Title	Level	Page Spreads	Synopsis
*The Three Little Pigs and a Big Bad Wolf**	F		This version of the traditional tale shows three clever pigs getting the best of the wolf.
The Lion and the Mouse	J		This tale shows the traditional conflict between the powerful or strong and the weak. The mouse teaches the lion a lesson.
The Fox and the Gulls	M		In this traditional tale, a mother gull successfully rescues her ducklings from a hungry fox.

* A variety of texts from Leveled Literacy Intervention (Heinemann 2009)

USING SERIES BOOKS TO BEST ADVANTAGE

Here are some suggestions for using series books productively:

- ❏ In the introduction to a new book in a series, make explicit connections between the new book and previously read books; remind students what a character was like or what happened in the stories they already read.

- ❏ With a nonfiction series, remind students of the ways information is presented in the series. Set expectations for the way information is organized in nonfiction.

- ❏ Have students reread one or two books from the series before they read a new book in the series so that the characters or the structure will be fresh in their mind.

- ❏ When students are reading a series book at their instructional level, have them read easier levels in the series on their own.

- ❏ Take a day to reread several or all the books in a series and talk about the characters (in a fiction series) or the way the texts are organized (in a nonfiction series).

- ❏ Do some writing about the series. Write about a character or create another story in the series.

- ❏ Use a nonfiction series as a model for children to write about something they know.

- ❏ As students become more advanced, have them try writing their own stories about a character. Or, create a group story using interactive writing.

- ❏ Have plenty of series books in accessible tubs or baskets so that students can choose them for independent reading.

Role of the Independent Level Text

It is important for students to read a great many independent level books—texts they can read with an accuracy rate of 95 percent or higher (Levels A through K) or 98 percent or higher (Levels L through Z). Against this backdrop of accurate reading, students are able to solve words more smoothly and their minds are free to think about what they are reading. For the struggling reader, quantity is essential. In the process of reading a large number of texts, they will increase their vocabulary, internalize new language structures, and develop fluency. Younger readers often read books independently that they have previously read at the instructional level. Thus, as readers gain proficiency, the text moves from challenging to easy. Rereading also improves fluency and comprehension.

Struggling readers also need to read *new* easier texts. You can help this process along by introducing an easier text in small-group reading instruction. You can also provide a box of lower-level books that you know these students have never seen before. (Remember, students should not be coached to attend to the levels of the books they are reading.) Selecting a book from this box, they have the experience of reading a text for the first time and finding it easy—a first!

Role of the Instructional Level Text

There is a wealth of information in this book about selecting and introducing instructional level texts to individuals and small groups of students. Instructional level texts are the rungs in a ladder of text that supports readers in taking on new texts that stretch their capabilities. Careful sequencing of instructional level texts assures that each rung is not so far above the next that readers' processing breaks down.

An instructional level text is used in conjunction with supportive teaching:

- ❏ You *demonstrate* behaviors and actions needed to meet the demands of the text.

- ❏ You *direct attention* to the information that will be most helpful to readers in processing the text effectively (background information, visual aspects of print, illustrations, story line, or category of information).

- ❏ You *prompt* readers to take action or engage in strategic activities (monitor their reading by searching for information and correct their errors based on this information).

- ❏ You *reinforce* the effective strategic activities that readers initiate and use successfully.

- ❏ You *discuss* the meaning of the text before and after reading to support students' active thinking.

▶ Suggestions for Professional Development

SELECTING AND SEQUENCING TEXTS TO SUPPORT LEARNING

1. Meet with your colleagues in the school bookroom or bring samples of books that you use for small-group instruction or intervention instruction. Limit the books to two or three levels (chosen with one group in mind). Try to include some series books.

2. Arrange the books by level. Talk about each one in terms of the ten characteristics discussed in this chapter. You may want to work in grade-level groups. Ask:

   a. How is the text supportive to readers?

   b. What are the challenges in the text?

3. After examining the books, create a viable instructional sequence. Think about these issues:

   a. Even though the books are the same level, some will be slightly more demanding, some less so.

   b. Even though the books are the same level, they will make different demands.

   c. Is there a way for the texts to build on each other in a powerful way? (Consider factors such as ideas, content, vocabulary, words, book and print features.)

   d. Are there connections that can be made between some of the texts?

4. Have some members of the group share their text sequences and explain them to the rest of the group.

5. Try out one of these sequences with your students over the next week or two and share the results with the group at the next meeting.

Language Systems and Literacy Learning

Reading and writing are language processes. Language plays a powerful role in children's acquisition of literacy. The systems of language—phonology, syntax, and semantics—are all critical to literacy learning. In this section, we take an in-depth look at the complex range of information that all readers must acquire and orchestrate to effectively process texts. Readers must build systems for acquiring vocabulary and intuitive knowledge of the alphabetic system that is basic to reading and writing. In this section, we present three chapters that explore the language base for literacy.

Language Matters: Talking, Reading, and Writing

CHAPTER

7

IN THIS CHAPTER, WE DESCRIBE THE POWERFUL ROLE LANGUAGE PLAYS in becoming literate. First, we take a look at the language system itself and at children as language learners. All children have internalized rules of oral language; but for some, the language of written texts is very difficult. We discuss how you can analyze the language of texts and, through conversation, make the language available to struggling readers as you introduce them to texts.

We accomplish the business of our world through language. Language permeates human relationships. It is integral to our identity as individuals, as groups, and as a society. Language is the most powerful tool of learning. It can be a barrier or a bridge. Through language we disagree, concur, negotiate, and arbitrate.

Almost three decades ago, building on studies of children's language learning, Clay (1979, 1998) proposed the powerful idea that teaching was a form of conversation. She explained that a teacher listens carefully before replying. Language interactions are the most important characteristic of teaching— more so than books, exercises, or any other type of material. Remember that it is the teacher who makes the difference through instructional interactions with children.

When we use the word *language*, we mean *speech*—the oral language that is acquired with speed and ease by virtually every child in the world. Oral language takes many forms. In some settings, it may be elaborate—storytelling or description, for example. In other settings, it may be spare but include rich nonverbal elements and demonstrations (the gestures we make, for example).

Oral language always adjusts itself to the purpose, the setting, and the speakers/listeners at any particular time. Think about how you talk differently with infants, elementary school children, and adults: your style, sentence structure, intonation patterns, and even vocabulary vary significantly. You talk differently with an old friend on the phone than you do with a parent in a conference about a student. You talk differently in a university class than you do at a neighborhood barbeque. Yet, in all its variations, oral language is the most powerful human tool. It is how we create our world; in turn, it shapes us as thinkers and doers.

Every child in the world, in about the same sequence and in about the same amount of time, develops language. Scientists suggest that our brains are "hard wired" for language. Children notice language all around them and begin to use it to interact with others. Clay (1991) has said that language is the first example of a "self-extending system," one that expands as it is used. She means that children construct an oral language system that expands itself and that, under natural conditions, all children are successful in doing this. The study of language learning provides convincing evidence that children engage in it creatively. They learn the underlying rules of language and apply them in new ways.

We are all familiar with children's first ways of talking and often find their expressions amusing. When two-year-old Lauren's mother tells her to "hold my hand," the child says firmly, "Me do it!" and clasps her hands together. Lauren has extracted meaning from the situation and applied it in new ways; likewise, she has created a language structure by putting together a subject, verb, and object. (She has not heard her parents say, "Me do it!" But Lauren does not say, "Do me it." That wouldn't follow the rules she currently understands.) Even primitive sentences are arranged in rule-governed ways. Lindfors (1987) provided some wonderful examples in her discussion of language and context:

❏   A teacher asked a four-year-old who was sweeping the nursery school floor, "Are you mopping?" The child replied, "No, I'm brooming." (161, attributed to Janet Rothschild)

❏   A four-year-old wanted her mother to put her to bed and said, "I need to get goodnighted." (161, attributed to Sally Means)

These children have used the rules pertaining to verb inflections to create new words.

There is ample evidence that children search for and respond to meaning in language and that parents participate as partners. For example, here is an inter-

action between a mother and her three-year-old daughter (Lindfors, p. 160):

MOTHER: People are always telling you to share, aren't they, Brenda? What does *share* mean?

BRENDA: It means I get to play with somebody else's toys.

Communication is present from birth. Infants prefer a real human face or image of it to a real or pictured object (Lindfors 1987). Smiling, laughing, waving arms, and playing turn-taking games are all signs that babies are learning the foundations of language. At about a year, we see words emerging. At first children make one-word utterances. Over the next couple of years, language increases steadily in complexity. (See Figure 7-1.)

Clay (1998) has reminded us that families are unconscious teachers. They engage in conversation with children. They speak, but they also listen, think about what the child understands, and reply carefully. Family members seem to know intuitively how to respond in ways that support children's language acquisition. Of course there are linguistic, cultural, and individual differences in just how these interactions take place, but there is also remarkable similarity.

When children enter school, they encounter new experiences, ideas, objects, and people. For many children, the number of individuals with whom they interact expands exponentially. Language expands with experience (Lindfors 1987):

1.   Language syntax (grammar) becomes increasingly complex and more like adult grammar.

2.   Children add new words to their vocabulary as well as ideas to expand their understanding.

3.   Children may refine their pronunciations as they see the need to make their meanings clear to many different speakers (this may require greater effort than speaking to their families).

4.   Children learn new uses for language. They learn to tailor their interactions to different speakers and specific contexts.

5.   Children learn to consider language—to talk about it. They start to use words like *word* and *sounds*.

Figure 7-1 The Growth of Language		
Pretalking	Smile Gestures "Peek-a-boo"	Infants have differentiated themselves as individuals and work to communicate with others. They learn turn-taking. They learn that their actions evoke responses from others.
One word	"Up" "Hi" "Hot "More"	Children use single words to convey a variety of meanings.
Telegraphic speech	"Allgone milk." "See doggie." "Bobby chair." "Eat bascetti." "Book Daddy." "Go bye-bye." "Mommy go?"	Children use mostly nouns, verbs, with some adverbs to express a variety of meanings. With two- and three-word sentences, children can direct attention, give commands, attribute ownership, and make requests and announcements. They can ask a question without varying the grammatical structure by using intonation.
Longer sentences	"No more cereal." "I no stay here now." "He no do that." "I no want pizza." "Where Sunny blankie?" "Why you do that?"	Children use slightly longer sentences with more detail. Their questions use both intonation and vocabulary specifically designed for questioning. They are more elaborate in the expression of negatives.
More complex speech	"Daddy came and he patted the doggie." "Watch me go riding." "I saw Bobby and he ate the cookie." "What's this gonna be?" "Does this be for me?" "Here she comes . . . wait for me!"	Sentences are longer and more complex. Children combine two clauses of a sentence, use more complex verb forms, and use articles and prepositional phrases.

Integral to this process is exposure to written language, which has entered the child's world much earlier. Children can hardly help noticing the print associated with their favorite foods, toys, or restaurants. And many very young children have been looking at print, experimenting with writing, and listening to written language that is read aloud. In school, however, attention to print is *required*. As they become immersed in texts, hearing them and beginning to write them, the consideration of language as a formal code becomes more visible.

All children have internalized rules of oral language, but for some, the language of written texts is very difficult. Teachers can analyze the language of texts and, through conversation, make the language available to struggling readers as they introduce texts.

▶ Language Systems

First, let's look at language itself. Linguists who study the language we speak have described it as several integrated systems (see Figure 7-2):

1. The phonological system refers to the sounds of the language.

2. The semantic system refers to the meanings that are carried by language.

3. The syntactic system refers to the rule-governed way words are put together in phrases and sentences to convey meaning.

Written language adds *graphemes* (letters) that represent all the systems of oral language. It is amazing that all the words and meanings of English are represented by only twenty-six characters (upper- and lowercase). Only one aspect of oral language is not easily represented in print—the intonation, stress, or emphasis on particular words and phrases that convey meaning through expression. The punctuation included in written language partially conveys the meanings that speakers communicate through expression.

Young children who have a well-developed knowledge of the systems of oral language have powerful tools for becoming literate. But every reader learns that there are some subtle but important differences between oral and written language. And every writer soon learns to construct those more formal sentences. If you have ever audiotaped yourself talking, even in a formal presentation, and then made a transcription, you realize that oral language has many stops, starts, interjections, repetitions, changes of tense, and partial sentences. Heavy editing is needed to turn it into readable prose. Let's look briefly at the three language systems and think about the differences and the connections between spoken and written language.

Figure 7-2 **Language Systems**	
Oral Language	**Written Language**
Phonological System	***Graphemic System***
The sounds that make up language.	The written symbols that represent phonemes.
Phonemes are the smallest units of sounds that speakers of a language understand.	Letters represent the phonological system.
Syllables are the breaks in words that speakers can hear.	Letters grouped together in syllables (but not defined by spaces) represent the breaks in words.
Semantic System	***Semantic System***
The meaning conveyed by language.	Morphemes are represented by letters and sequences of letters.
Morphemes are the smallest units of meaning.	Words are represented by sequences of letters in print and defined by white spaces.
Words are made up of sequences of phonemes.	
Syntactic System	***Syntactic System***
The structure of language—the rules by which words are put together in phrases and sentences that have meaning for speakers.	The words are sequenced from left to right and top to bottom in print to represent the rule-governed structure of the English language.

Sounds, Letters, and Words

Sounds and letters refer to the phonological system and the graphemes that represent it. When we talk, the sounds we make *mean something* to other speakers of the language. We parse (separate and identify) sounds into the individual words that make up the *lexicon* of the language.

ELEMENTS OF WORDS

The *phoneme* is the smallest unit of sound that can be identified. There are approximately forty-five phonemes in the English language. Each phoneme is really just a category of sounds that are enough alike that we can group them together. There are slight variations in the ways a single phoneme is pronounced within different words. There are also many geographic variations in the pronunciations of phonemes. But the phoneme is what we recognize as a sound, and a sequence of phonemes (usually two or more) makes up a word.

In written language, the letters represent sounds but not always in simple ways, so readers must learn to detect graphic patterns by the way they look and to connect those visual patterns with sounds in words. In English, for example, a single sound, like the lax (or "long") sound of *a* can be represented by many different letters and letter clusters: *a, ey, ay, eigh, ea, a(consonant)e, aigh,* and even *et.* Alternately, a single letter, such as *c,* can be connected to more than one sound: *cat, city.* The vowels in particular can be connected to many different sounds, and pairs of vowels often appear together. Consonants often appear in clusters as well: *st, str, sh.* Some letters appear in words but are "silent," that is, no sound is required. The reader is recognizing a visual pattern.

Recognizing letters is, in itself, a complex learning task. Readers must learn to recognize letters by their *distinctive features,* the small differences that make a letter different from every other letter. For example, a lowercase *h* and a lowercase *n* are different only in the length of the stick, while *n* and *u* are differentiated only by orientation. Readers learn that letters have short sticks, long sticks, circles, tunnels, dots, and tails

(see Appendix D for Verbal Path and letter descriptions; also see *Prompting Guide 1,* final page. There are efficient directional movements for forming each letter (the ones for *a* and *h* are shown in Figure 7-3). Knowing and using these movements helps young readers pick up the distinctive features of letters rapidly and effortlessly so they can recognize them in isolation and (a more difficult task) within words that appear in connected print.

An important component of oral language is the *morpheme,* the smallest unit that has meaning. For example, *play* is a *free morpheme*—it has meaning and can stand alone. *Play* can be a verb or a noun. You can add *-s, -er,* or *-ed* to *play;* these units are *bound morphemes.* They have meaning but cannot stand alone. They are added to words to indicate plurality, tense, or other variations in meaning. Morphemes are the building blocks of words. When readers are able to connect morphemes to the groups of letters that represent them, they can take words apart and not only speak them but have an idea of their meaning. For example, a speaker understands *play* as an action and *player* as one who performs the action. Connecting these meanings to the written word *play* and noticing the *-er* ending is the task of the reader.

The structure of words is also defined by *syllables,* which represent the way the sounds in the words are broken up. A syllable may be a morpheme, but a

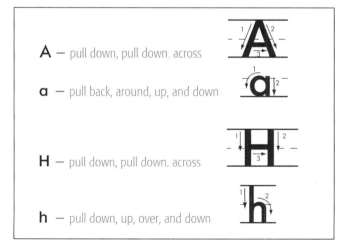

Figure 7-3 Verbal Path for Letter Formation *(Fountas and Pinnell Prompting Guide 1,* 2009)*

morpheme such as *-ible* may be composed of more than one syllable. Hearing the syllables and connecting them to the letters that represent them helps readers take apart longer words.

We all have a vocabulary we use in spoken language. This vocabulary varies by the context in which it is used. For example, you would hear and say many words at a professional conference that you would very seldom say at home with your family. Processing written language greatly expands vocabulary: there are words you read often but seldom use in speech, like *replied* and *exclaimed*. Every reader must acquire new vocabulary to process more difficult texts.

CHALLENGES FOR ENGLISH LANGUAGE LEARNERS

Sounds, letters, and words pose special challenges to English language learners. For one thing, they may have learned a phonological system that is very different from English. There are English sounds that do not appear in some other languages; there are sounds in other languages that do not appear in English. If you have learned to speak a second language, you know that the "accent" (using the phonology so that you pronounce the words as a native would) is challenging. Few speakers manage it unless they learned the second language as a child. English language learners will find some sound/letter relationships difficult, and phonics and reading lessons should take this into account. They may need to pay closer attention to the visual features of a word—how it *looks*—in relation to its approximated pronunciation.

Nonnative children who are learning to read in English may also find the vocabulary more challenging. If a word is not in the reader's oral vocabulary, it is much harder to read and understand. English language learners may find themselves saying words, cued by letters and sounds, but not understanding what they are reading—a recipe for disaster. These children will quickly become readers who perform mechanically without thinking.

SUPPORTING READERS WHO FIND LETTERS, SOUNDS, AND WORDS CHALLENGING

As all teachers know, even children who are native speakers of English can find letters, sounds, and words difficult. Children's oral vocabularies vary greatly; some children will encounter many words in texts that they either do not understand or do not often use. Others have difficulty pronouncing some of the sounds of the language and connecting them to letters and word parts.

The following are some essential teaching suggestions for helping children learn about letters, sounds, and words (see Figure 7-4). You will find more specific directions in Chapters 8, 9, 11, and 12.

Syntax

The words of a language are put together in grammatical patterns governed by rules. Here we are not talking about "proper grammar," as in a grammar handbook, but about the patterns of syntax that we all learn over the first years of life. For example, we could say, "I have a green scarf." We could even say, "Have I a green scarf?" But we would not say, "Scarf a I green have."

The way words are put together in rule-governed ways is the syntactic system, or structure, of language. By the time they begin to learn to read, most children have developed a strong inner knowledge of the structure of the language they speak. This sense of language structure helps them predict what the word order of a sentence is likely to be.

For example, the three-word sentence in the predictable text *Baby* (see Figure 7-5) is simple, a verb phrase following a noun. The pattern is within the control of most young beginners.

The seven-word sentence in *Hiding* (see Figure 7-6) is still simple, but the syntax is a little more complex. A proper noun begins the sentence, followed by a verb, an infinitive, and a prepositional phrase that includes the preposition, an article, and a noun.

The first sentence on page 10 of *The Trip* (see Figure 7-7) is even more complex, partly because it

Figure 7-4 **Suggestions for Helping Struggling Readers Learn about Letters, Sounds, and Words**	
Sounds **Connect sounds to other words (names) they know**	• Demonstrate and have children say words slowly to identify the sounds. • Teach letters and sounds together so that children have both auditory and visual signals. • Provide many opportunities to approximate sounds and match them to letters (pictures and letters) • Engage children in writing so that they say and hear words and represent them with letters. • Provide opportunities for children to say the words that are difficult for them and to locate them in the text before reading.
Letters	• Give children many opportunities to sort and match magnetic letters that provide a concrete example of the distinctive features that they can see and feel. • Demonstrate and give children many opportunities to write the letters using a Verbal Path.
Words **Opportunities to quickly build and write words left to right that they will read and write often**	• Demonstrate and have children build words left to right with magnetic letters. • Demonstrate and have children check the letter left-to-right sequence in words with a model. • Give children many opportunities to say words slowly and write them left to right. • Give children many opportunities to write words in sentences to notice the spaces. • Demonstrate and help children locate words within continuous print (first saying the word and predicting the first sound and letter). • Use unfamiliar words in conversation while introducing texts to children. • Have children say and talk about unfamiliar words before they read them in continuous print.
Syllables	• Demonstrate clapping syllables in words to help children hear them. • Have children clap words to hear the syllables. • Help children connect syllables to letters, letter clusters, and larger word parts they see in words. • Help children realize that every word has at least one vowel and every syllable has a vowel.

Baby is sleeping.

Figure 7-5 Page Spread from *Baby* from Leveled Literacy Intervention, Orange System (Heinemann 2009)

Puff likes to hide
in the box.

Figure 7-6 Page Spread from *Hiding* from Leveled Literacy Intervention, Orange System (Heinemann 2009)

"You will have so much fun on this trip!" said Froggy.
"I wish I could go with you."

"I wish you could, too," said Duck.

"Let's get your **big** bag," said Froggy.
"You have a lot to pack."

Figure 7-7 Page Spread from *The Trip* from Leveled Literacy Intervention, Blue System (Heinemann 2009)

includes dialogue. (Written dialogue is usually accompanied by attributive phrases not used in oral language; you would be much more likely to say, "Mary said we need to go now," than, "Mary said, 'It's time to go now.'") The clause in quotations starts with a pronoun, for which the reader must infer the referent; then there is a verb in future tense followed by an adverb, an adjective, a noun, and a prepositional phrase. The clause in quotations is followed by a verb and a noun identifying the speaker.

The third sentence on page 8 of *Bear's Birthday* (see Figure 7-8) contains even greater complexity. The clause in quotes is a question, in which the noun is inserted into the verb phrase. *Me* is the object of the

verb *ask* and there is a prepositional phrase. The speaker designation includes a noun, verb, and adverb.

Dialogue is not the only complexity that presents a challenge to young readers. The second sentence on page 23 of *Chester Greenwood's Big Idea* (see Figure 7-9) is very far from the oral language most people use: the compound predicate includes two embedded clauses.

There are an almost infinite number of examples of the syntactic complexity of English sentences. In general, the more complex the syntax, the harder the sentence will be for the reader to parse (identify the words in sequence and think what they mean).

CHALLENGES FOR ENGLISH LANGUAGE LEARNERS

Speakers of a language have been learning the rules of syntax from birth, internalizing them by listening to the language of the speakers around them. They progress from one-word utterances, to two- and three-word phrases, to simple sentences, and finally to complex sentences that include adjectives and embedded phrases and clauses. The syntax of oral language is learned without instruction because brains seem able to develop words and syntax simply by speaking and listening.

Children all over the world learn oral language in pretty much the same way. So English language learners *have* internalized grammar, but the rules they have learned will be different from the rules of English. They are in the process not only of acquiring English words but learning the patterns of English syntax. If you have learned a second language, you know that vocabulary is easier to learn than verb tenses and noun declensions. Syntax may not be a strong system for English language learners as they set out to read English.

HELPING READERS WHO STRUGGLE LEARN TO USE SYNTAX

The syntax of written language poses challenges for all children because of the significant differences from oral language. Some children come to school with underdeveloped oral language, which makes it difficult for them to process the complex sentences they read in texts. They try to recognize or sound out one word after another but have difficulty using language structure to check whether what they are reading sounds right. Other children have good control of language but simply do not realize that they need to think whether their reading sounds right. They neglect what they know about language structure and concentrate on letters and sounds alone. As a result, their reading sometimes sounds like nonsense; yet they move right along and gain little meaning. Still other children are fluid users of oral language but have little experience with the syntax of written language.

You always want to be thinking of ways to help students process language in all instructional contexts. We offer some general suggestions for helping children learn to use syntax while reading (see Figure 7-10). More specific suggestions for demonstrating and prompting students to use language structure are included in Chapter 14, Teaching for Problem-Solving While Reading Texts.

When he got home, Bear made the hats.

"These are good hats," said Bear. "Now I will blow up balloons. But I don't have any balloons."

So Bear went to Fox's house.

Bear thanked Beaver and took the paper. Then he went home.

"Why didn't Bear ask me to his party?" Beaver asked sadly. "I will ask Rabbit."

Figure 7-8 Page Spread from *Bear's Birthday* from Leveled Literacy Intervention, Green System (Heinemann 2009)

Soon Chester began to sell his ear protectors to people all over the world. The ear protectors got a new name. People called them earmuffs.

Chester became a famous inventor. He invented a special rake, a teakettle that didn't tip over, a mousetrap, a bed that folded up, and other things. Chester made more than 130 inventions. And it all began with earmuffs for his big ears!

Figure 7-9 Page Spread from *Chester Greenwood's Big Idea* from Leveled Literacy Intervention, Blue System (Heinemann 2009)

Meaning

The semantic, or meaning, system is the purpose and core of any language. Meaning is much more than vocabulary. The words and the syntax work together to convey the meaning we wish to communicate. The deeper meanings are mapped out in the syntax. The same meaning may be stated in different ways:

- ❏ She went to the kitchen to get the tea.

- ❏ To get the tea, she went to the kitchen.

- ❏ To the kitchen went she . . . to get the tea. (A somewhat poetic version!)

Figure 7-10 Suggestions for Helping Children Use Language Structure While Reading	
Interactive Read-Aloud and Shared Reading	• Read aloud daily and invite children to discuss the meaning of texts. Text-based talk will help children expand both vocabulary and knowledge of language structure. • Select texts with sentences that are within children's ability to understand. You can gradually increase complexity. • Select texts with content that is age appropriate so that children can both process the language structure and understand meaning. • Select some texts with repeating refrains, so that children hear the same language patterns over and over. • Repeat favorites and invite children to join in on some parts. • Pause to allow children to predict the ends of sentences or the next sentences so that they can try out their ability to use language structure.
Guided Reading Lessons or Small-Group Intervention	• Select texts that are within children's control with only a few new things to learn. • In the introduction to the text, have children repeat some of the language structures so that they will be familiar and they can immediately experience using language structure in combination with visual information and meaning. • Demonstrate using language structure to monitor whether reading sounds right. • Demonstrate using language structure in combination with visual information to solve words. • Prompt readers to use language structure to solve unknown words. • Reread whole texts and/or difficult parts of texts to understand and become familiar with the process of using language structure. • Help students become aware of punctuation to guide phrasing and intonation, which, in turn, will help them use syntax.
Interactive, Shared, or Independent Writing	• Model the composition of sentences that fit the requirements of written language. • Act as the students' memory to help them recall the words and syntactic patterns while they devote energy to spelling words one after another. • Help students say sentences several times before starting to write them. • Have students reread sentences they have written. They will be very familiar with the language and processing it again as a reading text will help them expand knowledge of syntax.

And the same sentence may have different meanings:

❏ It was cool this summer. (Describing weather.)

❏ You look cool. (Slang describing a good-looking person.)

The purpose of reading is comprehension. Starting with their very first attempts to process written texts, readers need to understand that reading must make sense. We want readers to actively search for meaning in the illustrations and in the print. They need to constantly use meaning to monitor their reading:

❏ Sentences must be consistent with what readers know. For example, a reader who is thinking knows that *see Sam* isn't a likely substitute for *said Sam* following a piece of dialogue.

❏ Sentences and illustrations should be consistent with each other. Readers should always be searching for a coherent whole and cross-referencing meaning from different sources.

❑ Sentences should make sense within the whole story or informational piece. Readers are always thinking of the overall story or topic in checking whether what they are reading is meaningful.

ENGLISH LANGUAGE LEARNERS

Many English language learners have a rich background of understanding and experience but lack the *labels* for what they know. And those who are new to this country may lack the experience and knowledge that are second nature to native English speakers. Many have not had a chance to immerse themselves in the culture, whether by watching television, listening to an adult read aloud, or reading independently.

HELPING READERS USE MEANING AS A RESOURCE WHILE READING

Many five-year-olds have limited background experiences. They may not have traveled beyond their own neighborhoods. They may watch television but not "educational" programs. They may not have had the opportunity to hear texts read aloud. Some readers have found reading so difficult that they don't realize that it has to make sense or that they should check their understanding. They have made a habit of mechanically processing the words, and this problem will be compounded as they progress through the grades.

Readers use meaning to monitor reading and to solve words. Chapter 14, Teaching for Problem Solving While Reading Texts, suggests specific ways to help children become aware of the meaning system of language as a powerful resource. You also want students to think actively as they process texts—to think beyond and about the text (see Chapter 2, Effective Readers: What Do They Do?). Chapter 17, Teaching for Comprehending: Thinking Before, During, and After Reading, suggests specific ways to encourage deeper comprehension. The more texts children read and understand, the more information they will bring with them when they read other texts. On the next page are some general suggestions for helping readers use meaning (Figure 7-11).

Interactive read-aloud is a powerful context for helping children think actively about the meaning of written texts, because children are freed from tracking print, decoding words, and using punctuation. Nevertheless, they still have a great deal of processing to do. As they listen, they need to parse long and sometimes quite complex sentences and deal with complicated and sometimes abstract words and ideas. It is important to select texts that stretch students but are not so complex that they cause confusion. It will not help students to hear and discuss texts that have ideas or language structure that is beyond them. You might want to select favorite texts with repeating refrains (*The Three Little Pigs*, for example) and invite children to join in. You can also pause and allow children to predict the ends of sentences that are exciting or poetic. Be sure that students can hear and say the separate words (and understand the meaning) of the phrases they are repeating.

In small-group reading, first analyze the text for vocabulary and concepts that will be challenging. Even simple ideas are sometimes not to be taken for granted, especially if you are working with English language learners. For example, they might understand one meaning of the word *pot* (as something for cooking) but be unfamiliar with the idea of a pot as a container for a plant. Similes (feeling like you're on *pins and needles*, for example) might be difficult. They might understand that chickens lay eggs but find the idea that animals such as snakes also lay eggs new and surprising information. Preview these concepts with the group, helping them use whatever they already know but providing as much information as needed to help them process the text with understanding. A good rule of thumb is, *don't wait until after reading to find out if they understood the text.* Bring comprehension to the forefront to ensure that students process the text with understanding.

Graphic organizers can help students see ways in which information is organized and presented: comparison and contrast, temporal sequence, cause and effect, problem and solution. A "map" of a story can help children remember the sequence of events and understand narrative structure. These organizational frameworks help their understanding. Figure 7-13 is a chart derived from the book *Elephant and Tiger* (see

Figure 7-11 Suggestions for Helping Children Use Meaning While Reading

Interactive Read-Aloud and Shared Reading	• Read aloud daily and invite children to discuss the meaning of texts. Text-based talk will help children understand that they need to bring their knowledge to the understanding of texts and at the same time articulate the new information they are gaining.
	• Select texts with familiar topics and concepts that are within children's ability to understand and that will expand their world. You can gradually increase the sophistication of topics.
	• Select texts with content that is age appropriate so that children can easily interpret the text and think beyond it.
	• Repeat favorites so that children can use prior knowledge to develop more insights.
	• Pause to allow children to predict what might happen next or what characters might be feeling or thinking.
Guided Reading Lessons or Small-Group Intervention	• Select texts that are within children's control with only a few new things to learn.
	• In the introduction to the text, discuss the meaning and help children understand the problem presented in the story or the way an informational text is organized.
	• Demonstrate using meaning to monitor whether reading sounds right.
	• Demonstrate using meaning in combination with visual information to solve words.
	• Prompt the readers to make sure their reading makes sense.
	• After reading, discuss the meaning of the text as a whole.
Interactive, Shared, or Independent Writing	• Model the composition of sentences that communicate the message that you want to communicate.
	• Compose writing that supports or extends the meaning of texts that children have read.
	• Use graphic organizers that help children understand and remember how information is presented in a text.
	• Use graphic organizers that help children understand and remember information from a text.

Figure 7-12 Cover of *Elephant and Tiger* from Leveled Literacy Intervention, Blue System (Heinemann 2009)

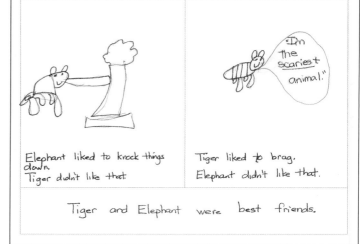

Figure 7-13 *Elephant and Tiger* Summary Chart

Figure 7-12). The students have described one attribute of each animal and then what they have in common.

Here is a very simple chart representing the central concept of *Play and Ride* (see Figure 7-14), the size comparison of "real" vehicles with corresponding toys (Figure 7-15).

When working with readers who struggle, an excellent strategy is to co-construct a chart using shared or interactive writing (see Chapter 1). It will not help them to try to fill out graphic organizers individually as if they were worksheets. True learning occurs during conversations in which you scaffold their thinking and help them express their ideas.

Figure 7-14 Cover of *Play and Ride* from Leveled Literacy Intervention, Orange System (Heinemann 2009)

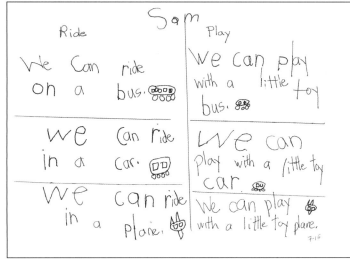

Figure 7-15 *Play and Ride* Summary Chart

▶ Analyzing Texts in Preparation for Small-Group Teaching

As you plan introductions for the texts you use in small-group reading instruction, analyze the language in the texts and the students' oral language proficiency:

- ❑ What oral language resources are these children able to bring to the reading of this text?
- ❑ What grammatical structures are different from the language children control and will be challenging?
- ❑ What words will be challenging to read and understand?
- ❑ What background information do I need to provide prior to reading?
- ❑ How can I help the children grasp the theme or main idea of the book?

In a brief conversation prior to reading, you can prepare children for new or unexpected language and help them understand the ideas. With this kind of support (along with careful text selection), you can help children process texts, making effective use of the elements of language, day after day.

Supporting Language Use in a Level C Text

Look at the cover of *Flap, Flap, Fly* (Figure 7-16) and the text characteristics of *Flap, Flap, Fly* (Figure 7-17). Notice that the text has rhythmic language and a repeating pattern. Even though the text is simple, the structure of the refrain "They can walk and walk" is different from oral language. It has a more literary quality, and most children will need support to be able read it. The text structure is simple too. Readers who understand that the little ducks always do what the mother duck does first will have a much better chance of understanding the text. Word challenges include the use of pronouns, one adjective, verbs, and prepositions. Readers will be expected to read words with inflectional endings (*eat, eats*), so knowing that structure will be helpful.

Review the sample of an introduction to *Flap, Flap, Fly* (Figure 7-18). The teacher drew attention to a couple of the words in the text but, more important, explicitly pointed out the unifying concept of the book and had the children say some of the language to help them process the structure.

Figure 7-16 Cover of *Flap, Flap, Fly* from Leveled Literacy Intervention, Orange System (Heinemann 2009)

Supporting Language Use in a Level H Text

Look at the cover of *Plants That Eat Bugs* (Figure 7-19) and the analysis of the book's text characteristics (Figure 7-20). The central concept of this informational text—the idea that plants can "eat" bugs—is fascinating to children but new information for most. The vocabulary related to the parts of plants could be challenging for some speakers, and action words like *rolls, traps, slides,* and *sticks* may be unfamiliar. The writer compares plant leaves to *cups,* which requires interpreting the accompanying picture and understanding the simile. Sentences are all in present tense, which is different from many narratives. There are sentences with prepositional phrases and clauses, as well as some compound sentences. There are some words with vowel combinations.

Analysis of New Book Characteristics   *Flap, Flap, Fly*, Level C

GENRE/FORM
- Narrative nonfiction

TEXT STRUCTURE
- Series of paired episodes in which little ducks repeat the mother duck's actions
- Builds to the end, when the little ducks learn to fly

CONTENT
- Familiar animals
- Concept of a mother duck teaching babies

THEMES AND IDEAS
- Adult and baby animals
- Caring for and teaching baby animals
- Baby animals learning and growing

LANGUAGE AND LITERARY FEATURES
- Rhythmic language
- Illustrations that communicate caring between the mother duck and babies and playfulness on the part of the young
- Suspenseful ending

SENTENCE COMPLEXITY
- One or two sentences on each page
- Sentences two or three words long
- Repeating pattern of meaning alternating between the mother's and the babies' activities
- Present tense
- Prepositional phrases

VOCABULARY
- Names of activities: *walk, swim, eat, fly*
- Pronouns: she, they
- Adjectives: *little*
- Prepositions: *in, by*

WORDS
- High-frequency words: *can, she, and, by, the*
- Words with inflectional endings: *coming, eats, swims*
- CVC words: *can*
- One-syllable words with some multisyllable words

ILLUSTRATIONS
- Soft pastel paintings across each page spread
- Close match between pictures and text

BOOK AND PRINT FEATURES
- Large font
- Ample space between words
- Three lines on each page of print except the last two
- Print on the left in a white box
- Periods, exclamation point, ellipses

Figure 7-17 Analysis of Text Charactistics in *Flap, Flap, Fly*

Figure 7-18 Introduction to *Flap, Flap, Fly*

Speaker	Interaction	What the Teacher Is Attending to
Ms. W	This book is called *Flap, Flap, Fly*. This is Mother Duck and these are her little ducks and they live by a pond. Can you see the pond?	*Draws attention to the picture and explains the setting.*
Charley	It's water.	
Alycia	There's a mommy duck and ducklings.	
Ms. W	Yes. In this book they call her a Mother Duck. In the story you will find out all the things Mother Duck can do. Her little ducks can do the same things.	*Says an important word from the text and explains the unifying concept of the book.*
Ms. W	Turn to pages 2 and 3. What can Mother Duck do?	
Marva	She is walking.	
Ms. W	Yes, she can walk. She walks by the pond.	*Uses some of the language.*
Ms. W	Say the word *she*. *She* starts with *sh*. The word *she* starts the sentence so it starts with an uppercase *S*. Find *she*. Put your finger under it and say it. Oh, you found it again. It is on the page two times.	*Draws attention to a word's letters and sounds. Prompts students to locate a word in the text.*
Ms. W	Turn to pages 4 and 5. Mother Duck can walk by the pond. She walks and walks by the pond.	*Uses language from the text.*
	[Children repeat teacher's language.]	
Ms. W	Now, what can her little ducks do?	*Draws attention to meaning in the pictures.*
Alycia	They can walk.	
Ms. W	Yes, they can walk by the pond, too. In this book it says "walk and walk by the pond." That sounds like a story, doesn't it? You say that.	*Helps children process literary language structure.*
Children	They walk and walk by the pond.	
Ms. W	Say the word *by*. What letter would come first in *by*? Yes, now put your finger under it and say it.	*Draws attention to a word and prompts students to locate it in the text.*
	[Children say *by* while locating the word.]	
Ms. W	Turn to pages 14 and 15. What can Mother Duck do?	*Asks for interpretation*
Charley	Mother Duck can fly.	
Marva	No.	
Charley	Yes.	
Ms. W	Well, turn the page. What are they doing?	*Draws attention to the picture.*
Alycia	They can fly!	
Ms. W	Yes, they can flap their wings. The little ducks can flap, flap, flap, fly! Can you say that?	*Helps them use book language.*
Children	The little ducks can flap, flap, flap, fly!	
Ms. W	Turn back to the beginning and read about Mother Duck and her little ducks and all the things they can do by the pond.	*Prompts thinking about the meaning of the story.*

Look at the sample introduction to *Plants That Eat Bugs* (Figure 7-21). The teacher drew attention to the words *leaf* and *leaves* and helped children understand why these words are important. She linked the book to word study by helping children notice vowel pairs and consonant clusters, but she also made sure they looked at the pictures and knew that the leaves trap the bugs. She frequently used language from the text, sometimes longer segments.

Supporting Language Use in a Level M Text

In Figure 7-22, you see the cover of *The Fox and the Gulls* and the book's text characteristics are shown in Figure 7-23. This traditional tale has literary quality; readers will therefore need to use their experience with complex written language structure. There are long stretches of dialogue and a traditional ending. Sentences are long and contain many embedded dependent and independent clauses. The vocabulary is more sophisticated than most children would use in oral language. There are some archaic concepts (*reed hut*) as well as expressions that would not be used in everyday language (*tasty feast*). This text is quite difficult for children who are inexperienced in processing literary language.

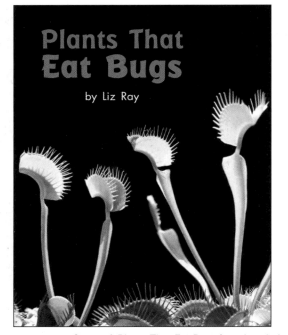

Figure 7-19 Cover of *Plants That Eat Bugs* from Leveled Literacy Intervention, Blue System (Heinemann 2009)

Analysis of New Book Characteristics — *Plants That Eat Bugs,* Level H

GENRE/FORM
- Nonfiction
- Informational text

TEXT STRUCTURE
- Different kind of plant every two pages (divided into sections)
- Description of how plants eat bugs
- Same sequence within each section Summary at the end

CONTENT
- Bug-eating plants
- Concept of parts of plants

THEMES AND IDEAS
- Nature
- Interdependence of plants and animals

LANGUAGE AND LITERARY FEATURES
- Interesting presentation of information
- Descriptive words

SENTENCE COMPLEXITY
- Present tense
- Varying sentence length, most seven to twelve words
- Prepositional phrases embedded within sentences
- Compound sentences
- Sentences with embedded clauses

VOCABULARY
- Technical words related to bug-eating plants

WORDS
- All one-syllable words
- Words with vowel combinations

ILLUSTRATIONS
- Photographs
- Close match between pictures and text but far more meaning in the text than can be carried by the pictures

BOOK AND PRINT FEATURES
- Pictures on right pages and print on the left
- Periods, exclamation point, commas
- Word and picture summary at the end

Figure 7-20 Analysis of Text Characteristics in *Plants That Eat Bugs*

Figure 7-21 Introduction to *Plants That Eat Bugs*

Speaker	Interaction	What the Teacher Is Attending to
Mr. V	You have another informational book; it's about plants that eat bugs. That's also the title: *Plants That Eat Bugs*. Have you ever heard of plants that eat bugs?	*Identifies genre and evokes background information.*
Natalie	It's like a flytrap plant.	
Spencer	I didn't know plants can eat bugs. How can they do it?	
Mr. V	Turn to page 4. On this page the writer talks about how the plant uses its leaves to trap bugs. You can see that happening in the picture. There are two leaves.	*Draws attention to the picture and uses vocabulary from the text.*
Clarissa	Are those the leaves with the little prickly things on them?	
Adam	Those are the leaves and they shut on the fly.	
Mr. V	Look at page 4. What would you expect to see at the beginning of the word *leaves?*	*Draws attention to the beginning letter of a word.*
Children	L. *[They locate* leaves.*]*	
Mr. V	The next two letters you see are *ea*, the two vowels that come together in words. We have been looking at words like that and we know that the two vowels have the sound of the first letter. Say *leaves* and see if that is true in this word.	*Makes a connection to word study lessons. Draws attention to a vowel pair.*
Children	*Leaves*. Yes.	
Mr. V	Turn to page 5 and find the word *leaf*—just one leaf.	*Draws attention to the singular form of a noun.*
Natalie	It's *ea*.	
Mr. V	Those leaves are very important because the leaf traps the bug. Look at page 8. The leaves on this plant are sticky. The bug sticks to the leaf. Stick!	*Explains a concept. Uses some of the language from the text.*
Spencer	It's stuck. That starts with *st*.	
Mr. V	You're right. It is the consonant cluster *st*.	*Reinforces child's noticing visual information.*
Mr. V	Turn the page and you will see a leaf that rolls up and traps the bug. Now look at page 14. This plant looks like a cup. It has smooth sides and the bug slides down inside.	*Explains a key concept. Uses some of the language of the text.*
Mr. V	What two letters would you expect to see at the beginning of *slide?*	*Draws attention to a consonant cluster at the beginning of a word*
Children	*S–l*. [They locate the word *slide*.]	
Adam	It's really sliding down in there. But how does the plant eat the bug?	
Mr. V	The juices of the plant sort of dissolve the bug and it soaks into the plant.	*Provides information beyond the text.*
Children	Oooh!	

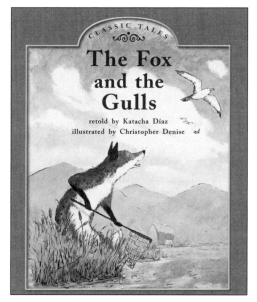

Figure 7-22 Cover of *The Fox and the Gulls* from Leveled Literacy Intervention, Blue System (Heinemann 2009)

Look at the sample introduction to *The Fox and the Gulls* (Figure 7-24). The teacher drew attention to the genre, which helped readers understand the underlying structure of a text, thus supporting comprehension. The children in the group had experience with traditional tales and could use this information to anticipate what the text would be like. The teacher also drew attention to the literary beginning of the story and pointed out some of the language, signaling that the children should expect the story to be quite different from informational texts or oral language. Several times during the introduction, the teacher repeated some of the language and used more difficult vocabulary in conversation. She also made sure children understood some of the trickier concepts.

Analysis of New Book Characteristics   *The Fox and the Gulls* Level M

GENRE/FORM
- Fiction
- Traditional literature
- Play

TEXT STRUCTURE
- Narrative
- Different episode on every page or page spread
- Problem and solution

CONTENT
- Historical context
- Country life
- Typical traits of traditional animal characters

THEMES AND IDEAS
- Danger and escape
- Cleverness of the weaker animals

LANGUAGE AND LITERARY FEATURES
- Literary language throughout *(long ago)*
- Long stretches of dialogue
- Setting, story problem, and satisfying ending
- Some rhyme
- Traditional ending *(never had to worry about Fox again)*

SENTENCE COMPLEXITY
- Past tense
- Varying sentence length, the longest sixteen words
- Sentences with many embedded dependent and independent phrases and clauses, some introductory
- Compound sentences
- Dialogue among several speakers, most of it split

VOCABULARY
- Many words that will be familiar to most children
- Wide variety of words assigning speech *(roared)*

WORDS
- One-, two-, and three-syllable words
- Words with *-ing* and *-ed* endings
- Adverbs with *-ly* endings and adjectives with *-y-* endings

ILLUSTRATIONS
- Drawings on most pages and on every page spread
- Variable placement of illustrations
- Illustrations showing emotions of characters

BOOK AND PRINT FEATURES
- Four to ten lines of print on every page
- Periods, exclamation point, commas, quotation marks, question mark
- Sentences beginning in the middle of the line
- Space to indicate paragraphing

Figure 7-23 Analysis of Text Characteristics in *The Fox and the Gulls*

Figure 7-24 Introduction to *The Fox and the Gulls*

Speaker	Interaction	What the Teacher Is Attending to
Ms. W	Today you have a classic tale called *The Fox and the Gulls.* You may not have heard this story, but it is an old tale like all the others you have been reading. Gulls are seagulls—birds that live near the sea. What are you thinking about foxes and gulls?	*Draws attention to genre. Activates background knowledge.*
Natasha	It's like in *Chicken Little?* The fox likes to eat the chicken and goose and birds.	
Bertie	They learn a lesson in stories.	
Ms. W	This story starts with the words *long ago.*	*Uses and draws attention to literary language.*
Martin	That's like a long time ago.	
Mary	Kind of like "once upon a time."	
Ms. W	Look at page 2. That is Fox. He lived in a little reed hut. Reed means a kind of grass. It had been a long winter and he didn't have much to eat. He would like to have a tasty feast. That means a meal that really tastes good—a tasty feast.	*Uses vocabulary and language structure from the text.*
Mary	He might be going to eat the gulls.	
Ms. W	You're right. Look at the second paragraph on this page. *[Reading]* "'The gulls are back!' Fox cried. 'It's been a long winter.' His stomach rumbled at the thought of a tasty gull breakfast." Find the word *stomach.* It's tricky.	*Reads some of the language from the text. Explains a new vocabulary word. Draws attention to the visual features of a new word.*
	[Children locate the word stomach *and say it.]*	
Ms. W	What do you think about that?	*Asks children to think about the story.*
Bertie	What does it mean "his stomach rumbled"?	
Natasha	Maybe you know like your stomach makes noises when you are hungry.	
Ms. W	Sometimes you say your stomach growls because it does make a noise, but in this book it says "his stomach rumbled." That's a good word to use to show how hungry Fox is. He wants a tasty gull breakfast.	*Draws attention to and explains a new vocabulary word.*
Bertie	He's going to get the birds.	
Ms. W	Look at page 4. Mother Gull was making a nest and Fox watched from a distance. Find the word *distance.* It means pretty far away. What are two parts of that word?	*Explains a new word and prompts children to take it apart.*
	[Children say the word in two parts and point to distance.*]*	

continues

Figure 7-24 Introduction to *The Fox and the Gulls, continued*

Speaker	Interaction	What the Teacher Is Attending to
Ms. W	Thinking about the parts of words will help you read it. Now look at page 6. What's happening?	*Draws attention to the meaning in the pictures.*
Natasha	He's getting the little babies!	
Bertie	He is going to eat them.	
Ms. W	He is taking them back to his little reed hut. Do you think he will eat them?	*Repeats vocabulary from the text.*
Children	Yes.	
Natasha	No, they'll get away.	
Ms. W	Look at page 11. There's Fox in the picture and he is reaching down to grab a chick, but you know all he got was a paw full of thorns—really sharp things like you find on roses. He knew that Mother Gull had tricked him, and he wants to teach her a lesson. So you are going to read to find out what happened.	*Uses language from the text. Explains a vocabulary word. Prompts prediction.*

▶ Using Language to Support Readers

Language plays a critical role in learning, especially in the process of becoming literate. All children come to school with an oral language system that does not precisely match written language. But some children have had broader experiences as well as opportunities to hear written language. They have assimilated some knowledge of language structure, concepts, and vocabulary as they conversed with adults and older children. Interacting with more advanced speakers gives children the information they need to extend language, and they do so intuitively—without explicit instruction. Children with more advanced language development have a powerful tool they can use in becoming literate. Although some highly verbal children do have difficulty with visual perception, and language knowledge does not guarantee success, it is one of the most important tools that children can have.

Having conversations about texts every day—during interactive read-aloud, literature discussion, small-group reading instruction, and writing about reading—will go a long way toward preventing reading difficulties, even in children whose knowledge of and experience with language is limited. Conversation is essential for English language learners. As children hear new vocabulary and structures, they can incorporate them into their own repertoire.

Some children may be making good progress in learning about and using language and yet not realize how to use this knowledge as a resource when reading. In addition to introducing the texts your students read, you can work alongside the children while they are reading and do some explicit teaching afterward to help them effectively use language structure, visual information, and meaning to develop an effective processing system. (More information about demonstrating, prompting, and reinforcing effective processing is presented in Chapter 14, Teaching for Problem Solving while Processing Texts.)

▶ Suggestions for Professional Development

EXPANDING LANGUAGE

1. Gather a collection of fiction and nonfiction texts that you would use for small-group reading. Choose several examples for each level (across a grade or several grades). (The gradient chart on page 45 links grade levels to text levels.)

2. In pairs or threesomes, examine each of the texts with language in mind. Ask:

   ❑ What oral language resources are the children able to bring to the reading of this text?

   ❑ What grammatical structures are different from the language children control and will be challenging?

   ❑ What words will be challenging to read and understand?

   ❑ What background information do I need to provide prior to reading?

   ❑ How can I help children grasp the theme or main idea of the book?

3. Write down some questions and comments to use in your introduction to the text. You cannot predict children's responses precisely, but you can plan some of the language you will use.

4. Repeat the process for children's literature you plan to read aloud to the whole class. Select several pieces to read over a number of weeks. Ask:

   ❑ Is this selection appropriate in terms of language complexity and ideas? (Children must still be able to understand selections that are read aloud.)

   ❑ What language may be difficult for the children?

   ❑ What will I need to stop and explain?

   ❑ What background will I need to provide before reading?

   ❑ What language learning opportunities does this text provide? What are the opportunities to expand language syntax? Vocabulary? Content knowledge?

   ❑ What should children discuss after the reading?

5. Prepare a few sentences to open the read-aloud session, mark several places to stop to invite brief discussion, and note some ways to get discussion going afterward. Frame your plan so that you are both demonstrating text talk and encouraging children to talk.

Words Matter: Building Power in Vocabulary

READING COMPREHENSION, WORD SOLVING, AND VOCABULARY KNOWLEDGE are deeply connected. If we are talking about reading instruction, particularly for struggling readers, then we must address the area of vocabulary, which is an important factor in both decoding and comprehension. In this chapter, we explore vocabulary development and the way texts make increasing demands on the reader's vocabulary knowledge. We also suggest ways to help students develop systems for word learning.

Vocabulary is important not only in early literacy but also in long-term proficiency in reading, writing, and speaking. Learning new words is a lifelong activity. We have systems of strategic activities for learning words, and we constantly apply these systems to expand our speaking, listening, reading, and writing vocabularies. It is a good thing that we can do so with great efficiency, because new words are being added to every language every day. We notice new words, puzzle out their meaning, and select some to add to our repertoire. Interestingly, unless we are preparing an academic paper or article or have avid curiosity about a word, we seldom consult a dictionary. When we do so, it is a purposeful activity; we use the dictionary as a tool for spelling and pronunciation and to check our predictions of a word's meaning.

When we think about reading instruction, particularly for readers who struggle, then we must address vocabulary, since it is an important factor in both decoding words and comprehension of texts. Certainly, readers can decode words without understanding them, and they can know the meaning of words but not recognize them in print. In general, however, children are much more likely to be able to solve a word if they already have it in their oral vocabulary (National Reading Panel 2000).

Reading comprehension and vocabulary are deeply connected (Baumann et al. 2003). It makes sense that knowing the meaning of words, while not the only factor in comprehending a text, is very important. Stahl (2003) found a high correlation between standardized measures of vocabulary knowledge and reading comprehension. But Nagy (1985) claims that superficial knowledge of words will not be enough to make a difference in reading comprehension.

Think about what it means to truly know a word, even a simple one like *home*. We might read the word in contexts like these:

Come **home** with me.
My **home** is in New York.
My **home** town is New York.
She comes from a broken **home.**
Welcome to our **home.**
The family **home** is in Saratoga.
She entered the nursing **home.**
Paris is the **home** of fashion.
He made it to **home** plate.
Bring **home** the bacon.
Home for the holidays.
This deal wasn't a **home** run after all.
*You Can't Go **Home** Again*
Drive **home** the point.
Sins will come **home** to roost.
I am at **home** in the great cities of the world.
Home is where the heart is.
We made it **home** free.
The Babe hit it **home.**

If we include inflectional endings or compound words, the meaning of *home* expands even more: *homebody, homebrew, homecoming, homely, homey, homemade, homemaker.* Clearly, word use is complex, and there is a lot to learn. But we are always building on what we already know. According to Nagy and Scott (2000), word learning is incremental. We deepen knowledge of a word and its meaning (both direct and connotative) as we encounter it again and again in many contexts.

Moats (2001) has presented evidence of significant gaps in the vocabularies of economically advantaged versus economically disadvantaged children—as much as a two-thousand-word difference around Grade 3. And once behind, it is extremely difficult to catch up (Biemiller and Slonim 2001). It is likely that

your students who find reading difficult are also the students who have limited vocabularies.

Most children enter school with oral vocabularies that include common labels like *pet, farm, zoo,* and names of wild animals; vehicles; all kinds of food; animal habitats; neighborhood landmarks; names of family members; things you might see in the city or country; and parts of human and animal bodies. Some children know a great many more labels. You may know a child who has learned the names of dinosaurs or whales: vocabulary grows when children develop interests and pursue them.

The children who know only a few labels will also include many children who are just learning English. These students do have a large vocabulary in another language—larger than many native English speakers. But they may need extra support to acquire enough English vocabulary to be able to read and write in their new language effectively.

Since the vocabulary gap naturally grows exponentially over the years, it makes sense to give specific attention to consciously developing vocabulary from the time children enter school. But as you know, time for instruction is limited. You want to do only what is most effective to help readers who struggle. For over a hundred years, vocabulary instruction has typically involved lists of words for which students are expected to write and memorize definitions. Nagy (1988) finds little value in learning words by studying definitions. A memorized dictionary definition will not make a difference in reading comprehension.

▶ Vocabulary Challenges in Texts

When you are planning to develop vocabulary in your lessons, it helps to think of three tiers of words (Beck et al. 2002):

1. First-tier words are very simple and basic. They are mostly learned without instruction. Examples are *summer, family, hungry.* This category includes simple verbs, nouns, articles, adverbs, prepositions, and possessives, although

nouns and verbs are usually the focus of vocabulary development.

2. Second-tier words appear frequently in the vocabularies of mature language users. They are not connected to a particular domain but rather are pervasive. Examples are *fascinate, unfortunate, enthralled, mentioned*. This category may also include words originally related to technical fields that have entered general conversation—*digital*, for example.

3. Third-tier words are specialized and are often related to scientific domains. They are usually learned through content area study and appear very frequently in the language. Examples are *ectoplasm* or *cabriolet*.

Significantly, all three tiers provide challenges for readers who do not bring a large vocabulary to becoming literate (see Figure 8-1).

Tier 1 Words

Tier 1 words are in the speaking, reading, and writing vocabularies of speakers of the language. Elementary age children are still developing their vocabulary of first-tier words. For example, they might know *ran* but not *dashed* or *sprinted*. Many of these first-tier words are easily learned through everyday conversation and by reading simple texts.

Some children enter school knowing few first-tier words. They may not know words like *chased* or

Figure 8-1 Vocabulary Challenges for Readers

Tiers of Words	Definition	Examples	Issues for Struggling Readers
1	Simple, basic words learned without instruction	*truck* *elephant* *bike* *winter* *arm* *music*	• Low repertoire of words • Need instruction to expand repertoire of tier 1 words (while many other students do not) • Comprehension undermined by lack of common labels
2	Words that appear in the vocabularies of mature language users and are pervasive across contexts (not connected to a particular discipline or domain of knowledge)	*serendipity* *unfortunate* *replied* *web* *hereditary* *petulant* *unexceptional*	• Devote problem-solving and attention to tier 1 words, with little left for tier 2 words • Find it difficult to take apart longer words • Have few known words or word parts to bring to the process • Cannot learn without instruction
3	Words that are specialized and often related to a scientific discipline	*ectoplasm* *eurhythmic* *phantasmagoria* *sabbatical* *sclerotic*	• Lack content knowledge and background experience for understanding words • Cannot build on a strong foundation of tier 1 and tier 2 words • Do not have ability to read a large number of tier 1 and 2 words easily and so cannot understand the language and content enough to take on technical words • Have difficulty learning even with instruction because the words are meaningless

sparkled. They may not have labels for things beyond their experience. Yet many books at early levels assume knowledge of these words. The Level B book *The Tide Pool*, for example, includes several vocabulary challenges. The concept of a tide pool might be familiar to children who live near a beach, have gone to an aquarium, or have traveled. Exposure through books or TV programs is also a possibility. All of the words in *The Tide Pool* are first-tier words, but they will not be familiar to all young readers, especially those with limited experiences. The words *fish* and *shell* would probably be familiar to most but not *jellyfish, crab, snail, starfish,* and *eel*. Many readers will need strong support to read even this simple text.

Although English language learners know many first-tier words in their first language, they need to learn first-tier words in their second language. They may understand concepts but not know the labels attached to them. They may be unaware of elements of language structure and therefore not know how to put endings on verbs, for example. These are the most vulnerable readers, because they learn to decode words without understanding their meaning and this makes their reading incomprehensible.

Just about all words in books you expect students to read while they are building a reading process should be tier 1 words; that is, they should be accessible to readers with teacher support. Through text introductions and discussions after reading, you can provide the strong support that readers need to add these words to their speaking and reading vocabularies.

But readers encounter a range of first-tier words, from the simple words used frequently in oral language to words that are used less frequently and tend to appear in written language. Also, words commonly used in oral language can have slightly different definitions in a written text. For example, *guard* and *watch* are usually tier 1 words—a security *guard* at an athletic event, sitting down to *watch* television. But look at both words in the context of page 8 of *The Roadrunners* (see Figure 8-3). Here they are used as synonyms, both conveying the sense of vigilant observation. Both words refer to the combination of acts needed to keep the eggs warm and protect them against predators. The text supports meaning through the illustrations and the explanations embedded in the body of the text.

Figure 8-2 Cover of *The Tide Pool* from Leveled Literacy Intervention, Blue System (Heinemann 2009)

Figure 8-3 Page Spread from *The Roadrunners* from Leveled Literacy Intervention, Blue System (Heinemann 2009)

Tier 2 Words

While readers are working hard to acquire first-tier words, they have little attention left to devote to second-tier words. Yet texts begin to include second-tier words, and readers need strategies to solve them. As in tier 1, tier 2 words range from more accessible to harder. Much depends on:

❑ How many times the reader has previously encountered the word.

❑ The reader's background information.

❑ How commonly the words are used in oral language.

❑ The accessibility of the content of the text to the reader.

❑ The sheer *number* of tier 2 words in the text (with too many, problem solving can break down).

❑ The supports provided within the text. Struggling readers need more than a glossary.

Friendly texts provide a great deal of support relative to the meaning of tier 2 words. For example, on page 7 of *The Fun Club Goes to the Aquarium* (see Figure 8-4), readers encounter the word *tentacles*, a word that is technical when applied to aquatic life but is used in many other contexts (sometimes figuratively).

You can make tier 2 words accessible to readers by building background knowledge in the introduction to a text, explaining the words and using them in conversation, and prompting readers to use the words themselves.

Tier 3 Words

Third-tier words provide significant challenges for readers as they begin to read texts with more complex content. Generally, the more tier 3 words a text has (and the more complex these words are), the harder the text (at least if the words are important to the meaning of the entire text). Most books from Level A through N will not have third-tier words. But keep in mind that a term like *zip code* in *The Fun Club Goes to the Post Office* (see Figure 8-5) can require this same kind of content knowledge and many readers will need extra support to understand it.

Without a strong foundation of tier 1 and tier 2 words, some readers will have difficulty comprehending texts that have many tier 3 words, even with instructional support.

Figure 8-4 Page Spread from *The Fun Club Goes to the Aquarium* from Leveled Literacy Intervention, Blue System (Heinemann 2009)

Figure 8-5 Page Spread from *The Fun Club Goes to the Post Office* from Leveled Literacy Intervention, Blue System (Heinemann 2009)

▶ What Do Readers Need to Be Able to Do to Understand Word Meanings?

Learning new words and adding them to your vocabulary is a complex process, but it is one that proficient readers and writers engage in automatically and efficiently. Readers may find each of the actions listed in Figure 8-6 difficult or hard to understand. Each action needs to be taught, and each is discussed individually below.

Monitor Understanding

Competent readers notice when they do not know the meaning of a word, because they are always monitoring their understanding. When readers encounter words they don't know, they may sound out a pronunciation and read on a little. If the lack of meaning

causes discontinuity, they are likely to reconsider the word and actively search for more meaning. In the search they may try to break down the word or use the structure and meaning of the text.

For example, Cecelia was reading *Playing with Blocks* (see the cover in Figure 8-7). As shown in a piece of her Reading Record (Figure 8-8), on page 8 she had difficulty with the word *tunnel*. She substituted *take* and read on, stopped after *I* and reread *this time*, which sounded right to her. She then read up to the word *blocks*, stopped, and reread from the beginning of the sentence, this time substituting *tube* for

---

> **Figure 8-6 What Readers Do to Derive the Meaning of Words**
>
> 1. Recognize when they do not understand the precise meaning of a word (monitor understanding).
> 2. Identify the important words in a text that must be understood and work on getting the meaning.
> 3. Use the context of the text to derive the meaning of words—the content of an informational text, the structure of the narrative, the meaning of the whole text, background information, and the language structure.
> 4. Make connections between the word and known words or word parts to solve them (a process that accelerates as more words are known).
> 5. Notice the morphology (word structure) and connect meaning to it.
> 6. Hypothesize word meaning and check with the language structure and the meaning of the whole text.
> 7. Decide whether the word is important to learn and record it.
> 8. Sometimes check the definition of the word in a dictionary or glossary.

Figure 8-7 Cover of *Playing with Blocks* from Leveled Literacy Intervention, Orange System (Heinemann 2009)

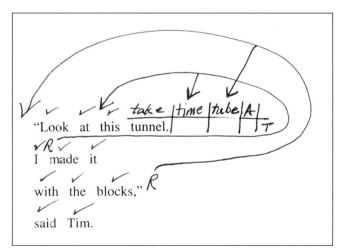

Figure 8-8 Section of Cecelia's Reading Record on *Playing with Blocks*

tunnel. Cecelia did check the object in the picture, but since it was made with blocks, it was abstract. Probably *tunnel* was not part of Cecelia's oral vocabulary, and the picture was not helpful. Finally, she hesitated again and appealed to the teacher. The important thing is that Cecelia was monitoring her reading and actively searching for what would make sense and sound right. She also used visual information (the first letter of the word). She may have reached the end of the quotation and remembered that everything in the book is made with blocks. Her final substitution even matched the shape of the object. Cecelia needed to know the word in order to understand the page.

After the reading, the teacher returned to the page and guided a conversation like this one:

TEACHER: Can you find the tricky part on this page? [*Cecelia points to the word* tunnel.] You did some good work on this page. You were looking at the first letter and thinking what would sound right and make sense. This word is *tunnel.* Say *tunnel.* A *tunnel* is like a tube. Tunnels are big enough for cars and trucks to drive through. But in this story, the children made a little tunnel on the road for their toy cars to go through. Put your finger on the tunnel in the picture and show where the cars go through. Now try the page again.

[*Cecelia reads correctly.*]

TEACHER: Have you ever been through a tunnel?

CECELIA: No, but it's kind of like the hall. Or it's like going under a bridge.

The teacher asked Cecelia to find the word that gave her trouble (which readers can usually do). She affirmed the work that Cecelia had done and then simply explained the word. If several children in the group had been shaky on the meaning of *tunnel,* the teacher could have taken everyone to the page to discuss the meaning.

Readers who struggle are sometimes so overwhelmed by the process that they give up on the search for meaning and keep on going with only superficial understanding. Be sure to reinforce children's monitoring and active searching even if they do not read the word correctly.

Identify the Important Words

Not all the words in a text are important for comprehension. Efficient readers give their attention to the words they need to understand to comprehend the text and work out the meaning of those words. Suppose, for example, as a proficient reader, you encounter a sentence like: "The aubergine curtains opened to reveal the entrance to the subterranean caverns concealing the crypt of the deviner." You would focus on *curtains, subterranean, crypt,* and *deviner* as key words in understanding the sentence. *Aubergine* might excite some curiosity, but the color of the curtains is not vital to the meaning (unless it surfaces later as an important clue to a mystery).

In one section of *The Wind and the Sun* shown (Figure 8-9), the reader needs to understand the words *contest, stronger,* and *breeze.* The reader can miss the word *agreed,* even substituting a word like *said,* and still understand the meaning.

"I win the contest!"
said Sun to Wind.
"I made the man take off his coat,
so I am stronger than you."

"Yes, you are," agreed Wind.
And he turned into a little breeze.

16

17

Figure 8-9 Page Spread from *The Wind and the Sun* from Leveled Literacy Intervention, Blue System (Heinemann 2009)

Readers who struggle tend to read one word after another, spending equal effort on almost every one. It will help them if you introduce a text by drawing attention to a few new or important words or using them in conversation and then make teaching points afterward. If children have difficulty with too many of the important words, then comprehension will be low. Select texts with only a few new words to solve.

Use Context to Derive Meaning

The concept of using context to derive word meaning involves more sophisticated and complex behavior than simply looking at a word in a sentence. To use context to solve a word, readers must simultaneously:

- ❑ Use background information.
- ❑ Notice the way the word functions in the sentence.
- ❑ Think about the meaning of the whole piece and what makes sense.
- ❑ Integrate contextual information with knowledge of morphemes and phonics.

In *The Skunk with No Stripes* (see Figure 8-10), readers might encounter several word challenges, among them *bushy, stubby,* and *spray.* Those three words are important for comprehending the story. The word *bushy* appears on many pages and on page 11 is contrasted to the word *stubby.* The word *spray* describes a key characteristic of a skunk and is also important for understanding the ending. A reader might compare *bushy* to a *bush* if that word is known, and might also notice the *-y* ending, which indicates the word is describing

something. Most important to understanding the meaning of these words in the text would be activating background information about skunks and about animals in general.

"That bear has a short, stubby tail," said Little Skunk. "I have a long, bushy tail. I am not a bear."

11

The bear followed Little Skunk home. "Go away!" cried Little Skunk. "Or I will spray you with a stinky smell."

12

Figure 8-10 Page Spreads from *The Skunk with No Stripes* from Leveled Literacy Intervention, Green System (Heinemann 2009)

This is a dolphin.
Dolphins live in the sea,
but they are not fish.

2

blowhole

Dolphins need to breathe air.
A dolphin breathes through a **blowhole**
on top of its head.

3

A dolphin has one **flipper**
on each side.
It has one **fin** on its back
and one fin on its tail.

The **tail fin** helps the dolphin
swim fast.
Some dolphins can swim
up to 25 miles an hour.

back fin

tail fin

flippers

4   5

Dolphins swim together in groups.
The groups are called **pods**.
A pod has baby dolphins
and grown-up dolphins.

calf

A baby dolphin is called a **calf**.
A calf stays with its mother
for two or three years.

6   pod   7

Figure 8-11 Page Spreads from *All About Dolphins* from Leveled Literacy Intervention,
Green System (Heinemann 2009)

While deriving the meaning of a word in a given context helps in understanding that text, the reader may still have only a superficial understanding of the word. Rich understanding is built across many contexts. Nevertheless, it would be impossible for children to learn every word in isolation. Readers need a range of strategies for using context.

Make Connections Between Words

The more words readers know, the easier it is for them to solve new words:

1. They have more resources for making connections.
2. They can generalize word parts across many words and can recognize them quicker.
3. They have developed systems for solving words because they have more experience.

It is obvious that struggling readers know fewer words; but they also may not even know that they should be making connections.

All About Dolphins (see Figure 8-11) has some technical word challenges.

On page 3, it is important for readers to understand the meaning of *blowhole*. Calling on background information, interpreting the illustration, and reading pages 2 and 3 will help. But the skillful word solver will also connect this compound word with either *blow* or *hole* (if known or easily solved words). The words *breathe* and *air* could clue the word *blow* even if *blow* is unfamiliar.

Notice and Use Word Parts

When readers are searching for clues to the meaning of a word, they immediately look for something about the word that they know. It might be a meaningful syllable or ending. For example, if you did not know the word *neologistical*, you could probably guess immediately that it is an adjective, based on the *-ical* ending. You might also connect the word with *neo* (*neo-Nazi, neophyte, neonatal*) or with *log* (*logistics, logic, geology, eulogy*). The word part *-ist* could also evoke meaning when connected with *pianist* or *realist*. By piecing together what you know about the parts, you can come closer to the real meaning of the word. Your key meanings might be *new, speaking, or study* and an adjective formed from something a person does. So a person who creates new meanings for an existing word would be a *neologist*. The *neologistical* meaning of a word is a new meaning (for example, "the net" means something different today than it did twenty years ago). The word *flipper* on page 4 has two word parts: *-er,* which means "doing something," and *flip,* which is an action like turning.

In combination with knowledge of word parts, a reader looking at pages 4 and 5 of *All About Dolphins* can use labeled illustrations as well as other resources to understand the key words, which are in bold.

Cross-Reference with Language Structure and Meaning

Proficient word solvers use language structure, background information, and textual meaning to check their understanding of words. For example, the word *fin* on pages 4 and 5 of *All About Dolphins* is easy to decode. Any reader who knows even a little about fish body parts would know the meaning—but would always be checking. *Fin* is a noun and sounds right in the sentence (modified by the adjective *one*). On page 4 the word can also be checked with labeled illustrations. Once the sentence on page 4 has been processed and understood, it is easy to understand the meaning of *tail fin* on page 5.

The word *pods* on page 6 is likely to be a new one. The reader can decode it easily and use the context to check the meaning. The sentence structure makes it clear that the word *pods* is a label for the group. The word *grown-up* is foreshadowed by the antonym *baby*. Continuing to read helps the reader check the predicted meaning.

Choose Which Words to Learn

After readers derive the meaning of a word in order to comprehend a particular text, they may or may not add the word to their vocabularies. Readers might use effective processing, work at understanding important words, and finish reading with good understanding. That does not mean that they "know" the word; they may have only an introductory awareness.

Sometimes readers find a new word interesting. It may reveal a new idea or concept. It may be a label for something they already now. They may understand a new meaning for an existing word and find that interesting. Depth of engagement may lead individuals (either consciously or unconsciously) to add the word to their collection of known words. They may write it down or plan to use it in some discussion or writing that they will do. You can make this process more deliberate by selecting some of the words you want students to learn and demonstrating some techniques for learning and remembering them (for example, writing the word, making connections among words, using word webs).

Check Understanding Using Tools

Readers sometimes use a dictionary to check their understanding of important and interesting words. Or if a baffling word is necessary to understand a text, readers may look up the meaning in a dictionary. In informational texts, a convenient glossary is often provided, and readers develop the habit of consulting it to learn the meaning of technical words used in the text.

The dictionary is a very valuable tool, and you should provide direct instruction in how to use it; but it is not the key to developing a large vocabulary. Rather, readers must become active word solvers, using many different kinds of information. You will want to demonstrate the use of dictionaries by first thinking of what the meaning might be. Usually, the definition includes "shades" of meaning or even several meanings. Using the dictionary should be an active process—readers need to compare their previous ideas with the dictionary definition.

▶ Building Vocabulary Instruction into Small-Group Reading Instruction

Simply reading an appropriate level of text will not ensure vocabulary expansion, especially for struggling

readers. Students need specific instruction to understand the words well enough to comprehend the text. Direct attention to vocabulary may take place any time you are working with small groups of readers at the same instructional text level using texts that have only a few new problems to solve: during the introduction, through prompting while reading, when discussing the text, as

All About Chimps
by Alex Gomez

All About Series

What Chimps Do

Chimps live in groups.
They make sounds to talk
to each other.
Chimps help each other
find food.

Chimps clean each other's
hair with their fingers.
This chimp looks for bugs
and dirt.
If he finds a bug,
he eats it!

6

7

Chimps

This is a chimp.
Chimps have dark hair.
They have big ears
and big hands.

Most chimps live
in the forest.
They spend a lot of time
in trees.

2

3

What Chimps Eat

Chimps eat fruit,
leaves, flowers,
and seeds.
They also
eat eggs
and bugs.

Some chimps work as
a team to find their food.
They share the food
they find.

8

9

Chimps have long arms.
Their arms are very strong.
Chimps can swing
from tree to tree.

This is a chimp's foot.
Look at the big toe!
It helps the chimp
climb trees.

4

5

Chimps use tools.
This chimp uses a stick
to catch bugs.
The chimp pokes the stick
into a hole.

Bugs crawl up the stick.
The chimp pulls the stick
out and eats the bugs.

10

11

FIGURE 8-12 Page Layout of *All About Chimps* from Leveled Literacy Intervention, Green System (Heinemann 2009)

teaching points, and as students extend their understanding of the text in writing. Vocabulary is also supported just about any time children discuss the meaning or you encourage them to think what makes sense.

In *All About Chimps* (see Figure 8-12), the words *team* and *tools* are used in a more generic sense than the definitions children may already know. The illustration

FIGURE 8-12 Page Layout of *All About Chimps, continued*

for *tools* is helpful, but the concept is somewhat abstract. *Nest*, too, may be an unexpected word if children connect the word only with birds. They may have a very specific definition connected to the kinds of nests birds make, and the illustration and context will provide little help. But the reader who stretches the definition of *nest* will construct a wider meaning for the word.

Look at the excerpts from a small-group reading lesson of *All About Chimps* shown in Figure 8-13. The teacher provided quite a bit of support in the introduction. She helped students build background information, explained or directed student attention to important concepts in the text, and used the words *forest, ears, long, arms, strong, groups, team, stick, nests,* and *tools* in conversation. She specifically pointed out the enlarged definitions of *groups, team, tool,* and *nest*.

During reading, the teacher interacted several times with all three children. In the two interactions shown, she prompted the children to think about what they know about the topic (some of this information had just been presented in the introduction) and to use meaning to monitor their reading. At times she also explicitly demonstrated the process of understanding the meaning of a word in the text.

After the reading, the teacher checked for understanding and again drew attention to the word *team*. She negotiated with the children to produce the five sentences, which she wrote on a chart as shared writing (Figure 8-14). They underlined the words *groups* and *team* as related. In this lesson, the students:

❑ Heard words in context.

❑ Used background knowledge to understand word meaning within the text.

❑ Made connections between words.

❑ Used words in oral language

❑ Read words.

❑ Used words in writing.

In this process, they expanded their understanding of the definitions of several words and/or learned the meaning of a new word (*tool*).

Figure 8-13 Introduction to *All About Chimps*

Speaker	Interaction	What the Teacher Is Attending to
Ms. D	What do you know about chimps?	*Evokes background knowledge.*
Owen	They are monkeys. I have a stuffed chimp.	
Melissa	They live in the zoo.	
Xandra	And sometimes they don't live in zoos but they are in the jungle.	
Ms. D	In this book you are going to learn more about them. Turn to page 3. What do you notice about how the chimp looks?	*Draws attention to meaning in the pictures.*
Xandra	They have hair.	
Melissa	They have big ears.	
Ms. D	You're right. Most chimps live in the forest and spend a lot of time in trees. Now, turn to page 4. What do you notice about the chimp's arms?	*Provides background information. Draws attention to meaning in the pictures.*
Owen	They really can just swing around on the trees.	
Ms. D	Those long arms are very strong. On page 5 what do you notice about its foot? The chimp's big toe helps the chimp and you are going to read to find out how. Turn to page 6. The chimps live in groups and they help each other. Can you say *groups?* Find it. Run your finger under it and say it.	*Uses language from the text. Points out a specific vocabulary word.*
Xandra	The groups are kind of like a family?	
Ms. D	It is like a family. They don't live just alone or in twos or threes. There is a whole group of chimps, kind of like our class. And you are going to find that the chimps in the group work together as a team to help each other.	*Uses two vocabulary words and explains them.*
Melissa	Like a football team?	
Ms. D	Any time people and animals work together and help each other, you could say they are working as a team. Like the way we work as a team to keep our classroom clean and to share our supplies. Look on page 7. They are helping to clean each other's hair by looking for bugs and dirt.	*Provides further information to explain vocabulary word.*
Ms. D	I would like to point out a couple more things to you. Do you see what the chimp is doing on page 10?	*Draws attention to meaning in the pictures.*
Owen	He's poking a little stick in a hole.	
Ms. D	You will read that he is using that stick to catch bugs. It is a tool— something you use to help you.	*Broadens the definition of a word.*
Xandra	Like a toolkit.	

continues

Figure 8-13 Introduction to *All About Chimps, continued*		
Speaker	**Interaction**	**What the Teacher Is Attending to**
Ms. D	Any time you use something besides your hand to help you do something, you can say you are using a tool—even a little stick like this one. Now, look at page 12. Look at the heading. What are you going to be reading about?	*Further clarifies expanded meaning.*
Xandra	How chimps live	
Ms. D	You will find out that they sleep in trees. They used the branches and the leaves to make a nest—a comfortable place to sleep. You may be thinking about a bird's nest for the eggs, but this is a new kind of nest—for chimps to sleep in. Now, turn back to the beginning and read all about chimps. When you finish we'll talk about what you found interesting about them.	*Points out a new meaning for a known word*
Melissa	*[Hesitates on* share *on page 9.]*	
Ms. D	Are you thinking about the meaning of the whole book? Think about what you know about chimps?	*Prompts for the use of background information from the introduction.*
Melissa	They work as a team.	
Ms. D	Try it again and think about what would make sense and look right.	*Prompts for connections between words by meaning.*
Melissa	Yes, because they are like a team.	
Owen	*[Substitutes* new *for* nests *and* break *for* branches *on page 12.]*	
Ms. D	You said, "they make news from break and leaves." Did that make sense?	*Prompts to check the word with meaning.*
Owen	No.	
Ms. D	Try it again and think about what you know about chimps.	*Probes for background knowledge.*
Owen	*[reading] Chimps make nests from [hesitates and appeals].*	
Ms. D	Could the picture help you think what would make sense?	*Draws attention to meaning in the picture.*
Owen	It isn't *trees.*	
Ms. D	Try branches. Would that look right and make sense?	*Prompts for use of two sources of information*
Owen	Oh, branches. *[Reads accurately.]*	
Ms. D	When I'm thinking about a word, I think about the topic or subject of the book. In this book, it helps to know a new kind of nest. Knowing that the word is *nests* helps me think about how they make nests from branches and leaves.	*Demonstrates process of figuring out words.*

continues

Figure 8-13 Introduction to *All About Chimps, continued*

Speaker	Interaction	What the Teacher Is Attending to
Ms. D	Did you learn something about chimps from this book?	*Draws attention to a word to extend meaning.*
Xandra	They live in groups and they eat bugs from each others' hair.	
Owen	They make nests in the trees.	
Melissa	But they just sleep in the nests and they make new nests all the time. They just really kind of sleep in leaves.	
Ms. D	You learned a lot! Teacher: Did you think more about the word *team?* What does that word tell you about chimps?	*Helps students expand understanding of a vocabulary word.*
Melissa	They can take care of each other and help each other get food.	
Ms. D	Do you think it's a good idea for them to live in groups?	*Asks for critical thinking.*
Owen	They can take care of their babies.	
Xandra	Yes, sometimes they have twins.	

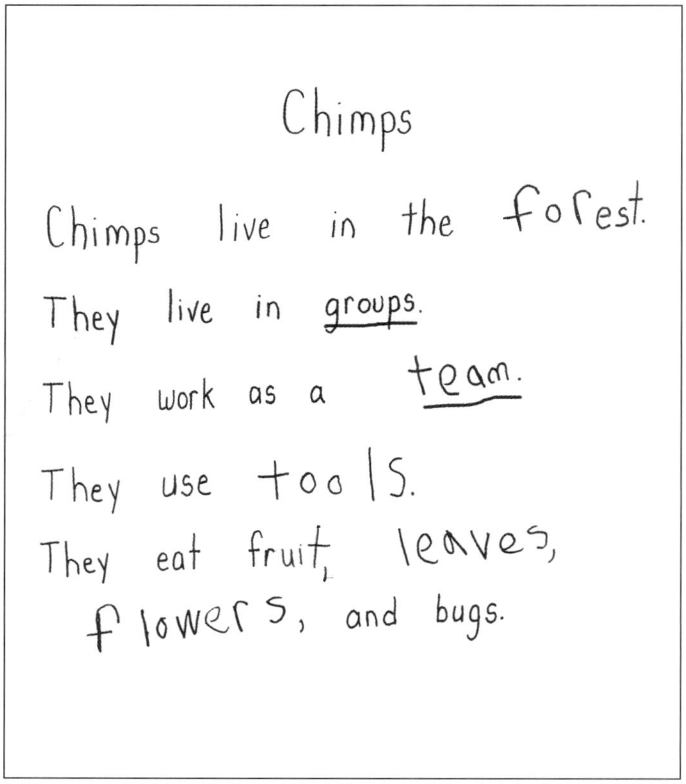

Chimps

Chimps live in the forest.
They live in groups.
They work as a team.
They use tools.
They eat fruit, leaves, flowers, and bugs.

FIGURE 8-14 Writing About the Text

▶ Ways of Increasing Vocabulary in Other Instructional Contexts

Vocabulary exists in our long-term memory. The process of learning a new word is first to notice and enter it into short-term memory and then to work with it in ways that will make it part of the lexicon stored in long-term memory. Sophisticated readers constantly add new words to their vocabularies through wide reading, and they probably also learn new words from watching television and going to the movies. But these sophisticated readers have been developing their vocabularies over many years. They have learned powerful strategies for noticing important new words and deriving their meaning. In your own vocabulary learning, you probably seldom encounter a new word. When you do, it stands out as important or intriguing. Possibly it is one of those new words that are constantly being created to label emerging concepts (a few years ago, *blog* was such a word). You may notice the new word several more times in oral or written language. (If you do not encounter it again, it will probably not be stored in long-term memory.)

You cannot expect less sophisticated readers, and certainly not struggling readers, to pick up all their vocabulary from context as they read or even when they hear texts read aloud. Nagy (1988) criticizes contextual approaches as seldom providing enough information to come to a precise definition. Reading *is* an important way to acquire vocabulary incidentally. Students who read more do have larger vocabularies (Nagy and Herman 1987; Stanovich 1986). For struggling readers, you need to encourage the random way they learn words but also provide some systematic ways of learning new words. Along with seeing to it that students read lots of texts, you can use some simple techniques to help them learn the meaning of words (see Figure 8-15).

Let's look at each of these techniques in a bit more detail:

1. *Introduce students to a wide range of words in interesting texts.* One of the reasons *All About Chimps* is accessible to readers is that the writer has used words they are likely to know, but used them in new ways. Children will not be interested in words if they do not read engaging texts (or hear them read aloud). It is a big mistake to restrict students to texts that are so simplistic and dull that they do not excite curiosity and are difficult to use as a basis for discussion or writing. Vocabulary is expanded through talk that enables children to use the new words they are encountering. They need to experience many genres, topics, and characters.

2. *Make sure students encounter a new word many times.* This does not mean you should use texts in which the language is artificially distorted. It

---

Figure 8-15 Fifteen Ways to Increase Your Students' Vocabulary

1. Introduce them to a wide range of words in interesting texts.
2. Make sure they encounter a new word many times.
3. Make sure they encounter a new word in many contexts.
4. Provide explicit vocabulary instruction related to each text they read.
5. Discuss word meanings with them.
6. Teach them how to recognize the important words in a text.
7. Help them recognize and use meaningful morphemes (word parts in longer words).
8. Teach them to use context to derive the meanings of words.
9. Teach them to use the dictionary or glossary as an aid to verifying meaning.
10. Help them integrate previously known definitions with new ones as they meet them in texts.
11. Help them use new words in discussion and in writing.
12. Teach them to make connections between words to understand their meaning.
13. Help them understand words that are used figuratively.
14. Help them develop deliberate strategies for learning words.
15. Encourage persistence and recognize success.

does mean that students should hear read or read for themselves books on similar topics. Whether books are related by topic, genre, or author or are part of a series, if wide reading is occurring, students are more likely to encounter words many times. You can increase the number of encounters by incorporating selected words into minilessons and writing assignments.

3. *Make sure students encounter a new word in many contexts.* Meeting a word in different contexts strengthens students' understanding of it. Whenever you run across a word students are learning, point it out. When reading a book aloud, for example, point out a word that is the same or means the same as a word that is part of your vocabulary or spelling instruction.

4. *Provide explicit vocabulary instruction related to each text students read.* If you give direct attention to words and their meanings in small-group reading lessons, students will have several encounters with the word in one lesson. Chances are, they will revisit the meaning again while rereading the text.

5. *Discuss word meanings with students.* Spend time discussing the meaning of words in many different contexts. It can be as simple as asking, "Were there any words that you didn't understand?" Or, "Were there any words in that book that were new to you?" Prompt students to talk about these words (and jot them down yourself so you can revisit them later).

6. *Teach students how to recognize the important words in a text.* By drawing attention to the words you know students need to understand to comprehend the text, you implicitly signal how to select important words. As they grow more sophisticated as readers, you can demonstrate how to identify these key words. They can use these words in their own writing.

7. *Help students recognize and use meaningful morphemes (word parts in longer words).* All readers need to be able to break down longer words. Base words have meaning; prefixes and endings add meaning. The more students connect and solve words by looking at the parts, the easier it will be for them to derive meaning. When students begin learning about word parts, their

vocabulary expands exponentially—for example, *fortune, fortunately, unfortunate, unfortunately.*

8. *Teach students to use context to derive the meanings of words.* Explicitly demonstrate, prompt for, and reinforce students' use of background knowledge, the meaning of the whole text, and language syntax to derive the meaning of words.

9. *Teach students to use the dictionary or glossary as an aid to verifying meaning.* Students can use dictionaries and glossaries as tools but should not do so as a static exercise. Using a dictionary should involve active thinking—hypothesizing the meaning of a word using many different sources of information.

10. *Help readers and writers integrate previously known definitions with new ones as they meet them in texts.* Readers and writers should always bring their background knowledge to the reading of new texts. But sometimes clinging to a narrow definition of a word can interfere with comprehension. You want your students to become flexible in their understanding of words. They need to realize that words can have shades of meaning—they need to understand slightly different meanings in different texts. Also help them to understand that words can have several definitions.

11. *Help students use new words in discussion and writing.* Surrounding literacy activities with talk—often intentionally directed at the meaning of words—will support vocabulary expansion. From talk, students can move to writing in ways that help them solidify their understanding.

12. *Teach students to make connections between words to understand their meaning.* Demonstrate how to make connections between words by constructing word webs or grids that show relationships. If you persistently call attention to connections between words, your students will start to do so automatically.

13. *Help students understand figurative use of words.* Understanding metaphors and idioms is one of the most difficult tasks English language learners face. Figurative language is also difficult for readers who have limited vocabularies. Often

the meaning is very difficult to derive. Provide support by explaining figurative meaning when it occurs and also by presenting some direct lessons. Students are often intrigued by these meanings of words and make collections of them.

14. *Help students develop deliberate strategies for learning words.* Young children can build a strong foundation by reading lots of texts and discussing words in these texts. As they become more conscious of words, you can teach some specific techniques (including writing) for adding words to their vocabulary. It may help older students to use the series of questions in Figure 8-16. These questions may be inserted in a reader's notebook or word study notebook, and students may use them during minilessons. (Exercise caution: answering a list of questions like these during independent reading would greatly interfere with comprehension.)

15. *Encourage persistence and recognize success.* Encourage and reinforce students when they notice words and try to use them. You may also want to have students note in the reader's notebook the new and interesting words they are

adding to those they already know. Students will take pride in using interesting words in their own writing. They need to feel the satisfaction of solving words to make a text meaningful, checking their own thoughts with a dictionary and glossary and finding that they were close or correct, and sharing new words they have noticed with their classmates.

Expanding Students' Vocabulary in Specific Instructional Contexts

The fifteen techniques can be implemented in three specific aspects of literacy instruction:

1. *Interactive read-aloud and literature discussion.* Here you have the opportunity to use intentional conversation to bring students attention to words and invite them to discuss words. The texts that you use for interactive read-aloud can extend vocabulary minilessons in which you have taught word-solving strategies. You can demonstrate how to derive meaning from context or look at word parts.

2. *Small-group reading instruction.* Here students have the opportunity to read for themselves with your support. In each instructional segment—introduction, reading, discussion, teaching points, and writing about reading—words can be examined, taken apart to identify meaningful parts, and discussed. Students are presented with examples in context and have the opportunity to apply word-solving strategies independently.

3. *Extending meaning through writing.* Here students have a chance to examine words more closely. You can extend understanding of the meaning of texts—and the words in them—by supporting students as they write about their reading. They can summarize their understanding, use organizational tools like graphic organizers to analyze the text, respond to specific language and the meaning they take from it, or write from the point of view of a character. As they write, they are considering and using the vocabulary from the text. In addition, they can focus on vocabulary directly using word webs, grids, or charts.

For specific suggestions, see Figure 8-17.

Figure 8-16 Ten Steps in Word Learning

1. Do I know this word?

2. Do I know what this word means in this sentence or book?

3. Is this word important for understanding the book?

4. What does the word have to do with the meaning of the book?

5. What about the word do I know or recognize?

6. Is this word like any other words I know?

7. What parts of the word do I know?

8. Does this meaning of a word make sense in the book and sound right in the sentence?

9. Should I write this word down to remember it?

10. Should I check my idea of the meaning with the definition in the dictionary?

From the very beginning, infants distinguish the human voice from every other sound. They respond to the nonverbal gestures that accompany words and enhance their meaning. Going from this stage of literacy to having and using a sophisticated adult vocabulary is quite a journey. Even children who initially struggle to acquire a rich vocabulary can become interested in learning new words. But we need to ensure that they find satisfaction and success in the process. Direct vocabulary instruction, integrated with many opportunities to read and write, has that potential.

Figure 8-17 Expanding Students' Vocabulary in Specific Instructional Contexts

Technique	Interactive Read-Aloud and Literature Discussion	Small-Group Reading Instruction	Extending Meaning Through Writing
1. Introduce students to a wide range of words.	• Read to students daily. • Talk about the text before, during, and after reading. • Point out interesting words.	• Have students participate daily in small-group reading instruction. • Vary genre and topic so that they will encounter many different words.	• Encourage students to use interesting words in their own writing. • Help students notice a writer's use of interesting words and note them for later use.
2. Make sure they encounter a new word many times.	• Sequence or group books on a topic so that related vocabulary will be encountered again.	• Keep a list of books members of the group have read so you can quickly connect new words as they appear.	• Encourage students to write about their reading and to use words from texts. Have them reread what they have written to make connections between texts.
3. Make sure they encounter a new word in many contexts.	• Make links to the same word encountered in other contexts.	• Make links to the same word encountered in other contexts.	• Make links to the same word encountered in other contexts.
4. Provide explicit vocabulary instruction related to each text read.	• Draw students' attention to words in the text, briefly providing meaning as needed. • After reading, revisit important new words.	• Introduce new words through conversation before reading, telling the definitions as needed. • Provide vocabulary instruction that focuses on important words after reading.	• Draw out interesting words from texts and encourage students to respond to them or use them in writing.
5. Discuss word meanings.	• Invite children to discuss new words during and after reading.	• In the introduction, invite students to discuss the meaning of a new word, using the context and pictures. • After reading, invite students to bring up new words and talk about their meaning.	• Have students write briefly after discussion to help them remember new words.

continues

Figure 8-17 Expanding Students' Vocabulary in Specific Instructional Contexts, *continued*

Technique	Interactive Read-Aloud and Literature Discussion	Small-Group Reading Instruction	Extending Meaning Through Writing
6. Teach how to recognize the important words in a text.	• Show students important words and talk about their meaning in the story or informational text.	• Draw students' attention to new and important words during the introduction. • Draw attention to words in bold or italics in nonfiction texts. • After reading, have students go back to words they found interesting.	• Give students copies of some of the texts they have read and have them highlight the important words.
7. Help them recognize and use meaningful morphemes.	• Write important words on a whiteboard after reading and help students notice their parts. • Help students learn new words by connecting them to the parts of words they know. • Help students think about the meaning of words by recognizing base words and affixes.	• Write new words on a whiteboard after reading and help students notice word parts. • Help students learn new words by connecting them to the parts of words they know. • Help students think about the meaning of words by recognizing base words and affixes.	• Have students write words and highlight word parts. • Have students write words and divide them by syllables. • Have students write words, separating the base words, prefixes, and suffixes.
8. Teach them to use context.	• Demonstrate how to use prior knowledge, syntax, and word parts to understand the meaning of a word in a text.	• Demonstrate, prompt for, and reinforce the use of prior knowledge, syntax, and word parts to understand the meaning of a word in a text.	• Have students write about their reading, using more complex words.
9. Teach them to use the dictionary or glossary.	• Demonstrate checking students' predictions about the meaning of a word by consulting the glossary or dictionary.	• Teach students how to use a glossary for an informational text. • Help them check their own understanding of a word with a dictionary.	• Have students write what they think a word means from context and then check it with the dictionary definition.
10. Help them integrate previously known definitions with new ones.	• Invite students to talk about what they already know about a word and then compare or contrast that with the word in a new context.	• Have students predict the meaning of words and then check their understanding after reading.	• Have students write new information they have learned about a word.

continues

Figure 8-17 Expanding Students' Vocabulary in Specific Instructional Contexts, *continued*

Technique	Interactive Read-Aloud and Literature Discussion	Small-Group Reading Instruction	Extending Meaning Through Writing
10. Help them integrate previously known definitions with new ones.		• After reading, invite children to talk about new words they've learned (or new meanings for words they know).	
11. Help students use new words in discussion and in writing (text-based talk and writing).	• Extend understanding by having students write about reading.	• After reading, give students the opportunity to write about their understandings of and responses to a text	• Make webs or grids (or other drawings) to show word meanings.
12. Teach students to make connections between words.	• Help students think of synonyms or antonyms for a word in a text. • Write a difficult word and demonstrate how it is connected with other known words.	• Demonstrate how to derive the meaning of a word by connecting it to a known word. • Help students understand a word by supplying a synonym.	• Make word webs to show connections between words. • Have students write words that look like, sound like, or mean the same or opposite of a word.
13. Help students understand words used figuratively.	• Select texts that include metaphors and idioms. • Ensure that students understand the figurative use of words (comparisons are usually understandable). • Explain the meaning of words used figuratively.	• Select accessible texts that use figurative language. • Explain figurative use of words in the introduction. • Clarify understandings of figurative use of words in the discussion.	• Use writing and drawing to illustrate the figurative meaning of words. • Have students collect examples of words used figuratively (in a writer's notebook or word study notebook). • Use diagrams to illustrate the contrasting definitions of words.
14. Develop deliberate strategies for learning words.	• Through discussion, help students engage in learning words from texts that are read aloud.	• Through discussion, help students engage in learning words from texts they are reading.	• Give older, more proficient students some key steps in word learning and have them glue them in a reader's notebook.
15. Encourage persistence and recognize success.	• Read highly engaging texts appropriate for and interesting to the group of students, so that they will find word learning easy and satisfying. • Have students keep a notebook that includes new words they have learned so that they can see progress.	• Match books to readers' abilities so that they encounter only a few new words. • Select "friendly" texts that provide the meaning of most new or technical words in context.	• Help students keep a list of words they have learned so that they can see their progress.

▶ Suggestions for Professional Development

PLANNING FOR VOCABULARY DEVELOPMENT IN READING LESSONS

1. Gather a group of read-aloud texts and several levels of texts for small-group reading instruction. (Tailor them to the grade levels of interest.)

2. Look at each interactive read-aloud book first and identify vocabulary challenges. Ask:

   ❑ What words are within students' control and need no explanation?

   ❑ What words need support and explanation before reading (in the introduction)?

   ❑ What words should be discussed or revisited after reading?

   ❑ What words might you encourage students to use in their writing?

   ❑ What words could be brought into vocabulary minilessons?

3. Repeat the process for the leveled books for small-group instruction.

4. You may want to compare your analyses with the continuum from *Teaching for Comprehending and Fluency, K–8: Talking, Thinking, and Writing about Reading* (Fountas & Pinnell 2008). Discuss how this continuum can inform direct lessons on vocabulary.

5. Plan a read-aloud (with intentional conversation) or a small-group reading lesson with vocabulary expansion in mind.

The Phonological Base for Learning to Read and Write

EVERY LANGUAGE HAS A PHONOLOGICAL SYSTEM, a syntactic system, and a semantic system. These systems, working together, enable people not only to communicate but to support thinking and knowledge construction in very complex ways. In this chapter, we discuss the sound system of language along with ways to help learners become more aware of and learn how to use sounds in words.

Speech is communicated through sounds that are meaningful to speakers of a language. Language has a phonological system, a syntactic system, and a semantic system (as explained in Chapter 7). These systems, working together, enable human beings not only to communicate but also to support thinking and knowledge construction in very complex ways.

The phonological system refers *only* to the sounds, not to sounds and letters. The orthographic system (letters and some other marks) was invented to represent the oral language, and there is a relationship between sounds and letters, although for English that relationship is not one to one. Historical changes in speech, including merging languages and borrowing words from other languages, have resulted in more complex relationships:

❑ A letter may be related to two or more sounds (/ā/-plate, /ă/–at; /k/-cat, /s/–nice).

❑ A sound may be related to more than one letter (/ə/nut, won); /j/–judge, giraffe)

❑ Two letters may represent a single sound and a sound may be represented by a cluster of letters (/wh/–wheel; /sh/–shell; /ō/ boat; /ā/–eight).

▶ Phonological Awareness

Phonological awareness has a very particular meaning with regard to literacy. *Phonological awareness* is the awareness of the constituent sounds (*phonemes*) of words in learning to read and spell (Harris and Hodges 1995). Even though the sounds and letters are not perfectly related, awareness of the sounds in words is still a very important factor in learning to read. Children need to be able to distinguish sounds so that they can attach them to letters. "Instruction in phonemic awareness

(PA) involves teaching children to focus on and manipulate phonemes in spoken syllables and words" (*Report of the National Reading Panel*, 7).

Children do not automatically identify sounds just because they can speak and understand language. There are barriers to developing phonemic awareness that cause difficulty for many students. "Speech is seamless and has no breaks signaling where one phoneme ends and the next begins. Also, phonemes overlap and are coarticulated, which further obscures their separate identities. . . . [S]peakers focus their attention on the meanings of utterances, not sounds. Unless they are trying to learn an alphabetic code, there is no reason to notice and ponder the phonemic level of language" (*Report of the National Reading Panel*, 2-32).

Supporting the phonological awareness of early readers (kindergarten and grade one) is very important. Some older readers may also need support because they either have not understood the concept of sounds used to convey meaning or have not fully grasped the important relationships between sounds and letters. But many older struggling readers *do* have good phonological awareness. It's often the only thing they use when they are having difficulty. They have received appropriate phonics instruction and are able to hear sounds and match them with letters but have developed other confusions. So while phonological awareness is an important area of instruction, it is not *the* answer to the problems of all readers who struggle.

What Is a Phoneme?

The smallest units composing spoken language are called *phonemes*. Each phoneme is in reality a *category* encompassing several sounds that are only slightly different from one another. For example, the /n/ in *nut, bent,* and *running* are each slightly different, but they are enough alike that we categorize them all as /n/.

There are forty-four phonemes. Their actual sounds in the language vary, because dialect, articulation, speech style, and other factors vary. Nevertheless, these differences are slight. Speakers of English can understand one another even if they have different regional accents. The common sounds associated with letters are shown in Figure 9-1.

▶ What Do Readers and Writers Need to Learn About the Sounds in Words?

Speech comes out in a stream of sounds. Children learn oral language easily and interactively within their homes and communities, but as they become literate, they need a heightened awareness of speech. Young readers need to be able to hear and be aware of:

❑ *Words.* Children need to be able to hear the individual words in the sentences they hear and speak. They parse streams of speech into individual words. There are humorous stories about children who think *macaroni'n'cheese* is one word because they hear those sounds together so much, but in general, they develop an internalized concept of words; we know this because they string words together in rule-governed ways to create sentences

---

Phoneme Chart

We examine forty-four phonemes. The actual sounds in the language can vary as dialect, articulation, and other factors in speech vary. The following are common sounds for the letters listed.

Consonant Sounds

b /b/ box	n /n/ nest	ch /ch/ chair
d /d/ dog	p /p/ pail	sh /sh/ ship
f /f/ fan	r /r/ rose	wh /hw/ what
g /g/ gate	s /s/ sun	th /th/ think
h /h/ house	t /t/ top	th /TH/ the
j /j/ jug	v /v/ vase	ng /ng/ sing
k /k/ kite	w /w/ was	zh /zh/ measure
l /l/ leaf	y /y/ yell	
m /m/ mop	z /z/ zoo	

Vowel Sounds

/ă/ hat	/ā/ gate	/o͞o/ moon	/û/ bird
/ĕ/ bed	/ē/ feet	/o͝o/ book	/ə/ about
/ĭ/ fish	/ī/ bike	/ou/ house	/ä/ car
/ŏ/ mop	/ō/ boat	/oi/ boy	/â/ chair
/ŭ/ nut	/ū/ mule	/ô/ tall	

Figure 9-1 Phoneme Chart

that they have never heard spoken (see Chapter 7). Remember that there are no spaces in oral language. While there are pauses, these pauses are related to meaningful phrases rather than individual words or sentences.

❑ *Rhymes.* Awareness of rhyme occurs when children begin to connect words by the way they sound. They learn to recognize words that sound alike in the ending part. Rhyme has natural appeal to users of a language. Children respond to the rhyme (as well as the rhythm and imagery) of poetry and song; and through exposure and participation, they internalize the ability to recognize rhyming words or sentences.

❑ *Syllables.* Breaking down words requires noticing the parts, or *syllables.* Young readers often confuse syllables and words simply because they are hearing these individual parts as they point to the words in print. They think each syllable is a word; but as they learn that words can have multiple parts, they quickly sort out that there is one group of letters (defined by space before and after) for each word. Saying words while hearing and clapping the syllables helps readers become aware that many words have multiple parts and that they can hear the parts when they say the words.

❑ *Onsets and rimes.* Words of one syllable may be broken into an opening part that consists of a letter or cluster of letters *(sl)* and an ending part. The opening part—the letter(s) before the vowel-bearing part—is called the *onset* and the ending part is called the *rime.* Words of two syllables can be broken into syllables, and the syllables broken into onsets and rimes *(p-ic, n-ic).* Sometimes a word will have only a rime *(a, an).* The word *rime* is not synonymous with *rhyme,* but if words have identical rimes *(foot, put)* then they rhyme. Speakers who can hear the onsets and rimes and can break words apart or blend them using these word parts will have an advantage in reading words or writing them.

❑ *Individual sounds or phonemes.* Readers need to be able to hear the individual phonemes in words. This can pose a challenge, because words are spoken in a smoothly articulated way. Once speakers can identify individual sounds, then they can connect them to the letters or letter clusters that represent them in words. Some phonemes are easier

to hear than others, and thinking about the position of the mouth and tongue is helpful. Speakers can "feel" the sound in the mouth.

❑ *Initial, final, and medial consonant sounds.* A group of twenty-five phonemes (see Figure 9-1) are connected with consonants and consonant clusters. Speakers who can hear these sounds and identify their position in words can more easily connect them to the sequence of letters that represent the sounds.

❑ *Initial, final, and medial vowel sounds.* A group of nineteen sounds are connected with vowels and vowel combinations. Vowels can appear in any position in words. They are in the middle position of a closed syllable (CVC); in this position, the vowel has a "short" or "terse" sound. In words that have a CVCe configuration, the vowel has a "long" or "lax" sound; that is, the vowel is articulated by making the sound of its name. The sounds of vowels can be combined with adjacent sounds (*moon, book, house, boy, tall*), especially *r (bird, car, chair),* and they can also be rendered by the *schwa,* or "uh," sound. With all this complexity, it is obvious that vowels are difficult for beginning spellers. Learning about vowels in the context of a good awareness of sounds as they relate to letters and words will help build readers' ability to use visual information.

❑ *Sounds in words in sequence.* A beginning reader who says the word *boat* may hear the /t/ and connect it with *t* as the most dominant sound in the word (and the last sound heard). But ultimately the reader must be able to hear the sounds in left to right sequence and connect them to letters. Think how many ways readers of text Levels A, B, and C can make use of the first sound of the word (especially if they can connect it to a letter): read up to the word and start it (putting together language structure, meaning, and visual information); notice mismatches (self-monitoring); correct themselves by using the first letter in combination with the picture.

❑ *Sounds that go together in words.* As children become more aware of the sounds in words, they notice that some sounds are often blended together. This realization usually comes as they notice letter clusters and hear the individual sounds within them (*string, slide, track,* and *drive,* for example).

The sounds of the English language are categorized in Figure 9-2.

Figure 9-2 Becoming Aware of the Sounds of the English Language

Words	The individual words (lexicon) of a language, which may have one or multiple syllables.
Syllables	A word part pronounced with a single, uninterrupted sounding of the voice. A word may have one or more syllables. Every syllable has a vowel.
Rhymes	Words that correspond with each other in sound, especially the ending sound.
Onsets and rimes	The onset is the first part of a one-syllable word (for example, *sh* in *ship* or *b* in *bat*). The rime is the rest of the syllable (for example *-ip* in *ship* or *-at* in *bat*). Breaking up a one-syllable word into onsets and rimes has great benefit for helping students use the parts of words.
Individual Sounds	The individual sounds of the word are the phonemes. The phoneme is the smallest unit of sound. There are 45 phonemes in English (see Figure 9-1). Phonemes are connected to consonants, vowels, and combinations of these letters.
Initial, final, and medial consonant sounds	The phonemes in a word are spoken in sequence. As readers learn to hear individual sounds, they also learn to identify their position in words (*/k/=cat, pickle, rack*). The consonants are more dominant and easier to identify, especially in initial or final position. Children can match pictures that start or end with the same sound.
Initial, final, and medial vowel sounds	The vowel sounds most often appear in the middle of words (*cat*), but may also be in initial (*along*), or final (*fiesta*) position. Vowels are influenced by the consonants around them (*art, orb*) and can be connected with several different sounds (*pen, feet, her*).
Sounds in words in sequence	To fully understand the structure of words and be able to read them or represent them with letters, it is necessary to hear sounds in sequence within each word. All words are made up of a sequence of phonemes, but some letters in a word are silent.
Sounds that go together often	Within words, some sounds appear often together (*/s/, /t/, /r/=string, stripe*).

▶ The Role of Phonemic Awareness in Learning to Read and Write

First, let's clarify some terms that are sometimes confused:

- ❏ A *phoneme* is a category of speech sounds.
- ❏ *Phonetics* refers to the scientific study of speech sounds—how the sounds are made vocally and

the relation of speech sounds to language as a process of communication.

- ❏ *Phonics*, as it is related to reading, uses a small portion of the body of knowledge that makes up *phonetics*. Phonics is a kind of instruction that helps children see the relationships between letters and sounds, both simple and complex.
- ❏ *Phonemic awareness*, or *phoneme awareness*, is the ability to hear sounds in words and to identify particular sounds. Phonemic awareness

instruction draws children's attention to particular sounds and helps them manipulate the sounds. Phonemic awareness instruction is not phonics unless it involves both sounds and letters.

According to the National Reading Panel, children who cannot hear and manipulate the sounds of spoken words will have a hard time relating these sounds to the letters in the written words (*Put Reading First*, 30). The panel recommends phonemic awareness instruction and cites studies showing that phonemic awareness training improves students' reading and spelling (*National Reading Panel Report*, 7).

Even before the panel's report, many states and districts were adopting phonemic awareness training as policy. It was seen as a "magic bullet" that would wipe out the obstacles to learning to read. After the No Child Left Behind legislation, phonemic awareness training was virtually required before educational funding proposals were approved. Educators started to see it as "inoculation" against reading failure.

Yet a careful reading of the panel's Summary Report indicates that caution be exercised. The kind of phonemic awareness training matters. The panel found that "characteristics of PA training found to be most effective . . . included explicitly and systematically teaching children to manipulate phonemes [in connection] with letters, focusing the instruction on one or two types of phoneme manipulations rather than multiple types, and teaching children in small groups" (*National Reading Panel Report*, 8). Children whose training focused on one or two phoneme/letter relationships at a time made better and faster progress than children who were taught three or more. Therefore, "it is prudent to teach one at a time until each is mastered before moving on to the next and to teach students how each skill applies in reading or spelling tasks" (*National Reading Panel Report*, 2–30, 31).

In addition, the panel advised caution in *how much* phonemic awareness training students need, recommending between five and eighteen hours. "Perhaps PA instruction is valuable mainly in helping children achieve basic alphabetic insight. Going beyond this by adding further nuances or complexities may . . . produc[e] confusion or boredom"

(*National Reading Panel Report*, 2–31). Their statement that "more is not necessarily better" (2–7) should not be ignored.

Phonemic awareness instruction is an important component, but *only* a component, of a comprehensive and integrated program for teaching beginning reading. It can provide some of the essential foundation children need for literacy and thus help prevent reading difficulties. We recommend that it be included in early intervention instruction for children who show signs of confusion. We include some guidelines for incorporating phonemic awareness instruction into a reading program—and specifically in an intervention system to help struggling readers (in Figure 9-3). Not all children need phonemic awareness training; if they are able to hear and identify sounds easily, they will probably benefit more from real reading and writing. Assessing whether phonemic awareness instruction is necessary is essential. Chances are, children who have difficulty learning to

---

Figure 9-3 Implementing Phonemic Awareness Instruction to Help Struggling Readers

- Provide a limited amount of phonemic awareness instruction in the absence of letters to help children focus on hearing the sounds.
- Integrate phonemic awareness with instruction using both sounds and letters, especially magnetic letters.
- Teach children a limited number of ways to manipulate phonemes (one or two) rather than many.
- Incorporate writing into phonemic awareness instruction.
- Provide phonemic awareness instruction not as an isolated activity but in combination with children's reading engaging texts and writing meaningful messages.
- Spend the majority of instructional time on reading and writing continuous, meaningful text.
- Realize that some children may not need phonemic awareness training (if, for example, they can hear sounds easily and write letters to represent them).
- Work with children individually or in small groups for greater effectiveness.

read *will* benefit from work with sounds, but it is important to identify all needs.

We also recommend presenting phonemic awareness instruction either to individual struggling readers or to struggling readers in small groups, so that you can be very specific in your demonstrations. Struggling readers won't "pick up" the ability to hear and manipulate sounds as you work with the whole group. (And the children who are able to respond quickly and successfully in that setting are probably the very ones who do not need the instruction.) Also, time spent on phonemic awareness instruction must be limited and include manipulation of letters as soon as possible.

▶ Finding Out What Children Know About Sounds

You can learn a great deal about children's knowledge just by observation. A list of questions to address as you observe children in literacy activities in the classroom is presented in Figure 9-4.

As you work with children in word study minilessons and application activities, interactive and independent writing, and shared and independent reading, you can gather quite a bit of evidence. The students who respond quickly and easily stand out; those who are confused or are having difficulty also stand out.

Notice how quickly and easily children can match pictures with rhyming words or the same initial or ending sounds. Observe children's responses in segmenting, blending, or manipulating games: which children can perform these tasks easily? Which ones are having trouble? Have children clap and tell the number of syllables in words.

During interactive and independent writing, look for evidence that children can say words slowly, artic-

Figure 9-4 **Observing for Evidence of Phonemic Awareness**	
Context	**How quickly and easily can children:**
Word Study	• Match pictures with rhyming words? • Match pictures with the same initial sound? • Match pictures with the same ending sound? • Match pictures with the initial letter? • Say the first sound of a word? • Segment words into individual phonemes? • Segment words into onsets and rimes? • Blend onsets and rimes to say a word? • Blend phonemes together to say a word? • Manipulate phonemes to make new words? • Manipulate onsets and rimes to make new words? • Clap words and tell the number of syllables?
Interactive and Independent Writing	• Say words slowly? • Identify sounds in words after saying them slowly? • Identify sounds in sequence • Represent specific phonemes with letters when writing words? • Identify syllables in words?
Shared and Independent Reading	• Start to say a word by making the first sound? • Locate a word by saying it slowly first and predicting the first letter? • Respond to and participate in saying in unison with others songs, rhymes, and poems? • Recognize rhyming words in a poem (for example, clap at the rhyming word)?

ulate the sounds, and connect the sounds with some letters. In shared and independent reading, look for evidence that children can start a word by making the first sound and use this information to find a word in a familiar or new text. Notice children's response to poems, rhymes, and songs. Do they pick up rhymes quickly and participate actively? Can they identify the words that rhyme?

You may want to make a list of children to whom you want to pay close attention. It is probably wise to assess them individually, since sometimes children just watch and imitate others around them without really understanding the task. A few quick and easy assessments will help you learn what children know about the sounds in words (see below). You don't need to administer all these assessments, and not every child should be assessed unless you are documenting grade-level progress. Select assessments that provide the information you need to inform your instruction. (Directions and materials for these assessments are included in *Fountas and Pinnell Benchmark Assessment System 1: Optional Assessments* or the *Phonics Lessons CD, Grades K and 1.*)

Rhyming

This assessment will help you learn the degree to which children can hear and make connections between words that rhyme. Have them match pictures that represent pairs of words that rhyme, saying the

words to check them. You can use a set of picture cards for a thorough individual assessment, or you can do a quick group assessment as shown in Figure 9-5. Start by demonstrating with one or two easy examples to help children understand the task.

Let's look at four children, Kirsten, Alex, Juliette, and Chuck. Assessed mid-kindergarten, Kirsten was able to match *bee* and *tree*, *fan* and *van*, and *ring* and *swing*. She incorrectly matched *star* and *socks*, perhaps focusing on the first letter. Kirsten understands the concept of rhyming but is not yet working with it quickly and automatically. She may occasionally confuse rhyming with beginning sounds. Incidentally, this indicates *more* rather than less knowledge, even though she is not clear about the concept of rhyme.

Alex, on the other hand, matched all pictures quickly and easily. Of course, this task becomes easier as pictures are eliminated, but a performance like Alex's indicates that he does not need to work on rhyming words.

Figure 9-5 Rhyming Assessment Sheets 1 and 2, *Fountas and Pinnell Benchmark Assessment System 1* (Heinemann 2011, 2008)

Juliette matched eight of the ten pictures quickly and easily. She had incorrectly matched *car* and *crown* and then hesitantly matched the two remaining pictures, *clown* and *star*. Probably, she understands the concept of rhyme but lost control momentarily because she was focusing on the *r*.

Chuck also matched all rhymes accurately. Of the members of this group, Kirsten could benefit from some quick, active work on rhyming words.

Initial Sounds

This assessment (see Figure 9-6) tells you how easily children can hear and match initial sounds of words. Begin by showing the child four picture cards: *bear, hat, dog,* and *milk*. Say the name of each picture. Then, hold up *bird* and ask the child to find the other picture card that starts with the same sound as *bird*. Repeat with *horse, desk,* and *mouse*. Then say the name of each of the four original pictures and ask the child to say the first sound in isolation. Record the child's correct responses as well as substitutions. Repeat using eight more picture cards (*cat, fan, ladder, pencil* and *cake, fire, lion, penguin*). Notice the number of sounds the child can match correctly as well as whether children can orally produce the initial sound of a word they have heard pronounced.

Kirsten was able to match picture cards for *b, m,* and *c/k* (her name). She was also able to articulate sounds for *bear, milk, cat,* and *pencil*. She substituted the /b/ sound for *dog* and heard the *t* at the end of *hat* but did not understand it as an initial sound.

Figure 9-6 Initial Sounds Picture Cards, *Fountas and Pinnell Benchmark Assessment System 1* (Heinemann 2011, 2008)

Alex and Chuck matched all pictures easily and were able to articulate the first sound. Juliette did not match any sounds except the *m* but she could articulate about half of the sounds.

Blending Sounds

In this assessment, children hear and say the individual sounds in a word and then blend the sounds to say the word. This ability helps children take words apart to solve them. You can use this assessment to determine how much experience children need in blending sounds.

Tell the child you are going to say the sounds of a word. "I will say the sounds of a word. Then you say the whole word smoothly." Use /m/-/ă/-/t/, *mat*, as an example. Continue with /h/-/ĭ/-/d/, *hid*; /w/-/ĭ/-/sh/, *wish*; /p/-/ŏ/-/t/, *pot*; /f/-/ē/-/t/, *feet*; /l/-/ōō/-/k/, *look*; /t/-/ā/-/k/, *take*; /m/-/ōō/-/n/, *moon*; /n/-/ŭ/-/t/, *nut*; /r/-/ă/-/p/, *rap*; /ch/-/ĭ/-/l/, *chill*. Notice the child's ability to listen to and understand the task and to blend the sounds. Record the results. (Consider the task mastered if a child can blend eight of the ten words.)

Kirsten was able to blend the sounds in *hid, feet, take, nut,* and *rap*. She seemed to understand the task, and also blended sounds to make *wish*, although her pronunciation was somewhat immature. (The same may be true for *chill*, although the teacher was uncertain.) Alex and Chuck had no difficulty with the task. Juliette was hesitant but after another demonstration was able to blend eight of the ten words.

Segmenting Words

In this assessment, children say a word and then say the individual sounds separately, but in sequence. The ability to segment words into sounds helps children spell and decode. Say a word and ask the child to say the segmented sounds in the word: "I am going to say a word. Then you say the sounds in the word, like this: *fan*, /f/-/ă/-/n/." Continue with *wet* [/w/-/ĕ/-/t/]; *vase* [/v/-/ā/-/s/]; *trip* [/t/-/r/-/ĭ/-/p/]; *miss* [/m/-/ĭ/-/s/]; *duck* [/d/-/ŭ/-/k/]; *pad* [/p/-/ă/-/d/]; *fast* [/f/-/ă/-/s/-/t/]; *kick* [/k/-/ĭ/-/k/]; *tool* [/t/-/ōō/-/l/]; *boat* [/b/-/ō/-/t/]. Notice children's ability to listen to and understand the task, say each sound, and say sounds in sequence.

Both Kirsten and Juliette found this task very difficult, and possibly did not understand it, even with the demonstration. Kirsten did produce initial sounds for several of the words and Juliette was able to segment four of the words. Alex and Chuck had no problems performing the task.

Writing Picture Names

You can administer this assessment to a whole class of students, although it would be easier in a small group. Hold up a picture and say the word that represents it. Ask children to say the word slowly themselves, think about the sounds in the word, and record some of the sounds by writing the letters. This is a complicated task. Children are being asked to say and hear a sound, associate it with a letter and the directional movements needed to write the letter, and then use these movements to write the letter in a legible form. A child may be able to hear and identify the sound (phonemic awareness) and yet find it difficult to write the letter. Suggested words:

1. *cat* (3 phonemes); *mug* (3 phonemes); *nine* (3 phonemes); *bed* (3 phonemes); *lock* (3 phonemes); *apple* (3 phonemes); *pin* (3 phonemes); and *doll* (3 phonemes).

2. *truck* (4 phonemes); *feet* (3 phonemes); *bag* (3 phonemes); *five* (3 phonemes); *nose* (3 phonemes); *gum* (3 phonemes); *map* (3 phonemes); and *seal* (3 phonemes).

Alternatively you can give children a sheet of picture names (see Figure 9-7).

You can administer this assessment to an entire class very quickly. Go over the names of the objects with the children once to be sure they understand the label. Then have them, on their own, write as much of each word as they can. This assessment provides additional valuable information about children's ability to hear and represent sounds. The score is not as important as the behavior you observe.

What you are looking for here is not correct spelling, although the child who can spell the words

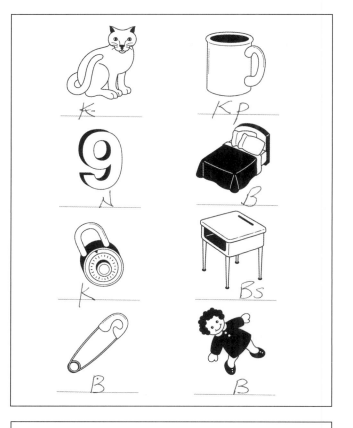

Figure 9-7 Writing Picture Names, *Fountas and Pinnell Benchmark Assessment System 1* (Heinemann 2011, 2008)

accurately has certainly progressed well beyond rudimentary phonemic awareness. Notice children's ability to identify labels for objects represented by pictures; say words very slowly to hear each of the sounds; say, hear, and identify individual sounds; associate sounds with letters; form letters; and write the letters in sequence. Kirsten's paper indicates that she is able to write some consonants to represent sounds in words. She made an attempt at every one.

▶ Making Decisions About Phonemic Awareness Instruction

Kirsten's individual scores are shown (Figure 9-8); the scores of all four children assessed are summarized (Figure 9-9). It is easy to see that of these four, Kirsten is the one most in need of phonemic awareness instruction. Juliette would benefit from some intensive instruction in writing so that she can learn to hear and represent sounds in sequence. Alex and Chuck do not need phonemic awareness instruction; they should be receiving more advanced instruction in phonics.

▶ The Great Potential of Poetry

One of the most enjoyable and effective ways to help children develop phonemic awareness is through the shared reading of songs, chants, rhymes, and poems. Simply reading and enjoying them is helpful, but that will not be enough to help struggling readers. You also need to do some specific teaching that draws children's attention to the sounds in words and also to the letters. After a poem has been read several times, you have a familiar text that can be "mined" for a great deal of learning (see Figure 9-10). Review the examples of a teacher using poetry to develop phonemic awareness (Figure 9-11). Examples 3 and 4 focus on children's awareness of sounds in connection with visual features of words.

"Phonological Awareness" Assessment—**Individual Record**

Name Kirsten Grade K Date

Initial Sounds Assessment

	Matching (✓ or substitutions)	Oral (✓ or substitutions)
b /b/	✓	✓
h /h/	–	/t/
d /d/	–	/b/
m /m/	✓	✓
c /k/	✓	✓
f /f/	–	–
l /l/	–	–
p /p/	–	✓
Total	3	4

Blending Assessment

	Scoring (✓)
/h/-/ĭ/-/d/ [hid]	✓
/w/-/ĭ/-/sh/ [wish]	✓ (w·i·s)
/p/-/ŏ/-/t/ [pot]	–
/f/-/ē/-/t/ [feet]	✓
/l/-/ŏŏ/-/k/ [look]	–
/t/-/ā/-/k/ [take]	✓
/m/-/ōō/-/n/ [moon]	–
/n/-/ŭ/-/t/ [nut]	✓
/r/-/ă/-/p/ [rap]	✓
/ch/-/ĭ/-/l/ [chill]	– (t·i·l)
Total	6

Segmenting Assessment

	Scoring (✓)
wet [/w/-/ĕ/-/t/]	w –
vase [/v/-/ā/-/s/]	–
trip [/t/-/r/-/ĭ/-/p/]	–
miss [/m/-/ĭ/-/s/]	–
duck [/d/-/ŭ/-/k/]	–
pad [/p/-/ă/-/d/]	p –
fast [/f/-/ă/-/s/-/t/]	–
kick [/k/-/ĭ/-/k/]	k –
tool [/t/-/ōō/-/l/]	–
boat [/b/-/ō/-/t/]	–
Total	0

Rhyming Assessment

	Scoring (✓)
bee/tree	✓
fish/dish	–
fan/van	✓
box/socks	–
star/car	–
rose/nose	✓
pen/hen	–
bat/hat	– (box)
crown/clown	–
ring/swing	✓
Total	4

Figure 9-8 Kristen's scores, *Benchmark Assessment System 1* (Heinemann 2011, 2008)

Phonological Awareness Assessment—**Class Record**

Name	Initial Sounds Assessment	Blending Assessment	Segmenting Assessment	Rhyming Assessment
1. Kirsten	3/8 4/8	6/10	9/10	4/10
2. Alex	8/8 8/8	10/10	10/10	10/10
3. Juliette	1/8 3/8	8/10	4/10	8/10
4. Chuck	8/8 8/8	10/10	10/10	10/10
5.				
6.				
7.				
8.				
9.				
10.				
11.				
12.				
13.				
14.				
15.				
16.				
17.				
18.				
19.				
20.				
21.				
22.				
23.				
24.				
25.				
26.				
27.				

Notes

Figure 9-9 Children's scores, *Benchmark Assessment System 1* (Heinemann 2011, 2008)

Figure 9-10 **Ways to Use Poetry to Develop Phonemic Awareness**

- Draw attention to rhyming words by having children clap on the rhymes or locate and highlight rhyming words.
- Have them say the poems and then say words that start or end the same.
- Help children notice the sounds of different word endings.
- Have them clap words to hear and count the syllables.
- Help them develop a core of words that they can use as examples in learning sound-to-letter relationships.

Example 1: Recognizing Rhyme

In this example, the teacher revisits a familiar poem to raise children's awareness of words that rhyme. The children probably have an implicit sense of the rhyme in the poem, but the teacher wants them to be more conscious of rhyme and its definition so that they can use it later to make connections to visual features of words. Notice that the poem has only two rhyming words, *tree* and *me.* The teacher clearly demonstrates by saying the words several times and having the children repeat them. Then they read the poem, highlighting the rhyming words. Finally they locate the words in the text and highlight them.

Example 2: Hearing Syllables in Words

The teacher revisits a simple poem with a multi-syllable word in it, *chocolate,* which is part of the children's oral vocabulary. She demonstrates saying the word and clapping for each syllable. After children have been introduced to the task, they substitute other words and clap the syllables.

Example 3: Recognizing That Rhyming Words Sound the Same at the End and Often Look the Same at the End

After many experiences, children will be accustomed to hearing and identifying rhyming words and can do so easily. They will now able to use this area of phonemic awareness to notice more about how words look. Example 3 shows a more complex task. There are three different pairs of rhyming words in the poem—but the advantage is that children can generalize a principle. They are able to notice that these pairs of rhyming words not only sound alike at the end but also look alike, not just in the last letter but in a word part. Notice that the teacher cautions that not all rhyming words look alike at the end but some do. Knowing that when words rhyme, they are likely to have the same word part at the end will help children use larger parts of words to read and spell them.

Example 4: Breaking Rhyming Words into Onsets and Rimes

As in example 3, the children in example 4 already demonstrate phonemic awareness. They can easily hear and identify rhyme. The teacher is helping them use their sense of rhymes and also their ability to break words into onsets and rimes to see large parts of words, vowel pairs, and letter clusters.

▶ Direct Teaching About Sounds

You will want to provide brief, powerful lessons that directly and explicitly teach children about the sounds in words. You can teach these lessons to the whole class, but if you have children who are confused or lagging behind others in phonemic awareness, you can take them aside and work with them in small groups. These lessons are very short; they can be attached to small-group reading instruction or presented by an intervention teacher as supplemental lessons.

Hearing Syllables in Words

You can help children work with syllables in the absence of letters by using picture cards. Children can say and clap the words, clapping once for each syllable. Here is an example:

- ❑ Place *cat, turtle,* and *banana* picture cards on the top line of the pocket chart. One picture at a time, demonstrate how to say the word and clap

Figure 9-11 Examples of Using Poetry to Hear Sounds in Words

■ **EXAMPLE 1**
Recognizing Rhyme

> ### Rain
>
> **Rain on the rooftop,**
> **Rain on the tree,**
> **Rain on the green grass,**
> **But not on me!**

After several readings of the poem "Rain," with pointing, the teacher chose to revisit it.

Speaker	Interaction	What the *Teacher Is Attending to*
Mr. P	You have been reading the poem "Rain." You know that the poems we have been reading have words in them that rhyme. They sound the same at the end. Listen while I read this poem. I am going to clap when I say the two rhyming words in this poem.	*Demonstrates reading and clapping once on* tree *and once on* me.
Mr. P	Now let's read it together and clap on the words that rhyme.	*Prompts to notice the syllables.*
	[Children read and clap.]	
Mr. P	The rhyming words in this poem are *tree* and *me.* They sound alike at the end. Let's say them.	*Demonstrates rhyme*
Tony	They both have *e.*	
Mr. P	Yes, you noticed that. Words that rhyme sometimes have the same letters at the end.	*Reinforces noticing graphic features of words.*
Mr. P	Let's highlight the two words that rhyme in the poem.	*Draws attention to graphic features.*
	[A child locates and highlights tree *and* me. *They read the poem once more and clap.]*	
Mr. P	Now look at page 9 in *My Poetry Book.* Let's read it together and point to each word.	*Hands out the books and yellow highlighters.*
Mr. P	Now you can highlight the words that rhyme, *tree* and *me.*	*Draws attention to graphic features.*
	[The teacher gives children an extra copy of the poem to take home and illustrate.]	

continues

Figure 9-11 **Examples of Using Poetry to Hear Sounds in Words,** *continued*

■ **EXAMPLE 2**
Hearing Syllables
in Words

> ### I Love Chocolate
>
> I love chocolate.
> Yum, yum, yum.
> I love chocolate.
> In my tum.

After reading the poem to the children and then inviting them to read in a shared way, with the teacher pointing, the children revisit the poem. A version of the poem is on sentence strips in the pocket chart.

Speaker	Interaction	What the *Teacher Is Attending to*
Ms. Z	Let's read the poem again.	*Invites reading.*
	[Children read the poem.]	
Ms. Z	*Chocolate* is a long word, isn't it? Listen while I say the word. I am going to clap the word to show the parts. You help me think how many parts are in the word.	*Demonstrates saying* chocolate, *clapping for each syllable. Draws attention to syllables.*
Ms. Z	You say the word with me and we will clap the parts. (Children join in.) How many parts does *chocolate* have?	*Prompts to notice syllables.*
Children	Three.	
Ms. Z	Now let's put another kind of food in the poem.	*Substitutes the word* pizza *for* chocolate. *They read the poem and* clap pizza.

continues

Figure 9-11 **Examples of Using Poetry to Hear Sounds in Words,** *continued*

▪ **EXAMPLE 3**
Recognizing that
Rhyming Words Sound
the Same at the End and
Often Look the Same

Little Frog

A little green frog.
sat on a log.
Eating a most delicious bug.
Ug!
He jumped in the pool
where it was nice and cool.
Good-by
Little green frog.

After reading the poem several times, with pointing, the teacher has children revisit it.

Speaker	Interaction	What the *Teacher Is Attending to*
Mr. V	This poem has some rhyming words in it. Those words sound the same at the end. Let's read the poem again and listen for the rhyming words. Now let's read the first two lines and clap on the words that rhyme.	*Prompts to notice rhyming words.*
	[Children read the line and clap on frog *and* log.*]*	
Sarah	*Frog* and *log.* [Sarah locates and highlights frog *and* log *in yellow.]*	
Mr. V	Who can read the next two lines and clap on the rhyming words?	*Prompts to notice rhymes.*
Evan	*[Evan reads the two lines.]* Bug *and* ug. *[He highlights* bug *and* ug.*]*	
Mr. V	Who can read the next two lines and clap on the rhyming words?	*Prompts to notice rhymes.*
Hannah	*[Hannah reads the two lines].* Pool and cool. *[She highlights the words.]*	
Mr. V	Now let's read it again with our rhyming words highlighted.	*Prompts to notice visual information.*
	[Children read as the teacher points.]	
Mr. V	Take a look at the words that rhyme. What do you notice about the way they look?	*Prompts to notice visual information.*
Sarah	*Frog* and *log* both end in *g.*	
Hannah	They end in -*o* and -*g.*	
Mr. V	*Frog* and *log* sound alike at the end and they look alike at the end. Is that true for other rhyming words? What do you notice, Evan?	*Underlines the* -og *in each word. Draws attention to visual information.*
Evan	*Pool* and *cool* both have -*ool.*	
Mr. V	You're right. Come up and underline the -*ool* in *pool* and *cool. (Evan underlines.)* How about *bug* and *ug*?	*Draws attention to visual information.*
Hannah	All of *ug* is in *bug.*	
Mr. V	They do rhyme because they sound the same at the end and they look the same, too. They both have the *ug* part. I'm going to underline those parts. Not all rhyming words look the same at the end, but these do.	*Demonstrates concept of rhyme.*

continues

Figure 9-11 **Examples of Using Poetry to Hear Sounds in Words,** *continued*

■ **EXAMPLE 4**
Breaking Rhyming Words
into Onsets and Rimes

Ice Cream

I scream.
You scream.
We all scream
For ice cream.

After reading the poem several times, with pointing, the teacher has children revisit it.

Speaker	Interaction	What the *Teacher Is Attending to*
Ms. A	What are the rhyming words in this poem?	*Hands out individual books and yellow highlighters*
Harry	*Cream* and *scream. Scream* is in three times and *cream* is in there two times.	
Ms. A	I want to highlight the parts of the rhyming words *cream* and *scream* that look alike. What should I highlight?	*Draws attention to visual information.*
Dialana	It's -*eam.*	
Carson	No, it's the *c* too.	
Ms. A	These two words are special. I'm going to highlight the -*eam* in each word and then we will talk about *the* c. You can do the same thing in your poetry book on page 25. I'll do it on my big copy. Then you can check what you have highlighted.	*Draws attention to visual information.*
	[*Children highlight* -eam *in each of the words. The teacher writes* cream *and* scream *on the whiteboard.*]	
Carson	You can just hear *e*, not the *a.*	
Ms. A	That's right. In this word pattern -*eam*, the two vowels, *e a*, make the long sound of *e.* Let's say all of the words to hear the *e* sound.	*Draws attention to letter-sound relationships.*
	[*Children say all of the rhyming words.*]	
Ms. A	You have been noticing the endings of words and learning to look at the first part and the rest of the word. Listen while I say these two words. I'm going to say the first part and stop and then say the last part. *cr-eam, scr-eam.* Now you say them.	*Draws attention to word endings.*
Children	*cr-eam, scr-eam.*	
Ms. A	The first part of *cream* is a letter cluster, *c-r.* It's like *cracker* or *crab.* What's the first part of *scream*?	*Draws attention to letter clusters.*
Dialana:	*Scr-, s-c-r.*	
Ms. A	You hear those sounds together a lot in words and they are called consonant clusters. *Cream* starts with the *cr* cluster, and *scream* starts with the *scr* cluster. They both look the same and sound the same at the end. They rhyme. Not all rhyming words look the same at the end but these do.	*Explains letter clusters.*

it. Children respond by saying how many syllables are in each word.

- ❑ Then present additional picture cards one at a time and invite children to say them and clap for each syllable. Additional pictures include *dog, goat, bird, bus, balloon, carrot, toothbrush, spider, snake, ball, toothbrush, tricycle, butterfly, elephant,* and *umbrella.*

- ❑ After identifying the number of syllables, children decide where to place it—under the *cat, turtle,* or *banana,* according to the number of syllables.

- ❑ Repeat the exercise so children can say, clap, and sort the pictures quickly.

This type of exercise can be integrated into independent classroom activities or assigned as homework.

You can teach children about syllables—and help them use their knowledge of syllables—as part of activities designed to:

- ❑ Help them pronounce a longer word in interactive read-aloud or shared reading.

- ❑ Help them point accurately during shared reading (to match voice to print, keeping the pointer on the word for two- or three-syllable words).

- ❑ Work out voice-print matching when reading independently.

- ❑ Identify the parts of words during small-group reading instruction.

- ❑ Break a word down in order to write it during interactive or independent writing.

Learning to Hear and Break Words into Onsets and Rimes

Through demonstration, you can help children separate the first part of the word from the last part of a one-syllable word. For example:

MR. W: We are going to play a game. I'll say the first part of the word and then I'll say the rest of the word. This word is *bear. [He holds up a picture of a bear.]* I'm going to say it in a tricky way: *b-ear, bear.* Now I'll say another word. I'll say the first part and the rest of the word. You say the whole word smoothly. Then I'll hold up

the picture so that you can check to see if you were right! *B-at.*

CHILDREN: *Bat.*

The teacher holds up the picture of a bat. He says the word again, segmenting the onset and rime and having children repeat the word. He then does this with g-oat, b-ird, t-op, t-ack, n-est, n-ut, s-ock, m-ouse, m-at, s-un, b-ug, *and* g-ate.

Because the children seem to understand the task, he invites them to do their own segmenting of first letters and the rest of the word so that the other children can guess.

Learning to Hear Individual Sounds in Words (Phonemes)

To quickly solve words in reading and spell them in writing, children must be able to hear the individual phonemes in words, which they then connect with letters, letter clusters, and sequential parts of words.

BLENDING AND SEGMENTING

Asking children to blend, segment, and manipulate phonemes can be very helpful. The National Reading Panel cautions that two or three versions of these activities are sufficient and not a lot of time should be spent on them. (Longer programs may have little benefit or even be confusing to children.) In the oral activity below, the teacher demonstrates segmenting words and asks children to blend them. (In Chapter 10, the manipulation of phonemes is accompanied by moving magnetic letters, which is more productive and more easily understood.)

MR. W: You have been thinking about the sounds in words. Today we are going to play a game. I am going to say the separate sounds of this word, *bat* *[holds up a picture of a bat].* Listen while I say the sounds and then put the sounds together to say the word smoothly: *b-a-t, bat.* Now, I'll say the sounds in this word and you say it smoothly: *c-a-t* *[holds up a picture of a cat].*

CHILDREN: *Cat.*

The teacher continues holding up pictures and saying the word in a segmented way, but after two or three words, he stops holding up the picture and has the children respond only to the segmented words. Since children seem to understand the task, he holds up pictures for another group of children and asks them first to say the word in a segmented way, then smoothly. Finally, groups of children try saying some of their own choices in a segmented way and asking someone else in the group to say the word smoothly.

USING SOUND BOXES

Elkonin, a Russian psychologist working in the 1960s, developed a productive way to help children hear the individual sounds in words. These boxes (see Figure 9-12), which were used by Clay (1976) in the Reading Recovery program and Fountas and Pinnell (Leveled Literacy Intervention 2009), help children become more aware of the sequence of sounds in words. Demonstrate the process to children first. Begin by teaching children how to say words slowly.

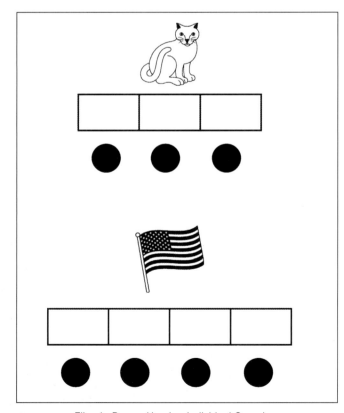

Figure 9-12 Elkonin Boxes, Hearing Individual Sounds

Here's an example:

Mr. W: I am going to say a word slowly. Listen and watch my mouth while I say it.

[He holds up a picture of a bat and says the word slowly, without segmentation but so that each sound can be heard.] Bat. Now you say it slowly.

Children: *Bat.*

After demonstrating with several more pictures and having children repeat the word, the teacher holds up pictures and asks the children to say the words slowly. Then children take turns selecting a picture and saying the word slowly.

If children have difficulty with the task, encourage them to watch your lips and feel their own lips and tongue as they say the word. In the example below, the teacher began to use sound boxes to help children think about sounds in sequence. He uses one box for each *phoneme* rather than each letter.

Mr. W: Today you are going to use boxes to help you hear the sounds in words. *[He places a picture card of a cat on the table and below it shows three boxes.]* Watch how I say the word *cat* slowly while I push these counters into the boxes. *[He demonstrates.]* Each of these counters helps me think of a sound. Watch. *[He demonstrates again.]*

The teacher then invites children to say the word slowly with him as he pushes the counters into the boxes. Finally, he gives each child in the group the Elkonin boxes for words with three sounds, as well as three counters. They continue to practice this task in brief sessions until it's easy for them to do. Soon, the teacher moves on to four boxes for words with four phonemes.

Saying words slowly using Elkonin boxes is an effective way to help your students become aware of the sounds in words. Most important, it will help them hear and identify the sounds when words are said smoothly, without the artificial segmentation that makes it easy to hear the sounds. (Chapter 10 includes examples in which Elkonin sound boxes are used in conjunction with letters.)

Learning to Hear and Recognize Initial Sounds

Recognizing initial sounds is very helpful to beginning readers; they can use that information to begin to notice mismatches and monitor their reading. For children who find hearing sounds difficult, you may want to do a few lessons in the absence of letters. In this example, the teacher is helping children focus on initial sounds using picture cards (see Figure 9-13). These same key words are used in the Alphabet Linking Chart (see Chapters 7 and 10).

> **MR. W:** I have some pictures at the top of our chart. Let's say the words for these pictures. [*The pocket chart has four key pictures along the top:* cat, bear, dog, moon.
>
> *The teacher helps the children say the words, placing slight emphasis on the first sound.*]
>
> **MR. W:** Now I'm going to take a picture and say its name. *Bat.* What picture starts like *bat?*
>
> **DUKE:** *Bear.*
>
> **MR. W:** Let's say the words to check: *bat, bear.* Are you thinking about the first sound you say?
>
> *The students match more cards in the deck of picture cards:* cow, can, boat, banana, duck, dish, mouse, match. *After the lesson, the teacher gives each child a set of picture cards (on a sheet of paper that they can cut apart) and a four-way sort card with key pictures at the top. They sort the pictures by sound and affix them in the right column.*

The activity described in this example may be repeated for many different initial sounds. You can also focus this kind of activity on ending sounds or on middle sounds (vowels). Soon, though, you will want to move on to relating sounds and letters.

Learning to Match Initial Sounds with Letters

There is strong evidence that sounds and letters are best learned when they are presented together. An intervention that helps children become aware of sounds may spend some time on activities dealing with sound alone, but the time should be short. In the example below, the teacher is helping children match letters and sounds in initial position (see Figure 9-14).

> **MR. W:** You are learning about letters and sounds. Today, we are going to say some words and think about the first sound. We are going to think, "What letter would I expect to see at the beginning of this word?"
>
> *He says the word* dog, *asks the question, and places the picture in the* d *column. He shows children more picture cards—*dog, moon, monkey, cat, sun, sandwich, top—*and has them place the pictures under a letter. After pictures are sorted, the children read the chart—the letter, the sound associated with it, and objects beginning with it.*

This sorting activity can be used with many other letters. At first, choose letters and sounds that are quite different from each other and are easily distinguished. You can also "speed up" the activity as

Figure 9-13 Sorting Initial Sounds

Figure 9-14 Matching Sounds with Letters

children work more easily with letter and sound connections. In the example below, children are sorting pictures very quickly.

The teacher has placed the letters j, l, r, c, h *in a line at the top of the pocket chart. He has pictures representing* jar, jam, jelly; lock, lake, lamp; rake, rat, rose; car, cap, cart; *and* harp, hand, ham.

Mr. W: You are very good at matching the first sound of a word with a letter. Today, I am going to give each of you some pictures. And you are going to say the name of the picture like this, *j-am, jam,* and place it under the right letter.

Children: *J.*

Mr. W: I'll put this one under the letter.

The teacher deals out all the pictures to the children so that they are randomly distributed. Children take turns saying the name of the picture (saying the sound first: j-jam*) and then putting the picture under the appropriate letter.*

Picture cards and letter cards can also be used for final and middle sounds in words.

▶ Teaching About Sounds Through Writing

Writing is a very powerful context in which to help children become aware of the sounds in words. Within the context of writing, you can help children:

- ❏ Learn to hear the words in sentences so that they can be read and written separately.
- ❏ Say words slowly and think about the sounds.
- ❏ Clap words to break them down for easier spelling.
- ❏ Notice initial sounds and think how to start a word.
- ❏ Reread writing to notice the sounds and letters.

We advocate including a strong writing component as part of any intervention to help struggling readers at every level. Shared and interactive writing, dictated writing, and independent writing are all beneficial.

Shared and Interactive Writing

We have provided descriptions and examples of both shared and interactive writing (Chapters 1, 10, and 13). Here are the definitions:

- ❏ In *shared writing,* the teacher and students compose a text together. The teacher is the scribe. Often, especially with younger children, the teacher works on a chart displayed on an easel. Children participate in the composition of the text word by word and reread it many times. Sometimes, the teacher has the children say a word slowly and think about how it is spelled. With more proficient children, the teacher writes quickly on the chart with student input. Students consider and examine the text. The text becomes a model, example, or reference for student writing and discussion.

- ❏ *Interactive writing* is identical to and proceeds in exactly the same way as shared writing, with one exception: occasionally the teacher, while making teaching points that help children attend to various features of letters and words, invites a student to come up to the easel and contribute a letter, word, or part of a word.

In both shared and interactive writing, you have the opportunity to help children produce meaningful texts and at the same time direct very specific attention to the sounds in words. By working interactive writing into small-group reading instruction or group intervention lessons, you can help children write a meaningful message about a text that extends their understanding and also gives you the chance to teach about sounds. In the example below, the children have read the Level B book *Bubbles* (some pages from the book are reproduced in Figure 9-15). The piece the children wrote is shown in Figure 9-16.

Mr. W: Your new book yesterday was *Bubbles.* What are all of the places you can see bubbles?

Stetson: In the soap bubbles when you put it in water.

Diamond: In bubble gum. And the fish make bubbles in the water.

Mr. W: Today we are going to write about some of the things you know about bubbles. What is one

See the bubbles
on the dog.

Figure 9-15 Page Spread from *Bubbles* from Leveled Literacy Intervention, Green System (Heinemann 2009)

Bubbles

We can see bubbles
in the fish bowl.
We can see bubbles
in the dog's bath.
We can see a big bubble
in the gum.
Pop!

Figure 9-16 Interactive Writing

thing we could write? Let's get several ideas. See if you can make a sentence like the ones you read.

DIAMOND: The dog has bubbles when he has a bath.

STETSON: We can see bubbles in the fish bowl.

MICHAEL: We can see a big bubble in bubble gum.

MR. W: You all have good ideas. Maybe we will have time to write all of them. Let's start with the fish bowl. Stetson, can you say your sentence again?

Stetson repeats We can see bubbles in the fish bowl *and the teacher then asks all the children to say it. They start with the first word, saying it slowly to think about the first sound. They say w- w-.*

MR. W: It's a *w*. Stetson can you write the *w* for *we?*

Stetson comes up and writes the w. *Then the teacher asks the children to say the word again and listen for the last sound (e). Stetson writes the e. They write the rest of the sentence, with Diamond writing the s at the beginning of see and at the end of bubbles. Each time they write a new word, they reread the sentence.*

They go on to write the other sentences. The group decides to change Diamond's sentence to follow the pattern set by Stetson. When they come to the third sentence, they vary the pattern slightly.

In this example, the teacher moves the writing along by doing most of it himself, but he engages the children to a high degree. They are consistently saying words slowly and rereading the text, in the process becoming aware of individual words and the sounds within them.

Dictated Writing

In *dictated writing*, the teacher reads a sentence aloud and children write it in their books with the teacher's support. Some of the words are known; the teacher helps children solve unknown words by using sound boxes, prompting them to analyze the sounds related to letters, and reminding them of words they know. The teacher sometimes writes a word on a whiteboard, which children copy or use to check their own attempt. Children reread their sentences when finished (and may draw a picture if there is time). The teacher may have them highlight words or word parts.

Through this structured activity, children:

❑ Learn how to turn oral language into written language.

❑ Solve words in the context of a meaningful sentence.

❑ Reread and check their work.

In the following example, a teacher uses dictated writing to extend children's understanding of the

Level B book *Orson's Tummy Ache* (some pages are reproduced in Figure 9-17). One child's writing is shown in Figure 9-18.

> **MR. W:** You have just read *Orson's Tummy Ache*. That was another book in the series about Orson, the big dog, and Taco, the little dog. What do you remember about the big dog Orson and what he did to get a tummy ache?
>
> **NATASHA:** He ate his food and then he ate a lot of other things.
>
> **DAMION:** He even ate a stick.
>
> **SHARA:** He ate a big bone and then he had a tummy ache.
>
> **NATASHA:** He was funny, and he ate grass.
>
> **MR. W:** Let's write some sentences in your writing book. Everybody take your writing books and turn to a new page.

The teacher dictates the sentences to the children, prompting them to say words like big, dog, *and* bugs *and listen for and write the letters. On the word* little, *he has children clap the word and shows them how to write it. He also prompts them how to start* ate *and tells them to add an* e. *After writing, children reread the sentences they have written. The teacher also has each child put together a cut-up sentence strip.*

Figure 9-18 *My Writing Book*

Figure 9-17 Pages from *Orson's Tummy Ache* from Leveled Literacy Intervention, Green System (Heinemann 2009)

Independent Writing

In *independent writing*, children write a text independently. The text may be a list, a message, labels for pictures, or any other type of writing. Because the text is meant to be reread, the teacher provides support as needed to help the children write in conventional form. Children develop independent control of early writing strategies, they learn to represent ideas in different ways, and they learn to monitor their own writing.

In the example below, children have read a book called *Family Pictures* (several pages from the book are reproduced in Figure 9-19). Cecelia's writing book is shown in Figure 9-20.

> **Mr. W:** You read *Family Pictures*. Think about the family pictures the little boy put in his book.
>
> **Dansen:** They were all of his family.
>
> **Martha:** It was like a scrapbook that my mom does.
>
> *After more conversation about children's family members, the teacher hands out children's writing books.*
>
> **Mr. W:** All of you have families, and you are going to write about them just like the boy did in the story. I am going to divide a page in your writing books. Watch me.
>
> *The teacher takes each child's writing book and divides it into four boxes with two crossed lines. Children write about a family member in each box. They write easy high-frequency words accurately and approximate the other words. The teacher prompts them to take words apart by syllables, listen for the*

Figure 9-20 Cecelia's Writing Book

sounds, and say the word slowly, listening for the first sound, the middle sound, and the ending sound.

▶ Teacher's Language During Writing Activities

When helping children with their writing, you can use very specific language to teach for, prompt for, and reinforce sound analysis. (Language like this is also explored in Chapter 13.) Here are some examples from the *Fountas and Pinnell Prompting Guide 1* (Heinemann 2009):

1. To draw attention to syllables and help children use them to take words apart:
   - ❑ *Listen while I clap the parts of the word.*
   - ❑ *Listen for the parts.*

Figure 9-19 Pages from *Family Pictures* from Leveled Literacy Intervention, Green System (Heinemann 2009)

❑ *Clap the parts you hear.*

❑ *You heard the parts.*

2. To draw attention to initial sounds:

❑ *Listen while I say the first part.*

❑ *Listen for the sounds you hear in the first part.*

3. To draw attention to sounds in sequence:

❑ *Listen for the first sound.*

❑ *Listen while I say the next sound.*

❑ *Listen while I say the last sound.*

❑ *Listen for the sound you hear next.*

❑ *Listen for the sound you hear at the end.*

❑ *Listen for the ending.*

4. To help children say words slowly to hear sounds:

❑ *Listen while I say the word slowly.*

❑ *Say the word slowly.*

❑ *You said the word slowly.*

❑ *Say the word slowly. What sound do you hear first? Next? Last?*

❑ *Say the word slowly. How many sounds do you hear?*

5. To help children make connections by sound:

❑ *This word sounds like ____ at the beginning [in the middle, at the end].*

❑ *Do you know another word that starts like that [ends like that]?*

6. To draw attention to letter-sound relationships:

❑ *What letter do you expect to see at the beginning [end]?*

❑ *Write the first sound you hear, the next sound, the last sound.*

❑ *You heard those sounds.*

❑ *You heard the sounds and wrote the letters.*

You can demonstrate what you mean by this language in the specific lessons you provide. You will find that very specific language will be quite helpful to writers as they become more aware of the sounds in words.

▶ Games and Independent Activities

Once you have provided instruction to help children notice and work with sounds, you can extend their learning by making sounds the basis for games like Follow the Path, Lotto, Snap, Concentration, or Go Fish. (Appendix F includes basic directions for these games.) Two or three students playing one of these games for even a short while get a great deal of practice saying and hearing the sounds in words. Examples include:

❑ *Sort pictures according to sounds.* Children have a sorting card with three key pictures down the left column (see Figure 9-21). They find other picture cards that rhyme with the key words and make rhyming pairs. Or you can put key pictures at the top of three columns. Have children look through a set of picture cards and sort them under pictures with the same first sound (or last sound).

Figure 9-21 Sorting Pictures by Sound

❑ *Write the words represented by picture cards.* Children take a picture card, say the word slowly, and write a letter for each sound they hear. (Figure 9-22)

Figure 9-22 Writing Words from Pictures

❑ *Play a version of Follow the Path with a picture in each space.* Children throw a die to determine the number of spaces to move forward. When they land on a space, they say the word the picture represents, then say the first and last parts of the word separately, and finally say the word again (*string, str-ing, string*). The first player to get to the end of the path wins. You can vary this activity by putting a one-syllable word in each space; the children say the word, segment it into individual phonemes, and then say the word again. (Figure 9-23)

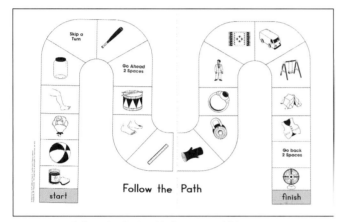

Figure 9-23 Follow the Path with Onsets and Rimes

❑ *Play Lotto using picture cards.* Students have Lotto cards with pictures on them. They draw from a deck. If they have a picture that starts with the same sound, they take the card and cover the space. The first player to cover the card wins. (Figure 9-24)

Figure 9-24 Lotto with Initial Sounds

❑ *Play Go Fish using a deck of cards that includes several sets of matching pictures.* Each player is given five cards to start. In turn, each player asks one of the other players for a card that matches one of the cards she is holding, saying the word in parts: "Do you have *f-ish?*" If the other child has a picture of a fish, he responds by blending the parts together and saying *fish.* He gives the card to the first player. The first player now has a match and puts it down on the table. If the second player does not have a match, he says, "Go Fish," and the first player takes a picture card from the deck. The first player with no cards wins the game. This game can be varied by using picture cards with three phonemes. Children segment and blend them into words. (Figure 9-25)

Figure 9-25 Go Fish with Onsets and Rimes

❑ *Play a word game with a partner.* One child takes a picture from a pile of fifteen or twenty picture cards and pronounces the first part and the last part of the word the picture represents. The partner blends the parts together and says the word smoothly. They proceed through all the cards in the pile. Then they mix up the cards and reverse roles. (Figure 9-26)

❑ *Play Snap! With two or three matching decks of cards, depending on the number of players.* When two players play, they look for a match between two cards. When three players play, they look for a three-way match. Each player has a deck of cards. The players simultaneously turn over a

Figure 9-26 Word Game, Blending Onsets and Rimes

card from their decks. The objective of the game is to notice matching cards quickly and say "Snap!" to win the cards that match. The player must also tell how the cards are alike. When all the cards have been dispersed, the player with the most cards wins. (Figure 9-27)

Figure 9-27 Snap! Matching Initial Sounds

▶ The Important Role of Phonological Awareness

It is critical for children to develop a strong foundation of phonological awareness through reading, writing, oral games, and other games that build sensitivity to the sounds of language and the letters that represent them. You can find numerous opportunities in your teaching throughout the day to help your students enjoy learning about the sound systems in language.

▶ Suggestions for Professional Development

ANALYZING EVIDENCE OF PHONOLOGICAL AWARENESS

Student writing provides strong evidence of phonological awareness.

1. Gather a group of grade-level and across-grade-level colleagues.

2. Ask each to select two writing samples from a low-achieving reader and bring enough copies for each member of the group.

3. Working in pairs or threes, talk about what aspects of hearing sounds and parts in words are evident in the writing. Use the following questions to guide your analysis:

   ❑ Can the child hear and write the first (last, middle) sound?

   ❑ Can the child hear the sounds for the letter clusters at the beginning and end of words?

   ❑ Can the child hear vowel sounds? Which ones?

   ❑ Can the child hear sounds in sequence?

4. Then discuss what other aspects of the alphabetic system they understand.

Learning Written Language Systems

Virtually every child learns oral language. It emerges naturally from interactions in the home. However, written language must be learned, and this is what literacy education is all about. This section focuses on the challenges of learning how written language works. We first focus on early reading behaviors—those essential understandings that young children must develop in order to understand how print works—for example, matching one spoken word to one written word or moving left to right across print. We then describe the important role of phonics as an instructional tool in helping readers. Chapter 12 focuses on how we can help readers learn words, particularly high-frequency words, and how those readers can use their known words as resources.

Learning About Print: Early Reading Behaviors

IN THIS CHAPTER, WE LOOK AT SOME IMPORTANT EARLY READING and writing behaviors that are essential understandings on which to build literacy. Many struggling readers were initially confused about some of these important concepts in their first years of school. By the time they figure them out, other children have moved on to much more sophisticated learning. If children have difficulty with these concepts, then they need early intervention. First, we look at a few simple assessments for checking children's knowledge of conventions. Then, we explore different ways of helping children take on the visual aspects of reading.

Children vary greatly in the amount and type of literacy experiences they have had before they start school. Almost every child will have had some experience with print, because the world we live in is full of it! Just look at these examples (Figure 10-1) and consider how many times a young child may have seen them.

Print is available just about everywhere; the key is attending to it, and that takes adult support. For example, when Jim gets on an elevator with his four-year-old grandson Mike, the child gets the chance to look for and push the right button. (Jim always helps, especially if there are other passengers, but the habit

of visual search has been established.) Sarah asks her five-year-old to find the right box of breakfast cereal in the market. (There is a reason store managers place the sugary cereals on the lowest shelves!) Three-year-old Mitchell picks out the *M* from an array of magnetic letters on the refrigerator door and loves seeing the McDonald's sign. Four-year-old Margaret takes a small notepad and felt-tipped pen and goes around "taking orders" for snacks. Four-year-old Britney moves the cursor to open her favorite computer game. Experiences like these are invaluable in the process of becoming literate, and many children have thousands of them before they step foot in a school.

While they are learning language, children experience print in very personal ways.

This learning is especially powerful when an adult is there to engage and guide the child's attention. When an adult reads to a child, that child has an opportunity to learn the structure of written language (as described in Chapter 7). But the child also notices that you read the print, not the pictures. When Virginia reads to her year-old grandson Mark, he sometimes puts a hand over the print, and she moves it to the side before reading on. Mark soon learns that Virginia needs to look at the print to read it, and he begins to distinguish print from pictures. Mark may also learn that:

❑ The story is the same every time you read it.

❑ Written language sounds different from the way people talk.

❑ You get information from the pictures and the print.

❑ You move through the book in a certain way, turning the pages.

❑ You read the left-hand page before the right-hand page, and you read from top to bottom.

❑ The marks on the page contain some letters that appear over and over.

❑ The same letter can appear in different words.

❑ Some letters look alike (sticks, curves, circles).

Learning is also powerful when a child pretends to write or shares a writing task with an adult. When Julia's mom writes a shopping list, for example, Julia likes to make her own. She places squiggles right under each other! But when she writes a letter to her grandmother, she places her marks, which include some letters and letter-like forms, in lines. (See Figure 10-2.) Through writing, Julia has the opportunity to learn much about how written language works:

❑ When you write, you want to communicate or remember something.

❑ Writing and pictures are different, but you can use both to say what you mean.

❑ You make marks on paper when you write.

❑ Some marks appear over and over and look alike.

❑ When you write you make letters.

❑ You can write for different purposes—lists, signs, letters, email, stories.

Figure 10-1 Environmental Print

❑ When you write, you make letters in a particular order to make a word.

❑ When you write your name, it always has the same letters in the same order.

❑ It matters which way you write a letter (not backwards; right side up).

❑ The letters that are in your name can be in other words.

❑ Your name can start like other names or words you know.

❑ When you write, you put marks on the page in some kind of order (top to bottom, left to right).

Usually, adults demonstrate and show processes. (That is why reading aloud is so important. A young observer cannot possibly tell what a silent reader is doing!) As children gain experience, they constantly refine their knowledge of print and they use the resources at their disposal. A three-year-old, Iris, makes letter-like forms that are different from her "picture," and she places them carefully on the page (see Figure 10-3). And notice how Madeleine makes the letter *M* to represent a whole message (see Figure 10-4).

In the past, when children entered school, we used to talk about whether they were "ready." Readiness was dependent on "maturation" or "development." Children were kept out of school or held back because they were immature or "young." The message was that we needed to wait until they were *ready* to read and write; meanwhile, children were often given exercises such as coloring, cutting, or tracing. This idea of readiness has long since been revised to accommodate the powerful role of experience in becoming literate. We now recognize the "emerging" literacy behaviors that indicate what the

child is noticing (Clay 1979; Fountas and Pinnell 1996; Pinnell and Fountas 1999). The term *emergent* in this context means that knowledge of reading and writing and their purposes gradually *emerges* during children's preschool learning experiences and opportunities to engage with print.

Emergent readers rely on language and meaning as they read simple texts having only one or two lines of print. They are just beginning to control early behaviors such as matching spoken words one by one with written words, being aware of how print is arranged on the page, and moving left to right in reading. They are learning what a word really is, how letters go together, and how letters are different from one another. They may know one or two high-frequency words they can use as anchors.

Figure 10-2 Julia's List and Letter

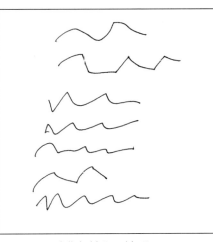

Figure 10-3 Iris's Writing

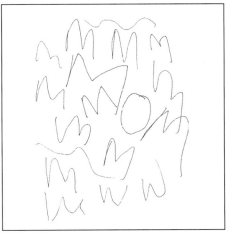

Figure 10-4 Madeleine's Writing

Emergent writers are learning that what they say and think can be expressed in written language. They are also beginning to understand that writing naturally accompanies human activity and can be used for different purposes. They approximate the "look" of writing and begin to produce both scribbling and letter-like forms, but they are moving toward conventional forms. They are proud of their written products; sometimes they impart meaning to the writing and sometimes they indicate that they simply want to "do writing." Emergent writers are also beginning to realize that writing letters and words is essential in order to produce a message that someone else can read, and they may learn to represent their names (or parts of names) and a few high-frequency words.

When we think of literacy learning in early childhood, nothing stands out quite so prominently as learning the ABCs. Emergent readers and writers are also learning a great deal about letters and their associated sounds. They may give specific attention to the alphabet when reading ABC books, singing the alphabet song, playing with magnetic letters, or playing simple computer games. More important, though, they are simultaneously learning the *purpose* and *use* of letters for communication, and this makes a huge difference.

Of course, not all students enter school with a rich background of literacy experiences. Some have been part of families that have little time to devote to literacy activities and/or that do not realize the importance of playing around with print. Some families feel, with some justification, that it is the school's job to teach children to read and write. Still other children must deal with issues such as poverty, family instability, or illness that stand in the way of early literacy learning. Even children who do have opportunities to experience forms of literacy may not attend to them—may find it difficult to focus on what must look like tiny, bewildering squiggles. Some families, with the best intentions, buy games that drill students on letters and sounds in ways that are meaningless and not very interesting. These kinds of experiences, especially if not balanced by hearing books read aloud and having access to pencils and paper with which to pretend to write, can undermine a child's motivation.

When a child enters kindergarten with little exposure to literacy, it is not too late to enrich his experience. By being immersed in activities such as interactive read-aloud, interactive writing, and letter and word manipulation, children can very quickly learn a great deal about how print works. Children who reach midpoint in kindergarten and still do not show significant signs that they are learning early reading and writing behaviors need intervention to help them notice significant information about letters and words.

In first grade, many children are quickly moving on to read simple texts independently. Children who enter first grade with little control of early reading and writing behaviors will find the instruction they receive confusing. Not knowing how to look at print, move left-to-right across a line of text and across a word, or match voice to print makes reading difficult, especially when the class begins reading texts with multiple lines of print and many high-frequency words. These children may try to "remember" the text—and they can often do so if the teacher goes over it several times—but this is not real reading.

It is important to identify children who are having early difficulty and then to clear up their confusions. In this chapter, we discuss a few simple assessments you can make and explore ways to help children internalize the visual aspects of reading. Many struggling readers in their first years of school are confused about some or all of the important early reading and writing behaviors (Figure 10-5). By the time they figure them out, other children have moved on to much more sophisticated learning. If children have difficulty with these concepts, then they need early intervention.

▶ Finding Out What Children Know About Print

You can gather a great deal of information by observing children engage with letters, words, and the simple texts you use for shared reading. You can identify the children who:

❑ Notice visual signposts.

❑ Follow print left to right.

Figure 10-5 Early Reading and Writing Behaviors

1. You read the print—not the pictures.
2. You read the words to know what the writer is saying.
3. You write words so readers will understand what you want to say.
4. You read and write left to right along a line of print and across a word.
5. At the end of the line, you return to the left and read or write from left to right again.
6. You turn pages left to right as you go through a book.
7. You read the left-hand page before the right-hand page.
8. A word is a group of letters that means something.
9. There is white space on each side of a word (left and right) and no spaces between the letters in a word.
10. You match one spoken word to one written word.
11. A sentence is a group of words in a line, left to right, that means something. The sentence ends when you see a period.
12. The first word in a sentence is the one on the left or the word immediately after a period and a space.
13. The first letter of a word is the one on the left, immediately after the space. The last letter of a word is the one on the right, immediately before the space.
14. The letters in a word are always in the same left-to-right order every time you read or write it.
15. A letter is one mark, A/a through Z/z.
16. For every letter there is an uppercase form and a lowercase form.
17. Most of the words you read and write are in lowercase form.
18. You use an uppercase form for the first letter in a name or for the first letter of the word that begins a sentence.
19. The same letters are in many different words.
20. You stop at a period, a question mark, and an exclamation point.
21. You write a period, question mark, or exclamation point to show the sentence ends. You use an exclamation point to show strong feelings, such as excitement, fear, joy, and so on.
22. You take a breath at a comma.
23. You get information from pictures and the print.
24. A name is a word. You can use your name to learn about other words.
25. You can find a word by looking for the letters in it.

- ❏ Point at words.
- ❏ Can come up with letters and write them when they attempt to spell words.
- ❏ Are able to focus on print.
- ❏ Are rapidly learning the names of letters and beginning to connect them to sounds.

You will also notice some danger signs. If you observe some of the following behaviors, you will want to intervene:

- ❏ The child chants along with others but is often not looking at the print.
- ❏ The child's writing goes all over the page, and letters don't exhibit many distinctive features.
- ❏ The child's writing shows little relation to sounds (many random letters).
- ❏ The child tries to memorize the text and looks at the pictures to produce it.
- ❏ The child has difficulty paying attention while reading.
- ❏ The child does not use language structure to monitor and solve problems.
- ❏ The child cannot point to the words while reading left to right (but may slide the finger along or not use it at all).

When you identify children who are exhibiting some confusion, you will want to administer some systematic assessments to provide more information. (You'll also want to use some of these assessments with your entire class to identify those who need small-group or individual intervention.)

Letter Recognition

This assessment reveals the letter forms children can associate with the corresponding letter name. You can use this information to identify children who need extra help and also as a basis for planning lessons. Look carefully at the results to decide what letters and letter features to bring to children's attention during interactive writing or shared reading. (Because you need to record each child's responses, administer the assessment individually. It won't take much time. Start with uppercase letters and then assess lowercase letters.)

1. Give the child the Uppercase Letter Recognition Sheet (see Figure 10-6 and Appendix G). Cover all but the top row. Point to each letter in the top row and ask, "What's this? " Once the child understands the procedure, have him or her continue reading across each successive row. If the child pauses more than four or five seconds, tell him or her to go on to the next letter on the right. Repeat using the Lowercase Letter Recognition Sheet.

2. Record responses on the child's individual record.

3. Notice:
   - ❑ The number of letters named accurately.
   - ❑ Unknown letter names.
   - ❑ Speed in letter recognition.
   - ❑ Letter confusions and substitutions.

Look at Ardis's individual record (Figure 10-7). Her score at the beginning of grade 1 is 19 of the 52 letters—less than half. Her knowledge of uppercase letters is slightly higher than her knowledge of lowercase letters. This assessment provides evidence that Ardis can notice the distinctive features of letters. Not only does she correctly identify 19 of them, but her substitutions are similar in shape to the correct letter (*m* for *w*, for example). She correctly identifies all the letters in her name except *i*. This assessment alone does not indicate that Ardis is at risk; however, she had good exposure to letters in kindergarten, and is still behind her class. Most of the other children

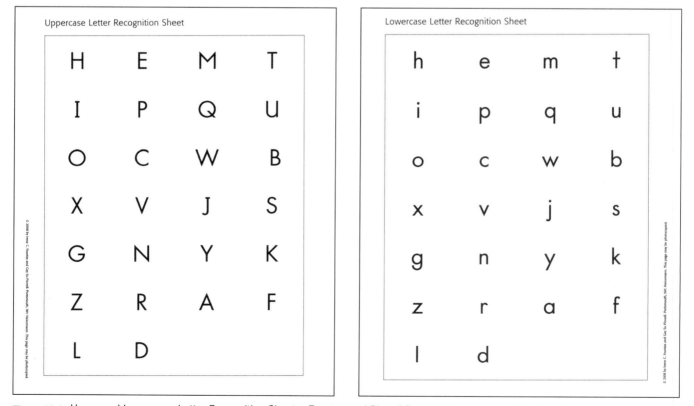

Figure 10-6 Upper and Lowercase Letter Recognition Sheets, *Fountas and Pinnell Benchmark Assessment System 1*

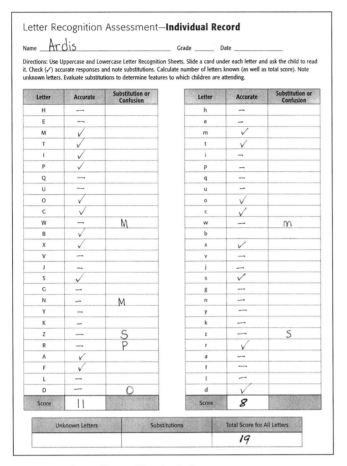

Figure 10-7 Letter Recognition for Ardis

scored at least 30 out of 48. She will need greater letter knowledge to be able to learn words and establish the visual signposts she needs to monitor her reading of easy texts. It will be necessary to "tidy up" her knowledge of letters.

Early Literacy Behaviors

We highly recommend the *Concepts About Print Assessment* by Marie Clay (1993). This assessment has been used for three decades to document children's early understandings of print. In lieu of this assessment, you can take any Level B or C book and ask the reader a series of simple questions. For example, a teacher used *The Puppets* (Level C—Figure 10-8) to assess Ardis's knowledge of how print works. (The assessment is shown in Figure 10-9).

Ardis's score was 6. She could identify where to start and where to go next, indicating that she knew about return sweep. She was able to locate a known word (*me*) and the unknown word *frog*, but she did not locate *fish*. When asked to point while the teacher read, Ardis slid her finger along the line. She was moving left to right, but there was no indication of voice-print matching. She located the letter *s* (a known letter) and found a word that starts with *p* (not a known letter). When asked to locate *l*, she pointed to *k*, another letter with a tall stick. There was no evidence of knowledge of punctuation. This assessment provided further evidence that Ardis needs to know more letters. Another high priority for her is matching voice to print.

When you administer this simple individual test, notice:

- ❏ Behaviors that seem quick and automatic.
- ❏ Speed in locating words and letters.
- ❏ Ability to connect letters, sounds, and words.
- ❏ Ability to match one spoken word with one written word.
- ❏ Ability to distinguish letter features when they are embedded in words.
- ❏ Ability to understand the difference between letters and words.
- ❏ Ability to read left to right and return to the left margin.

All of these early reading behaviors are important, and they should quickly become smooth and automatic so that they do not require conscious attention.

Word Writing

You can gain a great deal of information by having children write all the words they can within a designated time. Examining the result will tell you not only the words children can spell accurately but also what they are thinking about words and how they work. You can note attempts as well as evidence that children are placing words into categories. You can think about how their strengths in writing words can support reading.

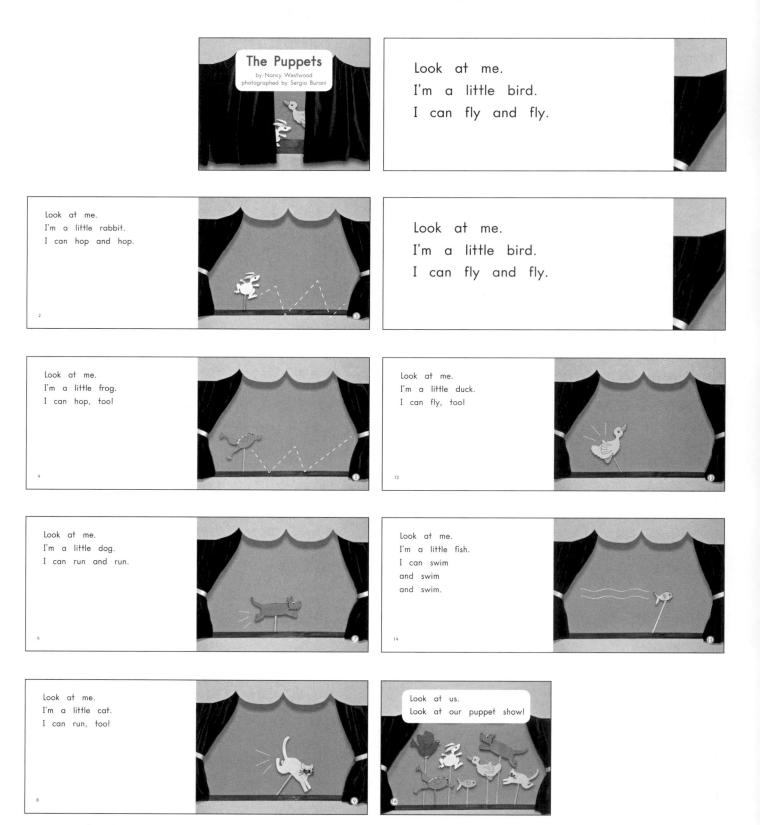

FIGURE 10-8 Page Layout of *The Puppets* from Leveled Literacy Intervention, Green System (Heinemann 2009)

Figure 10-9 Early Literacy Behaviors—Ardis

Teacher	Response	
1. Where do I start reading?	Pointed to left margin.	✓
2. Where do I go after that?	Pointed to left margin on line 2.	✓
3. Find *me* on this page *(page 2).*	Pointed to the word *me.*	✓
4. Find *frog* on this page *(page 4).*	Looked at the picture. Pointed to *frog.*	✓
5. Say *swim.* Find *swim* on this page *(page 14).*	Looked at the picture. Pointed to fish.	—
6. Point while I read. *(Reads page 14.)*	Slid finger along the line.	—
7. Find the letter *l* *(on page 16).*	Pointed to *k.*	—
8. Find the letter *s* *(on page 16).*	Pointed to *s* in *show.*	✓
9. Find a word that starts with *p* (On page 16).	Pointed to *puppet.*	✓
10. What's this? *(Points to period)*	Shook head.	—

Early in the year, you may want to administer this assessment individually so that you can prompt children with familiar words—*I, the, it, is, in* (refer to the list of high-frequency words in Appendix H). But even if you give this assessment to a small group of children at the same time, you will still get valuable information.

At your signal, children write their names and then write all the words they know until you tell them to stop. (Give them between five and ten minutes.) Encourage children to try words even if they think they don't know how to spell them with all the letters. You can make this assessment informal. For example, you do not need to hide all the print on the walls (it's interesting to see how children make use of their environment). But if you need systematic, more formal assessment, take the child into a room with no print resources. Analyze the child's writing, noticing what

letter/sound relationships and spelling patterns he or she controls. Look for:

- ❑ Knowledge of the way one word leads to another, connections between words, and categories of words.
- ❑ Use of phonograms and spelling patterns.
- ❑ Ease and fluency in constructing words.
- ❑ Use of endings to make several words from a root word.
- ❑ Ability to hear the sounds in words.
- ❑ Ability to represent sound with letters.
- ❑ Knowledge of high-frequency word patterns.
- ❑ Ability to use and connect word parts.

Word writing assessments for two children in the middle of first grade are shown in Figure 10-10 and Figure 10-11, along with analyses (Figure 10-12). There is quite a contrast between the knowledge of Andrew and Jessica. Andrew has benefited greatly from the instruction in his classroom. He has a flexible range of ways to work with words. But Jessica has also benefited.

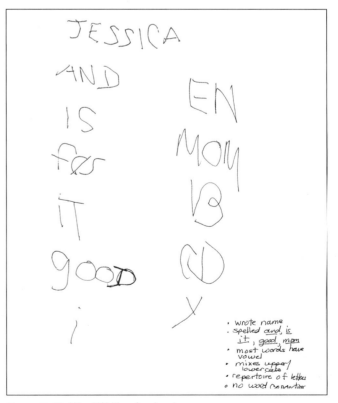

Figure 10-10 Word Writing for Jessica

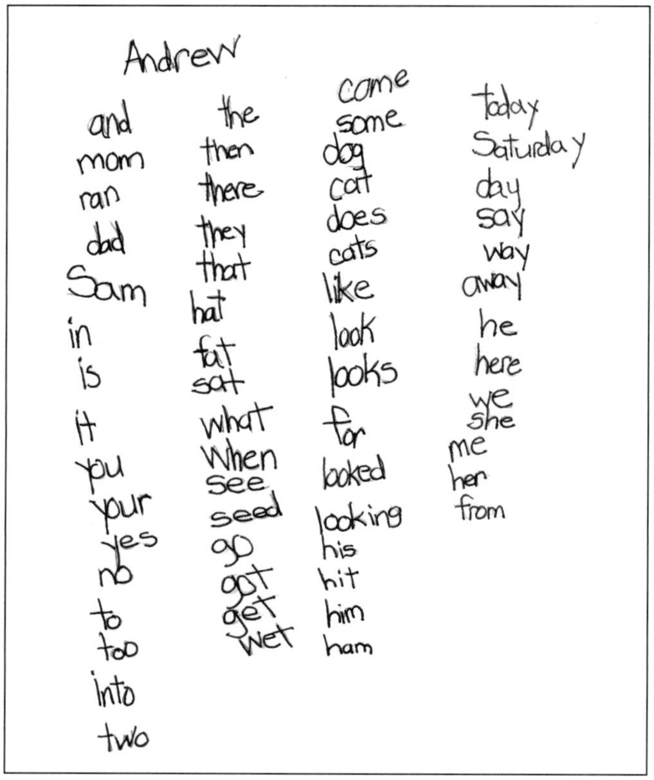

```
                Andrew

and      the      come      today
mom      than     some      Saturday
ran      there    dog       day
dad      they     cat       say
Sam      that     does      way
in       hat      cats      away
is       fat      like      he
it       sat      look      here
you      what     looks     we
your     When     for       she
yes      see      looked    me
no       seed     looking   her
to       go       his       from
too      got      hit
into     get      him
two      wet      ham
```

Figure 10-11 Word Writing for Andrew

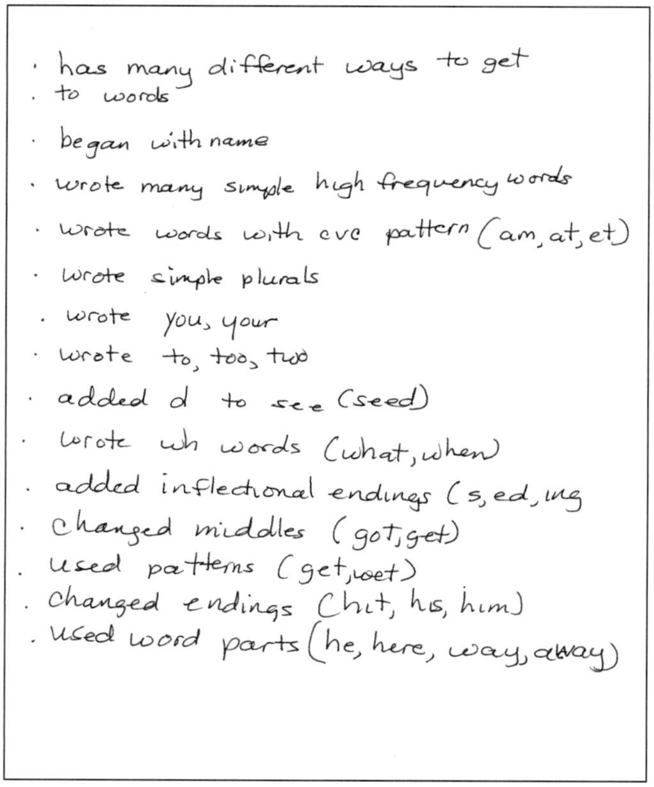

```
· has many different ways to get
· to words
· began with name
· wrote many simple high frequency words
· wrote words with cvc pattern (am, at, et)
· wrote simple plurals
· wrote you, your
· wrote to, too, two
· added d to see (seed)
· wrote wh words (what, when)
· added inflectional endings (s, ed, ing)
· changed middles (got, get)
· used patterns (get, wet)
· changed endings (hit, his, him)
· used word parts (he, here, way, away)
```

Figure 10-12 Teacher Analysis

She can write her name, knows a few high-frequency words, and has a repertoire of known letters. However, she needs some strong instruction to help her make the transition to written language.

▶ Letter Learning

Knowing the letters of the alphabet is necessary to learn to read and write. In the previous chapter we discussed phonological awareness as sensitivity to *sounds*. Orthographic awareness is the key in moving from oral to written language. Orthographic awareness is awareness of the symbols (*graphemes*) that represent sounds in a writing system (Harris and Hodges 1995). It's what you *see*. In order to recognize letters and use letter knowledge, children have to learn that:

❑ A letter has features that distinguish it from every other letter.

❑ Letters have names.

❑ Directional movements are required to make letters.

❑ Each letter has two forms—uppercase and lowercase.

❑ Some letters look different in different kinds of print *(a, a)*.

❑ There is a limited set of letters (twenty-six, all with upper- and lowercase forms).

❑ The letters come in a certain order in the alphabet.

❑ Letters are related to sounds you can hear.

There is some evidence that when letters and sounds are taught together, the learning is accelerated (Bradley and Bryant 1983; National Reading Panel 2000). As children learn letters and begin to notice words, their knowledge of sounds expands; and as children learn more about sounds in words, it becomes easier for them to notice letters.

Making Experiences with Letters Count

Children who are having difficulty learning letters also have problems using visual information to monitor and correct their reading. Confusions may persist. Children may even exhibit behaviors that block learning and create further confusion. Sometimes, children know a few letters but constantly miss or confuse others. This is not necessarily a problem of "seeing" a letter wrong or backward, and it may not be a physical problem with the brain or eyes, although parents will certainly want to have vision checked. All children occasionally reverse letters before they learn how important directionality is. Many children have not learned *how to look at letters,* and some develop confusions that persist.

You need to make your instruction count when you are helping struggling readers learn how to look at letters. We list some general suggestions you can use during word study, reading, or writing (Figure 10-13). Use these ideas every time there is an opportunity.

Figure 10-13 Making Letter Learning Effective for Struggling Readers

1. Be sure that letters are clearly printed in black or dark print on white or cream paper.

2. Be sure that readers are at all times able to see the print in word study lessons or in shared or interactive writing.

3. For beginning readers and writers (and children who are having difficulty), select texts with a consistent and clear font.

4. Use a verbal description of letter formation (the "verbal path") to help children learn features of letters.

5. Use a variety of ways to draw children's attention to the features of letters.

6. Provide kinesthetic experiences that help children learn directionality and the distinctive features of letters. (colored plastic letters, making letters in sand or salt, sandpaper letters)

7. Use magnetic letters to help children feel letter features as they sort them and build words.

8. Vary the ways children view letters as they read or write them.

9. Emphasize looking at the letters in words from left to right.

10. Create strong references that will help children keep the letter and a key word beginning with the letter in mind. (Alphabet Linking Chart)

---

1. *Be sure that letters are clearly printed in black or dark print on white or cream paper.* There should be a good contrast between the background and the print so that the print is easy to see. Avoid distracting or busy patterns under or close to the print. Also, avoid "dressing up" the letters with polka dots, stripes, or hats. Children who are having difficulty perceiving print need very plain, clear letters.

2. *Be sure that readers are able at all times to see the print in word study lessons or in shared or interactive writing.* Every time you focus children's attention on print—isolated letters, isolated words, or continuous print—be sure they can see clearly. Readers who are sitting far to the side or right in front of a raised easel, for example, may be getting a distorted view of the letters.

3. *For beginning readers and writers (and children who are having difficulty), select texts with a consistent and clear font.* With the large numbers of guided reading books being published today, it is easy to find texts with print in a very clear and consistent font. Avoid texts that have tricky things like print in a circle or print that pops up from the page. (You may want to read texts like this aloud.) Texts should be printed in a clear font with good space between words and lines to give readers maximum opportunity to perceive the letters.

4. *Use a verbal description of letter formation to help children learn features of letters.* You will find that it helps to establish a consistent way of talking about the directional movements needed to make a letter (see Chapter 7). You can use these "verbal paths" whenever, and as long as, needed to help children make letters efficiently. In the process they will learn how to look at letters.

5. *Use a variety of ways to draw children's attention to the distinctive features of letters.* There are very small differences between some letters, and some children find it extraordinarily difficult to detect them. You can talk about distinctive features and invite children to notice features of letters both in isolation and when

embedded in text. You can also help children focus on the features by inviting them to sort and match letters.

6. *Provide kinesthetic experiences that help children learn directionality and the distinctive features of letters.* Give children sandpaper, felt, or foam letters they can feel while reciting the verbal path followed in forming them. You can also have children form letters with their fingers in a tray of sand or salt.

7. *Use magnetic letters to help children feel the features as they sort them and build words.* Whenever possible, have children manipulate magnetic letters. These letters can be used for many purposes—sorting, building words, manipulating words, changing letters to make new words, as models for writing the letters, etc.

8. *Vary the ways children view letters as they read or write them.* It is easy for children to get into the habit of looking at letters in only one way (on a whiteboard or on the table in front of them, for example). Children need to see the same letters in different planes—on a vertical easel, chalkboard, or pocket chart; on a white-board or book page lying horizontally in front of them. They can work with magnetic letters looking down at them on a table but also standing in front of them at the chalkboard (and therefore looking directly at them at eye level).

9. *Emphasize looking at the letters in words from left to right.* This makes it easier to notice letters' distinctive features. It is critical to get the child's eye processing left to right across words.

10. *Create strong references that will help children keep the letter and a key word beginning with that letter in mind.* A tool like the Alphabet Linking Chart (see Chapter 7) is a valuable reference for children who are learning about letters and sounds. The chart includes a clear depiction of each upper- and lowercase letter and a picture of something whose l abel begins with the sound associated with the letter.

Using the Alphabet Linking Chart and Consonant Cluster Linking Chart

There are many powerful ways to develop print knowledge with two charts, the Alphabet Linking Chart and Consonant Cluster Linking Chart (see Figure 10-14 and Appendix I and J). You can have the children read the chart in a variety of ways—the letters and the pictures, just the pictures, just the letters, just the uppercase letters, just the lowercase letters, the consonants only, the two sounds of the vowels, backwards, every other letter, randomly as you point, and so on. They can sing the alphabet song while pointing

---

Figure 10-14 Ways to Use the Alphabet Linking Chart and Consonant Cluster Linking Chart

Reading the chart
- Read the entire chart, saying the names of the letters and the pictures *(a, apple; b, bear; etc.)*.
- Read the "known" letters (that have been taught in lessons).
- Read every other letter.
- Read just the consonants.
- Read just the vowels.
- Read while singing the alphabet song.
- Reading just the uppercase letters or just the lowercase letters.
- Read it backward.
- Read it randomly as you quickly touch letters.

Using the chart as a resource while writing
- Use the chart to find the letter for a sound (using key words).
- Use the chart to help in writing a letter accurately.
- Consult the chart to find the lowercase (or uppercase) form of the letter
- Use the chart to help in writing CVC words, particularly the vowel sounds.

Using the chart as a resource while reading
- Consult the chart to relate the letter to the initial sound in a word.
- Use the chart to help in using vowel sounds to solve words.

to the letters. This chart will help tidy up all the children's knowledge related to letters.

The Consonant Cluster Linking Chart includes pictures whose labels begin with two consonant letters (including the consonant digraphs). It is designed to help children recognize and smoothly articulate initial consonant clusters and can be used in the same ways as the Alphabet Linking Chart.

You can place several enlarged versions of these charts in the classroom or resource room. You can also give children their own copies to take home and/or put in their writing folders. A good way to get children to pay close attention to the Alphabet Linking Chart is to "make" it with them when you first introduce it:

1. On an easel place an enlarged version of the Alphabet Linking Chart that includes the letters but on which the picture boxes are blank. (Prepare a picture card for each letter, sized to fit in the box.)

2. Demonstrate saying the label for what a picture represents, saying the beginning sound (in isolation) and then finding that letter. Glue the picture in the box.

3. Ask children to look at one or two other pictures, one at a time, and say the label for each. Have them isolate the beginning sound and think about the letter that represents that sound. (Children can take turns finding the letter on the chart and gluing the picture in the box.)

4. Add one or two pictures to the chart over a period of a few weeks.

5. Each day "read" the alphabet chart in order, saying the names of the letters and the labels of whichever pictures are included at that time.

Having the children participate in preparing the chart gives them a sense of ownership and adds to the excitement when they receive their individual copies of the completed chart.

Sorting and Matching Letters

One of the most powerful ways to draw children's attention to the features of letters is to sort or match them in various ways. A simple way to begin is to put out three or four kinds of letters that can be manipulated, draw a circle on a paper, and put one letter in the middle—for example, *b* (see Figure 10-15). The child finds all of the letters that are just like that one (from a limited choice). Avoid putting in confusing letters, such as *d*. You can also place a group of letters along the top of a board and have children find a letter that matches each (see Figure 10-16).

Another helpful task is to build a simple high-frequency word—*to*, for example—using letters that can be manipulated, and have children build the word underneath it (see Figure 10-17). (Give children the precise right letters at first.) Show them how to make the word left to right and to check letter by letter with pointing: *t, t, o, o, to.*

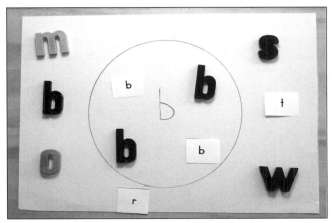

Figure 10-15 Matching One Letter

Figure 10-16 Matching Letters

Figure 10-17 Making a Word and Checking It

From these simple exercises, you can move to sorting. For example, give the child a group of letters, some with tall sticks and some with short sticks (see Figure 10-18). Put a key letter for each (for example, *h*

Figure 10-18 Letter Sorting Tall and Short Sticks

and *n*) at the top of the paper or on the chalkboard. Have the child sort letters with tall and short sticks under the key letters.

A number of suggestions for matching and sorting letters are listed in Figure 10-19. You can use these as part of phonics or word study minilessons or intervention lessons. Keep the task easy so that children can work quickly and confidently. For example:

- ❑ Use only one feature at first, then increase to two.
- ❑ Use clear examples (letters that are not easily confused) until children can notice many details.
- ❑ Use letters that are included in children's names.

Figure 10-19 **Ways to Sort and Match Letters**

Sort by feature	Picture
• Color • Slanted and straight lines • Upper- and lowercase pairs • Consonants and vowels • Tails and no tails • Circles and no circles • Tunnels and no tunnels • Long sticks and short sticks • Tall letters and short letters • Dots and no dots • Letters with similar upper- and lowercase forms and letters with forms that are not alike • Same letters in a group	
Sort by Function	**Picture**
• Consonants and vowels • Letters that you see doubled in words and letters you don't • Letters that are in consonant clusters and letters that are not • Letters in consonant blends and letters in digraphs • Letters in alphabetical order	

Increase the difficulty when you see that children are beginning to notice features. Sorting continues to be a very valuable activity long after children have learned the names of the letters. Many struggling readers need to attend closely to print, and they must become automatic in their recognition not just of letters in isolation but of letters embedded in continuous print.

Letter Minibooks

Letter minibooks (see Figure 10-20) are short books focused on a particular letter (or letter cluster) and its relation to a sound. When "reading" a letter minibook, children get a great deal of practice saying the name of the letter or letter cluster, hearing and feeling themselves say several words that start with the associated sound, and recognizing a series of key examples of concrete objects that illustrate the sound. They also get a great deal of experience looking at the letter or letter cluster. Describing the motions needed to form the letter or letter cluster helps children notice the distinctive features.

When using letter minibooks:

1. Introduce the letter minibook by saying, "This is a book that is all about the letter [name of letter]. [Name of letter] makes the sound, [make the sound]."

2. "Let's make the letter right on top of the [name of letter] on the front."

Figure 10-20 Letter Minibook, Leveled Literacy Intervention, Orange and Green Systems (Heinemann 2009)

3. Show children how to trace over the letter using the verbal path description (see Appendix D and *Fountas and Pinnell Prompting Guide 1*).

4. Have children trace the letter using the verbal path description, then say the name of the letter.

5. Show children how to "read" each page of the letter minibook by saying the labels for the objects. Draw their attention to the word that represents the object. They can also highlight the first letter in yellow.

After children know the routines for reading letter minibooks, they can read several of them quickly.

▶ Early Word Learning

Many struggling readers do not have a large repertoire of words. They cannot use known words as visual signposts to monitor their reading, and they have fewer resources to help them learn new words. Struggling readers need to build a core of words that they know quickly and automatically—that they can recognize without effort. They also need to develop a system for *learning how to learn words*. Ideas for ways to help children look at and learn a new word are listed in Figure 10-21.

It may be hard for children to learn this first core of words. Keep the task easy and go over the words every day. You don't need to spend a lot of time on this. It is better to spend a little time every day than to embark on long periods of drill. Some "big ideas" running through these suggestions are:

❑ Use clear and specific language when talking to children about words, but don't "overtalk." Sometimes you just need to say the word clearly while running a finger under it to draw attention to the visual features of the word.

❑ Combine word building and word writing.

❑ Offer many opportunities to notice the word, building the first collection slowly to be sure children have overlearned some of the words. Learning will accelerate as the child learns ways of looking at words.

❑ Always work left to right when building, writing, or checking words. It will help children to notice the letters in the proper order.

Figure 10-21 Ideas for Ways to Help Children Learn a New Word

1. Use language that makes it clear you are talking about a word: "This word is *[word]*." (Some children confuse letters and words.)

2. Tell children to look at the beginning of the word and show them what that means (first letter on the left).

3. Read the word to children as you run your finger under the word, left to right.

4. Ask children to look closely at the word and say what they notice at the beginning.

5. Ask them to look at the word and then read it as they use a finger to check it, left to right.

6. Remind them of another word that will help them remember a new word: *an, and; the, then.*

7. Help children notice the first letter and then look at the rest of the letters in the word, left to right, to notice more.

8. Give children magnetic letters in order to build the word left to right.

9. After building the word, have children take it apart and build it several times.

10. After building the word several times, have children write the word.

11. Show children how to check the word they have written letter by letter: *a, a, n, n, d, d.*

12. Have children, using magnetic letters, break the word apart by pulling down the first letter *(s)* and then the rest of the letters, e.g., *s-ee, th-e.*

▶ Using High-Frequency Word Cards

Once children have acquired a repertoire of known words, they can then use them as a resource for further learning. For beginning readers, a known word stands out from the rest of the print. A known word is recognizable; the reader can be certain of it. They can use known words to help them understand the concept of a word as letters with white space on either side. They can use them to monitor and correct their reading. For example, coming upon a known word helps readers keep track of where they are in the sentence and may alert them to possible mismatches.

When a word is known, it becomes phonologically available to the reader. Of course, many of the first words children learn are not "regular" in terms of letter-to-sound relationships (*the*, for example), but we don't want children to think that every single word is "decodable" by sounding out the letters. Known words help children begin to notice letter-sound relationships and word parts. Children can write known words quickly, leaving their attention free for problem-solving. They can also use known words to solve a new word. For example:

DAVID *[reading]*: We can play in the *[stops at the word sand]*.

MRS. S: *[David shakes his head. The teacher covers up the first letter.]* You can look for a part of the word that you know.

DAVID: *And!*

MRS. S: Now try it. *[Teacher uncovers the s.]*

DAVID: *S–sand.*

MRS. S: Read it again and see if *sand* makes sense and looks right.

You'll want to work with struggling readers in very specific ways to help them learn and recognize words:

1. Have each student keep a collection of word cards for words they know in a bag or box and add to it constantly.

2. Have children turn over word cards one at a time and read them. Then they place them in two piles: (1) words they know and (2) words they are learning. Ask them to choose one word from "words they are learning" and read it, make it with magnetic letters, and write it. (They can highlight the beginning letter or another part of the word to help them remember it as they write it.)

3. Ask children to lay out their collection of words they know face up in front of them. Play a game: "Find a word that starts with the letter *a*." (You can choose any word feature— a phonogram, letter cluster, vowel, ending). Children find the word, read it, and put it away.

4. Have children lay out a collection of word cards face down in front of them. They turn over a word and read it, leaving it face up. If they do not know a word, they turn it over again. They continue until (with help) all words are face up.

5. Deal out three identical sets of word cards to three children. Two children turn their cards face up in front of them. The third child keeps the cards face down in a stack, draws the top card, and reads it. The other two find the word in their set of cards and the three cards are set aside. This continues until all the words have been matched.

6. Have children choose a word card, make the word left to right with magnetic letters, read the word by running a finger under it, and then check it letter by letter against the word card (*c-c, a-a, n-n*). Then ask them to write the word, read it by running a finger under it, and check it letter by letter against the word card.

7. Have children choose a word card and look at it carefully. Then tell them to put the card face down and try to make the word with magnetic letters (or write it). Then ask them to check the model and make corrections if necessary.

8. Have children take their known words and lay them out face up. Ask them to find two words that are connected in some way (same first letter, same number of letters, same ending, etc.). They then show the words to the rest of the group, who try to guess how the words are connected.

► Early Connections Between Sounds and Letters

Two key principles for children to learn as they begin to acquire literacy are:

❑ *You can hear the sound at the beginning of a word.*

❑ *You can match letters and sounds at the beginning of a word.*

Many of the activities mentioned so far in this chapter will help children learn *the alphabetic principle*—that letters and sounds have systematic relationships. You will also want to teach these relationships directly.

The lesson below focuses children's attention on letter-sound relationships. The teacher can place pictures of a penguin, a horse, a feather, a duck, a kangaroo, a rope, a doll, and a basket down the left side of a pocket chart, with letter cards of the corresponding first letters in scrambled order down the right side. The Alphabet Linking Chart is to the right. (See Figure 10-22.)

MRS. S: I am going to say the words for the pictures on the chart. You say them after me. *[She says the label for each picture and children repeat it.]* You can use the alphabet chart to help you

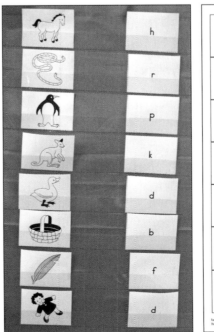
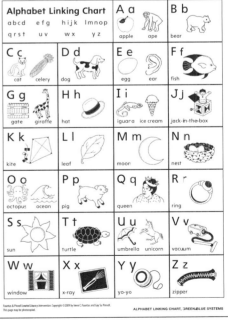

Figure 10-22 Pocket Chart and Alphabet Linking Chart

think of the letter that you would expect to see first at the beginning of each word. Okay, what picture on the alphabet chart has a name that starts with the same sound as *doll*? Dog sounds the same at the beginning. Both start with the letter *d*. *[Places the* d *letter card next to the picture of the doll.]* Now, say the name of this picture, *horse*.

CHILDREN: *Horse.*

MRS. S: Can you see a picture on the alphabet chart that starts like *horse*?

[This continues until all the pictures are matched with the corresponding letters.]

MRS. S: Now let's read all the pictures and letters.

This lesson can be varied as children learn more. For example, you can put letters along the top of the chart, lay out pictures whose labels start with those letters, and have children place them under the corresponding letter. You can also give children their own collections of picture cards and letter cards to match and sort. They can do this kind of activity at home as well, but be sure that the task is easy enough to perform successfully. As they develop more knowledge, they can begin to sort and match pictures and letters by ending sound.

▶ Learning to Connect Letters and Sounds in Sequence

Beginning readers and writers have to make a time/space transformation to understand the relationship between sounds and letters and how they work in sequence in words. The sounds are said in time and the letters are arranged in space. If children have previously learned how to use Elkonin boxes, you can use the boxes to help children make this transformation (see Figure 10-23).

In the first example, the teacher used the boxes to help children move from sound to letters:

MRS. S: You know how to say words slowly and push counters in the boxes. I'm going to do the same thing without the counters. *[She demon-*

strates by saying a few words and simply pointing to the boxes. She then has the children try it.]* Now I am going to say the word slowly and think of the letters I need to write. *Run.*

[She says the word in three segments and writes the r, *the* u, *and the* n.*]* Now let's try it with another word—*mop. [She asks the children to say the word as she points to the boxes.]*

JORDAN: *P.*

MRS. S: There is a *p* and I will write it here. All of you think of how to make a *p* and trace it with your finger on the table. *[She writes the* p *in the last box. The children say the word again to think of more sounds.]* Now I'm going to give you some boxes so that you can write words.

The teacher hands out a sheet with three sets of Elkonin boxes, each set accommodating three sounds. Next she holds up pictures of a fox, a pig, and a pen. Children first say the word, sliding a finger under the boxes, then writing in the letters they can hear. The teacher provides support as needed. After the words have been written in the boxes, the teacher has children read each one, left to right, while running a finger under it and thinking about the sounds.

In this example, the teacher accepted any sound the children could produce and wrote it in the box. After they learned this task well, she began to ask for the sounds in sequence.

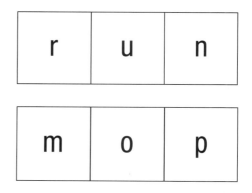

Figure 10-23 Using Elkonin Boxes to Connect Sounds and Letters in Words

In subsequent lessons, the teacher supported children's use of four and five boxes so that children could write longer words: *swim, went, belt,* and *milk.* Later, they will continue to use sound analysis boxes until they can easily identify the letters for the sounds in sequence. She also introduced them to the idea that two letters can stand for one sound, as in *seat* or *duck.* Both of those letters would be placed in a single box, which is also true for consonant digraphs and double letters because they stand for a single phoneme (Figure 10-24). She will also help them see the role of silent letters. Her emphasis will shift from "What can you hear" to "What would you see?"

While the first words children write using Elkonin boxes can be familiar so that they understand the task, they soon need to apply this technique with unfamiliar words. The goal is to give them an approach to spelling new words in their writing and,

in turn, help them use visual information more effectively in reading. Once children understand the tool, you can use these boxes on a whiteboard or piece of chart paper during interactive writing or on a practice space in independent writing. This will demonstrate to children how a writer stops to think about how to spell a word.

▶ Learning How Print Works

Children can learn a great deal about sounds, letters, and words and still have difficulty effectively processing continuous print. They do need this "item knowledge," but you must also help them apply it to actual reading and writing.

Locating a Word in a Text

It is beneficial for children to look through a text and locate specific words. The real challenge to the beginning reader is not to memorize a word in isolation but to read it within continuous text while keeping the meaning of the text in mind. Locating *both known and unknown* words will help them develop this ability.

Locating a word is a complex operation. Locating a known word means that the children can look for any part of the word they recognize. It is helpful to notice any word feature but ultimately they must be able to work left to right across words. To locate unknown words, readers systematically analyze sounds and connect them to letters. To locate a word, children must think about:

- ❑ How the word sounds at the beginning.
- ❑ The letter that is connected to the sound.
- ❑ How that letter looks.

Locating known words helps children recognize the word rapidly and without a great deal of effort while reading. Locating unknown words helps them think about and predict the beginning letter and remember other visual details about a word.

While introducing a text, you can ask the child to locate one or two known words and/or one or two

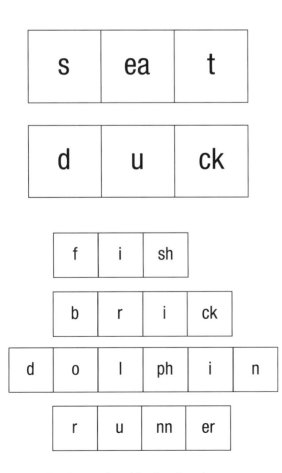

Figure 10-24 Two Letters Stand for One Sound

new words that are important to reading and understanding the text. For example:

> Say *see.* [Children respond.] What letter would you expect to see at the beginning of *see?* [Children respond.] Find *see* and put your finger under it.

Or, to help children recognize high-frequency words:

> You know the word *the.* Think how it looks. [Tell them the first two letters or show a model on the whiteboard if you think they need it.] Find *the* on this page and put your finger under it. [Children respond.] Turn the page and find *the* on the next page and put your finger under it. [Notice how quickly children can locate the word.]

Using Shared Reading to Promote Close Attention to Print

Shared reading is a way to demonstrate to children how print works. All the early reading behaviors can be taught through the powerful demonstration of shared reading of a common text. Examine the layout of an engaging text for shared reading (Figure 10-25). Review the example of a teacher helping children understand some of the important early reading behaviors during shared reading (Figure 10-26). (In this example, the teacher used specific language to teach for, prompt for, and reinforce the concept of matching voice to print.

Using Independent Reading to Support Early Reading Behaviors

Asking beginning readers to start reading for themselves helps establish early reading behaviors. You do not need to wait until children "know all their letters and sounds" or "know a lot of words." Beginning to read very simple texts, such as *Mom* (see Figure 10-27), will give them the opportunity to sort out confusions, especially when accompanied by strong teaching. Notice how the teacher is teaching for, prompting, for, and reinforcing early reading behaviors (Figure 10-28).

Ardis was just learning how to match voice to print. She used her pointing finger but tended to place her finger squarely on top of the words, effectively blocking her view of the print. This is evidence that Ardis did not fully realize that she needed to look at the *letters* in the words. Her memorization of a simple pattern and her use of pictures and finger pointing allowed her to "read" the easy text. But this behavior did not take her far! The teacher demonstrated and prompted her to point under each word. Ardis was then able to sustain this pointing behavior throughout the rest of the text. On page 8, she immediately appealed when she saw the word *swimming,* and the teacher prompted her to use the first letter and also the picture, finally telling her the word. On page 10, Ardis substituted *running* for *riding,* and the teacher prompted her to cross-check using meaning and visual information. This time, Ardis made the correction successfully. She also corrected her pointing on page 16 by matching voice to print. Ardis was beginning to learn about words with two syllables.

Using Shared and Interactive Writing to Promote Close Attention to Print

Group writing is a powerful way to help children attend closely to print and develop understanding of early reading behaviors (see Chapter 13). In shared and interactive writing, you "share the task" with children. When you are doing the scribing on the easel, you involve the children by talking. When you invite individual children to come to the easel to add a letter or word, some punctuation, or reserve space between words, the writing is interactive. Through group writing, children have the opportunity to understand the "code" of print, including:

- ❑ Difference between print and pictures.
- ❑ How pictures and print are connected.
- ❑ Left-to-right directional movement along a line of text.
- ❑ Returning to the left to start a new line of text.
- ❑ Letters—their shape and formation.
- ❑ Relationship of letters and sounds in writing words.

FIGURE 10-25 Page Layout of *Frog Food* from Leveled Literacy Intervention, Green System (Heinemann 2009)

Figure 10-26 Shared Reading of *Frog Food* (Level A)

Speaker	Interaction	What the *Teacher Is Attending to*
Ms. G	Let's read *Frog Food* again. Do you remember Froggy and what he likes to eat?	*Prompts access to background information.*
Jared	He likes bugs on everything!	
Ms. G	Yes, he does. I am going to read this book to you. Look how I point and read. [*Reads the book using a pointer.*] What did you notice?	*Demonstrates matching voice to print, using left-to-right directionality, and making the return sweep.*
Karin	You pointed under each word.	
Ms. G	I made it match, because every time I read a word out loud, I pointed to a word. Now, let's all read it.	*Explicitly describes matching voice to print.*
	[*They read the text together as the teacher points under each word left to right.*]	
Ms. G	You made it match!	*Reinforces matching voice to print.*
Ms. G	I am now going to give you your own copy of *Frog Food*. Here it is. Read it with your finger. Put your finger under each word just like I did.	*Prompts children to match voice to print.*
Michelle	This is Froggy.	
Ms. G	You found Froggy in your book! Now read it with your finger.	*Prompts and reinforces matching voice to print (points under words).*
	Children read as the teacher prompts individuals: • Read this page with your finger. • Don't cover up the words with your finger. • Try again with your finger. • You made it match. • You pointed under each word.	
Ms. G	That was a funny story, wasn't it?	*Asks for comment.*
	[*The children have a brief discussion of the weird food that Froggy likes.*]	
Ms. G	Aiden pointed under each word. On this page *(indicates page 2 on the enlarged copy of the text)* he read *I like bugs on my . . .* and then he stopped because he ran out of words. He needed to read *pancake*. So he went back and made it match, *I like bugs on pancakes.* If you have too many words, just go back and make it match. Let's all find that page and read it again.	*Demonstrates how to monitor reading by matching voice to print.*
	[*The children read page 2.*]	
Ms. G	You had just enough words. You made it match	*Reinforces monitoring reading by matching voice to print.*

❑ Upper- and lowercase letters.

❑ Letters in clusters (forming a word).

❑ Punctuation.

❑ Spacing between words and between lines.

❑ Arrangement of text on a page, left to right, top to bottom, in paragraphs continuing over successive pages.

While helping children construct text as a group, you can use very specific language, including terms like *letter, word, period, sentence, capital, letter,* and *space.* Children can carry this language over to other literacy learning contexts, such as independent writing. As they reread their group-created pieces, they engage in early reading behaviors. Because it is a text that they have composed and helped to commit to paper, there is a powerful sense of ownership and motivation. Often, the interactive text they produce and read is more complex than the books they are able to read independently.

Extending children's understanding of texts through interactive writing also helps them summarize and represent the important ideas. The interactive writing in the following example is based on *The Hat* (see Figures 10-29, text in Figure 5-3). The interactive writing is shown in Figure 10-30.

The teacher made a quick sketch of the hat to remind the three children in the group of the story. The children decided to write about the bear, the fox, and the ant. They wrote the first sentence, with Justin writing *the* and Lucy contributing the *b* and *r* for *bear.* Wade wrote the *w* for *went* and the teacher finished the word. Then Wade wrote *the,* with the teacher pointing out that the first *The* in the sentence had an uppercase *T* and this word was *the* with a lowercase *t.* The teacher used Elkonin boxes (on a small whiteboard) to have children generate the spelling of *hat,* and Lucy wrote the word at the end of the sentence and placed a period there.

Once the first sentence was written, the next two went quickly. The teacher used Elkonin boxes to spell *fox, ant,* and *pop.* She chose to quickly write all the words in the rest of the sentences herself; however, each time a word was added, the group reread

the sentence up to the next word. The teacher quickly revisited the text after writing it, locating *the* several times; noticing the upper- and lowercase letters at the beginning of *the*; locating *went* several times, after saying the word and predicting the first letter; and reading the entire message while pointing under each word.

Throughout the writing, children had the opportunity to attend to letters and associate them with sounds, notice the spaces between words, and read left to right while matching voice to print. The teacher prompted using language like:

❑ *Find a word that begins with an uppercase letter.*

❑ *Find a place where we used good spacing to divide the words.*

❑ *Find the word* the.

❑ *Say* went. *What letter would you expect to see at the beginning of* went? *Find* went.

❑ *Find a word that begins with the letter* p.

Using Dictated Writing to Support Early Reading Behaviors

Dictated writing also provides powerful support, especially for readers who are having difficulty with reading, writing, and phonics. When you dictate a sentence, you can select the exact words you want to use, and you can use the same kind of prompts you use in independent writing and shared/interactive writing. Here's how it works. You read a sentence aloud and the children write it with your support:

❑ Some of the words are known.

❑ You help children solve unknown words in several ways (using Elkonin boxes, using sound analysis or visual analysis, or thinking of words they know that are like the word they want to write). You may also write the word on a whiteboard so that children can check their attempt and correct it or simply copy the word.

❑ Children reread their sentences when finished and may draw a picture if there is time.

❑ You may have them highlight words or word parts of interest.

Figure 10-27 Cover of *Mom* from Leveled Literacy Intervention, Orange System (Heinemann 2009)

Figure 10-28 Ardis's Independent Reading of *Mom*

Reading Behavior	Teacher Prompts	Teaching Points
✓ ✓ ✓ **Mom is walking.** *Covers words with finger while reading.* *Reads again, moving finger under each word.* **2**	• When I read, I put my finger under each word. *[Reads.]* "Mom is walking." Now you read it with your finger. • Was your finger under the word? • Try it again and put your finger under each word.	• Demonstrates voice-print match and left to right directionality. • Prompts Ardis to match voice to print.
✓ ✓ ✓ **Mom is reading.** **4**	• You read it with your finger and made it match.	• Reinforces voice-print match.
✓ ✓ ✓ **Mom is jumping.** *Reads* jump, *then points to white space to read the second syllable.* *Rereads, pointing accurately.* **6**	• Did you have enough words? (*Demonstrates reading, leaving the finger under* jumping *for both syllables.*)	• Prompts Ardis to monitor her reading using voice-print match.
✓ ✓ A| **Mom is swimming.**|T *Appeals and is told the word.* **8**	• Can the picture help you think about this part of the story? • Would *swimming* make sense? Check the first part of the word *-s*.	• Prompts Ardis to use meaning. • Tells the word within a prompt to use meaning.
✓ ✓ running |SC **Mom is riding.** | *Substituted* running *for* riding *and self-corrected the error.* **10**	• Do you know a word that would make sense and start like that? • You made it look right and make sense.	• Prompts Ardis to cross-check meaning and visual information. • Reinforces cross-checking meaning with visual information.
✓ ✓ ✓ **Mom is shopping.** *Repeat to confirm.* **12**		• Observes correct responding
✓ ✓ ✓R **Mom is eating.** **14**		• Observes repetition to confirm
✓ ✓ ✓ RSC **Mom is hugging me.** **16**	• Try that again and make it match.	• Prompts Ardis to correct her reading by matching voice to print.
	• You made it match.	• Reinforces voice-print match.

Figure 10-29 Cover of *The Hat* from Leveled Literacy Intervention, Orange System (Heinemann 2009)

The bear Went in the hat.
The fox went in the hat.
The ant went in the hat.

Pop!

Figure 10-30 Interactive Writing in Response to *The Hat*

MOM IS EATING.

Mom is riding.

Mom is eating.

Figure 10-31 Dictated Writing in Response to *Mom*

Dictated writing in response to *Mom* is shown for Denise and Terry in Figure 10-31. The teacher assisted a small group of children to write the two sentences. You can see some differences in the use of capital and lowercase letters, but the spelling is conventional, and all children can reread their work. Through dictated writing, children learn how to transform oral language into written language, solve words within a meaningful sentence, and reread and check their work.

Using Independent Writing to Support Early Reading Behaviors

Children learn a great deal about letters, sounds, and how print works when they attempt their own writing. A very effective way to build a bridge between reading and spelling is to have children invent more complete spellings of words. Typically, kindergartners who know some letter names and sounds spell words using just the letters for the more prominent sounds in words, such as beginning and ending sounds. For example, they'll write *B* for *beaver* or *R* for *arm*. Although these spellings are not conventional, they indicate that these children can distinguish sounds in words. Once children can do this, you can help them detect additional sounds in words and learn conventional spellings for those sounds (National Reading Panel, 2000, 2-39).

Children who are having difficulty learning about print need classroom opportunities to write every day. But they do not need to write every word correctly (a practice that stifles young writers and makes them dependent on the teacher). Attempting spelling has more instructional value than copying. When children are working independently, encourage them to use every resource at their disposal and to attempt words. Teach them how to say words slowly and represent the sounds (perhaps using Elkonin boxes).

Working closely with an intervention group or an individual child, you can provide the support children need to spell conventionally. The children produce everything they can as they work to hear the sounds and represent them. You judiciously fill in the rest, and the text becomes one the children can read.

Jayden wrote a sentence in response to the book *At the Zoo* (Figure 10-32). His sentence is shown in Figure 10-33. As he wrote the sentence,

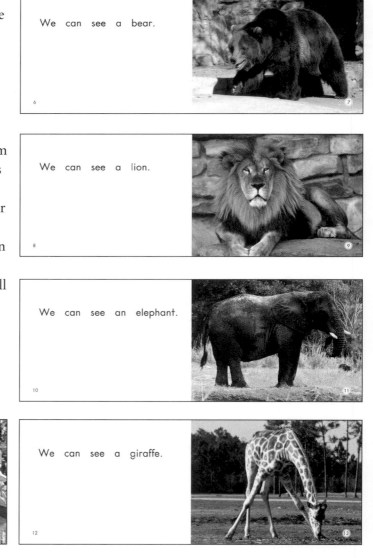

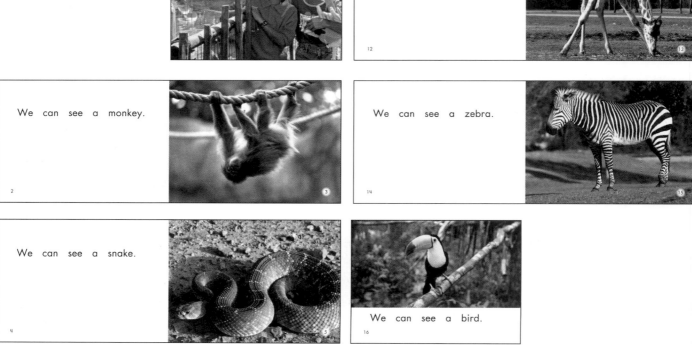

FIGURE 10-32 Page Layout of *At the Zoo* from Leveled Literacy Intervention, Orange System (Heinemann 2009)

he was able to reflect on one of the parts of the story. He also paid attention to spacing. When he wrote *can* too close after *we*, this interchange occurred:

> **Mr. K:** Leave some space before you start the next word. I'll cover the *c* with tape. *[Jayden places his finger after* we *and looks carefully at the spot where he will start* can.*]* You can feel the space with your finger. Say the word *can*. What can you hear?

> **Jayden:** C. *[He writes the* c *and then says the word again, emphasizing* /n/.*]*

> **Mr. K:** There is an *a* after *c*. I'll write it in. Now you write the *n*. *Can*. Leave some space before you start the next word.

> *Jayden now leaves good spaces between words. He writes the* s *and final* e *in* see. *The teacher writes the article* a *and the* e *and a in* bear. *Jayden produces the* b *and* r, *and draws a picture.*

> **Mr. K:** Look at all the good spaces. Show a place where you left a good space.

This supportive teaching helps Jayden produce a text he can revisit. He has created his own model for defining words with spaces. Every time he rereads the message, he can use voice-print matching.

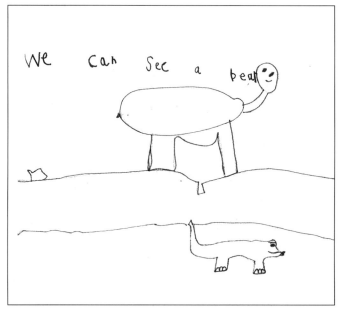

Figure 10-33 Independent Writing in Response to *At the Zoo*

Using a Cut-Up Sentence to Support Early Reading and Writing Behaviors

Often you will want to take one further step to bridge reading and writing as you work to help children develop early literacy behaviors. The cut-up sentence can be extremely helpful to beginners, especially those who find literacy learning challenging.

The teacher who helped the three students with their earlier interactive writing in response to *The Hat* created the sentence strips shown in Figure 10-34. She cut the sentences apart word by word and gave each child a sentence, mixed up the words (making sure they remained right side up), and had the children put the sentences back together. While they worked, she offered help and support. She also wrote each sentence quickly on an envelope. After assembling and checking their sentences, each child put the sentence in the envelope to take home and put together again.

Putting together a cut-up sentence involves:

- ❑ Remembering the sentence and its meaning.
- ❑ Remembering and using the language structure.
- ❑ Putting the sentence together left to right, word by word.
- ❑ Visually searching for the next word (thinking about letter-sound relationships).
- ❑ Rereading to check.
- ❑ Checking with the model (on the chart).
- ❑ Using voice-print match throughout the process.

The	bear	went	in	the	hat.
The	fox	went	in	the	hat.
The	ant	went	in	the	hat.

Figure 10-34 Cut-Up Sentences for *The Hat*

► Early Writing Strategies

At the same time you use writing to help children develop knowledge of print and learn about letters and sounds, you want to help children write to express their own meanings. Emergent writers need to be able to use writing strategies to go from their ideas to written messages.

There are a wealth of opportunities for helping your writers attend to early strategies for turning their thoughts into written words. The potential for learning is much more than getting the symbols down for others to read. It includes thinking about many different aspects of the writing process—purpose, form, language, message and craft.

For now, let's focus only on moving from the writer's thinking to getting the message down on the page. Children who are having difficulty acquiring early reading and writing behaviors can benefit from *daily* opportunities to write messages with explicit

---

Figure 10-35 **Teaching for Early Writing Strategies**

1. Writers use language to compose a message.
2. Writers hear the individual words in a sentence.
3. Writers use white space to show readers each word in the sentence.
4. Writers place letters and words on a page to show the kind of writing (e.g., list, letter, story).
5. Writers say words slowly to hear each sound.
6. Writers listen for the order of the sounds in each word.
7. Writers think about the letter or letters that represent each sound.
8. Writers think about what the letter that represents each sound looks like.
9. Writers use what they know about how the letters look to make their forms on paper.
10. Writers can write some words they know quickly to produce the message.
11. Writers use what they know about words to write new words.
12. Writers have a variety of ways to construct words.

---

instruction. As a teacher of writing, you help young children learn "how to write" by engaging them in doing what writers do (Figure 10-35). Using interactive writing, you create temporary scaffolds that allow children to participate in the early writing process with you so they can then apply what they learned as they work independently. As you "share the pen" with your students, they will learn the following strategies:

1. *Writers use language to compose a message.* Young writers formulate thoughts about a topic and make a decision about the message they want to convey. They put their thoughts into language by putting words together, or "composing" the message. As a teacher you help small groups or individuals compose, help them put together the purpose and decide on the form of the writing, and guide them to string words together in acceptable English structures that they, as readers, understand.

2. *Writers hear the individual words in a sentence.* Young children have developed an oral language system. As they talk, they produce a speech stream, putting their words together in a way in which space between each word is not evident. To begin to think about segmenting the speech stream into individual words, children need to first hear the boundaries of each word. Sentences like "I like pizza" become three separate sound units rather than one continuous stream of sound.

3. *Writers use white space to show readers each word in the sentence.* Once children are able to listen for the individual words that make up a sentence, show them how to place each cluster of symbols on the page so there is some white space between each word. Readers know where a word starts and ends because of white space on each side.

4. *Writers place letters and words on a page to show the kind of writing (e.g., list, letter, story).* Writers use space on the page in different ways. Stories are usually written in paragraphs with continuous sentences. The print for a list is positioned with one word or phrase under the previous one. A letter has an opening greeting, sentences below it, and a closing phrase at the end. Show young writers how to think about where they

will place the print so readers will understand if it is a list, letter, or story.

5. *Writers say words slowly to hear each sound.* To be able to record the symbols as writers, young children need to be able to listen for the sounds in words. To hear them, children first learn to slow speech down. The word *make* becomes *m-a-k,* as children say the word very slowly to hear each of the three sounds. You may want to have children watch your mouth as you say the word slowly and then have them say it slowly with you. The final step is for the children to say the word independently. When children say a word slowly, they can listen for the individual sounds, or *phonemes.* They can take the sounds they hear and connect them to the letters that represent them. You will want to be sure children can say the words slowly for themselves so they can then listen for each sound when they are working alone.

6. *Writers listen for the order of the sounds in each word.* As children say words slowly and listen for the individual sounds, they need to learn how to notice the order of the sounds in words. Each word is made up of a precise sequence of sounds. Some are easy to identify and connect to letters and others are more difficult.

7. *Writers think about the letter or letters that represent each sound.* As children listen for the sounds, they begin to think about how to represent the sounds with symbols. For some sounds there is one letter and for others there are several. For example, *make* has four letters and three sounds, *ate* has three letters and two sounds, and *eight* has five letters and two sounds.

8. *Writers think about what the letter looks like.* Once children know the sounds they want to write and the letters that represent them, they think about the written symbol and its features. For example /b/ is represented by a symbol that looks like a tall stick and a circle attached.

9. *Writers use what they know about how the letters look to make their forms on paper.* When children are able to perceive the letter form, they can then use their motor skills to construct it.

They may know what a *b* looks like, and now they need to form it efficiently. Sometimes you will want to use language that temporarily helps children with the motions (for example, "pull down, up, and around" for the letter *b*).

10. *Writers write some words they know quickly to produce the message.* Some words occur frequently in the language (e.g., *the, to, we*). Since there are some words that children will use frequently in their writing, teach them to write the words quickly, from beginning to end. Then they will be able to slow down and attend to the words that are new. They can also use what they know about these high-frequency words to help them write other words.

11. *Writers use what they know about words to write new words.* There are over 600,000 words in the English language and children could never learn them one by one. They need to learn words and then use what they know about these words to help them learn new words. For example, if children want to write *stay* and know the word *stop* and the word *day,* they can use the word parts they know. They can think, "It starts like *stop* and ends like *day—stay.*" They develop a network of knowledge about words that expands as they apply known principles to new words.

12. *Writers have a variety of ways to construct words.* Writers rely not only on sounds to construct words but also on their knowledge of letter patterns and what they know about other words. With a strategic approach, they can construct hundreds of new words. Over time, you will no longer need to create scaffolds for any of these strategies, because your writers will be in control. They will be able to get their thinking down on paper, attending to the many aspects of the writing process.

The understandings listed above are basic to the development of a writing process that will move toward achieving voice, writing in different genres, selecting interesting words, communicating about important experiences and topics, and using the conventions of written language. Early writing is critical to the process.

▶ Reciprocity of Writing and Reading in Establishing Early Understandings

Throughout this chapter, we have discussed some of the critical early understandings that emerge as very young children interact with print. It was essential to discuss both writing and reading because participating in one process fuels learning in both areas. Kindergarten classrooms that are alive with purposeful talk, drawing, reading, and writing draw children naturally into the world of print. We do not advocate boring drill or tedious copying exercises. But children will delight in hearing simple stories and beginning to read them with pointing. They will feel satisfaction at seeing their own words represented by print—either in group writing or working on their own.

In their reading and writing, young children will demonstrate a great deal of approximation as they gain control of the complex range of concepts. And, some may become confused, especially if the instruction is pitched at a level that is too complex for them to follow. Small group instruction that provides clear demonstrations and an opportunity to try out reading and writing with support can clear up these confusions and prevent later difficulties. We recommend that kindergarten children (especially those who are inexperienced or confused) read many easy books at Levels A, B, and C to establish a strong foundation of letter and word knowledge and early reading behaviors. Likewise, they should have daily opportunities to work with letters in a concrete way and to form letters as part of writing. Enjoyable participation in literacy, with success, will be the best preparation for the challenges of later grades.

▶ Suggestions for Professional Development

CONNECTING EARLY WRITING AND READING BEHAVIORS

1. Gather a group of grade level and across-level colleagues who are teaching kindergarten or grade 1 children.

2. Use the writing samples you collected in the last professional development session (Chapter 9).

3. Write the name of each child at the top of a column on chart paper and number 1 to 12 along the left side. Using Figure 10-35, make notes about what each child controls in early writing strategies.

4. Repeat the process for several samples and discuss your insights. Talk about what the child needs to learn how to control as a writer.

5. Refer to the *Fountas and Pinnell Prompting Guide 1*, Early Writing Behaviors. Select language you would use with each child to support their development or early writing strategies.

6. Then discuss the reading levels for each child and how this evidence informs what the child can do as a reader in terms of early reading behaviors.

Learning to Solve Words: Effective and Efficient Phonics

IT IS OBVIOUS THAT READERS MUST BE ABLE to take apart words and parse sentences into grammatical units while keeping their attention on the meaning of a text. Reading and writing require proficiency in many categories of phonics learning; any of them can create gaps for children who are struggling in becoming literate. In this chapter, we focus on phonics, the relationships between individual letters, letter clusters and sounds; spelling patterns, the simple to complex larger patterns we can see in words; and word structure, the ways words are put together with base words and affixes. These three areas, in combination, account for the way skillful readers and writers break down words. The operations related to word solving must be rapid and largely unconscious so that the reader can maintain attention to the meaning of a text.

*Learn to look
then
look to learn*

Learning the connections between sounds and letters in an alphabetic system is a long and complex process. The meanings of a language are delivered in oral language which is in turn represented by written language. Of course, literate people move directly from thinking to writing and from print to thought without voicing the language, but the link is always there. The relationships among meaning, sound, and written language are more complex than sound-to-letter correspondence. As readers, we recognize the structural components of words (*-er,* for example) that tell the function of the word in the sentence. We parse sentences into separate words as we read, but at the same time we note grammatical relationships among phrases and clauses and, from these, deduce the meaning of the sentence.

Readers need to be able to take apart words and parse sentences into grammatical units, while simultaneously keeping their attention on meaning. Take a look at this quotation:

> I could not help laughing at the resemblance, and mentioning it to my friend. He broke, as was his wont, into a fond eulogium of his sire, wished he could be like him—worked himself up into another state of excitement, in which he averred that, if his father wanted him to marry, he would marry that instant. "And why not Rosey? She is a dear little thing. Or why not that splendid Miss Sherrick? What a head!—a regular Titian! I was looking at the difference of their colour at Uncle Honeyman's that day of the *dejeuner.*"
>
> —Reissue of William Makepeace Thackery's *The Newcomes: Memoirs of a Most Respectable Family.* Published in parts October, 1852, to August, 1855. Edited by Arthur Pendennis Esq. This volume edited by D.J. Taylor. London: Everyman' Library, 1994. P. 241.

As a proficient reader, your mind focuses on the attitude of the young man speaking, even though this passage demands advanced decoding skills. You have to process some syllables with regular sound patterns as well as affixes. At the same time, you must access background knowledge (Titian) and possibly some knowledge of French (*dejeuner*). The reader must be able to process print with just this kind of efficiency in order to have enough attention remaining to think about the meaning. That means that readers must constantly develop a flexible range of word-solving strategies, and for that they need instruction in phonics.

Phonics is an instructional approach designed to help children understand the simple and complex relationships between sounds and letters in words. Explicit and systematic phonics instruction is a necessary and important component of an effective reading program and certainly of an intervention program. It is neither the only component nor the most important, but it is essential. As students learn more about the complexity of language, we refer to *word study* to

indicate that the understandings readers and writers need go beyond sound to letter relationships.

We have identified nine areas of learning in the process of developing efficient systems for word solving (see Figure 11-1). Reading and writing require proficiency in all these areas; any of them can create gaps for children who are struggling in becoming literate.

We have explored several of these areas in other chapters. The linguistic base for reading and writing is described in Chapter 7, and the area of vocabulary development in Chapter 8. A limited oral vocabulary will make even simple texts harder, because the reader is trying to learn the meaning of new words while at the same time building a reading process. We discuss phonological awareness and phonemic awareness instruction in Chapter 9. Children who cannot hear the sounds in words lack an important foundation for other learning. We address the area of early reading behaviors in Chapter 10. Children who are not oriented to print and do not know how it "works" are likely to become confused in early instruction that assumes they have established directionality and other early concepts. By the time they become oriented to print, instruction has moved on to more complex phonics, and they become more confused.

In this chapter, we focus on three areas of learning: (1) phonics, or letter-sound relationships; (2) spelling patterns; and (3) word structure. These three areas, in combination, account for the way skillful readers and writers take words apart. Readers and writers know the simple and more complex ways that sounds are represented by letters and letter clusters within words. The process of relating sounds to letters must be rapid and largely unconscious so that the reader can focus on meaning. Readers who have only partial (or very simplistic) understanding of letter-sound relationships will laboriously try to "sound out" words letter by letter or use only part of the word (the first letter, for example) and end up making a guess that may have little relationship to the meaning and does not take into account the precise sequence of letters in a word.

Efficient readers learn to use the spelling patterns in words. One way to look at word patterns is to

Figure 11-1 Developing Word-Solving Systems: Nine Areas of Learning

Early Literacy Concepts	Early literacy concepts include understandings such as knowing to read from left to right and matching voice to print. Many children enter kindergarten with good knowledge of early literacy concepts. If they do not, explicit and systematic instruction can help them become oriented quickly. While most of these early literacy concepts are not "phonics," they are basic to the child's understanding of print and should be mastered early.
Phonological Awareness	A key to becoming literate is the ability to hear the sounds in words. Hearing individual sounds allows the learner to connect sounds and letters. A general response to language is called phonological awareness. As children become more aware of language, they notice sounds in a more detailed way. Phonemic awareness involves recognizing the individual sounds in words and eventually being able to identify, isolate, and manipulate them. Children who can hear sounds in words have an advantage in that they can connect them with letters.
Letter Knowledge	Letter knowledge refers to what children need to learn about the graphic characters— how they look, how to distinguish one from another, how to detect them within continuous text, how to use them in words. A finite set of twenty-six letters, two forms of each, is related to all the sounds of the English language (approximately forty-four phonemes). The sounds in the language change as dialect, articulation, and other speech factors vary. Children will also encounter alternative forms of some letters—*a* and **ɑ**, for example—and will eventually learn to recognize letters in cursive writing. Children need to learn the names and purposes of letters, as well as the distinguishing features (the small differences that help you separate a *d* from an **ɑ**, for example). When children can identify letters, they can associate them with sounds, and the alphabetic principle is mastered.
Letter-Sound Relationships (Phonics)	The sounds of oral language are related in both simple and complex ways to the twenty-six letters of the alphabet. Learning the connections between letters and sounds is basic to understanding written language. Children tend to learn the "regular" connections between letters and sounds (*b* for the first sound in *bat*) first. But they also must learn that often letters appear together; for example, it is efficient to think of the two sounds at the beginning of *black* together. Sometimes a sound like */sh/* is connected to two letters; sometimes a cluster of letters is connected to one sound, for example */a/* for *eigh*. Children learn to look for and recognize these letter combinations as units, which makes their word solving more efficient.
Spelling Patterns	Efficient word solvers look for and find patterns in the way words are constructed. Knowing spelling patterns helps children notice and use larger parts of words, thus making word solving faster and easier. Patterns are also helpful to children in writing words, because they can quickly write down the patterns rather than laboriously working with individual sounds and letters.

Figure 11-1 Developing Word-Solving Systems: Nine Areas of Learning, *continued*

High-Frequency Words	A core of high-frequency words is a valuable resource as children build their reading and writing processing systems. We can also call them "high utility" words because they appear often and can sometimes be used to help solve other words. Making recognition of high-frequency words automatic frees the attention to understand meaning as well as solve other new words. In general, children learn the simpler words and in the process develop efficient systems for learning more words; the process accelerates. They continuously add to the core of high-frequency words they know. Lessons on high-frequency words can develop automaticity and help children look more carefully at the features of words.
Word Meaning Vocabulary	Vocabulary refers to the words one knows as part of language. For comprehension and coherence, students need to know the meaning of the words in the texts they read and write. It is important for them constantly to expand their listening, speaking, reading, and writing vocabularies and to develop more complex understanding of words they already know (for example, words may have multiple meanings or be used figuratively).
Word Structure	Words are built in rule-governed ways. Looking at the structure of words will help students learn how words are related to one another and how they can be changed by adding letters, letter clusters, and larger word parts. Readers who can break down words into syllables and can notice categories of word parts can apply their word-solving strategies efficiently.
Word-Solving Actions	Word solving is related to all the categories of learning previously described; but we have also created a separate category for it that focuses on the strategic moves readers and writers make when they use their knowledge of the language system while reading and writing continuous text. These strategies are "in-the-head" actions that are invisible, although we can often infer them from overt behaviors.

examine the way simple words and syllables are put together. In the consonant-vowel-consonant (CVC) pattern, the vowel is usually a short (terse) sound, as in *tap*, for example. In the consonant-vowel-consonant-silent *e* (CVCe) pattern, the vowel usually has a long (lax) sound. Many of these patterns in words occur over and over again. But readers will struggle if they work on words only as strings of letters. They must learn to make connections between words rather than see each as an isolated unit to be memorized.

Phonograms are spelling patterns that represent the sounds of *rimes* (parts of words or syllables within words that begin with a vowel). Words connected by rimes are sometimes called "word families." Some examples are *-at, -am, -ot.* When you add the *onset*

(first part of the word or syllable) to a phonogram like *-ot,* you can make *pot, plot,* or *slot.* A word like *ransom* has two onsets (*r-* and *s-*) and two rimes *-an* and *-om*). Young readers do not need to learn every phonogram as a separate item. Once children understand that there are patterns in one-syllable words and learn how to look for them, they will quickly discover more for themselves. Poor readers, on the other hand, may not be pattern seekers.

Efficient readers and writers are familiar with the way words are put together. Looking at the parts not only provides useful information for decoding but also provides clues to the meaning of words. Affixes are parts added before or after a word to change its function and meaning. An affix can be a prefix or a suffix. A *base word* is a complete word; a *root word* is the part that may have Greek or Latin origins (such as *ped* in *pedal*). It will not be necessary for young children to make this distinction when they are beginning to learn about simple affixes, but noticing these word parts will help children read and understand words as well as spell them correctly. Word parts that are added to base words signal meaning. For example, they may signal relationships (*tall, taller, tallest*) or chronology (*working, worked*). Principles related to word structure include understanding the meaning and structure of compound words, contractions, plurals, and possessives.

When helping children learn about phonics, spelling patterns, and word structure, we should not forget that the most important area of learning is the ability to apply word knowledge "on the run" while reading and writing continuous text. We call this learning area "word-solving actions." This chapter presents examples of word-solving actions with information on how to demonstrate and prompt for word solving at the end (also see Chapter 14).

▶ Change in Word-Solving Actions Over Time

Word solvers develop increasing proficiency over time as they encounter more demanding words in increasingly complex texts. This progression from print awareness to the ability to solve complex words is represented graphically in Figure 11-2. A key word in the path of learning is flexibility. Poor readers are rigid, applying one or two techniques over and over again even when they do not work. Proficient readers have a repertoire of ways to solve words, and they apply them in the most efficient way possible.

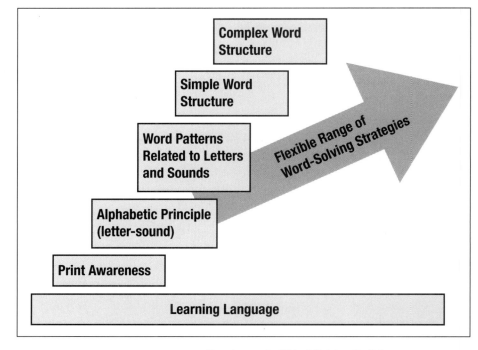

Figure 11-2 Development of Word-Solving Proficiency

Let's look at the development over time of Aiden, a flexible word solver. The composite in Figure 11-3, drawn from his readings of increasingly challenging texts, shows the growth of his word-solving ability. The checkmarks above the word show accurate reading. When the child reads a word different from the word in the text, it is written above the word. The letters SC mean the child corrected the word himself.

Here we focus on word solving in terms of using letters, sounds, and parts of words, but over and above this, readers are always:

❑ Predicting words using the meaning of the text and language structure.

❑ Checking on the accuracy of words using meaning and language structure.

❑ Searching for and using more information to make all sources of information fit (letters and sounds, word inflections, meaning, language structure).

When proficient readers process texts, they are not solving words in isolation. They use all the information available to them in continuous print. Ultimately, they must be able to take words apart, even in isolation, but using all the information from sentence

Figure 11-3 Aiden as a Word Solver at Nine Points in Time

Entry to Kindergarten	✓ <u>am</u> – <u>reading</u> – – I like to read at school. ✓ <u>am</u> – <u>writing</u> <u>something</u> – I like to write at school.	• Uses language patterns with little attention to print. • Uses a known high-frequency word.
Early Grade 1 **Level B**	✓ ✓ <u>w·w·</u>✓ The lion went ✓ ✓ <u>road</u> down the path. ✓ ✓ ✓ The tiger went ✓ ✓ <u>ro</u>|<u>sc</u> down the path. <del>the</del>|sc ✓R ✓ A monkey went ✓ ✓ ✓ down the path.	• Uses some known high-frequency words. • Self-corrects using high-frequency words. • Uses first letter and related sound. • Uses voice-print match to monitor accuracy. • Recognizes visual signposts. • Self-corrects using visual information.
Mid Grade 1 **Level E**	✓ <u>b·ar·</u>✓ <u>a·a·</u>✓ Taco barked again. ✓ ✓ ✓ ✓ He barked and barked ✓ ✓ ✓ ✓ ✓ at the big red thing. ✓ ✓ <u>n·no</u>|<u>nose</u>|A| <u>did not</u>|sc <u>st·op</u>✓ But the <del>noise</del> T didn't stop.	• Recognizes and uses some known words. • Uses first letters. • Notices and uses word parts. • Makes attempt using first letters before appealing. • Self-monitors using visual information. • Notices and uses consonant clusters to solve words. • Uses onsets and rimes. • Works through visual information until he needs help.

continues

Figure 11-3 Aiden as a Word Solver at Nine Points in Time, *continued*

End Grade 1 Level I		

End Grade 1

Level I

✓ ✓ War.✓ sunny|sc ✓
On a warm summer day

✓ ✓ ✓ ✓ s·o·ng ✓ ✓
you can hear the sound of bees

✓ ✓ ✓
in the garden.

✓ ✓ ✓
Buzz buzz buzz

✓ ✓ ✓
Little honeybees fly

and|sc ✓ ✓ R
around the flowers.

✓ ✓ ✓ work.✓
These bees are working!

- Notices and uses consonant clusters at the beginning of words.
- Notices and uses first letters.
- Goes beyond the first letter in some instances.
- Notices and uses word parts.
- Self-corrects using visual information.
- Notices and uses vowel digraphs that make other sounds.
- Uses word endings.
- Recognizes many words rapidly and automatically.

End Grade 2

Level N

✓ th|through|sc ✓ ✓ ✓ ✓
Chester thought and thought. He needed

✓ ✓ ✓ ✓ ✓ ✓ ✓ ✓
to put something warm over his ears. A scarf

✓ ✓ ✓ ✓ ✓ ✓
was too itchy. What could he use?

✓ ✓ ✓ ✓ ✓ ✓
Then he had an idea. Socks!

✓ ✓ ✓ ✓ ✓ ✓ ✓
He found two socks. Next, he got some

Wire|sc ✓ ✓ ✓ throw|sc ✓ ✓ ✓ ✓
wire and put it through the socks. Then he

tired|sc ✓ ✓ in·ven·✓R ✓ ✓ ✓ ✓
tried on his invention. His ears felt warm.

- Recognizes many words rapidly and automatically.
- Notices and uses word parts.
- Recognizes or quickly solves longer words with vowel and consonant combinations.
- Takes apart longer, multi-syllable words.
- Recognizes and uses word endings.
- Self-corrects quickly close to the point of error.
- Notices details of print within words.
- Self-corrects at point of error.
- Takes apart two- and three-syllable words quickly.

continues

Figure 11-3 Aiden as a Word Solver at Nine Points in Time, *continued*

End Grade 3

Level S

✓ ✓ ✓ ✓ ✓ ✓ ✓ ✓ ✓ ✓
Jaguars have large heads and powerful jaws that allow them

✓ ✓ ~~fearful~~|sc|R ✓ ✓ ✓ ✓ ✓
to be fearsome hunters. They are also skilled

✓ ✓ ✓ ✓ ✓ ✓ ✓
swimmers, able to snatch fish, turtles, and

a|sc ✓ alli·✓|R ✓ ✓ ✓ ✓ ✓
~~even~~ small ~~alligators~~ from the water in the

✓ ✓ rainy|sc ✓ R ✓ ✓ ✓
wet ~~rain~~ forests where they live.

- Recognizes many words quickly and automatically.
- Takes apart two- and three-syllable words quickly.
- Self-corrects at the point of error.
- Keeps word solving going over longer, more complex sentences.
- Uses knowledge of word structure to gain precise meaning.

End Grade 4

Level T

✓ ✓ ✓ ✓ ✓ ✓ ✓ deet·roit|sc ✓
The year was 1904, and everybody in Detroit had

✓ ✓ ✓ ✓ ✓ ✓ ✓ ✓
been talking about the horseless ~~carriage~~ that Henry

✓ ✓ ✓ ✓ ✓ ✓ ✓ ✓
Ford had invented. Ford called it the automobile

✓ ✓ ✓ ✓ ✓ ✓ ✓ ✓ received|sc
because it moved on its own. No horse was required.

✓ ✓ ✓ ✓ ✓ ✓ ✓ ✓ require·place|sc
Ford said that the automobile was going to replace

✓ ✓ ✓ ✓ ✓ ✓ ✓ ✓
the horse and carriage, but most people didn't

✓ ✓
believe it.

- Recognizes many words quickly and automatically.
- Solves words rapidly and unconsciously while keeping longer, more complex sentences in mind.
- Self-corrects for pronunciation.
- Uses known words to connect to unfamiliar words.
- Connects words by prefixes.
- Uses word solving to clarify meaning.
- Recognizes figurative use of words.

continues

Figure 11-3 Aiden as a Word Solver at Nine Points in Time, *continued*

End Grade 5 Level W	King encouraged African Americans to boycott the bus company because the buses in Montevey/Montgomery were segregated/segree. The boycotters walked instead of riding the buses. It was the beginning of one of the most important periods in American history—the Civil Rights Movement.	• Recognizes a large number of words quickly and automatically. • Searches for the meaning of words while reading. • Takes apart longer multisyllable words while reading longer, more complex sentences. • Derives the meaning of words from reading.
End Grade 6 Level Z	The cat that stalked us was fearsome, in·dis·criminal/indiscriminate, deadly, and could strike at any moment, yet my parents always remained calm and comforting, somehow managing to make the most gutter·deep/gut-deep fright tolerable, even as bombs blasted and we cowered in the dark.	• Recognizes a large number of words quickly and automatically. • Uses background knowledge to check on the meaning of words. • Uses known words to solve new words. • Use prefixes and suffixes to solve words. • Self-corrects using sentence structure within complex sentences. • Self-corrects using precise visual information. • Keeps word solving going over very long, complex sentences.

structure and context fuels the process. Readers also derive the meaning of words from context, and over time they add words to their repertoires through the act of reading them in many texts.

When Aiden entered kindergarten, he was aware of print as a source of meaning and he understood that there is a relationship between pictures and the words of a text. He knew a few high-frequency words, which he could use to monitor his reading, although he did not do so with consistency. He did not control voice-print match but relied on repetitious language

patterns. In general, Aiden used a few visual signposts, ran his finger under the print left to right, and produced language that made sense with the message in the pictures.

By the time he entered grade 1, Aiden had made significant progress in word solving. We can see evidence that he knew more high-frequency words. He noticed mismatches by using known words and first letters, showing that he had learned to monitor his reading. He also noticed first letters and used them to start the words. By now, Aiden recognized words as clusters of letters defined by spaces and he had control of voice-print match, which helped him monitor his reading accuracy and notice the visual features of words.

By the middle of grade 1, Aiden had learned much more about words. He could use the first letter in the word, but he could also go beyond the first letter to notice other parts of the word. He made attempts at words, again going beyond the first letter (for example *no, nose* for *noise*), but his appeal on that error showed that he was also monitoring using meaning. Notice that he used the letter cluster (*st*) and the rime (*op*) to solve the word *stop*.

Aiden's reading at the end of grade 1 showed a flexible range of word-solving strategies. He could use both first letters and letter clusters. He could work through a word using sounds and letters in sequence. He monitored his reading using meaning and language structure. It is evident that he also knew many more high-frequency words. Aiden's problem solving took place against a background of accuracy.

Grade 2 data shows that Aiden had long stretches of accurate reading. He recognized almost all easy one-syllable high-frequency words and was able to solve more difficult words like *thought*. He could work out words by saying parts in sequence. He used letter clusters at the beginnings of words and made connections between the parts of longer words. He could take apart multisyllable words. Generally, he self-corrected at the point of error using visual information in combination with meaning.

A year later, at the end of grade 3, Aiden's repertoire of high-frequency words had grown considerably. He could read most simple one- and two-syllable words, leaving him free to concentrate on multisyllable and new words. He used parts of words not only to decode new words but to derive the meaning of words. He was aware of syllables and used them to take words apart while reading for meaning. He had long stretches of accurate reading.

Let's look at Aiden's word solving at the end of grade 4. Here we see evidence that Aiden was processing longer and more complex sentences while at the same time taking words apart. He self-corrected pronunciation. There is evidence that he was able to derive the meaning of unknown words not only by looking at the parts but by learning from context.

By the end of grade 5, Aiden again showed that he could take apart unfamiliar words and derive their meaning from context. He used background information to self-correct both substitutions and intonation. He could take apart difficult, multisyllable words.

In grade 6, Aiden's problem solving allowed him to read for meaning as he processed very long and complex sentences. He realized that simple words can have figurative meaning, which he derived from the context. He self-corrected to assure consistent use of syntax. He showed that he could take apart long words, often connecting them to known words.

Looking at Aiden's progress in using visual information along with meaning and structure in the reading process over time, we see steady progress. He was able to expand his knowledge of words to meet the demands of increasingly difficult texts. By about grade 3, he had acquired a flexible range of word-solving skills as well as the ability to learn new words by reading.

But for many other children, the word-solving story is different. They:

❏ Find it difficult to notice and use letter-sound relationships.

❏ Do not learn to break down longer words into parts.

❏ Use *only* first letters (or only sound out) and so do not have a variety of tools for solving words.

❏ Use visual features of words but do not coordinate the information with meaning and language structure.

❏ Use the same approach over and over even if it is not working.

❏ Are content to produce reading that does not make sense or sound right just to get through a text.

Readers who struggle and have difficulty in solving words need intervention so that they not only acquire knowledge but learn how to use it while reading and writing.

▶ Helping Struggling Readers Become Effective Word Solvers

Helping struggling readers become competent word solvers involves a varied approach that includes:

1. Demonstrating and teaching word-solving principles through whole group or small group minilessons and supportive individual interactions.

2. Providing opportunities for readers to apply these principles as they engage in hands-on work with words in application activities.

3. Teaching for, prompting for, and reinforcing problem solving while readers are processing continuous text.

It will be necessary to give struggling readers explicit instruction—that is, to show them how words work. There are several contexts for doing so.

Explicit Phonics Lessons in Large and Small Groups

Minilessons are brief and specific; they are focused on a principle that readers can apply to many different kinds of words (see Pinnell and Fountas 2008). Usually, classroom teachers present a minilesson to the large group of children and then tailor it to individual needs through multilevel application activities (independent, partner, or small group) and in word work in small group reading lessons. For readers who struggle, we suggest that you also work in small groups to build systematic understandings. Select the principles they need, teach the lesson, and then provide opportunities for hands-on work and sharing of their learning.

An effective minilesson usually involves:

❑ *A brief statement of the principle in concise and clear language.* It is important to use very clear language when describing the principle, and to say it about the same way each time it is stated. This helps children keep the principle in mind as they apply it. It is also helpful if the intervention teacher and classroom teacher are using the same language to state phonics principles.

❑ *A clear demonstration of the principle, usually with a visual display of some kind.* Writing the principle with examples on a chart or whiteboard will help students remember it and also help you keep the language concise and clear. You can also use magnetic letters or letter cards, picture cards, or word cards in a pocket chart.

❑ *Active student participation.* Students learn best when they can contribute to the examples, do some of the writing, handle the magnetic letters, make the words in sand, or work with picture cards and word cards. Active participation during the lesson will prepare them for independent application of the principle.

While there is no rigid sequence in which to introduce phonics principles, there is a continuum of learning; and in general, phonics principles build on one another (see *The Continuum of Literacy Learning, Grades Prek–8, 2011, 2008*). Struggling readers often find it difficult to grasp a minilesson principle that is pitched to the majority of a class, because they do not have prerequisite understandings. For example, if you do not know quite a few of the consonant letters and related sounds, it will be hard to understand consonant clusters (blends and digraphs). If you do not understand that there are patterns in words (simple phonograms, for example) or how to look for them, it will be hard to grasp complex relationships such as the *-ough* in *rough* and *thought*.

Use clear and specific language to establish an important principle of word solving (as in the example in Figure 11-4). This teacher uses specific language to help students understand that they can use word parts in flexible ways.

Let's look at some examples of clear language that will help your students internalize important understandings about how words work.

Here is another example of the specific language that teachers can use in lessons (see Figure 11-5). This time the teacher is helping children learn something more advanced about words—the idea that vowels frequently occur in clusters that are connected to specific sounds.

Another lesson example (Figure 11-6) focuses on an aspect of word structure—adding *-er* and *-r* to words to tell about a person who can do something.

Figure 11-4 Magnetic Letters Illustrating the Principle, "You can make new words by putting a letter before the word part or pattern."

Figure 11-5 Magnetic Letters Illustrating the Principle, "Some words have two vowels together (vowel combinations). The vowel sound is usually the name of the first vowel *(mail, boat)*."

Add -er to a word to talk
about a person who can do
something.
Add -r to words that end
in silent e to make the -er
ending.

read   reader
play   player
hike   hiker
drive   driver

Figure 11-6 *—er* Chart Illustrating the Principles, "Add *-er* to a word to tell about a person who can do something *(John can read. John is a reader.)*." "Add *-er* to words that end in silent *e* to make the *er* ending."

Here the larger idea (that the ending has meaning) is communicated, along with two subcategories of the rules for adding the *-r* or *-er* ending. Notice that only a few examples are needed to make the comparison clear. You could follow up this lesson by asking your students to write words and add endings or sort word cards that follow one principle or the other.

These three minilessons illustrate some of the principles that readers and writers need to learn about the features of words. But more important, they illustrate the kind of specific language and demonstration that will be helpful to readers and writers who have difficulty. When you are working with an individual or a small group, your clear language is still important. Settle on some precise language and use the same language every time.

Application Activities

Students now need to apply the principle to more examples, either independently or with your support. Application activities may be pitched at easier and more complex levels for the same principle. Typically, an application activity involves the types of routines listed in Figure 11-7.

SORTING

Sorting is an engaging activity that helps students look closely at features of letters or words and make connections between them. As they encounter different examples, the features and patterns they are looking for become clearer. Making comparisons also helps them internalize patterns and features and form categories that give them ready access to examples rather than trying to apply principles as abstract and isolated "rules." Adults solve words in just that way: we make connections to words that we know. It doesn't always work, but it can be very helpful, especially when you are also using the context of the sentence. (For example, "The new baby *propitiated* family members previously opposed to the marriage.") It probably wouldn't help with a word like *paradiddle*, which has specific meaning in the field of music. But in general, categories help learners remember features and patterns of words.

Figure 11-7 Word Study Routines for Application Activities

Routine	Description	Learning Opportunities
Sorting	Students sort picture, letter, or word cards according to the criteria demonstrated. For example, they may sort by: • Similar features. • First sound or letter. • Rhymes. • Letter clusters (blends and digraphs). • Word pattern. • Affixes (prefixes and suffixes). • Syllables.	• Attend closely to the sound, letter feature, or word feature. • Notice letter clusters and word patterns that occur often. • Connect words by sound, feature, word pattern, or word part. • Compare sounds and letter features. • Form categories of words that are similar by sound, feature, word pattern, or word part.
Elkonin Boxes (sound and letter boxes)	Teachers work with children to illustrate the structure of words by drawing one box for each sound or each letter in the sequence. Students say the words and make connections to sounds, writing one or more letters in boxes (see Chapter 9).	• Learn to say words slowly, focusing on the sounds. • Feel the sound in the mouth (position of tongue and lips). • Connect sounds to letters within words. • Notice how words look. • Learn the features of letters while writing them.
Building/Making and Manipulating Words	Students use magnetic letters (or letter cards or tiles) to make words. They make new words by changing the beginning, middle, or ends of words. Teachers may illustrate writing and changing letters by using a chart or whiteboard. Students can also write words on small whiteboards and make changes, but it is very beneficial to readers to manipulate the letters.	• Internalize the idea that you can make new words by changing letters, letter clusters, and larger word parts. • Focus on working with parts of words. • Make connections among words to solve them. • Feel the features of letters while manipulating them. • Attend to important word parts (letters, letter clusters, patterns, affixes) while building and manipulating them.
Writing Words	Students write on paper, chart paper, or small whiteboards. The teacher may use writing to demonstrate the principle, and students either write at the teacher's direction or produce their own examples. They write words that are connected by feature, word pattern, or word part. They make new words by changing letters at the beginning, middle, or end or make new words by adding letters and/or longer word parts.	• Notice the features of words while writing them. • Think about the connections between known words. • Make new words by using word patterns or parts. • Develop flexibility in making new words.

continues

Figure 11-7 Word Study Routines for Application Activities, *continued*

Routine	Description	Learning Opportunities
Working with Words in Continuous Print	Students work with continuous print to identify words, word patterns, letters and letter clusters, and other parts of words. They are asked to quickly locate specific words in a text.	• Learn to search print quickly to identify words, word patterns, letters and letter clusters, and word parts. • Learn to use word-solving skills within continuous print.
Letter/ Word Games	Students engage in games with each other and in the process focus on a word study principle. A description of games is included in Appendix F.	• Engage students in interesting and fast processing of print in words. • Increase ability to identify word patterns and features quickly. • Develop quick recognition of letters, words, or word parts.

Young children who have difficulty learning to relate letters and sounds may not be looking efficiently at print. The simple sort shown in Figure 11-8 is designed to help children notice the parts of letters by sorting them into groups with tall sticks, short sticks, and no sticks. Sorting letters in this way will help children notice the small differences, the *distinctive features,* that make a letter different from every other letter. That in turn will make it possible for them to attach a letter to a name or a sound.

Children can use their knowledge of phonogram patterns to sort words (see Figure 11-9). This kind of sorting trains the eye to notice word parts rapidly and make connections between words. If readers can learn to recognize patterns like these quickly and effortlessly, reading will be more efficient.

Variations in sorting raise the level of challenge for children. The feature observed in Figure 11-10 is the presence of double consonants at the end of words. It follows a lesson about double letters. The double consonant appears at the end of the base word. The principle to apply in the other columns is related to the vowel sounds.

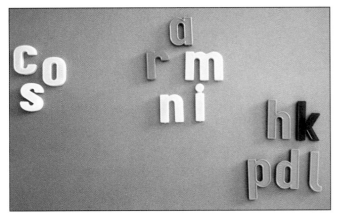

Figure 11-8 Letter Sorting

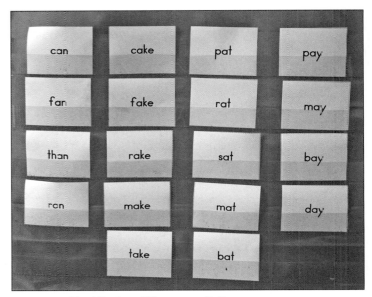

Figure 11-9 Word Sorting of Phonogram Patterns

bean	call	toy
clean	off	coin
seat	shell	boil
feet	fill	boy
key	wall	

Figure 11-10 Blind Sort—Double *l* in Words

In this "blind sort" (Figure 11-10), one partner draws a card and reads the word aloud without showing it to the other. The second partner points to the correct column and then places the card in that column. This activity requires the players to think about how the word looks, predict the pattern, and then connect it to other words.

Afterward, each student writes some words as examples for each category (see above). This sort requires complex word-solving strategies (that is, noticing more than one feature in the word). To write and read more complex words, students will need to learn principles that usually apply, with some exceptions. Making connections among these more unusual words will also be helpful.

SOUND AND LETTER BOXES (ELKONIN BOXES)

Using "sound boxes" (Clay 2005; Elkonin 1975) to help children learn to hear the individual sounds or phonemes in words is discussed in Chapter 9. The ability to hear sounds in sequence is essential if children are to connect them with letters to solve words. These boxes frame the word and make it easier to identify the sounds. Using "letter boxes" to help children connect sounds with letters and write them in sequence is discussed in Chapter 10. We recommend you use these boxes extensively with children who have difficulty using sound-to-letter relationships in

reading or writing. When using Elkonin boxes, keep the simple sequence shown in Figure 11-11 in mind.

At first, draw a box for every sound and work without letters. This helps children focus on saying and hearing the sounds in words. It is important for them to begin to identify the individual sounds. They can feel the position of the lips and tongue as they say the words and differentiate the sounds. Once children are able to say and hear sounds, pushing markers into boxes as they say the individual sounds helps them separate the sounds mentally.

When children can say words and push markers into boxes easily and you see evidence that children can identify one letter for each sound in a word they write (in sequence), move on to writing letters in the boxes and helping children understand that some sounds are represented by more than one letter

or some letters represent no sound in a word

m	a	ke

They can push the markers into the boxes while saying words and identifying the letter that goes with any specific sound that they hear. They then need to think about the way the letter looks and write it in the box.

When children can easily write letters in boxes for individual sounds, and with your support fill in letter clusters that represent them, move on to letter boxes. Here, you draw a box for every letter in the word, regardless of the number of phonemes. The boxes help children notice the discrepancies between number of sounds and number of letters. (In English, there is not a one-to-one correspondence between sounds and letters.) The boxes signal to the writer that more than one letter might be required—or that several letters might represent one sound. This process helps students begin to understand the complex letter-sound relationships in English spelling.

As children become skilled at working with sound or letter boxes, they can transfer that ability to spelling while writing stories or informational pieces. They can say words slowly and represent sounds in

Figure 11-11 Using Elkonin Boxes to Help Children Learn About Sounds and Letters in Words

Sound Boxes	Children use boxes in the absence of letters. They may not yet hear the sounds in sequential order.

Sound Boxes with Letters (Sound Analysis)	Children say words slowly and write letters in sequence (L to R) in boxes to represent sounds.		

c	a	t		s	k	a	te

s	n	ow		b	ee	t	le

Letter Boxes (Visual Analysis)	Children say words slowly and write letters in boxes. They know that there is one box for each letter, which helps them attend to spelling patterns.

c	a	t		s	k	a	t	e

s	n	o	w		b	e	e	t	l	e

Working Without Boxes	Children use sound analysis while writing new words. They say words slowly to hear sounds and write letters and letter clusters.

Working with Multisyllable Words	Occasionally use boxes to identify syllables in multisyllable words and analyze them for sounds and letters (e.g., *actually*). The child wrote *ac* and the teacher helped him clap each syllable and then write the letters in the boxes.

ac	t	u	a	l	l	y

sequence. As they grow more sophisticated, they can consider alternatives in representing a sound and will also develop the ability to use visual information to make the word "look right." Accurate spelling goes well beyond simple sound analysis. Writers also learn to take apart multisyllable words in order to write each syllable, and students may occasionally find it helpful to use letter boxes to write complex syllables.

BUILDING AND MANIPULATING WORDS

Using magnetic letters to build and manipulate words provides a concrete demonstration of how words work, which includes the teacher's language (Figure 11-12). Notice that the teacher provides a clear demonstration. She shows and tells rather than expecting children to guess and uses words the children already know. After demonstrating *me* and *be*, she involves children more as

Figure 11-12 **Changing the First Letter or Letters of a Word to Make a New Word**

Speaker	Interaction
T	I'm going to show you how to use a word you know to make a new word. *[Shows them the word* me *in magnetic letters.]* What is this word?
T	When you say a word, you can hear the sounds, can't you? Say *me*.
T	When you look at the word *me*, you can see the first letter. When you read the word *me*, you can hear the first sound, /m/, and the rest of the word. Now watch what I am going to do with the word *me*. I'm going to take away the first letter, the *m*, and put a *b* at the beginning of the word. What does it say now?
S	*be*
T	Now I'll take away the *b* and put the *m* first. What is the word now?
S	*me*

she works with *cat, mat,* and *fat* and with *by* and *my*—all words that are easy and familiar to the group. Then she gives children magnetic letters and has them repeat the operations themselves. Her goal is not to teach children these particular words, but to help them understand the substitution principle, that they can change the first letter of a word to make a new word.

Now look at a teacher who is working in a slightly more advanced way with children who have previously learned to change the first letter (see Figure 11-13). The teacher helps them understand that you can change the last part of a word to make a new word. Later, the goal will be flexibility in changing any letters or word parts to make new words. Working with magnetic letters will help children become fast and flexible in working with the parts of words.

You can also transfer the operation to writing (see Figure 11-14). This example is simple, but notice that this child has begun to notice letter clusters. We recommend using magnetic letters to help struggling readers and writers. It takes only a few minutes to demonstrate the principle and to turn the task over to students.

Finally let's look at a more advanced example (Figure 11-15). Here the teacher and children are exploring the use of the letter *r* in different words. As the children make new words, they observe how the sound of the vowel changes when blended with *r*. They are dealing with complex spelling and decoding problems, but building and manipulating the letters helps them understand these inner workings.

Another way to demonstrate making and manipulating words is by using a chalkboard or whiteboard (either a large one or individual handheld ones) to demonstrate word connections and make new words (Figure 11-16). Have students write words and change them to make other words. In general, at-risk students should work with magnetic letters before being expected to write words, but both activities can be very effective.

Students can achieve a great deal of sophistication and flexibility in their ability to connect words (see Figure 11-17). In changing only one letter at the

Figure 11-13 Changing Letters

bring   cloud

             clay

brown

Figure 11-14 Writing-Changing Letters

Figure 11-15 "Practice Test"

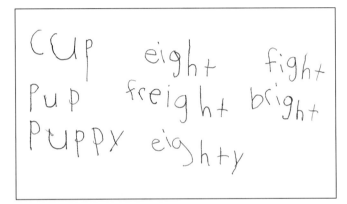

Figure 11-16 Writing and Connecting Words

beginning of a word, Matt demonstrates excellent knowledge of words and how they work. After students have had much experience in making and manipulating words with magnetic letters, they can transfer this ability to their own writing and reading.

WRITING WORDS

Just about everyone uses writing to support memory. When we are learning something new, we often make notes. When learning new words (or thinking about parts of words) the motor act of writing will support struggling readers and writers. We are not talking about the old practice of writing a word ten or twenty times. That does not work. Writers typically take the efficient route, writing the first letter ten times, then the second ten times, and so on. They get the task done but learn nothing about the internal structure of the word. You need to use writing in a much more strategic way.

After a lesson on using known words to learn new words, the children first made the word with magnetic letters and then wrote new words as an additional activity (see Figure 11-18). The act of writing helped them look even more closely at the visual features of the words.

You can also use writing to help children study or learn new words. In the process, they give very close attention to the visual features of words. Look at an

	Word Pairs Sheet
Name: Matt	Date:

chair	→	hair
at	→	fat
glow	→	low
speak	→	peak
it	→	spit
on	→	won
lip	→	flip
flower	→	lower
ground	→	round
eat	→	pleat

Figure 11-17 Changing First Letter

example of the study technique called Look, Say, Cover, Write, Check (see Figure 11-19).

Children use a lined check sheet in a folder that has three flaps. They follow these steps:

❏ In the first column, write each word to be learned and then check it to make sure it is written accu-

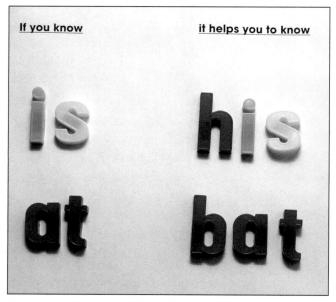

Figure 11-18 Making and Writing Connected Words

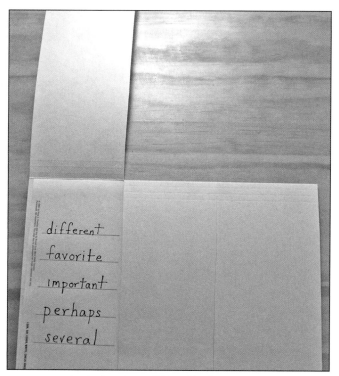

Figure 11-19 Look, Say, Cover, Write, Check

rately. (Younger students should check letter by letter; older students can look at letter clusters.)

❏ Then get a good look at the first word and say it.

❏ Close flap 1 to cover the word and open flap 2.

❏ Write the word in the second column and then open flap 1.

❏ Check the word written in the second column with the correct word in the first column—letter by letter.

❏ Repeat the process by closing flap 2, looking at the word in column 1, saying it, covering it, and writing it in column 3.

❏ Open flap 1 to check the word in column 3, letter by letter.

You can give students five or ten words at a time, and the learning is very effective. It is important that children are working with words that are part of their oral vocabularies. The words can be recently acquired from reading. This systematic process is helpful to struggling writers and carries over to their reading.

Another way to learn words by writing is for a pair of students to take a "practice test." In the example in Figure 11-20, one student makes a first attempt at four words on the right side of the page. The buddy checks it. The student takes a good look and tries again; the buddy checks it again. Finally, on the left side of the page, the student writes precisely what he needs to remember. In this way, the writer acknowledges what he already knows about a word as well as what he needs to know.

Connecting words is a powerful way to solve them in reading and in writing. We have successfully used making connections with many struggling readers and writers to help them learn more about how words work (see Figure 11-21); it is an engaging way to help them study words. Over time students become very adept and increasingly sophisticated at making connections. They can make any kind of connection:

❏ First, last, or middle letter.

❏ Letter clusters in beginning, last, or medial position.

❏ Inflectional ending.

❏ Affix.

❏ Base or root word.

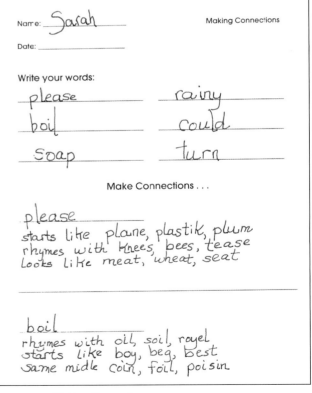

Write the words misspelled correctly; highlight parts to remember.

getting

wreck

Tell why they were misspelled and what you will need to remember.

it has 2 t's

it has a silent w and ends in ck

Buddy Check Sheet

Name: _____ Date: _____

Words	Try Again	Correct Spelling
shadow ✓		Highlight parts to remember and make the word with magnetic letters.
geting ✗	getting ✓	
chance ✓		
reck ✗	rek ✗	wreck

Score: /   Score: /   Over ——→

Figure 11-20 Practice Test

❏ Structure (contraction or compound).

❏ Meaning.

You can also use writing to help students work on a word feature they might be studying. The act of writing creates a personal record, and the children think about the feature every time they write a new example. In the example in Figure 11-22, the children have been studying vowel combinations in mini-lessons presented by their teacher. The task is to use word cards and magnetic letters to identify and make five words containing the vowel combinations *ea, ee, oa, ai, ay,* and *ow.* They consolidate their knowledge by writing words on two three-way word sheets. After writing, they circle the vowel combination.

It is mystifying why it takes students so long to internalize a simple concept like plurals, but the concept can be very confusing to struggling writers and readers. We suspect that many children try to learn plurals as individual words rather than applying a few related principles. The example in Figure 11-23 followed quite a few lessons on simple and more complex

Name: Sarah   Making Connections

Date: _____

Write your words:

please   rainy

boil   could

soap   turn

Make Connections . . .

please
starts like plane, plastik, plum
rhymes with knees, bees, tease
looks like meat, wheat, seat

boil
rhymes with oil, soil, royel
starts like boy, beg, best
same midle coin, foil, poisin

Figure 11-21 Making Connections

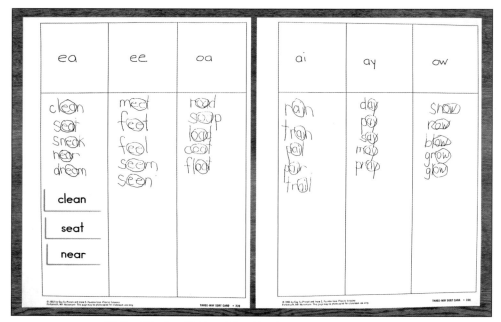

Figure 11-22 Writing Words with Vowel Combinations

Name: Matt   Two-Column Sheet   Date: _____

leaf	leaves
half	halves
hoof	hooves
shelf	shelves
elf	elves
wolf	wolves
life	lives
knife	knives
scarf	scarves
self	selves
wife	wives

Figure 11-23 Writing Plurals

plurals. The children take twelve word cards and make each singular word with magnetic letters. Then they write it in the first column on a two-column sheet. Next, they make the plural form with magnetic letters and write the plural form in the second column. Finally, they read their lists to a partner. As with the other examples, conscious attention to words helps children closely attend to the features of words.

WORKING WITH WORDS IN CONTINUOUS PRINT IN READING

The real challenge is helping children attend to the features of words "on the run" while reading continuous print for meaning. No amount of practice on words in isolation will be sufficient to help them develop the strategic actions that readers must use to quickly and unconsciously decode words while reading. Of course, readers use several sources of information in addition to the visual information in print. For example, they use context and language structure to access meaning; but they also must have the basic strategies to take words apart. Word solving includes recognizing words by any visual feature whatsoever to locate it.

One technique is to locate words within continuous text. For example, after reading a book together, the teacher asks children to locate the word *play* on the page shown in Figure 11-24:

TEACHER: Turn to page 2. What did the dog want the very busy hen to do?

JOSH: Play with him.

GENENE: Come and play but she wouldn't.

TEACHER: Say the word *play*.

STUDENTS: *play*

TEACHER: What two letters would you expect to see at the beginning of *play*?

Josh: *p*

Genene: *p* and *l*

Teacher: Quickly point under the word *play*. Run your finger under the word and say it. *[Students quickly find the word and say it.]* Now let's read what the dog said and make it sound like talking.

The general sequence of instruction is:

❑ Teacher: Say *play*.

❑ Student: *play*

❑ Teacher: What two letters would you expect to see at the beginning of the word *play*?

❑ Student: *p*

❑ Student: *p* and *l*

❑ Teacher: /Pl/. Now find *play* and point to it with your finger.

❑ Students find *play*.

❑ Teacher: That's right. Run your finger under it slowly while you say it. *[Demonstrates.] Play*.

Locating words and attending to their features takes only a few seconds, but it is powerful. You will want to have early readers locate easy high-frequency words on several pages of each text they read.

Continuous print can also be used to help readers attend to the features in words. In the example in Figure 11-25, the teacher is using a poem the children have read several times while looking at the print. As a follow-up to a series of lessons on consonant clusters (blends and digraphs), the teacher invites students to identify words with clusters and underline the parts of the word they are emphasizing. While you would not want word study to get in the way of enjoying the poem, there are many learning opportunities when revisiting the text:

❑ First letters.

❑ Syllables in words.

❑ Endings (*y* and *ing*).

❑ Rhyming words.

"Come and play," said the dog. "No," said the hen. "I am very busy. I am planting the wheat."

Figure 11-24 Page Spread from *The Very Busy Hen* from Leveled Literacy Intervention, Green System (Heinemann 2009)

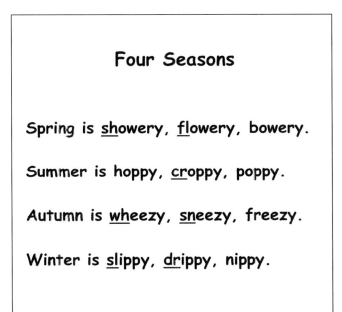

Four Seasons

Spring is <u>sh</u>owery, <u>fl</u>owery, bowery.

Summer is hoppy, <u>cr</u>oppy, poppy.

Autumn is <u>wh</u>eezy, <u>sn</u>eezy, freezy.

Winter is <u>sl</u>ippy, <u>dr</u>ippy, nippy.

Figure 11-25 Noticing Features of Words Within Continuous Text

❑ Long and short vowels.

❑ Vowel combinations.

❑ Double letters—vowels and consonants.

❑ Adjectives.

Children can also use individual copies of poems to notice and highlight features of words (as in

Figure 11-26). Here again, children are revisiting a text they have read many times. They search for consonant clusters and use a highlighter to identify them. In a later sharing session, they can report their findings. Notice that this poem can also be used to highlight letter clusters representing the *ow* sound. This activity is engaging and requires close visual attention to features of words. It will also help students connect words.

Here is a partial list of suggestions for revisiting texts to help children learn more about words (Figure 11-27). (There is a comprehensive list in *The Fountas and Pinnell Prompting Guide 1* 2009.) These prompts can be used on just about any text that children have read several times—a book, a poem, or a piece of interactive or shared writing. You can prompt children to find only one example of the feature (for example, a word that begins with *b*) or several examples.

The Itsy Bitsy Spider

The itsy bitsy spider

went up the water spout.

Down came the rain and

washed the spider out.

Out came the sun and

dried up all the rain.

And the itsy bitsy spider

went up the spout again.

Figure 11-26 Application Activity

Figure 11-27 **Revisiting the Text for Word Study**

Use these prompts after the writing of any text to reinforce understandings about words and how they work.

Teach

Model finding words and noticing different patterns or parts of words in a text.

Prompt

Find the word _____.

Find a little word.

Find a big word.

Find the letter _____.

Find a word that begins with a capital letter.

Find a word that begins with a lowercase letter.

Find a word that begins with (letter or letter cluster).

Find a word that begins like (word).

Find a word that begins with a consonant cluster or a vowel.

Find a word that ends like (word).

Find a word with two sounds (three, four, etc.).

Find a word that has more letters than sounds.

Find a word that has one syllable (two, more than two, etc.).

Find a word that has parts that can be removed.

Find a word that sounds exactly like it looks.

Find a word that could be spelled another way but sounds the same.

Find a word that has a tricky (interesting, hard, new) pattern (spelling).

Find a word that has a special pattern (spelling) that shows what it means.

Find a word that is a compound word (contraction, word with ending, word with prefix, etc.).

Find a word that is tricky (hard, new) for you to read. What will you want to remember about it?

LETTER/WORD GAMES

Children do not learn how words work by playing games. They need explicit teaching and prompting and reinforcing during reading. But games can help struggling readers develop automaticity in word solving. Overlearning some principles by playing games leads to quick, automatic visual searching and word solving. Once children clearly understand a few games, you can modify them to focus on:

❑ Letters at the beginning, ending, or middle of words.

❑ High-frequency words.

❑ Letter clusters (digraphs and blends) at the beginning or ending of words.

❑ Word patterns.

❑ Prefixes or suffixes.

The version of Lotto shown in Figure 11-28 focuses on ending consonant clusters. Students take a word card, read the word, and say the ending consonant cluster. If they have a word on the game card that ends the same, they cover it with a marker. The first player to cover all the words on the card wins. After playing, children may write and then share one or two of the words and identify the consonant cluster.

The Follow the Path game shown in Figure 11-29, used as a follow-up to a lesson on the spelling pattern -*ight*, helps develop letter/word analysis. The pronunciation of this spelling pattern is different if the letter *e* is before the -*ight* (*weight*). Children play Follow the Path using -*ight* word cards and word cards containing other patterns they know. They take a card and read it, and then they throw the dice to move their markers the indicated number of spaces. This game requires readers to search for the visual information in the word quickly, looking for patterns (including the -*ight* pattern), and then reading the word accurately.

Another classic game is Go Fish. Players have a deck of cards with four matching cards in each category of word features. They deal eight cards and leave the rest in a deck for drawing. They lay down any four-way matches they have. They ask the other player(s) if they have a word with a certain feature, who respond by giving the asker their cards. If there is no response, then the player must "go fish" by taking a card from the draw deck. The winner is the first to "go out" by laying down all the cards. The Go Fish game in Figure 11-30 focuses on words that include vowel combinations.

The Word Grid in Figure 11-31 is a more complicated game. This game could be used after a lesson on the principle, *You blend the vowel sound with* r *in some words.* The first player rolls a die with word parts on

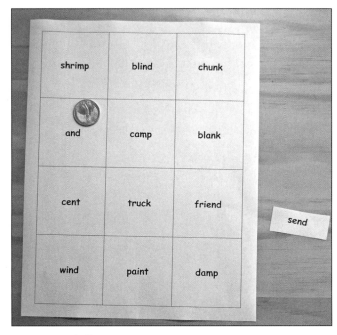

Figure 11-28 Lotto

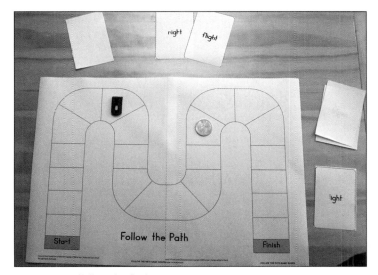

Figure 11-29 Follow the Path

Figure 11-30 Go Fish

it. He looks for a word on his grid that contains the same word part shown on the die, reads the word aloud, and crosses the word out on the sheet. Then the next player takes a turn. The first player to cross off all words wins.

As in other games, this one helps readers learn to search for very specific visual information. Games are useful only for overlearning and reinforcing, but they

Figure 11-31 Word Grid

can be very important for struggling readers who need more practice in searching for the visual features of words. Appendix F contains a complete list of games and their directions.

Teaching, Prompting For, and Reinforcing Word-Solving Actions

Struggling readers will benefit from direct study of words and their features through minilessons and applications, as well as from revisiting texts. But to help them become effective word solvers, you will need to go one step further. Often, struggling readers learn about letters and sounds but do not understand how to apply their knowledge while actually reading texts. As you work alongside these readers and observe them closely, you will see opportunities to teach for, prompt for, and reinforce effective word solving actions. The examples below include specific language that will be clear and helpful to students as you listen to them read.

"LISTEN TO HOW I START IT"

Here's an example of *teaching*. The student stopped at the word *stick* (the object this label represents was shown clearly in the picture; see Figure 11-32). The teacher could have directed the student to look at the picture and think what would make sense, but her goal for this reader was to help him use visual information in combination with meaning.

> **TEACHER:** Listen to how I start it. *[Reading.]* "The big dog ate a little st–."
>
> **STUDENT:** Stick!
>
> **TEACHER:** And check the picture. Does *stick* make sense?
>
> **STUDENT:** He's eating a little stick in the picture.
>
> **TEACHER:** Try *stick* to see if it makes sense and looks right.
>
> **STUDENT** *[reading]*: "The big dog ate a little stick."

The teacher demonstrated how to start the word, and the student immediately came up with the word.

But instead of just saying, "Right!" the teacher asked the student to check the picture with the prompt. She was promoting cross-checking behavior.

"DO YOU KNOW A WORD THAT STARTS WITH…?"

In the next example, the student reading the page shown in Figure 11-33 stopped at the word *busy*.

> TEACHER: Do you know a word that starts like that and makes sense?
>
> STUDENT: *[Rereading.]* "I am very b-b- I am very b-b-."
>
> TEACHER: Try *busy*. See if it makes sense and looks right.
>
> STUDENT: "I am very busy."

Here the teacher prompted the student to think of another word that starts with the letter. When the student was still unable to solve the word, the teacher told her to consider a word and see if it would fit. But notice *how* she did this. She asked the reader to check whether *busy* would make sense and look right. In telling the word in this way, she helped the reader be active rather than passively accepting the word. It is helpful to ask the reader either to think about whether something would look right, sound right, or make sense or to reread and engage in that thinking.

"DO YOU KNOW A WORD LIKE THAT?"

This is a prompt that makes more demands on the reader. The student is reading the page shown in Figure 11-34.

> TEACHER: You try it.
>
> STUDENT: /S/. "Out came a sweet sound"? No.
>
> TEACHER *[points to the word* chirpy*]*: Do you know a word like that?

Figure 11-32 Page Spread from *Orson's Tummy Ache* from Leveled Literacy Intervention, Green System (Heinemann 2009)

Figure 11-33 Page Spread from *The Very Busy Hen* from Leveled Literacy Intervention, Green System (Heinemann 2009)

> STUDENT: *chip?*
>
> TEACHER: It starts like *chip*. The next part is *-ir*, like in *girl*. Say that much—the *ch* and *-ir*.
>
> STUDENT: *chirp?*
>
> TEACHER: Add the ending.
>
> STUDENT: *chirpy?*

Figure 11-34 Page Spread from *The Ladybug and the Cricket* from Leveled Literacy Intervention, Blue System (Heinemann 2009)

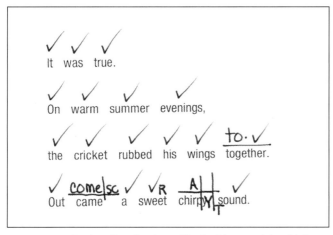

Figure 11-35 Student Reading from *The Ladybug and the Cricket* from Leveled Literacy Intervention, Blue System (Heinemann 2009)

TEACHER: Crickets chirp at night. That means they make a little sound.

STUDENT: Yes. Kind of like a chick.

TEACHER: Try that and see if it makes sense.

STUDENT: Out came a sweet chirpy sound.

TEACHER: And *chirpy* looks right too.

Notice that the reader may have been facing two or even three difficulties. He read very well up to the last part of line 4: notice his ability to read the first syllable and

then solve the word *together* (Figure 11-35). Also he self-corrected *come* to *came*. He stopped at the word *chirpy*. The teacher prompted, "Do you know a word like that?" The reader understood this prompt and came up with *chip*. But that didn't help in solving the word, possibly because it was not in the reader's oral vocabulary or he didn't know much about crickets or both. The teacher provided some information to help the reader put this word into perspective and then prompted for rereading to make sure it "looks right and sounds right."

LOOK AT THE SYLLABLES

In this example, the teacher supports word solving of a multisyllable word (Figure 11-36). The reader is working on the word *bumblebee*.

STUDENT: "Bum–b–." What's this word?

TEACHER: Look at the middle part of the word. [*shows* ble]

TEACHER: Put that together, *bumble*.

STUDENT: *bumble*

TEACHER: Look at the last part. *Bumble—[covers the first two syllables]*—what is it?

STUDENT: *Bumblebee*. Wow! The bat is as small as a bee?

TEACHER: Yes, it's hard to imagine a bat that little. It's like a bee. Look at the comparison of the bat with the person's hand.

Stopped at the word *bumblebee*, the reader demonstrated that she could take words apart by syllables and identify the first part, *bum*. (There is no picture support for this word.) The teacher prompted the reader to cover up the ending and focus on the middle part of the word. Then she changed the focus to the last syllable, and the reader solved the word.

Bats

This animal is a bat. Bats are not birds, but bats do have wings.

Bats do not have feathers. A bat's body is covered with fur. Its wings are covered with smooth skin.

12

Some bats have very big wings. The wings of the biggest bat are more than five feet long from tip to tip.

Some bats have very small wings. This small bat is about the size of a bumblebee.

13

Figure 11-36 Page Spread from *Animals with Wings* from Leveled Literacy Intervention, Blue System (Heinemann 2009)

SPECIFIC LANGUAGE FOR TEACHING, PROMPTING, AND REINFORCING WORD-SOLVING ACTIONS

It is important not to interrupt a child's reading in order to make long teaching points. Interrupting the flow of the story can result in a loss of meaning. It is preferable to conduct these brief interactions with students when a reader has stopped and is unable to proceed. Or, you can use them after the reading of the text. Some other general guidelines are:

❏ Be sure to *teach* or demonstrate before prompting. Prompting will not be effective if students do not know what you mean. Be sure that they understand the signal that your language is giving them.

❏ Modeling and prompting should always direct the reader's eyes from left to right across the word. Once this left-to-right way of looking is well established, you can direct attention to the middle and ending parts of the words.

❏ Teach for, prompt for, and reinforce only what readers have just learned or need to know how

to do next. Prompting for and reinforcing *everything* will interfere with learning. Prompting for and reinforcing at random or focusing on what readers already know is a waste of time and will interfere with reading fluency and comprehension. Prompting for actions that are far beyond readers' abilities will have no impact and, again, will interrupt reading.

This language specifically focuses on words, but, as in some of the examples above, you will realize more power by helping the reader cross-reference meaning and language structure. Effective readers are always searching for and using information from more than one source, and Chapter 14 presents more suggestions for teaching for, prompting for, and reinforcing strategic actions. A comprehensive list of prompts is included in *Fountas and Pinnell Prompting Guide 1* (2009).

▶ A Word in Conclusion

Learning to use phonics to solve words is a critical factor in helping readers who struggle. Just because it has sometimes been overemphasized in the past to the detriment of reading comprehension, we cannot ignore the processing of letter-sound information. Children need to learn the building blocks of word decoding, and this will not happen overnight. Struggling readers need teaching across instructional contexts. All the teaching approaches discussed in this chapter play an important role in helping readers attend closely to print. Subsequent chapters focus on helping them use letter-sound and word analysis while attending to the strategic actions they need to effectively process print.

▶ Suggestions for Professional Development

ANALYZING TEXTS AND SUPPORTING WORD ANALYSIS STRATEGIES

1. Gather a group of texts that your students will be expected to read during the next month or six weeks. Probably you will have several different levels of texts, but if you are using a basal or core program, you may have a section or sections of an anthology.

2. Work with colleagues to make a list of the word-solving demands of the texts. For example:

   ❑ Are there many simple CVC and CVCe words?

   ❑ Are there two- or three-syllable words?

   ❑ Are there words with affixes?

   ❑ Are there many easy high-frequency words?

   ❑ What support is there in this text for the tricky words?

3. Make the list as comprehensive as you can and share your lists across the group.

4. Analyze the lists to determine the principles that you think your students understand and those that will be hard for them. (This will be different for groups and varied levels.)

5. For a week or so, listen to individual students read these texts and make note of their errors. Check your findings with your analysis or the initial list.

6. Meet again with colleagues to share your findings. Work together to plan any of the following:

   ❑ Five to ten minilesson principles that will help your students.

   ❑ Word work for five to ten small group reading lessons (e.g., guiding reading). At the end of the lesson, spend one or two minutes on preplanned word work using magnet letters or writing on small white dry-erase boards or on paper.

   ❑ Small group intervention lessons for students who need extra help.

7. Look at the sample prompts in this chapter (and/or *The Fountas and Pinnell Prompting Guide 1*, 2009). Select language that you think will be especially helpful for a selected group of students. Make plans to use this language while interacting with students as they read.

Building and Using a Repertoire of Words

PROFICIENT READERS HAVE LEARNED MANY WORDS; but more important, they have developed powerful systems for learning words. They are able to problem-solve "on the run" while reading for meaning. Struggling readers generally have a lower repertoire of words that they can recognize effortlessly and their word solving is inefficient, slow, and tedious; sometimes they passively move through texts not even attempting to solve words that are hard for them. With a low repertoire of words, the reader has difficulty monitoring and correcting reading. Fluency and comprehension are affected. They tend to appeal rather than work actively at words. In this chapter, we explore ways of helping students build a core of words they recognize automatically, including many high-frequency words, as well as how to help them develop systems for learning words.

Readers process words rapidly and automatically as they construct the messages in texts. The ability to recognize words is necessary, although not sufficient in itself, for proficient reading. Mature adult readers recognize thousands of words instantly and without conscious attention, while their thinking is focused on the meaning of the text. Occasionally, they may use word-solving strategies (noticing an ending such as

-*tion*, for example), but even this happens rarely and so effortlessly that readers are often unconscious of their efforts. They are more likely to pause at a word that they can pronounce but don't know what it means.

Young readers continually construct their repertoire of known words and flexible ways of solving words, and progress is usually very rapid. Kaye (2007) analyzed proficient second graders' reading behaviors across a school year. In her examination of more than 2,500 text-reading behaviors, the twenty-one proficient readers demonstrated more than sixty ways (both one-step and multistep actions) to solve words (and these were only the problem-solving behaviors they displayed overtly). All words read correctly by students demonstrated their ability to recognize words instantly or engage in quick "covert" problem solving. These proficient second graders usually worked with large sub-word units. They *never* articulated words phoneme by phoneme. Presumably, they *could* "sound out" words when needed because they had excellent knowledge of letter-sound relationships. But they appeared to take more efficient or "economical" approaches, as described by Clay (2001). These readers were also extremely active in their problem solving; they *never* appealed to the teacher without first initiating an attempt. These proficient word solvers had learned many words; more important, they had developed powerful systems for learning words.

Proficient readers solve problems "on the run" while reading for meaning. They may be marginally aware of problem solving, but the process is largely transparent. Readers who struggle may have any of a number of difficulties reading words:

- ❏ The vocabulary they can recognize on sight isn't large enough for them to be able to read at expected levels of difficulty.

- ❏ They have a very limited range of strategies for solving words.

- ❏ The word solving they can do is slow and tedious, requiring much attention.

- ❏ They continue to apply one or two strategies even when the strategies do not work.

- ❏ They skip words or substitute words that are obviously nonsense or meaningless, especially when they are reading without teacher support.

- ❏ They do not or cannot use language structure and meaning to support their word solving.

- ❏ They do not or cannot check the accuracy of their solving by using language structure, meaning, and the visual information in print.

- ❏ They are passive, tending to appeal rather than work actively at solving words.

Chances are a struggling reader will exhibit one, several, or even all of these difficulties. Showing them how to attend to a range of visual features will help them extract cues from print. At the same time, they need to notice and use those features in coordination with other cues from language and meaning.

A word is a unit of language that has meaning. Words are made up of morphemes, which are the smallest units of meaning. Sometimes a morpheme is a word (*girl, green, run*); sometimes a word is made up of more than one morpheme (*girls, girlfriends, greener, running*). Understanding the concept represented by a word involves the internalization of meanings. In written language, a word is a pattern of letters that is a symbol for those same meanings; it is defined by white space on either side. (In oral language, there are no spaces between words.) The orientation of symbols is important; in English, letters are placed in a certain order and sequenced from left to right.

Just understanding the concept of a word is a challenge for very young children (Clay 1991); they often call a letter a word and vice versa. However, by the time they have learned their own names and a few high-frequency and/or important words, they understand the difference. Just imagine what confusion can persist if a child does not grasp these basic concepts!

Reading is in fact quite complicated. Children must mentally break speech into words, notice the visual patterns in the clusters of letters placed on lines, move the eyes from left to right while noticing the features, and coordinate all these actions (at first, assisted by the finger). As texts become more complex, the eyes must move along the print left to right automatically, picking up information needed to use a broad range of word features in a process that is largely unconscious. The more words readers know automatically, the easier this process will be, because not only will readers have to expend little energy on those words but they can also use these well-known examples as resources in solving new words.

The essential core of known words for the beginner consists of the high-frequency words that are ubiquitous in written language. Readers see a word, notice something about it, make connections with other words, form generalizations about patterns, solve the word, and then (after some familiarization) make it part of their repertoire of known words. For some words, this goal may be accomplished in a short time; other words may be trickier.

There are many ways to help struggling readers learn how to learn words. In Chapter 11, we examined ways of teaching phonics principles, which are highly useful in word solving. In this chapter, we address the acquisition of a sight-word vocabulary, using children's names as a starting point.

▶ Learning Through Names

A name is very powerful. It is often the first example of a written word a child sees. You can work with names in many different ways. Look at the two examples of name charts—a pocket chart and a chart with circles around names that start the same—in Figure 12-1.

Terms such as *first, last, letter,* and *word* have a technical meaning that some kindergartners and first graders do not understand. That means you may have difficulty directing their attention to the appropriate visual features of a word. They may be looking at a different part of the word or not looking at all. They may confuse isolated sounds and syllables with words. Remember that to the young child, many oral and most written words are unknown. Print can be bewildering. Through reading and working with name charts, you can:

❑ Help students learn how to look at words.

❑ Help them learn that a word is always made up of the same letters, arranged left to right.

❑ Direct their attention to reading left to right.

❑ Direct their attention to letter orientation across a word.

❑ Help them notice that names begin with an uppercase letter.

❑ Direct their attention to the first letters of words.

Figure 12-1 Name Charts

❑ Help them realize that words can have one or more syllables.

❑ Help them notice the distinguishing features of the letters in their names.

❑ Help them make connections to other words that have the same first letter or similar word parts *(Mary, my, me)*.

Children not only learn their own names but they will begin to learn the letters in the names of their friends. Here are some quick games you can play using a name chart:

1. Read the names in a shared way as you use a pointer to point to each (in order or randomly).

2. Have children line up, quickly touch their own names when they come to the chart, and then sit down.

3. "I'm thinking of someone who has a name that begins with *M*. Who can come up and find it?"

4. Deal out cards or slips of paper on which children's names are written. Call the names in alphabetical order. The child who has the name you called puts it in a pocket chart.

5. Place a set of name cards at the word study center. Have the children sort the names by first letter or match pairs of name cards.

6. Clap each name and have children tell the number of syllables they hear.

It is also useful for children to write their names. Look at the tracing card that the teacher has made for the child (see Figure 12-2).

Using directional movements that you have demonstrated, have children trace over the name several times and draw a picture. This will help them learn the features of letters within words.

Students need to see their names in many different contexts. Some teachers use a simple poem into which they can insert the names of students in the group (see Figure 12-3). Children enjoy reading poems like this over and over again as you insert different names. The poem can be on a wall chart or it can be on sentence strips in a pocket chart. In the latter case, children can put it together independently and insert their own names or those of their friends.

One teacher created sentences featuring children's names by generating a statement about each child and writing the words on separate cards (see Figure 12-4):

TEACHER: *Sujarta is the first word in the sentence. [Writes it on a card.] Let's say the sentence. [Children repeat the sentence they have composed.] What is the next word?*

CHILDREN: *loves*

The teacher writes the second word on a card and continues until the whole sentence is written on cards.

You may want to say the *next* word, which is a useful term for readers, or you can use words such as

Figure 12-2 Name Tracing Card

Apples on a Tree

One, two, three

Apples on a tree.

One for Sarah.

One for James.

And one for me!

| Apples on a Tree Name:_____ | One apple for _____ | One apple for _____ | One apple for me! |

Figure 12-3 Poem from *My Poetry Book* from Leveled Literacy Intervention, Orange System (Heinemann 2009)

first, *second*, and *third*. When you finish the sentence, place a period after the last word and have the children read the sentence all together. A simpler task for the children is to have the period attached to the last word card in the sentence. A more complex task involves putting the period (or other end mark) on its own card. Children can put the sentences together on a chart in a word study center. You can also write the sentence about a particular child on a sentence strip, cut it up, and have her put it back together.

A name puzzle is an excellent tool for helping children look closely at the features of words. You can create a name puzzle by providing a model of the name and the cut-up letters (see Figure 12-5). Children can work with this puzzle a number of times and you can increase the challenge:

1. Children put the puzzle together by matching each letter, left to right, under the model.

2. Children put the puzzle together left to right using the model, if needed.

3. Children put the puzzle together left to right, afterward checking letter by letter with the model.

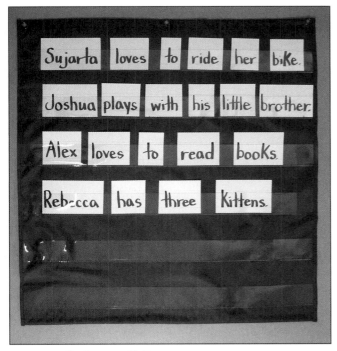

Figure 12-4 Sentences with Names

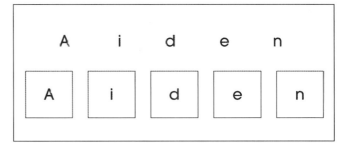

Figure 12-5 Name Puzzle

4. Children put the puzzle together without a model and check letter by letter with what they remember.

5. Children put together both their first and last names.

6. A name puzzle offers many opportunities to closely examine letters and words. Children must search for and use visual information in order to position each letter.

▶ The Role of Early Reading Texts

Many opportunities to read easy texts help children notice the regularities of word features. We recommend texts that use natural language and are carefully selected and sequenced. These texts are not identical to oral language, but they do contain words that occur frequently in spoken language.

Let's look at the sentences in several natural language texts (see Figure 12-6). Notice the repetition of high-frequency words. By the time children have read and reread each of these short, simple books several times, they will have had many exposures to the words *I*, *can*, *see*, *the*, *like*, *my*, *look*, *at*, *this*, and *is*.

These texts aren't very interesting when you look only at the words, but when you add interesting pictures (see Figure 12-7), they can be highly engaging for young readers. The illustrations carry a great deal of meaning, imply a story, and provide information that helps in reading words such as *flowers* and *tree*.

Froggy, the painter, is an engaging character that children will meet several more times as part of a

Figure 12-6 Text in the Early Reading Books

Page	Flying	Woof!	The Painter	Smells	Jesse
2	I can see a train.	Taco sees a bird.	I can paint my chair.	I can smell the flowers.	I like my purple shirt.
4	I can see a duck.	Taco sees a cat.	I can paint my bike.	I can smell the pizza.	I like my purple pants.
6	I can see a doll.	Taco sees a truck.	I can paint my house.	I can smell the soap.	I like my purple socks.
8	I can see a horse.	Taco sees a car.	I can paint my flowers.	I can smell the cookies.	I like my purple shoes.
10	I can see a pig.	Taco sees a squirrel.	I can paint my tree.	I can smell the popcorn.	I like my purple jacket.
12	I can see a bunny.	Taco sees a bike.	I can paint my swing.	I can smell the bread.	I like my purple cap.
14	I can see a car.	Taco sees a bug.	I can paint my friends.	I can smell the soup.	I like my purple glasses.
16	I can see a party.	Taco sees a dog!	I can paint myself!	I can smell the skunk!	I love purple!

Page	The Monkey	Oh, No!	Getting Dressed	Family Pictures	My Bath
2	The monkey can jump.	Look at the mail! Oh, no!	Look at my socks.	This is my mom.	This is my duck.
4	The monkey can eat.	Look at the water! Oh, no!	Look at my pants.	This is my dad.	This is my boat.
6	The monkey can climb.	Look at the trash! Oh, no!	Look at my shirt.	This is my brother.	This is my soap.
8	The monkey can sit.	Look at the paper! Oh, no!	Look at my shoes.	This is my sister.	This is my fish.
10	The monkey can walk.	Look at the flowers! Oh, no!	Look at my sweater.	This is my grandma.	This is my ball.
12	The monkey can ride.	Look at the pillow! Oh, no!	Look at my hat.	This is my cat.	This is my frog.
14	The monkey can hug.	Look at the paint! Oh, no!	Look at my backpack.	This is my bear.	This is my mom.
16	The monkey can sleep.	Look at the dog!	Look at me.	This is my family!	This is my bath!

series of early books. Children are reading highly patterned texts that make sense; at the same time they are noticing the features of words because they are matching one spoken word to one word in print. If readers encounter certain words successfully and are exposed to them numerous times in text, these words become familiar and easier to learn.

This early reading fuels word learning. You can teach young children words in isolation, but without the power of using them while reading continuous

text, the learning will be temporary. One school implemented an intervention program in which paraprofessionals, using word cards, taught children five words per week. They were perfect in reading these words by the end of the week. But two weeks later, the children had forgotten the words they had learned, because they did not have the opportunity to use them in a memorable way. If you teach words before children encounter them in texts, learning will be limited. Early word learning requires the combination of reading

Figure 12-7 Page Layout of *The Painter* from Leveled Literacy Intervention, Green System (Heinemann 2009)

and writing words within continuous print so that you can expose children to many repetitions of previously encountered words. At the same time, you need to:

❑ Draw children's attention to frequently occurring, high-utility words within texts.

❑ Systematically teach words children know so they can "learn how they work."

❑ Select words with letters that are known and that children have encountered.

❑ Use names to establish letter order and orientation.

High-frequency words, learned from reading texts, become an important foundation for understanding letter orientation and letter order within words. Building a rich collection of words that are known in every detail forms a foundation of knowledge that frees the reader's attention to solve new words.

Children's awareness of the features of the words is sharpened if you demonstrate and point out these features. After several encounters in different contexts, children begin to recognize patterns of print. It is easiest to find first, last, and repeated words. Below is a demonstration of how to locate an unknown word. (The cover of and a page spread from the related text is shown in Figure 12-8.)

TEACHER: You have been reading *Frog Food.* Froggy likes bugs on everything, doesn't he? I am going to show you how to find the word *like.* (Say *like.*) Now you say it with me.

CHILDREN: *like*

TEACHER: What letter do you expect to see at the beginning of *like?*

CHILDREN: *l!*

TEACHER: Yes, *like* starts like *leaf* with an *l.* *[Points out the leaf on the Alphabet Linking Chart (see Chapter 10).]* You can think about the first letter you expect to see and then look across the line from left to right and find *like* with an *l.* *[Demonstrates. Turn the page.]* Who can find the word *like?*

EMILY: Demonstrates on the lap book, page 4.

TEACHER: Did Emily find *like?* Check it by saying it and running your finger under it. Does it start with an *l? [Demonstrates]*

CHILDREN: Yes.

TEACHER: Yes, and he likes bugs on his pancakes, doesn't he? He really likes bugs.

CHILDREN: Take turns quickly locating *like* on several pages. Children say the word, think what letter they would expect to see first, find the word, and check it by running a finger under it left to right.

Here the teacher is using an enlarged version of the text called a *lap book* (ten by eighteen inches). Notice how explicit she is in helping children understand the series of actions (*say, think of the first sound and connect it to the letter, think how the letter looks, and search left to right for the word*). She demonstrates searching along the line, left to right, looking for the word. Then she says the word, running a finger under

I like bugs on pancakes.

Figure 12-8 Cover and Page Spread from *Frog Food* from Leveled Literacy Intervention, Green System (Heinemann 2009)

it left to right. When children become accustomed to locating words, they will be able to perform these searching actions quickly with their eyes, checking with the picture. *Like* is a key word in this text that will be highly useful to the children later, and they are learning the behaviors necessary to locate words.

Here's another example of a teacher prompting children to locate new and known words:

LOCATING AN UNKNOWN WORD

TEACHER: Say *can*.

CHILDREN: *can*

TEACHER: What letter would you expect to see at the beginning of *can*?

CHILDREN: *c*

TEACHER: Yes, it starts like *cat*, with a *c*.

TEACHER: Find *can* on this page. *[Children locate* can *on page 2.]* Say *can* and run your finger under it. *[Children do so.]* Now turn the page and find *can* on page 4. *[Children say and locate* can *on page 4 and again on another page.]*

LOCATING KNOWN WORDS

TEACHER: Turn to page 4. You know the word *my*. Say *my*.

CHILDREN: *my*

TEACHER: What letter do you expect to see first in *my*?

CHILDREN: *m*

TEACHER: Find *my* on this page. *[Children locate* my *on page 4.]* Now turn the page and find *my* on page 6. Find it quickly. *[Children say and locate* my *on pages 6, 8, and 10. Teacher emphasizes finding the word quickly.]* Look at the last page and say the word *myself*.

CHILDREN: *myself*

TEACHER: Find *myself* on this page. *[Children do so.]* Say *myself* and run your finger under it to check it. *[Children do so.]* What do you notice about *myself*?

BRODY: It has *my* at the beginning of it.

TEACHER: You noticed a part of the word that you know.

The operation is essentially the same. If needed, you can help the children refer to the name chart or the Alphabet Linking Chart to remember how the letter looks. Children may perform these actions step by step at first, but they will soon learn to search quickly for the visual information needed. In the process, they will be developing visual signposts that they can use strategically. Words like *can* and *my* will appear again and again in books at Levels A, B, and C.

A core of high-frequency words is a huge resource for beginning readers. For example, once a word is known, readers can:

- ❑ Recognize it quickly, leaving attention free to solve more difficult words.
- ❑ Use it to monitor (check on the accuracy) of their reading.
- ❑ Use it to correct their reading.
- ❑ Use it to predict or check on the accuracy of other words in a sentence.
- ❑ Use it as an example to deepen their knowledge of sounds and letters.
- ❑ Substitute, add, or delete letters to read new words (*can, ran; an, and; the, then*).
- ❑ Use it in analogies to get to new words (*can, man; my, cry*).

Of these, probably the most important function is monitoring. Learning their names and a few core words helps children develop the concept of a word and learn that a word is always written the same, left to right. While reading in connection with a pointing finger at Levels A and B, readers soon know that they must always say the same word when pointing under the same pattern of letters.

Many readers who struggle have difficulty even at these very beginning levels because they are not developing awareness of patterns and visual signposts. Each word they meet looks new and strange; they cannot monitor their reading using visual information. Some young readers ignore visual information because they find it so difficult. They may try to "remember" the language of a text instead of using the print and become more and more confused. Careful attention to words within print can be helpful to these learners, since they establish "footholds" to support new learning.

▶ Role of the Text Gradient

The ladder of support provided by a gradient of text (see Chapter 4) can be very helpful in working with struggling readers. First, a gradient helps you find a text that the child can read with high accuracy and thus be successful in processing. Remember that any person will look like a struggling reader if she is expected to process a text that is too hard. (Think about yourself reading Latin!) And the same person will look highly competent when reading a text that is easy. Place the reader in a text that she can read competently with teacher support and you make it possible for her to *look like a competent reader.*

It will do struggling readers no good to read text that is too hard. Day after day they will simply be reinforcing errors or experiencing frustration or becoming dependent on the teacher. Instead, shift the problem solving to the readers so they can experience solving words and thinking about meaning against a backdrop of accurate reading. You may find that some younger readers are not engaging with print at all. They know very few words (or none). They may even

be "inventing" text by making up something that sounds feasible. Have these readers process very simple Level A or B texts and use these early texts to build a core of known words.

Readers of higher-level texts may still need a great deal of work on words. After they have acquired a core of easy high-frequency words from word study and by reading early texts, readers move up the gradient to encounter texts with more difficult, less regular words. In the process, the network of strategic actions gets heavier use because of the more challenging texts (Clay 2001). For example, earlier in this chapter we presented two Level A texts in the Froggy and Friends series (see Figures 12-7 and 12-8). Another story in the Froggy series, *Baby Pictures* (see Figure 12-9), is Level E. Notice the increase in sentence complexity as well as the harder words.

Now look at another book in the series, *Good Friends*, this one at Level L (see Figure 12-10). Words like *foolish, peered, around, squeezed,* and *shrugged* are challenging, but by the time readers are processing texts at this level, they will have a reading vocabulary of several hundred words, enabling them to notice the structure of these more difficult words.

▶ Role of Teacher Interaction

Instruction is critical in helping children read increasingly challenging texts. The teacher arranges learning opportunities for the reader by selecting

Figure 12-9 Cover and Page Spread from *Baby Pictures* from Leveled Literacy Intervention, Green System (Heinemann 2009)

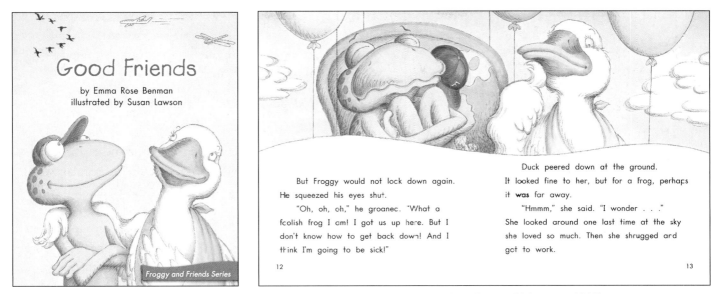

Figure 12-10 Cover and Page Spread from *Good Friends* from Leveled Literacy Intervention, Blue System (Heinemann 2009)

texts that are right for instruction. At the earliest levels, it is important for the children to see many of the same high-frequency words over and over again in the texts they read. Teacher interaction and assistance help readers expand their systems of strategic actions for word solving. It is important to know each of your students' current repertoire of known words so that you can arrange for more opportunities to read, write, and notice word features. Notice one teacher's systematic assessment of children's word reading of fifty high-frequency words that they are encountering in their books shown in Figure 12-11.

You can use the specific information from assessments like this to "tidy up" high-frequency word knowledge throughout the year by making personal sets of word cards for students and working with them and by using words that are nearly known in games and other activities (Chapter 11). Writing will also contribute greatly to word learning, and it is important to remember that the words children can read and those they can write are not precisely the same, although there is usually overlap. Most often, young children can read many more words than they can write in conventional spelling.

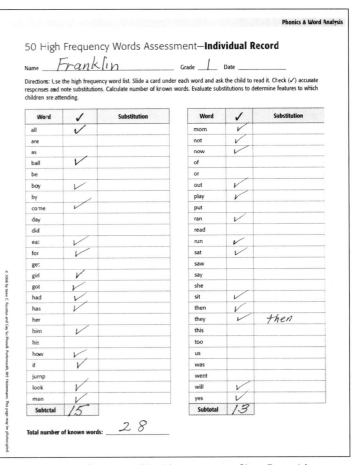

Figure 12-11 High-Frequency Word Assessment—Class Record from Fountas and Pinnell Benchmark Assessment System 1 (Heinemann 2008)

▶ Supporting Word Learning Within the Text

As mentioned above, in early texts, children become familiar with words that they read many times in different contexts. They continue to learn words as they read higher-level texts, and teacher interaction is vital to the process. When you engage children in reading texts, there are three contexts in which to help them learn how to learn words—in the book introduction, as you interact with them during the reading, and in the specific teaching points you make after observing their reading. The degree to which you emphasize word-solving actions within each of these contexts depends on the decisions you make based on the readers' processing strengths and needs.

Helping Children Learn Words Through Book Introductions

The support you provide in the book introduction is a scaffold that enables readers to process a more challenging text effectively. The introduction is a critical element in helping struggling readers experience effective processing. The main purpose of the introduction is to orient readers to the meaning of the whole text, engage their interest, and familiarize them with any tricky language structures they might encounter. You may also give some attention to words, helping readers notice patterns and features.

Earlier, we described specific ways to have children locate words in the early texts they read. You can continue to locate known and unknown words as they move up the text levels. Sometimes you'll help them notice content words—labels, actions, and other words that may pose difficulties. In introducing *The Trip* (see Figure 12-12), this teacher explained the idea of packing for a trip:

> TEACHER: You remember Froggy and all of his friends. This is another Froggy book. In this book his friend Duck is going on a trip to a big

lake. *[Pauses to let children volunteer what they know about a trip.]* Look at pages 2 and 3. Froggy asked Duck, "Where are you going?" Can you say that?

CHILDREN: "Where are you going?"

TEACHER: Duck told Froggy where she was going, and Froggy said, "I love lakes!" Froggy was going to help Duck pack for the trip to the lake, and he asked, "What are you going to do there?" Can you say that? Say *going. [Children say it.] Going* starts like *go.* Can you find it? *[Children locate* going.]

BARRY: It has *-ing* on the end.

TEACHER: Run you finger under it while you say it: *go-ing.*

CHILDREN: "What are you going to do there?"

TEACHER: Turn the page. Duck told Froggy all of the things she was going to do, and every time Froggy said, "I love to swim and hike," or, "I love to dance."

The teacher has the children look at several more pages to familiarize them with the story and language.

TEACHER: Now turn to page 10. Froggy said, "I wish I could go with you." Say the word *could.*

CHILDREN: *could*

TEACHER: What letter would you expect to see at the beginning of *could?*

CHILDREN: *c* like in *cat.*

TEACHER: It starts like *cat.* Find *could.*

Children locate could *twice on page 10.*

The real challenge to the beginning reader is not to memorize a word in isolation but to read it within continuous text while keeping the meaning in mind. Fast word recognition is important for smooth processing. Locating words engages children in the visual searching needed to recognize the word by its features. Locating *known* words helps

Figure 12-12 Cover and Page Spread from *The Trip* from Leveled Literacy Intervention, Blue System (Heinemann 2009)

them recognize the word rapidly and without a great deal of effort while reading. Locating *unknown* words helps them think about and predict the beginning letter and remember other visual details about a word.

Here are some suggestions for language to use when helping children locate a word:

❑ When children are recognizing known high-frequency words: "You know the word *the*. Think how it looks." [*Show a model on the whiteboard if you think they need it.*] "Find *the* on this page and put your finger under it." [*Children do.*] "Turn the page and find *the* on the next page and put your finger under it." [*Notice how quickly children can locate the word.*]

❑ When children are recognizing unknown words: "Say *but*." [*Children do.*] "What letter would you expect to see at the beginning of *but*?" [*Children say* b.] "Find it, run your finger under it, and say it."

❑ When children are recognizing more complex unknown words: "Say *trip*." [*Children do.*] "What two letters would you expect to see at the beginning of *trip*? [*Children identify the letters.*] "Find *trip* on this page." [*Notice how quickly children can locate the word.*]

Supporting Children While They Are Reading

While children are reading the text, you can teach for, prompt for, and reinforce word solving in ways that help them build systems for learning words. (We discuss this topic more comprehensively in Chapter 14.) Be aware of weak prompts, such as:

❑ "That's the new word you learned this morning."

❑ "Think of something that rhymes with *would*."

❑ "What do you wear on your feet?" (For *shoes*.)

These kinds of prompts might occasionally evoke the correct word, but they will not teach children *how* to solve words, and they will either confuse struggling readers or make them more dependent.

Following are some examples of teacher language directed toward helping children solve words. When helping children solve words while reading, the modeling and prompting should direct the reader's eyes from left to right across the word. Prompts like these are mainly used to help readers problem-solve when they have stopped and are unable to proceed.

TEACHING FOR STRATEGIC ACTIONS: WORD BEGINNINGS

Example 1: Teaching

The reader is stopped at *very.*

TEACHER: Look at the beginning of the word.

CHILD: *v*

TEACHER: Listen to how I start it: /v/. . . . I'm going to read up to the word and start it. [*Reading.*] Duck liked the lake /v/—

CHILD: *very*

TEACHER: Read that sentence again and see if that makes sense. [*Child reads.*] Now that makes sense and looks right.

Example 2: Prompting

The reader is stopped at *very.*

TEACHER: Get your mouth ready to start the word.

CHILD: /v/.

TEACHER: Now read it again and get your mouth ready to start the word.

CHILD [*reading*]: "Duck liked the lake very much."

TEACHER: Now that makes sense and looks right.

Example 3: Prompting

The reader is stopped at *very.*

TEACHER: Do you know a word that starts like that?

CHILD: *van*

TEACHER: It starts like *van.* Read it again and start the word.

Example 4: Reinforcing

The reader is stopped at *very* and then rereads, makes the first sound, and solves the word.

TEACHER: You noticed the first letter and made the sound. That makes sense and looks right.

As readers become more advanced, you can teach for, prompt for, and reinforce their using larger parts of words to solve them. Using these larger chunks of print makes the process more efficient. Here are a few examples.

TEACHING FOR STRATEGIC ACTIONS: WORD PARTS

Example 1: Teaching

The child is stopped at *foolish.*

TEACHER: Look how I cover the last part [*covers* -ish]. This first part starts like *food.*

CHILD: *fool.* . . .

TEACHER: *Fool.* The last part says *-ish.* Could this word be *foolish?*

CHILD: Yes.

TEACHER: Read it and see if *foolish* makes sense and looks right.

Example 2: Prompting

The child is stopped at *foolish.*

TEACHER [*covering the* -ish *ending*]: Is that like another word you know?

CHILD: It's like *food* at the beginning. *Foo.* . . .

TEACHER: Say the first part.

CHILD: *fool*

TEACHER: [*uncovering the ending*] Now look at the ending part of the word.

CHILD: *fool . . . ish*

Example 3: Prompting

The child is stopped at *foolish.*

TEACHER: Use your finger to break that word.

CHILD: *fool.* . . . [*Covers up* -ish.]

TEACHER: The first part is *fool* and the last part is?

CHILD: *-ish. foolish*

TEACHER: Read it again and see if *foolish* makes sense and looks right.

Example 4: Reinforcing

The child has stopped at *foolish,* then covered *-ish,* said *fool,* and then *foolish.*

TEACHER: You noticed the first part.

Attending to Words After Reading

Some teaching, prompting for, and reinforcing word solving can be in the form of teaching points after children have read and discussed the meaning of a text. You want to be cautious about intervening too much during reading. Prompt briefly and quickly and only when children have stopped and cannot move forward. (It is *not* helpful to tell children to skip the word and move on: struggling readers will lose the meaning of the story and the sense of the language structure. However, competent readers at much higher levels may be able to skip words and derive them from context.)

You can go back into the text *after* reading to demonstrate, prompt for, or reinforce word solving. Here, you are not trying to "fix" every error but are selecting teaching points that will help readers learn how to solve words. Below are three examples of teaching points after reading. Readers can almost always locate the word that was difficult for them.

Example 1: Teaching

TEACHER: Some of you found a tricky word on page 10. Turn to page 10. [*Children turn to page 10.*]

BARRY [*pointing to* could]: This is it.

TEACHER: You can look at the beginning of the word and think of another word that starts like that. *c*, like *can*. Then, go back to the beginning of the sentence and think what would make sense and look right. [*Reading.*] "I wish I /c/ . . . could go with you." Did that make sense?

CHILDREN: Yes.

TEACHER: And did it look right—start with a *c*, like *can*? [*Children say yes.*] Let's all read it together and get our mouths ready to start the word *could*.

Example 2: Prompting

TEACHER: Turn to page 15. There was a tricky word, wasn't there? See if you can find it. [*Children locate* very.] Think of the sound of the first letter.

CHILDREN: /v/.

TEACHER: Now let's all read the first sentence and say the first sound in the word.

CHILDREN [*reading*]: "Duck liked the lake very much."

TEACHER: So that word is *very*. Find it with your finger. Run your finger under it. What do you notice?

SARAH: It starts like *van*.

BARRY: It has an *-er* next.

BRESHA: It ends like *funny*.

TEACHER: You are noticing the parts of words. *Very* does have an *-er* like in *her*. And it does end in *-y* like *funny* and *happy*. The *y* sounds like *e*.

Example 3: Reinforcing

TEACHER: Barry helped himself when he came to a tricky word. He read the sentence again and made the sound of the first letter, *v*, and then he read *very*. It made sense and looked right. You can read the sentence again, start the tricky word, and think what would make sense in the sentence.

You can also locate words using enlarged texts (flipcharts, lap books, a pocket chart). When children have a great deal of difficulty locating words, it may help to use a mask to isolate a word—or you can use a highlighter or highlighter tape to identify it and make it stand out. Children enjoy placing tape on words or word parts. One way to draw attention to words is shown in Figure 12-13.

After children had read the poem "I Know Something" several times, the teacher had them say *can*, predict the first letter, and then locate the word and highlight it. You can use transparent highlighter tape that can be taken off and reused. One chart can then be reused to focus on different words. You can also teach children to use masking cards (rectangular pieces of tag with a "window" to show a word) to locate words and look at their details. In "Five Little Speckled Eggs," the teacher drew attention to word endings to help children recognize common endings and separate them from base words.

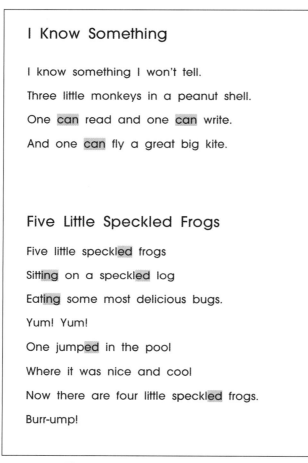

I Know Something

I know something I won't tell.

Three little monkeys in a peanut shell.

One can read and one can write.

And one can fly a great big kite.

Five Little Speckled Frogs

Five little speckled frogs

Sitting on a speckled log

Eating some most delicious bugs.

Yum! Yum!

One jumped in the pool

Where it was nice and cool

Now there are four little speckled frogs.

Burr-ump!

Figure 12-13 Highlighting Words ("I Know Something" and "Five Little Speckled Frogs")

Figure 12-14 Ten Suggestions for Teaching Words

1. Use language that makes it clear you are talking about a *word* (not a letter): "This word is *[can]*" (Some children confuse letters and words and may be focusing on only a *part*.)

2. Tell children to look at the beginning of the word, and show them what that means (first letter on the left).

3. Read the word to children as you run your finger under the word, left to right.

4. Ask children to look closely at the word and say what they notice at the beginning.

5. Ask them to look at the word and then read it as they run a finger under it, left to right.

6. Help children notice the first letter and then look across the word left to right to notice more.

7. Give children magnetic letters and have them build the word left to right. Then have them check against a model, letter by letter, left to right.

8. Have the children, using magnetic letters, break the word by pulling down the first letter and then the rest of the letters. Then have them put the word together again.

9. Connect the word to a simple word that children know. Sometimes another word will help children remember a new word: *an, and; the, then*.

10. Cover up endings to help children look at the base word. Connect the base word to a known word if possible.

▶ Supporting Word Learning Outside the Text

In addition to the kind of interactive support described above, readers need some very specific and systematic instruction to help them learn a core of high-frequency words and, ultimately, a system for learning more words. You'll want to establish some instructional routines that children learn and use. Ten general suggestions for introducing new words to children are included in Figure 12-14. (A general theme running through them is helping children look left to right across words and notice details in print.) Following, some of these suggestions are described in more detail.

Making and Writing Words

When working with readers at all levels, use magnetic letters to build and explore words (see Figure 12-15). Multicolored magnetic letters bring the details of a word to children in three dimensions. Children can touch the letters, feel them, and physically place them in order within the word

When you demonstrate building a word with magnetic letters, start on the left side of your chalkboard or metal plate (anything letters will stick to). Build the word left to right, always starting with the first letter. Once you have demonstrated a simple

Figure 12-15 Building the Word *like* with Magnetic Letters

word several times, give each child the letters (one at a time in order at first) and ask the child to make the word left to right and then compare it with a model. Try not to allow the child to act in error—establish left-to-right directionality and correct letter orientation. Children will soon learn to build words quickly.

Using magnetic letters to break words apart helps children see the parts of words (see Clay 2005). Words can be "broken" several ways (see Figure 12-16). After you demonstrate, children can learn to break words

Figure 12-16 Breaking Words Apart Using Magnetic Letters

into onsets and rimes, letters, and other word parts. Turn the task over to them. Remember to select very simple known words while they are learning this task.

Create a model for the word *can*. Suggested language: "Say the word *can*" [*while running a finger under it left to right*]. "Get a good look at it. Now we are going to break it into letters." [*Saying the word slowly, pull down the* c, *then the* a, *and then the* n.]

Make the word *can* and have children say it as you run a finger under it left to right. Suggested language: "Now, we are going to break *can* into parts."[*Say* c *and pull down the* c. *Say* -an *and pull down the rest of the word. Have children say the word, segmenting the onset and the rime:* c-an. *Then put* can *back together and break it into letters.*] "You can break a word two ways."

Segment several different words into onsets and rimes. Suggested language: "You can break a word into the first part and the rest of the word. Let's do that with some of the words you know." [*Using easy (CVC) words that begin with consonants, first make the whole word and have children say it. Then pull down the first letter, saying it, and then pull down the rest of the word, saying the rime.*]

Build an easy known word with an ending that children will recognize. Break it in the same way.

Some ways to teach children to break words are:
- ❏ Letters.
- ❏ Single consonant onsets and rimes (CVC).
- ❏ Letter cluster (digraphs and blends) onsets and rimes.
- ❏ Syllables.
- ❏ Inflectional endings (-*s*, -*ed*, -*ing*, -*er*, -*est*).
- ❏ Suffixes (-*ly*, -*ful*, -*ness*).
- ❏ Prefixes (*re-*, *un-*).

It's helpful for children to see (and manipulate) a new word in several different media. For example, Figure 12-17 shows the word *have* written on a whiteboard and made below with magnetic letters.

Looking at the same word made in slightly different ways helps children see the essential distinctive features of each letter and look more closely at the details of the word. One teacher provided three different ways for children to see the word *about* (see Figure 12-18). In

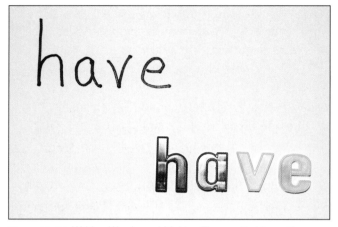

Figure 12-17 Writing Words and Making Them with Magnetic Letters

Figure 12-18 Different Ways to See the Word *About*

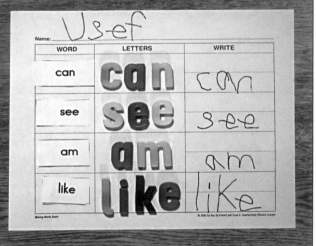

Figure 12-19 Take, Build, Write

Figure 12-19, the word on the card is a model for making the word with magnetic letters and for writing it.

When children understand the procedure for looking at a model to build a word left to right, they can practice this activity on their own. It is helpful to "overlearn" the core of high-frequency words so that they are known in every detail. Making and writing words in a very conscious way, always attending to the left-to-right nature of words, will help to establish a reading vocabulary that children can use as a resource.

Readers at higher levels can also benefit from using magnetic letters. Look at an example of building multisyllable words in Figure 12-20: the student uses a card on which five words are written. He chooses one and makes it left to right three times. By this time, readers have firmly established left-to-right order, but you should be sure to verify that they are building these longer words left to right. These words may also be broken into syllables to look at the parts.

Working with Word Cards

To encourage children to overlearn high-frequency words, give each child his own collection of word cards for words he has previously met in contin-

Figure 12-20 Building Multisyllable Words

uous text and is likely to meet again in the level of texts he is reading.

Look at the collections of simple and more complex words in Figure 12-21. You can place each card in a pocket chart one at a time, asking children to say the word as you run a finger under it. After all words are inserted in the chart, you can read down the columns using a pointer. Alternatively, you can write a list of simple and more complex words on a piece of chart paper. If you write the words, you can:

- ❏ Tell the children the word you are going to write, and ask them to watch as you say and write it left to right.

- ❏ Have children get a good look at the word and then say it as you run your finger under it left to right.

- ❏ Give children the word card and have them take a good look at the word as they say it while running their finger under it left to right.

When working with a small group, you will want to have a collection of high-frequency words that you have selected from the books you have introduced to them. Keep adding new words and taking out words all members of the group know well. There are several ways to familiarize children with words using word cards. For example:

- ❏ Lay all the word cards on the table. Call out each word and have a child say and locate the word card and then place it in the pocket chart (or reverse this action).

- ❏ Lay all word cards on the table and ask children to take turns saying and locating a word of their choice, then placing the word card in the pocket chart.

- ❏ Lay all word cards on the table and play a game: "I'm thinking of a word that begins with *f* [starts like *fan*]." Children take turns finding and saying the word, finding the word card, and placing it in the pocket chart.

- ❏ Place words in the pocket chart and ask children to look at a word, say it, and run a finger under the word.

Children can collect their own word cards in a small plastic tub, a small manila envelope, or a word bag (a one-quart plastic sealable bag). These words are enormously beneficial to the beginning reader, who can use them to:

- ❏ Understand the concept of a word in language.

- ❏ Understand the concept of a word as a sequence of letters with white space on either side.

- ❏ Monitor voice-print match.

- ❏ Monitor accuracy.

- ❏ Self-correct.

- ❏ Notice letter-sound relationships or word parts.

- ❏ Notice connections between words and use them to solve new words.

Figure 12-21 Collections of High-Frequency Words

❑ Begin to write words correctly.

❑ Help solve new words—for example, *the-then, is-in, an-and, an-man.*

To add a word to the collection:

1. Foreshadow the addition by having the children locate the word in the new book that they are reading (or rereading the next day).

2. Show children the word (on chart paper, with magnetic letters, on the whiteboard, or on a card) and read it while running your finger under it, left to right.

3. Have children read the word, saying it and running a finger under it left to right.

4. Have them read the word several times, make it with magnetic letters, or write it on the whiteboard.

5. Add it to the word collection.

Some ways they can work with the individual word card collection include:

1. Children turn over the word cards one at a time and read them. They place them in two piles: (1) words they know and (2) words they are learning. They then choose one word card from "words they are learning" and read it, make it with magnetic letters, and write it. (They can highlight the beginning letter or another part of the word to help them remember it.)

2. Children lay out their word cards face up in front of them and play a game: "Find a word that starts with the letter *a*." (You can choose any word feature—a phonogram, letter cluster, vowel, ending.) Children find the word, read it, and put it away.

3. Children lay out their word cards face down in front of them. They turn over a word card and read it, leaving it face up. If they do not know a word, they turn the card over again. They continue until (with help) all word cards are face up.

4. Two children lay out their word cards face up in front of them. A third child stacks his word cards and reads them one at a time. When the leader reads the word, the other two find their word cards and put them in a pile. They continue until all the word cards are in piles and then put them away.

5. Children choose a word, make it left to right with magnetic letters, read to check it by running a finger under it, and then check it letter by letter with the word card (pointing at each letter—*c-c, a-a, n-n*). Then they write the word, read to check it by running a finger under it, and check it letter by letter with the word card.

6. Children choose a word card and look at it carefully. Then, without looking at the word, they attempt to make it with magnetic letters or to write it. They check with the model and correct it, if needed.

7. Children take their group of word cards and lay them out face up. They find two words that are connected in some way. Then they show the words to the rest of the group, who try to guess how the words are connected (same first letter, same number of letters, same ending, etc.)

Word Sorting

A good way to help readers attend to and remember the features of words is by sorting them, an engaging activity that allows readers to make deep connections between words. After children recognize even a small body of words, they can begin to sort them. Start with simple examples, using words that children know. An example of a teacher's demonstration with very simple words like *and* and *go* is shown in Figure 12-22. Notice that *any* could go under *and*, as well, depending on what the sorter is noticing. Sorting is a powerful tool in helping readers notice parts of words. Scott's word sort, dividing words into those that start with a vowel, have the same middle sound, and have the same first letter, is shown in Figure 12-23. Word sorts by sound and by patterns are shown in Figure 12-24.

A comprehensive list of categories for word sorting is shown in Figure 12-25. As you can see, these ways of sorting will help readers notice the parts of words.

Figure 12-22 A Simple Word Sort

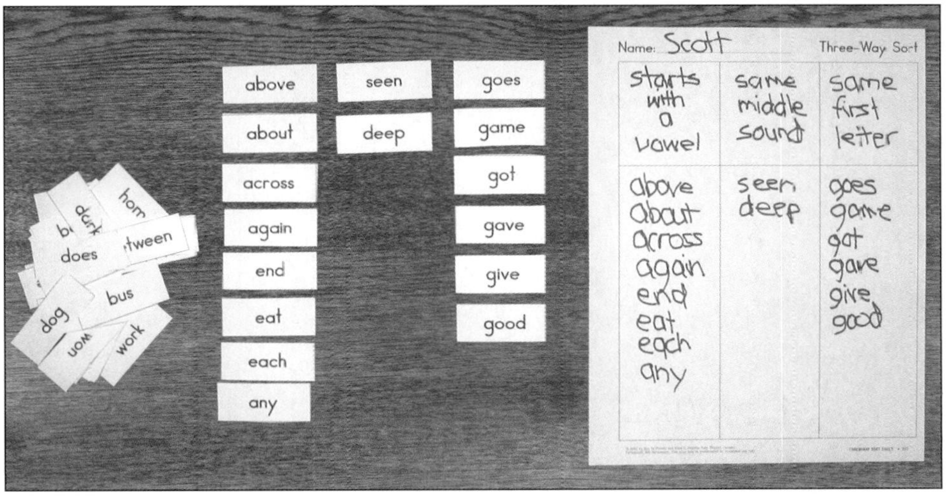

Figure 12-23 Scott's Word Sort

Writing Words

Writing plays an extremely important part in word learning. It supports the network of knowledge that children build around individual words. In addition, writing helps children learn orientation, sequence, and the details of words. The goal is to help children learn how words work. If they can develop a core of words that they know how to write in every detail, these words will fuel their literacy. The writing vocabulary will include known words as well as the words the child knows how to

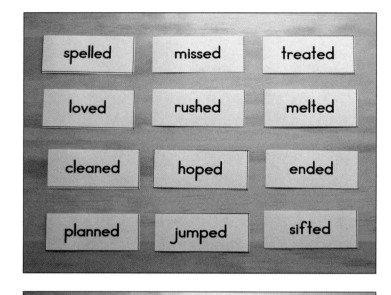

Figure 12-24 Word Sorting by Sound and by Pattern

construct by using sound-letter correspondence and word parts.

One teacher said to her students, "I'm going to say the word *cat* slowly to hear the sounds. *C-a-t*. Now I am going to write it." The teacher wrote this CVC word slowly as she said the sounds (see Figure 12-26). This action helped the children see the letters while associating them with the sounds. The children then wrote some other words they knew, associating the letters with the sounds.

A personal alphabet book that has a clear picture, letter, and word for every letter is a useful tool for letter learning and tidying up letter knowledge. Children can write in additional words that begin with the letter (see Figure 12-27).

In Chapters 10 and 11, we describe the process of using Elkonin boxes to write words. You will also find examples of using letter boxes in Chapter 13. Children say words slowly and think about the sounds in order to write the words, one box for each sound—see Figure 12-28. As their knowledge of words grows, they move on to use one box for each letter so that they understand how words *look*.

Children need to learn to construct words quickly as well as to write known words quickly. It is important to build up speed. This rapid recognition and writing of known words allows the reader to give more attention to new challenges. To help children achieve fluency in writing:

- ❑ Have them write words many times, noticing details.
- ❑ Have them write words bigger or smaller, with different tools (marker, pen, chalk pencil, water pen) and on different surfaces (poster board, paper, whiteboard, in sand, in salt).
- ❑ Give them new tools (for example, help them analyze the sounds in words, notice letter clusters, or use analogy).

The goal of writing words is not simply to learn specific words. You need to teach students *how* to do something—not memorization, but knowing how to construct words. You can help them to learn how to:

- ❑ Write words better.
- ❑ Write words faster.
- ❑ Link words to other words.
- ❑ Write words independently.

Child can then use what they already know as examples to dig deeper into print. Having children initiate the sequence of actions to produce the word from beginning to end is key. The goal is to give them the tools. They will start to initiate writing words because they have ways to construct them. It may start with writing the first letter, but it will move on to include other letters by virtue of visual and sound analysis and analogy. Look, Say, Cover, Write, Check (see Figure 12-29) is an excellent technique for learning words (see the discussion in Chapter 11).

Figure 12-25 **Categories for Word Sorts**

Categories related to sound or letter pattern

Words that begin/end with a particular consonants *(mom, mix, or, path, with)*
Words that start/end with consonant clusters *(spring, clap, soft)*
Words with double consonants *(zipper, mitten)*
Words with two consonants that make one sound *(shoe, chimney)*
Words with a vowel sound as in *apple (cat, map)*
Words with a vowel sound as in *egg (pet, then)*
Words with a vowel sound as in *iguana (sit, lip)*
Words with a vowel sound as in *octopus (hot, top)*
Words with a vowel sound as in *umbrella (under, up)*
Words with a vowel sound as in *cake (late, cape)*
Words with a vowel sound as in *feet (meat, keep)*
Words with a vowel sound as in *kite (sign, fight)*
Words with a vowel sound as in *goat (rope, soap)*
Words with a vowel sound as in *mule (cute, use)*
Words beginning with a vowel *(under, over)*
Words ending with a vowel *(tuba, solo)*
Words with the same vowel sound *(play, mail, take)*
Words with vowel combinations *(cream, boat, sail)*
Words with a vowel and *r (corn, first)*
Words that rhyme *(mail, sail)*
Words with a letter that makes a particular sound (the *s* sound in *see* and *bus* or *was* and *treasure)*
Words with silent letters *(make, seat)*
Words that can be paired with another word that sounds the same but means something different *(to, two, sail, sale)*
Words with one, two, or three syllables *(dog, rab-bit, to-ma-to)*
Words with an open syllable *(mo-tel, to-ken)*
Words with a closed syllable *(rob-in, cab-in)*

Categories related to structure or meaning

Words that have prefixes *(redo, unfasten)*
Words with endings *(smartest, looking, carried)*
Words with the same base *(write, rewrite, rewriting)*
Words that name people *(brother, friend)*
Words that name places *(home, yard)*
Words that are short or long *(to, reminder)*
Words in a category *(carrot, orange)*
Words that describe *(lovely, green)*
Words that mean the same *(fight, argument)*
Words that mean the opposite *(hot, cold)*
Words that can be spelled two different ways *(to, two)*
Words that are contractions *(haven't, wasn't)*
Words that are compounds *(someday, cannot)*
Words that have the same part *(fat, fatter, fattest)*
Words forms that are singular or plural *(calf, calves)*

The act of writing helps children look at the details of words and remember them. But the benefits of writing go far beyond learning words. Chapter 13 describes word writing in more detail and discusses several genres for writing about reading that can be helpful to struggling readers.

Figure 12-26 Saying Words Slowly and Writing Them

Figure 12-27 *S* for *Sun* in a Personal Alphabet Book, *My ABC Book* from Leveled Literacy Intervention

Figure 12-28 Writing *Like* Using Elkonin Boxes

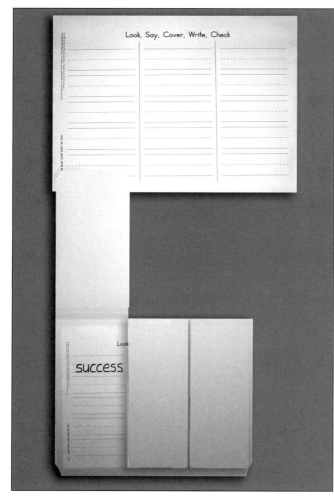

Figure 12-29 Look, Say, Cover, Write, Check

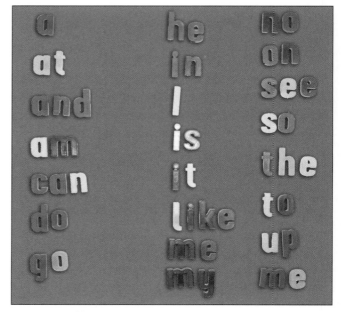

Figure 12-30 Making New Words

Figure 12-31 Erik Explores Plurals

Changing Words to Make New Words

You can use writing or magnetic letters to help children learn how to move from known words to unknown words. To do this they need to recognize significant word parts, and making connections is a very powerful way to help them see the parts of words. In Figure 12-30 a teacher uses magnetic letters to demonstrate making very simple words that children know.

Once children know the concept of substituting, adding, or deleting letters to make new words, they can use this principle to get to words. In the example in Figure 12-31, Erik used a base word and endings to explore simple plurals. Erik's teacher had previously presented several minilessons on plurals; the group

was learning about words that become plural by adding *-s* or *-es*. By looking at these examples, they began to generalize the idea that many words add *-s* but that when a word ends in *ch* or *x*, you add *-es* and it makes another syllable. Knowledge of this principle will be helpful in both reading and writing. Adding inflectional endings is not easy and is especially difficult for English language learners, but it does involve building on the known.

Children control a word when they learn that by adding endings they can make a new (and related) word. This knowledge is built over time through short lessons and clear examples. The example in Figure 12-32 shows the teacher's chart for the lesson and the student's independent work. The work reflects the following principles:

❑ You can add word parts to the end of a word to show when you did something in the present or past.

❑ You add -s to the end of a word to make it sound right in a sentence.

❑ Change y to i and add -es or -ed to words that end in a consonant and y.

❑ You add -ed to some words to show you did something in the past.

❑ Add -ed to words ending in silent e to make the -ed ending and show it was in the past.

❑ You add -ing to a word to show you are doing something now.

This activity encompasses a large amount of learning. The children are building new concepts from what they already know—always working from the base word. They soon learn to take a word apart by noticing the base word and using their knowledge of a limited set of inflectional endings. This knowledge is useful in reading and writing. If they understand this concept, you can prompt them to cover the ending, look at and solve the base word, and then say it with the ending—a much more efficient process than trying to sound out every word or memorize every word separately.

▶ Overlearning Through Games

The engaging activity of a game helps children develop the ability to process words quickly. (Appendix F includes detailed directions for several simple games.) Guidelines for using games as part of your instruction include:

❑ Have children play games with words that are *known* or that they can very easily solve. The idea is to develop automatic rapid recognition.

❑ Be sure that the materials (word cards, for example) used in the game are in very clear, standardized print so that children can recognize word features easily.

❑ Play a game *after* directly teaching children how to play it.

❑ Make sure that there is a cooperative spirit among the players (it's only a game).

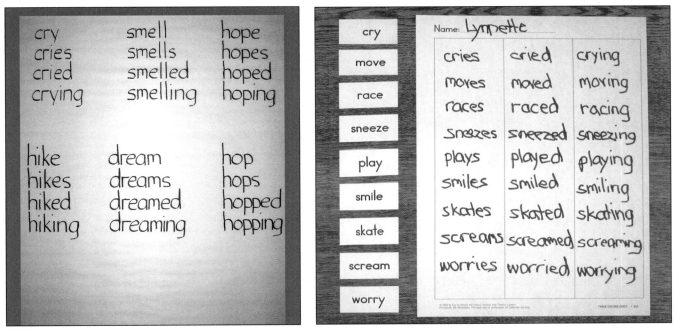

Figure 12-32 Teacher's Chart and Student's Independent Work.

Here are brief descriptions of a few games and their benefits:

1. *Snap!* (see Figure 12-33). Players each lay down a card with a word on it. They must quickly compare the words, which means they must notice and process the features. If the words are the same, a player says "Snap!" The first player who says it, must read the words. This game promotes quick comparison of word features.

2. *Concentration* (see Figure 12-34). Players lay out an array of words face down (from their collections of high-frequency words or other words). They turn over two cards. If the cards match, they can put them in a pile. If they don't match, they turn them over again. The game requires remembering features of particular words.

3. *Word Ladders* (Figure 12-35). This game is a mental puzzle. The idea is to build a ladder from

Figure 12-33 Snap!

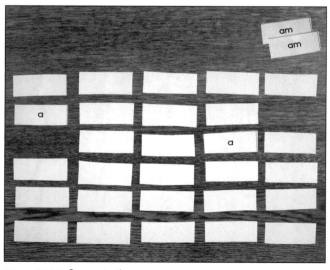

Figure 12-34 Concentration

Figure 12-35 Word Ladders

top to bottom by changing one or two letters in the word. In the first picture, the teacher has demonstrated the process using very simple examples. (The more letters you allow to be changed, the easier the game.) The students then start with a known word and see how far they can go (see Cecelia's word ladders). Children enjoy sharing their word ladders with other students. The game requires looking at a known word and making connections to another known word.

4. *Lotto* (see Figure 12-36). Lotto is similar to Bingo except that players put markers on the whole card. The game can be played at simpler and more complex levels. At the simplest level, a player draws a card with a word on it. If he has that word on his card, he places it on top. The first player to fill the card wins. To increase the difficulty, call out words and have players locate and read them and place markers on them. You can also play the game with any kind of word part—phonograms, inflectional endings, letter clusters, etc.

5. *Follow the Path* (Figure 12-37). Players throw a die and move a marker along the path. They must read the word written in the space on which they land or go back to the space they were on when they began their turn. The first player to reach the

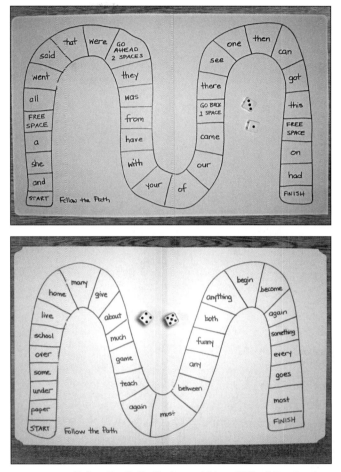

Figure 12-37 Follow the Path (Easier and More Difficult Versions)

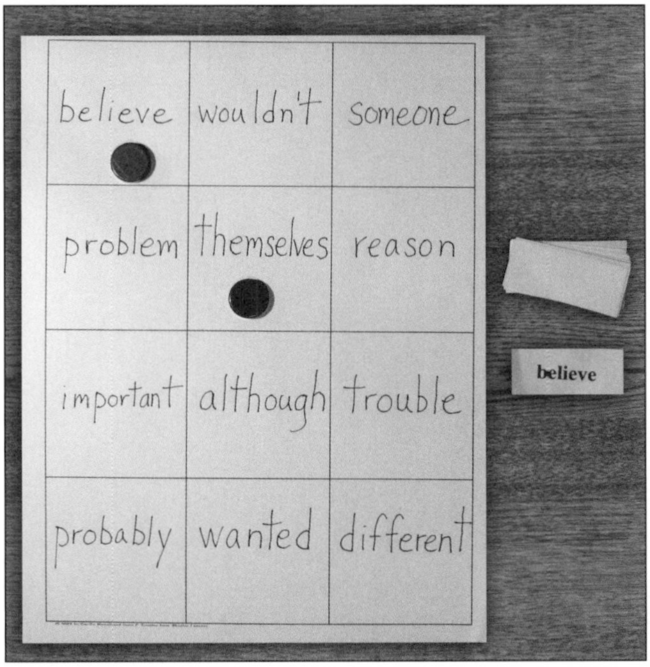

"finish" wins. The game gives children practice in reading high-frequency words. It can also be used in more complicated ways—for example, children can identify word parts or tell another word similar to the word in the box.

▶ Change Over Time in Teacher/Child Interactions

It is important to maintain a sequence of teaching actions in helping children learn about words. We recommend the following sequence:

1. Model writing a word and have children copy it. They need to see the correct form.

2. Have children write the beginning of the word and you finish the rest.

Figure 12-36 Lotto

3. Have children write the word while you prompt, remind, nod, facilitate.

4. The teacher talks more than shows. At this point, children just need occasional prompting.

▶ Building a System for Learning Words

When children are building their early core reading/writing vocabularies (which at first may overlap but are not exactly the same), words must be encountered many times before they are known. That is true for all of us. You seldom remember a difficult word like *obstreperous, puerile,* or *sanguine* simply by hearing it once. You need to use the word orally, read it in different contexts, and even write it for it to become a regular part of your repertoire. Of course, if a word is highly memorable for some reason (emotionally loaded, connected to a set of words you know), then the process is accelerated and you may not need so many exposures. It could move into your repertoire quickly, and you delight in using it. There are always shades in knowing a word from completely unknown and unrecognizable to deeply known, including the ability to use the word keeping in mind multiple meanings and any connotative meanings connected to it.

When we talk about developing early reading and writing vocabularies, the words are usually already in children's oral vocabularies. They are the simpler words that they have used in conversation for years. An exception is the child who is just learning to speak English and is simultaneously trying to establish an English reading and writing vocabulary. As a general principle, be sure these children understand the meaning of words they are trying to learn to read in English (you can provide this support through conversation). Knowledge of the English word's meaning will be strengthened as children learn to read and write it.

Children's knowledge of a word passes through shades of knowing, as shown in Figure 12-38. An easy word in a child's oral vocabulary may be anywhere along the spectrum of learning. Some will be unknown, some partially known, some known, and some flexibly known.

But as readers acquire a larger repertoire and more resources, the process is accelerated. For example:

- ❑ They may know many patterns and parts of words that they can use strategically. These larger parts take less attention and are used extensively by young proficient readers (Kaye 2007).
- ❑ They may connect the word to a known word (*can/cane*).
- ❑ They may use analogy, a form of word connection (*tree, my, try*).
- ❑ A word may be of intense interest to the children (*elephant, dinosaur,* a sports team).
- ❑ The child may be particularly motivated to learn a word (*grandma, football*).
- ❑ The word may have emotional impact (*sad, birthday party, died*).

Interest, motivation, and emotional impact overlap, and all three may be present. A word that has a higher impact has a better chance of being remembered and may make it into the known and flexibly known categories more quickly (Lyons 2003).

Readers may need many exposures to a word in different contexts. Use all the tools at your disposal in a systematic way to build your students' word knowledge. When readers find it hard to remember a word, keep in mind the continuum of learning a word and provide extra practice. Sometimes, children act very impulsively, saying or writing a word before really looking at it. In such cases, interactions like these are helpful:

READING

TEACHER: Take a good look at the word before you say anything. Run your finger under it like this *[demonstrate]* and take a good look at it.

CHILD: *from*

Teacher discusses details of the word—first letter, letter clusters, connection to another word.

TEACHER [*when working with the word in isolation*]: Run your finger under it and say the word. Does it look like *from*?

Extending Reading Power Through Writing

READING AND WRITING are reciprocal processes in that what is learned in one area can be used to strengthen and expand the other. Both reading and writing are part of a larger processing system, and they are related at every level of language learning. In this chapter, we discuss writing about reading as an essential component of an intervention effort and suggest ways that writing can benefit struggling readers.

When you work with children who are having difficulty becoming literate, you can build on the wonderful reciprocity between reading and writing. What is learned in one area can be used to strengthen and expand understanding in the other. Writing and reading are related at just about every level of language learning: letters, sounds, and words; syntactic patterns; mapping out meanings. It is amazing that some reading intervention programs do not include writing, because what is learned in writing powers the reading process. According to Clay (2001, 18), "When teachers do not include writing daily in early intervention lessons, they are severely limiting the child's opportunities to learn and they are contributing to slower progress overall, at a time when it is most important to learn quickly."

Reading and writing are both part of a larger literacy processing system. Readers and writers use the same sources of information, integrating them while processing continuous text. Of course there are important differences. Readers work with constructed text. They recognize written signs (visible information) and bring their own understandings (invisible information) to the process. Writers construct the text. They produce the written signs that map out the meanings they want to communicate. But readers often think like writers as they consider how to craft their ideas; and writers read their own material like readers as they reconsider the material and how it communicates (see Fountas and Pinnell 2006).

Writing is multifaceted in that it orchestrates thinking, language, and the motor movements required to produce the graphic signs representing meaning. For young children this means using directional movement to write letters, combine them into words, and lay the words out in lines of print. But the world of writing is different for today's young children. Increasingly, writing is created on computer keyboards, expediting the slow, mechanical act of handwriting. Don't bypass handwriting completely, however, because these early movements, full of tactile learning, help learners gain control of letter recognition.

Writing is a slowed-down process that allows children to attend to the details of letters and words. When they are writing, children must direct their attention to detail while simultaneously remembering the immediate message being encoded and keeping in mind the meaning and organization of the entire text (staying on the topic, for example).

Elsewhere, we have written about developing writers through the support of a variety of forms of writing (see Fountas and Pinnell 2001, 2006; Pinnell and Fountas 1999; McCarrier, Pinnell, and Fountas 2000). We have also described specific behaviors and understandings to notice, teach, and support with regard to conventions, craft, and writing process (see Pinnell and Fountas 2008). In this chapter, we focus on the role of writing in helping readers overcome difficulties.

▶ Reading Difficulties and Writing Difficulties

In many ways, children face similar requirements and have similar difficulties in reading and writing (see Figure 13-1). Critical processing behaviors required in both writing and reading include:

- ❑ Expectations about meaning.
- ❑ Motor coordination.
- ❑ Knowledge of how print works.
- ❑ Directional movement.
- ❑ Self-monitoring.
- ❑ Self-correction.
- ❑ Problem solving.
- ❑ Divided attention.

- ❑ Active thinking.
- ❑ Reflection.

Most likely, young children who are struggling with reading will also be having great difficulty with writing. They have trouble forming letters and placing them on the page. Often, when they focus on the mechanics of writing, they forget the intended message. They do not know how to check their writing for accuracy and have no tools for processing it as readers so that they know whether or not it makes sense. They may become so bogged down in writing accurately that they do not take risks and so do not engage in the word analysis that is so valuable for building their processing systems and that informs both writing and reading. Some children learn how to read but remain poor spellers; even children who learn to spell may not ever become skilled writers. The good news is that when you help learners use writing, you contribute to reading in a significant way.

▶ Contexts for Supporting Children as Writers

Everything you do to help writers develop effective writing strategies will also contribute to reading. In this book, we focus on *writing about reading* because the connections are closer; but you can also use these forms, genres, and supportive interactions in classroom lessons, writing conferences with individuals, and small-group instruction. Writing about reading is particularly effective in small-group intervention lessons for children who are having difficulty in either area or in both.

We use three specific forms of writing in intervention lessons (see Figure 13-2). Within each, you can use powerful interactions to teach, prompt, and support the writer. In the contexts we describe here, the teacher provides support for writing texts the children will reread; the text is therefore in conventional form. You may make a different decision. During regular classroom writing contexts (independent writing in a writing workshop, for example) you would not expect conventional form, as children learn through trying

Figure 13-1 Common Requirements of Writing and Reading

Writing	Reading
• The *expectation* that thoughts can be expressed in language that can be written.	• The *expectation* that print will be meaningful language.
• *Motor coordination*—eyes, hand, and fingers (writing or typing letters).	• *Motor coordination*—eyes and fingers (at first) and then eyes alone.
• Knowledge of *how print works*—early writing behaviors: using spaces, placing words in lines, starting on the left.	• Knowledge of *how print works*—early reading behaviors: voice-print match, starting on the left, etc.
• *Directional movement*—making letters, placing words across and down the page.	• *Directional movement*—looking left to right across words, letters, lines of print.
• *Self-monitoring* to determine if what was written is accurate (looks right, sounds right, and makes sense).	• *Self-monitoring* to determine if reading is accurate (looks right, sounds right, and makes sense).
• *Self-correction*—proofreading and revising to be sure the writing is accurate (looks right, sounds right, and makes sense).	• *Self-correction* to be sure that the reading is accurate (looks right, sounds right, and makes sense).
• *Problem solving*—selecting words and arranging them in meaningful strings; spelling words.	• *Problem solving*—working actively to solve words and search for information.
• *Divided attention*—remembering the message while using directional movements.	• *Divided attention*—keeping the meaning in mind while visually processing print.
• *Active thinking* to construct and reconstruct language in a way that communicates the desired meaning.	• *Active thinking* within, beyond, and about the text.
• *Reflection* on the meaning to consider revision and further editing.	• *Reflection* on the meaning to understand the text at a deeper level.

and/or approximating spelling on their way to conventional writing.

Shared and Interactive Writing

Shared and interactive writing are very similar. The only difference is whether or not individual children write some of the letters/words. In shared writing, children participate actively in composing the text, but the teacher is the scribe. Shared writing is a useful strategy to use when children know very little. As the scribe, the teacher can speed things along by writing the words that children already know well. There is no instructional value in having children write these words themselves.

Talk about the text. Throughout the writing process, conversation is very important. You begin by engaging in conversation with children about a text (or other experience).

Compose. Then, based on the conversation, negotiate the composition of each sentence of the text. Help the children make suggestions and then come to agreement. Guide this process so that the message is within students' control. In other words, don't just write down whatever individual children say; be sure it is meaningful to them as a group. You want the writers to own the message and be able to remember it. When writing about reading, you can encourage children to think about the meaning of the text and sometimes "borrow" from it. This is not the same as copying word for word. Ask them to consider and "try out" the messages. Hearing themselves saying and then writing sentences will help them learn more about language syntax, which is particularly helpful for English learners.

Write. In shared writing, the sentence is written word by word by the teacher on a chart that everyone can see. If you are working with a small intervention

Figure 13-2 Three Forms to Generate Writing about Reading

Format	Description	Value

Shared and Interactive Writing
 	
(handwritten margin note: teacher does all writing / Interactive students add)
	The teacher helps children compose a message or series of sentences that is written on a chart:
	
	1. There is conversation throughout the process that helps reveal the writing process.
	
	2. With teacher support, children negotiate the composition of the message sentence by sentence.
	
	3. The teacher writes the message in large print on a chart that everyone can see.
	
	4. In *interactive* writing, children take over the writing at particular points that have instructional value.
	
	5. The children reread the message in a shared way and sometimes individually.
	
	6. The writing students have produced becomes a resource:
	  • The teacher and children revisit the text for letter or word study.
	  • Children may have a typed copy to glue in their writing books and illustrate.
	  • The teacher may write the sentences on sentence strips to cut up and have the children reassemble and glue on paper.
		• Shared and interactive writing engages children in every aspect of the writing process.
		
		• Children receive a high level of support that enables them to look closely at letters, sounds, and words; use new vocabulary; and internalize English syntax.
		
		• The pieces of writing are saved and used in several ways.

Dictated Writing	The teacher reads aloud a sentence or series of sentences and children write them with teacher support:
	
	1. Some of the words will be known.
	
	2. The teacher helps children solve unknown words by having them use sound or letter boxes, prompting them to use sound analysis or visual analysis, helping them think of words they know, and/or writing the word on a whiteboard as a model for either checking their attempt or copying the word. The completed text is in conventional form.
	
	3. The teacher may use a verbal path to describe the movements needed to make a letter.
	
	4. The writing students have produced becomes a resource:
	  • The teacher and children revisit the text for letter or word study.
	  • They may use a highlighter to emphasize words or parts of words.
	  • The teacher may write the sentences on sentence strips to cut up and have the children reassemble and glue on paper.
	  • Children reread their sentences when finished and may draw a picture.
		• Children learn how to go from oral to written language.
		
		• They experience word solving within a meaningful sentence.
		
		• They reread and check their work.
		
		• They gain experience with English syntactic patterns and vocabulary.
		
		• They have a shared text to use as a resource.
		
		• They will enjoy taking their dictated sentences (or a copy) home.

continues

Figure 13-2 **Three Forms to Generate Writing about Reading,** *continued*		
Format	**Description**	**Value**
Independent Writing	After discussion, the children compose and then write their own sentences while the teacher supports them as needed: 1. The text may be a list, a message or sentence, labels for pictures, or any other type of writing. 2. The teacher provides support as needed to help the children write in conventional form. 3. The text becomes a resource: • Children may revisit the text to highlight parts of words they want to remember. • Children independently reread their sentences when finished and may draw a picture. • The teacher may write the sentences on sentence strips to cut up and have the children reassemble and glue on paper.	• Children develop independent control of early writing strategies. • They learn to represent ideas in different ways. • They learn to self-monitor their writing (check on themselves). • Composing and writing their own sentences about a text is highly motivating. • Children enjoy rereading their own compositions. • Children enjoy taking their compositions home.

group, you can use a chart approximately ten by fifteen or twenty inches. Some teachers find it works very well to use a large sketching tablet with no lines. The written pieces can be kept together in the coil-bound tablet, and it is easy to revisit them.

In interactive writing, the teacher may invite individual children to come up to the chart and write parts (or all) of some of the words. These words may:

❑ Be new and offer opportunities for sound analysis or visual analysis related to spelling.

❑ Be nearly known and offer opportunities for productive practice.

❑ Have parts that are useful to bring to children's attention.

For example, in the piece of interactive writing summarizing *The Mitten* (shown in Figure 13-3), the teacher wrote well-known words such as *the, of,* and *my.* Children contributed items such as the consonant cluster at the end of *lost,* the *w* in *went,* the *h* for *here,* and the word *is.* After the last sentence was read, the teacher went back and added quotation marks, explaining them.

The learning opportunities in this piece include:

❑ Print laid out using space and lines.

❑ Individual high-frequency words.

❑ A word in all capital letters for emphasis.

❑ A range of punctuation—periods, exclamation point, and quotation marks.

Reread. A piece of interactive writing is usually reread each time you add a word (or two or three). This rereading helps children get back to the whole message and it also provides important reading practice. Writers need to reread to check whether their writing sounds right and makes sense. You may wish to have the group read together or have individuals take turns reading lines.

The boy lost his mitten.

The animals went in the mitten.

The animals popped Out of the mitten.

POP!

Here is my mitten, the boy said.

Figure 13-3 Interactive Writing about *The Mitten*

Revisit. After it has been produced, a piece of shared or interactive writing becomes a valuable resource. It can be revisited for letter or word study. (Specific ideas for revisiting the text are presented in Chapter 11, Figure 11-27, and in *Prompting Guide 1.*) Children love to have a copy of the writing. If they have individual writing books, they can copy it there and draw a picture. Or you can give them a typed copy to glue in and illustrate. Another good use of the sentences is to write them on a sentence strip and cut them up (in phrases, words, or even some word parts). Children can reassemble the sentence, which requires the learner to search for and use visual information. (Cut-up sentences are discussed in more detail later in this chapter and also in Chapter 10).

You can use shared/interactive writing for just about any kind of writing you want to help children do. Sometimes you may generate a first sentence interactively and let students copy it and write a second sentence independently. (For an in-depth look at shared/interactive writing, see McCarrier, Pinnell, and Fountas 2000.)

Dictated Writing

Compose. You compose a sentence carefully to give children learning opportunities (to use new words from a text or help them gain control of new language structures) while not being so difficult that they do not understand it.

Read. You read the sentence aloud.

Write. Then you reread it word by word as the children write the sentence on their own papers or in writing books. You help them as necessary using any appropriate approach:

- ❑ Describing the verbal path for forming letters.
- ❑ Prompting them to say words slowly and think of the letters.
- ❑ Using Elkonin boxes (see Chapters 10, 12, and later in this chapter).
- ❑ Writing known words quickly.
- ❑ Highlighting words and parts of words they want to remember.

- ❑ Checking the word with a model (on a small whiteboard).

Reread. Reread the sentences every time a new word is added so that the readers can process the language. The sentences may closely echo the text writers are responding to. Rereading will provide more opportunity to internalize patterns of language structure. It will also give many children the opportunity to produce in writing more complex sentences than they can compose independently.

The dictated writing in Figure 13-4 was produced after children read a "hybrid" text from the Fun Club series, *The Fun Club Goes to a Dairy Farm* (pages 6 and 7 of the book are reproduced in Figure 13-5). The text contained concepts and vocabulary words that were unfamiliar to all the children in the group. The text was introduced, read, and discussed on one day. The next day, the children reread the book and talked a little more about it. Then they wrote these four sentences dictated by the teacher. They had the opportunity to use new vocabulary words such as *cud* and to solve words such as *lump* and *burp*. They also had the chance to write a word ending in *-ed, called*.

Revisit. When they have finished writing the dictated sentence(s), children can draw a picture to

Figure 13-4 Dictated Writing About *The Fun Club Goes to a Dairy Farm*

> "That cow looks like he's chewing gum!" said Rich.
>
> "She!" said Mr. Moody. "All these milk cows are females."

> "Cows burp up grass in little lumps called **cud**. Then they chew it again. These girls chew their cud all day."

Figure 13-5 Page Spread from *The Fun Club Goes to a Dairy Farm* from Leveled Literacy Intervention, Blue System (Heinemann 2009)

help them remember the content. The piece can be used as a resource in the same ways that you can use shared and interactive writing. Children may use highlighters to emphasize words and parts of words in their own writing books. They can also reread their writing books.

Independent Writing

Ultimately, you want children to compose and write their own response to reading independently.

Talk. Sometimes children have a very difficult time composing the sentences that they want to write. Writing about reading offers strong support, because they will have just processed a text effectively, using the words and language structure, and will have discussed the text before and after reading. Talking about the text will help fix language and meaning in their mind so that they can access it.

Compose. Help each child create a sentence. Once a child has composed a sentence, say it back to him and then have the child say it. During this process you can gently expand the composition, but be sure that it is a sentence the child can remember and reproduce. Act as the child's memory, as needed.

Write. As children write down their sentences, use all the teaching opportunities present in interactive and dictated writing. Supporting independent writing with a group is a little harder for you, because children are not necessarily working on the same words. But they will be working with similar words and concepts. Also, some children may write more than others.

Reread. As they write their sentences, encourage children to reread to help them remember the message and check on how their writing sounds. Rereading will also help them think of what to say next.

Revisit. Children will enjoy rereading their own compositions. You can revisit them in many of the same ways you did shared/interactive and dictated writing. Glancing quickly at the pages, you may want to use open-ended prompts such as:

- ❑ "Find a word that starts with a consonant cluster."
- ❑ "Find a word that means you are doing something."
- ❑ "Find a little word."
- ❑ "Find a long word."

Selecting the Form

Select shared/interactive, dictated, or independent writing according to your students' strengths and the goals of your instruction. If you want to focus children's attention closely on a single text or provide a strong demonstration of a concept, you might select shared/interactive writing, which is also excellent to promote shared reading. If you want students to spend more time writing and stretch their knowledge of language structure, you might use dictated writing. If you want to promote more independence in composition and spelling, you might have them write their own messages with your support.

▶ Genres for Writing About Reading

We use three basic genres for writing about reading in intervention lessons (see Figure 13-6). These genres are related to the purposes for writing and to learning goals. Each genre is very helpful to struggling readers, and within each you can use any of the three forms just discussed. You will find an extensive discussion of these genres in *Teaching for Comprehending and Fluency: Thinking, Talking, and Writing About Reading, K–8* (Fountas and Pinnell 2006) and detailed grade-by-grade goals for writing about reading in *The Continuum of Literacy Learning PreK–8: A Guide for Teaching* (Pinnell and Fountas 2011, 2008).

Functional Writing

Functional writing about reading helps the reader communicate, get something done, remember informa-tion, or bring analytic thinking to bear on a text. It includes:

❑ Notes and sketches—words, phrases, or sketches on sticky notes or in a notebook.

❑ "Short-writes"—a few sentences produced quickly in a notebook or on a large sticky note that is then placed in a notebook.

❑ Graphic organizers—words, phrases, sketches, or sentences.

❑ Notes and letters about reading.

Functional writing about reading goes on in the classroom all the time. In intervention lessons for early readers (text Levels A through N), you need to use very simple forms of functional writing and sur-round them with talk. An example based on the infor-mational text *Little Cat, Big Cat* (Level L; see the page spread in Figure 13-7) is presented in Figure 13-8.

The writer of *Little Cat, Big Cat* used the compare-and-contrast approach to present the information, so recognizing and understanding that structure is key to comprehending the text. The teacher and students discussed how house cats and lions are alike and dif-ferent. Then, using interactive writing, the teacher worked with the students to record information in the appropriate column. She kept the process moving by emphasizing thinking and talking rather than spend-ing a lot of time solving words. But the text can be revisited later.

Even with students reading at a fairly high level, you will want to produce complex graphic organizers like this in a supportive way. Graphic organizers have been shown to help readers (see National Reading Panel 2000); but they can be used in confusing ways. For example, just giving the organizer to students to fill out like a work sheet will not really help them understand—especially if they have struggled with the meaning of the text.

Sometimes you can follow up text discussion and writing with another activity that helps extend under-standing. Look at the sheet (for a take-home activity) the teacher has used based on reading, discussion, and group writing that the children have previously done (Figure 13-9). They worked on this sheet independ-

Figure 13-6 **Genres for Writing About Reading**	
Genre	**Helps the reader**
Functional Writing	• Communicate. • Get something done. • Remember information. • Bring analytic thinking to bear on a text.
Narrative Writing	• Retell some or all of a plot. • Recount significant events. • Tell a similar story from his own life.
Informational Writing	• Organize facts into a coherent whole. • Use categories and subcategories. • Use underlying structures such as compare and contrast, description, cause and effect, time sequence, and problem and solution.

ently as they read the text and drew pictures to represent the sequence in it.

Now look at the three simple examples of independent writing about reading shown in Figures 13-10, 13-11, and 13-12. In the first, children name and draw pictures of the characters in the Moosling series. In the second, they recall, draw pictures, and label the animals in *Things That Fly*. In the third, they reflect on a text they have read which points out the various parts of a police car. Labeling can help readers:

- ❏ Give close attention to the pictures.

- ❏ Understand and remember the important information in a text.

- ❏ Notice the relationships between information in a text.

Numbered lists also can help students understand a more complicated temporal sequence such as that in *Road Builders*. Look at the list that was produced through interactive writing after reading and discussion (see Figure 13-13). Putting items in order like this will help readers not only remember the processes in the informational text but also understand a bigger idea—that often tasks are presented in the order that you do them.

Sometimes, a graphic organizer can be used to reflect knowledge built over time. Series books are a way to help younger readers understand more facets of characters (see Chapter 6). Moosling is a young moose who is always having adventures. The example in Figure 13-14 shows different aspects of Moosling's character as encountered over time. Struggling readers benefit from this kind of help in connecting texts or remembering evidence within a text to get to the big ideas. When you ask readers to consider aspects of character like this, you are supporting inferring and analytic thinking.

Functional writing should not be overdone, but it is a strong framework for understanding a text. Ultimately, you want readers to form these organiza-

Figure 13-7 Page Spread from *Little Cat, Big Cat,* from Leveled Literacy Intervention, Blue System (Heinemann 2009)

Figure 13-8 Venn Diagram for *Little Cat, Big Cat*

tional patterns in their minds. Remember, conversation is the key learning element in using this kind of writing.

Narrative Writing

A narrative tells a story. Narrative writing about reading might retell some or all of a plot or recount significant events in the life of a biographical subject. Or, students might write a short narrative in response

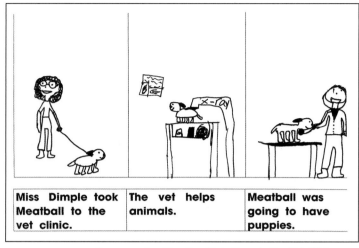

Miss Dimple took Meatball to the vet clinic. | **The vet helps animals.** | **Meatball was going to have puppies.**

Figure 13-9 Sequence for *The Fun Club Goes to the Vet Clinic*

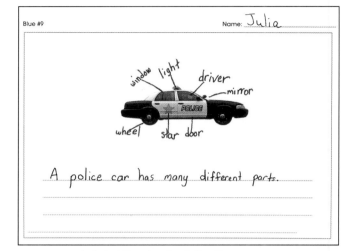

Blue #9   Name: Julia

A police car has many different parts.

Figure 13-12 Labeled Drawing for *Police Car*

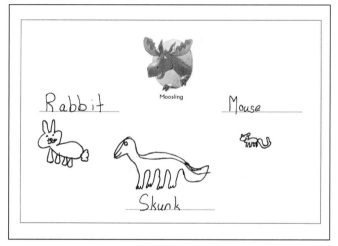

Figure 13-10 Labeling of Characters in the Moosling Series

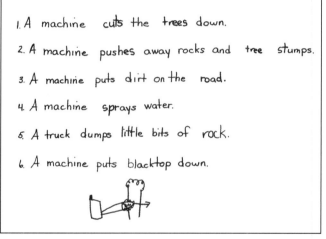

1. A machine cuts the trees down.
2. A machine pushes away rocks and tree stumps.
3. A machine puts dirt on the road.
4. A machine sprays water.
5. A truck dumps little bits of rock.
6. A machine puts blacktop down.

Figure 13-13 Sequence for *Road Builders*

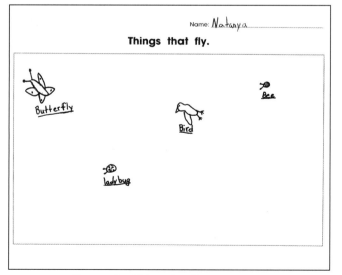

Name: Natanya

Things that fly.

Figure 13-11 Diagram for *Things that Fly*

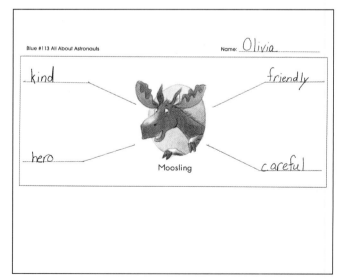

Blue #113 All About Astronauts   Name: Olivia

kind   friendly

hero   Moosling   careful

Figure 13-14 Character Web for *Moosling*

to a text—something in their own lives that the text reminds them of, for example. Also, they may draw pictures to represent the sequence of events in a story. All of this activity supports thinking about the sequence, the characters, and the events of a story.

You can be selective in narrative writing about reading. Choose a part of a story that the children found exciting and that offers opportunities to expand language syntax. Short pieces of interactive narrative writing that a teacher and her students have produced after reading *Bunny and the Monster* (see the page spread reproduced in Figure 13-15) are shown in Figure 13-16. They have written about just one significant event in the story.

After reading and discussing *The Costume Party* (see the page spread reproduced in Figure 13-17), children were asked to write independently about Moosling and how he felt about the costume party. The three sentences shown in Figure 13-18 reflect the writer's perspective about the important evidence from the text. She had to search for the ideas that seemed to convey the character's feelings.

A summary of *A Fast Fox* produced through interactive writing is shown in Figure 13-19. It too is a series of events, but, except for the ending, sequence is not important for the comprehension of the story. Most of the events could have happened in any order. What is important is the meaningful relationship between the animal Andy sees and the action he tries. Notice the complex sentences. Rereading this material will help readers expand syntactic patterns.

Now look at independent writing based on students' reading and discussion in intervention lessons using two other texts. One student read the beginning and ending of *The Ugly Duckling* and drew appropriate pictures (see Figure 13-20). Another student recorded four events from *The Coyote and the Rabbit*, also drawing pictures but adding speech bubbles (Figure 13-21). This cartoon-like way of representing the story supports understanding temporal sequence as well as the motivations of characters.

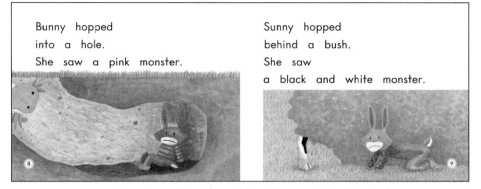

Figure 13-15 Page Spread from *Bunny and the Monster* from Leveled Literacy Intervention, Green System (Heinemann 2009)

Figure 13-16 Writing About Reading for *Bunny and the Monster*

When you involve students in narrative writing about reading, you are supporting their ability to notice important information (in sequence), understand narrative structure, and summarize.

Informational Writing

Informational writing about reading helps students organize facts into a coherent whole. The piece may reflect any of the underlying structures that are related to informational texts:

- ❏ Description.
- ❏ Temporal sequence.
- ❏ Cause and effect.
- ❏ Problem and solution.
- ❏ Comparison and contrast.

"Where is Moosling?" asked Mouse. "Why didn't Moosling come to the party?" Rabbit wanted to know.

"We want Moosling!" said the little skunks.

Uh–oh! Sorry!

Beaver and Pins didn't know who was in the dragon costume, so they peeked.

"I don't see Moosling," said Mouse.

"You're right," said Skunk. "Why isn't Moosling here?"

All the animals began to ask about their moose friend.

12

13

Figure 13-17 Page Spread from *The Costume Party* from Leveled Literacy Intervention, Blue System (Heinemann 2009)

Informational writing about reading may reflect the categories and subcategories into which the text has been organized, or it may reflect the reader's own perspective, such as what she found most interesting about a text (which would call for synthesis).

All About Robots is an informational text that presents information in categories (a page spread is reproduced in Figure 13-22). The text communicates some big ideas, which the children had discussed, offering details as evidence and examples. The summary shown in Figure 13-23 was produced through dictated writing.

The Roadrunners (see the cover reproduced in Figure 13-24) is also nonfiction but has within it some narrative showing the father and mother roadrunner making a nest and caring for the babies. The summary in Figure 13-25 reflects the text structure.

Moosling never went to a costume party.

He wanted to dress up like everyone else.

He surprised his friends with his costume.

Figure 13-18 Summary of *The Costume Party*

Andy saw a rabbit and he wanted to hop.

He saw a fish and he wanted to swim.

He saw a bird and he wanted to fly.

Andy ran as fast as a fox and he was happy.

Figure 13-19 Summary of *A Fast Fox*

Blue #80 The Boss   Name: Andre

| The big, gray duckling was sad because he did not look like the yellow ducklings. But Mother Duck loved him anyway. | The big, beautiful swan was happy because Mother Duck still loved him. |

Figure 13-20 Beginning and Ending Drawing for *The Ugly Duckling*

Eugenie Clark, Shark Lady is a beginning chapter book about a real scientist (a page spread is reproduced in Figure 13-26). The dictated summary statements for each of the short chapters (see Figure 13-27) are concise and reflect the main idea of the chapter. Remember that students have read and discussed the book. They will reread the text again and will also reread this dictated writing, increasing their familiarity with the vocabulary, language, and organization of this text.

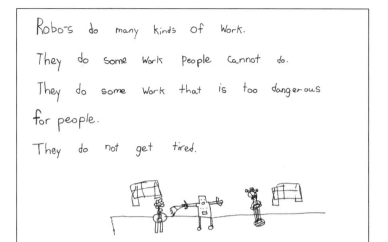

Figure 13-23 Summary of *All About Robots*

Figure 13-21 Cartoon of *The Coyote and the Rabbit*

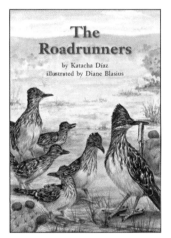

Figure 13-24 Cover of *The Roadrunners* from Leveled Literacy Intervention, Blue System (Heinemann 2009)

Figure 13-22 Page Spread from *All About Robots* from Leveled Literacy Intervention, Blue System (Heinemann 2009)

Figure 13-25 Summary of *The Roadrunners*

Figure 13-26 Page Spread from *Eugenie Clark, Shark Lady* from Leveled Literacy Intervention, Blue System (Heinemann 2009)

Figure 13-27 Chapter Summaries of *Eugenie Clark, Shark Lady*

Composing informational writing about reading helps readers learn that factual information is presented in an organized way. Understanding the organization of information helps readers comprehend texts. Ultimately you want readers to search for and recognize text structure quickly and automatically "in their heads" and use it as a support for reading.

▶ Interacting with Writers to Support Learning

In all the contexts discussed in this chapter, learning can be supported by teaching, prompting, and supporting writers while they are in the processes of composition, construction, and reflection. Below are examples of clear and specific language that will help writers express their thinking about the texts they are reading. (A comprehensive list of effective teacher language is included in *Prompting Guide 1.*)

Early Writing Behaviors

Writing helps children develop essential understandings about how print works—how to place print on a page, form letters, and compose sentences.

PLACING WORDS ON THE PAGE

Explicit language can be very helpful to children in solving the puzzle of print layout. Shared/interactive writing is a good context in which to demonstrate print placement. In the example below, the teacher and children are working on the summary of *The Mitten* (see Figure 13-3):

TEACHER: Jordan, come up and write the *l* for *lost*. Leave some space before you start the word.

TEACHER [*after writing the word* mitten]: I'm going to start our next sentence with the word *the*. When you get to the end, start here again.

Conferring with Jordan after writing:

TEACHER: Show a place where we left good space. [*Jordan points to a space.*] Look at all the good spaces.

LETTER FORMATION

In this chapter and Chapter 10, we recommend that you use a verbal path to help children make the proper directional movements to form letters effectively. You may want to model using large-scale movements at first. You can prompt students to say the language with you as they trace or write a letter. Once the path is learned, you can prompt or reinforce it:

- ❑ "You know how to start it."
- ❑ "Think about how to write it."
- ❑ "You knew how to write it."

Once students are making the letter easily with appropriate directional movements, the movement becomes automatic and they no longer need the verbal support. At this point, some quick practice will be helpful to make the movement automatic:

- ❑ "Write it again."
- ❑ "Write it here."
- ❑ "Write it quickly."

COMPOSING SENTENCES

Some children may talk fluently and easily and yet have difficulty coming up with a message to write. You can support early composition by inviting group composition during interactive writing:

TEACHER: Let's think about what Bunny was saying. She was always saying . . .

CHILDREN: "I can hop."

TEACHER: What were some of the places she hopped?

JULIE: Grass.

TEACHER: We can write what Bunny said.

WENDY: "I can hop."

TEACHER: We can write, "I can hop in the grass." Does that sound good? Let's all say that.

The complete piece of interactive writing is shown in Figure 13-28.

Participating in this strongly modeled process of generating sentences helps writers move from ideas to language. The key to composition is talk.

Figure 13-28 Interactive Writing for *Hop, Hop, Hop*

Conversation supports writers at all levels, beginner to adult. If children have had a good discussion of a text, they have used sentences to express their ideas. Then you can ask, "What do you want to write about that?" Or you might restate what the children said and ask, "What part do you want to tell about?" Also, they can draw from the models of language that they have seen in the text. Additional facilitative language includes:

- ❑ "Talk more about that."
- ❑ "How would they say that in the book?"
- ❑ "What happens first [next] [last]?
- ❑ "How would the character say that?"
- ❑ "That is an interesting way to say it."
- ❑ "That sounds like [name of character]."
- ❑ "That sounds interesting."

Constructing Words

As you work alongside writers in shared/interactive, dictated, or independent writing, you can teach them about how words are constructed. The level of teaching, prompting, and supporting writers need depends on what they already know, nearly know, and don't yet know about how words work.

USING SOUND ANALYSIS TO CONSTRUCT WORDS

If children do not fully grasp the idea that letters and sounds are related, they can learn the alphabetic principle as you help them construct a meaningful text. For example:

TEACHER: We are going to write what Hen asked everyone. What did she ask?

MOIRA: "Can you help me?"

TEACHER: "Can you help me?" said Hen. I am going to say *can* slowly and think how it starts: *c-a-n.*

JENNIFER: It's a *c.*

TEACHER: *Can* starts with *c* like *cat* on our chart. Jennifer, come and make the *c. [Jennifer makes the c.]* You heard the first sound. Let's say the word again and listen for the last part. *[They say the word and write the -an.]*

Strong demonstrations can help beginning word solvers learn to listen for the sounds in the word. As the easy-to-hear sounds become automatic, they can move on to representing more of the phonemes in the word, and they can give closer attention to the order of the sounds in words. Some examples of language that will be helpful as they learn more are:

❑ "Clap the parts you hear." (Listening for word parts.)

❑ "Listen for the sounds you hear in the first [last] part." (Listening for individual sounds.)

❑ "Say the word slowly. How many sounds do you hear?" (Saying words and listening for sounds.)

❑ "Write the first part [the next part] [the last part]." (Writing word parts.)

❑ "What letter do you expect to see at the beginning [end]?" (Listening for sounds and identifying letters.)

❑ "It sounds like [another word the writer knows]." (Using what is known to help write other words.)

❑ "It starts like [another word the writer knows]." (Using analogy.)

❑ "Do you know a word like that?" (Connecting words.)

❑ "You said that word slowly." (Reinforcing slow articulation.)

❑ "You heard the sounds and wrote the letters." (Reinforcing sound-letter relationships.)

USING VISUAL ANALYSIS TO CONSTRUCT WORDS

Writing is an important support to help readers understand that visual analysis is essential for reading and spelling. The grapheme-phoneme relationships in English are complex; the spelling of words often does not match simple phonemes because of how the word developed historically and other factors such as verb conjugation. Readers and writers need to learn how to think about how words look. Of course, it is helpful to beginning readers that many simple words do have regular sound-letter relationships, but you would not want to distort the language of texts by *only* using words like *not, hot, pot,* and *dot.* That would confuse readers even more and give a subliminal message that reading does not need to sound like language or make sense.

You can help them understand early on that in addition to thinking about the sounds, they need to think about how the word looks:

TEACHER: Let's say and clap the word *wanted.* *[Children say the word, clapping twice.]* That's right—*wanted.* I'll write the first part, *want.* Now let's clap again and listen for the last part.

CHILDREN: *-ed*

TEACHER: That's right; *-ed.* Now I'll put the ending on *wanted.* Now the word looks right.

They read from the beginning and Helena writes the h *for the word* her. *The teacher finishes* her. *The teacher writes* to *and they read again from the beginning.*

TEACHER: Say *come.* What do you hear at the beginning?

CHILDREN: *come; c*

TEACHER: Jordan, write the beginning of the word. *[Jordan writes* c.*]* Say *come* again. What else do you hear?

HELENA: *m*

TEACHER: I do hear an *m*. First a *c*, then I'll write an *o*, and then I'll write the *m*. I need to add an *e* to the word *come* to make it look right. We all know the word *and*. Watch how Helena writes it without stopping.

The following examples are more advanced:

Mark is writing the word painted—*he writes* pa *and stops.*

TEACHER: There are two vowels in the middle. The second vowel is silent.

Stephen has written "The animals pop out of the mitten."

TEACHER *[pointing to the word* pop]: It's almost right. Add the ending for *popped*.

Carole is writing the word very—ver.

TEACHER: Do you know a word that ends like that?

CAROLE: *happy [Adds the* y.*]*

TEACHER: You added the ending.

Sunni is writing the word acorn.

TEACHER: What do you know that might help?

SUNNI: *a [writes the* a *and the* c] Or is in the middle.

TEACHER: You used a part you know. *[Sunni writes* -orn.]You wrote it fast.

Additional language for helping writers use visual analysis to construct words includes:

- ❑ *Teach:* "Add this to make it look right."
- ❑ *Teach:* "You know this word."
- ❑ *Teach:* "You can think of a word you know."
- ❑ *Teach:* "You know [word]. Change the first letter[s] [middle] [end]."
- ❑ *Teach:* "Watch me write it like I know it."
- ❑ *Prompt:* "What would look right there?"
- ❑ *Prompt:* "Think of another word like that."
- ❑ *Prompt:* "There are [number] letters."
- ❑ *Prompt:* "What do you know that might help?"
- ❑ *Prompt:* "Write it without stopping."
- ❑ *Reinforce:* "You wrote it like you know it."
- ❑ *Reinforce:* "You added the ending."

MONITORING AND CORRECTING WORDS

We have already said that self-monitoring and self-correcting are very important reading behaviors; they are equally important writing behaviors. Writers need to learn how to check on themselves and to search for the information they need to spell accurately. In the process, they will be learning a great deal more about how words work. Here are some examples of ways to teach for, prompt for, and reinforce monitoring and correcting.

John is checking the word tomato.

TEACHER: Think about how the word looks. Check to see if all the sounds are there.

JOHN: Yes.

TEACHER: You checked it carefully.

Sarah has written craled *for* crawled.

TEACHER: You're almost right. Where's the tricky part? *[Sarah points to the* a *in* craled.*]* The middle sound is like the *aw* part in *saw*. *[She puts white tape over* -led. *Sarah writes* a w *and then* led.] Now you made it look right.

Greg has written, "Fire trucks can get water from" *and stops at swimming.*

TEACHER: Why did you stop?

GREG: It has to have two *m*'s.

Teacher explains doubling of middle consonant before *-ing*.

Other prompts and reinforcements that will help writers monitor and correct writing include:

- ❑ "You're nearly right. Change the middle [beginning] [ending].
- ❑ "Add a letter. Add the ending."
- ❑ "Find the part that's not quite right."
- ❑ "Check to see if all the sounds are there."
- ❑ "Check to see if that looks right."
- ❑ "There's a tricky word on this line."
- ❑ "Were you right?"
- ❑ "You worked that out all by yourself."
- ❑ "You made it look right."

USING CONVENTIONS OF PRINT

Like readers, writers need to understand, attend to, and use conventions of print such as punctuation. Even beginning writers sometimes need to use titles and headings. And they will enjoy inserting a different-size font or all capital letters for emphasis. Below are some examples of helping children use conventions.

The teacher and children are writing a summary of The Mitten *(see Figure 13-3).*

TEACHER: How can we make the word *pop* help the reader know to read it louder?

BRIDEY: Make it big?

SAM: You could do it with all uppercase letters like in the book.

TEACHER: Let's do it in all uppercase letters and that will make it look bigger too. Bridey, you can write this word. Remember to use all capital letters. *[Bridey writes the word.]* What do you think we should put at the end of *pop*?

MIKE: Exclamation point.

TEACHER: Bridey, you can do that, too.

They write the last sentence and then reread the entire text.

TEACHER: You made a good summary of the story, and the word *pop* looks like it should be said louder. Something is missing. Can you find the line on the page where the boy is talking?

MIKE *[reading]*: "Here is my mitten," the boy said.

TEACHER: Sam, can you use your hands to show what the boy said? *[Sam frames "Here is my mitten."]* You need to put quotation marks around that part. *[She puts in the marks.]* Now let's read it one more time. Make your voice sound like the boy.

Additional language to teach for, prompt for, and reinforce using conventions includes:

- ❑ "This is how to start the sentence." *[Show uppercase letters.]*
- ❑ "Start the sentence with an uppercase letter." *[Model]*
- ❑ "This is how to end the sentence. It's a period." *[Model]*
- ❑ "This is how to show excitement. It's an exclamation point." *[Model]*
- ❑ "This is how to show it is a question. It's a question mark." *[Model]*
- ❑ "This is how to show what the person is saying. These are speech marks [quotation marks]." *[Model]*
- ❑ "This is how to tell the reader to take a little breath." *[Model]*
- ❑ "This is how to tell the reader to read louder." *[Model bold, italics, all capital letters.]*
- ❑ "I'll think of a title [heading] that shows what my writing is about." *[Model]*
- ❑ "Think about how you always start the sentence." *[Prompt]*
- ❑ "Help your reader know where to stop." *[Prompt]*
- ❑ "Think about how to tell the reader where to stop." *[Prompt]*
- ❑ "Show the reader that you are asking a question." *[Prompt]*
- ❑ "How will you show what words [name of character] said?" *[Prompt]*

- "Show where the talking starts and ends with speech marks." *[Prompt]*
- "Do you want to tell the reader to take a little breath there?" *[Prompt]*
- "You started the sentence with an uppercase letter." *[Reinforce]*
- "You remembered to tell the reader where to stop." *[Reinforce]*

Selecting and Using Language

It's not easy to select language for teaching, prompting, and reinforcing. You are always making a judgment about what level is appropriate and will make the most difference for learners. You do not want to be telling children something that they already know; nor do you want to demand so much of them that they cannot act. If children know something very well and do it automatically, you don't want to clutter up the interaction by reinforcing it. The diagram in Figure 13-29 may be helpful in thinking about teaching, prompting, and reinforcing effective writing behaviors.

There is no firm way to categorize teaching and reinforcing prompts; each affects the reader a little differently. Let's think of the language in terms of level of support for the writer:

- A highly supportive statement gives the learner maximum information. It makes lower demands on the learner and shows the learner what to do. It assumes that the learner does not really have the knowledge or understand the concept. It *teaches.*
- A statement that is less supportive and more demanding assumes knowledge on the learner's part and may also assume some experience in performing the action. It directs the writer's attention to where it needs to go or reminds the reader to do something he knows how to do. It *prompts.*
- A minimally supportive statement gives very little information. It assumes that the learner already knows how to perform the operation; he already knows how to do it and the statement confirms the effective action. It *reinforces.*

Teaching statements provide a high level of information because the writer/reader has to be shown what to do before being prompted to do it. Supportive statements are helpful when the concept or operation is partially known. Prompting statements are helpful when readers know the concept but need to be reminded to do it. Reinforcing statements develop consistency in what the learner has learned how to do. Once a concept or operation is completely automatic, you will not need to comment on it. It has become its own reward—it is working for the reader/writer.

Figure 13-29 Selecting Language for Interacting During Writing

		Using Sound Analysis to Construct	Using Visual Analysis to Construct	Using Structural Analysis to Construct
H	**Teach**	You can say the word slowly and listen for the sounds. Watch me.	You can think about what looks right. Watch me write it.	You know a part of this word.
	Prompt	Say the word slowly. What do you hear first? Next? At the end?	Think about how the word looks.	Think about a part you know.
L	**Reinforce**	You heard all the sounds in order.	You made it look right.	You used a part you know.

Once you become accustomed to using this kind of language while interacting with children, it comes easily. If you use a prompt that provides too little support and the child does not understand it, you can quickly provide more information. As readers move to more challenging levels of text and as writers expand their abilities, you will constantly cycle through teaching for, prompting for, and reinforcing effective behaviors. This kind of interaction is not meant to correct every error; it is intended to be a call for action on the part of the learner.

▶ Using Children's Writing as a Resource

A written text that has been produced through shared/interactive, dictated, or independent writing is a very valuable resource for readers. These texts have been produced by:

- ❑ Thinking carefully before writing.
- ❑ Looking very closely at the details of every word.
- ❑ Saying the words and thinking about the sound-letter correspondence.
- ❑ Rereading to remember the message and check it.

A written text that has been produced in this way and is within the reader's control can promote powerful learning.

Cut-Up Sentences

One of the most productive activities for children who are having difficulty learning about letters, sounds, and words is the cut-up sentence. Often, these children seem to know letter-sound relationships, phonograms, or high-frequency words in isolation. But when writing or reading continuous print, they seem to forget what they know.

Write a sentence on a strip of paper about one inch by eleven or thirteen inches. The complexity of the sentence should be appropriate to the child's current language and word-solving understandings. Have the child read the sentence as you cut it into words.

Then, mix up the words, being sure that all words are in front of the child right side up and correctly oriented. Finally, ask the child to reconstruct the sentence while saying each word (and rereading often from the beginning) and then reread the entire sentence to check it. At first, you may want to have the child check the reconstruction with a model. Two examples are provided in Figure 13-30.

Reassembling a cut-up sentence requires learners to:

- ❑ Keep the whole sentence in their head.
- ❑ Attend to the order of words in sentences.
- ❑ Think about the first sound of a word and the corresponding letter or letter cluster.
- ❑ Search for and use visual information.
- ❑ Check by rereading.
- ❑ Use known words to monitor reconstruction and rereading.
- ❑ Attend to orientation.
- ❑ Attend to ending punctuation.
- ❑ Attend to capital letters at the beginning of a sentence.

All these behaviors are helpful to both writers and readers. You can apply this concept to more advanced texts and introduce new challenges (see Figure 13-44). For example:

- ❑ Have children reassemble more than one sentence and place punctuation in the appropriate place.
- ❑ Include all punctuation as part of the word previous to it.
- ❑ Attend to punctuation over longer sentences or several sentences.
- ❑ Attend to capital letters at the beginning of several sentences.

Sometimes, when children are very proficient at reassembling cut-up sentences, understand syllables in words, have a sense of the order of letters and sounds in words, and know about endings, you can vary the task by cutting a word into syllables or letter clusters or separating a base word from its ending. This will help writers attend more closely to the parts of words

Figure 13-30 Simple Cut-Up Sentences for *Orson's Tummy Ache* and *The New Puppy*

as they put together the sentence. (Caution: don't overdo it by making the sentence look like confetti!)

Reread Writing

Rereading what you have written is a different experience from rereading other texts, because you have a sense of ownership. Writers often reread their writing in progress to check it. Doing so develops their

ability to monitor and self-correct, as well as to remember the meaning. After the piece has been finished, learners can reread their writing over a period of time to help them remember the meaning of texts and rethink them. If you have students collect all their writing about reading in a notebook, they can quickly return to all of the texts they have read, which helps them make connections and build larger concepts.

Revisiting a Text for Word Study

A well-known text that the child has written and then reread several times is a useful context for looking more closely at words, because the reader must solve words within the context of connected print. You can use any of the pieces of shared/interactive, dictated, or independent writing in this chapter in connection with questions like those below. All of the actions should first be modeled, and they can be reinforced as needed.

Letters
"Find the letter [name of letter.]"
"Find a word that begins with a capital letter."
"Find a word that begins with a lowercase letter."

Arrangement of Print
"Find a place where you used good spacing to divide the words."
"Show where to start reading."

Words
"Find the word [*word*]."
"Find a little word."
"Find a big word."
"What's a new word you learned to write today?"

Letters and Sounds in Words
"What word begins with [letter] [letter cluster]?"
"What word begins like [*word*]?"

"What's a word with two [three] [four] sounds?"

"What word has more letters than sounds?"

"Which words begin with a consonant cluster [vowel]?"

"What words sound exactly like they look?"

Word Patterns and Structure

"What words have one syllable [two syllables] [three syllables] [four syllables]?"

"What words sound exactly like they look?"

"What word has parts that can be removed?"

"Which words have a tricky [interesting] [hard] [new] pattern [spelling]?"

"What words could be spelled another way but sound the same?"

"What word has a special pattern [spelling] that shows what it means?"

"Which word is a compound word [contraction] [word with an ending] [word with a prefix]?"

▶ How Does Writing Support Reading Development?

Writing is important for its own sake, and it also contributes to reading on several levels (see Figure 13-31), which is especially important to know when you are working with struggling readers.

The Contribution of Writing to Phonics and Word Learning

Writing allows children to work very closely with words and helps them understand how the code works.

LEARNING THE DISTINCTIVE FEATURES OF LETTERS

We describe the role of writing in helping beginners learn to look at print in Chapter 10. Using a verbal path helps children learn the directional

Figure 13-31	**How Writing Contributes to Reading**
Area of Learning	**Contributes to Reading**
Word Learning and Phonics	• Learning to recognize the distinctive features of letters. • Constructing words with letters in sequence. • Developing knowledge of sound-letter relationships by hearing and recording sounds in words. • Learning high-frequency words. • Using the parts of words (beginnings, endings, syllables) to spell them. • Recognizing and using patterns in words.
Early Reading Behaviors	• Placing print left to right across a line and top to bottom on the page. • Using spaces to define words.
Conventions of Print	• Using capital and lowercase letters correctly. • Using punctuation in a meaningful way. • Using titles, headings, and other text features.
Language	• Acquiring and using new vocabulary. • Learning the syntax of written language. • Expanding knowledge of language structure by writing more complex sentences.
Text Structure	• Thinking about the organization of a text to write it (sequence, categories). • Using narrative and diagrams to show text organization.
Literary Features	• Using narrative and diagrams to understand characters. • Selecting and using interesting language.
Memory	• Supporting the readers' memory of the information in the text. • Restating information to reflect organization. • Summarizing information.

movements for making letters. This process is very helpful to children because it helps them feel the letters in every detail, notice the features that make the letter different from every other letter, and become aware of the need for correct orientation.

CONSTRUCTING WORDS

Through writing, children learn how words are constructed. Words must be written letter by letter. There is no other way; and it is very important that the letters be in precise order. In intervention lessons, teachers help children write words letter by letter, often filling in the letters the children do not yet know. They may also invite them to "check" the word letter by letter (*n–n, o–o, t–t*) with a model. This process will help children make better approximations when they are working independently in the classroom.

It may be necessary to help children attend to letter formation as they write words. The first concept they need to learn is that a letter is made in the same way every time. Any given letter can vary in some ways (size, placement on the page, slight variations in style), but there are some features that do not vary—for example, orientation and distinctive features like the dot for the *i*. Uppercase and lowercase versions of letters have the same name but different graphic forms. Sometimes they look alike and sometimes they do not. So letter formation is often a challenge in constructing words. Children can get so caught up in making the letters that they lose track of the word.

Handwriting instruction will be helpful to children (see Chapter 10). Using a verbal path to get to letter formation will be very helpful. Let's observe Charley writing the word *hen* (see Figure 13-32). He is just beginning to hear sounds in words and control the directional movements to make letters and write words:

> TEACHER: You are writing *n*. [*She demonstrates writing the letter.*] Pull down, up, over, and down. You say that with me while you write the *n*.
>
> TEACHER AND CHARLEY: Pull down, up, over, and down. [*He slowly writes the letter.*]
>
> TEACHER: You're learning how to write it. Write another *n* over here [*on another piece of paper*]

Figure 13-32 Child-written *hen*

and say it again. [*Charley writes another* n *using the same language.*] Now, let's check the word.

Children can learn to write letters in isolation, but it is more challenging to switch from one letter to another while writing them in sequence to make a word. They need to use efficient directional movement that becomes automatic. Chapters 10, 11, and 12 include many suggestions for helping children learn to write words.

HEARING AND RECORDING SOUNDS IN WORDS

In Chapters 9, 10, and 12 we describe the use of Elkonin boxes (*sound boxes*) to help children learn how to hear sounds in words. It is essential for readers to learn how to identify the individual sounds and, ultimately, to hear them in sequence and record appropriate letters for them. But spellers and readers of English must learn that there will not necessarily be a one-to-one correspondence between sounds and letters. Once children know how to listen for sounds and record them in sequence using the Elkonin boxes, you will want to make the shift from *sound boxes* to *letter boxes*. This change signals to the children that we do not expect the number of sounds and letters in a word to be the same. In the example below, the teacher begins to make this shift with children:

> TEACHER: At first we used boxes to write letters for each sound you heard in words. Sometimes we put two letters in a box for one sound. Now I am going to draw a box for every letter. That will help you know how many letters there are in the word. I am going to write a word you know. [*The*

teacher draws six boxes (see Figure 13-33) and then asks the children to say mother.*] What letter would you expect to see in the first box?*

CRAIG: *m*

The teacher continues to demonstrate filling in the boxes, asking "What letter would you expect to see?" She reminds the children that there is now one box for each letter. She demonstrates that the t *and* h *are in two separate boxes even though they make one sound. The group experiments with the same words they looked at during the first part of the lesson. Then children propose their own words, and the teacher draws the correct number of boxes for each.*

Figure 13-33 Letter Boxes

You can use letter boxes effectively to help individuals write independently and also to demonstrate the process of spelling a word on a whiteboard. The goal is to enable children to spell words without boxes. Making the boxes in pencil and writing the letters with a dark-colored marker makes the boxes fade into the background.

LEARNING HIGH-FREQUENCY WORDS

Writing is a way to help children know some high-utility words in every detail. In Chapter 12 we discuss the value of developing a core of high-frequency words and describe how word writing can assist in the process. It is important to write high-frequency words quickly and automatically, using the appropriate directional movements.

While children are writing a piece of continuous text, you can have them quickly practice writing one or two useful high-frequency words. For example:

"Write it here." [*Indicate blank space on the page, or provide another piece of paper.*]

❑ "Write it again."

❑ "Write it quickly."

❑ "Write it big."

❑ "Write it smaller."

❑ "Write it faster."

Knowing a large number of words that can be written without effort contributes to fluency in writing, leaving one free to pay attention to the content and solve new words.

USING PARTS OF WORDS AND PATTERNS

As children learn more about words, they should begin to write *word parts* quickly. Chapter 11 includes suggestions for helping children use larger parts of words. This behavior is essential if they are to become proficient writers, and it contributes substantially to reading. For example, they learn to write consonant clusters, phonogram patterns, and word endings like *-ing* quickly and automatically. If this ability is well developed for the writing of one-syllable and simple two-syllable words, they will be better prepared to write and read longer and more complex words.

Early Reading Behaviors

The deliberate planning and close attention that beginning writers must give to print will build useful knowledge in reading. Yves wrote the piece shown in Figure 13-34 in response to *Three Little Pigs and a Big Bad Wolf* (a spread from the book is reproduced in Figure 13-35). He composed his own message and then constructed it with some teacher support on the words *couldn't* and *street*. The teacher chose not to correct his grammar on the word *blowed* or his spelling of *so*; but she will soon begin to help him sort out correct use of uppercase and lowercase letters.

PLACING PRINT ON THE PAGE

Notice how carefully Yves placed the words left to right across the page. This piece required him to return to the left margin twice. This slow examination of print placement is helping him cope with more lines of print in reading.

USING SPACES

One of the great challenges in both writing and reading is the use of spaces. Yves carefully left spaces between the words and even between the lines. It may be that drawing the line under the first line of print was his own way of reminding himself either to leave space or go back to the left.

Figure 13-34 Yves Writing About *The Three Little Pigs and a Big Bad Wolf*

Figure 13-35 Page Spread from *The Three Little Pigs and a Big Bad Wolf* from Leveled Literacy Intervention, Green System (Heinemann 2009)

Conventions of Print

Readers also need to learn to use punctuation and other print conventions to provide additional meaning and support fluency. Writing is helpful because it slows down the process. The writer has time to think about punctuation, print layout, and other conventions such as titles and headings. The discussion below relates to the writing shown in Figure 13-36, a piece of interactive writing that a teacher and her students produced together.

USE OF UPPERCASE AND LOWERCASE LETTERS

Capital letters give signals to readers. Either a new sentence is starting or the word is a name or other proper noun. A word in all capital letters is a title or heading or should be read with emphasis. Writing helps readers sort out these distinctions. Observe this interaction:

TEACHER *[after writing and rereading the first line]*: Next we decided to write, "He went down the chimney." I think I'll go back to the left to start writing the new sentence. "He went down the chimney." What's the first word?

TRISH: *He; h–e.*

TEACHER: Trish, can you write *he?* What will she be thinking about?

YVES: Writing the *h.*

TRISH: A capital *h.*

USE OF PUNCTUATION

The teacher helped the children give particular attention to ending punctuation:

TEACHER *[after the word* splash *has been written, with one child contributing the* spl *and the teacher writing the rest of the word]*: Let's read what we have so far. *[Teacher and children read the first two sentences*

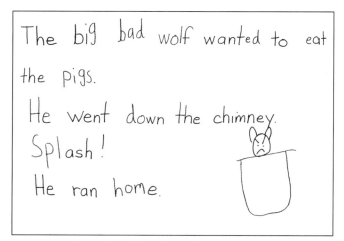

The big bad wolf wanted to eat the pigs.
He went down the chimney.
Splash!
He ran home.

Figure 13-36 Interactive Writing from *The Three Little Pigs and a Big Bad Wolf*

up to the word splash.] That was exciting. How did our voices sound when we read the word *splash?*

YVES: Excited and kind of loud.

TEACHER: I think so, too. When you want the reader to sound excited, or when you have an exciting part of the story, you can use an exclamation point. Should we do that to tell the readers to say *splash* with excitement?

USING TEXT FEATURES

Informational texts often convey that information in headings, insets, legends, labels, and graphics as well as in the body of the text. As texts' level of difficulty increases, graphics become increasingly complex and may be confusing to readers. It will help children to produce simple graphics themselves from the beginning, as in the piece of independent writing in Figure 13-37, composed in response to *All About Sharks.*

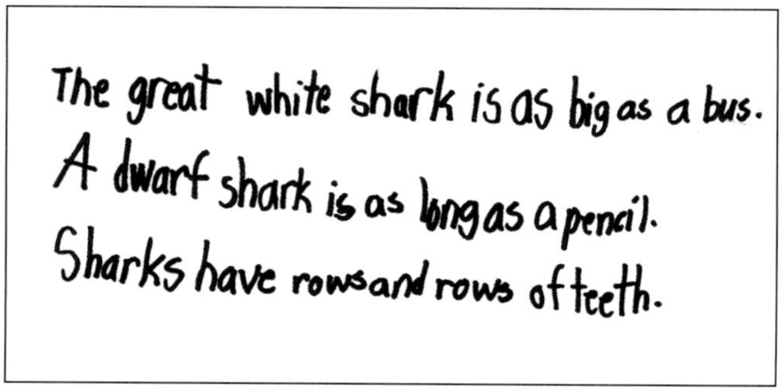

The great white shark is as big as a bus.
A dwarf shark is as long as a pencil.
Sharks have rows and rows of teeth.

Figure 13-37 Independent Writing About *All About Sharks*

Language

By producing their own sentences and larger pieces, which they reread many times, children have not only looked at the details but internalized language structure. In the writing in Figure 13-37, the student recorded three facts about sharks. Notice complex patterns such as *as big as.* Phrases like this imply the underlying structure—the way the writer is conveying information—and being able to process them is important for comprehension.

In dictated writing about *The Ugly Duckling* in Figure 13-38, students are using very complex sentences. Children understand them because they have read and discussed the book. There is a strong foundation of meaning. Also, in the process of writing the sentences, they have reread them many times, providing an opportunity to internalize more complex language structure.

EXPANDING VOCABULARY

Readers need several encounters with a new word before they can "own" it as part of their vocabulary—see the discussion of tier 1, 2, and 3 words in Chapter 8. Writing offers opportunities to build knowledge of all three of these kinds of words. The interactive writing about *Super Fox* (in which the character Roxy just has too much energy) shown in Figure 13-39 supports using action words, including the unusual word *twirl.*

The big gray duckling was sad because he did not look like the little yellow ducklings.
The big, beautiful swan was happy because Mother Duck loved him anyway.

Figure 13-38 Dictated Writing About *The Ugly Duckling*

Roxy ran and jumped and twirled in the house.
She broke the plant.
Her father took her to the park so she
could run and jump and twirl.

Figure 13-39 Interactive Writing About *Super Fox*

In the example of independent writing in Figure 13-40, you can see the emergence of tier 2 and 3 words. The writer uses difficult words like *erupt* as well as the technical word *lava*. When these words are used in writing, students have used them many times in reading and discussion. By including them in their own pieces (whether shared or independent writing), students have access to them again and again through rereading.

Learning Language Structure

Writing requires the learner to process language slowly and carefully, with attention to the meaning.

Saying the message, writing it, and rereading it several times, helps learners internalize examples of many different syntactic patterns. It makes language patterns available.

Text Structure

Text structure is an important factor in comprehension. Knowing the overall organizational pattern, as well as underlying structures such as comparison and contrast, provide a scaffold for deriving and understanding the information. Several of the previous examples for all three genres of writing show how writing helps children internalize text structure, because they require the writer not only to notice but to use them in producing a text.

Literary Features

Writing about reading gives children a chance to try out some of the literary features of texts in a highly supported way. For example, one teacher used the dictated writing shown in Figure 13-41 to help children attend to dialogue. In the process of producing this writing, readers said the dialogue several times. They could begin to grasp the nuances in intonation connected to reading and understanding dialogue, and they had an in-depth experience with one of the first challenges of written language—that dialogue is never

Some volcanoes erupt under the sea and some
erupt from under the ground.
Lava and rocks shoot out of a hole
in the earth.
The lava from Mt. Saint Helens was red, but
it turned into hard black rock.

Figure 13-40 Independent Writing About *All About Volcances*

"Can you help me?" said Hen.
"No, I can't," said Dog
and Cat
and Pig.

Figure 13-41 Dictated Writing About *The Little Red Hen*

exactly like spoken language because it usually includes a speaker designation.

SELECTING AND USING INTERESTING LANGUAGE

Writing about reading gives readers the opportunity to use some of the important and interesting language contained in texts. For example, the cut-up sentence in Figure 13-42 captures a key idea in the story *Moosling the Babysitter*—that the baby skunks spray when someone sings. Moosling, unfortunately, started singing, so the father skunk rushed up the path to tell Moosling what he had forgotten. This episode leads right into the climax and helps the reader predict it.

REPRESENTING LITERARY FEATURES

Through writing about reading, children can represent literary features of texts and learn more about them. For example, earlier in this chapter we showed the representation of characters in a series (see Figure 13-10). And the character web in Figure 13-14 shows the development of the character of Moosling as learned by reading several books in the series. You can use diagrams effectively to represent problem and solution, a series of events, or cause and effect. When you use graphic organizers like these, think of the conversation you have with readers as the central tool and the writing as representing (and bringing organization to) their thinking.

Memory

It is impossible to categorize all the ways that writing can support and extend children's thinking about the ideas in texts. The act of composing requires a reorganization of thinking, and in that process, memory is supported, freeing the reader to develop deeper insights. Many of us continue to use writing informally (notes, outlines) to support our thinking about texts and help us get back to points that we want to make.

SUMMARIZING INFORMATION/RESTATING INFORMATION TO REFLECT ORGANIZATION

When the framework of a text is easy to understand and remember, the conversation can move to a new level. Many readers struggle so hard to pick up the details and to remember and report them that they miss some of the important ideas.

The dictated writing in Figure 13-43 summarizes *The Trip*, a story about Froggy and his friend Duck. The goal is for children to mentally form summaries like this automatically.

Restating the events of the text helps children revisit the story and think about the meaning. It also helps them learn how to *select* and remember the important events. The piece of writing in Figure 13-44 (the cut-up sentence shown was prepared afterward) unpacks the complicated process of echolocation, which was one of the main points of the text.

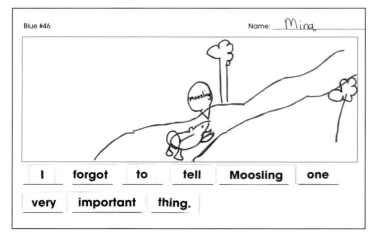

Figure 13-42 Cut-Up Sentence for *Moosling the Babysitter*

Duck was going on a trip to the lake.
Froggy helped her pack her bag.
Duck got on the bus.
Froggy hid in the bag and went to the lake too.

Figure 13-43 Summary of *The Trip*

Often, you will want to help readers by engaging them in two different forms of writing. Look at the interactive writing in Figure 13-45 that students have produced to summarize *How Frogs Grow*. (The teacher also gave them some work to do independently to help them review the life cycle, which is the central structure of the text.)

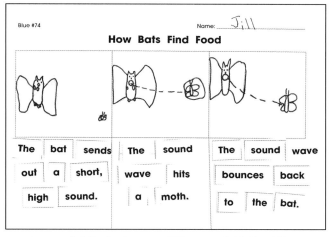

Figure 13-44 Cut-Up Sentence and Diagram of *All About Bats*

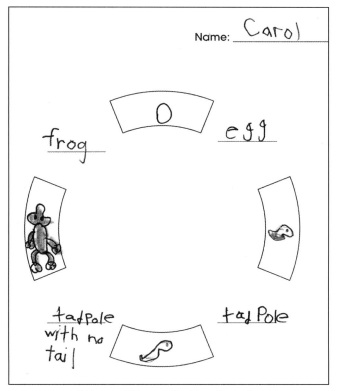

Figure 13-45 Writing and Diagram for *How Frogs Grow*

▶ In Conclusion

It is especially helpful—even essential—for learners who are finding reading difficult to engage in writing as often as possible. But just giving them the opportunity to write will not be sufficient. Often they do not have enough resources to make the activity productive, or they have learned a negative response to writing because they have had so much difficulty producing written pieces. Writing about reading provides a strong language base and good models for these writers. Demonstrations using shared/interactive writing and dictation also provide models of written products but, more important, of the process. Working alongside the writer to teach for, prompt for, and reinforce effective writing behaviors will give readers the support they need to use writing as a resource for building the system.

▶ Suggestions for Professional Development

ANALYZING EARLY WRITING STRATEGIES

1. Collect three writing samples from three early writers who are experiencing reading and/or writing difficulties.

2. With your colleagues, analyze one student's control of early writing strategies. Consider:
   - ❑ Use of meaning.
   - ❑ Use of language structures.
   - ❑ Use of spacing.
   - ❑ Use of print.
   - ❑ Use of the directionality of print.
   - ❑ Sound analysis (letter-sound relationships).
   - ❑ Visual analysis (how words look).
   - ❑ Use of punctuation.
   - ❑ Use of capitalization.

3. Use the following chart to list evidence of the writer's competencies.

4. Discuss the implications of the child's writing as it informs his reading.

5. Share your charts with other groups and compare your analyses.

6. Repeat the process for the remaining two writers.

7. Consider making a plan to include more writing about reading in your progress. You can embed it in small group reading lessons or intervention lessons for struggling readers.
   - ❑ Select a group of texts that you will use for instruction in the next two weeks.
   - ❑ Using the examples in this chapter, plan for writing about reading for each text.
   - ❑ Vary writing about reading to use functional, informational, and narrative writing.
   - ❑ For each piece of writing, look for potential opportunities to learn about words, language syntax, and text structure.

Behaviors the Writer Controls	Behaviors the Writer Almost Controls	Behaviors the Writer Does Not Yet Control

Teaching for Problem Solving While Processing Texts: Early Reading Behaviors and Searching for Information

CHAPTER
14

EFFECTIVE READERS ORCHESTRATE a range of cognitive actions while thinking about the meaning of the text (described in Chapter 2). This processing system can be built only through the experience of reading continuous text. Many high-progress readers develop and expand these systems of strategic actions spontaneously as they engage in reading a great many texts. Simply by reading, they learn more. Struggling readers need support to orchestrate effective strategies, and that needs to happen through strong teaching while they are reading continuous text. Lessons in phonics or reading strategies will not be sufficient to help readers who struggle. In this chapter and Chapter 15, we describe the kinds of conversations that you can have with readers to teach for, prompt for, and reinforce effective systems of strategic activities.

Effective readers orchestrate a range of cognitive actions while thinking about the meaning of the text; that is, they read with divided attention. We describe these systems of strategic actions in Chapter 2. In a smoothly operating system, effective readers solve words and search for and use different kinds of information. They remember important information in summary form and use it as background to gain momentum while moving through a text. They make

adjustments in the way they read based on their purpose for reading and the genre. They slow down to problem-solve and then speed up again. And they do all of this in a fluent, mostly unconscious way.

Children may learn some of the important information needed for reading (for example, sounds, letters, and words) in structured lessons such as those mentioned in Chapters 11 and 12, but the processing system can be built only through the experience of reading continuous text at an appropriate level of difficulty. Many high-progress readers develop and expand these systems of strategic actions spontaneously as they engage in reading a great many texts. Simply by reading, they learn more.

In contrast, readers who struggle:

❑ Have a lower repertoire of specific knowledge (letter-sound relationships, words).

❑ Spend less time reading continuous text and so have little experience in applying their processing systems.

❑ May have less content knowledge to bring to the reading of texts.

❑ May not have a strongly developed sense of language syntax.

❑ Need support in using effective strategic activities while reading continuous text.

Lessons in phonics or reading skills will not be sufficient to help readers who struggle. They need strong teaching to support their building of an efficient network of "in the head" systems for processing continuous text. You need to have conversations with these readers that teach for, prompt for, and reinforce effective strategic activities. For a succinct summary of language you can use to teach for, prompt for, and reinforce effective reading and writing behaviors, see *The Fountas and Pinnell Prompting Guide 1: A Tool for Literacy Teachers* (2009) and *The Fountas and Pinnell Prompting Guide 2: Supporting Comprehension* (in press).

The idea of "teaching as conversation" can be attributed to Marie Clay (1991). The term has figured strongly in her models for assessment and instruction. A conversation is an oral exchange in which the speakers take turns; each person listens carefully to the other before responding. Whatever behaviors the reader is demonstrating, the teacher is observing very carefully and making precise teaching moves that support the reader's ability to take action.

In this chapter we describe ways you can work alongside readers to help them establish early reading behaviors, match voice with print, and search for and use different kinds of information in the text. It also

provides examples of specific teaching points after children have read a text. In each example, the teacher is working with a small group of children using the lesson framework described in Chapter 18, in which you introduce a new text to the small group and all students read the entire text independently (rather than in unison or by taking turns as in "round robin reading"). While the students are reading the text, you observe and interact very briefly with each as needed. If students are reading silently (at about Level I or higher), you can ask the student you are observing to read aloud at whatever point he has reached in order to determine processing effectiveness.

▶ Teaching for Early Reading Behaviors

The early reading behaviors described in Chapter 4 are critical understandings for beginning readers. They must learn to work with print left to right and match voice to print in early oral reading. (Later, the eyes will take over the process.) This motor movement is essential for reading English. Often, classroom instruction assumes control of left-to-right directionality, voice-print match, and a return sweep to the left when starting a new line. However, many struggling readers are confused about how print works. They will not be attending to the relevant details of print if they cannot focus on the right pieces of information. Meanwhile, their classmates are moving on to decoding complex words.

Left-to-Right Directionality

Shared reading helps children understand left-to-right directionality. The following interaction, based on the page spreads of *Waking Up* reproduced in Figure 14–1, is typical in kindergarten and first grade:

The teacher first reads the entire text to the children, helping them think through the meaning. Then she goes back to the beginning to read the text with the children, demonstrating reading left to right and pointing crisply under each word.

TEACHER: I'll read this page to you. I start here *[points to first word]* and read this way. *[She reads the page.]* Now you read with me. Start here.

[Children read page 2 in unison as the teacher points.] "The rooster wakes up!" Let's read Cock-a-doodle-doo! just like the rooster said it.

[They go on to read the next page.]

At this point the children begin to read for themselves. They may recognize some words or parts of words, but they are also expending a great deal of energy engaging in the coordinated series of movements. The teacher continues to support left-to-right directionality by prompting for the children to engage in the action.

Return Sweep

Another challenge for young readers is understanding that while print moves from left to right, you have to return to the left margin each time you read a new line (return sweep). This print convention is purely arbitrary (as is reading from left to right). It was created when people invented writing. It has no natural basis; it's as arbitrary as the convention that in England drivers drive in the left lane and in Europe and the United States drivers stay to the right.

Young children can be helped to learn this concept early through shared reading. In this supportive context, they can engage in the movements necessary to process print that is more complex than they can read independently. In the following interaction, the teacher first teaches and then prompts:

TEACHER: When you are reading, start here and read this way *[demonstrates]*. When you finish

Figure 14-1 Page Spreads from *Waking Up* from Leveled Literacy Intervention, Green System (Heinemann 2009)

here, go back here *[points]*. Now you point and read. *[Child reads from left to right for two lines of text.]*

On the next page, the child hesitates at the end of the line and the teacher points at the left margin on the next line.

Even before children can read all the words independently, they can begin to internalize the motor behavior needed to read. In this interaction, children are reading a text with two lines of print (see the pages from *Bubbles* reproduced in Figure 14–2):

See the bubbles in the fish bowl.

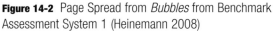

Figure 14-2 Page Spread from *Bubbles* from Benchmark Assessment System 1 (Heinemann 2008)

TEACHER: Let's read *Bubbles* again. Start here and read left to right. Remember that when you finish, go back here *[points to line 2, at the left].*

The teacher and children read the text together with return sweep. Then Jeffrey reads the book individually.

JEFFREY *[reading]:* "See the bubbles" *[He hesitates. The teacher points to the beginning of the second line.]* "in the fish bowl."

TEACHER: Good. When you finish here, remember to go back here.

The teacher's goal in this interaction is to be sure that the child is oriented to the way print works so that further teaching about visual features of words will be effective. The child is also learning some academic language, such as *left* and *right*.

Once left to right directionality and return sweep have become more established, there is no longer any need to comment on their behaviors.

Voice-Print Match

It is very important for children to understand the connection between oral and written language. Print is laid out left to right, and spaces define word boundaries. As proficient readers, we take this concept for granted, but it is not so easy for beginners. They need many experiences with print to establish firm voice-print match. Often, shared reading from big books involves multiple lines of print. Some children

can remember these predictable stories, but they do not know what to attend to with their eyes. When the teacher talks about the first word or the first line, they do not know where to look. These children may think that reading involves listening and trying to remember the language. Some children will even be resistant to pointing *because* it requires close attention to print.

Shared reading is an excellent context within which to teach voice-print match. Usually, you work with the whole class. Children will not establish voice-print match right away; but if they are still confused after several weeks of shared reading (you can detect the problem through assessment or by simply asking the child to read a small book that has been read a couple of times before), you will want to intervene with very strong teaching.

Try bringing children who are having difficulty learning voice-print match through whole-group shared reading together in a small group of three or four for a short time each day. This way you can engage their attention and involve them fully. Use a lap-size book (about eleven by fourteen inches) with very clear print. Start with only one line of print on each page, and move to two and then three lines, always checking to be sure children are able to track print left to right. Use a short, thin pointer to point precisely under each word. Be sure that children can *clearly* see each word. Keep moving along at a good rate so that children can understand meaning and syntax. Here is a good sequence to use (see Chapter 18 for a fuller description):

1. *Read to* the children. Ask them to watch while you point and read. Discuss the meaning of the story with them. Keep the emphasis on enjoyment. An engaging text like *Waking Up* (see Figure 14–3) is a good one to start with. You might use one of these teaching moves:

   ❏ "Look at how I point and read."

   ❏ "I made it match."

   ❏ "Look how I do it. I make it match."

2. Read *with* the children. Ask them to join in as you point and read.

3. Have the *children* read the text. Give each child a small copy of the same text and encourage them to point and read it for themselves. Offer support as needed. They can read this text again the following day as independent reading.

As children read books for themselves, you can prompt and reinforce voice-print match. You'll want to work very persistently to establish the behavior. Here are a few example interactions:

Figure 14-3 Pages from *Waking Up* from Leveled Literacy Intervention, Green System (Heinemann 2009)

The reader is pointing on top of each word and covering up the print.

TEACHER: Watch how I point under each word so I can see it.

The reader points under each word.
TEACHER: You pointed under each word.

The child is not pointing and is "inventing" some of the text.
TEACHER: Point to each word and read it with your finger.

The child is sliding a finger underneath the words without attending to them.
TEACHER: Put your finger under each word.

The reader gets mixed up in the reading and stops pointing.
TEACHER: Try it again with your finger.

The reader inserts extra words that aren't in the text.
TEACHER: Read this line with your finger. [*The reader reads the line accurately.*] You made it match.

The reader reads a text with crisp pointing, making it match.
TEACHER: You read it with your finger and made it match.

Having children begin with the aid of a finger allows you to establish voice-print match at early reading levels. But soon after this is established, you need to help children learn to use just the eyes. Many children spontaneously drop the finger because they find reading is smoother and more enjoyable without it, but readers who have difficulty may continue pointing with a finger far too long. Even some third and fourth graders may still point with a pencil. Pointing slows down reading, undermines fluency, and interferes with comprehension if you allow it to continue.

Some teachers and parents encourage pointing because they think it supports accuracy. Accuracy is very important, and that is why careful analysis of the student's reading level is needed. But pointing when the technique is no longer needed (usually around Level C) will not contribute to accuracy. Competent word solving and other strategies are needed. Interactions like these encourage children to let the eyes take over:

The child is reading the text accurately while pointing.
TEACHER: Now take your finger out and use your eyes.

OR

Read it with your eyes.

The child reads the text accurately without pointing.

TEACHER: You read it with your eyes.

Monitoring Voice-Print Match

One of the advantages of establishing voice-print match is that beginning readers can use it as an early way to monitor their reading—even readers who have only a beginning knowledge of letters and sounds have a way to detect whether their reading is accurate (see Figure 14-4). You can remind children using the following levels of support:

TEACHER: Go ahead and read *Eggs*. If you have too many words, go back and make it match. *[Demonstrates.]*

HALIMA *[reading page 4]*: "Mother *[pauses to look at the picture]* Snake laid a lot of eggs."

TEACHER: Did you have too many words? Go back and make it match.

HALIMA: "Mother snake laid s– some eggs."

TEACHER: You made it match.

BILL *[reading page 5]*: "The baby snakes came out of—"

TEACHER: Did you have too many words?

BILL: No.

TEACHER: You have too many words. Go back and make it match. *[Demonstrates.]*

RASHAWN *[reading page 2 of Sam and Papa (see Figure 14–5)]*: "I like to read with my Papa."

TEACHER: Did you run out of words? Go back and make it match.

RASHAWN: "I like to read books with my Papa."

TEACHER: You had just enough words.

Once these behaviors are firmly established, you can use a prompt that provides less support (one that prompts the reader to do what he already knows how to do):

SARAH *[reading page 2]*: "I like to read with my Papa." *[Omitted books.]*

TEACHER: Try that again and make it match.

SARAH *[reading]*: "I like to read books with my Papa."

TEACHER: You made it match.

One of the challenges of working with beginning readers is that they change over time along a continuum of learning. Four- and five-year-olds delight everyone by picking up their storybooks and "talking like a book" (Clay 1991). Remembering a story they have heard and enjoyed many times, they reconstruct it, often using the language of the text. They are not tracking print but using their knowledge of the meaning and pictures to create an oral text that resembles the actual text. If you are working with children reading texts at Levels A, B, and C, self-monitoring of voice-print match, or noticing one's own errors, is a top priority.

Mother Snake
laid some eggs.

4

Crack! Crack! Crack!
Baby snakes came out.

5

Figure 14-4 Page Spread from *Eggs* from Leveled Literacy Intervention, Green System (Heinemann 2009)

I like
to read books
with my Papa.

Figure 14-5 Page Spread from *Sam and Papa* from Leveled Literacy Intervention, Green System (Heinemann 2009)

▶ Teaching Children to Search For and Use Information

Readers are problem solvers who match up written signs with language that they process mentally to derive meaning. This happens very rapidly, usually without conscious attention, because word recognition is rapid and effortless. Readers also process visual images, punctuation, and features of print such as layout and font size or style—all play a part in the process of comprehending. When they do encounter something that doesn't make sense or match up, readers problem-solve using different kinds of information in a smoothly orchestrated way. They search actively, using both visible and invisible information (Clay 2001):

- ❑ Visible information includes the pictures, print, and all the conventions that make it easy to decode words—punctuation, spacing, layout, font size. It also includes graphics and symbols.

- ❑ Readers also use *invisible* information, which exists in their heads and may be prompted by

pictures if there are any. The invisible information readers use comes from background experiences, knowledge of the world, recognition of items, emotions, and the most powerful source—language.

Ultimately, readers must build ways of searching for and using information in their own heads; but you can teach for, prompt for, and reinforce behaviors in a way that supports the process.

Searching For and Using Meaning

We learn language because it is the primary way we communicate meaning to one another. While processing written language, proficient readers constantly check whether what they are reading makes sense. When they encounter problems, they think about what they know and about what they have read so far. They make predictions based on what they've read so far and read further to confirm these predictions. For beginning readers, the pictures not only make a text more engaging but also provide important information. They are a way to search for and use meaning. Consider this interaction during the introduction to *At the Market* (a page spread from the book is reproduced in Figure 14–6):

During the book introduction the teacher and children have looked at most pages of the text, used the

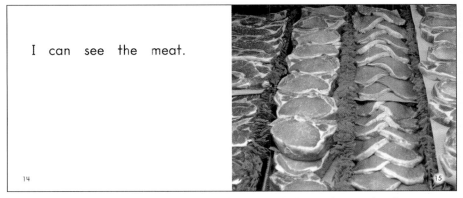

I can see the meat.

Figure 14-6 Page Spread from *At the Market* from Leveled Literacy Intervention, Orange System (Heinemann 2009)

predictable language, and said the labels of most of the food in the pictures.

TEACHER: Turn to page 14 and look at the picture.

SAM: It's where you get the meat.

TEACHER: So the writer is saying, "I can see—"

CHILDREN: The meat.

TEACHER: Let's check. What would you expect to see at the beginning of *meat?*

BECKIE: *m*

TEACHER: Find the word *meat.*

CHILDREN *[locating* meat *and reading]: meat*

TEACHER: You checked the picture and the word. Now point and read about all the things the boy says he can see at the market. *[Beckie hesitates at* milk *on page 10.]* Can the picture help you think about this part of the story?

BECKIE: *milk*

TEACHER: Try it again and see if *milk* makes sense.

The Reading Record (Figure 14–7) is a coding of Darcy's second reading of *Bubbles* (a page spread from the book is reproduced in Figure 14–8). Notice how she actively searched the pictures, once to check on her accuracy (at the word *tub*) and once to help her solve a word (*sea*) after she had started it.

After the reading and a short discussion, the teacher had Darcy turn back to page 10:

TEACHER: Show me the tricky part. *[Darcy points to the word* sea*].* Try it again and make it make sense.

DARCY *[reading]:* "See the bubbles in the sea." *[Looks puzzled.]*

TEACHER: Look at the picture.

DARCY: It's a lake?

TEACHER: It's like a lake, but it is called the sea. Have you ever heard of the sea?

DARCY: Yes.

TEACHER: There are bubbles in the sea. The picture will help you. Now turn to page 12. Read it

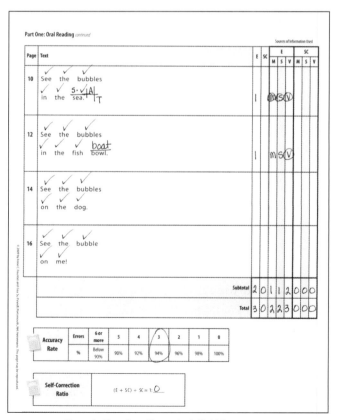

Figure 14-7 Darcy's Reading Record of *Bubbles*

again and think of what would make sense. The picture can help you.

DARCY [*reading*]: "See the bubbles in the fish b– fish bowl"?

TEACHER: Did that make sense?

DARCY: Yes. It's a fish bowl.

TEACHER: You were thinking about what would make sense and look right. You checked the picture and the words. [*Darcy reads page 14 accurately.*]

Here's another interaction during the reading of *All About Snakes*:

The text says: "Mother Snake laid some eggs."

DENNY: "Mother Snake like see eggs."

TEACHER: You said, "Mother Snake like see eggs." That doesn't make sense. In this part of the story, Mother Snake laid some eggs. Try that and see if it makes sense and looks right in the story.

DENNY [*reading*]: "Mother Snake laid some eggs."

TEACHER: That made sense and looked right.

And now let's look at an example featuring a higher-level text:

Simon is reading an informational text titled All About Chimps (pages 10 and 11 are reproduced in Figure 14–9).

SIMON [*reading*]: "Chimps use toys. This chimp used a stick to catch bugs. The chimp peeked in the hole."

TEACHER: You said, "Chimps use toys." That doesn't go with this part of the story. The writer is telling you that the chimp is using a stick like a tool to get bugs. Try it again. [*Simon reads pages 10 and 11 accurately.*] That's interesting, isn't it?

Figure 14-8 Page Spread from *Bubbles* from *Benchmark Assessment System* (Heinemann 2008)

SIMON: Yes, it's like he's digging the bugs out, kind of like a person would.

The meaning of the text is extremely important. Readers need to check on themselves constantly and not be content to produce nonsense. Even we as adults reading rapidly and silently hesitate and reread when something does not make sense. We are not willing to read nonsense. Young readers can try so hard to decode the words that they simply get through the sentence saying just about anything. Be persistent in helping them listen to themselves while they are reading orally.

Figure 14-9 Page Spread from *All About Chimps* from Leveled Literacy Intervention, Green System (Heinemann 2009)

Searching For and Using Language Structure

In Chapter 7, we explore language learning as well as the powerful role of language *in* learning. For most beginning readers, language structure is a very strong source of information, but it can also pose difficulties:

❑ Some readers have very little previous experience hearing written language read aloud. They can use their oral language as a source of information, but some written language patterns may be tricky for them. Without effective instruction, they may not fully use language structure to their benefit.

❑ Readers who spend a great deal of time reading texts that are too hard become so mired in solving words that what they are reading no longer sounds like language.

❑ English language learners may find the patterns of English syntax tricky and, consequently, be unable to access some language structures.

Proficient readers even at the lower levels are constantly checking to be sure that their reading "sounds right" (conforms to the syntactic patterns that are appropriate and meaningful in English). Children's knowledge of syntax can be strengthened by a dynamic literacy program that includes interactive read-aloud, shared reading, and independent reading. Helping students expand their knowledge of language structure makes it possible to teach for, prompt for, and reinforce the use of this information effectively in reading. Below are three interactions during the reading of *Making Soup* (see the pages reproduced in Figure 14–10):

SHANE [*reading page 6*]: "Here is . . . and . . . here and . . . here and the [*stops*].

TEACHER: Listen to this: "Here are the beans for the soup"—you try it.

SHANE [*reading*]: "Here are the beans for the soup."

TEACHER: That's how it would sound in this book.

DAISIA [*reading page 8*]: "Here and the put for the soup." [*Starts to turn the page.*]

TEACHER: You said, "Here and the put for the soup." That doesn't sound right. This word is *are* (*points to the word*). Look at the picture. What is he saying he is putting in the pot?

DAISIA: [*looks at the picture*]: "Here are the potatoes for the soup."

TEACHER: Now it sounds right and makes sense.

DAISIA [*reading page 10*]: "Here and . . . here are the one for the soup." No. "Here are the onions for the soup."

TEACHER: You made it make sense and sound right.

MARYANN [*reading page 14*]: "Here is the carrots for the soup."

TEACHER: Listen to this. "Here is the carrots for the soup." "Here are the carrots for the soup." Which one sounds better?

MARYANN: "Here are the carrots for the soup."

TEACHER: Now you made it sound right.

The Reading Record in Figure 14–11 captures Allen's reading of *Flap, Flap, Fly*, a Level C book. By the time Allen reached page 12, the teacher could see that the book was too hard and that he wasn't able to use language structure as a support. Of course, Allen will also need to learn to use phonics to look closely at words, but right now he needs support to be able to use language structure. They finished the book together using shared reading, a procedure that made it possible for Allen to use the language of the text. Then, the teacher had him return to page 2:

TEACHER: You said, "Mother Duck can walking." That's not the way the writer would say it in a book. The writer of this book said, "Mother Duck can walk." Try that and make it sound like the writer.

Reading and rereading a great many texts, with teacher support, will help children internalize some of the more challenging sentence patterns that appear even in simple texts. We have talked mostly about early readers here because that is when the behavior of using language structure should be established. But all readers use knowledge of language syntax, which becomes increasingly complex as texts increase in difficulty and move from oral to written language structures. Consider the complexity of some of the language structure in *A Trip to the Laundromutt* (pages 4 and 5 are reproduced in Figure 14–12).

First, this text has dialogue between two speakers. Dialogue always involves sentences with embedded independent clauses. But there are other complexities. Look at page 4. The reader has to process a sentence with "the look of" as the object of the verb, (understanding *look* as a noun) and then read another prepositional phrase after that. And, "the look of" is an expression that some readers may not have heard. On page 5, the sentence has three verbs joined by *and*, followed by a prepositional phrase. Page 8 has a compound sentence, with each part having two adverbs. As the book continues, there are signal words such as *next, then,* and *at last* embedded within the text to indicate sequence.

In the introduction to the book, the teacher supported some difficult language structures the reader would encounter:

Teacher: Have you ever heard someone say, "I don't like the look of something"? *[Children shake their heads no.]* Well, it just means that you see something and it makes you think something is going to happen that you won't like. When we are going to have a storm, I might look up at the sky and say, "I don't like the look of those clouds. It must be going to rain really hard." Or your mom might say, "I don't like the look of your room. You'd better clean it up."

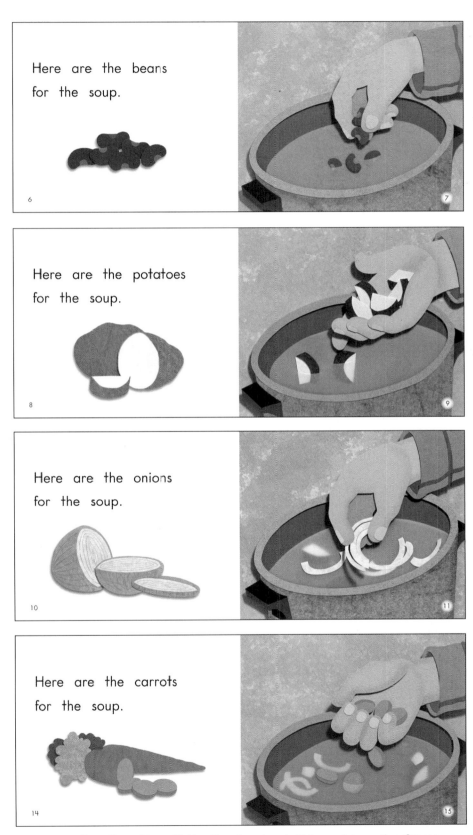

Figure 14-10 Page Spread from *Making Soup* from Leveled Literacy Intervention, Orange System (Heinemann 2009)

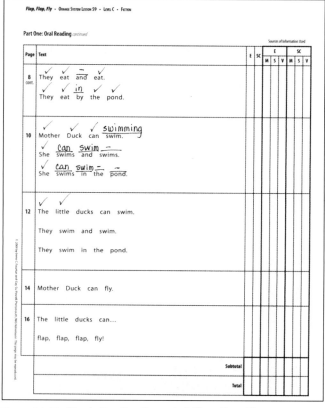

Figure 14-11 Allen's Reading Record of *Flap, Flap, Fly*

JAKE: Or, "I don't like the look of the mess on the floor."

TEACHER: That's right. Well in this book, Orson and Taco are really dirty and Mom and Jack take them to the Laundromutt. The Laundromutt is like the Laundromat, the place where you wash clothes, only this is a place where you wash dogs. Mutt is another name for a dog.

SAMMI: That's funny.

JONATHAN: Do they put them in washing machines?

TEACHER: No, they put them in big tubs like the one on the cover. Do you think Orson and Taco will like having a bath?

JONATHAN: No, dogs hate baths.

SAMMI: My dog doesn't.

TEACHER: You are right about Orson and Taco, Jonathan. Orson looked at those big tubs. He did not like the look of those big tubs. Let's take a look at some of the pages before we read.

During the reading, the teacher intervened to support children's use of more complex language syntax:

SAMMI [*reading page 6*]: "Soon Orson was wet, wet, wet. The big dog shakes and the Jack was too wet."

TEACHER: Try that again and think what would sound right.

SAMMI: "The big dog sh–oo–k and then Jack was wet, too."

TEACHER: That's how it should sound.

JAKE [*reading page 15*]: "But at last, little Taco look very good, too."

TEACHER: Try that again and think what would sound right.

JAKE: "But at last, little Taco looked very good, too."

TEACHER: He did, didn't he?

Language syntax will consume less attention as readers become more knowledgeable about this kind of grammar; soon they will be processing even complex sentences unconsciously. They are cued by the punctuation, which guides pausing and word stress. But even very proficient readers will sometimes reread a complex sentence to correct intonation, pausing, or word stress so their reading sounds meaningful.

Searching For and Using Visual Information

Pictures cue readers to search for and use meaning; of course, we look at pictures as we read, but within a processing system, visual information means the *print*. Ultimately, readers must process the individual words of a text, and that means looking at print (although they can cross-reference it with meaning and language structure).

Some readers need very specific and systematic instruction to learn about letters, sounds, and words and how to check them with the language and meaning in texts. In Chapter 9 we discuss the phonological basis for language, and in Chapter 11 we discuss phonemic awareness and phonics. Chapters 10 and 11 include ways to help children learn how words work. But they must be able to apply phonics to the processing of continuous print. Chapter 11 includes examples of using high-frequency words to help children monitor their reading and also provide a backdrop of accuracy when solving problems.

You can teach for, prompt for, and reinforce readers' ability to search for and use visual information as they read. Locating known words during the introduction to the text and supporting word solving during and after reading are important tools in this process.

THINKING ABOUT THE SOUNDS

Hearing the sounds in words is one of the first steps to take in breaking words apart. As soon as children can hear a few sounds and connect those sounds with some letters, they are using examples of

The Laundromutt had big tubs for the dogs. Taco did not like the look of those tubs!

4

"Let's wash Orson first," said Mom.
    She pushed and pulled and got Orson into a tub.

5

Figure 14-12 Page Spread from *A Trip to the Laundromutt* from Leveled Literacy Intervention, Green System (Heinemann 2009)

letter-sound relationships. Below are several interactions that support children's use of sounds connected to letters:

The teacher is introducing Baking *(see the pages reproduced in Figure 14–13).*

TEACHER: Turn to page 10. Oh, here's another thing that they baked.

CHILDREN: Cupcakes!

TEACHER: You see the cupcakes in the picture. Check the picture with the word. *Cupcakes* begins with a *c* like *cat*. [*Reading.*] "We baked the *c*. Does it start like *cupcakes*?

CHILDREN. Yes, it starts with *c*.

TEACHER: You can check the picture with the first sound of the word.

During the reading of Baking, *Shoshana stops at the word* brownies *on page 8. The picture may not offer enough support.*

SHOSHANA [*reading*]: "We baked the—" What's that word? "We baked the brownies."

TEACHER: Those look like brownies, and brownies begins with a *b*. Those brownies look good to eat.

Figure 14-13 Page Spread from *Baking* from Leveled Literacy Intervention, Orange System (Heinemann 2009)

Mouse is the story of a little mouse who likes to eat all kinds of things in bed. When she sleeps, she likes to dream of food (page 16 is reproduced in Figure 14–14).

ERNIE *[reading]*: "And Mouse likes to—" *[stops].*

TEACHER: Think about the story on this page as you say the first sound of that word. It looks like Mouse has fallen asleep. Read it again. And Mouse likes to d–.

ERNIE: Dream.

TEACHER: Now try that.

ERNIE *[reading]*: "And Mouse likes to dream in bed, t– too."

Figure 14-14 Page from *Mouse* from Leveled Literacy Intervention, Orange System (Heinemann 2009)

TEACHER: You thought about the story and used the first sound.

My Family is a simple Level B text in which Bunny, a repeating character in a series, introduces her family (pages from the book are reproduced in Figure 14–15).

ALAN *[reading page 2]*: "This is—" *[stops].* What's that word?

TEACHER: The bunny is telling us about her family. This is her mom. What would Bunny say?

ALAN: This is my mom. *[Reading.]* "This is my mom. My mom likes to dig."

TEACHER: That is the word *my*. It starts just like *mom*.

Sometimes, readers will encounter a new word at the beginning of a sentence. Without meaning or language structure to draw on, they must look at the letters and associate them with sounds. If you suspect such a word will be tricky and affect the rest of the reading of the text, it may be appropriate to locate the word during the introduction to the text.

The teacher is introducing Making Soup *(pages 2 and 3 are reproduced in Figure 14–16).*

TEACHER: In this book, the writer is going to tell about all the things we need to make soup. Look at page 2. What do you see in the picture?

JESSE: A spoon and a pot.

TEACHER: The writer is going to say, "Here is the pot for the soup." Say *here*. What letter do you expect to see at the beginning of *here*?

SUSAN: *h*

JESSE: *h*—here *[points to it].*

TEACHER: Jesse found the word. Now, everyone find the word. *[Children locate* here.*]* You found the word. "Here is the pot." It is going to say *here* on every page.

This is my mom.
My mom likes to dig.

2   3

This is my dad.
My dad likes to bake.

4   5

Figure 14-15 Page Spreads from *My Family* from Leveled Literacy Intervention, Orange System (Heinemann 2009)

Here is the pot
for the soup.

2   3

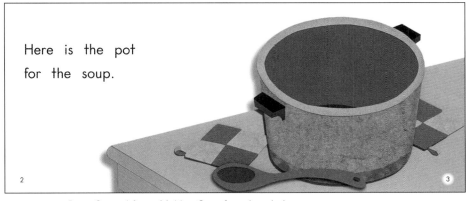

Figure 14-16 Page Spread from *Making Soup* from Leveled Literacy Intervention, Orange System (Heinemann 2009)

THINKING ABOUT HOW THE WORD LOOKS

It is important for beginning readers to realize that they need to check their predictions against how the word looks. They need to notice the letters. Their predictions may make sense and sound right, and they go right on; but to become proficient, they need to notice mismatches. Children need to stop when what they say does not match the visual information. Early on, the first letter of a word will be most helpful. They can use the words they know as resources. The interaction below focuses on thinking how the word looks:

Christine is reading page 4 of My Family *and has difficulty with the word* bake. *She is thinking about meaning and using language structure but not monitoring her reading using visual information.*

CHRISTINE [*reading page 4*]: "This is my dad. My dad likes to cook."

TEACHER: That makes sense, but look at the first letter [*points to the* b].

CHRISTINE: *b–*

TEACHER: Would *bake* look right? Try that.

CHRISTINE [*reading*]: "This is my dad. My dad likes to bake." It should say bake cookies!"

TEACHER: That would make sense, but there aren't enough words.

LOOKING MORE CLOSELY AT THE VISUAL INFORMATION IN WORDS

Readers' ability to search for and use visual information expands as they encounter more difficult words in texts and use known words as resources. Your phonics lessons will help children make connections between words. For example, you can take known words and add or substitute letters to make new words (*like, bike*). You can connect words that start the same (*me, my, make*). You can sort words by pattern (*not, pot, hot; stay, say, way*). Suggestions for these direct lessons are included in Chapter 11.

You can help children use those connections to solve words "on the run" while they are reading. In the interaction below, Brad is reading *Brave Taco*, a Level E text (see the page spreads reproduced in Figure 14–17):

BRAD *[reading]*: "A big red—" *[stops].*

Figure 14-17 Page Spreads from *Brave Taco* from Leveled Literacy Intervention, Green System (Heinemann 2009)

TEACHER: Do you know a word that starts like that?

BRAD: *the*

TEACHER: It does start like *the*

BRAD: And it has *-ing.*

TEACHER: So try it again.

BRAD *[reading]*: "A big red thing made a n–."

TEACHER: Would noise make sense and look right? Try it.

BRAD *[reading]*: "A big red thing made a noise."

TEACHER: Using parts you know can help you. The red vacuum did make a noise.

Notice that when the teacher told Brad a word, she prompted him to reread to check whether it made sense and looked right so that he would gain momentum and keep the meaning in mind.

On another page of *Brave Taco*, Tara had trouble with the word *more:*

TARA *[reading page 6]*: "The big red thing made made noise." *[Stops.]*

TEACHER: What did you notice?

TARA: I said *made* two times.

TEACHER: You're right, that wouldn't make sense, try that again.

TARA: "The big red thing made m–."

TEACHER: Do you know the next part of that word?

TARA *[reading]*: "The big red thing made more noise."

TEACHER: It helped when you used a part you know.

PROMPTING FOR A HIGHER LEVEL OF INDEPENDENCE

As readers gain strength in using known words to get to new words, you can make a less specific suggestion that calls for them to search for what they know. This kind of prompt calls for a higher level of independence. The following interactions occurred during the reading of *A Trip to the Laundromutt* (four pages are reproduced in Figure 14–18):

PATRICK [*reading page 3*]: "Mom looked at Orson. 'Orson—" [*stops*].

TEACHER: Think about what you know that might help.

PATRICK: Real. Really. [*Reading.*] "Mom looked at Orson. 'Orson really needs a bath,' said Mom. 'Let's go to the Laundromutt.'"

TEACHERS: You thought about a part you know.

At another place in the text, Patrick had difficulty again.

PATRICK [*reading page 11*]: "Taco ran— [*stops*].

TEACHER: What do you know that might help?

PATRICK: A–a–[*makes the sound of* r].

TEACHER: Try it again and use what you know.

PATRICK: "Taco ran around and around, and the floor got wet."

TEACHER: You used a part you know.

CONNECTING WORD SOLVING TO WRITING

In Chapters 11 and 13, we emphasize the powerful role writing plays in helping children learn how words work. You may want to teach and prompt children to connect the words they are trying to read with

Figure 14-18 Page Spreads from *A Trip to the Laundromutt* from Leveled Literacy Intervention, Green System (Heinemann 2009)

what they have learned in writing. In the following interactions, the teacher helps children make connections with how to write words:

The teacher is introducing All About Animal Babies *(pages 2 and 3 are reproduced in Figure 14–19).*

TEACHER: This book is all about how animal moms take care of their babies. Look at pages 2 and 3. In the picture, you see the mother robin feeding some worms to her babies.

Animal moms take care
of their babies.

This mother robin
feeds her babies.
The baby birds
eat worms.

2

3

Figure 14-19 Page Spread from *All About Animal Babies* from Leveled Literacy Intervention, Green System (Heinemann 2009)

LORI: Look how their mouths are all stretched open. They are really cute.

TEACHER: Say the word *feeds* and think how it starts.

CHILDREN: *feeds, f*

TEACHER: Find the word *feeds* on page 2. *[Children locate the word.]* I want you to look at this word. Let me show you how I can check it. I'll say it slowly like when we write it. *[Demonstrates saying the word slowly while running the finger under it.]* Now you do that. *[Children demonstrate the action.]* Could you hear the sounds and see the letters in the word *feeds?*

CHILDREN: Yes.

TEACHER: You can do that when you come to a word in a book that you are not sure about. The mother robin feeds her babies. Look at those worms!

Scott is reading At the Beach *(Level G; pages 4 and 5 are reproduced in Figure 14–20).*

SCOTT: " 'It's a good book,' Jesse said. 'It's about—" *[stops].*

TEACHER: Run your finger under it and say it slowly like when you write it.

SCOTT: *s–sh–ar–k, sharks*

TEACHER: Try it in the sentence. Does that make sense here?

SCOTT: Yes, there are fish in the book so it could be a shark. *[Reading.]* " 'It's about sharks.' "

TEACHER: It will help you to look through the whole word. *Sh–ar–k–s.*

An interaction like this helps readers look beyond the first letter in words. But be careful not to interrupt the reading too long or too often. Help children attend to the letters or word parts in order within the word, and if they can't solve it quickly, tell them the word.

"It's a good book,"
Jesse said.
"It's about sharks."

"Sharks can eat people,"
Sam said.

"The book didn't say that,"
Jesse said.

4

5

Figure 14-20 Page Spread from *At the Beach* from Leveled Literacy Intervention, Blue System (Heinemann 2009)

Using Multiple Sources of Information

Efficient problem solving involves the use of multiple sources of information in a smooth and flexible way. Readers are always:

❑ Searching for and using the kind of information they need to solve problems in the most efficient way.

❑ Checking one source of information against others.

❑ Using one source of information to help them find and use others.

❑ Thinking simultaneously about making all sources of information fit.

But the umbrella was too small.

Mouse wanted to have a picnic with Rabbit. But it was raining.

Figure 14-21 Page Spread from *A Picnic in the Rain* from Leveled Literacy Intervention, Blue System (Heinemann 2009)

These actions happen with such speed that we are seldom aware of the process.

Struggling readers, on the other hand, sometimes have difficulty using even one source of information. Even when a technique does not work in helping them solve problems, they use it again and again. As you help them learn to take words apart, learn about language syntax, and keep focused on the meaning of the text, you also need to help them develop a wider range of strategic actions for word solving that they can use in a flexible way.

If you notice that children are attending only to one source of information, you need to broaden the sources they attend to while reading. Let's look at the teaching after Zack's reading of *A Picnic in the Rain*. (Pages 6 and 7 of the book are reproduced in Figure 14–21; His Reading Record is shown in Figure 14–22).

Zack read with 92 percent accuracy and had a self-correction ratio of 1:4. His fluency rating was 2. Zack showed many strengths in processing this text, which he had read for the first time the day before. Yet once he substituted *top* for *tent*, he continued to make that error throughout the text. He remained satisfied with his response, even though it made little sense. Although the word and picture had been emphasized in the introduction, his teacher wondered whether Zack knew what a tent was.

Teacher: Let's go back to page 9. *[They turn to page 9.]* Find the tricky part. *[Zack points to* tent.*]* Look at the picture. Do you see Skunk? He is in his tent—something you put up in your yard or a park when you want to camp out. How do you think that tent helps Skunk?

Zack: It keeps the rain out.

Teacher: So read this sentence again and see if you can make it make sense and look right.

Zack *[reading]*: "'Come and sit in my tent,' said Skunk."

Teacher: Did that make sense and sound right?

Zack: Yes.

Zack: "Skunk wanted to have a picnic with Mouse and Rabbit. But it was raining hard."

Teacher: You made it all fit together.

In the interaction that follows, Salli is reading *Taking Care of Meli* (the page Salli is reading is reproduced in Figure 14–23):

Salli *[reading]*: "Ron brushes Meli every day. Dogs need to have careful fur. 'You're so pretty, Meli!' says Ron."

Teacher: Try that again. You are almost right. Think about Meli's fur.

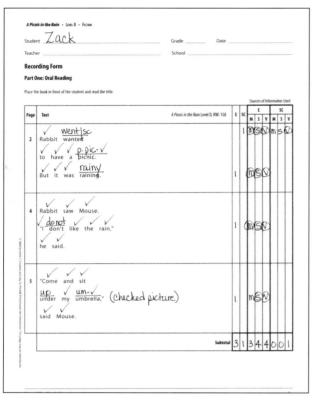

Figure 14-22 Reading Record of Zack Reading *A Picnic in the Rain,* p. 1

Figure 14-22 Zack's Reading Record, p. 2

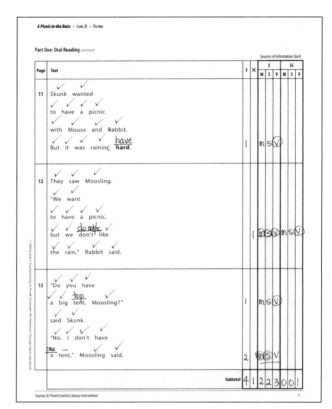

Figure 14-22 Zack's Reading Record, p. 3

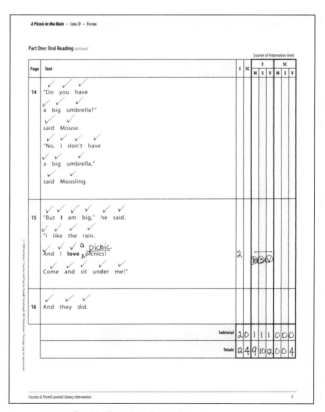

Figure 14-22 Zack's Reading Record, p. 4

SALLI: "Dogs need to have cl–[*stops*].

TEACHER: You started the word. Think what would make sense there.

SALLI: *clean?*

TEACHER: Try *clean* and see if it makes sense, sounds right, and looks right.

SALLI: "Dogs need to have clean fur. 'You're so pretty, Meli!' says Ron."

TEACHER: Now it all fits together.

SALLI: He uses that brush to clean her fur?

TEACHER: He sure does.

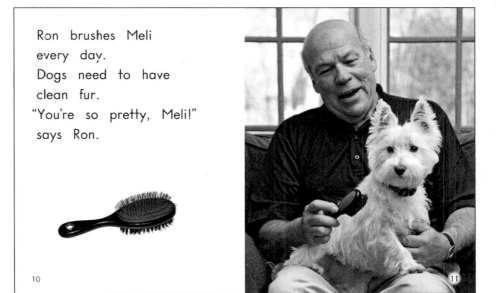

Ron brushes Meli every day.
Dogs need to have clean fur.
"You're so pretty, Meli!" says Ron.

10   11

Figure 14-23 Page Spread from *Taking Care of Meli* from Leveled Literacy Intervention, Blue System (Heinemann 2009)

▶ Problem Solving Over Time

It is important that beginning readers learn how print works as well as how to search for and use different kinds of information, with the goal of using all sources of information together. An amazing amount of learning takes place over the first books that children read (Levels A to about I). One of the reasons to intervene early when you first notice that children are having difficulty is to establish flexible ways of searching for and using information before readers become rigidly entrenched in the ineffective ways they are using print. As we discussed, your language in supporting the reader's ability to establish early reading behaviors and use multiple sources of information is critical to his success in building an efficient processing system.

Of course, readers need to take their problem solving to a much higher level. They need to become independent in initiating strategic actions. In the next chapter, you will find suggestions for specific language to support independence in problem solving while reading.

▶ Suggestions for Professional Development

USING LANGUAGE TO SUPPORT PROBLEM-SOLVING

1. The best way to expand your repertoire for teaching, prompting, and reinforcing effective reading behaviors is to reflect on Reading Records.

2. Prepare for a meeting with colleagues by taking Reading Records (with printed text) or running records (on a blank form) of the reading of about ten of your students. Vary the sample by reading level.

3. Bring the records to the meeting and share your insights into your reader's strengths and needs, particularly after errors or at difficulty. What strategic activities do they engage in?

4. Use the examples in this chapter to state language (teach, prompt, reinforce) that would have been appropriate to help readers solve the problem if you had not been engaged in assessment.

5. Then decide on some teaching points after reading the text that would have been helpful to readers. What language would you use?

6. Finally, make a list of some language that you think would be especially helpful to each reader. As you work with the reader individually or in a group, keep this language handy.

7. If you have it, you can also consult the *Fountas and Pinnell Prompting Guide 1* as a resource.

Teaching for Independence in Processing Texts: Solving Words, Self-Monitoring and Self-Correcting Behaviors

CHAPTER
15

Our goal for all readers is independence in smoothly processing texts. When you teach and prompt for effective reading behaviors, your goal is to help the reader learn to do something strategic that she can do whenever she reads. We want readers to be flexible in the way they engage in problem solving while maintaining a focus on the meaning of the text. Struggling readers tend to be rigid and slow; often they are dependent on the teacher. In this chapter, we continue the discussion of conversations that will support readers in independently using strategic actions. Our goal as teachers is to use powerful and explicit language that will help readers develop the fast and independent processing strategies they need.

The goal for all readers is the ability to read texts independently. Kaye's (2008) study of second-grade readers (discussed in Chapter 12) provided evidence of the independence and active problem-solving on the part of young proficient readers. A highlight of the study is that in all these readings, the proficient readers *never appealed for help without initiating attempts to solve words.*

Think about the struggling readers you teach. What patterns of behavior do they exhibit? Now contrast the Reading Records in Figures 15-1 and 15-2.

Kent read *All About Snakes* at 92 percent accuracy, which indicates that the book was a good instructional level for him. He made eleven errors and corrected four of them, a ratio of 1:3. His reading was accurate, but more important, Kent was *active* as a reader. Before appealing, he tried something. He monitored his reading using first letters and letter clusters. His attempts reveal he was aware of more than one source of information. He corrected himself using visual information and language structure. On occasion, when he made a good attempt (on page 14,

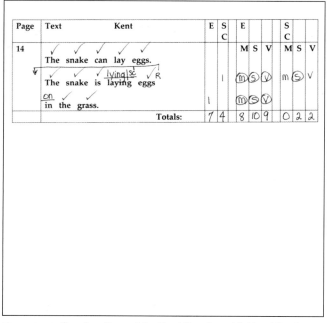

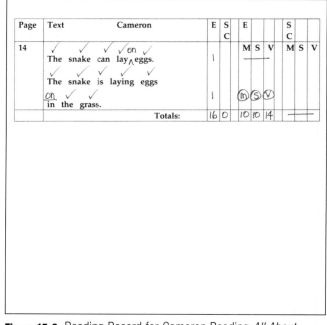

Figure 15-1 Reading Record for Kent Reading *All About Snakes*

Figure 15-2 Reading Record for Cameron Reading *All About Snakes*

for example) and read on to find that it didn't sound right, he repeated and corrected the phrase. Kent is just beginning to build a reading processing system, but he is demonstrating an emerging set of flexible strategic activities that he can use effectively.

Cameron read the same text. He made sixteen errors, reading at 82 percent accuracy. He made no self-corrections. It is obvious that the text was too hard for Cameron, but this is not uncommon; struggling readers are almost always reading texts that are too hard for them. What is of even greater concern is that Cameron was not working actively as a reader. His first move when a word was unfamiliar was to appeal for help. Only when prompted ("you try it") did he make an attempt. He does know some letter-sound relationships, as evidenced by substitutions like *crawling* for *climbing*, but he did not use them effectively to solve problems. He made repeated errors (*the* for *this* and *on* for *in*) without checking the details of the print. He does need phonics instruction, but if Cameron continues to read like this daily, no amount of isolated work with words will turn him into a proficient reader. Cameron's teacher needs to take three more actions: (1) giving him texts that are right for him instructionally; (2) presenting strong instruction while he reads continuous text; and (3) prompting him to use what he knows in an active way.

▶ Helping Readers Take Words Apart

We've already discussed (in Chapter 14) how readers use visual information to monitor and problem-solve while reading. Noticing mismatches is a critical early behavior: it shows that readers are beginning to use visual information in a coordinated way with other sources of information, like meaning and language structure. Teachers can use powerful language to teach for, prompt for, and reinforce beginning readers' use of visual information (see Figure 15-3).

The Fountas and Pinnell Prompting Guide 1 (2009) includes examples of a large range of language for teaching, prompting, and reinforcing readers' actions. The prompts may be used at any time in a lesson—to draw children's attention to important information during the text introduction, for example, or to do some specific teaching after the students have read a text. They can also be used to support learners when they are in the process of reading a text. When used during reading, these interactions should:

- ❏ Be very brief, so as not to interrupt the readers' grasp of the meaning of the story.

- ❏ Assist learners in using what they already know.

Figure 15-3 Supporting Strategic Actions During Reading

Teach	Prompt	Reinforce
The teacher demonstrates an effective action, telling or showing the reader what to do or say.	The teacher directs the reader's attention to the information that will help him solve the problem.	The teacher confirms what the reader did to solve the problem.
Examples:	*Examples:*	*Examples:*
"Look at the beginning part." *[point]*	"Say the first part. It starts like this *[say sound]*."	"You said the first part and it helped you."
"You can get your mouth ready to start the tricky word."	"Get your mouth ready for the first sound."	"You got your mouth ready to start the word."
"Listen to how I start it."	"Look at the first letter and say the sound."	"You noticed the first letter and made the sound."

❏ Draw readers' attention to the precise information they need to solve the problem.

❏ Be carefully selected—not too many during the reading of any one text.

❏ Promote fast processing.

Long interactions trying to elicit a word from a reader will interrupt comprehension and fluency. If readers cannot solve a word with one or two quick prompts, then it is best to tell them the word. If you have to tell too many words, then either the text is too hard or you did not provide enough support in the introduction.

In addition, it is important to support *fast processing* (Clay 2005). Your goal is to help readers develop "fast brainwork." You don't want to slow down the reading. In Chapter 12 we emphasize the importance of fast word recognition and describe how to help children locate words quickly. Learning to scan print, searching for visual features they remember, helps readers recognize words quickly, which contributes to fluency and frees attention for solving new words and thinking about the meaning of the text.

Word solving requires more than visual information, so often teachers use prompts such as those in Figure 15-3 in combination with language that directs readers' attention to other sources of information: "Try that again and see if it looks right and sounds right."

As students begin reading more difficult texts, they need to expand their strategic systems in order to be able to take apart and solve complex words. Teaching readers how to solve words as they are reading continuous print is directly related to the daily instruction they continue to receive in phonics and word study.

When you teach for, prompt for, and reinforce effective reading behaviors, your goal is to help readers learn how to do something that they can do when they read any text. It is not simply to "get the word right." Sometimes teachers fall into the trap of trying to elicit the correct word:

❏ "That's the word you learned yesterday."

❏ "It's on our chart."

❏ "You know that word!"

❏ "Remember you read that word this morning."

❏ "That's the word I was showing you."

❏ "You have that word on your spelling list."

❏ "What are you sitting on?" [For *chair.*]

❏ "That's what you say when someone does something nice for you." [For *thank you.*]

❏ "What would you say if you want to be polite?" [For *please.*]

Readers may read that word correctly but are not building in-the-head strategic activities for solving words using visual information, meaning, and language structure. This kind of teaching depends on idiosyncratic circumstances and increases dependence rather than promoting problem solving. All of us occasionally resort to hints like the above, and they may have some value in the moment; but in general they come from outside the text in ways that would not be available to the child when reading independently.

▶ Helping Readers Use Word Parts

Powerful instructional language draws readers' attention to the information that will be most useful for solving the word. This chapter includes quite a few examples of interactions with readers using language that helps them use parts of words to solve them. Keep in mind that these are very quick interactions, and you should also expect children to respond as fast as possible. The way you demonstrate or teach will make it easy for the reader to follow your prompts. When readers demonstrate they can perform the action, keep prompting until they are responding quickly. The ultimate goal is to promote *automatic* actions readers don't have to think about.

Telling the Word

It is better and more efficient to tell the word in a way that helps the reader attend to important information. For example, here are a couple of interactions during the reading of *Meli on the Stairs* (Level C; see the page spreads reproduced in Figure 15-4):

> **ELI** *[reading page 2]*: "Look at Meli. Meli likes to play on the s–." What's that word?
>
> **TEACHER:** You got your mouth ready to start the word. Now try it again and think what would make sense in the story and start with that sound.
>
> **ELI:** "Look at Meli. Meli likes to play on the s– steps"? *[Stops.]*
>
> **TEACHER:** That makes sense and it starts like that. In this story they are called *stairs*.

The teacher recognized a real strength. Eli could notice and make the sound of the first letter of a word. She prompted him to reread and access both visual information and meaning to read the word. Eli made an excellent attempt with *steps*. At this point, the teacher needed to help him move on: Eli had used all his resources, and the teacher did not want to interrupt the reading further. She told him the word. Then, to regain momentum, she prompted him to read it again, putting together all sources of information.

> **BOBBY** *[reading page 12]*: "Meli likes to go—." No. *[Stops.]*
>
> **TEACHER:** Why did you stop?
>
> **BOBBY:** It's not *go*.
>
> **TEACHER:** You noticed it didn't look right. Try that again and think what would make sense and start like that.

Figure 15-4 Page Spreads from *Meli on the Stairs* from Leveled Literacy Intervention, Green System (Heinemann 2009)

> **BOBBY:** "Meli likes to take her dog up the stairs and down the stairs. Up and down. Down and up."

In this interaction, the teacher reinforced Bobby's monitoring; he had noticed a mismatch, possibly because he knew the word *go* or because of the first letter. She wanted him to use the meaning, and she knew he could get his mouth ready to start the word.

Use Understandings Gained from Writing

In the following interactions, the teacher helped Rory access knowledge that he had gained through writing:

Rory is reading page 4 of The Red Pajamas, *pages of which are reproduced in Figure 15-5.*

RORY: "Froggy looked in his closet. He saw b– b–.

TEACHER: You can say it slowly like when you write it.

RORY: b–a–t. Bat, bats. [Reads the rest of the page accurately.]

TEACHER: It helped to say it slowly like when you write it.

Rory is reading page 14 of The Red Pajamas.

RORY: "He saw a fan and a cl– closet [stops].

TEACHER: It starts like that. Look through the word and say it slowly like when you write it.

RORY: cl–ock, clock.

TEACHER: Now try it from the beginning.

RORY: "He saw a fan and a clock and his cr– [checks picture] crayons. Then he saw his red pajamas."

Rory knows how to say a word slowly and write the letters that represent the sounds he hears. Also, while writing, he has learned how to run a finger under the word while saying it slowly to check it. When children have a repertoire of letter-sound relationships, they can use this technique in reading either to help them solve a word or to check on their accuracy. It is especially helpful when working with relatively simple words that have regular letter-sound patterns.

Looking at Word Parts in Sequence

In the next interaction, the teacher helped the reader look at the various parts in a word while reading *Taking Care of Meli* (see the page spreads reproduced in Figure 15-6):

IVIE [reading]: "Here is Meli. Meli lives with Ron. Ron takes good care of her. Meli is a—." [Stops.]

TEACHER: Say the first part.

IVIE: /v/.

TEACHER: Now say more.

IVIE: Ver–. [Pronounces it like the -er in her.]

TEACHER: Now say the ending.

IVIE [still pronouncing er as in her]: Ver–y. [Corrects the pronunciation.] Very! "Very lucky dog."

TEACHER: That makes sense and it looks right. Meli is a lucky dog.

IVIE: Yes.

Proficient readers attend to larger word parts. In the following interaction, the teacher worked with Karin to help her attend to the parts of words while

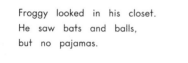

Froggy looked in his closet.
He saw bats and balls,
but no pajamas.

4   5

He saw a fan
and a clock
and his crayons.
Then he saw
his red pajamas!

14   15

Figure 15-5 Page Spreads from *The Red Pajamas* from Leveled Literacy Intervention, Blue System (Heinemann 2009)

reading *Super Fox* (pages from the book are reproduced in Figure 15-7).

> *Karin is stopped at the word* faster. *The teacher covers up the* -er.

TEACHER: You can say the first part.

KARIN: Fast . . . faster! *[Reading.]* "Roxy ran faster and faster. 'I can run faster than any fox!' said Roxy. 'I am Super Fox!'" That has an *-er,* too *[points to* Super*]*.

In an interaction like the one below, the teacher might not even have to orally prompt the reader to say the first part. Just covering the ending is a way of teaching a way to solve the word:

> **RICHARD** *[reading page 9]*: "Roxy—." *[Stops at the word* twirled *and covers the ending but does not read the word.]*

TEACHER: Say the first two letters.

RICHARD: /Tw/.

TEACHER: Look at the middle part.

RICHARD *[spelling]*: i–r. Like *girl.*

TEACHER: Would *twirl* look right there?

RICHARD: Yes.

TEACHER: *Twirl* means to turn around and around. That's what Roxy is doing.

Make Connections Between Words

Readers can also solve a word by making a connection with another word that may have similar letters. In the following example, Kyra is reading page 3 of *Moosling the Babysitter* (pages 2 and 3 are reproduced in Figure 15-8):

> **KYRA** *[reading]*: "He—." *[Stops at the word* let.*]*

TEACHER: It's like *get.*

KYRA: Let. "He let them climb up his legs."

Here is Meli.
Meli lives with Ron.
Ron takes good care
of her.
Meli is a very lucky dog.

Figure 15-6 Page Spread from *Taking Care of Meli* from Leveled Literacy Intervention, Blue System (Heinemann 2009)

Roxy jumped on a chair.
She jumped up and down.
She jumped very high.

Roxy jumped higher and higher.
"I can jump higher
than any fox!" said Roxy.
"I am Super Fox!"

"Roxy," said Father.
"We don't jump inside.
Please stop that."

"Okay," said Roxy.
"I won't jump any more."

Roxy twirled next.
She twirled on her toes.
She twirled faster and faster.
She twirled around
and around and around.

Figure 15-7 Page Spreads from *Super Fox* from Leveled Literacy Intervention, Blue System (Heinemann 2009)

Moosling liked baby animals,
and baby animals loved Moosling.

He let them climb up his legs.
He let them ride on his back.
He let them hang
on his antlers.

Figure 15-8 Page Spread from *Moosling the Babysitter* from Leveled Literacy Intervention, Blue System (Heinemann 2009)

clusters, phonogram patterns, and endings. She has located words by thinking about word parts and other features. She needs to use this information "on the run" while processing continuous print.

In the example below, Adam was reading pages 8 and 9 of *Wide Awake* (see Figure 15-10):

ADAM [*reading*]: "'Father!' Roxy called. Father ran in. 'I'm this, this—.'"

TEACHER: It starts like *this*, but it has an *r* before the *s*. Thirs–.

ADAM: Thir– s. Thirsty!

Lila is reading pages 6 and 7 of *Venus, the Flytrap Who Wouldn't Eat Flies* (the pages are reproduced in Figure 15-9):

LILA [*reading*]: "'How about a buzz, buzzy bee?' asked Mason. He showed her one as it flew past the w– window. 'Uh-uh!' said Venus. She snap– snapped her jaw shut. 'A w–'" What's that word?

TEACHER: Look for a part you know. [*Lila hesitates and the teacher covers the -ly in wiggly.*]

LILA: W– ig. Like *big*.

TEACHER: Yes. Now read the whole word.

LILA: "'A wiggly spider?' Mason asked. He wiggly, wiggled his fingers."

TEACHER: You checked the ending.

In this example, the teacher helped Lila use what she knows about words. Lila has sorted words, built them with magnetic letters, and worked with word cards in ways that have helped her notice word parts—letter

Other prompts that help readers use known words or word parts to solve other words include:

- ❑ "That's like [*word*]."
- ❑ "Do you know a word that starts with those letters?"
- ❑ "Do you know a word that ends with those letters?"
- ❑ "Look for a part you know."
- ❑ "Do you see a part that might help?"
- ❑ "Look for something you know."

"How about a buzzy bee?" asked Mason.
He showed her one as it flew
past the window.

"Uh-uh!" said Venus.
She snapped her jaws shut.

"A wiggly spider?" Mason asked.
He wiggled his fingers.

"No!" cried Venus, covering her eyes.

"Mom, I don't understand why Venus doesn't eat flies," said Mason.
"Flytraps aren't like other plants.
Flytraps can't make their own food.
They must eat meat to live."

"You mean bugs, right?"
asked Mom.

Figure 15-9 Page Spread from *Venus the Flytrap Who Wouldn't Eat Flies* from Leveled Literacy Intervention, Blue System (Heinemann 2009)

"Father!" Roxy called. Father ran in.

"I'm thirsty," said Roxy. "Maybe a glass of milk will help me go to sleep."

Father got a glass of warm milk, and Roxy drank every drop.
"Goodnight, Roxy," said Father.
"Go to sleep now."

8

9

Figure 15-10 Page Spread from *Wide Awake* from Leveled Literacy Intervention, Blue System (Heinemann 2009)

The list of prompts ranges from giving more to less help. Saying, "That's like *big*," when a reader is stopped at *wiggly* provides the less experienced reader just enough information to solve the word, provided she knows *big* and, more important, knows how to mentally compare *big* with the first syllable of *wiggly*. Even with the information, the reading work is complex. A prompt like, "Look for a part you know," gives less information: the reader then needs to search the word for similarities to other words in her repertoire. "Look for something you know" provides even less information. It is the teacher's complex task to decide the level of prompt that will help the reader solve the word.

Take Apart Words by Syllables

As readers grapple with more difficult texts, they will encounter multisyllable words. They will already know how to hear the syllable breaks in words, and they should have a range of strategies for solving one-syllable words. Struggling readers are often intimidated when they

meet a longer word and do not see that they can break down the word into smaller parts.

For example, look at the record of Natalie's reading of *All About the Sonoran Desert* (pages 8 and 9 are reproduced in Figure 15-11). Natalie read the text with 93 percent accuracy, indicating that it is an instructional level for her (see Figure 15-12). She was using visual information, as evidenced by the fact that she usually made the sound of the first letter before appealing on an unknown word.

While taking the Reading Record, the teacher looked for opportunities to teach. One option is to help Natalie look further so that she is sampling visual information beyond the first letter; she also needs to look at the parts of unknown words. The teacher decided to help Natalie learn more about taking words apart using syllables. She started by reminding Natalie that she was

This desert plant has no leaves.
The plant dropped its leaves to save water.

Here is the same kind of plant after the rain.
Now the plant is covered with new green leaves.

ocotillo (oh ko TEE oh) plant before the rain

ocotillo plant after the rain

8

9

Figure 15-11 Page Spread from *All About the Sonoran Desert* from Leveled Literacy Intervention, Blue System (Heinemann 2009)

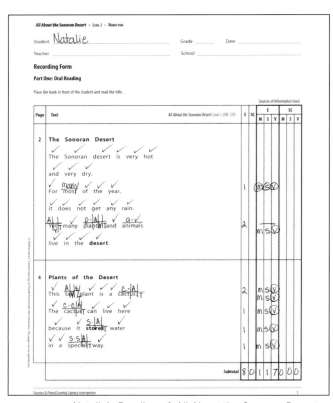

Figure 15-12 Natalie's Reading of *All About the Sonoran Desert*, p. 1

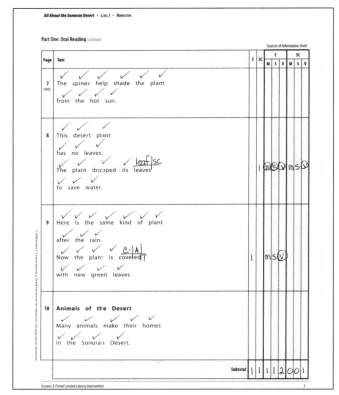

Figure 15-12 Natalie's Reading Record, p. 3

Figure 15-12 Natalie's Reading Record, p. 2

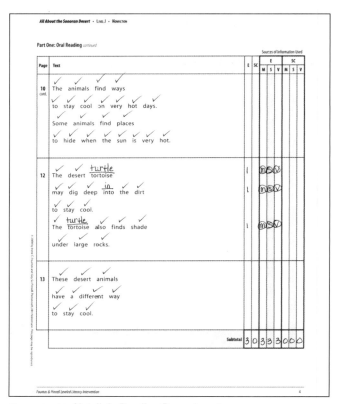

Figure 15-12 Natalie's Reading Record, p. 4

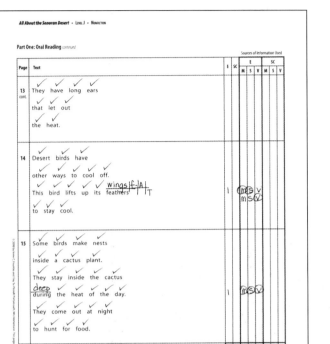

Figure 15-12 Natalie's Reading Record, p. 5

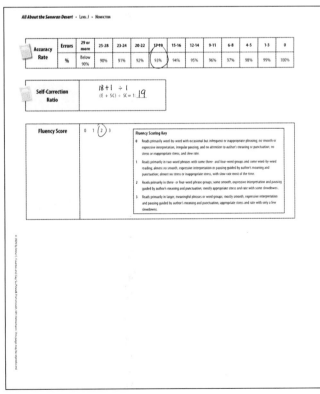

Figure 15-12 Natalie's Reading Record, p. 6

able to read the one-syllable word *tall* by noticing the part *-all*.

As shown in the interaction below, the teacher made two additional teaching points after the reading:

TEACHER: Let's go back to page 9. There was a tricky word here. You only used the first sound. *[She covers the word with her finger.]* You can look at the first part *[exposes the first part]: cov-*. Say the first part: */cov/*. Then you can look at the next part *[exposes the next part]: -er*. Say that part: */er/*. Then you can look at the last part *[exposes the last part]: -ed*. Say that part: */ed/*. Now go back to the beginning and try that when you come to the tricky word. *[Natalie rereads the sentence and successfully works her way through the word.]* That makes sense—that after the rain the plant would be covered with new green leaves. Now let's go to page 15 where the birds made a nest inside the cactus. There was something that didn't look right in this sentence. See if you can find it and use the parts to help you. *[Natalie rereads and when she gets to* during, *she covers the last part and says /dur/ and quickly adds /ing/. She finishes reading the sentence accurately.]*

TEACHER: Now does that makes sense and look right?

NATALIE: Yes.

TEACHER: You used your finger to break the word apart and you helped yourself.

Now let's look at the book Meredith was reading, *The Wind and the Sun*. Pages 2 and 3 are reproduced in Figure 15-13. Meredith's Reading Record taken on this book is shown in Figure 15-14. Looking at the record, the teacher noticed many strengths. For example, Meredith gave close attention to print (*stranger* for *stronger*, taking apart *idea* letter by letter, and attempting *traveler* with close approximation). She decided that a quick reinforcement of Meredith's ability to use base words and inflectional endings would be helpful:

TEACHER: Let's go back to the beginning of the story. Look at page 2 and find the word that was

One day, Wind and Sun
were bragging to each other.

"I am stronger than you,"
Wind bragged.
"When I blow, I can bend trees!
I can turn umbrellas inside out!"

2

"I am stronger than you,"
bragged Sun.

"When I shine,
I make plants grow.
I can melt snow and ice!"

3

Figure 15-13 Page Spread from *The Wind and the Sun* from Leveled Literacy Intervention, Blue System (Heinemann 2009)

tricky. *[Meredith points to* bragging.*]* Let me show you where to break the word. *[Puts her finger over* -ging.*]* You can figure out that first syllable by

thinking about the letters and sounds. It's a word all by itself. It's the base word, just like we have been talking about.

MEREDITH: brag

TEACHER: Do you know what *brag* means?

MEREDITH: It's to say what you've got is the best or you are the best at something.

TEACHER: That's right. To brag about yourself. Now when you put an ending on the word, it still means the same but it means you are doing it. You know this ending *[uncovers* -ing.*]*

MEREDITH: Bragging.

TEACHER: What were the Wind and the Sun bragging about?

MEREDITH: Who could make the man take off his coat.

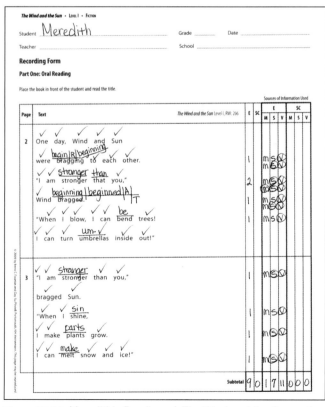

Figure 15-14 Meredith's Reading of *The Wind and the Sun,* p. 1

Figure 15-14 Meredith's Reading Record, p. 2

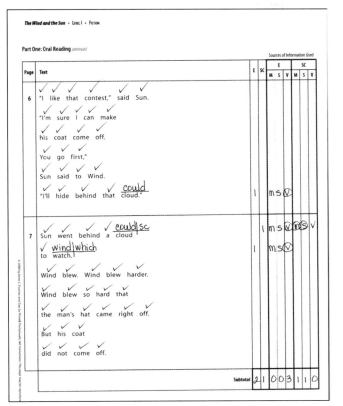

Figure 15-14 Meredith's Reading Record, p. 3

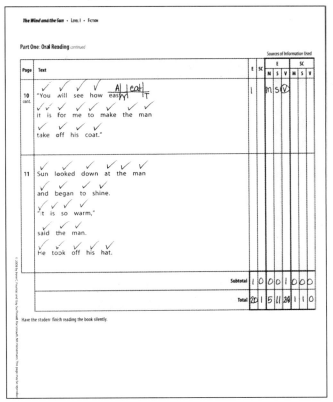

Figure 15-14 Meredith's Reading Record, p. 5

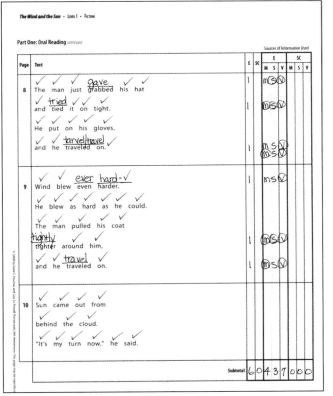

Figure 15-14 Meredith's Reading Record, p. 4

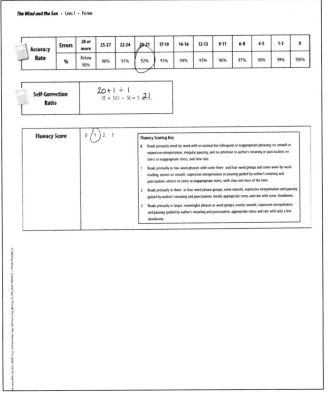

Figure 15-14 Meredith's Reading Record, p. 6

TEACHER: They were bragging about who was stronger, and they had a contest about who could make the man take off his coat. Now read from the beginning.

MEREDITH [*reading*]: "One day, Wind and Sun were bragging to each other. 'I am stronger than you,' Wind bragged."

TEACHER: Find the word *bragged*. [*Meredith locates* bragged.] Now find *bragging*.

MEREDITH [*locates* bragging]: It's the same word with two different endings.

TEACHER: That's right. Show me *stronger*. [*Meredith locates* stronger.] Are they bragging that they are stranger or stronger?

MEREDITH: *stronger*

TEACHER: You thought about the meaning. I'll bet you can cover up the ending and see the base word.

MEREDITH [*covers up* -er]: *strong stronger*

The teacher knows that Meredith has been working with base words and endings and has excellent strategies for using sounds and letters. She read the text at 92 percent accuracy and good comprehension, so it was within her instructional range. The reading provided an opportunity to help Meredith not only use what she knows about word structure but also think about the meaning.

▶ Self-Monitoring and Self-Correcting

One of the most important actions for struggling readers to take is to begin to monitor their reading—to notice the mismatches. For example, look at the record of Carlos's reading of *Funny Things* in Figure 15-16 (pages 14, 15, and 16 from the book are reproduced in Figure 15-15).

Throughout, Carlos read *I have a* for *look at the* without noticing the mismatches. On the last page, he used a different language structure. He used his knowl-

edge of the labels and the word *funny*; he matched voice to print; he understood that the language of the text was patterned and he said something consistently that made sense. This seems curious because he does know many letters and their accompanying sounds; for example, he knows *s* and connected it to *shoe* and *sock*; also, there is an *s* in his name.

This kind of behavior often takes place when children are confused about the processing of continuous print. If the behavior persists, then so will the confusion. Carlos will profit little from shared reading lessons in the classroom; he may even resist looking at the print. In the following interaction, the teacher helps Carlos begin to self-monitor using visual information:

TEACHER: Go to page 14. Take a look at the first word and listen how I start it [*makes the* /l/ *sound.*] It's like the first sound in *leaf*. Could this word be *look*? [*Carlos nods.*] In this book, the writer is telling us to look at all of the funny things on the clown. Say *look*.

CARLOS: *look*

TEACHER: What letter would you expect to see at the beginning of *look*?

CARLOS: *look l*

TEACHER: Find the word *look*. [*Carlos locates* look.]

TEACHER: Now read it.

CARLOS [*reading*]: "Look at the funny hat."

TEACHER: Were you right? Is that word *look*?

CARLOS: Yes.

TEACHER: Keep reading.

Carlos reads page 14 accurately. On page 16 he reads "I am" and stops.

TEACHER: Why did you stop? [*Carlos points to* look.] You knew something was wrong.

Carlos: *look*

Since Carlos is only beginning to use letters and sounds, the teacher avoids having him repeat wrong responses. She needs to move him into a position of

Figure 15-15 Pages from *Funny Things* from Leveled Literacy Intervention, Orange System (Heinemann 2009)

reading accurately while at the same time attending to print features. Carlos was using meaning and language structure but not monitoring his reading using visual information. His stopping when he noticed the mismatch on page 16 conveyed important information.

Often, readers use visual information very well but do not attend to the other sources of information. You can help children monitor their reading using visual information, meaning, or language structure.

Carlos' Reading of *Funny Things*, Level A

I have a ✓ shoe.
2 Look at the funny shoes.

I have a ✓ sock.
4 Look at the funny socks.

I have a ✓ ✓
6 Look at the funny pants.

I have a ✓ ✓
8 Look at the funny shirt.

I have a ✓ ✓
10 Look at the funny coat.

I have a ✓ head.
12 Look at the funny wig.

I have a ✓ ✓
14 Look at the funny hat.

I am a ✓ man
16 Look at the funny clown!

Figure 15-16 Carlos's Reading of *Funny Things*

Self-Monitoring and Self-Correcting Using Visual Information

In many of the examples in the word-solving section of this chapter, the teacher began by asking the reader to find the tricky part or the hard word. Readers who can do this are monitoring their reading. They realized something was not right but went on because they didn't know what to do about it. The prompts below help you find out whether your readers are monitoring their reading and let them know that it is important to notice errors:

- ❑ "Why did you stop?"
- ❑ "What did you notice?"
- ❑ "What is wrong?"
- ❑ "Were you right?"
- ❑ "Was that okay?"
- ❑ "Find the part that is not quite right."
- ❑ "Where is the tricky part?"

In the interaction below, Debra is reading page 16 of *Meli at the Vet* (see Figure 15-17):

DEBRA *[reading]*: "Then it is make—." *[Stops.]*

TEACHER: What's wrong?

DEBRA: It didn't sound right.

TEACHER: Where is the tricky part? *[Debra points to the word* time.*]* Watch me check it. *[Runs her finger under the first letter and says* /t/.*]* Now try it again and you say the first sound.

DEBRA: "Then it is t– time for Meli to go home."

Figure 15-17 Page from *Meli at the Vet* from Leveled Literacy Intervention, Blue System (Heinemann 2009)

Then it is time for Meli
to go home.
Meli likes that, too!

TEACHER: Are you right? Would *time* make sense and look right there?

DEBRA: Yes.

TEACHER: Read the whole page.

DEBRA: "Then it is time for Meli to go home. Meli likes that, too."

TEACHER: Were you right?

DEBRA: Yes!

Often, readers' errors tell us that they have noticed part of the word, and that means they are monitoring their reading to some degree. In the following interaction, in which Tabitha was reading pages 6 and 7 of *Taking Care of Meli* (see Figure 15-18), her teacher helped her use more of a word.

TABITHA [reading]: "Ron gives Meli clip—" [stops].

TEACHER: It starts like that. Now check the last part.

TABITHA: *clean*

TEACHER: Read the whole sentence and see if *clean* makes sense and looks right.

TABITHA: "Ron gives Meli clean water in her bowl ev– every day. Dogs need to drink free— [stops]. Dogs need to drink fresh water. Meli is a little monkey." No. "Meli is a little messy. She spills a little water on the floor.

TEACHER: You knew something wasn't quite right and you fixed it.

If readers are not using more than one source of information, you will want to prompt for it.

Self-Monitoring and Self-Correcting Using Language Structure

When you ask children to think about whether what they read "sounds right," you are asking them to think about the syntactic (or grammatical) patterns of the language. Young children begin learning simple language patterns when they are toddlers, and they continue to develop more complex language patterns throughout childhood. Syntax, which we call *structure* when we analyze reading behavior, is important because meaning is communicated not just by the words but by how they are arranged in sentences. (In the next chapter, we will discuss how sentences are arranged in paragraphs and longer stretches of texts.

Ron gives Meli clean water
in her bowl every day.
Dogs need to drink
fresh water.
Meli is a little messy.
She spills a little water
on the floor.

Figure 15-18 Page Spread from *Taking Care of Meli* from Leveled Literacy Intervention, Blue System (Heinemann 2009)

The overall organization of longer texts—*text structure*—also communicates deeper meaning and is critical to comprehension.)

To detect whether reading "sounds right," speakers rely on implicit knowledge, built from using the language. Most cannot explicitly state the "rules" by which they know a sentence like "I red the like hat" is not acceptable, while a sentence like "I like the red hat" is. They didn't learn this distinction by first learning a rule: it was built through years of using language; the knowledge is deeply held. Language syntax is a very powerful system for beginning readers. In fact, it can override attention to print. Your task is to help readers use language structure in a way that is coordinated with visual information and that helps them build a system for comprehending.

Struggling readers can have difficulty using language structure for many different reasons:

1. Some children may have limited language development. While they can speak and be understood, they are not familiar with the more complex sentence patterns. They need a great deal of oral language interaction; they also need to hear written texts read aloud.

2. Children may have a sense of language structure but be so focused on their struggle to decode print that they do not access and use their language knowledge. Their reading sounds nonsensical at times. They need to listen to themselves as they read and think about how the language sounds.

3. English language learners may be just beginning to learn the syntax of English. They may have a strong sense of the rules of syntax in their first language but make errors in English. This makes it harder for them to check on how their reading sounds. It may sound all right to them! They need many opportunities to say, read, and write English language patterns.

4. Some children may speak nonstandard patterns of English (regional dialects, for example). Some have heard written language read aloud only rarely. Book language may be strange to them, even the very simple sentences in early levels such as B and C. Immersion in hearing

written language read aloud and reading texts for themselves will enable them to rapidly expand their systems of language.

Given supportive interactions, children are very rapid language learners. There is no need to drill or correct them. They benefit from having supportive conversations with adults, hearing written language read aloud, and expanding their repertoire through reading.

In small-group reading, the introduction of a book is one of the most powerful instructional settings for supporting children's use of language structure. Look at the introduction to *Pictures of Hugs* in Figure 15-19. The teacher is very carefully using some of the more difficult language structure of this Level F book. This introduction requires a little more time than most, because the teacher is deliberately ensuring that readers will be familiar with the text's language structures. She not only repeats difficult language patterns herself but also has children either say or read them. She does no unnecessary talking that would interfere with children's understanding of the longer and more difficult sentences. They will read the text immediately after the introduction with no interfering directions or tasks.

In addition, you can teach for, prompt for, and support children's use of language structure while they are reading. One of the keys to effective prompting for language structure is to decide what elements readers know and are using. For example, look at the Reading Records of page 2 of *The Very Busy Hen* (Figure 15-20) provided in Figure 15-21.

Cody was using visual information and some meaning, but was not attending to language structure. In this case, it might be helpful to use interactions such as these:

- ❑ "That didn't sound right. You need to stop when it doesn't sound right."

- ❑ "Watch me check. You said [*repeat the child's error*]. That doesn't sound right."

- ❑ "You said [*repeat the child's error*]. Does that sound right?"

April was using meaning and language structure most of the time but not attending to visual information. It would not be productive to ask her if her

Figure 15-19 Introduction to *Pictures of Hugs* (Level F)

Speaker	Interaction	What the Teacher Is Attending to
Mrs. S	Do you remember Meg and Hugs? This story is called *Pictures of Hugs*.	*Evokes prior knowledge of a series book.*
Xavier	It's about Meg and her cat.	
Arvinia	She has a grandma.	
Mrs. S	Turn to pages 2 and 3. It was Pet Week at school, and Meg was trying to make a picture of her cat, Hugs, to share with her class. What was she using to make her picture?	*Provides information about the setting and the problem.*
Rick	She was drawing it with crayons.	
Mrs. S	Turn to page 5. Well, she doesn't like her picture. So Gram said, "Do you want my camera? I can show you how to use it."	*Conversationally uses the language of the text.*
Tawnia	The camera is better.	
Mrs. S	Turn to page 6. What was Hugs doing?	*Draws attention to the picture.*
Tawnia	Playing with a mouse.	
Mrs. S	Meg leaned over to take the picture. Click! Say *leaned*. (Children respond.). Do you know what *leaned* means?	*Uses language from the text. Prompts attention to a vocabulary word.*
Tawnia	To kind of bend over.	
Rick	She looked down at Hugs.	
Mrs. S	That's right. She leaned over to take the picture. Find *leaned*. Run your finger under it and say it.	*Uses language from the text. Draws attention to visual features of a word.*
Children	*(Find and say the word.)*	
Mrs. S	Look at the picture in the camera on page 7. Does that look like Hugs?	*Draws attention to the pictures and expands the problem.*
Xavier	No, it's just his tail.	
Arvinia	And the shoe is in the picture, but she wants Hugs.	
Mrs. S	Look at page 8. On this page, Hugs moved again. And look over at page 9. There is a long sentence on this page. Listen to me say it. *Hugs chased his mouse all around the room.* Have you heard people say that—"all around the room"?	*Repeats the language of the text. Clarifies a phrase.*
Arvinia	Yes, my dog does that.	
Mrs. S	Your dog runs all around the room?	*Repeats the phrase.*
Arvinia	All around the yard!	
Mrs. S	Let's all read that first sentence.	*Prompts children to practice the language structure.*
Children	Hugs chased his mouse all around the room.	
Mrs. S	Find *chased* and look at the ending of the word. It's an *-ed*. You say that word *chased*.	*Draws attention to the endings of past tense words.*
Children	It sounds like *t*.	
Mrs. S	It sounds like *t* in this word. We have to read the ending of the word to be sure that the reading sounds right. Does that sound right? Hugs chased his mouse all around the room. Meg kept chasing Hugs and taking pictures, but she could only get little parts of him. So read to find out how Gram solves the problem.	*Explains why endings are important. Repeats the language of the text. Prompts thinking about the meaning.*

"Come and play,"
said the dog.
"No," said the hen.
"I am very busy.
I am planting
the wheat."

2   3

Figure 15-20 Page Spread from *The Very Busy Hen* from Leveled Literacy Intervention, Green System (Heinemann 2009)

reading "sounds right." It does. If you were not looking at the print, you would think the reading was correct! Suppose April had read *come and put* for the first line. That would still indicate that she is using language structure. Remember that when you analyze the error, you think about the substitution not in the context of the whole sentence but *up to and including* the error. April has a strong grasp of language structure, but it may be overriding her attention to print. You want her to continue to use language structure but notice the mismatches. Prompts like these might be helpful:

❑   "Watch me check it. [*Reread 'Come and see,' pausing on the word* play.] It sounds right, but it

doesn't look right. I need to look at the first letter and make the sound—/p/. 'Come and *play*.' Does that sound right and look right?"

❑   "You said [*repeat the child's error*]. Does that look right?"

❑   "It could be [*provide the word*], but check to see if that looks right."

❑   "Check to see if that looks right."

Forest was using visual information but not consistently or closely monitoring meaning or language structure. *Every* is very close visually to *very*. He went on to substitute *be* for *busy*. At that point, he should have realized that the reading did not sound right. Effective behavior for him would be to reread to problem-solve. Prompts like these might be helpful:

❑   "You said, 'I am every be.' Does that sound right?"

❑   "Find the tricky part. [*Child points to* very busy.] Could it say *very busy*? Read to see if that sounds right and looks right."

❑   "You made a mistake on that page. Can you find it?"

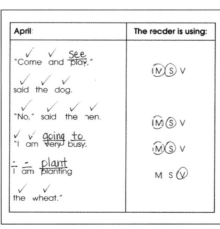

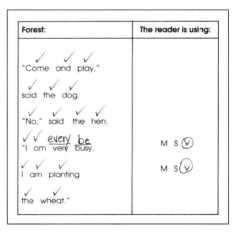

Figure 15-21 Cody, April, and Forest's Reading of *The Very Busy Hen*

Accurate reading indicates self-monitoring. Stretches of accurate reading like those in Forest's reading are evidence that he is monitoring using all sources of information.

In the following interactions, the teachers were supporting self-monitoring and self-correcting. The introduction to *Pictures of Hugs* is in Figure 15-19. Pages 6–7 and 12–13 are shown in Figure 15-22.

ROBERTA *[reading page 6]:* "Hugs was play with a toy—" *[stops].*

TEACHER: Could it be a toy mouse?

ROBERTA: Yes, it's there in the picture.

TEACHER: Would you say, "Hugs was play with a toy mouse" or "Hugs was playing with a toy mouse"? Which sounds better?

ROBERTA: *playing*

TEACHER: And look at the word *playing*. Find it. *[Roberta locates* playing.*]* Try it again and make sure it sounds right and looks right. *[Roberta reads accurately.]* You made it sound right and look right.

JOSEPH *[reading page 12]:* "But maybe I can use them after one, like a piece of a puzzle."

TEACHER: She is trying to think of it like a puzzle. Try that again and be sure that it sounds right.

JOSEPH: "But maybe I can use them *[hesitates]* all at *[hesitates]* one, once, all at once, like a puzzle."

TEACHER: You made it sound right and look right.

Figure 15-22 Page Spreads from *Pictures of Hugs* from Leveled Literacy Intervention, Green System (Heinemann 2009)

Joseph's reading of page 12 was quite complex. It may be that he noticed the word *all*, a phoneme pattern he knows. But it may also be that he thought about the phrase *all at once* as a whole, thus using language structure.

One of the most disastrous things that can happen to a young struggling reader is to think that language structure doesn't matter. Our knowledge of language syntax is very deeply held. It is how we map out the meanings that we want to communicate (see Chapter 7). If in our zeal to make readers attend to phonics cues we somehow communicate to them not to attend to language structure, we are contributing to reading that is not strategic. You may not always need to prompt readers to use language structure, but you will always want to support their doing so.

Self-Monitoring and Self-Correcting Using Meaning

As discussed in Chapter 7, the semantic system of language comprises the meanings that we communicate through words arranged in syntactic patterns. Meaning is the heart of the system. Communicating meaning is the purpose of human language. There is no other reason to read, and we need to ensure that students are accessing meaning every single time they engage with a text.

Readers should always monitor their reading to be sure it makes sense; as much as possible, they should also self-correct. Older readers may not display overt self-correction behavior. For example, when you realize that you do not understand what you are reading, you stop and think or search back in the text, but someone observing you would notice no change in your behavior. The proficient reader is always actively working to be sure that the reading makes sense.

When reading aloud, proficient readers self-correct with the listeners in mind, for example:

❑ Not correcting minor errors that make no difference in meaning.

❑ Reworking sentences after an error to make the syntax "sound right."

❑ Correcting an improper word stress or punctuation miscue so the reading will sound right.

❑ Correcting significant errors that change the meaning of the text.

These actions are signs of proficiency and flexibility. Struggling readers often become passive—either moving on, content to produce reading that does not sound right, or tolerating a loss of meaning.

Children who have heard a lot of written language read aloud know from the beginning that a text should make sense. They expect to gain meaning from every page and even more meaning from the text as a whole. They expand their understanding by discussing the text with others. Reading aloud to children is an essential component of a literacy program and is even more important for struggling readers.

In small-group reading instruction, the book introduction plays a major role in supporting readers' use of meaning. The introduction is not simply to help readers solve individual words. You want to orient them to the meaning of the text as a whole—the content and structure (the way it is organized) as well as some of the language and the words.

For example, take a look at *Time for Lunch*, a Level D text (see Figure 15-23).

To prepare to introduce this book, ask yourself, *What do readers need to know about the text to support understanding? How can I ensure they will read the text with understanding?* You might want to establish the following points:

❑ This is a story about a bear family. You can tell because of the names—Mother Bear, Baby Bear, Little Bear, and Father Bear. (Readers who grasp this idea will recognize all the names.)

❑ Mother Bear is gathering food for lunch. (Knowing this, readers will expect to read food names as well as the word *lunch*.)

❑ Even though these bears dress in clothes and talk, they still eat the kinds of food that bears like—berries, nuts, fish, honey. (Readers who understand this will have a smaller set of possible food words to check for meaning.)

❑ Mother Bear gets one kind of food after another, always because someone in the family likes it. (Readers who understand this will expect a sequence of actions, each one focusing on a new kind of food.)

❑ When you get honey in the woods, there are likely to be bees there, and bees are dangerous. (Readers who have this background knowledge, cued by the picture, are likely to predict and understand the ending.)

It takes only a minute or two to analyze a text. If *Time for Lunch* is at the appropriate instructional level (a little more challenging than children can read independently), struggling readers would need to

FIGURE 15-23 Page Layout of *Time for Lunch* from Leveled Literacy Intervention, Green System (Heinemann 2009)

understand *all* the information above before reading the text. Do not think of this as "giving it all away." Do not withhold information to "see if they get it." If they do not "get it," you will have provided another meaningless reading experience.

Proficient readers will have grasped these ideas within the first page or two of the text and may even predict that sooner or later Mother Bear will be going for honey. They know that stories have to have surprises and tension. When you provide this kind of information through conversation, readers can immediately access meaning in a way that will help them monitor and correct their reading.

During individual interactions with readers, you can support their use of meaning by teaching for, prompting for, and reinforcing effective behaviors. For example, see the interactions below:

RENEE *[reading page 2]*: "'It's time for lunch,' said Mother Bear. 'Baby Bear likes bushes. I will get some bushes.'"

TEACHER: You said, "Baby Bear likes bushes. I will get some bushes." That doesn't make sense in this story. Mother Bear is going to get Baby Bear something good to eat for lunch. So think what would make sense.

RENEE: *strawberries*

TEACHER: That's almost right. The author calls them berries. Say *berries*. What letter would you expect to see at the beginning of *berries*?

RENEE: *b*

TEACHER: Find *berries*. *[Renee locates and says* berries.*]* Now, find it again. Now try that again and see if it makes sense and looks right. *[Renee reads page 2 accurately.]* I'll bet Mother Bear likes berries, too. Remember in this book everything Mother Bear gets will be something good for lunch.

THERON *[reading page 4]*: "Mother Bear got some berries. 'Yes, yes,' see Mother Bear." *[Stops.]*

TEACHER: Why did you stop?

THERON: It doesn't make sense.

TEACHER: You knew something wasn't quite right. Try it again and think what Mother Bear might be saying as she eats those delicious berries. *[Theron reads accurately.]*

PAUL *[reading page 10]*: "'Father Bear likes to fish,' said Mother Bear. 'I will get so many—. *[Stops and rereads.]* 'Father Bear likes fish,' said Mother Bear. 'I will get some fish.'"

TEACHER: You found out what was wrong and fixed it all by yourself.

BRENDA *[reading page 16]*: "'Yum, yum,' said Mother Bear. 'I like honey. But I like bees!'"

TEACHER: You said, "But I like bees." Does that make sense in this story?

BRENDA: I do not like bees!

TEACHER: Now try it again and make sure it looks right.

In these interactions, the teacher directed readers' attention to the meaning of the text. Renee used visual information (first letter), and her response did fit with the picture, but she was not really thinking about the deeper meaning. Her teacher helped Renee think about the overall content of the story to help her eliminate possibilities. Theron's response sounded right in terms of language structure, and he too used visual information (the first letter). His stopping was significant—it showed he wasn't satisfied with his reading. His teacher provided a little support for his rereading. Paul's stopping was evidence that he sensed a subtle change in meaning. His reading sounded right and made sense. Also all of the words were read correctly except for the insertion of the word *to*. His response did not fit with the overall structure of the text, which is all about the things the family likes to *eat*. He reread to reflect the precise meaning. Brenda read quickly and in doing so, omitted the words *do not*. These words are the important closing to the story. This careless error sounded right to Brenda but did not make sense. The teacher brought it to Brenda's attention in a way that asked her to check the meaning.

▶ Self-Monitoring and Self-Correcting Using Multiple Sources of Information

In most of the interactions described above, the teacher was supporting the reader's use of more than one source of information. Proficient readers use multiple cues in a smoothly orchestrated way. At the lowest text levels (A, B, and C), you will want to keep your prompts simple. A complex prompt (for example, "It has to make sense, sound right, and look right") asks too much of the reader. You could be wasting your breath, because the reader does not understand what it means to use even one of these sources of information.

One of the first behaviors to emerge is noticing mismatches using one source of information, but very soon, readers will learn to cross-check one source of information with another. You may need to teach cross-checking in very explicit ways. In the interaction below, Darlene read *Funny Things*, a Level A text (pages 4 and 5 are reproduced in Figure 15-24):

> DARLENE *[reading page 4]*: "Look at the funny feet." *[Stops, checks picture, looks back at the word, and rereads.]* "Look at the funny socks."
>
> TEACHER: Were you right?
>
> DARLENE: Yes.
>
> TEACHER: It could be *feet*, but you looked at the word and saw it started with *s*. You found two ways to check the word—the picture and the first letter.

Look at the funny socks.

4

5

Figure 15-24 Page Spread from *Funny Things* from Leveled Literacy Intervention, Orange System (Heinemann 2009)

As readers grow in their ability to read more complex texts, you can continue to support the use of multiple sources of information through language like the following:

- ❑ "You can try it again and think what would look right and sound right."
- ❑ "You can try it again and think what would look right and make sense."
- ❑ "It has to make sense and sound right."
- ❑ "You are nearly right. Try that again and think, what would look right, sound right, and make sense." (Here the reader has already used one or more sources of information. You are prompting the use of another.)
- ❑ "You noticed that [*word or phrase*] didn't make sense [look right] [sound right]."

Once a problem has been solved using one kind of information, it is often helpful to have the child reread to check. This puts the reader in the position of "putting it all together."

▶ General Problem Solving

Children who know a lot about words and also have had some experience using many different ways to solve words have a repertoire that they need to learn to access without being reminded. In the following interactions, the teacher did not point the readers to a specific kind of information but rather reminded them to use what they know:

> *Marta is reading page 15 of* The Ladybug and the Cricket. *Pages 14 and 15 are shown in Figure 15-25.*
>
> MARTA: "'I have a surprise for you, too!' said the cricket. He pull, pulled out a t– violin."
>
> TEACHER: Do you see something that might help?
>
> MARTA: T–in–y. Tiny. It's a little violin.
>
> TEACHER: You thought about what you knew. Read it again and check to

Figure 15-25 Page Spread from *The Ladybug and the Cricket* from Leveled Literacy Intervention, Blue System (Heinemann 2009)

see if it looks right and sounds right. *[Marta reads accurately.]*

Jeremy is reading page 10 of All About Dolphins. *Pages 10 and 11 are reproduced in Figure 15-26.*

Jeremy: "Dolphins are nosy animals. They slap their tail fins on top of the water. They cl– click s– s–." *[Stops.]*

Teacher: Say the next part.

Jeremy: Squ–ea–k.

Teacher: Try it again from the beginning.

Jeremy: "Dolphins are n–o–sy." Nosy?

Teacher: Look carefully and think what you know about dolphins.

Jeremy: Noisy.

Teacher: Try it again and make sure it looks right and makes sense in the book.

Kevin is reading The Hot Day. *Pages 4 and 5 are reproduced in Figure 15-27.*

Kevin *[reading page 4]:* "Yes, but the egg just sat there. It didn't cook. It didn't even turn white around the eggs, eggs." That isn't eggs.

Teacher: How can you help yourself?

Kevin [covers up the s]: Ed, edge. Edges? *[He reads the rest of the page accurately.]*

Teacher: You worked that out.

Kevin *[reading page 5]:* "As Sam and Jesse started to leave, Papa asked, 'Are there any eggs left?' 'Two,' said Jesse. 'That should be enough,' Papa said. 'And Jesse, stay out of the room, r–e–f, re–from, r–.'"

Teacher: Stop for a minute. Read that again and try something else that will make sense there.

Kevin: "'That should be enough,' Papa said. 'And Jesse, stay out of the—.'" *(eggs in the refrigerator.)* *[Reading.]* "'That should be enough,' Papa said. 'And Jesse, stay out of the refrigerator, all right?'"

Teacher: You thought about what you knew.

Figure 15-26 Page Spread from *All About Dolphins* from Leveled Literacy Intervention, Green System (Heinemann 2009)

He came back a few minutes later.
"Actually," said Jesse, "it isn't."
"What isn't?" Sam asked.
"It isn't hot enough to fry an egg on the sidewalk," Jesse said.
Papa looked up from his work. "Did you try to do that?" he asked.
"Yes, but the egg just sat there. It didn't cook. It didn't even turn white around the edges," Jesse said.

Papa looked at his stack of papers. "I need to work just a little longer, boys, and I'll be done."
"Show me the egg, Jesse," Sam said.
As Sam and Jesse started to leave, Papa asked, "Are there any eggs left?"
"Two," said Jesse.
"That should be enough," Papa said. "And Jesse, stay out of the refrigerator, all right?"

Figure 15-27 Page Spread from *The Hot Day* from Leveled Literacy Intervention, Blue System (Heinemann 2009)

Using prompts to help readers solve problems pushes them to independence. Examples of higher-level prompts and reinforcements include:

- ❑ "You can read that again and try something else." [*Model another technique.*]
- ❑ "What can you do?"
- ❑ "Try it another way."
- ❑ "Look for something that will help you."
- ❑ "You tried to work that out. Do you see something that might help?"
- ❑ "What could you try?"
- ❑ "What do you already know?"
- ❑ "You can work that out."
- ❑ "Try something."
- ❑ "Try that again."
- ❑ "You worked hard on that."
- ❑ "You tried that again."
- ❑ "You tried another way."
- ❑ "You thought what it could be."

As readers learn more about the process and internalize some of your prompts, you won't need to verbalize them. For example, look at this interaction during a reading of *The Bird Feeders* (pages 4 and 5 are reproduced in Figure 15-28):

CELINA [*reading page 4*]: "'We can fix that,' said Rose. 'We'll make a bird feed, said Matt. Rose and Matt made a bird feed. They set it up outside in the yard." [*Teacher points to the -er ending on* feeder *in line 2. Celina rereads the page accurately.*]

The point of teaching, prompting and reinforcing effective reading behaviors is to create an *active reader*. Remember that Kaye's (2008) proficient second-grade readers *always* tried something before appealing. Your ultimate goal is for readers to use a flexible range of strategies without prompting. Eventually, they will internalize these strategic actions so that they don't realize they are using them and can give full attention to thinking about meaning.

"We can fix that," said Rose. "We'll make a bird feeder," said Matt.
Rose and Matt made a bird feeder. They set it up outside in the yard.

"Now you can watch the birds again," Rose said.

Figure 15-28 Pages from *The Bird Feeders* from Leveled Literacy Intervention, Blue System (Heinemann 2009)

▶ Suggestions for Professional Development

ANALYZING CHANGES IN SELF-REGULATING BEHAVIOR OVER TIME

Self-monitoring and self-correcting as well as flexible word-solving skills are important strategic actions that readers develop over time. Your ability to analyze how a reader who struggles is building these important aspects of the system will be critical to their success in processing.

1. For one reader, select three or four Reading Records taken at different points in the year. Consider the key questions from the Guide for Observing and Noting Reading Behaviors in Figure 15-29 and in Appendix B.

2. Analyze the patterns you notice in the reader's success or difficulty in noticing and correcting errors and in solving words in flexible ways.

3. If you are working with a colleague or colleagues, discuss these patterns and the implications for your teaching.

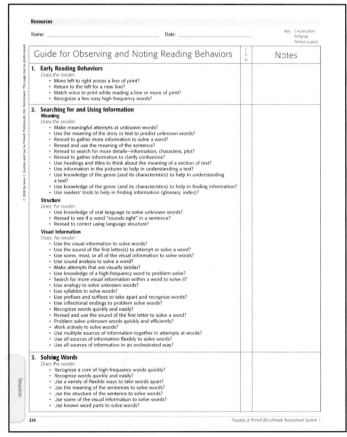

Figure 15-29 Guide for Observing and Noting Reading Behaviors

Teaching for Fluency in Processing Texts: Six Dimensions

ONE OF THE MOST SALIENT CHARACTERISTICS *of a struggling reader is dysfluency. Struggling readers sound terrible when they read aloud, partly because they are being expected to read texts that are far too difficult for them; but that is not the only reason. Many struggling readers, even young ones, have developed deeply ingrained habits of reading slowly without expression. Our job as teachers is to help them sound good, and that means not only matching texts to their ability but doing some very explicit teaching. They can only develop fluency by reading fluently. In this chapter, we discuss fluency in processing texts and describe ways you can work with struggling readers to help them become fluent readers.*

Fluency is almost always an issue when working with struggling readers. Most have a long history of dysfluent reading. Day after day, they have read texts that are too difficult; their reading is characterized by stops and starts, repetition, appealing to the teacher (if present), and skipping words (if the teacher is not present). They do not reap the reward of constructing meaning; consequently, they become disengaged and unmotivated.

These readers were not like this at the beginning of their literacy careers. Most of them talked as fluently as anyone else. If they had the opportunity, they listened to stories and thought about them. Early readers may even have sounded quite fluent as they "pretended" to read while looking at the pictures. Then somewhere in the process of learning to read, they also learned to read very slowly. The meaning seemed to die out of their voices.

Fluency is not a simple matter of speed; it has many dimensions. Compare the behaviors of fluent and nonfluent readers (Figure 16-1). There are vast differences in word-solving strategies, in expression,

Figure 16-1 Observable Behaviors of Fluent and Nonfluent Readers

Nonfluent Readers	Fluent Readers
Observable behaviors	**Observable behaviors**
• Fails to reflect punctuation with variation in the voice.	• Reflects punctuation with variation in the voice—pausing, intonation, pitch, stress.
• Pauses randomly, not reflecting logical phrase units.	• Pauses appropriately to reflect meaningful phrase units (although not always) in response to punctuation.
• Reads in a choppy or word-by-word way.	• Groups words into phrases that reflect meaning.
• Uses few rising and falling tones or monotonously applies rising and falling tones to produce "droning."	• Uses rising and falling tones in a way that is related to text meaning and punctuation (is not monotonous).
• Stresses few words, or places inappropriate stress on words.	• Places stress on words in a way that reflects meaning.
• Uses little or no expression, sometimes uses inappropriate expression.	• Uses expression to reflect his interpretation of the meaning of the text.
• Reads slowly.	• Reads with good momentum, although not so fast that phrasing is lost.
• Fails to vary speed or varies it in an inconsistent and unpredictable way.	• Varies speed, slowing down and speeding up for various purposes.
• Fails to differentiate dialogue from other forms of text.	• Reads dialogue in a way that reflects aspects of characters, their ways of expressing themselves, and oral language.
• Reads slowly or stops in an attempt to pick up and remember all the details.	• Focuses on meaning, doesn't get bogged down in details."
• Reads in a way that does not reflect awareness of language system.	• Reads in a way that reflects awareness of language syntax, with error behavior indicating such awareness.
Underlying strategic actions	**Underlying strategic actions**
• Processes visual information slowly with many attempts at words and many overt self-corrections.	• Processes visual information rapidly and efficiently.
• Has inefficient word-solving strategies, tends to "sound out" words using the smallest units (individual letters).	• Understands how pauses, pitch, and stress communicate the author's intended meaning.
• Reads one word at a time instead of word groups.	• Recognizes features of known words and uses these features to get to words that are unknown.
	• Reads word groups instead of single words.
• Reads as if not aware of oral language, with errors that do not indicate knowledge of structure.	• Uses oral language to anticipate what may happen next in the text.
• Tends to ignore punctuation as a tool for constructing meaning.	• Uses punctuation to construct meaning.
• Does not differentiate dialogue from other text.	• Notices dialogue and processes it as the character's voice, including hypotheses of intonation patterns and quality.
• Tends to stop often or to read very slowly even when accurate.	• Easily solves problems "on the run," slowing down but speeding up again in a smooth process.
• Reads slowly or stops in an attempt to pick up and remember all the details.	• Doesn't get bogged down in details.
• Misses much of the meaning and has to slow down to consider meaning.	• Rapidly accesses meaning.
• Gives so much attention to word solving that there is little left to give to prior knowledge, doesn't anticipate meaning.	• Uses prior knowledge and understanding of the world to anticipate what will happen in the story.

in pacing, and most important, in comprehension. "Nothing destroys the meaning more rapidly than droning through the phrases and punctuation marks, pausing at points which break up the syntactic group and the sense" (Clay 1991).

An important point related to fluency is that it is highly dependent on the type of text that the reader is trying to process. Many of us would sound dysfluent if expected to process a complex legal document or a scientific treatise outside our field of interest or study. We looked at Kulsum reading three texts, one at her independent level, one at her instructional level, and one at a hard level (Chapter 6). On the third text, she looked and sounded like a struggling reader, but in fact she is not. She reads well on her grade level.

One of the goals of literacy intervention is to get those students who exhibit difficulty to read fluently. When they read, they need to sound good. With leveled texts and powerful teaching, there is no reason for the struggling group to sound different from the high-progress group. When you are working with an individual or a small group of students, the casual observer should not be able to detect that they are struggling readers. When readers struggle with grade-level material, you need to provide an intervention lesson in which they can perform with proficiency, and that will help them become fluent readers. (You will need to be quite persistent in this teaching, because many struggling readers, even young ones, have the deeply ingrained habit of reading slowly without expression.)

▶ What Is Fluency in Literacy?

Fluency in reading and writing involves:
- ❏ Performing motor actions rapidly, easily, and without conscious attention (eyes in reading and hand movements and eyes in writing).
- ❏ Using the conventions of print (left-to-right directionality, spaces between words, etc.) with automaticity.
- ❏ Being able to navigate all levels of language— letter, word, sentence, paragraph, text.
- ❏ Using processing systems with automaticity.
- ❏ Achieving comprehension, expression, and voice.

We discuss the important reciprocal roles of reading and writing as well as how fluency in writing can be of value in helping readers learn the features of letters and words in Chapter 13.

It is also useful to think about what fluency is not—and that is speed. Much emphasis has been placed on "fast reading" and a fast rate becomes the single focus. We caution that this view may take you down the wrong path in working with struggling readers. Of course, fast processing is important. We examine that concept in Chapters 13, 14, and 15 and will revisit it in the next section. But if you think of fluency only as speed, you will miss the important dimensions of fluency that connect fluency to reading comprehension (see Figure 16-2).

Pausing

Readers respond to punctuation, most notably by pausing. In written language, punctuation helps the reader understand the intonation patterns that reflect the writer's meaning. The reader is guided by the punctuation to take short breaths at commas, longer breaths at a mark like a dash, and come to a full stop after a period. Young readers may be guided by print, as many early books have a "friendly layout" of the lines of print to support pausing.

Phrasing

The reader uses both pauses and intonation to parse sentences into meaningful phrases. The phrase breaks should sound natural, as in talking. These phrases reflect the writer's meaning. Think about the way you would say this sentence while reading aloud from a thriller:

Playing for time, I circled the van, closing in slowly, and finally saying, "Come out now, or we are coming in after you!"

You would pause after *time, van, slowly, saying, now,* and possibly after *are* and *in.* Your voice would convey

Figure 16-2 **Dimensions of Fluency**	
1. Pausing	The reader pauses at appropriate points in the text to reflect the punctuation. Punctuation provides visual information that cues the reader and adds to comprehension.
2. Phrasing	The placement and length of the reader's pauses parse the language into meaningful units. This kind of pausing goes beyond acknowledging the punctuation. In good reading, the pauses are logically and well paced; in oral reading, they help the listener.
3. Intonation/ Rhythm	The reader employs a rhythmic tonal quality that is not monotonous but captures the patterns of the language. The voice goes up and down, reflecting the punctuation and the meaning. There may be variations in the way individuals interpret a text.
4. Stress	Variations in the reader's voice contribute to fluency. The reader stresses words by saying them slightly louder to indicate his interpretation of the meaning of the text.
5. Rate	The reader moves along at an appropriate pace for the purpose of the reading, varying pace as needed. The reading is not too fast and not too slow.
6. Integration	The reader moves smoothly from one word to another and from one sentence to another, incorporating pauses that are just long enough to perform their function. There is no space between words except as part of meaningful interpretation. When all dimensions of fluency—pausing, phrasing, intonation/rhythm, stress, and pace—are working together, the reader is reading with expression, clearly showing evidence of understanding and thinking beyond the meaning of the text.

that the dialogue is a unit separate and different from the rest of the sentence. Different readers would offer different interpretations, but there are a limited number of possibilities.

Intonation

Intonation refers to the rising and falling tones of the voice and the way the reader varies the voice using tone, pitch, and volume to reflect the meaning of the text. Reading the example sentence above, your voice would probably remain at a suspenseful steady tone saying the words *time, van,* and *slowly.* It might rise slightly on *saying.* The dialogue might be slightly louder and possibly be at a different pitch. Your voice would sound excited at *you.* Intonation is very close to what we usually call *expression,* but all the dimensions of fluency are related to the expression we use when reading aloud for an audience.

Stress

Usually one or two words within a sentence are appropriate to stress; that is, to say a little louder than the other words. Stress figures into intonation or expression when reading aloud for an audience. But stress also reflects the meaning of any text, and it plays a role even when the reader is not performing. Read the following passage aloud:

1. This is a fireboat.
2. The fireboat helps
3. put out fires
4. on little boats
5. and big ships.
6. The boat sprays water
7. at the fire.
   —*All About Boats*

Possibly, you stressed the following words: line 1—*fireboat;* line 2—*fireboat;* line 3—*fires;* line 4—*boats;* line 5—*ships;* line 6—*water;* line 7—*fire.* Here, again, there might be some variation—some readers might also stress *this* in line 1—but the variations are not infinite. For example, stressing the word *little* in line 4 would imply that fireboats only put out fires on little boats (not big ones). *Little* is a modifier and not important enough to the meaning to be stressed. The same would be true of *sprays*; to stress this word would imply that some other means of getting water on the fire had been considered. Readers do not usually think consciously about the words they stress; they do it because they are reflecting the meaning. But occasionally when you read a text aloud—especially one you have not read before—you might correct word stress to be sure you are conveying the precise meaning. Word stress is a key factor in drama and comedy routines.

Rate

You want readers to move along at a good rate of speed. Failure to use pauses, phrasing, intonation, and appropriate word stress—accompanied by a very slow pace—will severely undermine comprehension. But it is a mistake simply to work for speed. Readers who have been drilled on speed can read pretty fast but sound robotic and still not think actively enough for good comprehension. And sometimes they read too fast, slurring over the words without giving enough attention to meaning.

When they read silently, most proficient readers go at a much faster pace than when they read orally. It takes much more time to say the words than it does to move the eyes over them and think them, especially when the process is unconscious and the reader is deeply engaged in the text. Processing requires much less effort, and this is great motivation for silent reading. Good oral reading is not too fast and not too slow. It is appropriate to the genre and to the reader's purpose.

Integration

All of the above dimensions are interrelated. The reader consistently and evenly orchestrates pausing, phrasing, intonation, stress, and rate. Struggling readers usually have great difficulty integrating these processes. And, in our experience, this integration is

paramount because it helps them to think about the meaning of the text. Explicitly demonstrating how to use pausing, phrasing, intonation, and stress is essential; pace will improve as the reader internalizes and integrates these dimensions of fluency.

▶ Change in Fluency Over Time

Fluency is not a "stage" in development. It changes over time and also varies with purpose and with the type of texts the individual is reading. It is important to describe the transitions in fluency over time.

Pointing with Precision and Matching Voice to Print (Levels A, B)

Young children who have heard many stories read aloud will often pretend to read. They can sound astonishingly fluent and expressive during these convincing performances. When they truly begin to engage with print, they slow down considerably. Most of them go through a phase of precise pointing and reading word by word.

Some children persist in "inventing" text long after they should have achieved voice-print match. They may even resist pointing, because at first it makes reading more difficult and they do not understand that they need to notice the mismatches. You will want to strongly encourage pointing and matching voice to print to get the process under way (see Chapter 14) so that beginning readers are careful and precise, leaving space between each word. When concentrating on coordinating directionality, readers have little attention to give to phrasing, intonation, or word stress. Children who are highly engaged, however, may begin to reflect meaning in their voices, through word stress and intonation, especially on a second reading, and this emerging behavior is very important.

For example, Nicky read page 14 of *Jesse* (see Figure 16-3) word by word, stopping at the period. His voice went down on the word *glasses*, indicating that he knew the period was coming. On page 16, his voice changed. It got louder on the word *love* (sig-

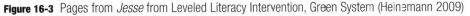

I like my purple glasses.

Figure 16-3 Pages from *Jesse* from Leveled Literacy Intervention, Green System (Heinemann 2009)

naled by the bold, enlarged print in the text) and went slightly up on the word *purple*, sounding excited. You can model this behavior and have students try it for themselves immediately after the demonstration.

When Melissa read *Orson's Tummy Ache* (pages 4 and 5 are reproduced in Figure 16-4), she paused slightly at the end of line 1 and then (still pointing) she read line 2 a little faster, putting her words together. Her teacher said, "You are making it sound like talking."

Langdon was reading *Over the River* (see Figure 16-5). He had learned in shared reading that it was significant that the bear did not go over the river on the log as all of the previous animals had. Instead the bear broke the log and went *in* the river. He read this page with stress on the word *in* and, although pointing, said the prepositional phrase *in the river* faster and smoother than the other words in the sentence. Langdon was not cued only by the bold print; discussion of meaning and teacher modeling played a strong role in his emerging fluency.

When children are reading at early text levels, the kinds of behaviors described above are very encouraging. Although students are pointing and assimilating other early reading behaviors, they are also exhibiting evidence of the important transitions (Figure 16-6). They go from slow, careful, precise pointing, a sometimes robotic voice, and frequent

The big dog ate
a little grass.

Figure 16-4 Page Spread from *Orson's Tummy Ache* from Leveled Literacy Intervention, Green System (Heinemann 2009)

We can see the bear go **in** the river!

Figure 16-5 Page from *Over the River* from Leveled Literacy Intervention, Orange System (Heinemann 2009)

stops to pointing occasionally, putting words together in phrases, obviously responding to the meaning, and using some expression. Soon, they will begin to drop finger pointing, although the voice may still reflect pointing behavior.

Figure 16-6 **Important Transitions**

From: ——————————————————→ **To:**

→ Slow, careful, and precise pointing.	→ Pointing but moving along the line quickly.	→ Occasional pointing and sometimes sliding the finger or removing it altogether on easy parts of the text.
→ Space between each word, coordinated with pointing.	→ Less space heard between words, with some following one another smoothly.	→ Putting many words together in groups with little space heard between.
→ Frequent repeating to correct when pointing is "off" (for example, running out of words).	→ Making pointing match most of the time without needing to self-correct.	→ Automatic pointing with more attention to checking with visual information within words than with matching.
→ "Sing-song" quality to reading, monotonous most of the time.	→ Evidence of putting words together on easy-to-say phrases like "said David" or "to the zoo."	→ Phrasing within most sentences, reflecting the meaning of the text.
→ Little stress on words or change of pitch.	→ Stress on important words and some change of pitch.	→ Using stress and variation in pitch to convey the meaning of the story.
→ Some voice reflection of basic punctuation such as periods and question marks.	→ Consistent voice reflection of basic punctuation such as periods and question marks.	→ Automatic voice reflection of a range of punctuation.
→ Emphasis on "reading" for its own sake.	→ More attention to and emphasis on the story.	→ Overt signs of enjoyment or interest in the story.
→ Stopping frequently to check on reading, solve words slowly, and assure matching.	→ Forward movement, stopping less frequently.	→ Few stops for problem solving; matching is automatic and does not need correction even when slightly "off."
Likely to happen on new texts that are challenging.	*Likely to happen on texts that are easy or when rereading familiar texts.*	

From *Guiding Readers and Writers: Teaching Comprehension, Genre, and Content Literacy*, p. 77, Irene C. Fountas and Gay Su Pinnell 2001.

Fluent and Phrased Oral Reading (Levels C to Z)

As the eyes take over the process, readers are able to see words grouped together in phrases. If texts are at an appropriate level, readers can reflect meaning with their voices. Some readers, very concerned with accuracy, persist in pointing much longer than they should. The pointing makes it easier and/or they do not realize that they can follow along with the eyes.

Sometimes teachers and parents encourage them to continue pointing because they either associate it with greater accuracy or think they need to "know where the reader is." Even older readers may still point with a pencil. Of course, anyone might use a finger to hold the place or help them puzzle out a very difficult new word. But habitual finger or pencil pointing that continues past Level C will slow reading down, undermine fluency, and increase dependency. Prompt readers to use their eyes (as described in Chapter 14). For those who have great difficulty, you can use transitions like sliding the finger, using a transparent marker to slide down the print, or moving a thumb down the side of the page to track the lines of print; however, the sooner these props can be dropped, the better.

Proficient readers begin to track print with their eyes; they know more and more words and so are able to recognize words rapidly or solve them quickly. They read faster and in phrase units that show an awareness of meaning and syntax. On new instructional-level texts, they may stop to problem-solve or reread in order to search for information. They are not perfectly fluent, but they sound good when they read aloud. They use appropriate word stress and intonation. On a second reading or when reading easy texts, they exhibit the dimensions of fluency to a higher degree.

We expect this kind of reading of easy texts independently and instructional-level texts with teacher support. Of course, any reader will be dysfluent on a text that is too hard.

▶ The Role of Fast Processing

Proficient readers increasingly raise the level of their performance. They change rapidly, making systems work together as they move from parsing sentences word by word to taking on larger pieces of text. As the level of text difficulty increases, the processing becomes faster. Most of what is processed is correct. Intervention must create this progression of change for struggling readers (Clay 2001).

Historically, we have slowed down instruction for struggling readers. A week like the following—described by a reading teacher—is typical:

- ❏ Monday—work on the words that will be in the story.
- ❏ Tuesday—practice skills.
- ❏ Wednesday—read the story (or part of it) slowly.
- ❏ Thursday—finish the story and reread it.
- ❏ Friday—work on skills.

These students will have worked an entire week on an eight- to sixteen-page story. The processing may

happen—but slowly and inefficiently. In intervention lessons, processing systems must develop faster.

Look back at the Reading Records of Kent and Cameron discussed in Chapter 15, both of whom are just beginning to read. In reading *All About Snakes*, Kent is active and independent. He corrects himself. He rereads to search for more information and has several ways of solving problems. He checks on himself. Cameron is passive, usually appealing when he does not know a word right away. His only evident word-solving strategy is making the sound of the first letter of the word.

If you could listen to the two readers, you would notice even more differences (see Figure 16-7).

Kent problem-solves rapidly. In spite of some stops and starts on this first reading, he puts his words together in phrases. He utters many two-word phrases and reads prepositional phrases as a unit. He pauses at periods and places appropriate stress on words. He reads without his finger for the most part, bringing it in when needed. He is not yet fluent, but fluency is beginning to emerge.

Cameron's reading sounds quite different. Still pointing throughout the text, he reads each word as a separate unit, stressing each equally. Only twice does he demonstrate a two-word phrase. His reading is slow and very choppy. He can attend to only one item at a time. He may slowly increase the number of words he knows and develop better word-solving strategies, but he is not establishing the network of strategic actions he needs to do rapid processing. The more he practices reading slowly, the more habitual dysfluency will become.

Both Kent and Cameron are just beginning to process print visually. They know some words as whole units and they can also use individual letters. Kent appears to notice letter clusters and word endings. We want both readers to become more efficient in word solving and to increase fluency, but speed is not the issue. In fact, it would be a mistake to try to speed up these readers before they are able to see and use patterns while reading.

At this point in the development of the reading process, children are learning to recognize words in all their detail, while at the same time beginning to

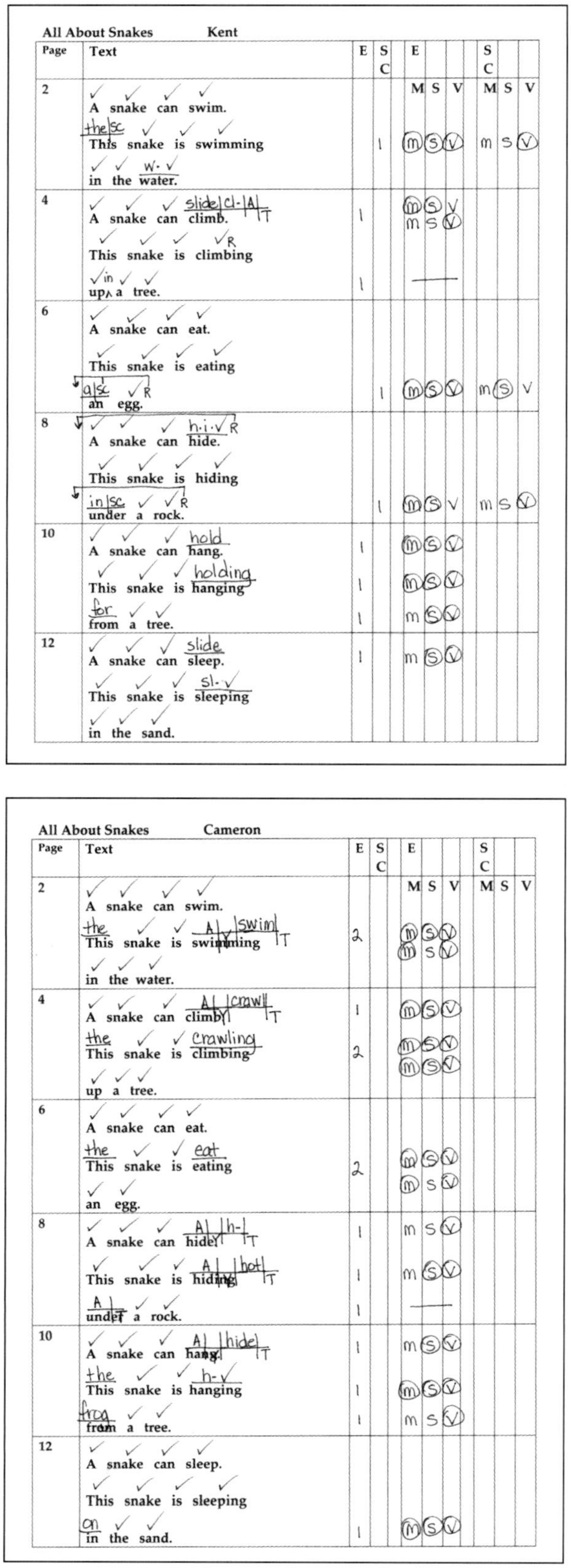

Figure 16-7 Reading Records for Kent and Cameron Reading *All About Snakes*

perceive some clusters of features as single units or patterns. These rough patterns help emerging readers make good attempts while they are learning more.

Proficient readers, on the other hand, work primarily with these larger units. When necessary, however, they can shift to smaller units, such as letters, and they usually do so automatically, without paying conscious attention. While proficient readers *can* look letter by letter through a word and probably see every letter, most of the time they work with whole words, clusters, word parts, or even short phrases. That is why some minor errors (*a* for *the* or *that* for *this*) go unnoticed (or at least uncorrected) unless they change the meaning. According to Clay (1991):

> The visual perception of print becomes more detailed, more differentiated, and then more richly patterned (chunked or clustered or unitized), and we may be conscious or not conscious of the patterning. (167)

As children have more encounters with print, the processing becomes more economical and therefore faster, and they pick up visual information more rapidly. But it would be a mistake to speed them up artificially before they own and can use a rich repertoire of larger units.

Readers acquire units through successive encounters (Clay 1991). A new unit (the *-ing* ending, for example) may be pointed out in word study lessons or as part of small-group instruction (*playing, running*). Readers then begin to recognize the unit again and again in different contexts (I can *swim*, I like *swimming*) and it becomes well known. Finally, the reader can use the unit to problem-solve in a wide variety of contexts, even when it varies from the original form (*fingernail, ingot, swimmingly*).

▶ Working for Fluency with English Language Learners

When you are helping English language learners develop fluency, it is important to recognize that they may produce word stress, phrasing, and intonation that reflect their own oral English speech, and it may vary from the patterns native speakers would use. These variations are not important and often make a speaker's language interesting. What is important is whether these readers are using phrasing, intonation, and word stress in ways that makes sense to them. As students have more opportunities to process texts that are accessible to them, their English will sound more fluid and expressive.

▶ The Role of Text

The type of text a reader is asked to process plays an important role in the development of reading fluency. An array of page spreads from the kinds of texts students might be expected to read from kindergarten through the beginning of grade 3 is shown in Figure 16-8. It's easy to see the growing demands. A number of text factors support developing readers.

Level

Providing accessible texts is one of the most important factors in creating a setting in which a student can read with fluency and phrasing. Many schools use sets of leveled texts for small-group reading instruction. Teachers assess students' reading levels and select texts that are within their reach. An accessible text will not guarantee fluency, but it is impossible to teach for fluency when a text is too hard.

General text factors such as genre, structure, content, themes and ideas, vocabulary, and language and literary features have an impact on fluency because they are related to the difficulty of the text and the challenge to the reader. (See Chapter 6 for a discussion of text factors.) The more the reader knows about these factors, the easier it will be to read fluently. Sentence complexity is a major factor in processing demands. In general the longer the sentence (and the more embedded clauses), the harder it is to reflect the meaning with the voice. The reader has to keep going over many long clauses, keeping the whole meaning in mind, and attending to the punctuation. Think about the challenges of comprehensibly rendering this sentence from a classic adult novel when reading aloud:

> Her wide light hazel eyes had the look of blind diffused excitement he knew best; she was probably talking already about the most personal things, telling her thoughts such as they were: for even when Jenny seemed intelligent, or sincere, he still distrusted her female mind, crooked and cloudy by nature: she was no doubt asking questions designed to lead the man to talk about himself, meaning to trap him into small confidences and confessions that later she could use as a weapon against him when needed.

> —Katherine Anne Porter, *Ship of Fools*, 27

Of course sentences in children's books are more simply constructed, but longer and more complex sentences can challenge the younger reader or a struggling reader just as much as the one above challenges the adult reader.

Instruction

There is always a place of tension in reading instruction. Students can develop fluency if they read a great many easy texts, although some struggling readers require instruction for fluency even if the text is at the independent level. But they will not grow in the reading process unless they take on more challenging texts. The instruction teachers provide enables students to read harder texts with phrasing, intonation, and appropriate word stress.

Engagement

Students need the opportunity to read texts that engage them, that are inherently interesting in terms of topic, characters, or plot. (See Chapter 20 for a discussion of the role of engagement.) To read with expression, you must think about the meaning, and for that to happen, there must be engagement. Interest in a topic is built if students can make connections between and among texts. The nonfiction texts shown in Figures 16-9 and 16-10 are connected by topic. *Animals That Go Fast* (Level C) has engaging photographs of animals that have the ability to go

I like bugs on pizza.

Frog Food from Leveled Literacy Intervention, Level A, Green System (Heinemann 2009)

"Mommy, was I a cute baby?" Froggy asked.

"Yes, yes, yes!" his mom said. "You were a cute baby frog."

"Can I see my baby pictures?" Froggy asked.

Baby Pictures from Leveled Literacy Intervention, Level E, Green System (Heinemann 2009)

Bunny ran to Hoppy. She ran very fast.

Then she ran back. The thunder went **Boom! Bam! BAM!**

Boom! Bam! BAM!

The Big Storm from Leveled Literacy Intervention, Level E, Green System (Heinemann 2009)

Soon Taco was wet, wet, wet. Taco did not like that! The little dog jumped out of the tub.

No, Taco!

Taco! No!

Taco ran around and around, and the floor got wet. Taco shook, and the walls got wet.

A Trip to the Laundromutt from Leveled Literacy Intervention, Level H, Green System (Heinemann 2009)

"I know!" said Hoot. "We can have a costume party!"

"What is a costume party?" Moosling asked.

"It's a dress-up party," Hoot told him. "You dress up as someone else. You can even dress up as a thing! Mouse dressed up as a carrot last time."

"It will be fun!" Mouse said. "I can choose the best costume. I'll even give a prize!"

"Can we still have dancing?" asked Skunk.

"And games?" asked Rabbit.

"And food?" Moosling asked.

"Yes, yes, yes," said Hoot. "And guess what! I have a trunk full of old clothes and other things. You can all come and get what you want to use for costumes."

The Costume Party from Leveled Literacy Intervention, Level M, Blue System (Heinemann 2009)

I can paint myself!

The Painter from Leveled Literacy Intervention, Level A, Green System (Heinemann 2009)

The big dog ate a little stick.

Orson's Tummy Ache from Leveled Literacy Intervention, Level B, Green System (Heinemann 2009)

Next, Moosling followed some very little footprints.

And there was Skunk! "Skunk, I found you!" said Moosling. "I followed your footprints!"

"Good for you!" said Skunk.

Footprints from Leveled Literacy Intervention, Level H, Blue System (Heinemann 2009)

But along came Skunk. "Hello, Skunk!" shouted Moosling. "Hi, Moosling," said Skunk. "I came to say good-bye."

"Oh, no! Are you going away, too?" Moosling asked. "Will you fly away like the birds? Or will you sleep in the mud like Frog?"

"I don't fly. And mud is not for me," said Skunk. "I have a nice little den under a log. I'll sleep there until it's warm again."

Then off he went to his den.

Moosling in Winter from Leveled Literacy Intervention, Level K, Blue System (Heinemann 2009)

Figure 16-8 Texts to Support Readers

fast. *Things That Go Fast* (Level A) explores the concept of going fast more broadly using familiar things. Notice that the drawing of a race car is enhanced by an inset photograph of the real thing! Both are examples of informational texts for very early readers. Accessing the meaning of these texts will provide clues to word stress and intonation.

Dialogue

The texts shown in Figure 16-8 are all books in series that feature interesting animal characters. (The role of series books in supporting readers is discussed in Chapters 6 and 20.) These engaging characters offer many opportunities for using expression. In addition, many of these texts contain dialogue. It is natural for readers to be motivated to read dialogue in a way that sounds like talking.

Layout

Many high-quality texts are especially designed to help readers use phrasing. Notice in Figure 16-8 how the layout changes from Level A (*Frog Food*) to Level E (*Baby Pictures*). The Level A texts are the simplest and easiest to process. The single row of print supports readers in matching voice to print. But the engaging texts also allow readers to enjoy the story and stress words appropriately. By Level E, dialogue is present. Notice that the text is laid out so that the phrase unit is often on a new line. The two speakers on page 12 of *Baby Pictures* are separated by extra space. The layout signals readers to pause. The texts from the Orson and Taco series also support phrasing. In *The Big Storm*, Level E, the line is broken just where you would pause and then read line 2 as a unit. By Level H, *A Trip to the Laundromutt*, although the layout is still friendly, the reader is expected to pause at a period in the middle of a line on page 11. Selections from the Moosling series reveal more layout challenges. *Footprints,* Level H, includes divided dialogue and space between speakers. At Level K, most sentences begin on the left, but that is not the case at Level M.

This animal is a big cat.
The cat can run very fast.

Animals That Go Fast from Leveled Literacy Intervention, Level C, Orange System (Heinemann 2009)

A car can go fast.

Things That Go Fast from Leveled Literacy Intervention, Level A, Orange System (Heinemann 2009)

Figure 16-9 Connecting Texts by Concept

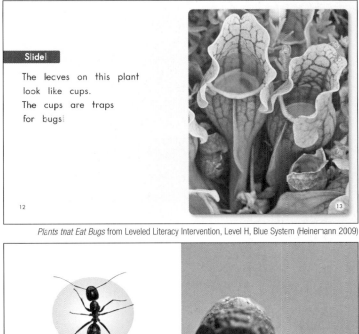

Slide1

The leaves on this plant look like cups.
The cups are traps for bugs.

Plants that Eat Bugs from Leveled Literacy Intervention, Level H, Blue System (Heinemann 2009)

This is an ant.
Ants crawl on the ground.
A little ant can carry
a very big load.

All About Bugs from Leveled Literacy Intervention, Level F, Blue System (Heinemann 2009)

Figure 16-10 Connecting Texts by Concept

All of these texts have a clear font and friendly layout. Gradually, they scaffold the reader toward a familiarity and ease with conventional layout. You must be very careful when you select texts for struggling readers, and leveled texts allow you to be.

▶ The Role of Self-Correction

Self-correction fuels the development of the early reading process. Each substitution is a decision based on current information. Stopping, checking the word, and either making another attempt or decoding the correct word are all decisions that involve hypotheses based on meaning, language structure, and visual patterns. As readers move through the text, what has come before provides background information that influences monitoring and self-correction. Hypotheses are easier to make because meaning and text structure support the thinking. Readers often gain momentum and pick up fluency towards the end of the text.

Having a wide range of word-solving strategies—including the flexible use of meaning and language structure—allows readers to make decisions more rapidly. Kent's self-corrections (see Figure 16-7) are overt; that's why we can tell so much from looking at his Reading Record. But over the next year and a half, the process will change. Self-correction begins to take place before the reader says the word aloud. Or the reader may note the self-correction in passing but not bother to correct it. This covert self-correction adds to the reader's ability to produce the language in phrases. Don't expect to hear very much overt self-correction from highly proficient first graders reading easy books independently.

The relationship between self-correction and reading progress is not linear. As children progress to higher text levels, observable self-correction decreases and may become nonexistent. A 1:1 or 1:2 self-correction ratio in highly accurate reading is too high, because readers should be ignoring small errors or mentally correcting their responses before saying them aloud. We can assume that proficient readers are

self-regulating both their oral and silent reading, but we will not be able to observe it. That's why when we assess reading at Levels L through Z, we report the number of self-corrections and omit the ratio.

▶ Teaching for Fluency

As we've said, supporting pausing, phrasing, word stress, and intonation is the most powerful way to teach children to read fluently and ultimately affects the pace and the way readers integrate the dimensions of fluency. In this section, we present language that will support readers in using each dimension. You will find a comprehensive list of similar language in *The Fountas and Pinnell Prompting Guide 1: A Tool for Literacy Teachers* (2009).

Pausing

A very concrete way to teach pausing is to help children notice and use the punctuation, as shown in the following interaction after a second reading of *What Is Very Long?* (page 16 of this Level C book is reproduced in Figure 16-11). Ms. M is calling attention to some of the important transitions described in Figure 16-6, Important Transitions.

> **Ms. M:** Listen to me read this. Can you hear my voice go down at the period? *[Reading.]* "He is a hippopotamus. The hippopotamus has a very long name!" Did you notice I made a full stop after the period? Did you notice I made my voice excited at the end? Now you read it just that way. *[Jacob reads the page with appropriate intonation—a full stop at the period and an excited voice at the end.]* You made your voice go down at the full stop and you made your reading sound excited at the end, too.

In the next interaction (see Figure 16-12), Mr. F is teaching how to read dialogue and pause at punctuation (pages 2-3, *A Visit from Aunt Bee*).

> **Mr. F:** On this page you see an exclamation point. Mom is excited because Aunt Bee is coming. I'm

going to make it sound excited. *[Reads.]* "'Aunt Bee is coming!' said Mom." What did you notice?

JACOB: You read it like she was excited.

MR. F: What did my voice do at the end of the whole sentence?

JACOB: Your voice sounded excited.

MR. F: My voice was excited at the end and I made a full stop. Listen to me read it again. *[Does so.]* Now you read it. Read the punctuation. *[The children read in unison and show excitement.]*

On longer texts, readers have many different punctuation marks to process within a single sentence or paragraph. In the interaction below, Mrs. C worked with Haleema on punctuation (pages 6 and 7 of *Too Many Teeth* are reproduced in Figure 16-13). We placed one slash (/) to show a short pause and two slashes (//) to show a longer pause.

> **MRS. C:** Go back to page 6. Read it again and be sure to read the punctuation.
>
> **HALEEMA** *[reading]*: "Don't forget," / Mom said on Friday morning. "I will pick you up / after school, // so you can visit the dentist." "Oh, no!" Annie / said / to / herself. "The dentist will say // I have too many teeth. I have / a lot more teeth / than my friends."
>
> **MRS. C:** You took a breath when you saw commas in the first sentence. And you made your voice sound excited when Annie said, "Oh, no!" Look at the rest of the sentence. Listen to how I put my words together. "'Oh, no!' Annie said to herself." She is talking to herself. You try that. *[Haleema reads the sentence with no pauses on* Annie said to herself.*]* You read the punctuation and you put your words together.

Here is a
hippopotamus.
The hippopotamus has
a very long name!

Figure 16-11 Page from *What is Very Long?* from Leveled Literacy Intervention, Orange System (Heinemann 2009)

Phrasing

In the previoius interaction, Mrs. C was helping Haleema read the punctuation but was also teaching her about phrasing. In addition to using punctuation, readers need to think about the natural breaks in language so that they can make the reading understandable. This process is closely connected to comprehension. Here's another example of teaching phrasing, based on pages 14 and 15 of *The Good Dog* (see Figure 16-14).

"Aunt Bee is coming!"
said Mom.

Figure 16-12 Page Spread from *A Visit from Aunt Bee* from Leveled Literacy Intervention, Orange System (Heinemann 2009)

"Don't forget," Mom said on Friday morning. "I will pick you up after school, so you can visit the dentist."

"Oh, no!" Annie said to herself. "The dentist will say I have too many teeth. I have a lot more teeth than my friends."

Annie felt more and more worried. She started to count her teeth again.

Figure 16-13 Page Spread from *Too Many Teeth* from Leveled Literacy Intervention, Blue System (Heinemann 2009)

CARSON [*reading*]: "Then / Jack / said, / 'Get / the / ball, / Orson!' Orson / was / very good. He / got / the ball / for / Jack."

MR. T [*covers up everything except* then Jack said]: These words make sense together. Read them together.

CARSON [*reading*]: "Then Jack said."

MR. T [*uncovers the next line*]: Read it all. Be sure to make what Jack said sound like talking.

CARSON: "Then Jack said, / 'Get the ball, / Orson.'"

MR. T: You made it sound like talking. Now look at the rest of the page. Listen to how I put my words together on this whole page. [*Reads the entire page with phrasing.*] You try it

and listen to how your reading sounds.

CARSON: Then Jack said, / "Get the ball, / Orson!" Orson was / very good. He got the ball / for Jack.

MR. T: You put your words together. You made it sound like talking.

When you have worked with children so that they understand what you are asking them to do, you can use prompts such as:

❑ "Try that again and put your words together so it sounds like talking."

❑ "Are you listening to how your reading sounds?"

These prompts assume the reader has been taught what to do, knows how to do it, and is reminded to accomplish it.

Stress

Proper stress on words is directly related to the reader's construction of meaning. You can, in fact, communicate different meanings by word stress. Consider the slightly different implications of stress-

Then Jack said, "Get the ball, Orson!" Orson was very good. He got the ball for Jack.

Oh, no!

Figure 16-14 Page Spread from *The Good Dog* from Leveled Literacy Intervention, Green System (Heinemann 2009)

ing different words in this sentence (words that are stressed are underlined):

- ❑ <u>Now</u> they look like frogs. (They didn't before.)
- ❑ Now <u>they</u> look like frogs. (As opposed to other animals that look like frogs.)
- ❑ Now they look like <u>frogs</u>. (As opposed to other things they might have looked like.)

Certainly different interpretations of a text are possible because readers bring different meanings to it. So you don't want to communicate that there is *one* right way to stress words; that is only sometimes true. But you will want to demonstrate word stress so that the reader knows the concept of saying one word (or perhaps more if the sentence is complex) louder than others in the sentence.

In fiction, print conventions such as all capitals, a larger type size, italics, and boldface let readers know which words to stress when reading out loud. In non-fiction, these conventions are used to highlight key words or important concepts, but they are also related to stress at least most of the time. In this interaction, Mrs. L teaches early readers how to use the bold print that appears in *Talent Show* (pages 14, 15, and 16 of the book are reproduced in Figure 16-15):

MRS. L: Just look at the pictures on pages 14 and 15. Horse was doing everything, wasn't he?

RICHARD: It's funny.

FRANCESCA: They are singing and the notes are coming out.

MRS. L: Did you think it was a good show?

CHILDREN: Yes.

MRS. L: Turn the page. Listen to how this sounds. *[Reads.]* "It was a very good show!" Did you see how I made my voice sound when I read *very?*

FRANCESCA: You said *very* louder.

MRS. L: Look at the word *very.* Do you see how it is darker than the other words? That's called bold print. When you see that dark, bold print, make the word sound important. You read the page and make it sound like a very good show.

CHILDREN *[reading]:* "It was a very good show!"

MRS. L: You made it sound like a very good show.

Here is an interaction centered on *How Frogs Grow,* an informational text (pages 12 and 13 are reproduced in Figure 16-16)

Marik has just finished reading page 12 in a robotic voice. Just about every word was stressed in the same way, although he tended to say words louder when they were harder for him to decode.

Figure 16-15 Pages from *Talent Show* from Leveled Literacy Intervention, Green System (Heinemann 2009)

Figure 16-16 Page Spread from *How Frogs Grow* from Leveled Literacy Intervention, Green System (Heinemann 2009)

Prompt children to stress appropriate words in dialogue so they carry the meaning of the text. In *The Fun Club Goes to the Vet Clinic,* a group of children visit a clinic with Miss Dimple and her dog Meatball because Meatball has been getting fatter. The surprise comes at the end of the story when the doctor discovers that Meatball is fine but is going to have puppies. (Pages 14, 15, and 16 are reproduced in Figure 16-17.)

MARIK [*reading*]: "The little tadpoles grow up. They have very long legs and no tails. Now they look like frogs."

Ms. S: I'll read the last sentence to you. [*Covers up the first three lines.*] Listen to how this sounds. [*Reading.*] "Now they look like frogs." Which word did I say louder? [*Marik points to* now.] When you read, think about the story. They were little tadpoles. They grow up and have long legs [*pointing to picture*] and no tails. Now they are frogs. Listen to me read and think about how my voice is helping show how the tadpoles changed. [*Reads again.*] "The little tadpoles grow up. They have very long legs and no tails. Now they look like frogs." Now you try it.

MARIK: "The little tadpoles grow up. They have very long legs and no tails. Now they look like frogs."

Bobbie has just read the last sentence on page 14.

Ms. N: Try that again and make that word [*points to* fine] sound important. Bobbie [*reading*]: "'No,' said Dr. Grimes. 'Meatball is fine.' [*Turns the page.*] 'But she's going to have puppies!' he said.

Ms. N: Try that again and make that word [*points to* but] sound important.

BOBBIE: "No. Meatball is fine. 'But she's going to have puppies!' he said."

Ms. N: You made some of the words sound important.

Intonation

Intonation refers to the modulation of the voice. Pausing, phrasing, and stress are all related to meaning, but it is through intonation that readers truly interpret the text and make an impression on listen-

Figure 16-17 Pages from *The Fun Club Goes to the Vet Clinic* from Leveled Literacy Intervention, Blue System (Heinemann 2009)

ers. You can cue intonation with prompts related to punctuation, like these:

- ❏ "Make your voice go down when you see the period."
- ❏ "Make your voice go down at the period. Then stop."
- ❏ "Make your voice go up when you see the question mark."
- ❏ "In this part, [character] is asking a question. How would [character] ask the question?"
- ❏ "Use emphasis when you see the exclamation point."
- ❏ "Make your voice show excitement when you see the exclamation point."

Dialogue is a wonderful opportunity to prompt readers to use intonation:

- ❏ "Make your voice sound like the character is talking when you see the quotation marks."
- ❏ "Make it sound like the characters are talking."
- ❏ "Make your voice sound like the character is talking."
- ❏ "In this part, [character] is very excited. How would [character] say that?"

Readers can also be asked to think about the writer's craft:

- ❏ "Make it sound like a story you listen to."
- ❏ "Make your voice show what you think the author meant."
- ❏ "Make your voice show that you understand what the author means."

Your on-the-run observations while taking a Reading Record will give you great information about intonation and other aspects of fluency and tell you more than the fluency score you finally decide to give the reading. For example, look at the section of Emma's Reading Record in Figure 16-18. (Pages 6, 7, 14, and 15 of *The Three Little Pigs and a Big Bad Wolf* are reproduced in Figure 16-19.) Emma read the text at above 90 percent accuracy, but her reading was slow and choppy with poor intonation. Based on the nature of her miscues, Mr. D hypothesized that Emma might be losing meaning. In fact, her slow, plodding reading was undermining her sense of language struc-

ture. She was trying to make meaningful attempts but not really listening to herself read. After the reading, Mr. D worked with Emma for a minute or two to support her use of intonation.

MR. D: Let's go back to page 6. On this page, what's happening?

EMMA: He built the house with bricks and then the wolf came.

MR. D: How do you think the third little pig felt about his fine brick house?

EMMA: Happy.

MR. D: He was really happy and proud, too. Read that last sentence. Make your voice sound like the character is talking. Show how he felt.

EMMA [*reading*]: "'What a fine house!' he said."

MR. D: You made it sound like the third little pig was talking. There are two characters talking on the next page.

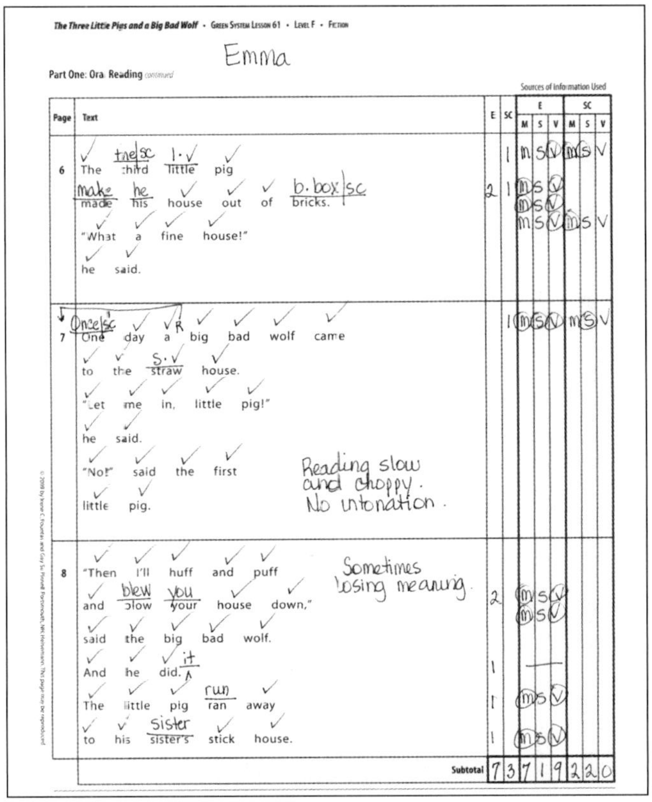

Figure 16-18 Emma's Reading of *The Three Little Pigs and a Big Bad Wolf*

Figure 16-19 Page Spreads from *The Three Little Pigs and a Big Bad Wolf* from Leveled Literacy Intervention, Green System (Heinemann 2009)

EMMA: Yes.

MR. D: I think the author meant to have the wolf sound scary and the little pig sound excited or scared. So I read it a little louder and also made my voice sound interesting. You read this page and make your voice show what you think the author meant.

EMMA: "One day a big bad wolf came to the straw house. 'Let me in, little pig!' he said. 'No!' said the first little pig."

MR. D: Did you listen to yourself? Did it sound good?

EMMA: Yes.

MR. D: Let's go to a really exciting part. Turn to page 14.

EMMA: He's trying to get in!

MR. D: Read this page and make it sound like the characters are talking.

EMMA [*reading with intonation*]: "The wolf said, 'Let me in!' 'No, no, no!' said the three little pigs."

MR. D: How do you think your reading sounds?

EMMA: Like a story.

MR. D: You made it sound interesting like a story.

EMMA: The wolf and the pig.

MR. D: Try this page and make it sound like a story you listen to.

EMMA [*reading, but without intonation*]: "One day a big bad wolf came to the straw house. 'Let me in, little pig!' he said."

MR. D: Listen to me read this. Can you hear how I sound like the wolf is talking? [*Reads the first four lines with expression.*] Do you think I made the wolf sound bad?

Rate

Sometimes readers will use fairly good intonation and word stress but fall into the habit of reading quite slowly. They will not be fully able to use language structure and meaning if they constantly read too slowly. It may be necessary to help readers move at a quicker rate. For some intensive work on rate, first be sure that the text is accessible when reading independently—on the easy side but not so easy that there is nothing to work on. During a second reading of *The Three Little Pigs and a Big Bad*

Wolf, Mr. D had this interaction with Manira:

Mr. D: I am going to read this faster. Listen to how I read this. [*Reads page 6 at a good rate.*] Can you read this quickly? [*Manira reads it moderately fast.*] Now can you read this quickly? [*Reads the first two lines of page 7 at a good rate. Manira reads it slowly.*] Move your eyes forward quickly so that you can read more words together. [*While Manira reads, Mr. D pushes a card across the line of text to help her eyes move.*] You read it faster that time. Read the whole page quickly. [*Manira reads faster without the card.*]

Notice that Mr. D is helping Manira understand the purpose of the task—that when you read quickly, you can put more words together.

For most readers, you will not need to use props like pushing a small white card across the print; but it can sometimes be useful in breaking the habit of slow reading. Once faster reading is established, you need to insist on it, always given that the reader is not engaged in too much problem solving.

Integration

Integration is the orchestrated use of all dimensions of fluency. You will want to prompt for integration even on lower-level texts so that readers get the feel of "putting it all together." Once readers understand what you mean by a word like *smooth*, you need only remind them. Two interactions after reading *Baby Pictures*, Level E, are presented below. (Pages 4 and 5 are reproduced in Figure 16-20.)

Ms. P: Make your reading sound smooth like this. [*Reads pages 4 and 5 with appropriate rate, pausing, phrasing, word stress, and intonation.*] Can you read it the same way? [*Niles reads with accuracy and all aspects of fluency.*] You sounded smooth that time.

Figure 16-20 Page Spreads from *Baby Pictures* from Leveled Literacy Intervention, Green System (Heinemann 2009)

Ms. P: Read pages 4 and 5 like the author is telling the story. [*Gracie reads slowly.*] Listen to how I read this. I am telling the story with my voice. [*Reads with intonation and word stress. Gracie reads faster but without intonation.*] How do you think your reading sounds?

Gracie: Not too much like a story.

Ms. P: Listen to how I read this. [*Reads just page 5 with expression.*]

Gracie [*reading with intonation, word stress, and phrasing*]: "Yes, / you were a cute baby," // said Froggy.

Ms. P: You made your reading sound interesting that time. Keep going.

As readers attempt more difficult texts, they will need constant encouragement to integrate the dimensions of fluency. The interaction below took place after reading *Chester Greenwood's Big Idea*, a Level N text (pages 22 and 23 are reproduced in Figure 16-21):

Mrs. J: Let's go back to page 22 and 23. On page 22, what were you learning?

Austin: He got famous all over the world and sold a lot of earmuffs.

Mrs. J: Yes. This picture shows the country of Russia, where it is very cold. And look at all of the people wearing his ear protectors, or earmuffs, which is what we call them. On the next page, we

Soon Chester began to sell his ear protectors to people all over the world. The ear protectors got a new name. People called them earmuffs.

22

Chester became a famous inventor. He invented a special rake, a teakettle that didn't tip over, a mousetrap, a bed that folded up, and other things. Chester made more than 130 inventions. And it all began with earmuffs for his big ears!

23

Figure 16-21 Page Spread from *Chester Greenwood's Big Idea* from Leveled Literacy Intervention, Blue System (Heinemann 2009)

read a list of all the other things Chester invented.

JAKE: He was famous.

MRS. J: Sometimes it's tricky to read a sentence with a long list of things. Listen to my voice and tell me what I do with it. [*Reading.*] "Chester became a <u>famous</u> inventor. He invented a special <u>rake</u>, / a <u>teakettle</u> that didn't tip over, / a <u>mouse-trap</u>, / a <u>bed</u> that folded up, / and <u>other</u> things. // Chester made <u>more</u> than 130 inventions. And it

all began with <u>earmuffs</u> for his <u>big</u> <u>ears</u>! // What did you notice?

JAKE: You stopped a little after every time you said something he invented.

MRS. J: Yes, just a short pause but my voice did not drop. It just stayed the same. What else?

CHARLEY: You made it sound smooth.

JAKE: You said some words louder.

AUSTIN: You sounded excited at the end.

SADIE: You made your voice stop at the period.

MRS. J: So I'm going to listen to each of you read this page and I want you to make your reading sound smooth and interesting. Use your voice and the punctuation to show there is a list.

Sometimes readers encounter different kinds of texts within a book and you will want them to use integrated aspects of fluency for each. For example, here's an interaction that took place after reading *Pen Pals*, Level K (pages 14, 15, and 16 are reproduced in Figure 16-22).

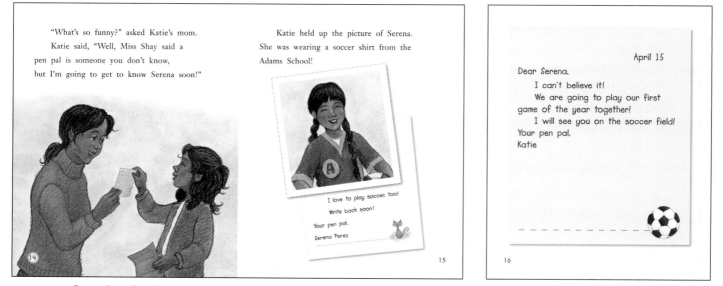

"What's so funny?" asked Katie's mom. Katie said, "Well, Miss Shay said a pen pal is someone you don't know, but I'm going to get to know Serena soon!"

14

Katie held up the picture of Serena. She was wearing a soccer shirt from the Adams School!

I love to play soccer too!
Write back soon!
Your pen pal,
Serena Perez

15

April 15

Dear Serena,
   I can't believe it!
   We are going to play our first game of the year together!
   I will see you on the soccer field!
Your pen pal,
Katie

16

Figure 16-22 Pages from *Pen Pals* from Leveled Literacy Intervention, Blue System (Heinemann 2009)

Mrs. G: Go back to page 14. Read this page and make your reading sound interesting. [*Tanya reads pages 14 and 15 with all aspects of fluency.*] You are reading it like you are telling a story. What have you learned about Katie and her pen pal, Serena?

Tanya: They both play soccer and they are going to play each other!

Mrs. G: That is interesting! So, on the next page, we will read the letter that Katie wrote back to Serena. Listen while I read it in an interesting way and notice what I do with my voice. [*Reads the letter with pauses after* Dear Serena *and* Your pen pal, *and appropriate pace, pausing, phrasing, word stress, and intonation.*] What did you notice?

Tanya: Your voice sounded kind of different. You stopped some places.

Mrs. G: That's right. Can you read it the same way? [*Tanya reads the letter with all aspects of fluency.*]

Remember that none of these prompts will work if the text is too hard for the reader. But given good book selection and introductions, you can improve a reader's fluency within a very short time.

▶ The Role of Shared and Performance Reading

Shared and performance reading provide an authentic reason for students to read aloud. Students are in a context in which they are motivated to reflect meaning with their voices. As they read poetry in a shared way or read enlarged books together, they can use the support of others to get the feel of reading fluently.

Ms. H: Do you notice the word *in*? It's darker than the other words. That means that we say it a little louder and that makes it sound like an interesting story. *In* is an important word, isn't it? That's what we thought would happen in this story—that the bear wouldn't go over the river.

Instead, he broke the log and went in the river. Let's read this last page and make it sound like a story. [*Children read, stressing* in.]

The interaction below took place after reading the poem "There Once Was a Queen" (see Figure 16-23).

Ms. R: Here is the poem that we read yesterday. Listen while I read the first two lines. [*Reads.*] Did you notice that I said the two rhyming words, *queen* and *green*, just a little louder? Let's all read these two lines. [*Children read, stressing the words.*] Now listen to me read the rest of it. [*Reads.*] What did you notice about the way I read it?

Jonno: It sounded good.

Ms. R: It sounded good because I put my words together. Watch. I will read "And got up in the morning" all together and then stop. Then I'll read "To go to bed" all together. [*Demonstrates.*] Now let's all read that and put our words together. [*Children read, using appropriate phrasing.*] You read it smoothly. Now let's read the whole poem like that.

Readers' theater is a very enjoyable and powerful way to help readers read with fluency. After students

---

There Once Was a Queen

There once was a queen
Whose face was green.
She ate her milk
And drank her bread,
And got up in the morning
To go to bed.

Figure 16-23 Poem "There Once Was a Queen"

have read any text that includes dialogue, you can turn the texts into scripts featuring the speaking characters and a narrator. More sophisticated readers can learn just to read the dialogue, without saying the words that identify the speaker (*said City Mouse*, for example). You don't need to use the entire text for readers' theater—just the most exciting part. See the examples in Figures 16-24 and 16-25.

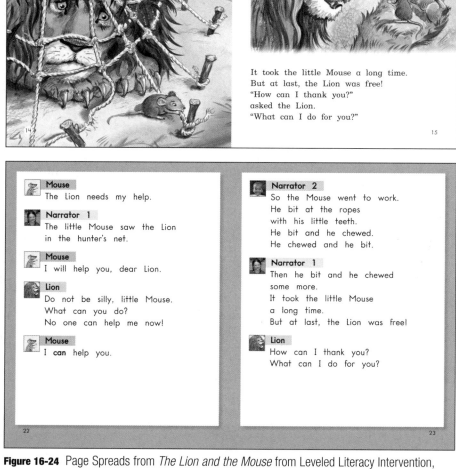

Figure 16-24 Page Spreads from *The Lion and the Mouse* from Leveled Literacy Intervention, Green System (Heinemann 2009)

▶ Teaching Hard for Fluency

As you are working with struggling readers, you will need to be very persistent in teaching for, prompting for, and reinforcing fluency. None of the teaching moves described here will work if the text is too hard for the reader. You have to first create a setting in which the reader is *capable* of fluency, then teach hard for it. The following actions combine both classroom and small-group instruction:

1. Provide many models of fluent reading through interactive read-aloud and shared reading.

2. Invite students to read with you so that you can support fluency.

3. Tell students what you and they are doing when they read fluently in shared reading.

4. Demonstrate and teach aspects of fluency before expecting students to use them as prompted.

5. Give students books that are accessible, so that students have the potential for fluent reading.

6. Teach aspects of fluency using a text that students have demonstrated they can read with high accuracy.

7. Prompt for aspects of fluency when you know students can do it. If they are not able to follow your prompt, show them what you mean through teaching.

8. Reinforce students' fluent reading as necessary (just after they have learned to do something).

9. Make short readers' theater pieces from the texts that students read in small-group instruction.

10. For small-group instruction, select engaging texts that students will find interesting and want to read with expression.

11. Be careful about increasing text levels. Have students demonstrate fluent, phrased reading to your satisfaction before going on to the next higher level.

12. Be very persistent in the pursuit of fluent reading.

Helping struggling readers process print fluently can be some of the hardest teaching you will ever do. But it will have a big payoff for your students. Many of them have never had the experience of performing like a proficient reader who is putting everything together in a fluid way. Being able to do so will encourage them to keep working.

Just then, City Mouse squeaked, "Run!"

"What's wrong?" cried Country Mouse.

"The people are here!" yelled City Mouse. "Run into that hole!"

The little mice ran as fast as they could into a hole in the wall. Country Mouse was shaking with fear.

"That was terrible!" said Country Mouse. "Does that happen all the time?"

"Oh," said City Mouse. "You get used to it after a while."

Country Mouse did not think that she could ever get used to it. City life was just too scary for her.

The mice sat inside the wall.

"We can have a nap here," said City Mouse. "This is nicer than your scratchy old hay bed."

Country Mouse didn't agree. But, tired from so much running, she closed her eyes and slept.

When the mice woke up, it was quiet.

"Let's go back out!" said City Mouse.

In the kitchen, the mice saw big plates of food everywhere.

Country Mouse sniffed and nibbled one delicious dish after another.

Then Country Mouse saw a beautiful piece of cheese in the corner.

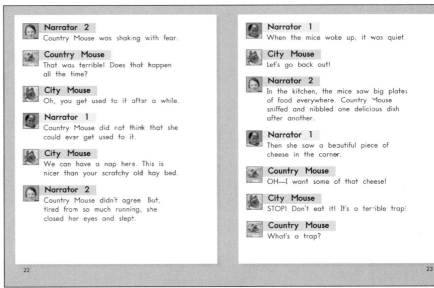

Narrator 2
Country Mouse was shaking with fear.

Country Mouse
That was terrible! Does that happen all the time?

City Mouse
Oh, you get used to it after a while.

Narrator 1
Country Mouse did not think that she could ever get used to it.

City Mouse
We can have a nap here. This is nicer than your scratchy old hay bed.

Narrator 2
Country Mouse didn't agree But, tired from so much running, she closed her eyes and slept.

Narrator 1
When the mice woke up, it was quiet.

City Mouse
Let's go back out!

Narrator 2
In the kitchen, the mice saw big plates of food everywhere. Country Mouse sniffed and nibbled one delicious dish after another.

Narrator 1
Then she saw a beautiful piece of cheese in the corner.

Country Mouse
OH—I want some of that cheese!

City Mouse
STOP! Don't eat it! It's a terrible trap!

Country Mouse
What's a trap?

Figure 16-25 Page Spreads from *The Lion and the Mouse* from Leveled Literacy Intervention, Green System (Heinemann 2009)

▶ Suggestions for Professional Development

ANALYZING THE DIMENSIONS OF FLUENCY

1. Set a challenge for your group! Prepare for a professional development meeting by recording about two minutes of reading for each of the students in one of your reading groups (or in your class). Record them on the second reading of a text but do not "rehearse" the reading.

2. At the beginning of the meeting, review the six dimensions of fluency (under the heading, Teaching for Fluency). If you have not previously read the section, you can "jig-saw read" it for a quick start. Divide the material into small parts, assign each part to a person, and take 10 or 15 minutes to individually read the assigned parts. Then, moving quickly, have each person share the information gained.

3. Then, listen to a few readers that no one knows. If you have *Fountas and Pinnell Benchmark Assessment System*, you will find readers on the DVDs that are included. Alternatively, if you have *Teaching for Comprehending and Fluency: Thinking, Talking, and Writing about Reading*, you will find a selection of readers on the DVD that is included with the book.

4. Then work as partners or in grade level groups to listen to and discuss the fluency of the readers you have taped.

5. Finally, select some areas of needed improvement. From the prompts in this chapter (or in *Prompting Guide 1*), select some that you may want to use with your students. Make some notes on your teaching plan so that you will have them handy.

Teaching for Comprehending: Thinking Before, During, and After Reading

READING MEANS READING WITH UNDERSTANDING. If lack of fluency is one characteristic of struggling readers, then limited comprehension is certainly another and is the more serious problem of the two. With struggling readers, we need to teach hard for understanding. In this chapter, we discuss the active process of comprehending texts and the role of attention. We provide suggestions for helping children deeply understand texts. Our goal is to help them think actively while reading: making predictions, inferring and connecting, synthesizing new information, and analyzing and critiquing the texts that they read.

Understanding reading comprehension is a journey in understanding the human mind.

Our human mind is both embodied—it involves a flow of energy and information that occurs within the body, including the brain—and relational, the dimension of the mind that involves the flow of energy and information occurring between people—from the writer to the reader, for example. Right now this flow from me as I type these words to you as you read them is shaping our minds—yours and mine. Even as I am imagining who you might be and your possible response, I am changing the flow of energy and information in my brain and body as a whole. As you absorb these words your mind is embodying this flow of energy and information as well.

—Daniel Siegel, *The Mindful Brain*, 5

Siegel sees mindful awareness as reflection that allows us to make choices and change: how we focus attention helps shape the activity and growth of the brain. He bases this thinking on Langer's concept of "mindful learning," which suggests that learning is more effective and enjoyable if it has a *conditional* rather than an *absolute* quality. Thinking is tentative, ready to change in response to new information. This suggests that the learner is active, creating and testing hypotheses in an ever changing network of understandings. As Langer says, we need to appreciate "the value of uncertainty" (Langer, p. 15).

Uncertainty is healthy and prevents individuals from falling into the trap of premature conclusions and habits that block learning. Their thinking is characterized by:

- ❏ Being open to the unexpected.
- ❏ Being aware of multiple perspectives.
- ❏ Being alert to what is happening in the present.
- ❏ Holding ideas conditionally.
- ❏ Noticing new things.
- ❏ Being sensitive to context.
- ❏ Being flexible about interpretation.

It is not that mindful learners do not come to conclusions and make decisions; they do. And they necessarily convert some actions into routines that require less attention. But they are always ready to detect anomalies. At any moment they see details with new eyes; they can shift gears, find new options, form new conjectures and questions.

Can we apply this idea to reading continuous text? "Reading continuous text is a sequential solving process involving a network of interacting systems. Working on texts, in either reading or writing, provides opportunities to develop this network" (Clay 2005, 89). Readers are flexible decision makers. They notice anomalies and search for information to make things fit. If readers do not solve the problem in one way, they try something else. They hold information tentatively, prepared to change ideas as they gather or communicate information. They process language in ways that create images and ideas. They ask and search for answers to questions, and they interpret information in the light of setting and circumstances. They pull together everything they know in order to make decisions as they move through continuous text. They have many resources on which they can draw, and they are

strategic in using their energy and resources. Every time they engage in this successful processing, they increase the capability of the neural network they are using. Their "brainwork" becomes faster and more proficient because they are building in-the-head systems. They actively notice things and have an effective way to remember what they notice:

> You relate what you hear or see to things you already understand. The moment of truth is the moment of input: how you attend, how much you care, how you encode, what you do with it, and how you organize it. How well you access it depends on how well you stored it in the first place. How do you become more savvy about the way you remember things? Have a good system. Notice your errors and try to fix them. (Squire, 1996, Dana Foundation Video, cited by Clay, 2006)

For proficient readers, *the act of reading actually changes the brain*. And working on errors is part of the process of learning. Duckworth (1987) says that "we must come to accept surprise, puzzlement, excitement, patience, caution, honest attempts and wrong outcomes as legitimate and important elements of learning" (69).

That doesn't sound like struggling readers, does it? Struggling readers are often passive, unable to call on resources, waiting for help, or trying the same ineffective strategy over and over again. Too often, remedial teaching has focused on "getting the reader through the book," "helping the reader remember the book," or "reading the words correctly." Even helping a reader understand a particular text falls far short of where we need to pitch our instruction. Our goal as teachers is to help readers build the neural network so that it becomes "smart enough" to expand on its own (Clay 2005). Readers need to be able to initiate problem-solving activities and become active and proficient.

That instructional focus is important for all readers, but it is critical for those who are having difficulty. Intervention instruction must be directed toward the creation of efficient processing networks—

ideally early on, because mechanical learning based on absolutes will lead to the habits that block learning and result in learned helplessness, poor self-esteem, or a variety of defense mechanisms, including off-task behavior. Clay (1972) argued for early intervention to prevent the downward spiral that is a likely possibility for struggling readers:

> An even greater problem is that the child has not failed to learn in his three years at school; he has tried to do his work, he has practised his primitive skills and he has habituated, daily, the wrong responses. He has learned; and all that learning stands like a block wall between the remedial teacher and the responses that she is trying to get established. A remedial programme must take what has to be unlearned into account. (11)

We are advocates of early intervention: this book and the Leveled Literacy Intervention Systems (Heinemann 2009) are directed toward readers who are having difficulty and need intervention to be able to read with competence and enjoyment. In a layered system such as that described in Chapter 21, timely intervention can greatly reduce the number of struggling readers in schools. Ideally a great deal of intervention work would be concentrated at grades K and 1, when only a little effort may put the child back on track (Reading Recovery is a powerful example of an intervention that addresses the problem in first grade). But we sometimes meet older learners who have been struggling for years. In that case, we need to intervene *immediately* using the kind of instruction that alters attention.

It is commonly accepted that attention is not a fixed entity. There are several different kinds of attention, and it is possible to influence attention through instruction. Siegel (2007) has described three dimensions of attention (see Figure 17-1):

1. *Alertness* refers to the degree to which the mind is open, prepared, and ready to respond to stimuli. Ideally, we would like readers to sustain a highly alert state so that they are able to notice the information they need. They do not search actively partly because they do not know how to

attend in this alert way. They either do not know that the information they need is there, or they do not know how to access and use it. This makes it very difficult for them to fix their errors; passivity is the result.

2. *Orientation* refers to the capacity of the brain to select information. Proficient readers choose, from a variety of options, the information that will be most helpful to them.

3. *Executive attention* means the way the brain functions to regulate thought. This kind of attention determines a focus, regulates emotions, and allows decision making. It comes into play when the reader "nearly knows" a response and tentatively tests it.

4. It detects and works on errors.

Looking at these three kinds of attention helps us to understand how much we can learn about readers by looking at what they do at a point of difficulty as they read—and it is there that we can be of most help to them. Enhancing executive attention has the power to break through the wall of habitual thinking.

Some of the early investigations of teacher-child interactions during Reading Recovery lessons showed that successful teachers tended to prompt and reinforce the child's search for and use of the full range of information needed for reading: meaning, language syntax, and visual information (see Lyons, Pinnell, and DeFord 1993). Less successful teachers tended to overemphasize the use of one kind of information and did not work for flexibility. Successful teachers tended to require independent

Figure 17-1	**Dimensions of Attention**
Alertness	Openness, readiness to respond, awareness of anticipated stimuli or arousal level.
Orientation	Capacity to select information and voluntarily shift attention.
Executive Attention	The general processes related to decision making, conflict resolution, error detection, and regulation of thoughts and feelings.

action and offer many opportunities for the student to negotiate meaning through talk. They observed closely and selected teaching points in ways that helped children build systems of understanding. As Clay (1985) has said:

> Sensitive and systematic observation of young children's reading and writing behaviors provides teachers with feedback which can shape their next teaching moves. Teaching can then be likened to a conversation in which you listen to the speaker carefully before you reply. (6)

Readers and writers make imperfect, approximate attempts, but the teacher helps learners expand and refine the response. In doing so, they integrate information. This can happen only when individuals are reading continuous text, which provides the opportunity to build the network, or assemble "working systems" they can apply to increasingly challenging tasks.

Deeper thinking begins when children hear stories. They gather information, make predictions, laugh, shiver, and feel satisfied. Most young children enter school believing that learning to read will be as easy as everything else they have done (eating, walking, talking). They expect reading will be meaningful, and you want to be sure those expectations are met as they begin to read easy texts.

▶ Text Choice

We recently had the opportunity to think in a different way about the structure of texts. We worked with authors, illustrators, and a publishing company to create hundreds of books that would:

❏ Appeal to children and engage their attention.

❏ Provide a ladder of progress that would support readers in doing effective processing from Levels A to N.

❏ Provide the variety that allows readers to become flexible.

❏ Draw readers into the texts and provoke deeper thinking.

❏ Offer opportunities for building the network of strategic in-the-head actions, *even for readers who previously were having great difficulty.*

Over several years we worked on every detail of these texts. We moved from first drafts to fully illustrated publications, and in the process, we added a great deal to our understanding of text selection to support readers. It was a major advantage to be able to control some of the factors that influence readers' decision making.

First, we asked authors to come up with appealing stories rather than to "write for a level." This direction made the process take much longer but it underscored how important it is to create interesting texts that children want to read. Refining the texts for reading instruction taught us a lot (see Figure 17-2).

Figure 17-2 **Thinking About Text Choices for Readers Who Struggle**
• Engage the readers with delightful texts.
• Think about the way the child will understand the text.
• Use books that have print features that support rather than impede comprehension.
• Use texts with language that is accessible to the reader.
• Use books with text structures that the reader can access and understand.
• Use texts with illustrations that support meaning and do not confuse the readers.

Engage Readers with Delightful Texts

Every reader needs engagement. As adults we have wonderful control over what we read. Except for a few job-related texts, we can simply put down one that does not interest us. Children in school have no such control, although we would like for them to have some choice. They must read, so we need to make sure that what we offer will make them want to read more.

Readers who struggle have an even greater need for wonderful texts. The first book in the Orson and Taco series, for example (see Figure 17-3), sets the scene for reading more about these appealing characters. *Friends* is not a narrative in the truest sense. (There is no problem or resolution.) But meaning does build to the ending in which a twist of perspective adds interest.

Figure 17-3 Page Layout of *Friends* from Leveled Literacy Intervention, Green System (Heinemann 2009)

Think About the Way the Child Will Understand the Text

Consider the meaning of the text from the child's perspective. Children need something they can relate to their own lives and understandings. As teachers think about what readers can take from the text they might ask, *does the text have enough support to allow them to predict, to make inferences, to learn something new?* Notice that *Eggs* is quite easy, but there is information to interest the reader (see Figure 17-4). And it is presented in a very simple categorical structure. This informational text is *not* a story. Instead a different example of a unifying concept is presented on each page. This book is a very simple example of presenting information in categories.

We cannot underestimate the role of early books. Through them, children learn how to process information while using print. They rely heavily on their own language knowledge and on your introduction, in which you can give them the information they need. You enable them to use background knowledge; you give them tools they can use to search for and use the information in the text. You set them up for a successful reading experience by removing the obstacles.

Use Books That Have Print Features That Support Rather Than Impede Comprehension

If you look at the layout of *Friends*, you see a simple font with clear spaces between words and lines. This very easy text does not even require the beginning reader to return to the left margin after reading a line. The print is on an otherwise blank page against a white background. When choosing texts for beginning readers, especially those who have confusions, everything needs to be easy to perceive. *Eggs*, too, is a very friendly layout (a simple font with clear spaces), although a little harder than *Friends*.

As you progress up the gradient, the layout of print gradually becomes more complex, but even in higher-level texts, you do not want a lot of "noise." It is amazing how a text that seems accessible can be confusing. All readers need to learn to deal with complex text features, but like everything else, gradual exposure is key.

Use Texts with Language That Is Accessible to the Reader

Think about the match between children's oral language and the language in the texts you are offering them. Written language will always be different from oral language, but at earlier levels, it needs to be close. Early texts must have very simple sentences such as those in *Friends* and *Eggs*. Midlevel texts like *All About Sled Dogs* (see Figure 17-5) and *The Great Big Enormous Turnip* (see Figure 17-6) have language patterns that are fairly consistent with typical oral language patterns, although as written language they have a more formal quality.

As children move to reading higher levels of text, written language becomes much more complex and exceeds the oral language complexity of most children—see the pages from *A Dragon's Lullaby* reproduced in Figure 17-7, for example. Readers come to expect this complexity and have built the knowledge they need to process the language over many readings of texts that gradually become more challenging. This gradual increase is essential for building the network; the challenge is not so hard that it breaks down the processing system, but it is hard enough to expand the system. *All About Volcanoes* (see the pages reproduced in Figure 17-8) illustrates some of the very complex vocabulary, sentence structure, and graphic features that characterize informational texts as children move up the text gradient.

Use Books with Text Structures That the Reader Can Access and Understand

Think about the reader's current ability to follow a story or cope with different kinds of organization. It is easy to see how *Eggs* "works" as a text. *All About Sled*

Figure 17-4 Page Layout of *Eggs* from Leveled Literacy Intervention, Green System (Heinemann 2009)

Figure 17-5 Page Spread from *All About Sled Dogs,* from Leveled Literacy Intervention, Blue System (Heinemann 2009)

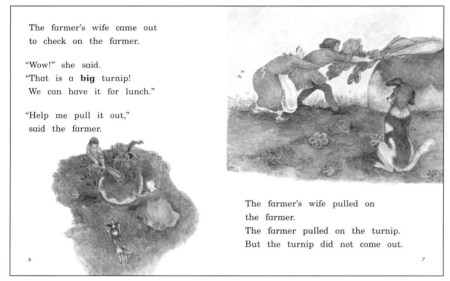

Figure 17-6 Page Spread from *The Great Big Enormous Turnip* from Leveled Literacy Intervention, Blue System (Heinemann 2009)

Figure 17-7 Page Spread from *A Dragon's Lullaby* from Leveled Literacy Intervention, Blue System (Heinemann 2009)

Dogs is more complicated. On each page you learn facts in a new category. *The Great Big Enormous Turnip* has a repeating pattern that makes the text more available. *A Dragon's Lullaby* has a more challenging text structure: a problem, a series of events, a climax, and an ending. Embedded within this fantasy are two other genres—a letter and poetry.

Readers become able to deal with text complexity by experiencing many different kinds of organization, always moving from simple to more complex, supported by teaching that reveals to them how the text "works." In doing this teaching, your goal is not so much to enable readers to process this particular text as to help them learn to figure out how texts are organized.

Use Texts with Illustrations That Support Meaning and Do Not Confuse the Reader

Oh, No!, another very easy book in the Orson and Taco series (see Figure 17-9), delivers a story line through the illustrations. Taco's owner encounters a number of disasters in the house and finally tracks down the source. Just think about how this story would sound if you read it aloud without the illustrations! Beginning readers can process only very simple sentences, but they still need a well-defined story. The illustrations carry the burden of meaning for readers at these levels. We discovered just how difficult it is to craft illustrations that appeal to readers, provide the information they need, and communicate meaning.

Guiding the construction of texts, we realized more fully just how impor-

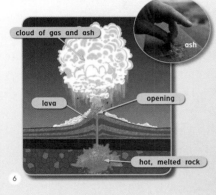

Chapter 2

How a Volcano Forms

Mount Saint Helens is a volcano. A volcano is an opening in the Earth through which lava, ash, and gases come out. Lava is hot, melted rock that comes from deep inside the Earth. Ash is small bits of lava and rock.

cloud of gas and ash

ash

lava

opening

hot, melted rock

6

Gas gets trapped in melted rock inside the Earth. The gas escapes when a volcano explodes. Then lava and rocks shoot out. This is a little like shaking a bottle of soda and then opening it. The gas in the soda causes the liquid to bubble up over the top of the bottle.

7

Figure 17-8 Page Spread from *All About Volcanoes* from Leveled Literacy Intervention, Blue System (Heinemann 2009)

tant illustrations are as well as how they can confuse struggling readers. In the early texts you choose, be sure that the illustrations are spare, with no distracting information. For example, suppose in the picture on page 5, you also saw a bone, some trash, and a sock. Or, suppose Taco's owner were not looking at the water. As it is, the reader can predict either *bowl* or *water* and use the print. Compare the "working copy" for pages 4 and 5 with the final page spread shown in Figure 17-10. Time and again, we had to delete details from the illustrations, move objects and characters, and change the appearance of characters to make the text accessible for emerging readers.

As they gain proficiency, readers can deal with much more complexity in the illustrations, and including more detail increases an illustration's appeal. At the same time, illustrations become less important because the text includes more information than can be conveyed in pictures. At this point, the illustrations enhance meaning and extend understanding, but they do not provide enough information to be able to read the text. Reading is

all about the print and will be for the rest of the readers' literate lives.

▶ Systems of Strategic Actions: All Roads Lead to Comprehension

The twelve categories of strategic actions (see Figure 2-1) that make up the language processing system are not separate from one another, nor are they linear. They occur in the head, simultaneously, and with speed—"fast brainwork." However, we categorize the systems to help us think about the complex cognitive actions that make up the network in the brain as we process text (see Figure 17-11).

All these actions are used by the reader; each makes its own contribution to comprehension. Cued by the language in print, the proficient reader integrates strategic activities, and this can happen only when processing continuous text. In the process, the network is expanded. We discuss these strategic actions further at the end of this chapter.

▶ Building the Neural Network Through Reading Texts

Several kinds of reading contribute to the expansion of the network of strategic actions.

Rereading Familiar Texts

Rereading texts provides the opportunity to practice smooth processing. Since students have already read the text with instructional support, they are reading with

Figure 17-9 Page Layout of *Oh No!* from Leveled Literacy Intervention, Green System (Heinemann 2009)

Figure 17-10 Working Copy and Final Pages for *Oh No!*

good understanding; they can notice more detail in the meaning and in the print. Rereading is a way to shape a fast, efficient processing system. If you take a Reading Record on students' second reading of an instructional level text, you will gain excellent insights into the way they are processing continuous print. Their behaviors will help you identify the information they are using and neglecting as they construct the messages of the text, and that will guide your teaching interactions.

Reading New Texts Independently

It is important for developing readers to learn how to take on new material independently. You can provide this opportunity by making previously unseen independent level texts available. Texts at a reader's independent level will need only a brief introduction. Ease in processing new texts builds confidence and makes reading more interesting and enjoyable. The reader feels competent.

Figure 17-11 **Strategic Activities Involved in Comprehending Texts** *(also see Figure 2-1 and the discussion in Chapter 2)*

Thinking Within the Text	Thinking Beyond the Text	Thinking About the Text
Solving Words	Predicting	Analyzing
Monitoring	Making Connections	Critiquing
Searching	Synthesizing	
Summarizing	Inferring	
Maintaining Fluency		
Adjusting		

Reading Instructional Level Texts

A new book at the instructional level introduces new requirements while taking advantage of what readers already know and can do. It provides the opportunity to "settle these new things into the integrated networks of knowledge that this child already controls" (Clay 2005, p. 90). Taking on a new book that is harder than their independent reading level has the highest instructional value for building students' processing network. In stretching to accomplish this task, readers must use everything in their repertoire. In the new book, there will be at least one and probably almost all of the following challenges:

❑ Unfamiliar words—longer, with more syllables or more complex patterns.

❑ More complex sentence structures with accompanying punctuation—dependent and independent phrases, lists divided by commas, various kinds of dialogue (assigned, unassigned, split).

❑ Less familiar vocabulary—harder tier 1 words (in common oral language) and some tier 2 words (less common).

❑ More complex text structures—longer stories, plots with more episodes, informational texts with categories and subcategories.

❑ Harder genres—historical fiction, biography, fantasy, hybrid texts.

❑ Less support from illustrations and/or more demanding graphics.

❑ Denser print with less space.

Chapter 6 includes a detailed description of text factors and how they make demands on readers. It is all-important that readers take on new instructional level texts with effective processing. Good text selection and sequencing *as well as* strong teaching support are the key to "making it easy" for struggling readers to learn.

▶ Supporting Readers Before, During, and After Reading

Through your teaching you help readers process instructional level texts by smoothly integrating all the strategic actions that proficient readers use. Your effective teaching surrounds the reading in a way that simultaneously challenges and supports readers. Think of it as helping readers use their processing network successfully. If that happens, good comprehension will be the outcome.

Introducing Texts in Ways That Assure Comprehension

The introduction is key in supporting readers' ability to construct meaning while reading a new instructional level text. In the introduction, you can recognize and evoke what children already know. You can direct the conversation to any aspect of the text that you think will be too challenging for children to understand without your help. Remember that the first reading is not a *test* of what the reader can do; instead, it should be an exercise in successful processing because you made sure readers had the tools to work it through. You want to help children understand the structure—how the whole text works. They need this framework to organize their thinking—it is a more powerful tool in supporting comprehension than pre-teaching words. Recognizing the theme, overarching concept, or patterns such as comparison and contrast or problem and solution provides strong support for constructing meaning.

Point out unfamiliar words (*musher* in *All About Sled Dogs*, for example), either showing how to solve the word or clarifying its meaning. New texts some- times present a familiar word in a new context with a different meaning—in *Down the River*, for example, the words *down* and *up* have different meanings from the ones children probably know. Knowing this new meaning is essential for understanding the story. Likewise, on page 4 of *A Dragon's Lullaby*, the text says, "The village was so still you could hear a star shoot across the sky." This is literary language in which *shoot* appears in a context the child might not immediately understand.

Help readers see the text from their own perspec- tive so that they can relate to it and make connec- tions. Drawing attention to the pictures is helpful, but the introduction is *not* a "picture walk"—it is about orienting the reader to the meaning of the whole text. You would not look at every picture, and it is not about the pictures. The *teaching* during the introduc- tion should help readers understand the text. It is not a time to have readers browse through the pictures on their own. Your moves will teach them what to do when they read a book. Look at the introduction to the lower-level text *Down the River* in Figure 17-12 (a number of pages from the book are reproduced in Figure 17-13). Ms. A used this text for shared reading first and then asked students to read it independently.

Ms. A was getting the students ready to listen to and learn from introductions. She moved from help- ing students become familiar with the language of the text to assisting word solving. At the end of the intro- duction, she encouraged children to make predictions based on the information she gave them. Also, she made clear the new meanings for *up* and *down* that children are meeting in the text.

In the introduction to *Eggs* (also a very easy text) in Figure 17-14, Mrs. B helped students predict and infer. The text is unified by the idea that some animals come out of eggs that are hatched. The babies that come out of the eggs are the same kind of animal as the mother who hatched them. Ms. B helped students access their background information and make con- nections. What they did not know, she provided. While prompting for meaning, she also assisted in word solving.

In introducing *The Great Big Enormous Turnip* (see Figure 17-15), Ms. C knew that children had good background knowledge. She affirmed their background knowledge and called attention to the genre and the literary language. She asked them to make inferences and predictions.

Most children are probably familiar with dogs, but the idea of sled dogs who race may be new. In the intro- duction to *All About Sled Dogs* in Figure 17-16, Mr. D provided quite a bit of background knowledge both to interest children and help them bring meaning to the text. Pictures are very important in the process. He used and explained vocabulary from the text and explained the meaning of a graphic. He also had children run a finger along the route of the sled dogs. One of his goals was to help children learn how to add new information to their funds of knowledge (to *synthesize*).

As mentioned earlier, *A Dragon's Lullaby* is a com- plex text that includes a great deal of literary language. In introducing the text (see Figure 17-17), Ms. E made sure to use and explain some difficult vocabulary words. She also used language from the text and was very explicit about helping children notice and identify the different genre (poetry) embedded within the text. She invited the children to make inferences and prompted them to think about problem and solution.

Students are fascinated by volcanoes. In intro- ducing *All About Volcanoes* (see Figure 17-18), Ms. F realized that students knew something about volca- noes but needed help with cause and effect. The text also required them to search for information in a more complicated graphic than they had previously interpreted.

Sometimes when reading nonfiction, students do not know where to look for information. Here, Ms. F did some very explicit teaching to help them know how to search for information on page 2. She told stu- dents what the section was about on page 6 and let them know how it would help them. She demon- strated figuring out the definition of a technical word by using context and reminded students to use text features such as headings.

What you do before reading has everything to do with the reader's fluent processing and comprehension

Figure 17-12 Introduction to *Down the River*

Speaker	Teaching Moves	Contributions to Comprehension
Ms. A	This book is called *Down the River*. Here you see a little girl and her mom and dad. They are going down the river in a canoe. Have any of you ever been in a boat or canoe?	*Uses language and vocabulary from the text.* *Checks for background knowledge.*
Jason	I've been in a boat. It's a little different.	
Irinia	A motorboat?	
Jason	With a motor on the lake.	
Ms. A	They are going down the river. That means they are going the same way the river is flowing. It's like saying "going down the hall" or "down the street." If they turn around, they would be going up the river.	*Uses language from the text.* *Clarifies a concept and new meaning for words. Foreshadows the ending.*
Ms. A	The girl is saying, "We went down the river." Say *went*.	*Assists word solving.*
Children	*Went.*	
Ms. A	What would you expect to see at the beginning of went?	*Assists word solving.*
Children	*W.*	
Ms. A	Find *went* on this page. *[Children locate the word.]* And look at Mom in the picture. She is telling them to look at the boat. See how she is pointing? All the time they are going down the river they are seeing different things and saying, "Look at that."	*Provides information.*
	Ms. A guides the children through the text as they name some of the things they see.	*Provides information.* *Checks vocabulary.*
Ms. A	You would see all of those things if you went down the river. But look at page 14. Do you know what that big animal is?	*Engages interest.*
Irinia	A moose!	
Ms. A	That moose is really big. Do you think they should turn around and go *up* the river?	*Encourages prediction.*
Jason	Yes!	
Irinia	I would.	
Ms. A	Go back to the beginning and read to see what happens.	*Raises expectations.*

of texts. It makes no sense to allow students to read page after page ineffectively. When you provide an introduction, you are not "giving away the text." You are making it possible for the reader to experience excellent understanding, which not only develops the neural network but satisfies the emotions, which is the heart of motivation and mediates all other thinking (see Chapters 19 and 20).

Interactions During Reading to Support Comprehension

In Chapters 14, 15, and 16, we describe ways that you can teach for, prompt for, and reinforce effective reading behaviors. Chapter 15 includes many examples of prompts you can use to help readers stay in touch with the meaning. Examples include:

Figure 17-13 Page Spreads from *Down the River* from Leveled Literacy Intervention, Blue System (Heinemann 2009)

❑ "The picture will help you think about this part of the story."

❑ "You can think about the story."

❑ You said [*repeat reader's miscue*]. That doesn't go with this part of the story."

❑ "Are you thinking about what will happen next?"

❑ "Are you thinking about the story?"

❑ "Think about what you have learned so far."

❑ "Think about what has happened in the story so far."

❑ "You were thinking about what you know."

Language like that above prompts readers to think about the meaning of the larger text rather than just the meaning of the sentence. But you will want to be very selective in teaching and prompting while children are engaged in the hard work of reading an instructional level text. Too much talking can interrupt processing and undermine comprehension. If the introduction was well done, you will have removed many obstacles, so there are just a few problems for the readers to solve.

Another way of interacting and encouraging readers to think is to use the "spaces" in the reading—when readers are turning pages or stopping to look at a picture. Sometimes, too, a reader will ask you an on-the-spot question. Here are some examples:

Tyler has just finished reading page 15 of A Dragon's Lullaby.

Ms. E: He looks happy, doesn't he? I wonder if he will sing to them again. *[Tyler turns the page and reads the ending.]*

Children are reading Down the River *in a shared way. They stop at page 15.*

Ms. A: Be thinking what they should do now. *[He turns the page and they read the ending.]*

Seiko turns to page 10 of The Great Big Enormous Turnip.

Ms. C: I'm noticing that the characters are getting smaller. Can the mouse really help?

Figure 17-14 Introduction to *Eggs*

Speaker	Teaching Moves	Contributions to Comprehension
Mrs. B	This book is about mothers and their babies. It is called *Eggs*, because lots of animals lay eggs and their babies grow inside the eggs. What did you notice about the mother on the cover?	*Provides background information. Asks children to search for information in the pictures.*
Waverly	She's sitting on the eggs. That keeps them warm.	
Mrs. B	Yes, this is Mother Hen and she laid some eggs. Are you thinking about what is happening inside the eggs?	*Prompts inference using background knowledge.*
Waverly	The little chicks are getting bigger.	
Mrs. B	Turn to page 2. There is Mother Hen. Point and read page 2. Look at the picture on page 3. So now what will happen to the eggs?	*Invites prediction.*
Waverly	The little birds will come out.	
Richard	The eggs hatch.	
Mrs. B	Baby chicks came out of those eggs. How do you suppose the chicks did that?	*Prompts inference using background information.*
Spencer	They peck with their beaks.	
Mrs. B	They peck the egg shell and it cracks. "Crack! Crack! Crack!" Look at the mark after the word *crack*. It's an exclamation point. When you see that mark, make your voice sound excited. It is exciting when the eggs crack open and the babies come out. Like this *[reads]*, "Crack! Crack! Crack!" Read that all together.	*Confirms inference using background information.* *Draws attention to punctuation and relates it to meaning.*
Children	"Crack! Crack! Crack!"	
Mrs. B	You sounded excited. Let's see what other kinds of babies came out of the eggs. Look at page 6.	*Reinforces fluency.* *Prompts searching for information.*
Waverly	Baby fish.	
Mrs. B	Those are baby fish. The eggs they came out of are really thin, so the babies just pop out of the eggs.	*Provides background information.*
	They browse through the text, identifying baby animals.	*Clarifies meaning.*
Mrs. B	What do you think those baby ducks will say?	*Asks for prediction using background information.*
Spencer	Quack, quack!	
Mrs. B	Turn the page and see if you are right? *Quack* would start like *queen* on our chart.	*Assists word solving.*

Figure 17-15 Introduction to *The Great Big Enormous Turnip*

Speaker	Teaching Actions	Contributions to Comprehension
Ms. C	The title of today's story is *The Great Big Enormous Turnip*. Have you ever heard a story with a title like that?	*Checks background knowledge.*
Natasha	The turnip is real big and they have to pull it out but it's really hard.	
Seiko	I think it was a watermelon.	
Janine	It came up and they all fell down.	
Ms. C	I see you all already know something about the story. This is the kind of story that you hear or read again and again. So now you get to read another version. Turn to page 2. This story starts with the words *one day*. Lots of these kinds of stories start with words like that. There is the farmer. He just planted a turnip seed. Then he went to bed. Look at page 3. Say and then find the word *night* on this page.	*Affirms background knowledge.* *Communicates something about the genre.* *Brings attention to literary language.* *Provides information.* *Assists word solving.*
	The children say and locate night.	
Ms. C	I want you to look closely at the word *night*. It has *igh* in the middle like *sight* and *might*.	*Assists word solving.*
Seiko	It says *i* in the middle.	
Ms. C	What else do you notice about page 3?	*Prompts attention to the layout.*
Janine	The print gets bigger.	
Ms. C	It gets bigger because the writer wants you to say it louder. Why do you suppose?	*Prompts inference.*
Natasha	Because the turnip is getting bigger?	
Ms. C	I think you might be right. Go to page 4. When the farmer came out to check on the turnip, he saw how big it was. I wonder what will happen.	*Affirms thinking.* *Invites prediction.*
Seiko	They are going to pull it up.	
Ms. C	Now go to pages 10 and 11. They are all pulling the turnip now. Turn the page and you will see that a little mouse ran up. At first they told him, "You are too little to help." But then look over on page 13. Does it look like the mouse can help?	*Provides information.* *Uses language from the text.* *Invites prediction.*
Janine	They're going to pull it up!	
Seiko	The mouse is the one who did it.	
Ms. C	Read to find out what happens.	*Prompts searching for information.*

Figure 17-16 Introduction to *All About Sled Dogs*

Speaker	Teaching Actions	Contributions to Comprehension
Mr. D	You have another informational book today. It is called *All About Sled Dogs*. What do you know about sled dogs?	*Checks background knowledge.*
Lila	*[Shakes head.]*	
Matt	You can have them pull something.	
Sheldon	*[Shakes head.]*	
Mr. D	The sled dogs can pull a sled. In this picture they are running in a race. Sled dogs love to run fast. Turn the page and say *strong*. What are the first three letters you expect to see?	*Provides background information.* *Assists word solving.*
Children	s–t–r	
Mr. D	*Str* is a consonant cluster. Let's look at page 6. Sled dogs are always out in the cold. They have thick fur to keep them warm and they wear booties on their feet. The booties protect their feet.	*Assists word solving.* *Provides background knowledge.* *Uses language from the text.* *Uses vocabulary.* *Explains concepts.*
	Mr. D has children say protect, *predict the consonant cluster, and locate the word.*	
Mr. D	Turn to page 8. The dogs that lead the team are up front. Now look at page 11. The dog team has a driver. The driver is called a musher. Put your finger on the word *musher*. You can see a musher in the picture. And in the box there are some words that mushers use. I'll read the word and you read what it means.	*Uses and explains vocabulary from the text.* *Prompts readers to search for meaning in the pictures.*
	Mr. D reads the words and children read and talk about the meaning.	
Mr. D	Turn to page 11. In some informational books you will find maps. This map shows a very important race in Alaska. Do you see the little drawing that shows the way the sled dog is going? Take your finger and move it from Anchorage to Nome. The dog teams race mile after mile on the ice and snow.	*Explains the meaning of a graphic in the text.* *Provides background information.*
Matt	That's a real long way.	
Lila	Do they run all the time?	
Mr. D	I have never seen it, but I think they do stop to rest sometimes. Go back to the beginning. You will be learning some new things in this book. So when we get back together, you can share something new that you have learned about sled dogs.	*Prompts readers to identify new information (synthesize).*

Figure 17-17	**Introduction to *A Dragon's Lullaby***	
Speaker	**Teaching Actions**	**Contributions to Comprehension**
Ms. E	Your new book is called *A Dragon's Lullaby*. It's about a kindly dragon named Dario. He was very kind, so in this story the writer calls him kindly.	*Uses language from the story. Connects a new vocabulary word to the base word.*
Molly	Dario the Dragon! Is a dragon like a dinosaur?	
Rashid	No, it's just something in stories.	
Ms. E	Turn to page 3 and you will see Dario's castle high on a mountain. Dario had golden wings, and every night he flew over the village below and sang lullabies. He sang to the villagers. That means the people who lived in the village—the villagers. Say that word—*villagers*.	*Provides information. Clarifies a new vocabulary word.*
Children	*Villagers.*	
Ms. E	The villagers are the people who live in the town—the village. Do you see the print that looks like a poem? Listen while I read it. [Reads the poem.]	*Explains a new vocabulary word. Draws attention to a new genre within the narrative text. Demonstrates how to read the poem.*
Tyler	It sounds kind of like a song.	
Rashid	It rhymes.	
Ms. E	So every night when Dario began to sing, the children would look for his long, golden wings that sparkled in the moonlight. And they got very sleepy. The lullabies were soothing. Do you know what that means?	*Provides background information. Uses language from the text. Uses vocabulary words from the text. Draws attention to a new vocabulary word and asks for derivation of meaning from context.*
Rashid	They put people to sleep.	
Lily	They kind of got sleepy listening to him sing and because he was so nice to them.	
Molly	It was night so they went to sleep. His lullabies were soothing. His wings were gold?	*Repeats vocabulary.*
Ms. E	He had golden wings. His lullabies sort of helped people settle down. They were soothing. It was peaceful and they could go to sleep easier. Dario would say, "Good night, sleep tight." But no one ever answered. Why do you think?"	*Clarifies meaning of a new vocabulary word. Uses language from the text. Invites inference.*
Rashid	Because they were all asleep!	
Lily	Or maybe they didn't even know he was there.	
Ms. E	We will find out. Turn to page 6. One night Dario did not appear. They couldn't fall asleep. They were unhappy. They were miserable. That's a long word. Find it and I'll show you how to take it apart.	*Invites searching for information. Provides information. Uses a new vocabulary word. Assists word solving.*
	Ms. E shows the children the four syllables on the whiteboard and has them notice the syllables in the word in the text.	

continues

Figure 17-17	**Introduction to *A Dragon's Lullaby, continued***	
Speaker	**Teaching Actions**	**Contributions to Comprehension**
Ms. E	On this page it says that Dario stopped singing. Why do you suppose?	*Invites inference.*
Molly	He got tired of it.	
Tyler	He thought they didn't appreciate him.	
Ms. E	Those could both be reasons. Remember how sad he was that they didn't answer him when he said good night, sleep tight. That could be a reason, too.	*Affirms inference and offers more information.*
Tyler	He thought they didn't like him?	
Ms. E	The villagers are going to have to do something to get Dario to sing those soothing lullabies again. Turn to page 12. So they wrote a special lullaby for Dario. Turn the page, and I'll read what they wrote. *[Reads the lullaby on page 14 and points out the word* soothing.*]* Turn back to the beginning and find out what happens. When you finish, we'll talk about what the problem was and how the villagers solved it.	*Identifies the problem and the solution. Demonstrates how to read the poem. Prompts children to think about the problem and the solution.*

SEIKO: He's little but he can help. *[Continues reading.]*

Dominic has just finished reading All About Volcanoes.

Ms. F: Wow, I wonder about that mountain.

DOMINIC: It could erupt again. It says it's door mat.

Ms. F: Close! Do you know what *dormant* means?

DOMINIC: I thought it was sort of still like a door mat.

Ms. F: You are thinking. *Dormant* means it is not active—kind of like sleeping. But….

DOMINIC: It could go off again.

Matt is reading page 8 of All About Sled Dogs.

MATT: "Sled dogs work as a team." It's like a soccer team?

MR. D: "Team" means any time people or animals work together. These dogs are a racing team. They pull the sled together and race other teams. *[Matt continues reading.]*

Katie is reading page 6 of All About Volcanoes.

KATIE: "Lava is hot, melted rock that comes from deep inside the Earth. Ash is small bits of lava and rock." How can ash be the same as lava?

Ms. F: See the part that says "very small bits"? That means really, really small, even smaller than sand. Like very fine dust. You can see it in the inset picture.

KATIE: Yes. *[Continues reading.]*

Interactions like these take only seconds and prompt the reader to stay connected to the meaning and think a little more deeply about the stories or informational texts.

Teaching After Reading

The discussion after reading a text can be brief, *but it is essential.* You have attended to the deeper meaning of the text in the introduction and sometimes in brief interactions during reading. There may be little left to say, but now you have an opportunity to return briefly to the text and ratchet up the understanding. Students may have comments to offer. There may be further insights you want to elicit. As in the introduction, you are always working to help

Figure 17-18	**Introduction to *All About Volcanoes***	
Speaker	**Teaching Actions**	**Contributions to Comprehension**
Ms. F	You have an informational text today called *All About Volcanoes*. There is a picture of a volcano on the cover. What do you know about volcanoes?	*Checks background knowledge.*
Katie	They happen in mountains. The lava builds up and then it just blows out the top. It kills a lot of people.	
Lorenzo	There was one on TV and it made everything turn all black like it was burned or ashy or something.	
Dominic	It's like a big bomb or something—an explosion.	
Ms. F	I see that you know a lot. You will find out more about volcanoes from this book. Turn to page 2. This heading says *Mount Saint Helens* and you see a photograph of it. In 1980 this mountaintop exploded. Turn the page and you can see the destruction. The print in the red inset box gives you more information. In that box you will see that scientists saw clues that Mount Saint Helens was about to erupt and so they could save lives by telling people to leave. What are you thinking?	*Recognizes background knowledge.* *Provides information.* *Points out the function of text features.* *Invites thinking.*
Dominic	It's really good they found it out because a lot of people could get killed if it erupts.	
Ms. F	Let's go to page 6. This section will help you understand what causes a volcano to erupt. Remember if you don't know what something is, look for the definition in the print. It says that lava comes out of the opening. I can read that lava is hot, melted rock that comes from deep inside the Earth.	*Draws attention to cause and effect.* *Demonstrates how to figure out the definition of a vocabulary word from context.*
Katie	You read us another book about a whole city that was covered with lava.	
Ms. F	That's right! It was Pompeii. I want you to look quickly through the book and read the headings. There are two headings on this page.	*Recognizes connection.* *Draws attention to the organization of the text.* *Draws attention to text features.*
Lorenzo	*[Reading.]* Chapter One. Mount Saint Helens.	
Ms. F	When you get to page 10, stop.	
	Children read to page 10.	
Ms. F	Dominic, you said that the volcano can erupt, meaning that it explodes out the top. Find *erupt* on this page. *[Children do.]* Now find *erupted*. Turn back to the beginning and look at the Table of Contents.	*Assists in word solving.* *Draws attention to text organization and the text feature.*
Katie	They are like the headings.	
Ms. F	Remember that the heading will help you know what the section is about. When you are finished, we are going to talk about what makes a volcano erupt.	*Reminds readers how to use text structure. Prompts readers to search for information about cause and effect.*

readers orchestrate the systems of strategic actions. You are also looking for evidence of their understanding through the talk.

In the discussion of *All About Volcanoes* in Figure 17-19, Ms. F did not ask for a "retelling." Instead, she asked a question that helped her get evidence of student understanding. "What did you learn about volcanoes that was interesting to you?" is fundamentally different from, "Tell me the information in this text." Ms. F was tapping into what engaged students, but also

what was new to them. They were able to *synthesize* this knowledge because it engaged them. Notice, too, that Ms. F prompted students to interpret the diagram and asked for evidence from the text. This helps prepare students for rigorous tests of their comprehension that may not be as user friendly as a conversation.

A Dragon's Lullaby offers significant challenges to young readers. The patterns of cause and effect or problem and solution require deeper thinking. A brief discussion after the reading (see Figure 17-20)

Figure 17-19 Excerpt from the Discussion of *All About Volcanoes*

Speaker	Teaching Actions	Contributions to Comprehension
Ms. F	What did you learn about volcanoes that was interesting to you?	*Asks for selected information.*
Katie	It's a good thing that scientists can tell when they are going to erupt. They are really dangerous.	
Lorenzo	The most interesting page was where they showed you what the mountain looks like inside.	
Ms. F	Take us to that page and let's all look at it.	*Draws attention to evidence in the text.*
Lorenzo	The lava is down here and it goes up this tunnel and blows out the top.	
Katie	I think it's the gas that blows the top off and the melted rock pours out, too.	
Dominic	Yeah, and when it cools off it's just rock again but it looks kind of like water.	
Ms. F	That diagram is really helpful, isn't it? Anything else?	*Asks for interpretation of the diagram.*
Dominic	When it pops, it's like a soda can that sprays all over you.	*Affirms understanding.*
Ms. F	Like a pretty big one!	
Katie	And it burns everything up.	
Ms. F	It was surprising to me to learn that volcanoes can do some good. Do you remember that part?	*Prompts for key understanding.*
Lorenzo	They make islands.	
Ms. F	Let's look at page 12.	*Prompts to search in the text.*
Katie	The ashes make the ground good for growing things.	
Dominic	And they can make hot water.	
Ms. F	So I guess there are good things and bad things about volcanoes.	*States a key understanding.*

helped Ms. E know if the students understood the nuances. She prompted children to offer evidence from the text and consider text structure (problem and solution). She also drew attention to the literary language.

Making Teaching Points to Support Comprehending

The purpose of making teaching points after reading is *not* to fix up mistakes readers made while

Figure 17-20	**Excerpt from the Discussion of *A Dragon's Lullaby***	
Speaker	**Teaching Actions**	**Contributions to Comprehension**
Ms. E	Well, what do you think about Dario?	*Invites comments.*
Rashid	He was happy at the end.	
Molly	He started singing songs again.	
Ms. E	Yes, he did. But I'm wondering why.	*Probes for inference (cause and effect).*
Tyler	Because they sang to him.	
Ms. E	Well, how did that help him ?	*Probes for more evidence.*
Molly	Because he knew they liked him.	
Rashid	No, it's because he thought they were asleep and so they couldn't say good night.	
Ms. E	Take us to the part in the text that makes you think that.	*Asks for evidence from the text.*
Lily	It's on the last page. Page 16. See, he was sad because they didn't say good night. But now he knows they were just asleep. Because he didn't say good night to them.	
Tyler	He was asleep.	
Rashid	It says *[reading]*, "But this time Dario knew why. His lullabies had put all the villagers to sleep!"	
Lily	And he will probably keep on singing.	
Ms. E	Okay, that's good evidence. So the villagers problem was—?	*Asks for identification of the problem (text structure).*
Lily	Dario stopped singing to them because they never answered him.	
Tyler	They couldn't sleep without the lullabies.	
Ms. E	They solved it by—?	*Asks for problem solution (text structure).*
Rashid	They sang to him and then he knew that they didn't answer because they were asleep.	
Ms. E	Sounds right. Take a look at the language on page 14. The top part is telling the story and the second paragraph is the villagers' song. Rashid, you read the first paragraph out loud and, Lily, you read the song. Let's listen and think about how they are different.	*Draws attention to language (analysis).*
	They read the passage and talk briefly about the differences in language.	

reading. The teaching points you select do depend on what you noticed caused readers difficulty and what they did well. But you have a larger goal—to help students expand the processing system. The behaviors and understandings to notice, teach, and support at each text level in *The Continuum of Literacy Learning, Grades PreK–8* (Pinnell and Fountas 2011, 2008) will help you think about what your readers need *to learn how to do* as they read this text *in order to read other texts.*

In the discussion of *All About Volcanoes* (Figure 17-21), Ms. F drew attention to text structure and asked students to extend their understandings in writing.

Remember that teaching points are brief and explicit. They are selective, keeping in mind what readers need to know. Look at the quick teaching point after the discussion of *A Dragon's Lullaby* (see Figure 17-22). Ms. E focused on genre and probed for evidence from the text. She also helped readers notice aspects of the writer's craft.

Now let's go back to a very simple example—a teaching point after the reading of *Oh, No!* (see Figure 17-23). Here Ms. P helped learners give a great deal of attention to the pictures to support comprehension of the text.

As you can see, the text in these first reading books is quite limited. Reading it aloud without picture support makes it sound ridiculous and meaningless. For the young child, the meaning is created through the pictures.

Figure 17-21 **Teaching Point for *All About Volcanoes***		
Speaker	**Teaching Actions**	**Contributions to Comprehension**
Ms. F	You know it's interesting how the writer of this book used cause and effect to help us understand volcanoes. Turn back to pages 6 and 7. On these two pages it tells us what causes a volcano. You talked a lot about it.	*Draws attention to text structure (analysis).*
Dominic	It's gas exploding from inside the earth.	
Ms. F	Yes, the center of the earth is hot melted rock. That's the cause of the volcano. The effect is the big explosion—what happens afterwards. What are some of the other effects? Everyone find something and show us where it is in the text.	*Provides information.* *Identifies cause (text structure).* *Asks students to identify effect.*
Katie	On page 4 it shows how it covered everything with mud.	
Dominic	On page 12 and 13 it tells the good things that come from volcanoes.	
Lorenzo	It covers everything.	
Ms. F	And on page 10, it shows how volcanoes under the sea can form an island. Lorenzo what are you thinking about that?	*Provides information.* *Probes for thinking.*
Lorenzo	That's Hawaii.	
Ms. F	So what do you think about volcanoes?	*Probes for comments.*
Katie	They can really do a lot of stuff.	
Ms. F	Take a piece of paper and divide it in half. Then write the cause of volcanoes in the first column and the effect in the second column.	*Asks students to write about cause and effect.*

Speaker	Teaching Actions	Contributions to Comprehension
Figure 17-22 Teaching Point for *A Dragon's Lullaby*		
Ms. E	This is an interesting book because it is a fantasy. How do you know it is a fantasy?	*Asks for characteristics of genre. Probes for evidence.*
Tyler	It's make-believe.	
Molly	There really aren't any dragons.	
Lily	It just kind of sounds like a fantasy.	
Ms. E	Can you give an example of that?	*Probes for evidence.*
Rashid	Just the way it starts. *[Reading.]* "In a castle high on a mountain lived a kindly dragon called Dario." It's like some of the sentences are turned around—not like talking.	
Ms. E	No, it isn't like talking. You know it reminds me of some of the stories we have read like *The Wind and the Sun.* So this is fantasy and inside this story there are two other kinds of texts. Do you know what they are?	*Offers a connection. Identifies main genre. Probes for identification of other genres.*
Molly	There's a song.	
Ms. E	Yes, on two pages there is a song, which is the same as poetry. We read that. And on page 11—turn to it—there is an invitation. Why do you think the writer did that?	*Identifies embedded genre. Probes for analysis of the writer's craft.*
Lily	It shows exactly what they did.	
Ms. E	It does do that, and it makes it interesting.	*Points out something about the writer's craft.*

▶ Teaching for Strategic Actions

Now let's go back to the categories of strategic actions (see Figure 17-11) and think about how each of them is related to processing the meaning of a text. The above examples demonstrate that teaching support can direct readers' attention in ways that help them engage in the actions or activities that build complex in-the-head systems. Through engagement, they learn how to expand thinking. This is not the same as teaching a skill ("I want you to make an inference"), and it does not mean labeling thinking ("You made an inference"). Effective processing of any text worth reading will involve the simultaneous orchestration of all strategic actions in the pursuit of meaning. The teachers in the examples above all directed read-

ers' attention to the content of the story and prompted them to engage in a range of strategic actions so that they can think more deeply about the text.

Word Solving

A principle to keep in mind is that word solving should take as little energy as possible. The proficient reader engages in many ways of solving words and works with larger units whenever possible (Kaye 2007). While we have emphasized focused, efficient phonics lessons elsewhere in this book (see Chapters 11 and 12), we know that learners will never achieve this fast, effortless word solving without accessing their knowledge while reading continuous text. Observing children read, you'll gather evidence about the efficiency of the word solving. Are students reading accurately but working too hard to be able to read

Figure 17-23 **Teaching Point for *Oh No!***

Speaker	Teaching Actions	Contributions to Comprehension
Ms. P	You know the pictures in this book really help us understand it. Let's go back to page 2. Mom comes in the door and says, "Look at the mail!" But it isn't just the mail, is it? What do the pictures tell you?	*Draws attention to the pictures and asks readers to search for information.*
Tyra	It's a mess.	
David	It's all torn up.	
Ms. P	And look at the next page.	*Prompts searching for information.*
Samuel	The water is all spilled.	
Ms. P	Do you notice anything else?	*Prompts searching for information*
Tyra	It's a bowl turned over.	
Ms. P	This is a clue. That bowl says *Taco* on it. That's the name of her dog and that is his water bowl. Look at some more pages. They tell a story.	*Provides information. Explains how the pictures help you gain meaning.*
Samuel	He turned over the trash.	
Tyra	He tore up the paper.	
Samuel	He chewed up the pillow.	
Ms. P	So when you noticed his bowl was turned over, you started thinking that maybe Taco did all this damage. Look at page 15. There is another clue.	*Tells students how they are using the pictures to gain meaning. Prompts searching for meaning.*
David	There's his footprints. He walked in the paint.	
Ms. P	So you see how the pictures can really help you understand what is happening in the story. You need to look at them and think about them.	*Summarizes teaching point.*
David	This page [16] shows that he did it all.	
Ms. P	Why do you say that?	*Asks for evidence.*
David	There's a flower and little bits of everything he tore up.	
Ms. P	You are really thinking about the pictures.	*Affirms thinking.*

fluently? Is word solving taking so much time that comprehension is undermined?

Teaching efficient word solving is just one factor in creating a setting in which the reader can comprehend. As you work alongside readers and make teaching points, teach and prompt for flexible word solving. Show children how to look at parts of words and also how to check whether the word they solve sounds right and makes sense. The goal is to use all sources of information—meaning, language, and print—together as they read. When a reader does some good work on a word and solves it correctly but with effort, that may be a good place to make a teaching point. Watch for evidence that the behavior is learned and becoming automatic.

Monitoring and Correcting

Often we think of monitoring and correcting as actions at the word level, but these are actually broader terms that also apply to comprehending. Proficient readers monitor their understanding all the time, especially as language becomes more complex. Are they "reading" the punctuation correctly? For example, reading commas (in dialogue, lists of items, direct address, setting off clauses and words like *too*) requires thinking about the meaning. Misreading commas can seriously undermine understanding. When processing dialogue, readers need to know who is speaking. Even adults sometimes have to back up when reading strings of unassigned dialogue. Recognizing the correct antecedent to a pronoun is essential to understanding a text, and although the behavior is unconscious, readers will stop when they lose correct relationships between pronouns and referents. Sometimes you may even want to make a list of characters as readers meet them so they can refer to it. They also should know whether they are getting essential information or not. When reading about a difficult topic, readers often gather information by searching back through the text or taking notes. By leading discussions before and after reading, you can help readers learn how to monitor themselves in this larger sense.

Searching For and Using Information

Readers search for the information they need to gather from a text. They know that they must have enough information to follow a plot or expand their knowledge of content. Throughout this book we have stressed how readers search for meaning, language structure, and visual information. These three larger categories encompass the whole of the reader's resources. Each contributes essential information. The visual information in print represents language; meaning is mapped out in the words and how they are arranged in syntactic patterns. Your teaching must support the reader in using all sources simultaneously.

Summarizing

When talking about summarizing, we too often think of the discrete "test-taking" skill of writing a short synopsis after reading a text or passage. Summarizing really means:

- ❑ Searching for and using information.
- ❑ Identifying essential information.
- ❑ Carrying the important information forward when reading a text.
- ❑ Using the important information to interpret the meaning of the text and solve problems.
- ❑ Remembering the important information after reading.
- ❑ Reflecting on the text to reorganize the information in a logical way.
- ❑ Recalling, in logical order, *only* the important events or major points, supported by evidence.
- ❑ Recalling the essence of a text long after reading.

You can teach this kind of summarizing by introducing a text in a way that helps students know what it is about as a whole, supporting the identification of important information while students are reading the text, and discussing the text afterward.

Writing about reading is also very helpful in helping readers understand the role of summarizing (see Chapter 13).

Some prompts that will help students understand the text as an organized whole include:

- ❑ "The most important ideas are. . . ."
- ❑ "This book is about. . . ."
- ❑ "This part is about. . . ."
- ❑ "First . . . next . . . finally."
- ❑ "Three things we want to know are. . . ."
- ❑ "Three things we learned are. . . ."
- ❑ "Tell the steps in order."
- ❑ "Let's label the parts of this drawing [diagram] [paragraph]."
- ❑ "What was the problem? What was the solution to the problem?"
- ❑ "What were the main ideas in this book?"
- ❑ "Let's think about or write a summary of this chapter."

All the above can be used in conjunction with oral discussion, writing, or graphic organizers (see

Chapter 13). The best way to learn summarizing is not to practice it for a test but to engage in it orally and in writing each time a group reads a text.

Maintaining Fluency

The strong connection between fluent reading and comprehension is examined in Chapter 16. One of the great things about engaging students in reading continuous print is that just about everything you do to support fluency also contributes to reading comprehension. When you use prompts like "make it sound like talking" or "think of how he would say that," you are requiring students to think about the meaning. A deeper look at fluency suggests it is more than just reading smoothly so that it sounds good. Even in silent reading there is an element of fluency that means ideas are flowing freely, with all information fitting together in a satisfying way. The truly fluent reader flies through the book or article, intent on and absorbed in meaning.

Adjusting

The proficient reader instantly and without effort shifts strategic actions to meet the different demands of texts. Here again, readers must work with continuous text in flexible ways to develop the strategic actions needed to make transitions such as those demanded by *A Dragon's Lullaby.* You can support the ability to adjust strategic actions by:

❑ Ensuring quantity. Readers need to process a large amount of text to develop the power to shift.

❑ Ensuring variety. Readers need the experience of many different genres, writing styles, and ways of organizing texts.

❑ Teaching readers what to look for. You can draw their attention to text characteristics as you introduce them and discuss them after reading.

❑ Developing academic language. Give students labels for the important concepts they need to recognize in order to strategically shift action.

Predicting

Because it is so often a part of instruction, predicting has become a somewhat mechanical process; for example, "let's make two predictions and then read to see if we are right." A technique like this, used over and over, will not spark readers' interest. We do not predict just to "do predictions." Predicting is a dynamic cognitive action that is essential for physical survival. We cannot stop our brains from predicting and then either confirming or rejecting predictions; we do it with lightning speed and in multiple ways.

You'll engage readers in making predictions simply by helping them focus on using what they know to think about what might happen next in a story (for example, when the family sees the moose in *Down the River* or what the writer might tell about next). Model for your students how to think about what is happening and how to anticipate what will follow:

❑ "I am wondering. . . ."

❑ "I think such-and-such will happen."

❑ "I imagine. . . ."

❑ "Maybe. . . ."

❑ "I predict. . . ."

Prediction requires many kinds of thinking and is a good example of the way cognitive actions are simultaneous and related. To predict, you must gather information, remember it (which in turn requires all the strategies for thinking within the text), and make inferences about what will happen.

Making Connections

Making connections, too, is often taught in a way that makes readers think it is an end in itself. You don't read in order to "make a connection" of some kind. Rather, your memories and sources of knowledge simply come alive; they are summoned as cued by the text. When you prompt students to use what they know (background knowledge), other books they have read (text knowledge), or their previous experiences, you are helping them use this knowledge to further their understanding of the text they are reading.

Synthesizing

Synthesizing means learning—expanding one's knowledge. It is easiest to think about synthesizing in relation to nonfiction, because you are adding information and revising what you know. But fiction also changes the reader; you may gain new information, think in new ways, see other perspectives, or experience vicarious emotions. Synthesizing requires:

- ❏ Evoking present knowledge.
- ❏ Gathering and storing information in memory.
- ❏ Adjusting what you already know.
- ❏ Seeing or understanding ideas in a new way.

In many of the sample introductions in this chapter, the teacher invites students to talk about their own experiences or knowledge. Often, their responses help teachers decide what background information they need to provide. The goal of the introduction is not to tell students everything they will read in the book but to provide just enough information so that they will be able to process it with comprehension and sufficient accuracy. Whether you evoke students' own background knowledge or provide it, they can then experience synthesis. You may want to provide a framework for this process by listing what is known and thinking about what you would like to know. You call for synthesis every time you ask students to talk about:

- ❏ "Something new that you learned."
- ❏ "Something interesting in this book."
- ❏ "New ideas you noticed."
- ❏ "Surprises?"
- ❏ "Something you are going to think more about later."
- ❏ "Something you want to remember."
- ❏ "The author's messages."

Inferring

Inference is at the heart of comprehending. "Reading between the lines" (finding hidden meaning in something said or written; insightful thinking) has become a universally understood English idiom.

Inference operates at every level. For example, you use your understanding of syntax to infer the pronoun referent. Inferring character attitudes supports you in following unassigned dialogue. Your inferences about what is currently happening in a story help you predict what might come next (for example, inferring character motivations or the logical outcome of an event).

But inference is even more complex than these examples. From your experience with the whole text—language, images, structure—you infer the deeper meanings that the writer wants to convey. The theme is not just the "answer" on a test. It involves grappling with the hidden messages in the text. In reading informational texts, you infer the underlying attitudes of the writer and thus are able to read critically. Inference allows you to gain insight into the perspectives of people who are far distant from yourself in time and space. It is one of the reasons you read (or listen to actors speak) dialogue. You can demonstrate or call for inference with language like this:

- ❏ "I wonder if the writer is trying to say. . . ."
- ❏ "What is [character] really like?"
- ❏ "How do you think [character] is feeling?"
- ❏ "I wonder why the writer. . . ."
- ❏ "The real message of this book is. . . ."

Analyzing

Inferring something like the author's messages moves readers toward analyzing a text. You want readers to be able to think analytically about how the writer is presenting ideas and using language to communicate meaning. In the texts that beginners read (Levels A, B, C), the themes are extremely simple, yet they can recognize sequence or understand when two things are compared. As they read texts that are a little more complicated (Levels D to H), children start to encounter real stories with simple plots. They can talk about the problem in the story and how it is resolved. They start to get to know characters who, while still one dimensional, have appealing characteristics. The variety of genres of still higher-level texts (Levels I to

Figure 17-24 **Prompting for Successful Comprehending**

Activity	Helps readers learn how to:	Sample Prompts Related to Comprehending
Word Solving	• Use letter/sound relationships to take words apart while thinking about the meaning. • Make meaningful attempts at unknown words. • Use sentence and context to monitor reading and problem-solve words. • Notice word parts that are related to meaning of individual words (base words, affixes). • Predict what a word might mean and check it with the sentence or story. • Think of the meaning of the whole text in deriving the meaning of a word. • Understand connotative meanings of words.	• Think about what would make sense. • Think about what would sound right. • Look at the first part. (Show base word, cover ending). • Think about what that word means in *this* sentence (in *this* story). • That means the same as (synonym).
Monitoring and Correcting	• Notice when something doesn't make sense. • Notice when something does not sound right in terms of language structure. • Try another word that makes sense or sounds right and check with the letters. • Reread or read on to clarify meaning. • Make multiple attempts at words that fit meaning.	• Does that make sense? Sound right? • Try _____. Would that make sense? Sound right? • Try that again and think what would make sense (sound right). • Read on and think about what that means. • Does that make sense in this whole story? • Be sure it makes sense in this book.
Searching for and Using Information	• Notice important information while reading. • Reread to search for and use information. • Use text meaning and structure to solve new words. • Relate information in one part of the text to the information in other parts. • Search for and find specific facts and other information in a text. • Use readers' tools (glossary, table of contents, headings) to clarify or add information. • Process a range of dialogue. • Find and use information in graphics.	• Try that again and think what would make sense. • Try that again and think what would sound right. • Try looking back for the information you need. • Think about who is talking now. • And what did _____ say? • Look back to find where the writer tells about _____. • What will you expect to learn about _____? • What do you learn about _____ from this (e.g. table of contents)? • What additional information did you learn from this (graphic)? • What were some of the important facts (ideas) that the writer presented in this book?

continues

Figure 17-24 **Prompting for Successful Comprehending,** *continued*		
Activity	**Helps readers learn how to:**	**Sample Prompts Related to Comprehending**
Summarizing	• Notice,remember, and carry forward the important information. • Report events in a logical sequence, when needed. • Recall previously read information. • Recall information that serves as evidence for summary points as needed. • Provide an oral summary of the text that is concise, logical, and informative. • Provide an oral summary that reflects the big ideas of a text rather than a few details.	• Think about what you know so far. • Think about what has happened so far. • Tell what you know so far in the story. • What were the most important things this writer had to say? • What do you want to remember about this book? • What is your evidence for that idea? • Tell about the whole story.
Maintaining Fluency	• Notice and use meaningful phrase units. • Read a variety of punctuation. • Use the meaning to stress the right word. • Use intonation patterns and pausing to reflect interpretation of the text when reading aloud. • Reflect the meaning of dialogue with the voice. • Use the voice to interpret the meaning of the text. • Use text features such as italics to guide word stress and intonation.	• Put these words together. • Make your voice go down at the period (or up at a question mark and excited at an exclamation point). • Think about how to say that. • Think how _____ would say that. • Read it like you're telling the story. • Make your voice show what the writer means there. • What do you notice about those words that makes sense in this part of the story (italics, bold, headings)?
Adjusting	• Vary reading pace across the reading of the text as needed (e.g. to problem-solve). • Have expectations for reading different types of texts e.g. fantasy, information books. • Adjust reading to process dialogue. • Adjust speed and processing to the different demands of a text—pace, content, sentence structure, complexity. • Reread to confirm complex text structures such as stories within stories or multiple story lines.	• You can slow down to figure it out and then move on. • Think about what you know about _____ (e.g. fantasy) books as you read. • When you notice something tricky like that, go back and figure out how the story works. • Did you find yourself reading faster during the exciting part? • Did you find you were stopping to think more during this part of the text?

continues

Think Beyond Text

Figure 17-24 Prompting for Successful Comprehending, *continued*

Activity	Helps readers learn how to:	Sample Prompts Related to Comprehending
Predicting	• Raise expectations based on prior experience prior to reading a text (author, genre, content). • Capture important information at the beginning of the text and remember it to use as a basis for prediction. • Throughout the reading of a text, use previous information to anticipate what will follow. • Make predictions based on knowledge of characters or type of story. • Predict what characters will do based on traits. • Predict solution to the problem of a story.	• You are already thinking about what this book might be like because you know _____ (author, genre, content). • What do you think will happen? • So now what are you thinking? • I'm thinking that… • Based on what you know about [character, story], are you wondering what will happen? • Think about what you know. What do you think will happen?
Making Connections	• Think about how the text content relates to your own life. • Relate background knowledge to reading. • Think about how the text content relates to what is known about the world. • Think about how the text content is like other books. • Think about how the text is like or different from other books (fiction and nonfiction, plot, genre, writing style).	• What does this remind you of? • This book reminds me of [known example]. Can you think why? • What do you know about that that helps you think about _____? • Think of another book you read that is like this. • Think about what you already know about _____. • Have you read about other characters like this? • Do you know a place like this? • Do you know anyone who is like a character in this book? • How does that (e.g., book, character, place) help you think about this book, character, place? • What do you think the writer will teach you about _____?
Synthesizing	• Use information from the text to create new understandings. • Identify new learning. • Compare previous understandings to new information. • Express changes in ideas after reading a text. • Relate background knowledge to reading.	• What was the writer teaching you about _____? • Think about what you learned that was new (interesting, surprising). • What was new information for you? • How is what you learned different from what you knew before? • How did your thinking change?

continues

Figure 17-24 **Prompting for Successful Comprehending,** *continued*

Activity	Helps readers learn how to:	Sample Prompts Related to Comprehending
Inferring	• Think about what is not there in the text but is implied. • Use background information to interpret the actions in a text. • Infer the big ideas or messages of a text. • Show evidence in print or illustrations to support inference. • Notice how characters change and make hypotheses as to why. • Interpret illustrations. • Identify characters' feelings, motivations, actions, attributes. • Identify what the author thinks is important. • Identify the author's message.	• That's what the writer said. What do you think he means? • That's what the character said. What did she mean? • What was the writer trying to say? • What made you think that? • How do you know _____ has changed? • What do you know about _____? • Why do you think _____ did that? • What do the illustrations make you think? • You can think about what the character says and what that makes you think about him (how character looks, thinks, what others say about him).
Analyzing	• Understand how the text is constructed or "how the book works." • Notice how the writer uses language to construct meaning. • Notice the writer's style. • Notice how ideas are related to each other. • Identify and appreciate humor. • Notice how writer uses dialogue to add to meaning. • Understand the structure of a story. • Understand categories and subcategories in informational texts. • Notice how headings reveal categories of information. • Notice the patterns in exposition (e.g. compare/contrast, sequence, description). • Recognize difference between fiction and nonfiction. • Identify the genre and its characteristics. • Discuss whether a story could be true. • Understand the relationship between setting and plot. • Notice how setting is important to a story. • Notice and interpret figurative language.	• What did you notice about the writer's language? • What did the writer do to make the story funny? (interesting, sad?) • What was the writer's purpose in writing this book? • Who are the characters? • What is the problem? • How was the problem solved? • Who were the important characters in the story? • What did you notice about the place they were? • What kind of book is this? (Fiction or nonfiction; realistic or fantasy). • What did the writer do to make the characters (animals or human) seem like they were real? • Look at this section. What kind of information will you find here? How can you tell? • How did the writer start the story? What do you think about that? • What did the writer tell first about (content). Why do you think the writer chose that to be first? • Where did the writer tell something in just the right order? Why?

continues

Figure 17-24	**Prompting for Successful Comprehending,** *continued*	
Activity	**Helps readers learn how to:**	**Sample Prompts Related to Comprehending**
Analyzing, *continued*	• Notice and understand combined genres in a text. • Identify literary elements such as beginning and ending, character, plot or story problem, setting.	• I noticed this language (read). What did the writer mean by that? (Figurative language, metaphor, idiom). • What do you notice about how the writer did that?
Critiquing	• Evaluate the text based on personal knowledge. • Provide evidence for evaluative comments. • Form opinions about the book or illustrations. • Describe the text and support with evidence (e.g. interesting, humorous, exciting, well written). • Agree or disagree with ideas from the text. • Hypothesize how characters might have behaved differently to make the text better, more interesting, more real. • Evaluate whether the text sounds "true" or not. • Evaluate the illustrations and whether they are interesting or provide good information.	• What are you thinking about this book? • What makes this a good _____ (e.g. biography, fantasy, etc.)? • What did the writer say to make you think that? • How else might _____ have behaved? • What else might _____ have done? • Do you think this book sounds real? Or true? What makes you think that? • What do you think about the illustrations?

N) offer the opportunity for deeper analytic thinking. *Chester Greenwood's Big Idea* is a biography about the inventor of earmuffs. (See Chapter 13 for writing about this text.).

It is hard to develop a sense of character from very early books, but reading books in a series can support deeper understanding even at these levels. For example, over several books in the Moosling series, readers learn that he is curious, friendly, helpful, and brave. (See Chapter 13 for writing about this text.) Some characteristics are repeated across texts; others emerge as new understandings in successive stories.

Talking and thinking in an analytic way about texts is assisted by learning "academic language." Chapter 16 of our book *Teaching for Comprehending and Fluency: Thinking, Talking, and Writing about Reading, K–8* (2006) includes an extensive discussion of the vocabu-lary for talking about texts at each grade level, as well as a continuum for development. Over time, as children become more sophisticated, you move from a simple statement of the concept to the *label* for the concept, from meaningful general terms to specific and technical terms. For example, when you first start talking about characters, you just refer to the people (by name) or animals in the story; soon you can begin to call them characters. When you first start talking about the plot, you talk about the problem in the story and what happened. Interactive read-aloud is the ideal place to begin to help students use this kind of language, but you can also bring it into the introduction and discussion of texts in small-group reading instruction.

When working with younger students, especially those who are struggling, don't clutter up the conversation with too much technical language. The important thing is to get the thinking going. You call for analysis when you use language like this:

- ❏ "This story happened. . . ."
- ❏ "Where does the story take place?"
- ❏ "Who are the characters [people/animals] in the story?"
- ❏ "I can tell [name of character] is [trait] because…"
- ❏ "What did the writer do to make [name of person/animal] seem interesting?"
- ❏ "In this story we're going to read about [name or type of character]."
- ❏ "Let's look at the illustrations to see what we can tell about [name of character]."
- ❏ "Who is the most important character in the story?"
- ❏ "What problem does [name of character] have?"
- ❏ "How did they solve the problem?"
- ❏ "When you have read a story, you can think about what the writer was really trying to tell you. I think that in this story the writer was telling us.…"
- ❏ "This is a fiction story. I know that because.…"
- ❏ "This is a book that gives us information. It is nonfiction."
- ❏ "Where in the book did the writer say something really interesting?"
- ❏ "On this page, I think the writer said something in a very interesting way."
- ❏ "On this page, the writer was comparing.…"
- ❏ "What caused the problem?"
- ❏ "This is a biography—a true story about a real person. Why do you think the writer chose this person to write about?"
- ❏ "Some parts of this biography are fact. The writer probably imagined a few things to make it more interesting. Let me show you some."
- ❏ "How did the writer make the information interesting?"
- ❏ "What part is fact?"
- ❏ "What part was probably imagined?"

Critiquing

We live in an era when it is more important than ever to read and listen critically. To read critically, individuals must not only orchestrate all other strategic actions but also add a layer of thinking that questions and evaluates the writing of the text to detect point of view, bias, or persuasion. Texts at Levels A through N do not require much critical thinking, but we still want readers to think critically. Even beginning readers can tell you whether or not they liked a story or nonfiction book and why. They can also bring some critical thinking to the illustrations, evaluating them and talking about what makes them interesting. They can be aware of how photographs illustrate the points in nonfiction texts and make them seem real; they can notice sections like a glossary that help to support the information in the text.

▶ Questioning for Construction

Questioning is a primary teaching tool. There are two kinds of questions: (1) questions that test and (2) questions that prompt construction. Often, we think we are using the latter, but we fall into the trap of using the former. For example:

> The teacher provides the students little introduction to the text, thinking "I want to see if they can get it by themselves." The students process the text inefficiently. They get through it. Then the teacher asks them what they "got." The answers are unsatisfactory, so she probes deeper with questions that "lead" so strongly that she finally elicits (or tells) the "answer." The bell rings for lunch. The students are unengaged and the teacher is exhausted. She goes to lunch and tells her colleagues that teaching is like "pulling teeth."

We have all been there and done that. Questions that test have their place. We do need to probe students' understanding.

But we can often do so in more effective ways when we engage learners in constructive dialogue. They will not only learn more but also find reading more satisfying. You can gain substantial information about your students' comprehension by observing discussions in which they reveal:

❑ Evidence of thinking processes.

❑ Their perspective.

❑ The information they select and use.

❑ Their preferences.

❑ Their emotions.

❑ Their interests.

❑ The aspects of texts that engage them or confuse them.

The answer to the question, "Did they get it?" is seldom yes or no. We want to know *what* they understand and *how* they understand it. We want to know the nuances they did not grasp, what puzzled them, what they questioned or wondered about. To get at this kind of discussion, it is important to ask questions that prompt construction. This kind of question nudges the reader to think differently or more deeply. This chapter contains many examples of constructive questions.

Remember, too, that the probe doesn't have to be in the precise form of a question. "Wondering" statements imply a question and invite thinking while at the same time modeling the process. Once students learn how to engage in the thinking, talking, and writing that are part of the constructive process of making meaning, you will find that teaching readers to comprehend is less exhausting and more fun.

A sampling of comments and questions related to the systems of strategic actions that you might use in your interactions with children in thinking, talking, and writing about their reading is provided in Figure 17-24. Notice how your language can help readers think within, beyond, and about the text. The key is to ensure that active thinking about the writer's message is an integral part of all reading.

▶ Suggestions for Professional Development

SUPPORTING COMPREHENSION ACROSS THE LESSON

1. Prepare for a professional development meeting by choosing one of your guided reading or intervention groups and select three texts that you will be guiding them to read within the next week. Take to the meeting the texts and any other information you have on the children. If you have *The Continuum of Literacy Learning, Grades PreK–8* (Pinnell & Fountas 2011, 2008), take it to the meeting so that you can refer to the level for Text Characteristics and Behaviors to Notice, Teach, and Support. Or if you are working with Leveled Literacy Intervention, take your lesson guide because that will have the same information for the level.

2. At the beginning of the meeting, "jigsaw read" the section under the heading "Systems of Strategic Actions" in Chapter 2, page 16. Share and discuss some of the points you have learned relative to analyzing and introducing texts, prompting for strategic actions, and making teaching points following your observations of the reading.

3. Work with a partner or grade level colleagues. For each text (considering the needs of your group),

   ❑ Analyze the text. What aspects will challenge readers? What aspects will be supportive to readers?

   ❑ Plan the introduction to the text. (Make some notes that you can use next week.) Consider important aspects of comprehension that you will need to support.

   ❑ Considering your readers, think what you need to demonstrate, prompt for, and reinforce during the reading to assure successful comprehension. (Use *The Fountas and Pinnell Prompting Guide 1* if you have it. You can also use all of the prompts listed in this chapter.)

   ❑ Plan for some Writing about Reading that will extend students' thinking about the text.

4. Schedule a follow-up meeting to share insights about comprehension that you gained from your lesson.

Working Successfully with English Language Learners

MULTI-FACETED EARLY INTERVENTION IS ESSENTIAL for English language learners because a literacy problem can very quickly develop when children are faced with the dual task of learning a new language and learning to read in English. These students do not necessarily have a literacy problem. They may have a language problem that is related to the environment they are in. We must remember that all of these children are bilingual; they speak two languages and, often, more and that must be viewed as a strength. In this chapter, we provide specific suggestions for working with English language learners who are having trouble learning to read and write in English.

The populations of most of today's classrooms are richly diverse. It is not unusual to find speakers of a dozen or more different languages in a single school. Their *primary language* is the first language they learn—the language they speak at home and in the community—but most of these students are being taught to read in English. These *English language learners*:

❑ Speak a primary language different from English.

❑ Are still developing their primary language.

❑ Are at the same time learning to speak English.

❑ Are expected to learn to read and write English while still learning to speak it.

Being an English language learner is quite a challenge. Young children amaze us every day by taking on so much new learning at once.

It makes the best sense for a young child first to become literate in the language he has learned at home. In that case, all the information derived from language structure, vocabulary, and meaning will be available as a resource in developing proficient systems for reading and writing. Once these processes have been established, the student knows *what reading and writing are* and can take on English written language more easily. For this reason, bilingual education is highly effective.

Unfortunately, bilingual education is simply not available to most English language learners. Often, no teachers or other staff members who speak the child's home language are available. (In some schools, students simply speak too many different languages.) Parents and community members provide valuable assistance in communicating with students who are only beginning to learn English, but literacy instruction takes place in English. All teachers must meet the challenge of serving these students because literacy is essential for school success and citizenry. And, we must remember that there is a great deal of variation among English language learners and their English proficiency level is not a reflection of their cognitive level (Menyuk and Brisk, p. 205).

It is not surprising that some English learners have difficulty becoming literate in English. They have a rich background of language that does not readily match up with the print they are expected to process. It is important that we remember that this mismatch is a unique source of difficulty. The learners are not "disabled" or "slow." They are simply learning two huge bodies of information simultaneously, and that presents an enormous challenge.

All of these children are bilingual; they speak at least one language and are learning to speak one more. Some of them have had experiences that would daunt adults: some have coped with serious issues of survival; others are fast becoming the interpreters for their families. Most juggle two cultures—the one at home and the one they brush up against at school. English learners are exceptional, flexible, and bright, and we need to appreciate their strengths while supporting language and literacy learning. Every English language learner is unique, with a different set of language, cultural, and school experiences.

Appreciating languages other than English is an essential feature of a supportive learning environment. If at all possible, include some labels and signs in other languages. Have everyone in the class learn to say phrases like "good morning" in several languages. It is effective to expand rather than "correct" language; everyone makes errors as they take on the syntax of a new language. And, it is very easy to make mistakes when you are adjusting to new cultural understandings. You can easily create situations in which children have the chance to repeat appropriate grammatical patterns in an enjoyable way. Language is so much a part of us; the language we speak shapes our actions, customs, and lives.

As teachers we need to be sensitive to the fact that the language we speak shapes our actions, customs, and lives. We use it to express our deepest feelings, our beliefs, and our values. We share its nuances with other speakers of the language. When someone criticizes the way we use language, it undermines our sense of self. When we take on a new language, we must also acquire a large body of cultural understandings, and these take years to develop.

Multifaceted early intervention is essential, because a literacy problem may develop when children are faced with the dual task of learning the language and learning to read in English. Some children become confused about the task of reading, engaging in it mechanically without expecting it to make much sense. They may learn to decode, but comprehension may be severely undermined. How interesting would you find reading if you understood very little and were engaging in rote learning? It would be hard to build any kind of motivation. We need to give students the gift of reading and writing as language processes, and that means learning language while at the same time becoming literate.

Fortunately, children are very fast language learners. After all, they learned their home language with no instruction at all other than interactions with family members. The human brain is programmed to learn language (Lindfors, 1999). Clay (1998) argues that "it is important that children develop rich control of their home language as their first language, even when the language of the school is English; schools can build from there. Teachers and caregivers must talk to particular children one to one more often." It is eminently possible to work with English language learners successfully.

▶ Language Facets English Learners Must Acquire

Here's a brief look at some essential aspects of language to help you understand the complexity of the task you are helping English learners accomplish. These aspects reflect the characteristics of language. We include vocabulary, grammar, and pragmatics.

Vocabulary

The first thing that monolingual speakers usually think about is vocabulary. English learners must learn the words, particularly the nouns and verbs, of a language. This is a serious task when you consider that English speakers enter school knowing an average of 4,000 words; they leave elementary school with about 80,000 words and enter college with about 120,000 (Brisk 2008). Elsewhere in this book we have emphasized that readers should know or be able to solve about 95 percent of the words for a text to be accessible; they also should *understand the meaning* of about 95 percent of the words. The words children understand and those they can recognize or solve using the visual information may not entirely overlap, but in general children need to know the meaning of a word to truly solve it.

Some characteristics of vocabulary words may confuse English learners (Menyuk and Brisk 2005, Brisk 2008). They may (as many of us do) confuse words that sound alike (*leaf* and *leave, concomitant* and *continent*). They may have difficulty with long words or those that are difficult to pronounce. Homophones (*cent, sent, scent; idle, idol*) and homographs (*read, read*) are even more confusing to English learners than they are to native speakers. Words have multiple meanings that sometimes are related but in abstract ways (*fold a handkerchief; fold in a poker game; fold his wing; fold in the cream*). And

English has shortened words like *burger* and *exam* and blended words like *brunch*. The most difficult vocabulary to grasp for any individual learning another language is the idiom. Language is a creative, growing entity. It is always changing; words are combined and used in new ways and gradually enter the traditional lexicon—the shared knowledge of a language that we have without realizing its origin. Think how difficult the following idioms would be to explain to English language learners: *two peas in a pod; as right as rain; beat around the bush; apple of my eye; raining cats and dogs; go over it with a fine tooth comb; pay the piper.*

English language learners often learn one vocabulary word and then use it extensively, either in isolated ways or in sentences with incorrect grammar. You have to listen very hard and infer their meaning. When reading, they search for the meaning of individual words, but tend to think about the word as an isolated entity in the sentence they are reading. Often, a word has different or expanded meaning within the whole text. Even if a word is known in some sense, comprehension can be lost.

Grammar

If you have traveled in a country where you don't speak the language, you have probably found a pocket dictionary helpful only in limited ways because you do not know how to string together meaningful sentences. The same is true for your English language learners. Conjugating verbs (*work, works, worked, will work, will have worked*) is daunting. When verbs are irregular (and many are) you will hear things like *I seed* (for *I saw*) or *I lookted.* Learners may have difficulty switching from one form of a verb to another (the present tense with auxiliary *I can play* and the present participle *I am playing*, for example). It is very difficult to explain these differences, and learners have to internalize them through many examples. Plurals, too, are challenging because they are formed differently in the various languages. And speakers often talk without articles or prepositions as they begin to frame phrases and sentences. Acquiring the grammar of a language takes place over time as learners have rich experiences and opportunities to interact with native speakers.

Pragmatics

Pragmatics refers to the meaning of sentences in terms of the speaker's intentions; in other words, meaning has a *context* and requires interpretation. Pragmatic knowledge is gained as children have the opportunity to use language within a social context. We seldom think about teaching children the cultural knowledge that influences the appropriate use of language. For example, in some cultures, children may be taught that it is impolite to disagree or to answer a question directly. They may not know the appropriate and polite way to ask for help. Pragmatic knowledge means thinking about the speaker's intentions; for example, knowing the difference between "I think" and "I know" or between "should" and "could" (Menyuk and Brisk 2005, 87). Engaging in connected discourse on a topic takes time; all speakers take a long time to develop sophisticated pragmatic knowledge, but learning the pragmatics of a new language is especially challenging.

Young children develop much pragmatic knowledge before they enter school. They learn to speak in a different way to adults than to other children. They learn to speak differently in public places than at home. All of this is equally true for English language learners. It's just that we forget to teach the pragmatics to these emerging English speakers. An added difficulty is that the "rules" may not match in every case.

Many new speakers of English are learning oral English primarily from other children in the home and community, and they may be learning vocabulary, language syntax, and pragmatics only from you. Therefore:

❏ It will take time.

❏ You will need to provide many models to assist learning.

❏ They will require explicit instruction in all three areas.

❏ They will need rich exposure to language.

▶ Classroom Environment

This book focuses on small-group intervention for children having difficulty learning to read and write. Intervention may not be needed for all English language learners, but all of them must have a rich language environment in the classroom. They need to be surrounded by language that is meaningful (or that can become so with good teaching). They need to interact with English language users in meaningful and appealing ways. They need access to texts that will enrich their English vocabularies, help them learn about English language syntax, and understand how texts are structured.

A comprehensive classroom language and literacy program offers a great deal of support to English language learners. Three aspects (see Figure 18-1) are critical:

1. *Language base.* All students need the opportunity to interact through language, and you as the teacher are the one who can give students the greatest lift. But it is also very helpful for

Figure 18-1 **Critical Factors in Creating Classrooms to Support English Language Learners**	
Language Base	• Students use language in meaningful ways in all instructional contexts. • Interactions take place surrounding text. • Students have opportunities to "try out" language in a safe environment.
Coherence	• Activities are consistent and form a coherent whole. • Children are getting the same messages every time they engage with text, which is often! • One instructional activity extends and contributes to another.
Multiple Modes of Communication	• Communication doesn't depend solely on oral language—information is also conveyed by actions, through pictures, in writing.

English learners to interact with English-speaking peers. First, the classroom must be permeated with respect. Everyone there is in the process of learning, and attempts at talking, reading, and writing should be valued. There must be many opportunities for talking, because students learn more about language each and every time they use language. Give students the opportunity to use language in a highly supported way. Consider modeling language that they can then take on and use as their own. Base the talk on text.

2. *Coherence.* English language learners are often the victims of a fragmented curriculum. They will have one lesson with one focus and then an entirely unrelated lesson about something else. They have no opportunity to build strong concepts *across* reading, writing, and word study. They need to see strong connections between reading and writing; phonics should make sense to them because they are applying what they learn to processing connected text. All readers and writers need coherence, but English language learners need it even more, and we probably need to make the connections more explicit to them. The activities in which students engage should be consistent. They need to get the same message in all their lessons:

   ❏ Reading is an experience with meaning. What you read needs to make sense, sound right, and look right. This takes into account the phonics they need but also the vision of meaningful reading in English.

   ❏ Writing is a way to communicate meaning. It involves hearing sounds and writing words that go together in a message. This takes into account the task of saying words, relating the sounds to letters, and writing words letter by letter, but also the vision of keeping a meaningful message in mind.

Coherence is important for student motivation (Chapter 20). It is even more important for English learners. Everything children experience should fit into this framework that combines meaning, visual information, and language structure.

3. *Multiple modes of communication.* You will not want to depend solely on oral language, especially with children who have newly arrived from another country and have very limited understanding of English. Think what it is like to listen to a string of directions and remember them; then think what it would be like to listen to it in a language that you are only beginning to learn. Use other means of communication:

   ❏ Act it out.

   ❏ Demonstrate explicitly what you want students to do.

   ❏ If it's complicated, have them "walk through it," acting out what they will do (or have a few students demonstrate while others watch).

   ❏ Seek the support of another student who also speaks the student's primary language (if possible).

   ❏ Use pictures and symbols.

   ❏ Provide it in simple writing accompanied by illustrations if necessary.

   ❏ If at all possible, learn some key words in the child's language.

These three overarching concepts are important for all learners. Many native English speakers have not developed the vocabulary and language syntax they need to meet grade-level expectations in the language arts. For all of these learners, you will want to set up a classroom that provides high support (see Figure 18-2).

Know Them as Learners

With the pressures teachers face, you may sometimes fail to learn some very important linguistic and cultural characteristics of the children you teach. Be sure you know:

   ❏ The country the child or his family is from and what that place is like today.

   ❏ The language that is spoken in the child's home.

   ❏ Something about the language users in the child's home. Does he have siblings who speak more English? Does he have non-English speakers in the family?

- Give children access to storybook reading.
- Ground talk in texts.
- Select texts that reflect diversity in language and culture.
- Teach academic language.
- Use shared reading and readers' theater.
- Make lessons clear and explicit.
- Establish predictable routines.
- Make expectations clear and check for understanding.
- Remember that being an ELL is not a deficit.

❑ Some of the names for family members in the child's language (*mother, dad, grandmother*).

❑ Some of the characteristics of the culture to which the child's family belongs.

❑ Something about typical syntactic patterns of the language they speak so you can anticipate English patterns that will be tricky.

❑ Content that will be familiar to students (and that which will not be).

❑ The amount and nature of any formal schooling.

The more you know, the easier it will be to work effectively with the learners.

Provide a Rich Language Environment

Learning is facilitated through talk—children learn their first language through social interaction. Throughout all learning activities, encourage children to enter into the give and take of conversation. Even though children are hesitant, you will want to create a safe environment within which they feel free to talk. Clay (1991) provides the following caution:

It is misplaced sympathy to do his talking for him. Instead, put your ear closer, concentrate more sharply, smile more rewardingly, and spend more time in genuine conversation, difficult though it is. To foster children's lan-guage development, create opportunities for them to talk, and then talk with them (not at them)." (69)

In your conversation with children, listen carefully to their responses. Occasionally take the opportunity to expand their ideas without correcting them. For example:

ANTWON: This rabbit he play trick.

Ms. A: You're right. He did play a trick. He got his brothers to help him. What was the trick?

You will also want to monitor students' understanding of your language. We recommend asking students to try to answer in sentences instead of just nodding or saying yes. This gives you more feedback on what the child understands. You will certainly not want to evaluate or correct what the child says, and you'll want to ask questions that elicit talk. Another valuable technique is to ask the child to repeat or paraphrase what you have said.

If you see signs that students do not understand, you may need to restate in a simpler or clearer way. But don't flood them with talk by saying everything three or four times in different ways. Students just beginning to use English need natural, clear, simple sentences. It will help to use gestures and pictures as well as words. Act out what you want students to try to do.

Read Stories Aloud

Reading to children has been shown to increase vocabulary and strengthen literacy concepts, and talking about the stories enhances this development (Snow et al. 1998; Teale 1984). Roberts (2008) reports on a recent study in which preschool English language learners were read stories at home in Hmong, Spanish, or English and were read stories and given vocabulary instruction in English in the classroom. Half the children were read stories at home in their primary language, half in English, the groups switching midway. *Both groups* made significant gains in English vocabulary recognition after storybook reading and again after classroom storybook reading and vocabulary instruction. So sending home books, whether in their native language or in English, for family caregivers to read to children will be a great benefit. Another way to give children access to texts is to build up a collection of CDs that can be tucked inside the books, especially when no family members read English.

Ground Talk in Texts

One of the best ways to expand children's knowledge about language is to talk with them about the texts you have read aloud to them or they have read for themselves. This is true for all students, not just English learners. As they discuss the texts, they intuitively repeat some of the language and in the process expand their knowledge of syntactical patterns.

Elsewhere we have called text talk an "intentional conversation" (Fountas and Pinnell 2006). These conversations, which can take place before and after reading and even briefly during the reading, should be genuine and encompass some or all of the following types of interactions:

❑ *Questioning.* Questioning children about what they read is an effective way to help children develop vocabulary (Sénéchal, Thomas, and Monker 1995). We don't mean you should ask questions for students to answer as a kind of test, but it is easy to work real questions into a discussion of high-quality children's literature. For example:

"How do you think Little Bear felt when he saw his chair?"

"What were you thinking when the fox was creeping up on them?"

"Do you think they will get off the tracks before the train comes?"

❑ *Expanding.* As part of conversation, you can also restate and expand the comments children make about texts. For example:

Mrs. R: Let's tell about the story. What do you think we could write?

Sira: Coyote want to win race.

Mrs. R: We could write that Coyote wanted to win the race. Do you think that we should also say why? Coyote wanted to win the race because....

Adding to and/or restating children's language gives them a model based on something they already understand (Pemberton and Watkins 1987; Valdez-Menchaca and Whitehurst 1992).

Select Texts That Reflect Diversity in Language and Culture

You will want to read aloud and discuss a wide variety of texts that will expand children's language and background knowledge. Be sure to look for texts that reflect the many languages and cultures represented in your school. (Even if you do not have great diversity in your own classroom, you will want your students to recognize many languages and cultures.) In Chapter 20, we describe the role of appealing texts in increasing student motivation: *Tortillas and Lullabies: Tortillas y cancioncitas* (Reiser 1998) is an example of the kind of books you can read aloud to English language learners. *Charlotte Huck's Children's Literature with Literature Database CD-ROM* (Kiefer, Hepler, and Hickman 2006) lists many other recommendations. The website of the IRA Children's Literature and Reading Special Interest Group— *http://www.tcnj.edu/~childlit/index.htm*—is another good resource. Finally, on our website *fountasandpinnellleveledbooks.com* we regularly introduce new, culturally diverse books to read aloud. We also provide suggestions for using each book with children, including ways to extend ideas through writing.

Teach Academic Language

When English language learners enter school for instruction in English, they not only face a whole new language, but that language contains vocabulary and ways of talking that they may not have yet experienced in their primary language. (This is also true for most English speakers.) Some will have received adequate schooling in their native country, but others' schooling will have been limited or interrupted. Children who have been in the United States for more than seven years may still be reading below grade level (Freeman and Freeman 2002). These students have the very difficult task of learning *academic language* related to the tasks they are expected to do, as well as words that have specific technical meaning in the content areas (math, language arts, social studies, and science). They need to comprehend, speak, read, and write when the context is not rich and the topic is cognitively demanding.

Every content area has its own specialized vocabulary. This is most evident to adults in college courses. For young children, words like *lab, scientist, flippers, wings, feathers,* or *gravity* are challenging technical words when they appear in nonfiction books. Beginning readers, including English language learners, often do not understand the meaning of words related to print, like *first* (on the top left), *letter, word, sentence, period, comma, exclamation point, question mark,* and other labels. When it comes to understanding directions, they may be challenged by words such as *bottom* and *top* when it refers to a piece of paper or *complete* when it means to fill in the blanks on a piece of paper.

Accept Variety in Pronunciation and Intonation

Often, English learners can speak the language, but they still employ the phonology and intonation patterns of their primary language. This makes for great variety, and you do not want to correct them, especially not in front of others! After all, every one of us has some kind of "accent" as viewed by people in other regions and countries. Rather, respond to the meaning of what they say. You can do the same kind of teaching, prompting, and reinforcing for fluent reading as you do for all students (see Chapter 16). As English language learners gain more experience in speaking, reading, and writing, they will take on the complex intonation patterns that reflect meanings expressed in English.

Use Shared Reading and Readers' Theater

Shared and performance reading provide an authentic reason to read something over and over, become fluent with it, and think about the meaning. It is also an ideal way for children to use new language structure with support, and it promotes good articulation.

Make Lessons Clear and Explicit

You may feel frustrated when you teach an entire lesson and then find that students do not understand and cannot follow through in their independent work. This happens with many students if the work is too difficult; but for English language learners the reason may be trouble in understanding English. It will help all your students to be very clear in the language you use in lessons (see Pinnell and Fountas, 2003a, 2003b, 2003c, and 2003d for examples).

- ❑ State the principle in very clear language that you use several times during the lesson.
- ❑ Write the principle on a chart that children can see clearly.
- ❑ Provide very easy examples of the principle using words that children know.
- ❑ Leave the chart in view so that children can refer to it while engaged in independent work.
- ❑ If you see that the principle is too hard for many of the children, provide small-group support to build a foundation.

Establish Predictable Routines in the Learning Environment

It is tremendously helpful to English learners to have a predictable and organized environment—one in which they know what to do and are not required to follow *different* oral directions every day. If they know how to get materials and put them away and predict what will happen next, they feel competent. They can pay more attention to expanding language, reading, and writing.

Make Expectations Clear and Check for Understanding

Consider this set of directions:

First I want you to read the first chapter of the book. After you are finished, take this piece of paper. In the first box draw and write a sentence about something in the book. Then find something in the first chapter that the writer has compared to something else. Draw and write about it in the second box. Do the same thing in the remaining two boxes on the page. After that, finish the word study sheet on consonant clusters that begin a word.

All these activities may be valuable, but it's easy to see how English learners could be overwhelmed. If children have difficulty understanding and remembering directions, tell them about one task at a time and act out exactly what you want them to do. Use fewer words and show more. Over time, they will not only learn more language but they will be able to predict the actions expected.

▶ Small-Group Reading Instruction and Intervention Lessons

With good classroom practices as a foundation, be sure English language learners receive small-group reading instruction. Some may need an extra intervention group. Below are some suggestions related to small-group instruction.

Provide Lessons with Predictable Routines

Using a predictable lesson framework that includes subroutines will help all at-risk literacy learners develop confidence and a sense of security. They know what is expected of them in the different parts of the lesson. Lessons are not rote. The books change, the concepts vary, and the conversation takes different turns. As you begin guided reading or inter-

vention lessons, explain each part of the lesson carefully. Tell and show children what they will be doing. You will need to remind them at each point in the lesson for some time, but eventually they will begin to be comfortable with the framework and the routines will require little attention. It may also be important to tell children *why* they are engaging in different kinds of literacy tasks, for example:

- ❏ "Read this again to help make your reading sound smooth."

- ❏ "When you sort these words it will help you see the pattern."

- ❏ "Say the words slowly and it will help you hear the sounds."

Analyze Texts to Detect and Clarify Difficult Concepts

It is easiest for beginners to read about familiar topics; however, it's impossible to select texts that deal *only* with ideas that are completely familiar to children. What are the children's levels of background knowledge related to the topic? Think about the content, and vocabulary such as idioms, colloquialisms, contractions, and words with more than one meaning. Notice the language structure, illustrations, and the graphics. You will need to provide some background information to help children better process a text, and there is no better place to do this than in the book introduction.

Setting the Table is a very simple book (page 16 is reproduced in Figure 18-3). A boy is getting the table ready for dinner. On each page, the boy puts a new item on the table and tells what is here. On the first page he says, "Here is the mat." The pattern does not vary: "Here is the [item]." English language learners can read this perfectly with only an introduction to the structure, but you want to be sure they understand it. In many households, the table is never set like the one on page 16 (and even if it is, it might look very different). In some cultures, it is quite acceptable and mannerly to eat with your hands, or the implements may be different. The only other example children may have is the school cafeteria. Children do understand sitting down to eat with family members and know that things like plates and bowls are usually used. Simply explain that this is one way to get ready to eat, and go over the labels of the items.

Making a Snowman (see the pages reproduced in Figure 18-4) is also a very simple text. But millions of children have never seen snow or made a snowman! Still, snow needn't be left out of children's books altogether. Chances are, almost all children have seen snow in the media or at least in holiday decorations. Nevertheless, you will want to check their understanding and explain the concept if needed:

Mr. W: This book is about making a snowman. In some places in the winter, it is very cold and they have snow. Have any of you seen snow?

Jared: I saw Frosty the Snowman.

Linnet: It's like ice.

Mr. W: It is cold like ice. Just imagine that instead of rain, the water is frozen and fluffy. Look at page 3. The snowflakes are coming down, and it is piling up on the ground. You can pick it up and make big balls like the girl is going to do in this book. She is going to do some things to make the balls of snow look like a funny man.

Little Things (see Figure 18-5) is built around the concept of small things. This text is also repetitive and quite easy. But readers need to understand why the word *little* appears on every page. Point out that in comparison to the girl, the chair or table is *little*. Looking at page 16 before reading will put the entire book into perspective. Don't be afraid to give readers the information they need. It is far better to "know" the ending than to read the entire book without good comprehension. After reading this book a couple of

Figure 18-3 Page Spread from *Setting the Table* from Leveled Literacy Intervention, Orange System (Heinemann 2009)

Figure 18-4 Pages from *Making a Snowman* from Leveled Literacy Intervention, Orange System (Heinemann 2009)

times, children will not only understand the word *little* (and have a good chance of being able to read it in another text), but will also have practiced reading with the adjective *before* the noun. (In some languages, it usually appears after the noun.)

Often, illustrators and writers include significant information in the pictures. Be sure that readers absorb that information. Preview all texts for ways to help children gain meaning from illustrations; then draw children's attention to the pictures and support their interpretation. They need to notice labels, comparisons,

FIGURE 18-5 Page Layout of *Little Things* from Leveled Literacy Intervention, Orange System (Heinemann 2009)

insets, speech and thought bubbles, etc. In *Animals with Wings* (several pages are reproduced in Figure 18-6), for example, the writer and illustrator compare several kinds of birds and bats. Readers need to look at the illustrations in this text to comprehend the overall concept.

On page 16 of *Little Cub* (see Figure 18-7) readers need to understand that the illustration in the "thought bubble" means that Little Cub is dreaming about playing soccer:

> **Mrs. L:** And let's look at the last page. What is Little Cub doing now?
>
> **Julio:** He's sleeping.
>
> **Saundra:** He's kicking the ball, too.
>
> **Mrs. L:** He is asleep in his bed. The little bubble above his head shows you that he is dreaming—thinking about things in his head while he is asleep.
>
> **Charley:** Like bad dreams?
>
> **Mrs. L:** Well, this is a good dream, because it's about his favorite thing. See the little bubbles coming from Little Cub's head to the big bubble? That means he isn't saying anything, but he is thinking. He is dreaming that he is kicking the ball right into the net and that makes a score. And he is saying, "I am dreaming."

Analyze Texts for Tricky Language and Rehearse Children in Using It

The more you know about your English learners, the better you will be able to read books quickly and pick up vocabulary, concepts, and aspects of language structure that will be difficult for them. Of the three, language structure is probably the most challenging.

Figure 18-6 Page Spreads from *Animals with Wings* from Leveled Literacy Intervention, Blue System (Heinemann 2009)

Figure 18-7 Page from *Little Cub* from Leveled Literacy Intervention, Orange System (Heinemann 2009)

My Big Brother has syntactic patterns that many children will not have encountered before in written language (see Figure 18-8). In this segment of her introduction, Ms. P talks about the central concept—that in this book a boy talks about his big brother:

Ms. P: Look at page 14. On this page, the boy tells about his brother. He says, "My big brother likes to read books with me." What do you think about the big brother who likes to read books with his little brother? *[Points to the little brother and big brother while talking.]*

Hilda: It's nice he likes to read with him.

Ms. P: Let's read this all together.

Children and teacher together read, "My big brother likes to read books with me."

My big brother likes to read books with me.

Figure 18-8 Page Spread from *My Big Brother* from Leveled Literacy Intervention, Orange System (Heinemann 2009)

Ant met a frog.

"Can you hop?" said the frog.

"No, I can't," said the ant.

Figure 18-9 Page Spread from *Ant Can't* from Leveled Literacy Intervention, Green System (Heinemann 2009)

The question and answer format in *Ant Can't* (pages 6 and 7 are reproduced in Figure 18-9) is an example of difficult language. Mrs. J has read the book to the children twice and now invites them to use the language in preparation for shared reading:

Mrs. J: On page 6, Ant met a frog. The frog asks the same question. "Can you hop?" The ant says the same thing: "No, I can't." Let's say the question and the answer.

Children and Mrs. J: "Can you hop? No, I can't."

Mrs. J: Now Elena, you say the question, "Can you hop?" And Sonia and Jake, you say the answer, "No, I can't." Say it like the frog and the ant are talking.

Elena: "Can you hop?"

Sonia and Jake: "No, I can't."

Mrs. J: You sounded like you are talking. Now, let's read the rest of the book that way.

This may seem like a great deal of rehearsal, but if you have ever struggled to learn another language, you know that syntactic patterns and verb inflection are a big part of the task. The first texts children read have very simple, direct sentences (see Chapter 6), but just like all readers, English learners must learn to deal with more complex syntax.

Word endings can be quite challenging for students, and they cannot figure these endings out using phonics alone. It helps to have students look at a word like *coming* in two parts and to learn the *-ing* ending. But students also need a sense of the syntax so that they can tell if their reading sounds right. The example below is from a book introduction to *The Soccer Game* (pages 10 and 11 are reproduced in Figure 18-10):

Ms. B: On page 10, Sam yelled something to Jesse. Say *yelled.* What would you expect to see at the beginning of the word *yelled?*

Ignacio: It's like *yellow?* A *y?*

Ms. B: Yes. Find *yelled.* [*Children locate the word.*] Now look at the end of the word. It's an *-ed.* Cover the *-ed* with your finger and you see *yell.* [*Demonstrates.*] Read the whole word and it says—

Children: *yelled*

Ms. B: That means that he did it. He yelled. Let's read that whole sentence. Listen to how it sounds. [*They read in unison, then repeat this process with* looked *and* coming.] So, on all the pages of this book, you are going to see words with endings. Say the endings and be sure that your reading sounds right.

In this case, some independent work to take home reinforced the concept. The simple sheet in Figure 18-11 prompts children to draw pictures showing the comparison between two characters. At the same time they get more practice reading words with the *-ed* ending.

Another difficult syntactic pattern is shown on page 7 of *A Surprise for Mom* (see Figure 18-12). There are two challenges on this page—reading the word *too*, which is set off by commas, and reading a list that is separated by commas:

Ms. G: Look at page 7. There are a couple of tricky things here that I want to show you so that you can tell if your reading sounds right. Look at the first line and find this little mark—the comma. [*Writes a comma on the whiteboard. Children find the comma on the page.*] Now, listen while I read and tell me what my voice does at the comma. [*Demonstrates.*]

Henry: You stopped and took a breath.

Ms. G: The writer used *too* to tell us they got another thing. Yes, now let's all read that. [*They*

Figure 18-10 Page Spread from *The Soccer Game* from Leveled Literacy Intervention, Green System (Heinemann 2009)

Figure 18-11 Comparison in *The Soccer Game*

read in unison.] Take a little breath when you see a comma. Listen while I read the next sentence. [*Reads the second sentence.*] This time the comma tells us there will be more than two things in the sentence. The boy is saying that they like to eat corn and peppers and potatoes. But what do you see after *corn?*

Children: A comma.

Ms. G: Just a comma. So you read the sentence like this. [*Demonstrates again.*]

Figure 18-12 Page from *A Surprise for Mom* from Leveled Literacy Intervention, Green System (Heinemann 2009)

We got some corn, too.
We like to eat corn,
peppers, and potatoes.
We like carrots
and tomatoes, too.

7

The ability to understand this text was supported in the independent homework activity shown in Figure 18-13. Here the children have the opportunity to think about the meaning and read a longer sentence with an easier syntactic pattern. They illustrate each concept and read the words several times.

You can use punctuation and text features to help English language learners process more complex syntax and improve their intonation patterns. The challenges in *Bad Luck Day* include divided dialogue, phrases, idioms, a phrase set off by a dash, expressive

Green#78 A Surprise for Mom   Name: Paola

We like potatoes and tomatoes and peppers and corn and carrots. We like the soup.

Figure 18-13 Homework Activity for *A Surprise for Mom*

utterances that are not sentences, and words in italics to signal emphasis. As part of the introduction, the teacher worked to help students understand the role of the dash on page 13 (see Figure 18-14):

Ms. M: That little black cloud over Tia's head means she is really having a bad luck day. Look at page 13. In the first sentence, the writer wants to be sure that we understand just how bad Tia's day was getting to be. Her day is different from everyone else's. Do you see a little line right before the word *but?* [*Children locate the dash.*] That is called a dash, and it tells you to stop and then say the next part a little bit louder. Listen while I read it. [*Demonstrates.*] What are you thinking?

Liz: She isn't reading like everybody else.

Ms. M: That's right, and to be sure you know that, there is a dash.

Teach Text Structure

Perceiving text structure is a powerful factor in comprehension (see Chapters 2 and 6). Helping English language learners understand how the text is organized provides a framework that will support comprehension. For example:

❑ In reading *Little Things,* it will help to know that the girl first shows many of the little things that go in the house. At the end you see the whole house and it is little. The same text structure operates in *Setting the Table.*

❑ In reading *Animals with Wings,* the writer always shows you how the animals are alike (having wings) and how they are different (for example, swimming and flying).

❑ To read *Ant Can't,* it helps to understand the question and answer format.

❑ To read *Making a Snowman,* it helps to understand that the girl is doing things in a sequence and her finished snowman is shown on the last page.

Making a Pizza is also a book with sequential order, but it has a circular structure (five pages are reproduced in Figure 18-15). Comprehending even this simple text requires inference; knowing the text structure will support deeper thinking:

Mr. K: How many of you like to eat pizza? [*All raise their hands.*] In this book, you will learn how to make a pizza. Look at pages 2 and 3. Start with a pan. Take a good look at it and put your finger on the pan. The writer says, "Here is the pan." On every page the writer tells a new thing that goes on the pizza. [*Mr. K has children say and locate the word* here *on two pages. He moves through the book, drawing attention to the picture and touching the new item while saying the label.*] Now look at page 15. What is here now? Here is the what? "Here is the pizza." Right. Doesn't it look good? Do you think this is the end of the book?

Josh: No, there is one more page.

Mr. K: There's going to be a surprise on the next page. Turn it and see.

Rick: It's gone!

Josh: It's just the pan.

Rick: They ate it. But we didn't see them.

Mr. K: It looks like you might be right. But I can see some little crumbs, so that's probably what the pan looked like after they ate it all. So what will the writer say? Now go back to page 2. Point and read.

"A BUG!" Tia shrieked,
dropping the sandwich.

Gracie leaned down.
"It's just a plastic worm," she said.
"I *knew* Tony was up to something."

Back in class, everyone else was reading
—but not Tia.
Her stomach rumbled.
She searched her backpack
for something to eat.

Tia found an old candy bar.
Finally, some good luck!

Then a shadow fell across Tia's desk.

12   13

Figure 18-14 Page Spread from *Bad-Luck Day* from Leveled Literacy Intervention, Green System (Heinemann 2009)

Here is the pan.

2

Here is the pizza.

14

Here is the pan.

Figure 18-15 Page Spreads from *Making a Pizza* from Leveled Literacy Intervention, Orange System (Heinemann 2009)

Extend Understanding Through Writing

As part of your small-group instruction for English language learners, consider including a variety of genres of writing (see Chapter 13). Interactive and shared writing support English language learners by:

❑ Providing a model of English syntax.

❑ Showing students how to put thinking into words.

❑ Helping them use new vocabulary in context.

❑ Allowing them to compose standard English sentences as a group.

❑ Giving them a sense of ownership of the piece.

❑ Providing a reason to reread and re-experience the syntax.

After a group had read, discussed, and reread *All About Dolphins* (pages 6 and 7 are reproduced in Figure 18-16), Ms. O and the children together composed the piece of interactive writing shown in Figure 18-17. The children had the opportunity to produce two complex sentences, one that included a technical vocabulary word. The second sentence also has a prepositional phrase in it. They can revisit this text to reread it or attend to features of words.

A dolphin has a blowhole.
A baby dolphin stays with its mother two or three years.

Figure 18-17 Interactive Writing based on *All About Dolphins*

The idea of a temporal sequence is valuable information for English language learners, and this can be reinforced through writing as well as diagrams. For example, sequence—the life cycle—is key to the meaning of *All About Frogs* (page 16 is reproduced in Figure 18-18. The teacher used interactive writing to record understandings of the process in sequential order (see Figure 18-19); students contributed and wrote some of the letters/words. They then created the version of the life cycle shown in Figure 18-20).

You can also use dictated and independent writing to help English language learners learn about the formation of sentences and individual vocabulary words in English. Dictation relieves the writers of the act of composition. They can concentrate on constructing the words, one after another. They reread the sentence many times, which helps them internalize syntactic patterns that are acceptable in English.

Ultimately, English language learners need to write independently. One of the good things about small-group work is that you can support sentence construction. Be sure to stick with the child's own

Dolphins swim together in groups.
The groups are called **pods**.
A pod has baby dolphins
and grown-up dolphins.

calf

A baby dolphin is called a **calf**.
A calf stays with its mother
for two or three years.

pod

Figure 18-16 Page spread from *All About Dolphins* from Leveled Literacy Intervention, Green System (Heinemann 2009)

meaning and suggest only minor expansions. The child should be able to read back the sentence and find it meaningful.

Be Explicit in Teaching About Letters, Sounds, and Words

English language learners do need to learn about sounds and letters and how words "work." All of the

Figure 18-18 Page from *How Frogs Grow* from Leveled Literacy Intervention, Green System (Heinemann 2009)

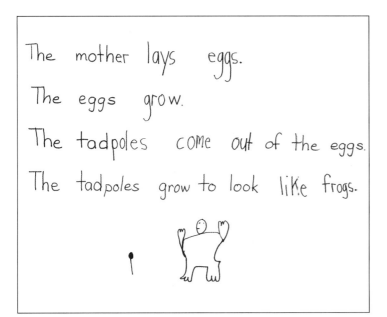

Figure 18-19 Interactive Writing based on *How Frogs Grow*

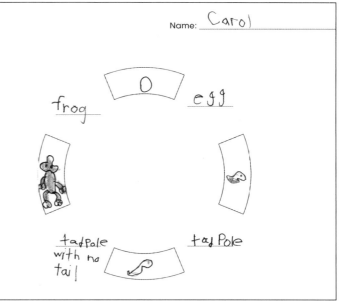

Figure 18-20 Student-Created Life Cycle for *How Frogs Grow*

suggestions in Chapters 11 and 12 will be helpful as you work with children in small groups. After each guided reading lesson, take a few minutes to focus on a specific kind of information by working with words. You can use a small whiteboard or chalkboard, the easel, or a chart. Tell children what you are doing and show them at the same time. Here's an example:

> **Mrs. N:** I want to write *hop*. I know /h/. [*Writes it.*] "I know /op/. [*Writes it.*] Now my word says *hop*. Say the sounds with me.
>
> **Children:** /h/ /op/
>
> **Mrs. N:** Now say the whole word with me.
>
> **Children:** *hop*

Children can learn to associate letters and sounds by sorting pictures (see the examples in Figures 18-21 and 18-22). These exercises help students learn the English label for the picture, but you may find that they use their first language occasionally as well. Spanish-speaking children often place the picture of a cat under *g* (as in *gato*). This indicates good understanding of the task you are trying to teach, but the child will also need to know the English word. (Some teachers place a few words in other languages on their wall charts. All children are interested in learning another language.) Be sure children know the labels for all of the pictures you use. Discard those that you think will be confusing.

Visual examples are helpful even when English language learners are working with higher-level phonics principles. The chart in Figure 18-23 can be used to draw attention to vowels with *r*. The word sort in

Figure 18-24 was completed by a student independently. Here, again, it is best to work with words children have in their speaking vocabularies. Otherwise, they are only saying meaningless words. You may also find that their pronunciation is not always helpful when they are sorting words. Don't drill too much on words that are hard for students to say. Instead, help them look at the words, say them, and understand their meaning. Most of all, help them recognize the patterns they are learning when they encounter words as they read or write continuous print.

Figure 18-21 Pocket Chart Sorting Pictures Under Letters

-ar	-ir	-ur	-er	-or
car	bird	burn	her	corn
barn	fir	fur	mother	for
far	first		better	torn

Figure 18-23 Words with a Vowel and *r*

Figure 18-22 Individual Picture Sort, Initial Consonants

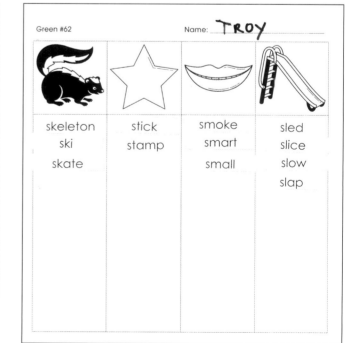

Figure 18-24 Consonant Cluster Sort

▶ Individual Interactions During Reading and Writing

Besides working with a small group, you should also have interactions with individuals. This individual work is important because you want children to become independent readers and writers. That means teaching them and providing support, but ultimately you must turn over the task and let them do it—with your help as necessary.

Individual Interactions During Reading

Teach, prompt, and reinforce effective behaviors as you work alongside children who are reading individually during small-group instruction. Support English language learners' understandings of the text—language, words, and organization. Also support word solving, but invite them to check with other sources of information (the meaning and language).

Individual interactions are highly effective. You may not have a great deal of time for such interactions, but to the extent you can work them in, they will have a big payoff. Below are some suggestions.

BE AWARE OF PLACES IN THE TEXT THAT MIGHT BE HARD FOR AN INDIVIDUAL READER

In your initial examination of a book before using it for instruction, make predictions about text factors that might be difficult for the English language learners in your group. This will vary according to their knowledge of English and their language backgrounds. For example, Ms. E looked at *The Soccer Game* (see Figure 18-10) and predicted that her students would have some difficulty noticing and using word endings even though they had studied them over a few weeks. So she focused on

word endings during the orientation. She then interacted with Julius while he was reading:

JULIUS [*reading page 11*]: "Jesse put his foot out. He stop the ball [*stops and looks at* stopped]. He stop—he—

Ms. E: Why did you stop? [*Julius points at the* -ed.] You saw something you know.

JULIUS: It says *stop–ed?*

Ms. E: *Try stopped.*

JULIUS: "He stopped the ball to save the ants."

Ms. E: Now it sounds right and looks right.

JULIUS: "Then he kick—kicked the ball back to Sam." Why does it sound like *t?*

Ms. E: Sometimes the *ed* sounds like *t—looked, stopped,* and *kicked.*

You can use individual interactions to clarify a student's understanding of words as well. *Into the Sea* is an informational text that includes some technical words (see the pages reproduced in Figure 18-25). In the interaction below, Mrs. S clarified a word that has a meaning other than the one Daniel knew:

DANIEL [*reading page 2*]: "My name is Emma— [*Appeals.*]

My name is Emma Hickerson.
I am a scientist.
I study plants and animals of the sea.

I use this little sub.
It is a special sub that can dive deep into the water.

Figure 18-25 Page Spread from *Into the Sea* from Leveled Literacy Intervention, Blue System (Heinemann 2009)

MRS. S: You try it.

DANIEL: "Hic— [*Stops.*]

MRS. S: You started it. Could it be Hickerson?

DANIEL: "My name is Emma Hickerson. I am a scientist. I study plants and animals of the sea. I use this little sub— [*stops and looks puzzled*]. Is it *sub*?

MRS. S: *Sub*. It is short for *submarine*, a boat that can dive under the water. See it in the picture? A sub is a sandwich that you eat, and it's called that because it sort of looks like that underwater boat.

Mrs. S helped Daniel make use of the pictures. She hypothesized that he did not know the vocabulary word *submarine* but might have familiarity with the sandwich. In this way she tried to make a connection. She also gave the reader a little boost for reading the language of the paragraph. The first pages of a text about a new concept are often hard. Once he knows some of the critical concepts, Daniel can gain momentum.

USE CLEAR LANGUAGE AND MONITOR UNDERSTANDING

There are many examples of the kind of clear language you can use to support readers in Chapters 14, 15, 16, and 17. Be sure that English language learners understand what you mean by the following kinds of prompt:

- ❑ "Make it sound right."
- ❑ "Try that again."
- ❑ "Start the word."
- ❑ "Something wasn't quite right on that page."
- ❑ "Read it with your eyes."
- ❑ "Make it sound like you're talking."

This is a new kind of academic language that you are helping them understand, and once they do, they can begin to internalize the behavior. If you find that a reader does not understand the prompt, go back and show what you mean. Be very explicit. Say the prompt and then demonstrate the behavior.

Individual Interactions During Writing

After providing directions and setting up the task, you can interact with children while they write. Remember that writing slows down the process so that children can give more attention to the details of print. In brief interactions, teach more using any of the language presented in Chapter 13. For example:

- ❑ "Start here."
- ❑ "Write here next."
- ❑ "Feel the space with your finger."
- ❑ "Show a place where you left good space."
- ❑ "You know how to start it."
- ❑ "Think about how to write it."
- ❑ "Clap the parts you hear."
- ❑ "Say the word slowly. How many sounds do you hear?"
- ❑ "Do you know another word that sounds like that?"
- ❑ "Think about a part you know."
- ❑ "You need a vowel next."

As with reading interactions, you will want to monitor children's understanding closely. Below are some general suggestions for helping English learners in writing:

- ❑ Value drawing—it will help children express understandings and rehearse language.
- ❑ Have children repeat the sentence several times before writing, so that they hold on to the language structure.
- ❑ Help children talk about familiar topics before being expected to write them.
- ❑ Help children use charts produced through interactive and shared writing as resources; allow them to imitate at first.
- ❑ Help them use their reading books as models.
- ❑ Learn something about the sound systems of children's first languages; you will gain valuable insights into the way they approximate spellings.
- ❑ Accept attempts at spellings that reflect the child's own pronunciations of words; they are showing phonics knowledge, and with support

they will learn to look at the words to help them use conventional spelling.

❑ Help them value their work by having them save it in a portfolio.

▶ Speaking Two or More Languages—A Gift, Not a Deficit

At the beginning of this chapter, we mentioned the tremendous challenges faced by English language learners, but we should also remember that, ultimately, they have a real advantage. If we can support these students in speaking, reading, and writing English while at the same time encouraging them to value and converse (or read and write) in their primary language, they will have linguistic resources that allow them a much broader access to vocabulary. Because of how languages mix, expand, and change, many word roots and parts cross languages; using different kinds of syntax makes the speaker flexible. Also

consider the tremendous amount of learning that has already taken place before children start school. That is evidence that children can take on much more. Of the new school entrant, Clay (1991a) says:

> He has learned how to learn language.
>
> It is important for teachers to remind themselves of this when they seem to hear differences in a particular child's speech. The child may not know as much about language as some of his peers, or he may find the rules for talking in school are different from those in his culture or ethnic group, or he may see little similarity between talking in his family and the more formal teacher-pupil talk of the classroom, or he may even speak a different language from the teacher's. Yet in all these cases the child has already learned how to learn language. (26–27)

Every language system is evidence of the tremendous learning power of every child. Except in severe cases, every child develops language. By building on children's strengths, we can help every one of them become literate.

▶ Suggestions for Professional Development

PROVIDING SPECIAL SUPPORT TO ENGLISH LANGUAGE LEARNERS

1. Make a list of English language learners in your classroom and the first language of each. Take the list to a meeting with colleagues.

2. For each language, brainstorm a list of grammatical structures and vocabulary words that these learners find difficult. Having a speaker of the native language at the meeting will also be helpful. That individual can describe some of the important differences between the children's first languages and English and can also tell you what speakers of the language find difficult about learning English.

3. Take a group of texts that your students are likely to read in the next few weeks. Examine each to determine language structures and vocabulary words that will be challenging.

4. Make a plan to use these grammatical structures and vocabulary words in several contexts (interactive read aloud, shared reading, discussion, dictated writing, and guided reading). Don't make an artificial situation; just look for opportunity.

5. Plan book introductions to several texts. Tailor the introductions to help children deal with tricky language structure and vocabulary. Discuss how your introductions provide special support to your language learners.

6. Schedule another meeting to discuss your results and insights you gained.

Engaging Readers' Attention and Memory in Successful Learning

CHAPTER

19

ATTENTION AND MEMORY ARE BOTH CRITICAL *to learning. Proficient readers and writers can selectively attend to important information, store it in short term memory, and evaluate it in terms of stored memory. These actions are required in order to learn. And these are the very actions that struggling readers almost always find difficult. In this chapter, we explore the role that attention plays in forming the memory and, in turn, the role of memory in learning literacy. We have discussed these factors in other chapters; here, we summarize them as fifteen important principles.*

Attention and memory feed each other; both are critical to learning. Through attention, we notice information; through memory, we store and recall it. Without the ability to selectively attend to important information, store it in our short-term memory, and evaluate it in relation to our stored memory, we cannot learn. Those requirements apply to all learning, including the ability to read and write. Teachers often are concerned that struggling readers:

❑ Cannot sustain attention.

❑ Don't know what to look for.

❑ Have trouble differentiating information when attending.

❑ Have difficulty remembering information.

❑ Have trouble recalling and using information they do remember.

❑ Are rigid, approaching a problem in the same way no matter how unsuccessful the attempt.

❑ Cannot attend to language and graphic information at the same time (losing meaning when they engage in word solving or reading inaccurately when they think about meaning).

It takes them longer to learn words; they are slower and forget more easily than other students. They seem to be struggling not just with one thing but with many. Soon they enter a downward spiral. Because they have fewer resources, they do not develop efficient strategic actions. They read slowly and with difficulty, so they do less reading. They become passive whenever they engage with print; they simply stop trying.

The longer this cycle persists, the harder it is to break. In general, we as teachers need to create situations in which readers do attend actively, know how to direct attention selectively, store information efficiently, and retrieve the information they need to read and write strategically.

▶ Attention

From their earliest days, babies pick up stimuli from the environment, gradually differentiating those things that are meaningful and deserve attention. Very quickly, they begin to attend selectively by paying less attention both to sounds and sights that are familiar and to those that are completely new. They give more attention to sounds and sights that are novel but not completely unfamiliar. Children's brains continue to develop as they begin to process more sensory information and learn to use language through interaction with others. At this point, children are able to focus attention purposefully—because they want to. The systems for attending become more and more complex.

Attention has an alertness aspect (availability) and a selectivity aspect (the ability to focus on the important piece of information and filter out the other stimuli) (see Figure 19–1). Both aspects must be present to store information in memory. All of us direct our attention all the time and selectively attend to what we consider to be important, ignoring many of the hundreds of pieces of information that bombard us at any given moment. Several regions of the brain work together to create the arousal that ensures we are ready to respond to stimulation. Other parts of the brain provide the feedback pathways between regions that make it possible to *select* what we attend to. So our brains constantly pick up stimuli and screen out stimuli.

Alertness means actively attending, searching for stimuli. Reading is a complex act requiring individu-

---

Figure 19-1 Factors in Attention

Alertness: The individual is ready to attend to stimuli—aroused, active, and alert to receive information.

Selectivity: The individual attends only to the stimuli that are important for the act he is attempting; other information is ignored.

---

als to sustain active attention for long periods of time, constantly taking in new stimuli. Selectivity means readers are attending only to the information needed to construct meaning from the text. Selectivity may be something relatively simple—distinguishing the word *can* from *cat*—or it may involve very sophisticated thinking processes—detecting propaganda by understanding its characteristics and comparing the ideas in a text with background knowledge.

Askew and Fountas (1998, 126) have described children as "active participants in their own literacy development." Children attend to and select information, using it to test hypotheses. Using all the sources of information available to them, they work at overcoming difficulty. Their resources include the meaning of the text, the language structures, the vocabulary, the details and features of print, and the illustrations. These young readers compare new information to what they already know and this, in turn, influences further active attention. In contrast, they say, some learners are passive, waiting for the teacher to direct the task and do the work. The more passive and dependent a reader becomes, the harder it will be to develop complex reading and writing processes. It is critical for such learners to learn to:

❑ Work at overcoming difficulty.

❑ Take some initiative.

❑ Make some links.

(Askew and Fountas 1998, 128)

Fostering active attention means engaging learners as they take on all aspects of reading. Many researchers describe a cycle of learning: take letter learning as an example. At first letters are a confusing mass of information. They look more alike than different. Learners must use visual stimuli to distinguish letters from each other. At first they may notice any one feature—the dot on the *i*, the tail on the *g*. But over time they begin to attend to finer details until they know the features of the letters. Their attention sharpens; by paying close attention they notice every detail, make connections, and form categories. Then they learn to distinguish letters faster. Finally, readers can move letters around—make words, write words, and decode words with little conscious attention, leaving the attention free for more learning.

We do not mean to imply that learning to read or write is a linear process in which the child first must learn letters and then begin to read. Simultaneously, in many different areas, children complete this learning cycle from undifferentiated attention to noticing some features to close attention to specific features and on to speed and automaticity. Efficient learners are linking these sets of information as they engage in the complex act of reading.

Remedial reading programs often teach a very narrow set of skills a reader has been diagnosed as being unable to do. By the time they get to grade 3 or 4, many struggling readers have a long history of trying to learn isolated sets of information, much of which is meaningless. They do not realize how concepts are connected to one another, and they have no sense of the overall "executive function" of planning, organizing, carrying out activities, and evaluating and modifying behavior in the process of problem solving.

Children do need to know and attend to some very specific information such as letters or sounds, or even some words; but the best way to break the downward spiral described above is to enable readers to operate effectively. They need items of knowledge, but they also need to develop powerful strategic actions that enable them to learn a great deal more. They need to be able to *use* information in the process of problem solving during the complex act of reading and writing (see Figure 19–2). Even items that are partially known can be used strategically. Through this problem solving, readers and writers learn to

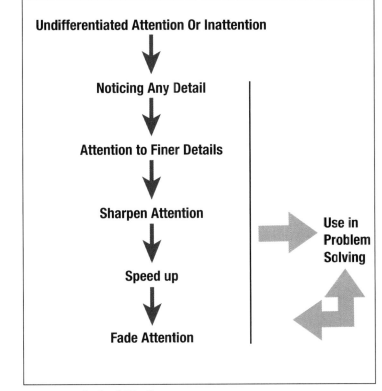

Figure 19-2 Cycle of Attention

weight attention; that is, to increase the attention paid to important dimensions and features and decrease attention to information that is either automatic or not needed.

Divided Attention

The role of attention is complex. As mentioned in Chapter 12, we once worked with a group of paraprofessionals who had been trained to teach each struggling first grader five new words each week. The words selected were those coming up in the stories in the basal reading series used in the school. Daily, they drilled the children using word cards, and by Friday every child was just about perfect in word recognition. However, the paraprofessionals were puzzled by two things: (1) teachers often reported that many children could not read these same words when they encountered them in continuous print and (2) children often had trouble recognizing words they had studied a couple of weeks before.

The problem may have been that the students' attention was directed toward just those features of words that would distinguish them from the other four being studied at the same time. When these readers met the same words in a text, the task was different. Now, they were required to recognize the word within a bewildering array of other visual forms and also process the language of the text. One of the characteristics of a proficient reader is the ability to shift attention in a rapid and flexible way, looking for the information that will be most helpful. Reading is always accomplished with *divided attention.*

According to Clay (2001), even the most proficient readers tend to give more attention to visual information when they are reading harder texts. That makes sense, because more word solving is required. There may be unfamiliar vocabulary, complex sentences with complicated punctuation, or difficult words. What distinguishes proficient from poor readers is that they are able to allocate this extra attention to print without losing the meaning or their sense of language. Ng's (1979) study of proficient young readers revealed their ability to change their word-solving and self-correction strategies to accommodate different kinds of texts. Kaye's (2008) more recent study of proficient second-grade readers revealed that they demonstrated more than sixty ways to overtly solve words. Both studies indicate the readers' ability to give different weights to different kinds of information as needed to accomplish the task at hand. They could "gear up" to do more heavy-duty decoding while still attending to language and meaning.

You must make it possible for your struggling readers to divide their attention like this as well—place them in a situation where they can attend to and make connections among the information they are noticing. Then you can help them engage in the cycle and expand it with levels of increasing complexity. "There is no simplified way to engage in the complex activities, but teachers and the public are typically presented with patently untrue simplifications in new commercial instruction kits" (Clay 1991, 224).

▶ Memory

Memory is all important. Without it, we cannot learn—cannot even function. Memory is strengthened through associations and connections. We remember best when we build a network of understandings that make sense to us. Here, too, the executive function plays an important role. Learners who have a "big picture" of the information or task will know why it is important to remember it. As they become more sophisticated, readers and writers become progressively more aware of how what they are learning will help them. They find this motivating.

According to Lyons (2003), there are several different kinds of memory, and "there is no single center for memory, no region of the brain responsible for locating and retrieving memories. Memories are made and stored in different networks of neurons throughout the brain" (66). The memory systems are outlined in Figure 19–3.

When a stimulus is noticed by your brain, it becomes an image. This moment of perception lasts only a second or two while your brain decides what is worthy of attention. Here, the selectivity of attention is evident. Some information is lost or ignored, and that is good and necessary. But some information that should be available may be lost because it is more complex than the learner can understand at the moment. It is just too hard. In this case, the perceiver does not have all the information needed.

Your *short-term memory* holds information for between fifteen and thirty seconds while you sort it and make decisions. What you decide to retain is temporarily stored in your *working memory*. Working memory is very active and lasts for several hours, which gives you the opportunity to enter selected information into *long-term memory*. Some of your working memory may become something you know extremely well; information that is not used does not remain. Long-term memory is stored in the hippocampus as a *memory trace* and is communicated back to other regions of the brain as needed. Long-

Figure 19-3 Memory Systems

"Buffer"	Perceives stimulus and holds it for a few seconds.
Short-Term Memory	Holds selected information for between 15 and 30 seconds while the individual makes decisions about what to put into working memory.
Working Memory	Holds selected information for a few hours while the individual makes decisions about whether it is meaningful (forming patterns in the brain).

Long-Term Memory

1. **Procedural Memory**	Skills such as motor movements related to a task. Procedures are consciously learned but become automatic.
2. **Episodic Memory**	Memory of information and events that the individual places at specific points of time in the past.
3. **Semantic Memory**	Memories that are impersonal; the foundation of knowledge that individuals acquire through learning that is not connected to personal experiences.
4. **Emotional Memory**	Memories that are associated with positive or negative emotions. May occur when forming procedural, episodic, or semantic memories.

term memory stores information indefinitely, ready to be recalled. (For a description of the brain and how it works, see Lyons 2003.)

Procedural Memory

Procedural memory allows us to perform all kinds of skilled tasks while paying minimal attention. Children acquire the skills of walking, running, and eating by first paying conscious attention and with much approximation; after a short time, they speed up and become more skilled; finally the procedure becomes automatic. In this way, we acquire thousands of processes, and there is variation among individuals. Some become highly skilled at typing or playing the piano; others at driving or playing a game. Many operations are composed of both highly automatic procedures and new learning (such as trying out a new recipe or driving your car through unfamiliar territory).

Procedural memory certainly plays a role in learning to read or write. Learning to match voice to print requires a great deal of effort for some young readers, but teacher support can make this action automatic in a fairly short time. The automatic aspects of reading that free attention for deeper thinking include:

- ❑ Being aware of left-to-right directionality and return sweep (finger, then eyes).
- ❑ Matching voice to print (finger, then eyes).
- ❑ Recognizing words (visual patterns).
- ❑ Recognizing patterns.
- ❑ Following punctuation cues.
- ❑ Using language structure.
- ❑ Interpreting illustrations.

Some readers and writers continue to struggle with things beyond the time they should be automatic, so their attention cannot be directed to other kinds of thinking. Other struggling readers may have turned counterproductive skills (reading each word as if it exists in isolation, for example) into habits that block learning. Confused by instruction, they may have internalized the wrong routines—the human brain is ready to learn and it will do so.

Many of the chapters in this book describe teaching actions that support readers as they practice an overt skill until it becomes automatic. Chapter 9 presents ways to help children automatically perceive the sounds in words; Chapter 10, to internalize early reading behaviors; and Chapters 11 and 12, to help children make word solving and word recognition automatic. Chapters 13, 14, 15, and 16 provide guidance in helping children engage in the problem solving that makes automatic responses faster and require little attention. Procedural memory acts to move the whole process forward.

Episodic Memory

Many of us can remember episodes from our past—a wedding, the senior prom, graduation, birth of children. If we have served in the military during a war, that period might stand out in vivid detail. Chances are, episodic memory is enhanced by emotional memory (in that we remember what we associate with happiness or sorrow). Episodic memory may be distorted, because all of us remember selectively and from our own perspectives. Siblings, for example, often remember their parents and events that took place in childhood very differently from each other.

Episodic memory also figures in learning to read and write. Embarrassing or successful experiences with texts may stand out in the learner's mind. Few of us remember the "moment" when we learned to read, but memories of that period of time are probably securely lodged in long-term memory. Gay has a childhood memory—well before starting school—of realizing that she could recognize some of the words in the adult books in her home. That realization kicked off a spree of circling all the known words with a pencil. She couldn't read the book, of course, but think about all the processes that contributed to that episode:

❑ *Procedural memory* of how to open a book and look across the print.

❑ *Storage* in long-term memory of the visual features of some words.

❑ *Recognition* and *retrieval* of items stored in long-term memory.

❑ *Searching* for more examples of what was known.

Helping children become readers should be a pleasant experience—in an authentic rather than artificial way. Giving empty praise and slowing down the process will not do it. Few things are more pleasurable than tackling a challenging but achievable task and being successful. We need to put struggling readers in a position where they feel the satisfaction of the whole process coming together. You can accomplish this by careful text selection and sharing tasks that are too complex.

Episodic memory can help readers comprehend texts. For example, having visited India would make reading *The Namesake* more memorable. Having served in Afghanistan in recent years would help a reader think more deeply while reading *A Thousand Splendid Suns.* We read novels that remind us of people in our lives. History is more meaningful if we have visited the region to which it pertains. In Chapter 2, we describe how readers make connections between what they are reading and their personal lives. Of course, we all also read texts that are distant from our own experiences. But we have a vast store of information that we have gained through books, film, and interactions with other people; we use this *semantic memory* (see below) to comprehend those texts.

Semantic Memory

Most of our knowledge is stored in what we call *semantic memory.* Semantic memory doesn't depend on personal experience. Of course, memory is complex and not so easily categorized as this discussion might suggest. A memory of something like the Grand Canyon might be composed of knowledge gained through reading geology books, the memory of reading Western novels, thousands of photographs seen over a lifetime, *and* the experience of riding a mule to the bottom or rafting along the river. This combination of different kinds of memory makes a rich fabric against which to learn more.

Our knowledge consists of semantic memory that we have organized in systematic ways. We store more semantic memory every time we learn something. Language (words, rules of grammar, intonation patterns) is stored in semantic memory. Language is a tool for learning information that we then store in the form of words. Language is also the means by which we hold on to semantic memory. Most of what we learn is richly contextualized. We form categories and networks of information that help us remember.

Thinking and learning are more efficient for readers who are forming a network of understandings rather than a collection of isolated bits of information. Think about the difference between a computer hard drive and the old Rolodex. The Rolodex was organized and ordered for its time. The information was coded, but searching was limited to one dimension, one category, and searching had to be sequential. A computer stores a varied array of information that is coded and connected in many ways. You have a search engine that can rapidly access what you want. It isn't perfect; retrieval can be difficult, especially if you have not been systematic about naming and storing files, but the information is there if you know how to search for it, even if you have deleted it! Yet a computer is nothing compared to a human brain. Your brain operates using highly complex networks that connect hundreds of thousands of neurons that interact simultaneously. Our brains are always working to find relationships and connections, and the maps become more complex over time (Lyons 2003).

Everything depends on semantic memory. Readers need the opportunity to use and expand the language knowledge they have, and they also need to build a large amount of content knowledge. In the classroom, reading aloud texts that engage children will greatly benefit struggling readers, because it allows them access to more complex language and concepts. Readers who are having difficulty need to hear *more* texts read aloud than proficient readers do. For small-group instruction and intervention, select texts that readers can process as language and that will expand the words and grammatical structures they know. Above all, readers should process texts with attention to meaning.

Emotional Memory

Emotional memory associates positive and negative feelings with experiences, ideas, and information. In recent years, the policy of assigning more and more homework—some of it too difficult for students to do independently—has led to many unhappy scenes in the family home. Parents find themselves having to force children to spend long hours struggling. They may gain some semantic memory, but emotional memory of a negative sort will also be stored.

Children not only store memories of their own emotions, but they also respond to the feelings of those around them. Children can sense disapproval (Lyons 2003). Holland (1991), in a long-term study of struggling first-grade readers, reported being present when one of her subjects brought home his first report card, which included a D in reading. The parent immediately changed their opinion of the child's ability from competent to incompetent. Such experiences are packed with emotion.

Emotional memory is the mediator of all other kinds of memory. The more emotionally upset a learner is, the harder it is to learn and to engage in effective problem solving. (We talk more about the role of emotion in Chapter 20.)

▶ In the "Zone"

Attention and memory are related to Vygotsky's (1962) concept of the "zone of proximal development," which is the "distance between the actual developmental level as determined by independent problem solving and the level of potential development as determined through problem solving under adult guidance or in collaboration with more capable peers" (86). This theory suggests that individuals learn best when they are working at the "edge" of their own knowledge, using current understandings as a resource to perform a more challenging task or take on new learning (see Figure 19–4). If the task is too easy, they will not learn more; if it is too hard, they are in such foreign territory that they cannot use their knowledge.

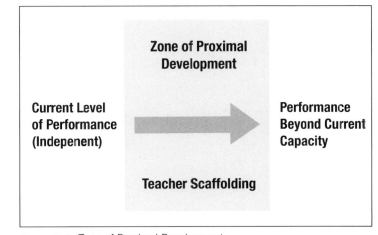

Figure 19-4 Zone of Proximal Development

The teacher's instructional scaffold plays an important role in helping a reader construct a proficient literacy system. Chapters 13 through 17 include many descriptions of ways you can work alongside the reader/writer to teach, prompt, and support the use of effective strategies. The language you select creates an ever changing scaffold that is continually adjusted in response to ongoing observation of the reader/writer.

Vygotsky's theory turns us away from just "waiting" for literacy to happen and toward very skillful intervention that has the student behaving like a successful reader/writer. As he states, "the only good kind of instruction is that which marches ahead of development and leads it; it must be aimed not so much at the ripe as at the ripening function" (1962, 104). This kind of instruction is desperately needed by readers to break the cycle of failure. The keys to helping struggling students work "in the zone" are:

❏ Carefully selecting the reading or writing task.

❏ Reminding the students what they already know.

❏ Sharing the task when needed to assist performance.

❏ Providing prompt feedback that guides performance.

Your instruction needs to provide just enough support to help students push the boundaries of their knowledge. According to Clay and Cazden (1990), "the nature of the scaffold provided in the instructional setting must change, continuing the support offered, always at the cutting edge of the child's competencies, in his or her continually changing zone of proximal development" (219).

▶ Fifteen Principles for Working with Struggling Readers

There are fifteen important principles related to teaching actions that direct readers' attention and support memory (see Figure 19–5):

1. *Provide daily supplemental instruction.* An extra lesson once or twice a week is not likely to help struggling readers. It's tempting to believe that

---

Figure 19-5 Engaging Attention and Memory: Principles for Working with Struggling Readers

1. Provide daily supplemental instruction.
2. Create an appropriate physical setting.
3. Establish predictable routines.
4. Show children how the task is organized.
5. Ensure that readers are focused.
6. Engage the senses.
7. Base teaching on observation of your learners.
8. Link instruction to what children know.
9. Create links among knowledge sources.
10. Make it easy to learn.
11. Share rather than simplify.
12. Avoid long detours.
13. Show and be clear about what to attend to.
14. Make children active.
15. Make the task a positive emotional experience.

---

bringing in volunteers occasionally will make the important difference for readers in trouble. It makes the volunteers feel good and may generate more support for schools; children may enjoy the attention they get from visitors. But no research supports turning over your at-risk students to volunteers. Students miss valuable instructional time when they work with volunteers. At-risk students need the best, most highly skilled teaching *in addition to good classroom instruction,* and they need it *daily.* Thinking about the way memory works, it's easy to see the value of this regular instruction; it allows children to hold and strengthen the memory trace of what they learned the day before.

2. *Create an appropriate, well-organized physical setting.* You will want to create a very organized work space for your work with struggling readers. If you are working in the corner of a classroom, have the students face you rather than the room. Have materials such as magnetic letters or markers well organized so that you will not distract students by searching for them. Students' materials also should be well organized. Teach them routines for storing and

retrieving their materials quickly so that they do not forget what they are learning. Displays that you want students to attend to closely (the alphabet linking chart, easel, or pocket chart) should be very clear and visible to everyone (see Chapters 10 and 11).

3. *Establish predictable routines.* Students can attend better when they know what to expect. Use a predictable routine for lessons so that they can anticipate what is coming. For example, knowing that the introduction to the text will help in reading it encourages students to pay attention to and remember what is being said. Knowing they are expected to talk about the meaning of the text afterward prompts them to try to remember more of what they read. Chapter 21 includes an example of a predictable framework that we have used very successfully. Depending on your students' needs, you can create your own, but predictability will free attention for thinking, talking, reading, and writing. You can of course vary lesson structures when necessary; just teach students explicitly that the lesson will be different and in what way.

4. *Show children how the task is organized.* The lesson framework you use is a "plan" within which children know what will happen. It builds within them a kind of vision of the behaviors they want to demonstrate. Tell students when the lesson begins, and as the task changes announce what you will be expecting them to do in each part of it. Help them remember what was accomplished yesterday, and let them know what they are learning today. Reinforce effective processing and let them know how everything they are doing will help them.

5. *Ensure that readers are focused before you begin.* Ask for students' attention before beginning a task. Avoid creating the situation where you have to repeat directions several times for students who were not paying attention. This will get in the way of other students' ability to attend and remember. You might touch a child's hand or ask him to direct his eyes toward you before you teach. Don't allow children to lie across the table or rest their chins on it. Their view of the features of words and letters will be distorted.

6. *Engage a variety of senses.* It is very helpful to struggling readers to have kinesthetic experiences while learning. Touch, sight, and hearing are all ways to attend and remember. In Chapters 10, 11, and 12, we describe the use of magnetic letters to build words. Forming letters using a verbal path helps children learn letter features (see Chapters 10 and 13). Having the support of a visual display (principles and examples) is also very helpful, because readers and writers can use it to recall information about word patterns (see Chapter 12).

7. *Base your teaching on precise observations of your learners.* What you think children are attending to may be different from what they are really attending to. Keep a constant eye on their precise reading and writing behaviors and what those behaviors suggest to you. In Chapters 4 and 5 we describe ways to observe children's reading behavior that help you not only monitor progress but gain insights into how the building of the processing system changes over time. From these observations, form hypotheses about what children are attending to and how to direct their attention. Without detailed observation, you can spend time on teaching that misses the mark.

8. *Link your instruction to what children know.* Research on attention and memory tells us that connecting information perceived and stored in short-term/working memory must be linked to information in long-term memory, forming networks of meaning in the brain. It is essential to help struggling readers activate background knowledge (gained from experiences and reading). Chapters 11 through 17 present many ways to teach and prompt children to use what they already know to get to what they do not know. This process operates at the letter, word, and text level and pertains to both decoding and comprehending.

9. *Create links among knowledge sources.* Do everything you can to help struggling readers retain the information they need to solve problems in different ways. For example, they need to see, build, read, and write a word in many contexts before it is fully known. Intervention lessons should involve not only word study and phonics

but also a large amount of reading and writing of continuous texts in many genres, so that children can make connections between and among all these literacy activities. Through supportive and specific teacher language (suggested in Chapters 13–17) you can bring these connections to children's attention, so they will notice and use them independently.

10. *Make it easy to learn.* Your role is to place the task within the grasp of your readers/writers. Keep the learning within the reach of children with your support. By using clear language you can offer the support that makes the task easier than it would be if the students were working alone or as part of a large group. Keep intervention groups small enough that you can be alert for signs that a reader is having trouble, practicing wrong responses, or becoming frustrated. Teach and prompt effective actions.

11. *Share rather than simplify.* Learning isolated bits of information will not help readers and writers "put it all together" or integrate information. They must experience the complexity of the reading and writing processes as they absorb additional information they can use to continue to develop. Yet, as point 10 suggests, you have to "make it easy." In the past, educational theorists have tried to simplify reading and writing by breaking it down to the smallest units—and when you directly teach phonics (see Chapter 11), you sometimes do that. Your purpose then is to help the children learn some valuable pieces of information and to form categories that will help them remember (connecting phonogram patterns, for example). But your ultimate purpose must be to help them use the information while reading and writing, and that has to happen every day. Sharing the task when it is too difficult (selecting texts carefully, providing a supportive introduction, teaching and prompting while children read, supporting them while they write) keeps the complexity there.

12. *Avoid long detours.* When working with struggling readers and writers you may be tempted to stop them and go into a long spiel of teaching. But if you've selected your texts carefully, provided an effective introduction, and thoroughly prepared them for the task, that shouldn't be

necessary. Interactions such as those described in Chapters 13 through 17 should be quick and interrupt the ongoing process as little as possible. Lengthy interruptions can destroy the momentum of your readers/writers and cause memory gaps. Readers forget what has gone on before, which should be helping them comprehend and solve words. Writers forget the message (something difficult enough to remember when spelling new words).

13. *Show and be clear about what to attend to.* As you work with struggling readers and writers, try to be very clear about what you want the children to attend to. If the attention is not focused where it should be with a quick prompt, show and tell the readers or writers what they need to notice. Chapters 13–17 contain many examples of ways to "tell" information that require readers or writers to attend to the information. Knowing where and how to focus attention is critical to the growth of independence.

14. *Make children active.* Some struggling readers and writers have learned a pattern of passivity and dependence. They know that if they wait long enough, you will become frustrated and do the work. So while making it easy and providing a strong scaffold is important, at the same time your challenge is to make the struggling reader independent. First, move the reader to a position where independence is possible and then insist on it through teaching, prompting, and reinforcing effective behaviors. In both reading and writing, the task is to help children learn and internalize not just information but strategic actions.

15. *Make the task a positive emotional experience.* There is nothing like success to create a positive emotional experience. Successfully processing new texts every day builds up emotional memory that supports readers in undertaking the task again and again. If you can use the appealing texts that engage children—drawing them into stories and pondering interesting information—they will be motivated to read. Achieving a body of writing (kept in a folder or writing book) helps writers understand and feel pleased with themselves about what they have learned.

▶ The Working of the Brain

It is obvious from this list of fifteen principles and information about attention and memory that cognitive actions are greatly influenced by emotional, or affective, factors. Attention, memory, emotion, and motivation cannot be separated. You may have years of experience "motivating" children to read and write, but you will not be successful if no true effective cognitive processing takes place. At the same time, you will not be successful in helping struggling readers process texts if the experience is negative.

▶ Suggestions for Professional Development

NOTICING THE LEARNER'S ATTENTION

1. From chapters in this book, select a specific instructional activity that involves directing the reader's or writer's attention. Some suggested contexts are:

    ❏ Letter sorting or word sorting (Chapter 11).

    ❏ Locating words in continuous text (Chapters 11 and 12).

    ❏ Look, Say, Cover, Write, Check (Chapters 11 and 12).

    ❏ Interactive writing (Chapter 13).

    ❏ Putting together a cut-up sentence (Chapter 13).

2. Work with an individual student using the activity. If you can, videotape the interaction so that you can watch it again. Or, take turns with a colleague, observing each other. Observe closely and make notes about where the reader directs attention. Notice when the attention changes. Think about teaching actions that:

    ❏ Directed the student's attention to important information.

    ❏ Distracted the student's attention.

3. Now follow up by having the student read a text. Again try to determine where the reader is directing attention. If you take a running record, you can note the sources of information (meaning, language structure, or visual information) that you think the reader used at point of error and self-correction. That will also give you an idea as to where the reader is directing attention. After the reading, work with a colleague to decide on a teaching point that would direct the reader's attention to the most useful information. You can also use the prompts in this book or *The Fountas and Pinnell Prompting Guide 1* to select potential language for working with this student in the future.

Engaging Readers' Emotion and Motivation in Successful Learning

CHAPTER
20

IN RECENT YEARS, THE ROLES MOTIVATION AND EMOTION play in children's ability to learn have been given little attention, yet these factors have a huge impact on achievement. In this chapter, we discuss how emotion and motivation impact struggling readers' ability to become deeply engaged with texts. We will describe the power of successful processing, shared understanding through talk, engaging texts, social motivation, and self-efficacy. We will also give some examples of how each of these can be fostered in classroom instruction and supplementary intervention lessons.

In the late 1980s, the Educational Testing Service asked a research team to assess the oral reading fluency of a nationwide sample of fourth graders (Pinnell et al. 1995). The team evaluated a thousand fourth graders from all over the United States, all of whom had taken the National Assessment of Educational Progress test. These students read aloud into a tape recorder and then were interviewed by a researcher. A team of trained evaluators listened to the tapes and rated students' oral reading.

Almost half of these readers were rated "dysfluent" on a reliable four-point scale; the grade-level texts were much too difficult for them. The remaining readers, for whom the texts were at an appropriate

level, had an average accuracy rate of 98 percent. Not surprisingly the students who read with high accuracy also had high reading comprehension scores on the NAEP test and high oral fluency ratings. In the interviews, these were also the students who said they read voluntarily and could name favorite books and authors. Most of the other students did not see reading as important in their lives.

Another study (Fielding et al. 1986), which tracked 155 fifth graders for at least eight weeks (some were observed for as long as twenty-six weeks), revealed that "among all the ways children spent their time, reading books was the best predictor of several measures of reading achievement between second and fifth grade. However, on most days, most children did little or no book reading [outside school]" (285). We have no reason to believe that this situation has changed for the next generation of students. On the contrary, it is getting harder and harder for children to find time to read even if they want to. Yet reading in quantity is necessary. For that to happen, children must read voluntarily—and that requires motivation.

In the years since these two studies were undertaken, the stresses on educators have increased tenfold. We are accountable for the reading achievement of every student, and there is special concern about learners reading below grade level. These are likely to be the least motivated readers in the school, and the problem is magnified as they grow older. However, student engagement and motivation receive little emphasis in the current conversation about raising achievement.

The *Report of the National Reading Panel* (NICHD 2000) and the subsequent influence of the No Child Left Behind Act have greatly influenced literacy education—even in schools not eligible for funding under the act. The researchers who wrote the original report listed motivation among the topics "neglected" by the survey. They called for research on how to motivate children to learn phonics and to apply it in reading and writing.

Phonics has always been an important component of an effective reading program and has certainly been emphasized in the early grades. NCLB has stepped up the emphasis on phonics, and struggling readers get an extra heavy dose of it. The National Reading Panel took care to caution that "phonics instruction is never a total reading program" and "should not become the dominant component in a reading program, neither in the amount of time devoted to it nor in the significance attached" (2–136).

The concern for accountability has led to a huge increase in testing. The intensive testing of children's knowledge of isolated units of language has reached an all-time high, and instruction has generally followed suit. What is tested is taught—often in the very same form as the test. We sometimes forget that a measure of progress that is easy to analyze statistically is not necessarily a measure of good instruction.

The title of a recent article by Nichols and Berliner (2008) says it all: "Testing the Joy Out of Learning." The writers claim that "there is no convincing evidence that student learning has increased in any significant way on tests other than the states' own tests…nor have achievement gaps between students of higher and lower socioeconomic classes narrowed." Instead, "a wealth of documentation indicates that the unintended and largely negative effects of high-stakes testing are pervasive and a cause for concern" (14).

We know that we need good, ongoing assessment if we are to help readers who struggle. Two chapters of this book (and many sections within others) are devoted to monitoring progress. And certainly we need excellent phonics instruction to help struggling readers. Many chapters in this book emphasize helping low-achieving readers learn letters and sounds as well as how to take words apart. Techniques like this can be interesting as children discover how words work—like a puzzle. If they are successful, they enjoy it. But true motivation that results in voluntary reading can only come from finding rewards in the act itself.

Emotion and motivation play a vital role in struggling readers' ability to become deeply engaged in texts. *Successful processing, shared understanding through talk, engaging texts, social motivation,* and *self-efficacy* are powerful means to that end and can and must be fostered in classroom instruction and supplementary intervention lessons.

▶ Classroom Contexts for Engaging Students with Texts

Most of this book focuses on the specific interventions we need to provide to help readers who struggle. But even for those readers, the most important instruction takes place in the classroom. Struggling readers need not only daily extra, specific assistance but also the opportunity to engage deeply with texts over time, talk with peers about their thinking, and be a member of a supportive learning community. It is what they do all day that makes the biggest difference. Classroom work has to be productive; intervention alone cannot make a struggling reader a successful one.

Figure 20-1 summarizes contexts in which you can support all the readers in your classroom. We have written extensively about these contexts elsewhere and provided many examples and suggestions (see Fountas and Pinnell 1996, 2001, 2006, 2008). Leveled texts along a gradient are used not only for guided reading instruction but also for intervention. In those two settings, learners are grouped for instruction so that you can precisely match texts to their abilities. In interactive read-alouds and book discussions, children need to be able to choose from a limited number of texts you have pre-selected. If a book is too hard for particular students, they can listen to a recording. For independent reading, students learn how to select books for themselves that interest them and that they can read with understanding and fluency. Implementing these contexts in your classroom will provide lots of opportunities for students to engage with texts successfully.

Figure 20-1 **Instructional Contexts for Engaging Students with Texts**		
Context	**Description**	**Texts**
Interactive Read-Aloud *Whole Class*	The teacher reads aloud, inviting discussion before, during, and after reading. Often, the teacher stops at a few points during the reading and invites quick comments or asks students to "turn and talk" to a partner. For younger children, read-alouds are often connected to interactive or shared writing.	• Teacher-selected texts. • Illustrated picture books in a variety of genres. • Shorter chapter books with issues and characters that engage readers. • Text sets.
Literature Discussion *Small Groups or Book Clubs (Heterogeneous)*	Students talk with each other about texts, basing discussion on texts they have heard read aloud or read themselves. Students prepare, discuss, and often summarize or evaluate the discussion.	• Student-selected texts (usually from a limited set that the teacher has pre-selected). • Illustrated picture books in a variety of genres. • Easy chapter books with issues and characters that engage readers.
Guided Reading *Small Temporary Homogenous Groups*	After assessment, the teacher brings together a group of students who are similar enough in their reading development that they can be taught together for a period of time. The teacher selects and introduces a text. Then each student reads the entire text or a unified part of it softly or silently while the teacher observes, listens in, and supports. They discuss the text and the teacher makes some specific teaching points.	• Teacher-selected texts. • Leveled books. • Variety of genres. • Illustrated texts. • Shorter chapter books.
Independent Reading *Whole-Class Minilesson and Sharing*	Students independently and individually read books. Independent reading for young children may include rereading several shorter books. Older students read silently and often write about their reading.	• Student-selected texts. • Variety of genres, topics, authors. • Many "little books" for younger children. • Combination of shorter nonfiction books and easy chapter books (fiction and biography).

▶ The Role of Emotion

Young children, to whom everything about reading is unique, will persist despite some setbacks and will even tolerate some pretty uninteresting texts. But, (especially if they are frustrated and confused) that won't last long. It doesn't take long for even younger readers to become discouraged. Lyons (2003) reminds us of the neurological roots of emotion and cognition. She has provided a detailed description of the brain and how it works, to include the strong role of emotion. (We urge you to read the full account.)

Lyons describes two structures inside the medial part of the temporal lobes of the brain—the *amygdala* (a site of basic emotional recall) and the *hippocampus* (which encodes information from working memory and transfers it to long-term memory). In the hippocampus we plan, solve problems, and reason regarding information, but the amygdala tells how we feel about information. Cognition occurs in the cortex and from there, stimuli go on to the hippocampus, which is linked to the amygdala. The amygdala has a large influence on how well something is remembered, because it determines whether it is emotionally important enough to be stored. Emotional responses to stimuli can even be stored without conscious cognitive perception. Some experiences, then, are tagged with emotion—both positive and negative. Even from this simplified description, you can see that it is extremely important for young children's experiences in reading and writing to be positive.

There is ample evidence that learning is not just a cognitive process, although we often treat it as such in school. According to Lyons, "the brain always gives priority to emotions" (66). Emotion is a factor in *whether* children learn to read and write. Emotions, wants, and intentions figure strongly into *how* readers process texts. Emotion can cloud the memory and get in the way of processing, or it can fuel the process. Have you ever fallen in love with a set of characters and felt deep satisfaction as you start to read a sequel? Have you ever been so worried about something that you literally could not concentrate enough to read a text or write something? Have you ever read a few pages of a

book and found the subject matter so difficult that, emotionally, you could not continue? You already know how to read and can put it aside. But imagine a struggling reader in the same situation. It is no wonder that teachers struggle to motivate some students.

▶ Motivation

Motivation plays a strong mediating role in the reader's engagement; in turn, engagement is strongly related to reading achievement (Cipielewski and Stanovich 1992; Campbell, Voelkl, and Donahue 1997). We've all read stories of people who have overcome poverty and other obstacles to achieve significant accomplishments. Often, reading (strongly motivated by personal need and enjoyment) is cited as a factor. Motivation rests on a constellation of emotional factors such as confidence and a sense of ownership, both related to engagement (Au 1997). Cambourne (1995) describes engagement as having elements such as reading for a purpose and believing in oneself and one's abilities.

Motivated and engaged readers usually have something personal at stake; they are invested in their reading. We have mentioned enjoyment, and that is important, but readers do not always have to find pleasure in their reading, unless you define learning as a form of pleasure. Readers may be intensely interested in the topic, pursuing information and revising theories as they read. It will sometimes be hard work; they have to search for understanding. Readers are purpose driven. There must be something much more authentic in the process than simply "practicing" reading to satisfy a requirement.

Motivation is different from interest, from beliefs, and from emotion, although all four may be related. Motivation can be either intrinsic or extrinsic, and both kinds of motivation influence the amount and frequency of children's reading (Miller and Meece 1997; Wigfield and Guthrie 1997). The intrinsically motivated reader is processing texts for the internal satisfaction it brings. But we can be extrinsically motivated as well. All of us have read texts and written treatises to pass tests, gain credentials, or receive rewards that bring us satisfaction. Extrinsic motivation appears to increase over time, which makes sense; it is related to one's educational and career decision making.

These kinds of rewards are quite different from the incentives that schools sometimes put in place in an attempt to motivate their students. Children read for "points" that result in prizes such as pizzas or hamburgers. People say, "Well at least they are reading." But we question the quality of the reading and the ultimate effect. In a review of research on motivation, Guthrie and Wigfield (2000, p. 407) write:

> However, extrinsic motivation is usually associated with the use of surface strategies for reading and the desire to complete a task rather than to understand or enjoy a text or a task (Meece and Miller, 1999). Further, extrinsic motivation can produce self-terminating behavior. When children win the incentive (e.g., the pizza) their reading often ceases. Extrinsic incentives often lead students increasingly to become dependent on rewards and recognition to energize their reading (Barrett and Boggiano 1988).

The message is clear. Engagement and motivation matter. Struggling readers must be willing to read and to read in quantity. That will not occur with assigned reading or with extrinsic motivation only. Readers must be internally motivated for reasons that seem real to them.

We also strongly discourage any attempt to use the text gradient as a motivator. We have been in classrooms in which students' reading levels are displayed on the wall, the idea being that students "feel good" or "feel in control" when they move up a level. The gradient is a teacher's tool—nothing more. Introducing competition from level to level can only undermine authentic reading and lead students to think that reading a harder text is more valuable than thinking deeply about texts and sharing your thoughts with others. We have never recommended that students choose their books by level or think of themselves as "on a level" (see Pinnell & Fountas 2006). Rather, we have described a variety of ways to help children select texts they can read with understanding and fluency without teacher support.

Factors Related to Emotion and Motivation

Motivation is based on emotion and is related to six factors (see Figure 20-2). By building children's intrinsic motivation, we can turn indifference or little commitment to reading into total engagement.

Figure 20-2 Factors Related to Motivation

Factors (Goals/Actions)	Definition
Self-efficacy	The confidence or belief that one can produce effects or intended results, make something happen, or be successful.
Successful processing	In reading, smooth, automatic processing of written texts that includes taking words apart while focusing on meaning. In writing, smooth operation of the reciprocal processes of composing and encoding a text to communicate meaning.
Engaging texts	Texts that engage readers' interests, provide enjoyment, and build background knowledge to support successful processing. There must be some texts that enthrall students and provide the deep engagement that is necessary for ongoing motivation.
Appropriate text level	Readers learn how to process texts better when the text allows for new learning—a text that is just right for supporting effective processing with appropriate teaching.
Shared understanding through talk	Readers and writers are part of a community in which they think and write about texts with the idea that they will talk about their understandings with others.
Social motivation	Learners are members of a reading and writing community; their opinions are valued and respected along with their peers' opinions.

Self-Efficacy

Self-efficacy is the belief in one's own capability to perform, or the degree to which a person expects and values success based on how he has performed in the past. According to Guthrie et al. (1999, cited in Guthrie and Wigfield 2000, 408), "students with high intrinsic motivation, a learning goal orientation, and high self-efficacy are relatively active readers and high achievers." Self-efficacy is not the same as motivation; you can have confidence or believe you can do something and yet be unwilling to do it because of other factors. But it probably is a necessary factor in motivation. The good news is that affective factors are even more amenable to instruction than cognitive factors.

Self-efficacy can be built through repeated successful experiences in reading and writing. Clear goals and specific feedback will help students become aware of what they are doing effectively. This builds the concept they have of their literate selves. You can specifically demonstrate what students are to do and then prompt them to take action. Reinforcing effective behaviors also has a place. Point out small steps forward so readers can begin to see evidence of their own growth. Total engagement is the result of an ability to maintain interest even when faced with obstacles. Learned helplessness or defense mechanisms such as poor behavior appear when readers face consistent failure. Affirm what the reader or writer has done rather than use the label *good*. Provide feedback that addresses the specific parts of students' efforts that have contributed to their success. Language you can use to provide effective instruction and feedback to readers and writers is suggested in *The Fountas and Pinnell Prompting Guide 1* (2009). The combination of assessment and strategy instruction increases reading self-efficacy (Schunk and Zimmerman 1997).

Successful Processing

We have long been convinced that nothing builds confidence and motivation as much as success. This does not mean "stars" or empty praise. Readers need to feel themselves moving through texts with ease and understanding; that is, with only a few problems to solve and with their attention free to think actively about meaning. With instructional level texts that require some problem solving, you can make that happen by providing supportive introductions and effective teaching. Students also need opportunities to process many texts independently with ease and success. For younger students, rereading helps build ease and fluency, and they will enjoy simply being able to do it. But beyond the first few levels of the gradient, you don't want students to reread a "too hard" text several times, finally "reading" it on the fourth or fifth try. Readers will soon tire of that and think that the only way they can read is to endure practice and repetition. Motivation will plummet.

CLASSROOM INSTRUCTION

As they engage in independent reading, students have many opportunities to process texts with ease and understanding. You'll want to guide struggling readers as they select books for themselves, but ultimately they must have the motivation of choice. Initially, they may wish to pretend to read harder books, but this is completely non-productive. Of all the students in the class, it is most important for struggling readers to successfully engage in independent processing. Here are several suggestions:

- ❑ Determine students' reading levels.

- ❑ Include in the classroom collection a good selection of books that are within students' reading ranges. Look for books that are interesting, and include a good variety. Informational texts may be especially helpful.

- ❑ Emphasize in minilessons the importance of selecting books that are interesting and "just right" for readers at the time.

- ❑ Create a supportive social environment in which individual selections are valued.

- ❑ Present both higher- and lower-level books in your "book talks" (short reviews to interest students in books).

- ❑ For students having special difficulty, pre-select some books from which these students then have a limited choice.

❑ Use individual conferences to support student reading and help students "rehearse" what to write about or talk about relative to their reading.

In guided reading lessons students, with your support, have the opportunity to read instructional level texts. Introduce the text in a way that:

❑ Provides support for the whole meaning of the text.

❑ Untangles any vocabulary that students may find difficult to derive from reading.

❑ Focuses attention on a few words that may be tricky.

❑ Shows children how the text works in terms of organization or structure.

❑ Draws attention to the genre of the text (if appropriate).

❑ Raises questions about the text in readers' minds.

While students read the text individually at their own pace in a whisper (younger students) and silently (those reading at or above Level H), the teacher "listens in" and supports readers through teaching for, prompting for, and reinforcing effective behaviors. After reading, give students the opportunity to discuss the meaning of the text and make a specific teaching point that demonstrates the effective employment of reading strategies. You also have the option of doing one or two minutes of word work or having children extend their understandings through writing about reading. Every moment of guided reading is directed toward helping students successfully process the text.

In writing, children need to experience the power of composing something that expresses their own ideas. Whether it is a piece about something they've read or a personal narrative or any other genre, successful writing includes the satisfaction of a concrete product. Children may throw away workbook pages, but they treasure their writer's notebooks, folders, and writing books. It is also beneficial for them to participate in creating shared and interactive writing. Here, you provide the support needed to help children pro-duce a written product for which they have ownership. Occasionally, you will want to dictate well-formed sentences to help children express the concepts in books they have read.

INTERVENTION INSTRUCTION

In Chapter 21, we describe frameworks for intervention lessons that feature book introductions and teaching similar to guided reading. The difference is that the intervention lessons are based on a specific sequence of texts, have a different structure, and include writing about reading. *Bear's Birthday* is a simple animal fantasy at Level I (about the end of first grade). A few pages of *Bear's Birthday* are reproduced in Figure 20-3. It poses a few challenges to the group in terms of word solving as well as following a plot that is a little more complex than they have previously read. A supported-reading lesson featuring this text is shown in Figure 20-4.

In her introduction, Mrs. W:

❑ Provided an introductory statement that explains the setting.

❑ Invited children to bring their background knowledge to understanding the setting.

❑ Drew attention to unfamiliar words and asks children to locate them in the text.

❑ Drew attention to the first letters and letter clusters of words.

❑ Provided two brief summaries of the action.

❑ Drew attention to the meaning conveyed by the illustrations.

❑ Asked children to infer characters' feelings.

During the reading, Mrs. W interacts with each of the children a couple of times. She:

❑ Helped readers solve words using both meaning and visual information.

❑ Reinforced effective reading behaviors.

After the reading of the text, Mrs. W:

❑ Communicated the expectation that children share their thinking.

❑ Asked them to think about causes for actions.

Figure 20-3 Cover and Page Spreads from *Bear's Birthday* from Leveled Literacy Intervention, Green System (Heinemann 2009)

> Bear went to Rabbit's house. Beaver and Fox were there.
>
> "I'm sad," Bear told them. "I made a cake and party hats. I blew up balloons. Why didn't you come to my birthday party?"
>
> "We did not come," said Bear's friends, "because you did not ask us!"
>
> "Oh," said Bear. "I planned a party. But I forgot to ask my friends to come."
>
> "We will come now!" said Fox.

14   15

> "Hello, Rabbit," said Bear. "Do you have any eggs? I want to bake a cake."
>
> "I have some eggs," said Rabbit. "What is the cake for?"
>
> "It's my birthday, and I'm having a party," said Bear.

> Bear thanked Rabbit and took the eggs. Then he went home.
>
> "Why didn't Bear ask me to his party?" Rabbit asked sadly.

4   5

> When he got home, Bear blew up the balloons. He put the cake and the hats on the table.
>
> "I am finished," Bear said. "Now I will wait for my friends."

> Bear waited and waited, but no friends came. Bear was sad. It was his birthday. Where were his friends?
>
> "I will go look for them," he said.

12   13

- ❏ Asked them to infer characters' feelings.
- ❏ Drew attention to punctuation and reinforced intonation.
- ❏ Helped children understand the meaning of the word *surprise* in the story (not the usual meaning).

The teaching in this example supports successful processing even at the instructional level. The children reread the text the next day, and Mrs. W checked on their processing. They reread the text one more time and then took the book home.

Rereading helps learners experience successful processing, but intervention lessons should also regularly include the reading of new texts at the independent level so that students experience relatively easy reading of texts they have never seen before.

Writing about reading also benefits struggling readers. After the second reading of the text on the next day, Jeremy wrote a summary of the book (see Figure 20-5). In this writing, produced with Mrs. W's support, Jeremy:

- ❏ Composed sentences summarizing the story in sequence.
- ❏ Practiced writing known high-frequency words.
- ❏ Used *and* as a conjunction.
- ❏ Used pronouns to substitute for nouns and as possessives.

Figure 20-4 Supported Reading of *Bear's Birthday*

Speaker	Interaction
Mrs. W	It is Bear's birthday and he wants to have a party. What do you think he will want to make for his party?
Jeremy	Birthday cake and candles.
William	A lot of cupcakes or ice cream.
Katie	I had a cake at my birthday.
Mrs. W	Well, the first thing he wants to make is a cake. Say *first*.
Children	*first*
Mrs. W	What letter would come first in the word *first*?
Children	*f*
Mrs. W	Find *first* and run your finger under it and say it.
Children	*[Finding the word.]* first
Mrs. W	Bear didn't have any eggs so he went to Rabbit's house to borrow the eggs. Look at page 4. When rabbit asked what the cake was for, what do you think Bear told her?
Katie	That he was making a birthday cake.
Jeremy	That there was a party.
Mrs. W	Look at page 5. What do you notice about Rabbit?
Katie	She's crying.
Mrs. W	Yes, she is sad. She asked, "Why didn't Bear ask me to his party?" Say *why*. What two letters come first in *why*?
Children	*[No response.]*
Mrs. W	It's a /wh/ word like *when* and *what* and *where*. Find *why*, that starts with *wh*, and run your finger under it and say it.
Children	*[Finding the word.]* why
Mrs. W	Every time Bear wanted to make something for his party, he went to one of his friends to borrow what he needed. Turn to page 13. When he was all done, he waited for his friends. Where were they?
William	They didn't know to come.
Mrs. W	Say *where*. *Where* starts like *why*. Find *where*. Run your finger under it and say it.
Children	*[Finding the word.]* where
Mrs. W	What do you think was wrong?
Katie	He didn't ask them and then they didn't come.
Mrs. W	Turn back to the beginning and read about what happened on Bear's birthday.

continues

- ❏ Used prepositional phrases.
- ❏ Spelled more complicated words like *friends*.
- ❏ Spelled a compound word.
- ❏ Spelled words containing consonant clusters.
- ❏ Used sound and word part analysis to write words like *blew* and *party*.

Intervention lessons should regularly include writing about reading to extend understanding, learn the conventions of writing, and help students experience success in writing.

Engaging Texts

Motivation will not happen without good books. No amount of incentives will persuade children to voluntarily read dull texts that leave no room for thinking. They may engage for a short time but will opt out in predictable ways—reading mechanically without thinking, sliding over the print just to get through it, remembering little about it afterwards. Every terrible text children read undermines motivation. But the children's stories being published today offer many opportunities to engage children.

CLASSROOM INSTRUCTION

The first way children encounter engaging texts is hearing them read aloud. Even if they have had few opportunities outside school, young children respond quickly to an interactive read-aloud. Sharing texts by hearing them read aloud is essential for all learners. Struggling readers need them even more.

Figure 20-4 **Supported Reading of *Bear's Birthday, continued***	
Speaker	**Interaction**
Discussion During Reading	
Mrs. W	*[Jeremy is stopped at the word* thanked *on page 5.]* Do you see a part that you know?
Jeremy	*T-h.* And there is *an* in it. *[Still unable to solve the word.]*
Mrs. W	Well, Rabbit gave Bear some eggs, so he would have said thank you. Try it again.
Jeremy	*[Reading.]* "Bear thank, thanked Rabbit and took some eggs."
Mrs. W	That made sense and it looked right. Keep reading.
Discussion After Reading	
Mrs. W	What are you thinking about Bear and how he felt about the party?
Jeremy	He was so silly 'cause he didn't even invite people to the party.
Katie	But, really he thought they didn't like him because they didn't come and then they came but he forgot to ask them.
Mrs. W	His friends felt kind of sad about the party, didn't they? Are you thinking about that, William?
William	He just asked them to give him things and then didn't ask them to come to the party.
Katie	But they had a nice party at the end.
Mrs. W	It was really a surprise at the end wasn't it? And I'll bet they had a good time.
Teaching Point	
Mrs. W	Go back to page 13. Bear is asking a question on this page. He is wondering where his friends are. Katie, can you read the question just like you think Bear said it?
Katie	*[Reading.]* "Where were his friends?"
Jeremy	He went to look for them.
Mrs. W	That was a good idea, wasn't it? Did you notice that Katie's voice went up at the end of that question? It sounded just like Bear was talking. Turn to page 15 and find the question Bear is asking now.
William	*[Reading.]* "Why didn't you come to my birthday party?"
Mrs. W	Look at the last page. Why did Bear say it was a surprise party when he knew about it all along?
William	Because he thought his friends wouldn't come and then he found out they wanted to come.
Katie	He remembered to ask them.
Mrs. W	It was a surprise party after all.

Wemberly Worried (Henkes 2000) is a highly engaging text for primary age children. In this story about Wemberly, a childlike young mouse who worries about everything, Kevin Henkes has captured many of the fears and worries that young children have. For example, Wemberly worries about the crack in the living room wall: "What if it gets bigger and something comes out of it?" (7). She worries about Petal, her doll: "Shouldn't Petal have a car seat, too?" (9). And when she worries, she rubs Petal's ears, and then she worries Petal will have no ears left! Most of all, she worries about the first day of school, but the problem is resolved when Wemberly meets a friend and has a good day, ending with her saying, "Don't worry" (27). Children identify with Wemberly's anxieties.

A book like *Wemberly Worried* will have an even greater effect if you connect it to other texts as part of a set (a group of books that are connected in some way—author, theme, content, illustrations, genre, writing style). If children hear and talk about several books by Kevin Henkes, for example, they will meet wonderful characters such as Lilly (*Lilly's Purple Plastic Purse*, 1996), Julius (*Julius, the Baby of the World*, 1990), and Chester (*Chester's Way*, 1988).

Even younger children can understand and think about deeper subjects if they have rich texts as a foundation. In *Grandma's Purple Flowers* (Burrowes 2000), a girl loves visiting her grandmother and is very sad when she dies. She learns that she can always remember her grandmother because her purple flowers

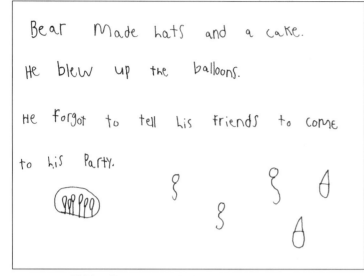

Bear made hats and a cake.

He blew up the balloons.

He forgot to tell his friends to come

to his Party.

Figure 20-5 Writing About *Bear's Birthday*

come up every spring. The story gives children the opportunity to think about serious topics such as death and to recognize a writer's use of symbolism. The same is true for *Annie and the Old One* (Miles 1985), in which a Native American girl removes the weaving on the rug each night because she fears her grandmother will die when the rug is finished. Another engaging text for a set like this is *Nana Upstairs and Nana Downstairs* (dePaola 2000).

The opportunity to listen to texts read aloud has increased greatly in recent years as so many books have become available on CDs. This will not take the place of your own reading aloud and encouraging literature discussion. But any way that students can hear engaging texts read aloud gives them access to age-appropriate material, which is highly motivating.

INTERVENTION INSTRUCTION

Texts used in intervention instruction must match readers' current abilities and be sequenced so that the readers can make strong connections among them. They must include a variety of genres and formats so readers can develop a flexible range of strategies. But first, they must be engaging. Just because books are leveled, they do not have to be dull. What makes children respond to a text? We describe some characteristics of books that will engage your readers (see Figure 20-6).

Figure 20-6 Characteristics of Leveled Texts that Engage Readers

Something Familiar
Interesting Information
Wonderful Characters
Interesting Plots
Great Illustrations

Something Familiar

If readers see something they recognize or can connect with themselves, they want to keep reading. All of us become instantly more interested in a text if it has a setting, problem, or character we already know. If it contains information on a topic that we already know something about, then we feel competent and empowered—ready to be intrigued by learning more.

It is difficult to write very easy books (Levels A and B) that engage readers, but it helps if they are about situations that are largely familiar to the readers, with only a few novel items inserted to make the book more interesting. *Friends* is a Level A book about two dogs—one little and one big (see Figure 20-7; for the full page layout, see Figure 17-3, page 401). The text is very simple and repetitive, but most children will recognize items related to dogs and appreciate the contrast and the twist at the end showing the two dogs as friends. *Orson's Tummy Ache,* another Orson and Taco book (see Figure 20-8) is only a little harder.

Whenever children meet familiar characters again in a series, they immediately realize that they already know something about the book; motivation and confidence are increased. *The Big Storm* is another Orson and Taco book, this one at Level F (see Figure 20-9). Notice how children's abilities have grown by the time they read *A Trip to the Laundromutt* (see Figure 20-10), yet another book in the series. You don't want to overdo series books, but meeting something familiar as they move up levels is a big boost to readers' motivation. Children have the immediate satisfaction of applying prior knowledge to a new text.

Figure 20-7 Cover and Page Spread from *Friends* from Leveled Literacy Intervention, Green System (Heinemann 2009)

Figure 20-8 Cover and Page Spread from *Orson's Tummy Ache* from Leveled Literacy Intervention, Green System (Heinemann 2009)

Figure 20-9 Cover and Page Spread from *The Big Storm* from Leveled Literacy Intervention, Green System (Heinemann 2009)

Figure 20-10 Cover and Page Spread from *A Trip to the Laundromutt* from Leveled Literacy Intervention, Green System (Heinemann 2009)

Another way to meet something familiar is in nonfiction books based on particular content. *Making a Pizza*, a very simple Level A book, shows the sequence of making a pizza (see Figure 20-11). This book has an elegant circular structure that helps very beginning readers not only follow a sequence but also infer that the pizza was not only made but eaten! Note the clean pan pictured on page 3 and the empty pan with crumbs pictured on the last page of the book, page 16.

A different kind of informational series features a real dog named Meli. After children first meet her in *The New Puppy* (see Figure 20-12), they will enjoy reading about Meli again as she plays on the stairs (*Meli on the Stairs*; see Figure 20-13), goes for a walk in (*A Walk with Meli*; see Figure 20-14), and gets a checkup (*Meli at the Vet*; see Figure 20-15).

Children can also find something familiar in classic tales such as *The Great Big, Enormous Turnip* (see Figure 20-16). If your school has an active read-aloud program, children will have heard many of these tales before in another form and bring strong background knowledge to the reading. In the case of *The Great*

Figure 20-11 Cover and Pages from *Making a Pizza* from Leveled Literacy Intervention, Orange System (Heinemann 2009)

I got a little dish.

Meli

2 3

Figure 20-12 Cover and Page Spread from *The New Puppy* from Leveled Literacy Intervention, Green System (Heinemann 2009)

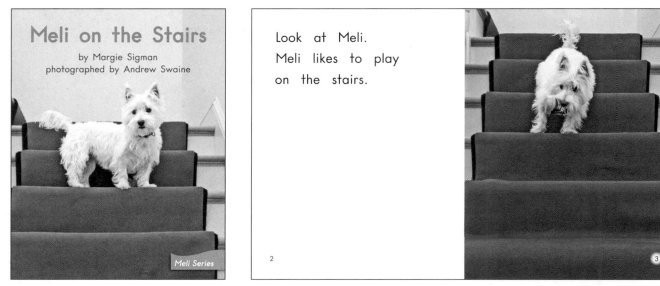

Look at Meli.
Meli likes to play
on the stairs.

2 3

Figure 20-13 Cover and Page Spread from *Meli on the Stairs* from Leveled Literacy Intervention, Green System (Heinemann 2009)

Here is Meli.
Meli is Ron's dog.

"It is time to go
for a walk," says Ron.
Ron gets Meli's red leash.
"Let's go, Meli," says Ron.

2 3

Figure 20-14 Cover and Page Spread from *A Walk with Meli* from Leveled Literacy Intervention, Green System (Heinemann 2009)

Meli at the Vet

by Margie Sigman
photographed by Andrew Swaine

Meli Series

Here is Meli.
Meli is Ron's dog.

Meli is going to the vet
with Ron.
A vet is a doctor
for pets.

Meli is a West Highland terrier.

2

3

Figure 20-15 Cover and Page Spread from *Meli at the Vet* from Leveled Literacy Intervention, Blue System (Heinemann 2009)

CLASSIC TALES

The Great Big Enormous Turnip

retold by M.C. Hall
illustrated by Johanna Westerman

Figure 20-16 Cover and Page Spreads from *The Great Big Enormous Turnip* from Leveled Literacy Intervention, Blue System (Heinemann 2009)

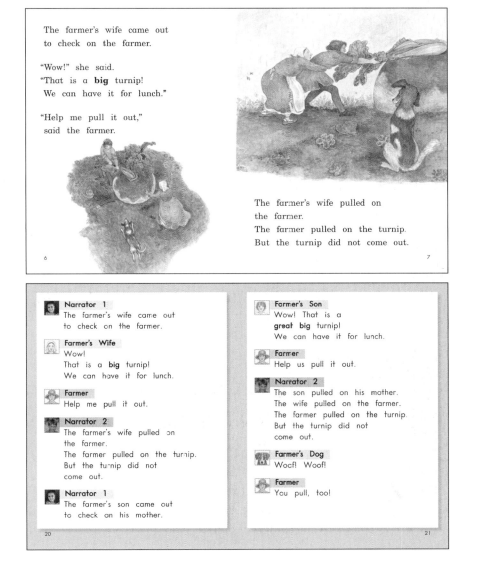

The farmer's wife came out
to check on the farmer.

"Wow!" she said.
"That is a **big** turnip!
We can have it for lunch."

"Help me pull it out,"
said the farmer.

The farmer's wife pulled on
the farmer.
The farmer pulled on the turnip.
But the turnip did not come out.

6

7

Narrator 1
The farmer's wife came out
to check on the farmer.

Farmer's Wife
Wow!
That is a **big** turnip!
We can have it for lunch.

Farmer
Help me pull it out.

Narrator 2
The farmer's wife pulled on
the farmer.
The farmer pulled on the turnip.
But the turnip did not
come out.

Narrator 1
The farmer's son came out
to check on his mother.

Farmer's Son
Wow! That is a
great big turnip!
We can have it for lunch.

Farmer
Help us pull it out.

Narrator 2
The son pulled on his mother.
The wife pulled on the farmer.
The farmer pulled on the turnip.
But the turnip did not
come out.

Farmer's Dog
Woof! Woof!

Farmer
You pull, too!

20

21

Big Enormous Turnip, the story appears again in the form of a play at the end of the book. Plays like these are highly motivating to readers. They provide an authentic reason to read aloud, and children grow in confidence as they hear themselves reflecting the meaning through expressive reading.

Interesting Information

Nonfiction texts on topics that interest readers can be very engaging. Children like to meet what they know in a text, but they are also motivated if they are learning something new and interesting. For example, *All About African Elephants* is about a familiar animal, but it provides interesting facts that readers may not know—for example, that elephant babies suck their trunks (see Figure 20-17). Another example, *Eugenie Clark, Shark Lady,* tells about sharks but also about a scientist who goes right in the water with them (see Figure 20-18).

Sometimes readers are engaged when a text puts together ideas in new ways. For example, in *Animals with Wings,* the writer compares and contrasts many different kinds of wings (see Figure 20-19).

Figure 20-17 Cover and Page Spread from *All About African Elephants* from Leveled Literacy Intervention, Blue System (Heinemann 2009)

Figure 20-18 Cover and Page Spread from *Eugenie Clark, Shark Lady* from Leveled Literacy Intervention, Blue System (Heinemann 2009)

Through the text and sensitive illustrations, *The Roadrunners* provides a vivid picture of the lives of these interesting birds in the desert (see Figure 20-20).

Another interesting way of presenting information is the hybrid text. In *The Fun Club Goes to the Aquarium* (see Figure 20-21), a fictional group of characters takes a trip to the aquarium. The book is filled with factual information nested within the narrative, but the information itself is in categories. The illustrations reflect the fact/fiction blend through the combination of photographs and drawings. The hybrid text reflects a "friendly" way for children to read factual texts.

Figure 20-19 Cover and Page Spread from *Animals with Wings* from Leveled Literacy Intervention, Blue System (Heinemann 2009)

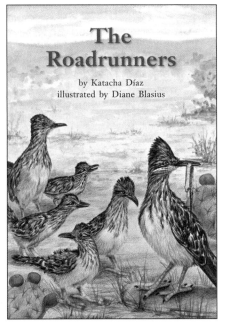

Figure 20-20 Cover and Page Spread from *The Roadrunners* from Leveled Literacy Intervention, Blue System (Heinemann 2009)

Figure 20-21 Cover and Page Spread from *The Fun Club Goes to the Aquarium* from Leveled Literacy Intervention, Blue System (Heinemann 2009)

Wonderful Characters

Fiction offers readers the opportunity to get to know wonderful characters. The Fox Family series depicts realistic family activities and issues, but the characters are foxes. In *Puddle Play* (see Figure 20-22), two little foxes can't resist getting really wet splashing around in puddles. The mother succumbs to the temptation as well and they all have a great time splashing together.

Another fanciful character readers will enjoy getting to know is Moosling, a young moose who is very caring and curious. In *Moosling the Babysitter* (see Figure 20-23), we learn that Moosling is very popular with younger animals, and they continue to like him even after he babysits for a family of skunks. In *Moosling the Hero* (see Figure 20-24), Moosling saves a nest of baby birds and then has to take care of them until they are ready to fly away.

Two realistic fiction characters we meet in *Papa's Birthday* are Sam and Jesse (see Figure 20-25). They have different interests. Sam likes race cars and sports; Jesse likes science and computers. But they both love their papa. Sam and Jesse have a quirky but great relationship.

Figure 20-22 Cover and Page Spread from *Puddle Play* from Leveled Literacy Intervention, Blue System (Heinemann 2009)

Figure 20-23 Cover and Page Spread from *Moosling the Babysitter* from Leveled Literacy Intervention, Blue System (Heinemann 2009)

Figure 20-24 Cover and Page Spread from *Moosling the Hero* from Leveled Literacy Intervention, Blue System (Heinemann 2009)

Figure 20-25 Cover and Page Spread from *Papa's Birthday* from Leveled Literacy Intervention, Green System (Heinemann 2009)

Interesting Plots

Whether fantasy or realistic fiction, a good story captures the reader's attention. In *Venus: The Flytrap Who Wouldn't Eat Flies* (see Figure 20-26) a very particular Venus flytrap plant suddenly begins talking and refuses to eat bugs and is in danger of dying. Like lots of children, she is finally persuaded to eat bugs on pizza. In *The Scream* (see Figure 20-27) Lizzie must get an injection from a doctor, and she learns from her grandmother how valuable a loud scream can be.

In Level A, B, and C texts, it is hard to create a true story line, because the books must be so simple and easy. But the illustrations can carry a great deal of meaning. In *Over the River* (see Figure 20-28), the illustrations show larger and larger animals walking on a log over a river. Suspense is built through the illustrations, and the ending is foreshadowed by the branch beginning to break.

Figure 20-26 Cover and Page Spread from *Venus: The Flytrap Who Wouldn't Eat Flies* from Leveled Literacy Intervention, Blue System (Heinemann 2009)

Figure 20-27 Cover and Page Spread from *The Scream* from Leveled Literacy Intervention, Blue System (Heinemann 2009)

Figure 20-28 Cover and Page Spread from *Over the River* from Leveled Literacy Intervention, Orange System (Heinemann 2009)

Great Illustrations

Illustrations can add greatly to student engagement with text. Barry Rockwell's simple and clear illustrations (see Figure 20-22) make the Fox Family come alive. Illustrations by Diane Blasius in *The Roadrunners* reflect the mood and tone of the story and help readers understand these unusual birds. The nature of the boasting coyote and the tricky rabbit are reflected in the illustrations for *The Coyote and the Rabbit* (see Figure 20-29). In *Too Many Teeth* (see Figure 20-30), a young crocodile is afraid to go to the dentist because, compared to other animals, she thinks she has "too many teeth." The happy ending is foreshadowed in the illustrations.

Illustrations can prompt deeper thinking. Informational texts are greatly enhanced by photographs that provide additional meaning. In *All About Honeybees* (see Figure 20-31), the illustrations help readers understand the text. Enjoyment is enhanced by the honeybees who fly throughout the text. Illustrations can also make it easier for children to comprehend text structure. In *Little Cat, Big Cat,* (see Figure 20-32), the writer uses comparison and contrast to help readers think about domestic cats and lions. Experiencing underlying structures such as comparison and contrast or cause and effect in these easier texts with powerful illustrations will build comprehending strategies over time.

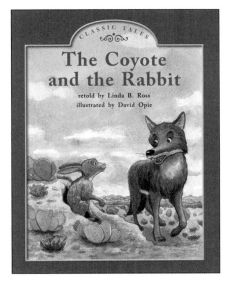

Figure 20-29 Cover and Page Spread from *The Coyote and the Rabbit* from Leveled Literacy Intervention, Blue System (Heinemann 2009)

Annie Alligator was worried.

"On Friday, Mom is taking me to see the dentist," thought Annie. "I've never been to the dentist before. What will Dr. Cobb do to my teeth?"

Annie looked at her teeth in the mirror. Then she started to count them. She counted her top teeth. She counted her bottom teeth. There were dozens of teeth to count.

Annie worried and worried.

"I have so many teeth," she thought. "What if Dr. Cobb wants to take some of them out?"

2

3

Figure 20-30 Cover and Page Spread from *Too Many Teeth* from Leveled Literacy Intervention, Blue System (Heinemann 2009)

In the Garden

The flowers bloom
on a warm summer day.
You can hear the sound of bees
in the garden.
Buzz, buzz, buzz.

Little honeybees fly
around the flowers.
These bees are working!

2

3

Figure 20-31 Cover and Page Spread from *All About Honeybees* from Leveled Literacy Intervention, Green System (Heinemann 2009)

Little Cat, Big Cat
by Maryann Dobeck

Lion

This is a lion. It has fur, claws and padded feet. A lion lives outdoors with its lion family.

Lions have soft fur that gets covered with dirt and mud. But lions clear their fur just like house cats do.

House Cat

This is a house cat. It has fur, claws, and padded feet. A house cat lives with a human family. House cats have soft fur. They lick their fur to keep it clean.

2

3

Figure 20-32 Cover and Page Spread from *Little Cat, Big Cat* from Leveled Literacy Intervention, Blue System (Heinemann 2009)

▶ Appropriate Text Level

You cannot simply ask readers to try harder while continually asking them to read texts that are too hard. They begin to feel that they are not smart or that no matter how hard they try they will never be able to succeed like their peers. The same is true when the texts are consistently too easy; readers feel they are being asked to do something anyone can do. The key is matching readers' ability to a text that is not too easy and offers enough challenge and support that they feel they are successful and learning with reasonable effort. When the text conditions are "just right," readers can develop pride and confidence.

Shared Understanding Through Talk

The meaningful talk that surrounds every literacy activity is interesting, enjoyable, and highly motivating for students. They read with greater interest when they know that other people care about what they are thinking. Discussing books during interactive read-aloud and in book clubs gives students the opportunity to think and talk about age-appropriate, interesting topics.

We all know children who have learned a lot about reading before starting school. Family members have read stories aloud to them and talked about those stories. But many children learn their love of books solely from teachers at school. You can engage children with texts in highly intentional ways too. A recent article by McGee and Schickendanz (2007) discusses a group of teachers working with preschoolers. They read specially selected children's literature several times and made sure to surround it with talk. The researchers found evidence of increased comprehension over the readings of a text. Engaging in talk makes the experience more satisfying. Participants in discussion feel their ideas are valued; they make more of an effort and consequently feel more successful. They are motivated because they want to participate.

CLASSROOM INSTRUCTION

Our earlier work includes many examples of "intentional conversation" during interactive read-aloud, in book discussions, in guided reading groups, and in individual conferences with students during independent reading (Fountas and Pinnell 2006). In the excerpt from a small-group discussion of *Wemberly Worried* (Henkes 2000), the children demonstrate their ability to infer a character's feelings and speculate on the underlying causes for them (see Figure 20-33). In a discussion of *Grandma's Purple Flowers* (Burrowes 2000), second graders also connect to their own experiences and to another text they have listened to and discussed (see Figure 20-34). Ms. L is playing an active role in the discussion by modeling some of her thinking and reminding children that it helps to connect to other texts.

Figure 20-33 Excerpt from a Small-Group Discussion of *Wemberly Worried*

Speaker	Interaction
Mary Ann	She was worried about everything. She always thought something bad was going to happen. I don't know why. It didn't say anything bad happened.
Spencer	Maybe she got scared when she was just a baby and then she was just scared of everything.
Daria	Her friend helped her.
Mrs. W	It did help to make a friend, didn't it? She rubbed her doll's ears when she was really worried. Did you notice that?
Daria	It's kind of like some little kids suck their thumbs.
Mrs. W	Or maybe have a blanket?
Spencer	I used to have a blanket.
Donnie	Like *Knuffle Bunny!*
Sandra	[Laughs.]

Figure 20-34 **Excerpt from a Discussion of** *Grandma's Purple Flowers*

Speaker	Interaction
Molly	The flowers helped her remember her grandma.
Ms. L	Can you say more about that?
Molly	Because she planted the flowers. Grandma planted them.
Jessica	The flowers always came up every spring and her grandmother really liked them.
Gerald	They were a pretty color.
Ms. L	So the flowers remind her of her grandma and all of the times she had with her?
Gerald	Yes, so every time she looks at them she feels like her grandma is still there.
Ms. L	This story reminds me a little of *Nana Upstairs, Nana Downstairs*
Daniel	Because the boy wanted something to help him remember his grandma, too.

Each of these one-minute excerpts is from a discussion that is less than five minutes long. Reading aloud and discussing texts does not take a great deal of time, and it is well worth the time spent on it. The language of school is different from the talk children experience at home and in their neighborhoods. Interacting around texts helps them learn the academic language used in schools (see Chapter 7). They learn to talk about texts with vocabulary such as *page, title, author, illustrator,* or *problem*. They learn directions for school tasks: *complete, selection, practice,* or *finish*. They learn the imperative clause that communicates expectations: "Finish your work by lunchtime." They also learn some indirect language that communicates expectations not clearly stated: "When we come back together, you can talk about your thinking about this character." Of course, you want to make your expectations clear and explicit, but children will always meet some of these oblique statements; struggling readers need to know how to interpret them.

INTERVENTION INSTRUCTION

In Chapter 21, we recommend that during intervention lessons children be invited to talk about texts as they read and write. An example is provided in Figure 20-35. On the previous day, children had read *The Lucky Penny* (summarized in the figure). On this second reading, Ms. F had an opportunity to support the children as they restated the key understandings of the text. Notice that she prompted one of the children to talk more and go a little deeper with her interpretation.

During the book introduction, there should be an opportunity for children to state their observations and talk about the pictures. Without letting the talk stray off to other topics or take too much time, you need to invite children to verbalize what they think the story or informational book will be about and discuss prior knowledge. This conversation continues after the reading (see Figure 20-35).

In this excerpt, Ms. F asked the children to think about what they had read and to state some of their understandings. The process helped them rehearse what they wanted to write (notice that Ms. F repeated Anne's sentence as a support). In this way, they shared understandings and questions; they also sorted out some of their questions. The next day, the children reread *All About Honeybees* and did some writing about the interesting facts (see Figure 20-36).

No intervention or classroom activity will be effective if students sit by passively. They will be engaged and motivated only if they take an active role in the conversations that support and expand learning. It is conversation, supported by you, that helps them extend their understandings and also creates the learning community.

Social Motivation

Motivation is closely connected to students' feeling of social support in the classroom and a sense of belonging (Wentzel 1997). Readers who struggle are often the least likely to have the support of a collaborative learning community. Our schools are generally

Figure 20-35 Talking About Texts in an Intervention Lesson

On the previous day, children read *The Lucky Penny*, in which a boy's mother gives him a penny. He loses the penny and several other people find it and then lose it; in the end, the boy finds the penny again. Today, they **reread** this book and then read a book about bees. First there is a quick interaction about *The Lucky Penny*.

Speaker	Interaction
Ms. F	Why did he call it his lucky penny?
Sandy	His mom said it was lucky.
Ms. F	Can you say more about that?
Philip	It wasn't so lucky really, because everyone just kept losing it.
Ms. F	I guess it might have been unlucky for everyone but the boy.
Sandy	It was lucky for him because it came back.
Ms. F	It sure did. Where in the story did you start to think he might get it back?

Excerpt from the book introduction to *All About Honeybees:*

Ms. F	The bees bring the nectar home to their hives. Turn to pages 8 and 9. What do you notice about the side of the hive?
Philip	It's all divided up—kind of like a house with a lot of little rooms.
Sandy	It looks more like little round boxes to me.
Anne	Kind of like you see with eggs at the store, only little.
Ms. F	The little boxes are called cells and the bees put honey in them. Turn to page 10 and 11. When the bees flap their wings, they dry the nectar and what do you think it becomes?
Children	Honey!
Ms. F	Yes, honey. Who do you think likes to eat the honey?

Excerpt from the discussion after reading:

Ms. F	Talk about what was most interesting to you.
Sandy	The way the honey came with a part of the place they put it in—the little boxes, only now it is honey instead of being just part of flowers.
Anne	They have to wear really a lot of clothes so the bees won't sting them when they take care of the hives.
Philip	I loved it when the bear got the honey, but didn't he get stung?
Ms. F	That's an interesting question. What do the rest of you think?
Philip	He probably has thick fur and they can't sting him.
Anne	No, it said that they sting him! And maybe he doesn't mind some stings so he can get the honey.
Ms. F	Did you notice how the bees use their wings?
Sandy	They kind of flap them and it dries out the stuff from the flower.
Ms. F	It dries the nectar and that turns it into honey.

Revisiting the text through writing:

Ms. F	Today you can write about what you found interesting about honeybees. Write two or three things. Let's think of some of the things you said yesterday.
Anne	The bees put the nectar in the—what were they?
Philip	cells
Anne	The bees put the nectar in the cells inside the hive.
Sandy	And they flap their wings to dry the nectar.
Philip	The bees make honey out of the nectar.
Ms. F	Anne, you said, "The bees put the nectar in the cells inside the hive." That's a sentence with interesting information. Okay, you can get started.

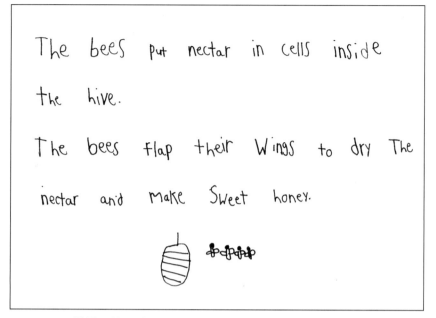

The bees put nectar in cells inside the hive.

The bees flap their Wings to dry The nectar and Make Sweet honey.

Figure 20-36 Writing About Reading—*Honeybees*

organized competitively, with students constantly evaluated to determine their performance compared with others. Struggling readers generally wind up on the low rung of the competitive ladder in just about every area. Grading is a reality in most schools; however, letter grades are meaningless to young children. Some school districts use letter grades in conjunction with conferences in the primary grades, so teachers can help parents understand their children's progress.

We have observed many classrooms that are based on cooperation and mutual respect rather than competition. The norms established in these classrooms demand mutual respect. Students are expected to support each other, and the goal is for every person to be productive during every school day. Reading and writing are valued for the acts themselves; all reading is valued regardless of level. Everyone in the class listens carefully as students explain their thinking about texts. Students volunteer to help each other; they feel recognized and affirmed by the teacher and their classmates. A classroom in which all members of the group want to read and believe that they can fosters a positive emotional climate and a collaborative spirit that results in intrinsic motivation and leads to greater amounts of reading (Oldfather and Dahl 1994).

▶ Suggestions for Professional Development

PROMOTING ENGAGEMENT IN READERS

1. Work with a group of colleagues to study emotional factors and level of motivation in your students. Have each person identify two or three students that they perceive as being "unmotivated" in reading.

2. Have a meeting to discuss these students and read the first part of this chapter.

3. Over the next couple of weeks, make the commitment to observe the selected students closely and engage them in conversation about anything, including books they are reading. Take some observational records to determine how difficult they are finding it to read the materials they are expected to process. Determine whether the problem is related to text difficulty. If not, make some hypotheses about these readers' lack of motivation. Make a list together and talk about causes for each.

4. Bring your results back to another meeting of the study group. Discuss your new insights about the behavior of these students. Refer to your list and work collaboratively to make a plan that will foster deeper engagement on the part of each child. It may involve finding more interesting texts at levels that they can read, making age appropriate texts accessible, or providing more time for discussion. It may involve using drawing and sketching more extensively prior to talking or writing about reading. Use the ideas in this chapter as well as those referenced.

5. Implement your plan over a designated period of time. Be sure to keep at it consistently for a fairly long period. The low motivation was not created overnight.

6. Have a follow-up meeting to talk about your successes and challenges.

Keys to Effective Intervention: Success For All Children

IN THIS FINAL CHAPTER, *we describe the multi-layered intervention systems that schools need if they are to serve all readers. The partnership of many expert professionals is necessary to accomplish the goal of helping every student develop an effective literacy processing system while learning to enjoy reading and writing. We describe fifteen keys to effective interventions as well as a framework for literacy lessons that you can use to help readers from Level A to N.*

Moving children who struggle with literacy along from grade to grade as the lowest achievers is easy but not acceptable. Students who make the lowest scores on tests year after year are always struggling at the bottom of the group or are tracked into the lowest-progress classes. They are likely to misbehave or drop out. Students with few literacy skills can overcome the odds and live quality lives, especially if they have highly supportive families. But in general their chances of success are undermined by the educational system that is supposed to help them. Their socioeconomic status is more likely to be lower than that of their average and high progress peers. For many, their school years, which

should be some of the happiest of their lives, are miserable.

Testing has been touted as the answer, but excessive testing may exacerbate the problem. The key tool of testing comes not from the future but from the past. Marshak (2003) points out that one hundred years ago schools were shaped to fit industrial models of efficient production. They sorted children. "These industrial schools were structured to maximize competition between students and to minimize the depth of relationships between students and their teachers." Public schools built on this industrial model were designed to leave many children behind, so they would drop out and go to work in what we now call low-skill jobs. Today, the dropout rate in many cities and poor urban areas is staggering. A report from America's Promise Alliance (Swanson, 2008) says:

> Only about one-half (52 percent) of students in the principal school systems of the 50 largest cities complete high school with a diploma. That rate is well below the national graduation rate of 70 percent, and even falls short of the average for urban districts across the country (60 percent)….[I]n the most extreme cases (Baltimore, Cleveland, Detroit, and Indianapolis), fewer than 35 percent of students graduate with a diploma.

It's hard to know why the general public is not more outraged by these statistics, but the problem gets little space in the national media and is sometimes covered by obfuscation and a great deal of selective reporting of "dropouts" while ignoring "attrition." For example, in 2003, just as the "Texas miracle" was being hailed, "hundreds of thousands of Texas students never made it to graduation from their high schools in the past seven years, but the reported dropout rates of many Texas school districts came through in small single digits" (McKenzie 2003, p. 1).

If students are not making progress teachers must be aware of it, and we need more than end-of-year test scores, which are of little use to inform teaching. When struggling students *are* identified, we need to intervene. We know that children who experience difficulty in the early grades fall further and further behind their peers (Stanovich 1986). Research shows that children who read below grade level at the end of grade 1 are likely to continue to read below grade level (Juel 1988). Many continue moving from grade to grade along with their peers, receiving token supplementary help if they're lucky. Others drop out of school as soon as they can. Many schools have long lists of students who are not progressing satisfactorily in regular classroom instruction. Even in educational settings where teachers are provided frequent professional development sessions and become ever more expert at what they do, some students fail to thrive. They need good classroom instruction, and they need more.

Intervention is the key to changing this picture, and early intervention is the best investment (Clay 2005a; Goldenberg 1994; Hiebert and Taylor 1994). When you intervene early, the chances of closing the gap between below-level and on-level performance are far greater. Before children fall behind and develop poor self-esteem, you can help them get back on track, able to benefit fully from reading and writing instruction. Intervention in kindergarten makes it possible for initially low-achieving children to start the next year with a strong foundation for literacy learning. Powerful early intervention can put struggling readers on the path to literacy.

But what about the students who have already had several years of schooling? If the students in front of you, whatever their age, are struggling to learn to read or write, you need to intervene. And to do that, you need carefully designed systems for working with the whole class, with small groups of children, and one on one.

The first line of instruction is always the classroom. No series of interventions—even highly effective ones—can take the place of good classroom instruction that builds a rich base and creates a community of learners (see Chapter 1). Effective intervention takes place in the classroom. You can use all the instructional support presented in this book as you work with struggling readers in the classroom in whole-class, small-group, and individual settings. Good assessment will help you identify students' strengths and needs and design instruction to meet them.

For students who need the most help, one-to-one tutoring is the strongest intervention. The Reading Recovery program is an outstanding example of teaching that is finely tuned to the needs of individuals. Used only in first grade, that critical period before a child having difficulty learning to read has fallen too far behind, its powerful results are well documented (see whatworksclearinghouse.com). Other tutoring approaches can effectively support older readers.

A common way of providing extra help is small-group instruction. Today almost all schools provide small-group instruction to low-achieving children in addition to classroom instruction; generally, however, these efforts are not systemic, and they are often not coordinated, not cohesive with the classroom program, and not tied to positive outcomes. Rarely do they close the achievement gap. They are also expensive: extra small-group support is required all year, every year. We need highly organized, easy-to-implement, intensive, effective small-group interventions that supplement classroom instruction and one-to-one interventions in flexible ways. We need to create a *coherent* new system—one that codifies:

❑ How students' strengths and needs are analyzed.

❑ The level of intervention offered.

❑ When the intervention takes place.

❑ How the intervention instruction is designed.

Readers who are struggling require the most skilled teaching. Many teachers who are expected to work with low-achieving readers receive very little training or support for doing so. Strongly designed instruction, carefully sequenced texts, and professional development that helps these teachers learn how to work with small groups of children who find literacy learning difficult can dramatically increase their expertise and confidence.

A single approach will not solve all problems. Schools need to provide many layers of assistance. The ultimate goal is for no one to slip through the cracks. To achieve that goal, you need a design that flexibly combines approaches and settings so that you can make the best use of what works. This chapter is a step toward that end.

▶ Fifteen Keys to a Successful Intervention Design

We will describe fifteen key characteristics of effective literacy interventions (Figure 21–1). Some have to do with the allocation of time and resources; others focus on what should be included in the lessons themselves. They are discussed in more detail below.

Figure 21-1 Fifteen Keys to Designing Effective Interventions

Intervention lessons must:

1. Be supplementary
2. Occur frequently
3. Have a low teacher/student ratio
4. Be short term
5. Be structured and systematic
6. Be fast paced
7. Develop comprehension strategies and vocabulary
8. Combine writing and reading
9. Include systematic phonics
10. Develop fluency
11. Be based on high-quality texts
12. Include ways to assess and monitor progress
13. Connect to the classroom
14. Connect to students' homes
15. Be developed and presented in connection with professional development

---

1. Provide Supplementary Lessons

Interventions must supplement, not supplant, effective classroom instruction. Differentiated instruction in the classroom lets you work more intensively with individuals and small groups; but many students need more. When children fall behind, they need "something extra" to make faster progress and catch up to their peers. Educational planners in the United States have experimented with supplementary pull-out and push-in small-group instruction, before-school and after-school programs, and computer-driven intervention. There are positive outcomes as well as drawbacks to each approach and each must be managed carefully. Some research has shown that readers spend a great deal of time "going down the hall" for pull-out programs, but there are ways to solve the problem through strategic location and teaching children to move quickly to places where they can have their lessons. Supplementary intervention lessons can be presented by another teacher working in the corner of a classroom, and that requires organization and collaborative planning, as well as a relatively quiet classroom. Whatever the decision for the time and location of the supplementary lessons, be sure they are effective and consider carefully the amount of time expended.

2. Provide Frequent Lessons

Struggling readers need a predictable, consistent schedule of instruction. *Daily* supplemental instruction helps them gain momentum; you can reinforce and build on what was learned the day before. They need to read and reread texts and engage in writing about reading with the fewest possible time gaps between lessons. We recommend a thirty-minute lesson that includes daily instruction in reading, writing, and phonics/word study so that learning can be reinforced and progress accelerated. (Fountas and Pinnell, Leveled Literacy Intervention, Heinemann 2009).

3. Keep the Teacher/Student Ratio Low

One teacher to three students is ideal in the primary grades. Three students provide enough varied conversation, you are able to match their reading levels more closely and keep them engaged, and you can still observe and interact closely with individuals. In the past, many supplemental reading teachers worked with groups of six, seven, or even eight children for forty-five minutes to an hour, all year. Working with three children for thirty minutes each day and staggering the groups so you work with groups for about half the year means you can provide intervention instruction to this same number of students as in the larger group served for a whole year. We will provide an example later in this chapter.

4. Provide Highly Effective Short-Term Services

You need to design systems of intervention that are flexible and highly effective so that students will not need extra support year after year, or even the whole year. If the intervention is early and effective,

eighteen to twenty weeks will be enough for most children. Children who are very far behind may need a year or even two years of effective supplementary instruction. Your layers of intervention should be flexible enough that you can group and regroup students or move from group to individual intervention.

5. Provide Highly Structured and Systematic Lessons

True efficiency depends on a carefully designed and highly structured instructional framework in which all the participants know what to expect and what is expected of them. In addition, struggling readers need predictability to help them build confidence. Design lessons carefully using a sequence of texts that build on each other in many ways—concepts, complexity, word difficulty, other relevant factors. The intervention lesson structure should include phonics principles, built systematically, as well as an emphasis on reading texts and writing about reading.

6. Provide Fast-Paced Lessons

Struggling readers are easily distracted. A fast-paced lesson will engage them and keep their attention focused on reading and writing. Too often, struggling readers are subjected to boring texts, nonsense words, and tedious drill. Everything is "slowed down" for them. In fact, what they need is to be very active, read interesting texts with fluency, engage in writing, and work quickly with words. A lively pace, within which they are behaving with competence, is a refreshing change for many struggling readers.

7. Focus on Comprehension Strategies and Vocabulary

Too often, reading becomes a mechanical and tedious task for students who are having difficulty, and writing becomes a matter of just spelling a few words. Because they have so often struggled through books that are too hard (and this can happen as early as the middle of grade 1), they develop the habit of giving all their attention to word solving. They do not think actively about the text meaning and, as a consequence, have great difficulty when they begin to read more complex texts. Even when these readers are matched with appropriate texts, they may still not be thinking actively. They need very supportive teaching to help them think about texts and talk about their thinking. They also need explicit vocabulary instruction to support their understanding of increasingly challenging texts.

8. Combine Writing and Reading

No thirty-minute early intervention that also addresses reading can fully develop a child's understanding of the writing process, writer's craft, and conventions. That must be done in the writing workshop in the classroom. But using writing in combination with reading is highly effective in supporting both reading and writing skills:

- ❑ Children learn how to go from thoughts or ideas to composing language.
- ❑ Children learn how to compose sentences that conceptually reflect the texts they have read.
- ❑ They learn how to write a large core of high-frequency words.
- ❑ They learn a variety of ways to notice and use word parts to construct words.
- ❑ They learn to hear the sounds in words and represent them with letters as they give close attention to visual information.
- ❑ They learn conventions of print such as left-to-right directionality, spacing, layout, capitalization, and the use of punctuation.
- ❑ They extend their thinking about texts.

9. Make Systematic Use of Phonics

Very often, struggling readers need to learn the building blocks of words—how words work. Phonics in itself is complex, and children need to build concepts in a very systematic way: phonological awareness, letter knowledge and formation, letter-sound relationships, word structure, spelling patterns, high-frequency words, and word-solving actions (see Chapters 8, 9, 11, 12).

Principles must be explicitly introduced, and students given the opportunity for "hands on" or kinesthetic practice and application. Students need to meet the same principles again and again and be prompted and reinforced as they apply them in reading and writing.

10. Develop Fluency in Reading and Writing

Fluency must be an important goal of intervention lessons, including attention to fluent, phrased reading as well as fluency in writing. In order to be perceived as successful by classroom peers as well as to process print effectively, readers and writers need to read smoothly and write quickly. It is especially important for low-achieving children to become fluent in language and literacy—before they become discouraged and habituate slow processing.

11. Center Your Instruction Around High-Quality Texts

It is imperative for children to read high-quality texts (see Chapters 6 and 20). Too often, texts for struggling readers are shockingly inferior or just boring. Readers who struggle need the same variety and quality as proficient readers. They need stories that engage them and nonfiction texts that offer interesting new information. They need to read challenging texts that stretch their processing systems and easy texts that build confidence and fluency. The success of any intervention program ultimately depends on children's being interested—even delighted—by the books they are reading and writing about.

12. Assess Difficulties and Monitor Progress in Valid and Reliable Ways

You need to make initial and final assessments, monitor progress continuously, and keep practical records that inform your day-to-day teaching. Assessments help you determine appropriate reading levels for guided reading and intervention instruction. They also help you understand the strategic actions readers control, partially control, and need to control, as well as their strengths and needs in decoding, fluency, and comprehension. Without ongoing assessment to inform your daily teaching, you cannot design highly effective instruction.

13. Connect the Intervention to the Classroom

Make strong, explicit, and cohesive links between your intervention lessons and your classroom literacy program. If you are the classroom teacher, have the intervention teacher collaborate with you to design activities that students can complete in the classroom—books to read, word activities to apply, and writing to reread. If you are the intervention teacher, work closely with the classroom teacher. Struggling readers/writers may have difficulty sustaining independent work. Extending the extra instruction into reading, writing, drawing, or working with phonics in the classroom gives it extra impact. It's also important for intervention and classroom teachers to continually discuss and share records of student progress. When you work as a team to support struggling readers, they will have the best chance for success. They will thrive when there is a cohesive, coordinated effort on their behalf.

14. Connect Intervention Instruction to Students' Homes

When children have many opportunities to share their successes with their families at home, their self-esteem is enhanced. In addition, they gain valuable reading and writing practice. Children should have many opportunities to take home phonics materials and writing. Allow students to take home books that they can read well so they increase their time reading texts. You may want to mark one book as a "read aloud" so it can be read to the child. The others can be for the child to read to family members. Parents, too, will grow in their confidence in their child and the school as they observe what their children can do.

15. Include High-Quality Professional Development

Excellent intervention requires a high level of professional development. You learn to teach by teaching, and you'll need a great deal of support as you work with struggling readers. You need to learn how to observe reading and writing behaviors and make effective decisions regarding each child. It will be helpful to watch video clips of teachers presenting effective lessons, to read and discuss theoretical texts, and to observe your colleagues as they teach. Professional development is the key to improved student achievement. Too often, it is nonspecific, espousing generalities without the specificity of lesson frameworks. Teachers are left to apply principles on their own without supportive materials. In the Leveled Literacy Intervention system (Fountas & Pinnell 2009), we have provided sequenced texts, lesson guides with a structured framework and specific suggestions, take-home books that children can keep, a prompting guide, video recordings of teaching and routines, a lesson resources CD, and an exciting data management tool for teachers. Those options make it easy to teach, but you will find that there are still many decisions that only you can make because only you know your students. Strong teaching is the result of strong professional development over time.

▶ Creating Multiple Layers of Intervention

In education, different specialties and services have been created over the years to help struggling readers, but the systems for coordinating and communicating about these services have often been weak. In many schools, students receive two or more types of intervention, with little interaction or conversation between the people providing this instruction. In recent years, however, many school districts or boards have begun to coordinate extra services and make a closer connection with classroom instruction. The goal is to provide many layers of intervention (see Figure 21–2). The concepts behind this approach are that:

- ❑ Effective classroom teaching is the essential base for all children's educational achievement.

- ❑ Intervention should begin early, when children are identified for extra support.

- ❑ Differentiated instruction to give students more intensive support should be provided in the classroom—usually by the classroom teacher but sometimes on a short-term basis by a specialist.

- ❑ Students who are the lowest achievers should receive a series of accelerated interventions before being referred to long-term special education services.

- ❑ Students who require ongoing support must have access to it over time.

The intervention plan for Leveled Literacy Intervention (Fountas & Pinnell 2009) is shown in Figure 21–3. This intervention provides intensive small group teaching for students who need to read up to Level N on the text gradient (see Chapter 6). Reading Recovery is recommended as the individual tutoring approach in grade 1. The process moves generally from in-classroom differentiation to special education serv-

ices, with coordinated, high-quality support along the way. The goal is to create a "fail safe" system so that children's needs are not neglected. This plan also suggests concentrated one-to-one support at a critical time—grade 1. Tutoring has a very high impact and an excellent record of success. The combination of tutoring for the neediest children in first grade and systematic small-group intervention at grades K, 1, 2, and 3 has great potential for reducing the numbers of children who need long-term specialized help and providing excellent diagnostic information to support long-term services. These specialized services can then be reserved for the children who need them most (in spite of previous intervention). Because students move from place to place, among other reasons, it will always be necessary to provide layers of intervention at every grade. Once the interventions are in place, clear communication procedures must be established. Closer collaboration between classroom teachers, reading/specialist teachers, and special education teachers is a positive move that can have great benefit for struggling readers.

▶ Selecting Children for Intervention

You may have many children who do not meet grade-level reading expectations—too many for you to provide intervention instruction to all of them. Begin with the children who need the most help and work with as many as you can. Suggested grade-level goals for reading are listed in Figure 21–4. (You can adjust them to coincide with standards in your school system.) If the majority of children in your classroom cannot fully participate and learn from grade-level classroom instruction, they can benefit from an intervention such as Leveled Literacy Intervention (LLI).[1]

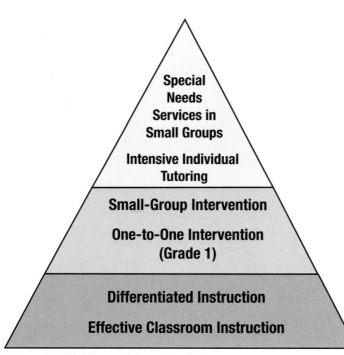

Figure 21-2 Multilayered Intervention Systems

---

[1] Leveled Literacy Intervention (LLI), designed and written by Irene Fountas and Gay Su Pinnell and published by Heinemann (2009) is a short-term intervention designed to help younger children (grades K, 1, and 2) who need extra help reading on grade level. It is also used with older students who need to read up to Level N. Using a structured framework, the teacher provides daily small group lessons that include reading, writing, and phonics/word study. The LLI system is supported by a specially designed set of 300 original texts. These texts are sequenced to build strategic actions across time. Recommended group size is three. For more information, see fountasandpinnell.com or heinemann.com.

Figure 21-3 Systems for Intervening to Help Readers

Assessment to Identify Students Who Need Intervention and to Inform Instruction

Kindergarten	Grade 1	Grade 2	Grade 3	Students who need to learn to read up to Level N
Comprehensive classroom instruction	Comprehensive classroom instruction	Comprehensive classroom instruction	Comprehensive classroom instruction	
Differentiation to meet individual needs	Differentiation to meet individual needs	Differentiation to meet individual needs	Differentiation to meet individual needs	
Small-group intervention instruction beginning midyear	One-to-one tutoring Small-group intervention instruction	Small-group intervention instruction	Small-group intervention instruction	Small-group intervention instruction Variety of special needs services

Ongoing progress monitoring for students receiving intervention

Most schools/districts have assessment systems for identifying children for intervention and then monitoring their progress. These assessments are applied at regular intervals and the results are entered into student records. In Chapter 4, we discuss the importance of such assessment and what observation can tell you about readers. Both ongoing observation and a systematic assessment at several points in time are necessary in order to provide strategic intervention. For example, November or December is a good time to formally evaluate kindergartners. At this time they should be beginning to read the very simple one-line texts at Level A, and they might know a few high-frequency words to use as signposts while moving through print. They should understand that there is a relationship between letters and sounds as well as the letter and sound associated with a few consonants. If that is not the case, intervene with some focused work in a small group. It may be that children are not engaging with print because they have difficulty attending in the large group; maybe they are confused. Sometimes these confusions can be sorted out in just a few weeks before they are compounded.

By March, kindergartners should know quite a few letter-sound relationships and be able to read easy texts at Level B (two or three lines of print). They should recognize between ten and twenty high-frequency words. By the end of the year, the goal for instructional reading is Level C. We are not advocating "pushing" children or drilling them. Most children engage with print through enjoyable

Figure 21-4 Suggested Grade-Level Reading Levels	
Grade Level	**Instructional Reading Level** (intervention is appropriate if the child is not reading at this level)
Kindergarten—early midyear (January)	A
Kindergarten—midyear (March)	B
Kindergarten—end of year (June)	C
Grade 1—Beginning of year (September)	C
Grade 1—November	D
Grade 1—December	E
Grade 1—January	F
Grade 1—February	G
Grade 1—March	H
Grade 1—April/May	I
Grade 1—end of year (June)	I/J
Grade 2—beginning of year (September)	I
Grade 2—midyear (December)	L/M
Grade 2—end of year (June)	M/N
Grade 3—beginning of year (September)	N

experiences such as shared reading; poetry; interesting work with letters, sounds, and words; and interactive and independent writing. Bringing them into a small group for more of these experiences can have a big payoff in the long run.

Intervention in kindergarten has high value in preventing further difficulties. You want children to establish a strong foundation in knowing how print "works," in recognizing and using visual information, in automatically using the motor movements needed for reading and writing continuous print, and in developing a core of known words. A first grader who enters reading strongly at Level C and knows letters, sounds, and many words can benefit from classroom instruction. In Leveled Literacy Intervention (LLI), one of the three systems is especially designed for this purpose. LLI teachers provide a maximum of 70 les-

sons between Levels A and C; this span of time makes it possible to firmly establish the early reading behaviors and the phonics knowledge they need.

In this same way for grades 1 through 3, if the child is not reading at the level indicated, we recommend some kind of intervention. Working with your school leadership team or your grade-level colleagues, decide the level of intervention needed. You may have children at higher grade levels who are reading below Level N; they definitely need intensive intervention. Make thoughtful decisions about the kinds of texts and lessons needed by these students. Many of the suggestions in the book will be helpful in working with them. (See fountasandpinnell.com for detailed maps to monitor progress using a range of systematic measures.)

▶ Forming Groups for Intervention and Allocating Teacher Time

Once you have identified children who need intervention and have determined their instructional levels, you can create small groups of readers who are similar enough that you can teach them together. After forming these groups, you (or perhaps a Title 1 or other supplementary reading teacher) can begin providing intervention lessons using texts appropriate for the group. These lessons can be taught in a quiet corner of the classroom or in a nearby room that doesn't take long to get to. We suggest you work with three children at a time for thirty minutes a day, for between fourteen to eighteen weeks. Then work with another group of three. From time to time, you may make other decisions; however, we recommend a group of three so that you can:

❑ Observe closely and provide strong individual support.

❑ Keep all children in the group highly engaged throughout the thirty-minute lesson.

❑ Prompt for effective strategic activities while listening to individual readers.

❑ Observe closely and interact with children as they write to support the development of writing strategies.

❑ Manage your time efficiently.

The scenario in Figure 21–5 shows how one teacher served thirty-six of the lowest achieving children across a school year with four 30-minute teaching slots a day. The numbers across the top of the chart indicate the number of weeks in the school year.

The teacher started the year with two groups of first graders and two groups of second graders who were determined by assessment to need intervention.

❑ About week 15 of the school year, the teacher started another group of first graders.

❑ About midyear, the teacher determined (based on ongoing assessment) that the two first grade groups were reading at grade level. She released them and picked up two groups of kindergartners.

❑ At about week 19, the teacher picked up another group of second graders after the first two second grade groups exited the program.

❑ Toward the end of the year, as groups exited, the teacher started two groups of kindergartners for six weeks and four weeks respectively, a group of first graders for four weeks, and a group of second graders for two weeks.

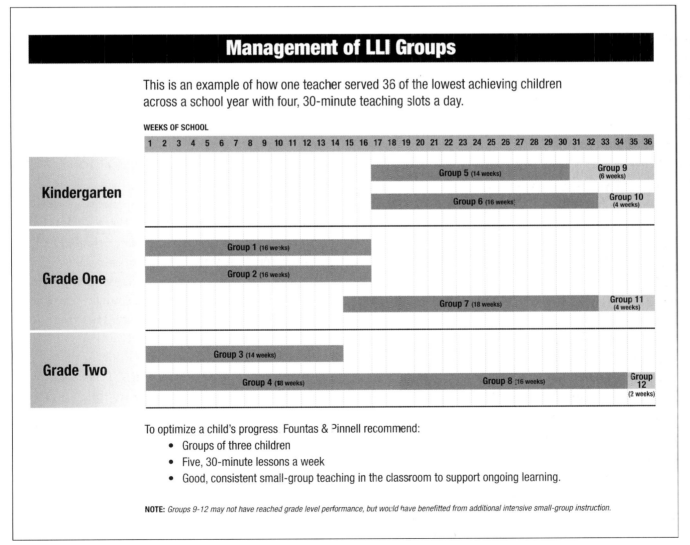

Figure 21-5 Management of LLI Groups

In this scenario (using the guideline of three children per group), the teacher has worked with a total of 36 children over the year, although her last "round" of lessons gives only a few weeks of service to "boost" the four groups. Some of these children, however, will benefit greatly from just a few weeks of intensive lessons. They would also benefit from additional intervention services the following year. Remember, the neediest children were served first. And, six weeks is plenty of time for kindergarten children to make progress to Level C. If needed, they can enter LLI immediately in the fall. If you have a teacher working all day with small groups, then you can add a potential six to nine students for every extra time slot provided.

Small-group intervention should be short-term, but a year of extra instruction may be appropriate for children who are having the most difficulty. Children will not progress at the same rate. You may move a child from one group to another at any time. The system needs to remain flexible so that the best decisions can be made for each student.

In many schools that use the Reading Recovery program, the Reading Recovery teacher works with four children individually for two hours of the day (four different children each half year). The rest of the day, the Reading Recovery teacher works with two or three additional groups for thirty minutes each. This is an excellent plan for giving intensive instruction to the neediest children, combining a tutorial and small-group instruction to reach large numbers of children.

▶ Our Framework for Literacy Intervention Lessons

We use three different instructional frameworks in our Leveled Literacy Intervention system (Fountas and Pinnell 2009), one designed to help children who are learning how print works (Getting Started lessons) and two others designed to support children as they grow as readers to Level N (about the beginning of grade 3). This program supplies a leveled set of children's books, sequenced from A to N, dedicated to

intervention. All the activities included in these frameworks have also been described in some detail in examples in other chapters of this book. You may need to adjust them to meet the needs of your particular readers.

A Framework to Support Early Reading and Writing Behaviors

This Getting Started framework (see Figure 21–6) is designed to be used daily with children (usually kindergartners or first graders) who are not making progress in attending to the visual features of print. Within the framework, children enjoy a great deal of your and group-member support as they engage with print, while you help them direct their attention to critical aspects of reading and writing. Four basic activities are the essential parts of lessons: rereading, phonics/word work, reading a new book, and writing about reading. There are three additional optional components: extra letter/word work, classroom connection, and home connection.

REREADING BOOKS

Rereading gives children the opportunity to participate in reading as a smooth and orchestrated process. They may still need to point precisely under the words while attending to the spaces and the first letters of words, but this process allows children to experience the process of reading. During this time, you can teach for, prompt for, and reinforce all early reading behaviors (see Chapter 10).

PHONICS/WORD WORK

Explicit phonics and word work is essential to help beginners learn to take words apart. You build these understandings systematically over time—see *The Continuum of Literacy Learning, Grades PreK–8* (Fountas and Pinnell 2011, 2008). Usually, you present a very clear visual demonstration. There is usually an active element; children need to work with letters and words using magnetic letters, word and picture cards, and other materials. You can find many suggestions in

Figure 21-6 Suggested Framework for Getting-Started Lessons

Lesson Component	Description	Approximate Time
Rereading Books	Children reread books they have previously read with others in a shared way (read to, with, and by).	5 minutes
Phonics/Word Work	You provide a brief, explicit lesson on a phonics principle appropriate to students' current understandings. There is an active "hands on" component to the lesson.	5 minutes
Reading a New Book	You introduce children to a new book in a highly supportive way. The first experience with the book uses an enlarged text (lap book). **Read to:** You read the text to the children and discuss the meaning. **Read with:** You invite the children to read the text in unison as you point. **Read by:** The children read an individual version of the text independently.	10 minutes
Writing About Reading	Children participate in group writing (shared or interactive). You help them compose and then write word by word a message that expresses something about the text they have read.	10 minutes
Additional Letter/Word Work	Children briefly work on letters, sounds, or words.	As time permits
Classroom Connection	Children have a specific task, related to their reading and writing, to work on independently.	Part of general classroom work
Home Connection	Children work with word cards, a writing/drawing task, and a "take home" book.	Done at home

Chapters 9 and 11. The emphasis is on phonemic awareness, letter identification, letter-sound relationships, and high-frequency words.

READING A NEW BOOK

You support reading a new book using a three-step process. (It helps to use a book with enlarged print, which we call a *lap book*. It is not as large as a typical "big book," and the text construction and print layout are carefully designed to support early reading behaviors. See Figure 21-7.)

❑ *Read to:* Read the text to the children and lead a conversation about it. (See Chapter 7 for suggestions on helping children use language structure and meaning.) Children's attention is freed to think about the meaning of the text and hear the language. They can enjoy the story while developing the familiarity they need to support their reading.

❑ *Read with:* Invite the children to join in on a second reading of the text. Supported by your voice and pointing, children experience reading the text while attending to the visual information. This provides another chance to talk about meaning. In addition, you can draw attention to words and their features (first letters, for example). Children can say and locate words. They are gradually unlocking the print of the text (see Chapters 11 and 12 for suggestions on applying principles to continuous print).

Figure 21-7 Lap Books from Leveled Literacy Intervention, Green System

❑ *Read by:* After the support of two readings, give each child a small version of the same book. (If the book is still difficult, do another shared reading before giving children the individual books.) This time, they use a whisper voice to read the book independently. Ask them to point crisply under each word while reading, and demonstrate and prompt as needed. (This book will be read again in tomorrow's lesson.)

▶ Writing About Reading

In interactive writing, the children as a group write about the text they have read. First, talk with them as you compose a simple text together. Ask them to suggest first letters as you write words. Then have them read the text several times and quickly draw a picture or two. You'll write most of the text, but you can share the pen with children at specific points by inviting individuals to write a letter or word ending. These moments have high instructional value.

In the example in Figure 21–8, based on a book about baby animals, the teacher and children composed the sentence, "Come and see the baby puppy":

[**MRS. C:** The first word of our sentence is *come*. Say *come*.

Children: *come*

MRS. C: *Come* starts like Carol's name. What let-

ter would you expect to see at the beginning of *come?*

GARETH: *c*

MRS. C: It's a *c*, like *Carol* and like *cat* on our chart [*points to the alphabet linking chart*]. Gareth, would you come up and write the *c* to start the word *come*.

In this case, Mrs. C wrote the rest of the word *come* and the word *and*. Different children wrote *see* and *the*, and Mrs. C finished the sentence. (In later lessons, Mrs. C will help the children switch to lowercase letters.) The whole sentence was written quickly and reread several times. Chapter 13 includes suggestions for different kinds of writing and for revisiting a written text for further learning

ADDITIONAL LETTER/WORD WORK

If time allows, give children the opportunity to do some additional, active letter/word work to extend the principle or work with high-frequency words.

Figure 21-8 Interactive Writing

CLASSROOM CONNECTION

Children complete a classroom activity that cues them to do a simple task independently, with your collaboration. (See the example in Figure 21–9. Each child has to read the sentence at the bottom and draw vegetables under the bowl to represent it.)

HOME CONNECTION

Children take home a previously read book to read to family members. They also can take home activity sheets, word cards, cut-up sentences, and other tasks they can perform successfully. This simple lesson structure works well within a thirty-minute period. Children should not need this level of support very long, because you are providing strong demonstrations of early reading and writing behaviors and prompting children to internalize them. After about ten of these Getting Started lessons, begin to alternate between the other two lesson frameworks we describe next.

Alternating Frameworks for Intervention Lessons

We have also designed two lesson frameworks you can alternate as you carry out an intervention program for a small group of students (Figure 21–10). These frameworks use specially designed sets of leveled texts based on the Fountas and Pinnell A-to-Z

Figure 21-9 Classroom Connection

gradient and form the basis of the Leveled Literacy Intervention systems. Based on your assessment of the child's instructional text level, you select and sequence texts within either framework. The components of these frameworks are described below.

TEXT SELECTION

After carefully assessing students' current instructional reading level, you'll know their instructional level (Pinnell and Fountas 1999), and you can start from there. In these alternating frameworks, the two texts provide different experiences for the students and different opportunities for you to teach. The instructional level text is just a little harder than we would expect the students to read independently, but with your strong teaching they can process it effectively, and in the process expand their reading powers. The independent level text provides the experience of reading a new book with ease—something struggling readers rarely experience. During the reading of both texts, you can teach for, prompt for, and reinforce problem solving (see Chapters 14 and 15).

REREADING BOOKS

Research provides evidence that "fluency develops as a result of many opportunities to practice reading with a high degree of success" (Armbruster et al. 2000, 27). At lower levels (A and B), children should be pointing while reading. This provides the opportunity to teach for, prompt for, and reinforce early reading behaviors. As children advance up text levels, the eyes take over the process.

Rereading is usually oral until about Level I or J, when students should be expected to read silently; even at higher levels, you'll need to sample some oral reading from each student so that you can make judgments about the processing. Through a few brief interactions during rereading, you'll support the readers, demonstrating and prompting for fluency—rapid word solving, phrasing, appropriate stress on words, intonation, and moving along at a good rate (not too slow and not too fast). Many suggestions for fostering fluency are included in Chapter 16.

Figure 21-10 Alternating Frameworks for Intervention Lessons in Leveled Literacy Intervention

LESSON COMPONENT	APPROXIMATE TIME
Framework 1	
1. **Rereading Books** *Children reread the two books that have been read in the previous lesson.*	5 minutes
2. **Phonics/Word Work** *You teach a phonics principle based on children's needs.*	5 minutes
3. **Reading a New Book** *Children read a new book at their **instructional level.***	15 minutes
4. **Letter/Word Work** *Children work with letters, sounds, or words.*	5 minutes
Classroom Connection *You introduce a reading or writing task children can perform independently in the classroom.*	Variable
Home Connection *Children take home something they can do with a family member: their classroom connection task, another similar task, word cards, etc. They also take home a previously read book.*	Variable
Framework 2	
1. **Rereading Books and Assessment** *Children reread the two books that have been read in the previous lesson. You take a Reading Record of one child's reading of the instructional level text read the day before.*	5 minutes
2. **Phonics/Word Work** *You teach a phonics principle based on children's needs. The lesson may build on the principle studied the previous day or explore a new one.*	5 minutes
3. **Writing About Reading** *With your support, children write to extend their understanding of the instructional level text they read the day before.*	15 minutes
4. **Reading a New Book** *Children read a new book at an **independent level** (slightly easier than the previous day's book).*	5 minutes
Extra Letter/Word Work *Children work with letters, sounds, or words.*	As time permits.
Classroom Connection *You introduce a reading or writing task children can perform independently in the classroom.*	Variable
Home Connection *Children take home something they can do with a family member: their classroom connection task, another similar task, word cards, etc. They also take home a previously read book.*	Variable

PHONICS/LETTER/WORD WORK

You'll provide phonics/letter/word work twice in every lesson for framework 1 and once for lessons using framework 2. (If you have time, you can provide extra phonics/letter/word work in framework 2). Within a lesson, the first instance of phonics teaching focuses on a particular principle, while the second includes "hands on" practice recognizing high-frequency words or work with principles children have previously learned.

Lessons at the early levels include systematic instruction in phonemic awareness and phoneme discrimination, critical elements in beginning reading (National Institute of Child Health and Human Development 2001, 2–33). You will want to include activities such as segmenting and blending. In addition to phonemes, children should work with rhymes, words, syllables, and onsets and rimes. While children are learning to hear and identify sounds in words, teach them the letters of the alphabet. Matching letters to phonemes helps children transfer this knowledge to reading and writing and see the usefulness of hearing sounds in words. "If children do not know letter names and shapes, they need to be taught them along with phonemic awareness" (Armbruster et al. 2000, 6).

As children progress, include phonics instruction—both simple and more complex relationships of sounds and letters, as well as word patterns and word structure. Include consonants, vowels, digraphs, blends, phonograms, prefixes and affixes, and multi-syllable words as appropriate to the level children are reading. These phonics lessons should be carefully sequenced so that children build knowledge systematically. They can immediately apply their new knowledge to the texts that they are reading and writing.

In this section of your lessons, you'll also want to help children build a core of known high-frequency words. Research indicates that "word recognition is a necessary but not sufficient condition for fluent reading" (Armbruster et al. 2000, 30). Automatically known words allow readers to begin to monitor and correct their reading; they also free readers' attention to think about meaning. Often, readers use phonics to solve a word several times and then it becomes

known; other words (like *the*) are learned using the visual features of the word.

You can use a variety of active ways to study words:

- ❑ Building words with magnetic letters.
- ❑ Writing words.
- ❑ Matching word cards and letter cards.
- ❑ Sorting pictures, letters, and words.
- ❑ Reviewing word cards.
- ❑ Playing letter and word games.

In phonics and letter/word work, emphasize looking from left to right. It takes a long time for some children to fully establish left-to-right directionality. You will find many suggestions for this component of the lesson framework in Chapters 11 and 12.

READING NEW TEXTS

In every lesson, readers process a new text supported by intensive teaching. For framework 1 the new book is at students' instructional level; for framework 2 the book is at the independent level—that is, a little easier. In either case, supportive conversation is important in helping children "learn new words and concepts and relate them to their prior knowledge and experience" (Armbruster et al. 2000, 35).

Instructional Level Text

An *instructional level text* is one that the reader, with instructional support, can successfully process with:

- ❑ 90 to 94 percent accuracy and satisfactory or excellent comprehension (Levels A–K).
- ❑ 95 to 97 percent accuracy and satisfactory or excellent comprehension (Levels L–Z).

You provide this support by:

- ❑ *Introducing the text.* Familiarize readers with the meaning of the entire text, with some of the language structure, and with some unfamiliar words. (For more information on introducing texts, see Chapters 7 and 20.)
- ❑ *Reading the text.* As each student reads the entire text softly or silently, observe and interact quickly to support effective reading strategies.

❏ *Discussing the text.* Lead students in a conversation about the meaning of the text.

❏ *Teaching for strategic actions.* Explicitly teach for, prompt for, or reinforce effective strategic actions.

Independent Level Text

An *independent level text* is one that the reader, with minimal instructional support, can process with:

❏ 95 to 100 percent accuracy and satisfactory or excellent comprehension (Levels A–K).

❏ 98 to 100 percent accuracy and satisfactory or excellent comprehension (Levels L–Z).

You still provide support, just less of it. Sequence books carefully so that children build a repertoire of words and phonics skills, develop reading strategies, and acquire content knowledge.

WRITING ABOUT READING

Framework 2 includes writing about the instructional level text children read in Framework 1. We recommend the three kinds of writing described below. Each is written in conventional form with your support so it becomes text for rereading.

Interactive Writing

You and the children compose a meaningful text they want to write. You write some of the text and share the pen at selected points. In interactive writing,

❏ You and the children engage in conversation as you compose and write the message.

❏ You and the children write the message in large print on a chart that everyone can see.

❏ You demonstrate, prompt for, and reinforce early writing strategies and letter formation, and help the children construct a text in conventional form. (See *The Fountas and Pinnell Prompting Guide 1*, 2009; see also Chapter 13).

❏ Children take over the writing at particular points that have instructional value. For example, you may ask a child to write a letter or word.

❏ The children reread the message. Sometimes you invite them to revisit the text for letter or word study.

You may also provide a typed copy for children to glue in their writing books and illustrate. Another very effective teaching move is to write the sentences on sentence strips to cut up and have the children assemble and glue on paper.

Dictated Writing

Writing sentences that you dictate helps children make the transition from oral to written language. They solve words within a meaningful sentence. They reread and check their work. The completed text is in conventional form. In dictated writing:

❏ You prompt children to write known words quickly.

❏ You help children solve unknown words by using sound or letter boxes, prompting them to use sound analysis or visual analysis, and helping them think of words they know. You may also write the word on a whiteboard and either have children copy it or compare their attempt with it.

❏ You may use verbal path descriptions (see *The Fountas and Pinnell Prompting Guide 1* [2009] and Chapter 10) to support letter formation.

❏ You invite children to reread their sentences when finished and to draw a picture if there is time.

❏ You may have children highlight words or word parts of interest.

Independent Writing

In independent writing, children compose and write their own sentences about the instructional level text they read the day before as you help them use the proper conventions. Through independent writing, children learn to control early writing strategies, represent ideas in different ways, and monitor their writing. In review,

❏ The children write a text independently.

❏ The text may be a list, a message or sentence, labels for pictures, or any other type of writing.

❏ You help them with the appropriate writing conventions so the text can be reread (see the *Fountas and Pinnell Prompting Guide 1* 2009).

CLASSROOM AND HOME CONNECTIONS

In the classroom connection, children receive materials and instructions for a productive literacy task they can do independently in the classroom. These tasks are designed to give children more experience in reading and writing and may include phonics or word work. They may be done in connection with rereading a book they have read at least twice before. The partnership between the classroom teacher and the intervention teacher (if these are different people) is critical in helping children make fast progress and catch up with their peers. If you have the assistance of an intervention teacher or are providing such assistance:

❏ Together, discuss the idea of classroom connections at the beginning of the program. Look over some examples of the activities and talk about how the tasks will be explained to children so they will be able to complete them independently.

❏ Together, choose the children who will receive intervention instruction and discuss how to make time for the classroom connection tasks. (Sometimes struggling readers have a great deal of difficulty working independently; the classroom connection tasks are helpful and necessary.)

❏ Share lesson plans, record-keeping forms, assessments, and observations so you both have the same information regarding children's progress.

Connections to students' homes are very important in supporting struggling readers. The intervention lessons include activities children can take home to do with their family members. Often, the activity is the same one children have done in the classroom. And children should always take home a book they have previously read with success. Home activities should:

❏ Allow the child to demonstrate success.

❏ Be very clear to families in terms of the routines and tasks (send a short letter home with each task).

❏ Demonstrate the child's ability to use phonics, write, and read continuous text.

▶ Sample Lessons

Figures 21–11 and 21–12 are sample lessons from the Leveled Literacy Intervention system (Fountas and Pinnell 2009). They illustrate specific procedures for Frameworks 1 and 2. The first page helps you think about the materials you will need, the goals of the lesson, and text characteristics. You can use these examples to plan your own lessons using leveled texts.

▶ Implementing Intervention Lessons

It is a challenge to design and implement intervention lessons that make a difference for readers who struggle. The resources listed in Figure 21–13 will help you. The chapters in this book also include specific examples of procedures you can use in your classroom instruction, within the components of the intervention lessons you design, or as you teach individuals.

As you work more with intervention lessons, you will find that you can use your basic frameworks over and over. Of course, you will make adjustments for each group of readers, and your conversations will be as varied as the children! They will always surprise you with their responses to texts. Our experience suggests that it is worthwhile to create a predictable sequence of events and stick to it. And, choose the best texts you can find.

Throughout this book, we have described an array of teaching actions and theoretical foundations that may seem overwhelming if you try to do everything at once. But, essentially, you will want to have a very broad repertoire from which you can draw to teach children who find literacy learning difficult. We encourage flexible use of this text. Start by reading the chapters you think will be most helpful. Use this chapter to get lessons going and establish routines. Look back for deeper understanding of language, reading and writing, and for specific teaching actions that will help. Take each area one at a time and hone your teaching skills. You will find that your students

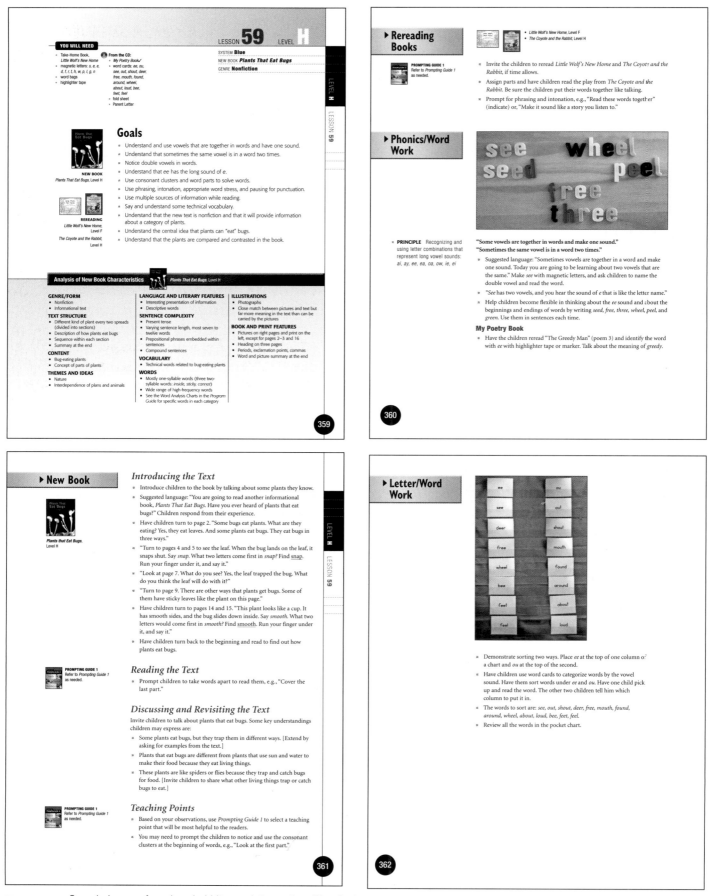

Figure 21-11 Sample Lesson from Leveled Literacy Intervention, Blue System

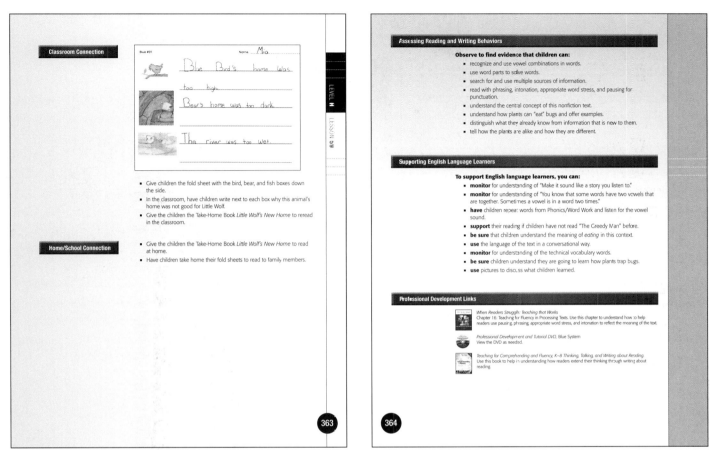

Figure 21-11 Sample Lesson from Leveled Literacy Intervention, Blue System, *continued*

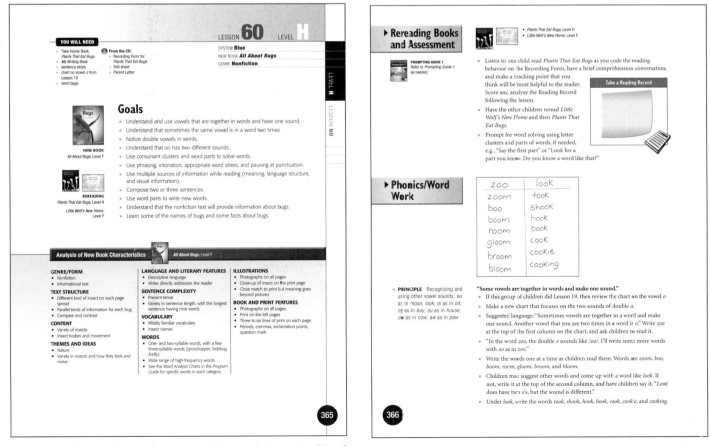

Figure 21-12 Sample Lesson from Leveled Literacy Intervention, Blue System

continues

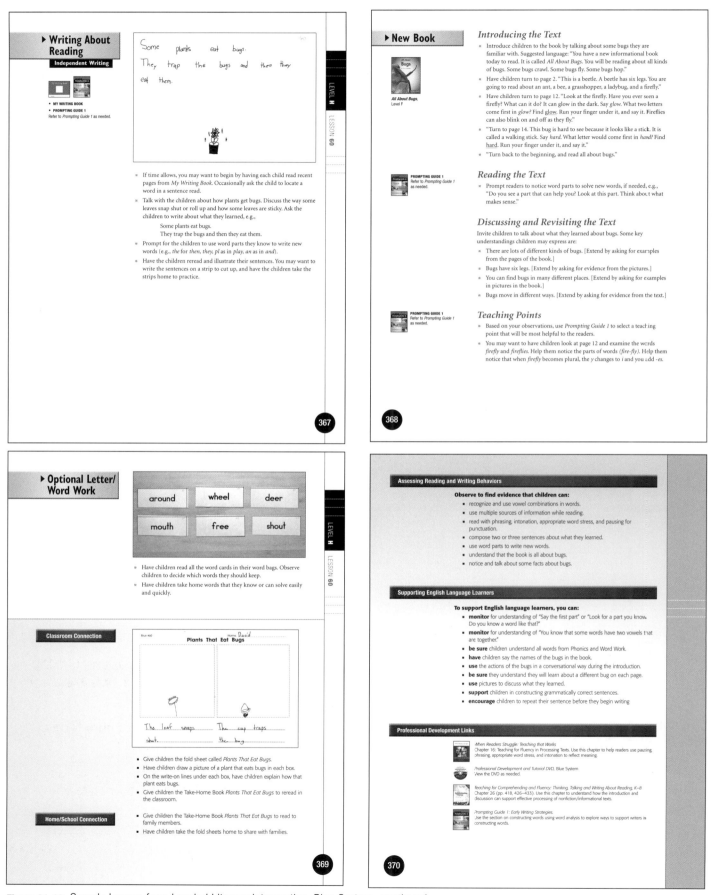

Figure 21-12 Sample Lesson from Leveled Literacy Intervention, Blue System, *continued*

will respond well. Your work with struggling readers is critical, and you will find it worthwhile and satisfying as you grow in your ability to understand and work with them effectively.

As educators, we have the ability to educate all children well. Schumaker challenges the inertia that sometimes exists in our schools. He argues, "We have an opportunity to blow the lid off school attainment, dramatically and swiftly reduce the achievement gap, and enhance the life chances of all children, regardless of their social or economic circumstances." The real question, according to Meier (2006) is, "Do we want

to do it badly enough?" If we do, then we will need to have the energy, courage, and humility to turn our caring into actions. The children's progress is limited only by our own limitations in teaching them.

Our goal in sharing the information in this book has been to develop our collective expertise in working effectively with struggling readers, as our belief is that effective instruction will have the biggest impact on literacy achievement. Effective teaching can only be measured by evidence of its influence on learning. Together, let us examine our teaching to assure that "it works" for every child.

Figure 21-13 **Resources for Planning Intervention Lessons**		
Area	**Resources in *When Readers Struggle: Teaching That Works***	**Other Resources** *(All publications from Heinemann.)*
Selection and Sequencing of Texts	**Chapter 6:** Text Matters: A Ladder to Success **Chapter 20:** Engaging Readers' Emotion and Motivation in Successful Learning	Pinnell, G.S., & Fountas, I.C. (2011, 2008). *The Continuum of Literacy Learning, Grades PreK–8: Behaviors and Understandings to Notice, Teach, and Support.* Fountas, I., & Pinnell, G.S. (1996). *Guided Reading: Good first teaching for all children* Fountas, I. & Pinnell, G.S. (2006) *Teaching for Comprehending and Fluency: Thinking, Talking, and Writing About Reading, K–8.* Fountas, I., & Pinnell, G.S. (2005). *Leveled Books, K–8: Matching Texts to Readers for Effective Teaching.*
Supporting Early Reading Behaviors	**Chapter 10:** Learning About Print: Early Reading Behaviors	McCarrier, A.M., Pinnell, G.S., & Fountas, I.C. (2000). *Interactive Writing: How Language and Literacy Come Together, K–2.* Fountas, I., & Pinnell, G.S. (1996). *Guided Reading: Good First Teaching for All Children.* Fountas, I., & Pinnell, G.S. (2009). *The Fountas and Pinnell Prompting Guide 1: A Tool for Literacy Teachers.*

continues

Figure 21-13 **Resources for Planning Intervention Lessons,** *continued*

Area	Resources in *When Readers Struggle: Teaching That Works*	Other Resources *(All publications from Heinemann.)*
Phonemic Awareness, Phonics, and Word Work	**Chapter 9:** The Phonological Base for Learning to Read and Write **Chapter 11:** Learning to Solve Words: Effective and Efficient Phonics **Chapter 12:** Building and Using a Repertoire of Words	Pinnell, G.S., & Fountas, I.C. (2011, 2008). *The Continuum of Literacy Learning, Grades PreK–8: Behaviors and Understandings to Notice, Teach, and Support.* Pinnell, G.S., & Fountas, I.C. (2003). *Phonics Lessons, Grade K: Letters, Words, and How They Work.* Pinnell, G.S., & Fountas, I.C. (2003). *Phonics Lessons, Grade 1: Letters, Words, and How They Work.* Pinnell, G.S., & Fountas, I.C. (2003). *Phonics Lessons, Grade 2: Letters, Words, and How They Work.* Pinnell, G.S., & Fountas, I.C. (1998). *Word Matters: Teaching Phonics and Spelling in the Reading/Writing Classroom.* Fountas, I., & Pinnell, G.S. (2009). *The Fountas & Pinnell Prompting Guide 1: A Tool for Literacy Teachers.* Pinnell, G.S., & Fountas, I.C. (2004). *Sing a Song of Poetry, Grade K: A Teaching Resource for Phonics, Word Study, and Fluency.* Pinnell, G.S., & Fountas, I.C. (2004). *Sing a Song of Poetry, Grade 1: A Teaching Resource for Phonics, Word Study, and Fluency.*
Interacting with Students to Support Strategic Processing While Reading	**Chapter 2:** Effective Readers: What Do They Do? **Chapter 7:** Language Matters: Talking, Reading, and Writing **Chapter 8:** Words Matter: Building Power in Vocabulary **Chapter 14:** Teaching for Problem Solving While Processing Texts: Early Reading Behaviors and Searching for Information **Chapter 15:** Teaching for Independence in Processing Texts: Solving Words, Self-Monitoring and Self-Correcting Behaviors **Chapter 16:** Teaching for Fluency in Processing Texts: Six Dimensions **Chapter 17:** Teaching for Comprehending: Thinking Before, During, and After Reading	Pinnell, G.S., & Fountas, I.C. (2011, 2008). *The Continuum of Literacy Learning, Grades PreK–8: Behaviors and Understandings to Notice, Teach, and Support.* Fountas, I.C., & Pinnell, G.S. (2006). *Teaching for Comprehending and Fluency: Thinking, Talking, and Writing About Reading, K–8.* Fountas, I., & Pinnell, G.S. (1996). *Guided Reading: Good First Teaching for All Children.* Fountas, I., & Pinnell, G.S. (2009). *The Fountas & Pinnell Prompting Guide 1: A Tool for Literacy Teachers.*

continues

Figure 21-13 Resources for Planning Intervention Lessons, *continued*

Area	Resources in *When Readers Struggle: Teaching That Works*	Other Resources *(All publications from Heinemann.)*
Writing about Reading	**Chapter 13:** Extending Reading Power Through Writing	Pinnell, G.S., & Fountas, I.C. (2011, 2008). *The Continuum of Literacy Learning, Grades PreK–8: Behaviors and Understandings to Notice, Teach, and Support.* McCarrier, A.M., Pinnell, G.S., & Fountas, I.C. (2000). *Interactive Writing: How Language and Literacy Come Together, K–2.* Fountas, I.C., & Pinnell, G.S. (2006). *Teaching for Comprehending and Fluency: Thinking, Talking, and Writing About Reading, K–8.*
Classroom and Home Connections	**Chapter 19:** Engaging Readers' Attention and Memory in Successful Learning	Pinnell, G.S., & Fountas, I.C. (2004). *Sing a Song of Poetry, Grade 2: A Teaching Resource for Phonics, Word Study, and Fluency.* Fountas, I., & Pinnell, G.S. (1996). *Guided Reading: Good First Teaching for All Children.*
Assessment and Progress Monitoring	**Chapter 4:** Reading Behavior: What Does It Tell Us? **Chapter 5:** Change Over Time: Processing Systems in the Making	Fountas, I.C., & Pinnell, G.S. (2007). *Fountas and Pinnell Benchmark Assessment System 1.*

▶ Suggestions for Professional Development

REFLECTING ON TEACHING

1. Read this chapter before coming to a meeting with colleagues. Gather some good texts at a level you think will work well for a group of struggling readers you teach. Ask participants to bring any student records that they have (for example, running records or benchmark assessment).

2. Talk together about the framework for lessons. Select one of the frameworks in this chapter. You can adjust it to meet your needs. Or, you can create your own framework.

3. Look at the texts you have selected. Discuss them with a partner or grade level team. Ask:

   ❏ What are the features of this text that will be challenging to students at this level?

   ❏ What are the opportunities to learn?

   ❏ What might you attend to in the introduction to the text?

4. Now plan a few consecutive lessons that you will try out next week.

5. Schedule a follow-up session to share your results.

6. After teaching the lessons, reflect on the one that went best. Use questions in the following figure to reflect on the effectiveness of your teaching (Figure 21-14).

7. Bring your reflections and any observational records you have to the follow-up session. You can make adjustments in your framework, share lessons, and choose new texts.

Figure 21-14 Guide to Effective Teaching

REREADING
- How did I support children's processing?
- How did I support phrasing and fluency?
- What evidence did I see of good problem solving?
- What problem solving did the readers initiate?

PHONICS/WORD WORK
- How did I organize materials so that the children work on letters/words independently?
- How fluent were readers in making words, taking them apart, and making them again?
- What were children noticing about words and how they work?

NEW BOOK

Before reading
- How did I help children expand language and vocabulary? What evidence did I see?
- How did I support readers' comprehending of the text?

During reading
- How did I support children's processing?
- What evidence did I see of good problem solving?

After reading
- How did I help children understand features of the text?
- How did I support effective processing strategies?
- What changes did I see in the readers' ability to initiate problem-solving actions?

WRITING ABOUT READING
- How did I engage children in composing the sentences?
- What are the characteristics of the two sentences children have composed (complexity, accuracy, etc.)?
- How did I draw children's attention to the construction of words?
- What links did I provide to help readers use previous knowledge?
- What evidence did I see of learning?

CLASSROOM AND HOME CONNECTION
- How did I help children work independently?
- How will the activity help the reader/writer?

Appendices

APPENDIX A

Ways of Thinking About Text Reading: Observing for Evidence

Thinking	Systems of Strategic Actions	✓	Evidence From Observation: Introduction, First Reading, Discussion, Running Record
Within the Text	Solving Words		
	Monitoring and Self-Correction		
	Searching For and Using Information		
	Summarizing		
	Maintaining Fluency		
	Adjusting		
Beyond the Text	Predicting		
	Making Connections • Personal • World • Text		
	Synthesizing		
	Inferring		
About the Text	Analyzing		
	Critiquing		

Name: _____   Date: _____

Guide for Observing and Noting Reading Behaviors	C P N	Notes
1. Early Reading Behaviors *Does the reader:* • Move left to right across a line of print? • Return to the left for a new line? • Match voice to print while reading a line or more of print? • Recognize a few easy high-frequency words?		
2. Searching for and Using Information **Meaning** *Does the reader:* • Make meaningful attempts at unknown words? • Use the meaning of the story or text to predict unknown words? • Reread to gather more information to solve a word? • Reread and use the meaning of the sentence? • Reread to search for more details—information, characters, plot? • Reread to gather information to clarify confusions? • Use headings and titles to think about the meaning of a section of text? • Use information in the pictures to help in understanding a text? • Use knowledge of the genre (and its characteristics) to help in understanding a text? • Use knowledge of the genre (and its characteristics) to help in finding information? • Use readers' tools to help in finding information (glossary, index)? **Structure** *Does the reader:* • Use knowledge of oral language to solve unknown words? • Reread to see if a word "sounds right" in a sentence? • Reread to correct using language structure? **Visual Information** *Does the reader:* • Use the visual information to solve words? • Use the sound of the first letter(s) to attempt or solve a word? • Use some, most, or all of the visual information to solve words? • Use sound analysis to solve a word? • Make attempts that are visually similar? • Use knowledge of a high-frequency word to problem solve? • Search for more visual information within a word to solve it? • Use analogy to solve unknown words? • Use syllables to solve words? • Use prefixes and suffixes to take apart and recognize words? • Use inflectional endings to problem solve words? • Recognize words quickly and easily? • Reread and use the sound of the first letter to solve a word? • Problem solve unknown words quickly and efficiently? • Work actively to solve words? • Use multiple sources of information together in attempts at words? • Use all sources of information flexibly to solve words? • Use all sources of information in an orchestrated way?		
3. Solving Words *Does the reader:* • Recognize a core of high-frequency words quickly? • Recognize words quickly and easily? • Use a variety of flexible ways to take words apart? • Use the meaning of the sentences to solve words? • Use the structure of the sentence to solve words? • Use some of the visual information to solve words? • Use known word parts to solve words?		

Key: C=Consistent
P=Partial
N=Not evicent

Guide for Observing . . . (cont.)	C P N	Notes
3. Solving Words *(cont.)* *Does the reader:* • Use sound analysis (sounding out)? • Use analogy to solve words? • Make attempts that are visually similar? • Use the sound of the first letter to solve words? • Work actively to solve words? • Use known words or parts to solve unknown words? • Use syllables to problem solve? • Use prefixes and suffixes to take words apart? • Use inflectional endings to take words apart? • Use sentence context to derive the meaning of words? • Use base words and root words to derive the meaning of words? • Make connections among words to understand their meaning?		
4. Self-Monitoring *Does the reader:* • Hesitate at an unknown word? • Stop at an unknown word? • Stop at an unknown word and appeal for help? • Stop after an error? • Notice mismatches? • Notice when an attempt does not look right? • Notice when an attempt does not sound right? • Notice when an attempt does not make sense? • Reread to confirm reading? • Use knowledge of some high-frequency words to check on reading? • Check one source of information with another? • Check an attempt that makes sense with language? • Check an attempt that makes sense with the letters (visual information)? • Use language structure to check on reading? • Request help after making several attempts?		
5. Self-Correcting *Does the reader:* • Reread and try again until accurate? • Stop after an error and make another attempt? • Stop after an error and make multiple attempts until accurate? • Reread to self-correct? • Work actively to solve mismatches? • Self-correct errors?		
6. Maintaining Fluency *Does the reader:* • Read without pointing? • Read word groups (phrases)? • Put words together? • Read smoothly? • Read the punctuation? • Make the voice go down at periods? • Make the voice go up at question marks? • Pause briefly at commas, dashes, and hyphens? • Read dialogue with intonation or expression? • Stress the appropriate words to convey accurate meaning? • Read at a good rate—not too fast and not too slow?		
7. Other Behaviors		

Resources

Coding Errors and Self-Corrections in Oral Reading

Behavior	Coding	Error Counting
Accurate reading	no mark OR environments ✓	No error
Substitution, not corrected	worry / wonder	One error
Substitution, self-corrected	worry |SC / wonder	No error; one SC
Multiple substitutions, not corrected	adopt | adopted / adapted	One error per word in the text
Missing the same word several times in a text	Speckles / Species Spiced / species	One error each time missed
Errors on names and proper nouns—repeated during the reading	area / Arctic ark / Arctic	One error the first time; no error after that even if different substitutions are made for the nouns
Contractions (reads as two words or reads two words as contraction)	Cannot / Can't they're / they are	One error
Multiple substitutions, self-corrected	adopt | adopted |SC / adapted	No error; one SC
Insertion of a word	✓ very ✓ / ∧	One error per word inserted
Omission of a word	✓ only ✓ / —	One error per word
Skipping a line	from the cold water	One error per word
Repetition	R R₂	No error
"You try it" followed by student reading correctly	environments|Y |✓ / A	No error
"You try it" followed by a substitution	environments|Y |endings / A	One error
Appeal followed by "You try it" and Told	environments|Y|T / A	One error
Told (teacher supplied word)	environments |T	One error
"Sounding out" followed by correct reading	o-n-ly ✓ / Only	No error; no SC
"Sounding out" followed by incorrect or no further reading	o-n-ly |once / only	One error
Sounding the first letter and then saying the word correctly	o ✓ / only sp ✓ / species	No error; no SC
Sounding the first letter incorrectly and then saying the word correctly	w |SC / only	No error; no SC

Verbal Path for the Formation of Letters

Sometimes it helps children to say aloud the directions for "making" a letter. This "verbal path" helps them to understand the directional movement that is essential. In addition, it gives the teacher and child a language to talk through the letter and its features. Here, we suggest language for creating a verbal path to the distinctive features of letters.

Lowercase Letter Formation

a — pull back, around, up, and down

b — pull down, up, around

c — pull back and around

d — pull back, around, up, and down

e — pull across, back, and around

f — pull back, down, and cross

g — pull back, around, up, down, and under

h — pull down, up, over, and down

i — pull down, dot

j — pull down, curve around, dot

k — pull down, pull in, pull out

l — pull down

m — pull down, up, over, down and up, over and down

n — pull down, up, over, and down

o — pull back and around

p — pull down, up, and around

q — pull back, around, up, and down

r — pull down, up, and over

s — pull back, in, around, and back around

t — pull down and cross

u — pull down, around, up and down

v — slant down, up

w — slant down, up, down, up

x — slant down, slant down

y — slant in, slant and down

z — across, slant down, across

Uppercase Letter Formation

A — slant down, slant down, across

B — pull down, up, around and in, back and around

C — pull back and around

D — pull down, up, around

E — pull down, across, across, and across

F — pull down, across, across

G — pull back, around, across

H — pull down, pull down, across

I — pull down, across, across

J — pull down, curve around, across

K — pull down, slant in, slant out

L — pull down, across

M — pull down, slant down, slant up, pull down

N — pull down, slant down, pull up

O — pull back and around

P — pull down, up, and around

Q — pull back and around and cross

R — pull down, up, around, in, and slant down

S — pull back, in, around, down, and back around

T — pull down, across

U — pull down, around, up, and down

V — slant down, slant up

W — slant down up, down up

X — slant down, slant down

Y — slant in, slant, and down

Z — across, slant down, across

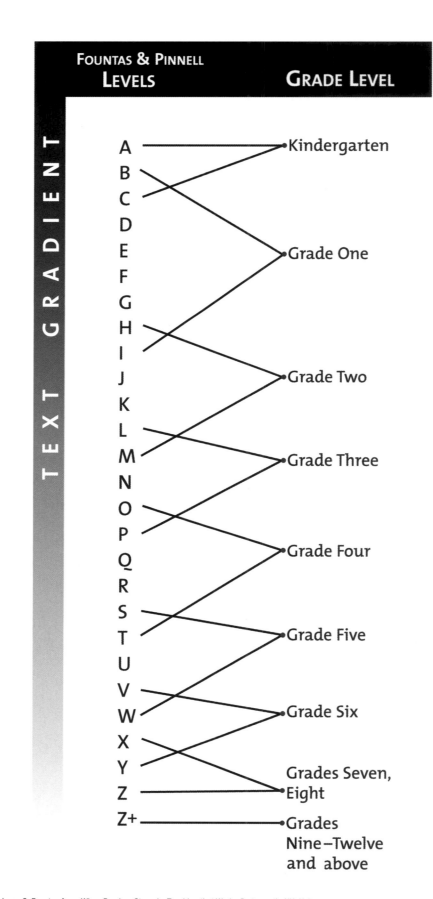

Directions for Concentration

The goal of the Concentration card game is to make matches between cards that display letters, pictures, or words. The letters, pictures, and words will vary according to the purpose of the application activity (for example, matching beginning sounds or ending sounds, letters and sounds, beginning consonant clusters and pictures, and so on). The objective is to gather the most pairs by the end of the game.

Making the Game

To make the game, prepare a collection of cards with letters, pictures, or words to be paired. You may want to draw a simple picture or place a sticker on the reverse side of the cards to create a uniform deck. If you make the back of each set of cards different, keeping cards in different decks and selecting different decks becomes easier. The total number of cards should be anywhere from twelve to twenty-four.

Playing the Game

To play the game,

1. Place the cards face down on the table in orderly rows.
2. Each player has a turn. The player turns two cards over to show the letter, picture, word or word part.
3. If the cards go together, the player takes the pair and takes another turn. If they don't match, the player turns the cards back over and the next player has a turn.
4   The player who has the most pairs at the end of the game is the winner.

This game requires players not only to make matches among sounds and letters but to remember the position of potential matches.

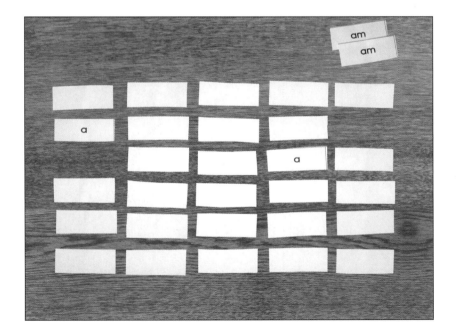

Directions for Follow the Path

In Follow the Path, players throw a die or draw a card to move a marker along a curved "path." Follow the Path games may also have names like Going to the Zoo, Trip to Outer Space, Race to the Finish, or Trip to the Ice Cream Store. The objective is to reach the destination (or end of the path) first.

Making the Game

To make the game board, draw a curved path on the inside of a colored file folder or on a poster or piece of tag paper (for example, 9" x 12" or 11" x 18"). Divide the path into approximately twenty spaces. You can glue or draw pictures of interest around the path and make an interesting "finish" box at the end (for example, the zoo, the moon, a finish line, or the ice cream store).

In each space on the board, write or glue a letter, picture, word, or word part as appropriate. Provide three or four game pieces such as colored markers or small, plastic animals. To generate movement along the path you will need a die or block with a 1, 2, or 3 on each side. Two alternatives to using the die or number block are:

- You can make a set of cards that have letters, pictures, words, or word parts that correspond to those on the board. When a player draws a card, he moves to the space with the corresponding letter, picture, word, or word part.

- You can make a set of number cards. When a player draws a card, he moves the number of spaces indicated on the card.

If you use either set of cards, you might include cards for "take an extra turn," "go back one space," "go forward one space," or "miss a turn." The cards and pieces can be kept in a sealable plastic bag.

Playing the Game

To play the game, each player shakes the die, lets it fall, and moves the corresponding number of spaces. If players are drawing cards, they draw the next card in the pile, read it aloud, and move to the next corresponding space. The player might also have to perform some action (such as saying the next letter of the alphabet, reading a word and saying the beginning or ending sound, looking at a picture and clapping syllables, and so on). The player who gets to the end of the path first wins the game.

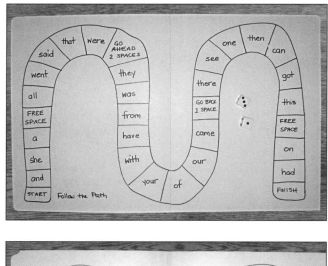

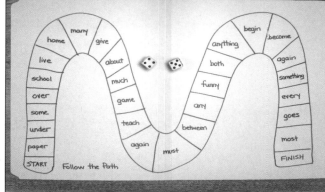

Directions for Go Fish

Go Fish is a card game played with letter, picture, or word cards. The object is to collect two, three, or four of the same card in order to discard all of the cards in your hand.

Making the Game

To make the game, make letter, picture, or word cards. A set of cards can focus on any principle you are teaching. For example, children can match pictures to learn the game but can progress to matching pictures that start with the same sound, matching pictures and letters, matching words, or matching words with similar features (such as *-ing* or *-ed* endings).

For a simple form of the game, have children match pairs; for a more difficult version, children must collect three or four cards to make a match.

To make the card sets, glue on pictures or write words or letters on the cards to create anywhere from twenty to forty cards in four-card "suits" (that is, cards that match).

Playing the Game

To play the game, all cards in the deck are shuffled. Each player is dealt five cards, and there is a "draw" pile. Players take turns.

The first player says, "Do you have a [picture of something that starts with _____; picture that starts like _____; word that starts with ___; word with (feature)]?"

The second player hands over the match or says "Go Fish!"

If the first player receives a match, she places the matching cards face up on the table and then gets another turn. If instructed to "Go Fish," the first player draws from the pile. If she then has a match, she places the matching cards face down on the table and draws another card. If the player does not draw a match, she keeps the card in her hand.

If players are required to match three or four cards before laying them down, they will have to "hold" cards until the proper number of matches is found.

The object of the game is to "go out" by laying down all your cards in matching pairs or groups.

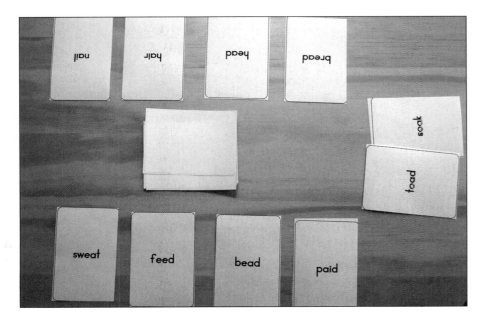

Directions for Lotto

Making the Game

You will need enough Lotto game boards made of card stock for the number of children who will participate. Typically there are between two and four players per game. The players' boards should all be different from one another. You may want to create sets of colored boards and then make sure each group has one of each color.

The basic game board has 12 squares, 3 across and 4 down. You can make a smaller board with 9 squares (3 across and 3 down) or an expanded board with 16 or 25 squares (4 x 4 grid or 5 x 5 grid). If you decide to use a game card with more than 12 squares, you will need to reduce the picture cards or cut out the pictures so they will fit within the game squares.

Randomly place the letters, pictures, or word cards in the boxes of each card. All of the cards are different from one another. You can write or paste one item in each box. You may want to put a free space in a different place on each card.

Make a set of letter, picture, or word cards appropriate to the game that players will use to match to their squares on the game card. Have plastic chips or some other way for players to mark the boxes on their game cards.

Playing the Game

Give each player a game card. Place the letter, picture, or word cards and the plastic chips or other markers in the middle of the table.

Players take turns drawing a card and saying what it is. All players search their game cards for a corresponding letter, picture, or word. They can mark any spaces that correspond.

For Lotto, the first player to cover the entire board wins the game. The game can then continue until others fill their cards if desirable. For the Bingo version, the player who covers one row across, down, or diagonally wins the game.

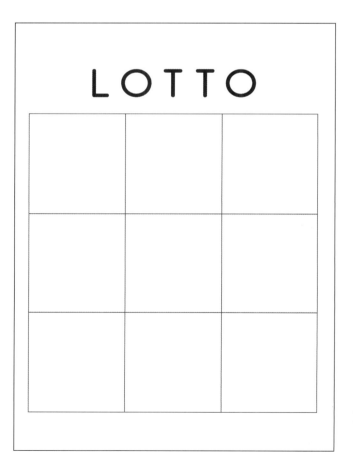

Directions for Snap!

This game works well with two or three players. The objective is to notice matching cards quickly and say "Snap!" to win the cards that match. The winner is the player with the most cards at the end.

Making the Game

Make a set or deck of cards for each player with words and pictures. The sets are either identical (with exact matches) or have elements that match. For example, the matching elements might be digraphs (chick, match, child) or word endings (swimming, cooking, reading). The sets may be constructed to help players focus on any element. When children really understand the game, several different ways of matching can be included in each game. The simplest task is to look for exact matches (for example, words). A more complex task is to look for the same element but different examples in words. The most complex task is for players to look for any kind of connection.

Playing the Game

When two players play, they look for a match between two cards. When three players play, they look for a three-way match. (You can make the game quicker by allowing any two-card match even when there are three players.)

Players shuffle their cards and place them in a face-down deck on the table. Each player has a deck. Simultaneously, they pick up a card and turn it over. They scan the cards (two or three), looking for a match. If there is a match, they say "Snap!" The first player to say "Snap!" gets to keep the matching cards. The player must tell how the cards are alike.

If there is no match, cards are placed face down in another deck. If two or three players say "Snap!" at the same time, you can say that no one will get a card, or each player can take one. When all the cards in the deck are turned over (minus the cards that each player has won), the players shuffle them, lay them face down in a deck and continue to play. (They will find more matches as the number of cards in the decks goes down.) The game is over when all of the cards are dispersed. The player with the most cards wins. You can shorten this game by having players turn over all of the cards only once and then counting to see who has the most cards.

Directions for Word Grids

Word Grids are pages of small boxes in which words or word parts are written. They can be used for a variety of purposes: independent practice for quick whole-word recognition; practice for taking words apart quickly; or individualized practice of words or word parts.

A Game for Principle Practice

Making the Game

You will want to design word grids related to lesson principles. Fill the boxes on the game board with words or word parts. For example, they might have high-frequency words, words with particular spelling patterns, words with suffixes or prefixes, words with particular vowel sounds, words with consonant clusters or consonant digraphs, or words that have synonyms, antonyms, or homophones.

On the sides of the die or on word cards are words or parts related to the principle that is the focus of the game. You may write consonant clusters, vowel configurations, phonograms, numbers (for syllables), endings, or any other category related to the lesson principle.

Playing the Game

- The game is designed for two to four players. To play the Word Grid game, a child rolls a die or draws a card and reads the word or word part.
- He looks for a related word (for example, a word with the same beginning cluster, a synonym, a word with the same spelling pattern) and places an X with a pencil over the word in the box.
- Players take turns, each time crossing out a word that matches. The first player to cross out all the words on the grid wins the game. Players can continue until all players but the final one cross out all the boxes.

Practice for Quick Word-Solving

To use the Word Grid for practice, the child reads the words across as quickly as possible. She reads it several times to gain speed (but not so fast as to distort articulation). She can read it different ways: for example, read columns down or start at the end box. The purpose is to develop quick recognition. You can create grids for any category of words: for example, create several high-frequency word grids for children to use for practice.

Personalized Practice Grids

Use a blank game board to list the specific words a child needs to practice. For example, list all the high-frequency words a child almost knows but has not yet mastered. You might involve the children in selecting words to place in the practice or game grids.

Directions for Word Ladders

Word Ladders is a technique for helping children learn how to manipulate letters and word parts to construct new words. You start with a word, then, change, add, or remove one or more letters to make a new word, for example, *can, many, any, and* or *hand, handy, handle.* You can show children the word to start with using magnetic letters. You can then have children identify the new words you make by adding or removing letters. You may want the children to suggest the letter changes, and you can make the changes and show them the new word. You will want children to say each new word and understand its meaning.

Uppercase Letter Recognition Sheet

H	E	M	T
I	P	Q	U
O	C	W	B
X	V	J	S
G	N	Y	K
Z	R	A	F
L	D		

Lowercase Letter Recognition Sheet

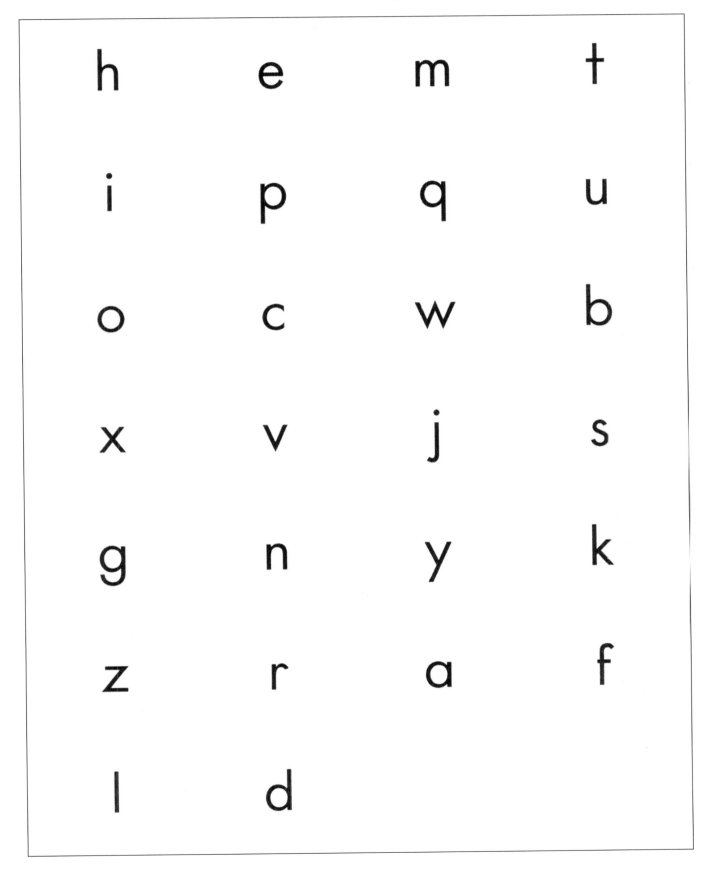

25 High-Frequency Words

no	so	go
is	on	it
can	in	do
me	up	an
you	am	the
and	we	my
he	like	to
at	see	
a	I	

50 High-Frequency Words

all	girl	not	she
are	got	now	sit
as	had	of	then
ball	has	or	they
be	her	out	this
boy	him	play	too
by	his	put	us
come	how	ran	was
day	if	read	went
did	jump	run	will
eat	look	sat	yes
for	man	saw	
get	mom	say	

100 High-Frequency Words

LIST 1	LIST 2	LIST 3
than	have	over
about	there	ride
back	any	don't
after	into	said
I'm	just	that
been	little	one
big	make	with
came	before	five
away	two	their
your	four	what
who	mother	but
when	where	here
them	very	going
because	could	our
from	were	three

LIST 4		LIST 5	
want	take	books	sleep
able	dad	good	love
bad	hide	help	much
give	almost	city	stay
today	dog	write	name
week	anything	top	new
something	home	room	paper
bus	down	under	rain
year	become	fast	door
can't	end	hill	fun
tell	behind	know	sky
across	fish	use	both
world	why	let	time
cat	car	place	

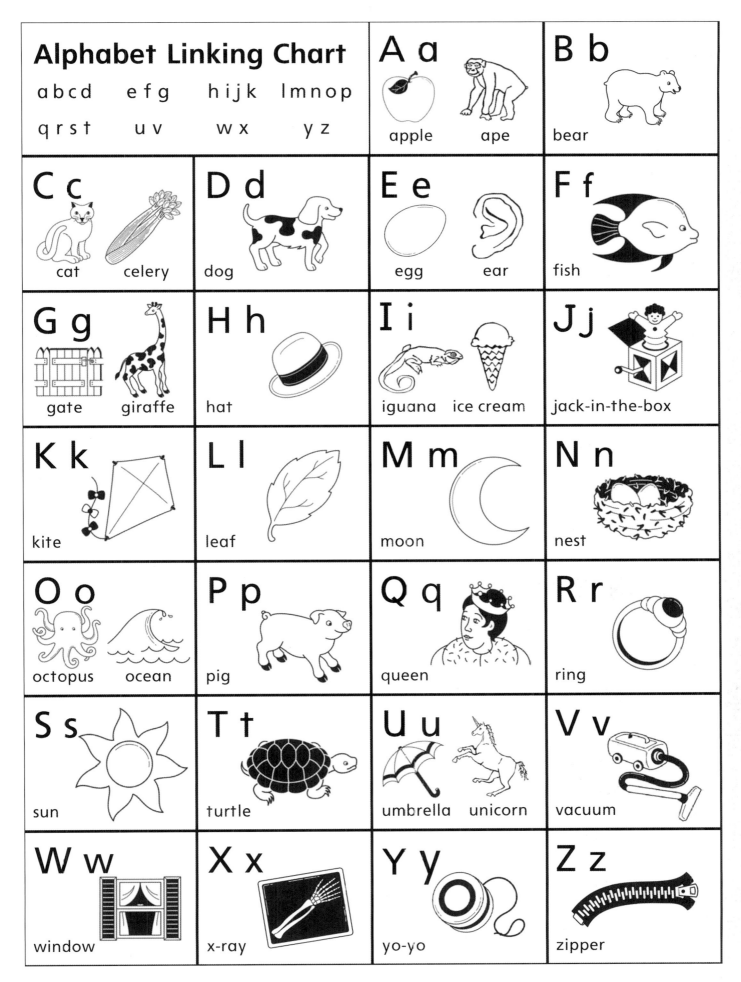

Alphabet Linking Chart

a b c d   e f g   h i j k   l m n o p

q r s t   u v   w x   y z

A a   apple   ape

B b   bear

C c   cat   celery

D d   dog

E e   egg   ear

F f   fish

G g   gate   giraffe

H h   hat

I i   iguana   ice cream

J j   jack-in-the-box

K k   kite

L l   leaf

M m   moon

N n   nest

O o   octopus   ocean

P p   pig

Q q   queen

R r   ring

S s   sun

T t   turtle

U u   umbrella   unicorn

V v   vacuum

W w   window

X x   x-ray

Y y   yo-yo

Z z   zipper

Consonant Cluster Linking Chart

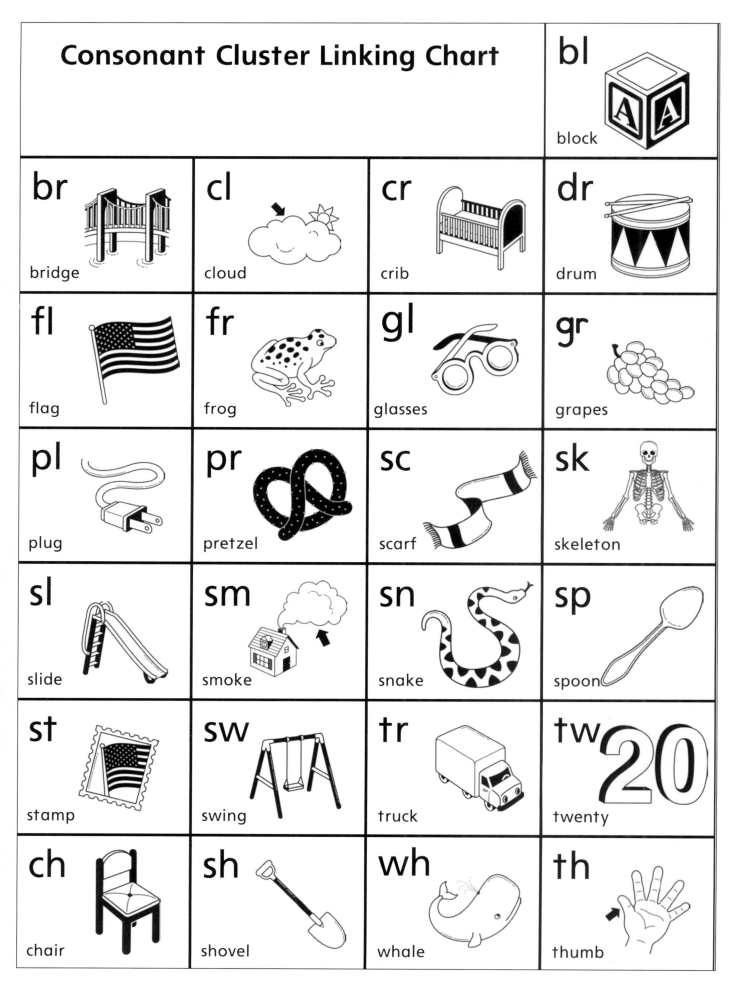

bl block

br bridge

cl cloud

cr crib

dr drum

fl flag

fr frog

gl glasses

gr grapes

pl plug

pr pretzel

sc scarf

sk skeleton

sl slide

sm smoke

sn snake

sp spoon

st stamp

sw swing

tr truck

tw twenty

ch chair

sh shovel

wh whale

th thumb

Glossary

accuracy (as in oral reading) or **accuracy rate** The percentage of words the child reads aloud correctly.

adjust (as a strategic action) To read in different ways as appropriate to the purpose for reading and type of text.

affix A part added to the beginning or ending of a base or root word to change its meaning or function (a prefix or a suffix).

alphabet book *(My ABC Book)* A book that helps children develop the concept and sequence of the alphabet by pairing alphabet letters with pictures of people, animals, or objects with labels related to the letters.

Alphabet Linking Chart A chart containing upper- and lowercase letters of the alphabet paired with pictures representing words beginning with each letter *(a, apple)*.

alphabetic principle The concept that there is a relationship between the spoken sounds in oral language and the graphic forms in written language.

analogy The resemblance of a known word to an unknown word that helps to solve the unknown word's meaning.

analyze (as a strategic action) To examine the elements of a text in order to know more about how it is constructed and to notice aspects of the writer's craft.

analyzing a Reading Record Looking at errors, self-corrections, and sources of information and strategic actions to plan instruction.

animal fantasy A make-believe story in which personified animals are the main characters.

assessment A means for gathering information or data that reveals what learners control, partially control, or do not yet control consistently.

automaticity Rapid, accurate, fluent word decoding without conscious effort or attention.

base word A whole word to which affixes can be added to create new word forms (for example, *wash* plus *-ing* becomes *washing*).

behaviors Actions that are observable as children read or write.

blend To combine sounds or word parts.

bold (boldface) Type that is heavier and darker than usual, often used for emphasis.

book and print features (as text characteristics) The physical attributes of a text (for example, font, layout, and length).

capitalization The use of capital letters, usually the first letter in a word, as a convention of written language (for example, for proper names and to begin sentences).

choral reading To read aloud in unison with a group.

code (a Reading Record) To record a child's oral reading errors, self-corrections, and other behaviors.

Coding and Scoring Errors at-a-Glance A chart containing a brief summary of how to code and score oral reading errors.

compound word A word made up of two or more words or morphemes (for example, *playground*). The meaning of a compound word can be a combination of the meanings of the words it contains or can be unrelated to the meanings of the combined units.

comprehension (as in reading) The process of constructing meaning while reading text.

concept words Words that represent abstract ideas or names. Categories of concept words include colors, numbers, months, days of the week, position words, and so on.

connecting strategies Ways of solving words by using connections or analogies with similar known words (for example, knowing *she* and *out* helps with *shout*).

consonant-vowel-consonant (CVC) A common sequence of sounds in a single syllable (for example, *hat*).

consonant A speech sound made by partial or complete closure of the airflow that causes friction at one or more points in the breath channel. The consonant sounds are represented by the letters *b, c, d, f, g, h, j, k, l, m, n, p, q, r, s, t, v, w* (in most uses), *x, y* (in most uses), and *z*.

consonant blend Two or more consonant letters that often appear together in words and represent sounds that are smoothly joined, although each of the sounds can be heard in the word (for example, *tr* in *trim*).

consonant cluster A sequence of two or three consonant letters that appear together in words (for example, *trim,chair*).

Consonant Cluster Linking Chart A chart of common consonant clusters paired with pictures representing words beginning with each cluster (for example, *bl, block*).

consonant digraph Two consonant letters that appear together and represent a single sound that is different from the sound of either letter (for example, *shell*).

content (as a text characteristic) The subject matter of a text.

contraction A shortening of a syllable, word, or word groups, usually by the omission of a sound or letters (for example, *didn't*).

conventions (in writing) Formal usage that has become customary in written language. Grammar, capitalization, and punctuation are three categories of conventions in writing.

critique (as a strategic action) To evaluate a text using one's personal, world, or text knowledge, and to think critically about the ideas in the text.

cumulative tale A story with many details repeated until the climax.

decoding Using letter-sound relationships to translate a word from a series of symbols to a unit of meaning.

dialect A regional variety of language. In most languages, including English and Spanish, dialects are mutually intelligible; the differences are actually minor.

dialogue Spoken words, usually set off with quotation marks in text.

dictated writing The teacher reads aloud a sentence, and children write it to learn how to go from oral to written language. The teacher provides support as needed.

directionality The orientation of print. In the English language, directionality is from left to right.

distinctive letter features Visual features that make every letter of the alphabet different from every other letter.

early literacy concepts Very early understandings related to how written language or print is organized and used.

English language learners People whose native language is not English and who are acquiring English as an additional language.

error A reader's response that is not consistent with the text and that is *not* self-corrected.

expository text A composition that explains a concept, using information and description.

F&P Calculator Stopwatch A device that will calculate the reading time, reading rate, accuracy rate, and self-correction ratio for a reading. (See Fountas and Pinnell's Benchmark Assessment System and Leveled Literacy Intervention.)

factual text (See **informational text.**)

fantasy An imaginative, fictional text containing elements that are highly unreal.

fiction An invented story, usually narrative.

figurative language Language that is filled with word images and metaphorical language to express more than a literal meaning.

fluency (as in oral reading) The way an oral reading sounds, including phrasing, intonation, pausing, stress, rate, and integration of the first five factors.

fluency in reading To read continuous text with good momentum, phrasing, appropriate pausing, intonation, and stress.

fluency in word solving Speed, accuracy, and flexibility in solving words.

folktale A traditional story, originally passed down orally.

font In printed text, the collection of type (letters) in a particular style.

form (as a text characteristic) A kind of text that is characterized by particular elements. Mystery, for example, is a form of writing within the narrative fiction genre.

genre A category of written text that is characterized by a particular style, form, or content.

gradient of reading difficulty (See **text gradient**.)

grammar Complex rules by which people can generate an unlimited number of phrases, sentences, and longer texts in a language. Conventional grammar reflects the accepted conventions in a society.

grapheme A letter or cluster of letters representing a single sound or phoneme (for example, *a, eigh, ay*).

Guide for Observing and Noting Reading Behaviors Lists questions a teacher should ask himself or herself about the ways a child is processing or problem solving texts.

hard reading level The level at which the child reads the text aloud with less than 90% accuracy (Levels A–K) or less than 95% accuracy (Levels L–Z).

high-frequency words Words that occur often in the spoken and written language (for example, *the*).

historical fiction An imagined story set in the realistically (and often factually) portrayed setting of a past era.

illustrations (as a text characteristic) Graphic representations of important content (for example, art, photos, maps, graphs, charts).

independent reading level The level at which the child reads the text with 95% or higher accuracy and excellent or satisfactory comprehension (Levels A–K) or 98% or higher accuracy with excellent or satisfactory comprehension (Levels L–Z).

independent writing Children write a text independently with teacher support as needed.

interactive writing The teacher and children compose and construct a text on chart paper for everyone to see and reread.

individual instruction The teacher working with one child.

infer (as a strategic action) To go beyond the literal meaning of a text; to think about what is not stated but is implied by the writer.

inflectional ending A suffix added to a base word to show tense, plurality, possession, or comparison (for example, -*er* in *darker*).

informational text A category of texts in which the purpose is to inform or to give facts about a topic. Nonfiction articles and essays are examples of informational text.

insertion (as an error in reading) A word added during oral reading that is not in the text.

instructional reading level At Levels A–K, the level at which the child reads the text with 90–94% accuracy and excellent or satisfactory comprehension; or 95% or higher accuracy and limited comprehension. At Levels L–Z, the level at which the child reads the text with 95–97% accuracy and excellent or satisfactory comprehension; or 98% or higher accuracy and limited comprehension.

interactive read-aloud The teacher reading aloud to a group of children and inviting them to think and talk about the text before, during, and after reading.

interactive writing A teaching context in which children cooperatively plan, compose, and write a group text; both teacher and children act as scribes (in turn).

intervention Intensive additional instruction for children not progressing as rapidly as expected; usually one-on-one tutoring or small group (one-on-three) teaching.

intonation The rise and fall in pitch of the voice in speech to convey meaning.

italic (italics) A type style that is characterized by slanted letters.

key understandings Important ideas within (literal), beyond (implied), or about (determined through critical analysis) the text that are necessary to comprehension.

label (in writing) Written word or phrase that names the content of an illustration.

label book A picture book consisting of illustrations with brief identifying text.

language and literary features (as text characteristics) Qualities particular to written language that are qualitatively different from spoken language (for example, dialogue; figurative language; and literary elements such as character, setting, and plot in fiction or description and technical language in nonfiction).

language use (in writing) The craft of using sentences, phrases, and expressions to describe events, actions, or information.

layout The way the print is arranged on a page.

letter and word games (Lotto, Follow the Path, and so on) Games that require children to look carefully at words, letters, and parts of words.

Letter Minibooks Short books, each of which is focused on a particular letter and its relation to a sound.

letter-sound correspondence Recognizing the corresponding sound of a specific letter when that letter is seen or heard.

letter-sound relationships (See **letter-sound correspondence**.)

letter knowledge The ability to recognize and label the graphic symbols of language.

letters Graphic symbols representing the sounds in a language. Each letter has particular distinctive features and may be identified by letter name or sound.

leveled books Texts designated along a gradient from Level A (easiest) to Level Z (hardest).

Leveled Literacy Intervention A short-term intervention designed to help younger children (grades K, 1, and 2) who need extra help reading on grade level (Fountas and Pinnell 2009).

lexicon Words that make up language.

long vowel The elongated vowel sound that is the same as the name of the vowel; it is sometimes represented by two or more letters (for example, c*a*ke, e*i*ght, m*ai*l).

lowercase letter A small-letter form that is usually different from its corresponding capital or uppercase form.

M (meaning) One of the sources of information that readers use (MSV: meaning, language structure, visual information). Meaning, the semantic system of language, refers to meaning derived from words, meaning across a text or texts, and meaning from personal experience or knowledge.

magnetic letters Multicolored upper- and lowercase letters that children manipulate to learn to read and form words.

maintain fluency (as a strategic action)

To integrate sources of information in a smoothly operating process that results in expressive, phrased reading.

make connections (as a strategic action) To search for and use connections to knowledge gained through personal experiences, learning about the world, and reading other texts.

monitor and correct (as a strategic action) To check whether the reading sounds right, looks right, and makes sense, and to solve problems when it doesn't.

My ABC Book A book containing upper- and lowercase letters on each page, along with a key word and a picture to develop children's knowledge of the alphabet, upper- and lowercase letters, features of letters, and letter/sound relationships.

name chart A tool for helping children learn about letters, sounds, and words. It is a list of names, usually in alphabetical order by the first letter. Some teachers write the first letter of each name in red and the rest of the name in black. The print should be clear, and names should not be jammed together.

name puzzle Using a set of letters, each child forms a puzzle of his or her own name in order to notice letters and their distinguishing characteristics.

narrative text A category of texts in which the purpose is to tell a story. Stories and biographies are kinds of narrative.

new word learning A variety of ways children learn new words, including looking at the first letter and then running their finger left to right as they scan the word with their eyes.

nonfiction A text whose primary purpose is to convey accurate information and facts.

omission (as in error) A word left out or skipped during oral reading.

onset-rime segmentation The identification and separation of onsets (first part) and rimes (last part, containing the vowel) in words (for example, *dr-ip*).

onset In a syllable, the part (consonant, consonant cluster, or consonant digraph) that comes before the vowel (for example, *cr*-eam).

oral games Games teachers can play with children to help them learn how to listen for and identify words in sentences, syllables, onsets and rimes, and individual phonemes.

orthographic awareness The knowledge of the visual features of written language, including distinctive features of letters, as well as spelling patterns in words.

orthography The representation of the sounds of a language with the proper letters according to standard usage (spelling).

phoneme The smallest unit of sound in spoken language. There are approximately forty-four units of speech sounds in English.

phoneme-grapheme correspondence The relationship between the sounds (phonemes) and letters (graphemes) of a language.

phoneme addition To add a beginning or ending sound to a word (for example, *h + and, an + t*).

phoneme blending To identify individual sounds and then to put them together smoothly to make a word (for example, *c-a-t = cat*).

phoneme deletion To omit a beginning, middle, or ending sound of a word (for example, *cart – c = art*).

phoneme isolation The identification of an individual sound (beginning, middle, or end) in a word.

phoneme manipulation To move sounds from one place in a word to another place in the word.

phoneme reversal The exchange of the first and last sounds of a word to make a different sound.

phoneme substitution The replacement of the beginning, middle, or ending sound of a word with a new sound.

phonemic (or phoneme) awareness The ability to hear individual sounds in words and to identify individual sounds.

phonemic strategies Ways of solving words that use how words sound and relationships between letters and letter clusters and phonemes in those words (for example, *cat, hat*).

phonetics The scientific study of speech sounds—how the sounds are made vocally and the relation of speech sounds to the total language process.

phonics The knowledge of letter-sound relationships and how they are used in reading and writing. Teaching phonics refers to helping children acquire this body of knowledge about the oral and written language systems; additionally, teaching phonics helps children use phonics knowledge as part of a reading and writing process. Phonics instruction uses a small portion of the body of knowledge that makes up phonetics.

phonogram A phonetic element represented by graphic characters or symbols. In word recognition, a graphic sequence composed of a vowel grapheme and an ending consonant grapheme (such as *-an* or *-it*) is sometimes called a word family.

phonological awareness The awareness of words, rhyming words, onsets and rimes, syllables, and individual sounds (phonemes).

phonological system The sounds of the language and how they work together in ways that are meaningful to the speakers of the language.

picture book A highly illustrated fiction or nonfiction text in which pictures work with the text to tell a story or provide information.

plural Of, relating to, or constituting more than one.

possessive Grammatical constructions used to show ownership (for example, *John's, his*).

predict (as a strategic action) To use what is known to think about what will follow while reading continuous text.

principle (in phonics) A generalization or a sound-spelling relationship that is predictable.

processing (as in reading) The mental operations involved in constructing meaning from written language.

prompt A question, direction, or statement designed to encourage the child to say more about a topic.

Prompting Guide 1: A Tool for Literacy Teachers A quick reference for specific language to teach for, prompt for, or reinforce effective reading and writing behaviors. The guide is organized in categories and color-coded so that you can turn quickly to the area needed and refer to it as you teach (Fountas and Pinnell 2009).

punctuation Marks used in written text to clarify meaning and separate structural units. The comma and the period are common punctuation marks.

reading graph A graph that charts individual or group progress through leveled books.

reading rate (words per minute, or WPM) The number of words a child reads per minute, either orally or silently.

Reading Record The transcript of the text on which oral reading is coded.

Recording Form The form on which oral reading, the comprehension conversation, and the "writing about reading" assessment for a text are coded and scored.

repetition (in oral reading) The reader saying a word, phrase, or section of the text more than once.

rhyme The ending part (rime) of a word that sounds like the ending part (rime) of another word (for example, m*ail,* t-*ale*).

rime The ending part of a word containing the vowel; the letters that represent the vowel sound and the consonant letters following it in a syllable (for example, dr-*eam*).

rubric A scoring tool that relies on descriptions of response categories for evaluation.

running words The number of words read aloud and coded.

S (structure) One of the sources of information that readers use (MSV: meaning, language structure, visual information). Language structure refers to the way words are put together in phrases and sentences (syntax or grammar).

scoring a Reading Record Counting coded errors and self-corrections, which allows you to calculate *accuracy rate* and *self-correction ratio* on the Recording Form. The form also provides space for a *fluency score* (Levels C–N) and *reading rate* (Levels J–N).

search for and use information (as a strategic action) To look for and to think about all kinds of content in order to make sense of text while reading.

searching The reader looking for information in order to read accurately, self-correct, or understand a text.

segment (as a strategic action) To divide into parts (for example, c-*at*).

self-correction ratio The proportion of errors the reader corrects himself.

semantic system The system by which speakers of a language communicate meaning though language.

sentence complexity (as a text characteristic) The complexity of the structure or syntax of a sentence. Addition of phrases and clauses to simple sentences increases complexity.

sentence strips Strips of oak tag on which sentences have been written and then cut up and mixed up so that children put the sentences back together.

series book One of a collection of books about the same character or characters and the different events or situations they encounter.

shared reading Teacher and children read a large-print text together after the teacher has read it aloud once to the children. The teacher points under each word and later places the pointer at the start of each line.

short vowel A brief-duration sound represented by a vowel letter (for example, c*a*t).

silent *e* The final *e* in a spelling pattern that usually signals a long vowel sound in the word and does not represent a sound itself (for example, mak*e*).

silent reading The reader reading the text to herself.

sketching and drawing (in writing) To create a rough (sketch) or finished (drawing) image of a person, a place, a thing, or an idea to capture, work with, and render the writer's ideas.

small-group reading instruction The teacher working with children brought together because they are similar enough in reading development to teach in a small group; guided reading.

solve words (as a strategic action) To use a range of strategies to take words apart and understand their meaning.

sound boxes and letter boxes (Elkonin Boxes) A tool for helping children to learn about the sounds and letters in words.

sounding out Pronouncing the sounds of the letters in a word as a step in reading the word.

sources of information The various cues in a written text that combine to make meaning (for example, syntax, meaning, and the physical shape and arrangement of type).

spelling aloud Naming the letters in a word rather than reading the word.

spelling patterns Beginning letters (onsets) and common phonograms (rimes) form the basis for the English syllable; knowing these patterns, a child can build countless words.

split dialogue Written dialogue in which a "said" phrase divides the speaker's words: for example, "Come on," said Mom, "let's go home."

standardized Remaining essentially the same across multiple instances.

strategic action Any one of many simultaneous, coordinated thinking activities that go on in a reader's head. See **thinking within, beyond, and about the text**.

stress The emphasis given to some syllables or words.

substitution (as in error in reading) The reader reading aloud one (incorrect) word for another.

suffix An affix or group of letters added at the end of a base word or root word to change its function or meaning (for example, hand*ful*, hope*less*).

summarize (as a strategic action) To put together and remember important information, while disregarding irrelevant information, during or after reading.

syllabication The division of words into syllables (for example, *pen-cil*).

synonym One of two or more words that have different sounds but the same meaning (for example, *chair, seat*).

syntactic awareness The knowledge of grammatical patterns or structures.

syntactic system Rules that govern the ways in which morphemes and words work together in sentence patterns. Not the same as proper grammar, which refers to the accepted grammatical conventions.

syntax The study of how sentences are formed and of the grammatical rules that govern their formation.

synthesize (as a strategic action) To combine new information or ideas from reading text with existing knowledge to create new understandings.

text gradient A twenty-six point (A–Z) text-rating scale of difficulty, in which each text level, from the easiest at Level A to the most challenging at Level Z, represents a small but significant increase in difficulty over the previous level. The gradient correlates these levels to grade levels.

text structure The overall architecture or organization of a piece of writing. Chronology (sequence) and description are two common text structures.

theme The central idea or concept in a story or the message that the author is conveying.

thinking within, beyond, and about the text Three ways of thinking about a text while reading. Thinking *within* the text involves efficiently and effectively understanding what it is on the page, the author's literal message. Thinking *beyond* the text requires making inferences and putting text ideas together in different ways to construct the text's meaning. In thinking *about* the text, readers analyze and critique the author's craft.

told The teacher telling the reader a word he cannot read.

topic The subject of a piece of writing.

understandings Basic concepts that are crucial to comprehending a particular area.

V (visual information) One of three sources of information that readers use (MSV: meaning, language structure, visual information). Visual information refers to the letters that represent the sounds of language and the way they are combined (spelling patterns) to create words; visual information at the sentence level includes punctuation.

Verbal Path Language used to help children get the hand moving the right way to form letters efficiently.

vocabulary (as a text characteristic) Words and their meanings.

voice-print match Usually applied to a beginning reader's ability to match one spoken word with one printed word while reading and pointing. In experienced readers, the eyes take over the process.

vowel A speech sound or phoneme made without stoppage of or friction in the airflow. The vowel sounds are represented by *a, e, i, o, u,* and sometimes *y* and *w.*

ways to sort and match letters Using magnetic letters or letter cards, children sort letters to learn their distinctive features.

word A unit of meaning in language.

word analysis To break apart words into parts or individual sounds in order to read and understand them.

word boundaries The white space that defines a word; the white space before the first letter and after the last letter of a word. It is important for beginning readers to learn to recognize word boundaries.

word family A term often used to designate words that are connected by phonograms or rimes (for example, *hot, not, pot, shot*). A word family can also be a series of words connected by meaning (affixes added to a base word; for example: *base, baseball, basement, baseman, basal, basis, baseless, baseline, baseboard, abase, abasement, off base, home base; precise, précis, precisely, precision*).

word ladders A technique for helping children learn how to manipulate letters and word parts to construct new words. You start with a word, then change, add, or remove one or more letters to make a new word.

word-solving actions (See **solve words**.)

words (as a text characteristic) The decodability of words in text; phonetic and structural features of words

words in text Children use their eyes to locate known and unknown words in text.

writing Children engaging in the writing process and producing pieces of their own writing in many genres.

writing about reading Children responding to reading a text by writing and sometimes drawing

writing words fluently Children learning to write words fast by writing a word several times.

"You Try It" A prompt given by the teacher that directs a child to make an attempt at reading a word during oral reading.

References

Leveled Literacy Intervention Children's Book References

The following titles, which are referenced throughout *When Readers Struggle: Teaching that Works* can be found in the Orange, Green, or Blue System of Leveled Literacy Intervention, as indicated below. LLI, designed and written by Irene Fountas and Gay Su Pinnell and published by Heinemann (2009), is a short-term intervention created to help younger children (grades K, 1, and 2) who need extra help reading on grade level. Each title is followed by its level designation and lesson number. There is a lesson based on each of these books in the LLI *Lesson Guides* for Orange, Green, and Blue Systems.

To review the complete LLI System, go to the Fountas and Pinnell website at *www.fountasandpinnell.com*

Leveled Literacy Intervention, ORANGE SYSTEM

A Visit from Aunt Bee, Level C, Lesson 57
Animals That Go Fast, Level C, Lesson 69
At the Market, Level A, Lesson 1
At the Zoo, Level A, Lesson 13
Baby, Level A, Lesson 18
Baking, Level A, Lesson 66
Flap, Flap, Fly, Level C, Lesson 59
Funny Things, Level A, Lesson 3
Hiding, Level B, Lesson 39
Hop, Hop, Hop, Level B, Lesson 41
Little Cub, Level A, Lesson 20
Little Things, Level A, Lesson 27
Making a Pizza, Level A, Lesson 56
Making a Snowman, Level A, Lesson 24
Making Soup, Level B, Lesson 7
Mom, Level A, Lesson 11
Mouse, Level C, Lesson 9
My Big Brother, Level B, Lesson 49
My Family, Level B, Lesson 8
Over the River, Level B, Lesson 5
Play and Ride, Level C, Lesson 51
Playing with Blocks, Level C, Lesson 63
Setting the Table, Level A, Lesson 29
The Hat, Level B, Lesson 35
Things That Go Fast, Level A, Lesson 70
What Is Very Long?, Level C, Lesson 53

Leveled Literacy Intervention, GREEN SYSTEM

A Surprise for Mom, Level E, Lesson 78
A Trip to the Laundromutt, Level H, Lesson 110
A Walk with Meli, Level E, Lesson 59
All About Animal Babies, Level F, Lesson 88
All About Chimps, Level H, Lesson 108
All About Dolphins, Level J, Lesson 103
All About Honeybees, Level I, Lesson 99
Ant Can't, Level C, Lesson 7
Baby Bird, Level G, Lesson 75
Baby Pictures, Level E, Lesson 57
Bad-Luck Day, Level J, Lesson 109
Bear's Birthday, Level I, Lesson 93
Brave Taco, Level E, Lesson 80
Bubbles, Level B, Lesson 23
Bunny and the Monster, Level F, Lesson 65
Eggs, Level C, Lesson 8
Family Pictures, Level A, Lesson 19
Friends, Level A, Lesson 4
Frog Food, Level A, Lesson 2
How Frogs Grow, Level G, Lesson 79
Jesse, Level A, Lesson 15
Looking for Taco, Level C, Lesson 33
Meli on the Stairs, Level C, Lesson 35
Oh, No!, Level A, Lesson 17
Orson's Tummy Ache, Level B, Lesson 21
Papa's Birthday, Level G, Lesson 73
Pictures of Hugs, Level F, Lesson 67
Sam and Papa, Level B, Lesson 5
Talent Show, Level E, Lesson 55
The Big Storm, Level F, Lesson 69
The Good Dog, Level D, Lesson 47
The Lion and the Mouse, Level J, Lesson 105
The New Puppy, Level A, Lesson 3
The Painter, Level A, Lesson 13
The Puppets, Level C, Lesson 52
The Skunk with No Stripes, Level H, Lesson 81
The Soccer Game, Level F, Lesson 63
The Three Little Pigs and a Big Bad Wolf, Level F, Lesson 61
The Very Busy Hen, Level D, Lesson 10
Time for Lunch, Level D, Lesson 45
Waking Up, Level A, Lesson 1

Leveled Literacy Intervention, BLUE SYSTEM

A Dragon's Lullaby, Level M, Lesson 109

Bibliography of Children's Books

Adler, D.A. 1999. Illus. T. Widener. *The Babe and I.* San Diego, CA: Gulliver Books of Harcourt Brace & Co.

Bahr, M. 1995. Illus. D. Cunningham. *The Memory Box.* New York: Albert Whitman & Company.

Boroson, M. 2008. *The Sleepover Party.* Benchmark Assessment System 1. Portsmouth, NH: Heinemann.

Burrowes, A.J. 2008. *Grandma's Purple Flowers.* New York: Lee & Low Books.

Cameron, A. 1997. *The Stories Huey Tells.* New York: Random House Books for Young Readers.

Crisp, M. 2002. *Private Captain: A Story of Gettysburg.* New York: Putnam Juvenile.

DePaola, T. 2000. *Nana Upstairs and Nana Downstairs.* New York: Putnam Juvenile.

Gary, R. 2008. *Playing.* Benchmark Assessment System 1. Portsmouth, NH: Heinemann.

George, L. 2008. *The Loose Tooth.* Benchmark Assessment System 1. Portsmouth, NH: Heinemann.

Heath, R. 2008. *My Little Dog.* Benchmark Assessment System 1. Portsmouth, NH: Heinemann.

Henkes, K. 1990. *Julius the Baby of the World.* New York: Greenwillow Books from HarperCollins.

Henkes, K. 1996. *Lilly's Purple Plastic Purse.* New York: Greenwillow Books from HarperCollins.

Henkes, K. 1988. *Chester's Way.* New York: Greenwillow Books from HarperCollins.

Levine, K. 2002. *Hana's Suitcase: A True Story.* New York: Albert Whitman & Company.

Meacham, A. 2008. *Anna's New Glasses.* Benchmark Assessment System 1. Portsmouth, NH: Heinemann.

Miles, M. 1972. Illus. P. Parnell. *Annie and the Old One.* New York: Little, Brown Young Readers.

Murphy, J. 1995. *The Great Fire.* New York: Scholastic.

Palacco, P. 1994. *My Rotten Redheaded Older Brother.* New York: Simon & Schuster Children's Publishing.

Reiser, L. 1998. Illus. V. Corazones. *Tortillas and Lullabies/ Tortillas y Cancioncitas.* New York: Rayo.

Ringgold, F. 1993. *Dinner at Aunt Connie's House.* New York: Hyperion.

Rodriguez, C. 2008. *Bubbles.* Benchmark Assessment System 1. Portsmouth, NH: Heinemann.

Rylant, C. 1985. Illus. S. Gammell. *The Relatives Came.* New York: Scholastic.

Uchida, Y. 1978. Illus. C. Robinson. *Journey Home.* New York: Margaret K. Elderry.

Professional References

Anderson, R.C., P.T. Wilson, and L.C. Fielding. 1988."Growth in Reading and How Children Spend their Time Outside of School." *Reading Research Quarterly* 23: 3: 285-303.

Anderson, R.C. and P. Freebody. 1981. "Vocabulary knowledge." In *Comprehension and Teaching: Research Reviews*, edited by J.T. Guthrie. Newark, DE: International Reading Association.

Armbruster, B. B., F. Lehr, and J. Osborn. 2001. *Put Reading First: The Research Building Blocks for Teaching Children to Read: Kindergarten through Grade 1.* Jessup, MD: National Institute for Literacy, 2001.

Armbruster, B.B., F. Lehr, and J. Osborn. 2003. *Put Reading First: The Research Building Blocks for Teaching Children to Read, K–3.* Jessup, MD: Center for the Improvement of Early Learning Achievement, 2003.

Askew, B.J., and I. C. Fountas. 1998. "Building an Early Reading Process: Active from the Start!" *The Reading Teacher,* 52: 126–134.

Au, K. H. 1997. "Ownership, Literacy Achievement, and Students of Diverse Cultural Backgrounds." In *Reading Engagement: Motivating Readers through Integrated Instruction*, edited by J.T. Guthrie and A. Wigfield. Newark, DE: International Reading Association.

Bartholomew, B. 2008. "Sustaining the Fire." *Educational Leadership,* 65: 55–60

Baumann, J.F., E.J Kame'enui, and G.E. Ask. 2003. "Research on Vocabulary Instruction: Voltaire Redux." In *Handbook of Research on Teaching the English Language Arts, 2nd edition*, edited by J. Flood, D. Lapp, J.R. Squire, and J.M. Jensen. Mahwah, NJ: Lawrence Erlbaum Associates.

Beck, I.L. and M.B. McKeown. 1991. "Conditions of Vocabulary Acquisition." In *Handbook of Reading Research* (Vol. 2), edited by R. Barr, M. Kamil, and P.D. Pearson. New York: Longman.

Brisk, M. Presentation to the Literacy Collaborative, May 28, 2008. Cambridge, MA: Lesley University.

Cambourne, B. 1995. "Toward an Educationally Relevant Theory of Literacy Learning: Twenty Years of Inquiry." *The Reading Teacher,* 49: 182–192.

Campbell, J.R., K.E. Voelkl, and P.L. Donahue. 1997. *NAEP 1996 Trends in Academic Progress* (NCES Publication No. 97-985). Washington, DC: U.S. Department of Education.

Cipielewski, J., and K.I. Stanovich. 1992. "Predicting Growth in Reading Ability from Children's Exposure to Print." *Journal of Experimental Child Psychology,* 54: 74–89.

Clarke, Lane W., and Jennifer Holwadel. 2007. "Help! What is Wrong with these Literature Circles and How Can We Fix Them?" *The Reading Teacher* 61(1): 20–29.

Clay, M.M. 2003. Afterword to *Research in Reading Recovery, Volume Two*, edited by S. Forbes and C. Briggs. Portsmouth, NH: Heinemann.

Clay, M.M. 1998. *By Different Paths to Common Outcomes.* Portland, ME: Stenhouse Publishers.

Clay, M.M. 1991. *Becoming Literate: the Construction of Inner Control.* Portsmouth, NH. Heinemann.

Clay, M.M. 2001. *Change Over Time in Children's Literacy Development.* Portsmouth, NH: Heinemann.

Clay, M.M. 1985. *The Early Detection of Reading Difficulties,* 3rd Ed. Portsmouth, NH: Heinemann.

Clay, M.M. 2006. *Literacy Lessons Designed for Individuals: Part Two, Teaching Procedures.* Portsmouth, NH: Heinemann.

Clay, M.M. 2005. *The Observation Survey of Early Literacy Achievement.* Chicago, IL: Heinemann Library.

Clay, M.M. and C.B. Cazden. 1990. "A Vygotskian Interpretation of Reading Recovery." In *Vygotsky and Education: Instructional Implications and Applications of Socio-historical Psychology*, edited by L.C. Moll. New York: Cambridge University Press.

Duckworth, E. 1987. *"The Having of Wonderful Ideas" and Other Essays on Teaching and Learning.* New York: Teachers College Press.

Elkonin, D.B. 1975. "U.S.S.R." In *Comparative Reading: Cross-National Studies of Behavior and Processes in Reading and Writing*, edited by J. Downing. New York: Macmillan.

Elley, W.B. 1989. "Vocabulary Acquisition from Listening to Stories." *Reading Research Quarterly*, 24: 174–187.

Fountas, I. C., and G.S. Pinnell. 2007. *Fountas and Pinnell Benchmark Assessment System 1: Grades K–2, Levels A–N.* Portsmouth, NH: Heinemann.

Fountas, I. C., and G.S. Pinnell. 2007. *Fountas and Pinnell Benchmark Assessment System 2: Grades 3–8, Levels L–Z.* Portsmouth, NH: Heinemann.

Fountas, I.C., and G.S. Pinnell. 2009. *The Fountas and Pinnell Prompting Guide 1: A Tool for Literacy Teachers.* Portsmouth, NH: Heinemann.

Fountas, I.C. and G.S. Pinnell. 2000. *Guiding Readers and Writers, K-8: Teaching Comprehension, Fluency, and Content Reading.* Portsmouth, NH: Heinemann.

Fountas, I.C. and G.S. Pinnell. 1996. *Guided Reading: Good First Teaching for All Students.* Portsmouth, NH: Heinemann.

Fountas, I.C. and G.S. Pinnell. 2009a. *Leveled Literacy Intervention: Orange, Green, and Blue Systems.* Portsmouth, NH: Heinemann.

Fountas, I. C., and G.S. Pinnell. 2006. *Teaching for Comprehending and Fluency: Thinking, Talking, and Writing about Reading, K–8.* Portsmouth, NH: Heinemann.

Fountas, I.C. and G.S. Pinnell. 2009a. *When Readers Struggle: Teaching that Works.* Portsmouth, NH: Heinemann.

Goldenberg, C. N. 1994. "Promoting Early Literacy Development among Spanish-Speaking Children: Lessons from Two Studies." In *Getting Ready Right from the Start: Effective Early Literacy Interventions*, edited by E. H. Hiebert and B. M. Taylor. Needham, MA: Allyn and Bacon.

Guthrie, J.T., A. Wigfield, J.L. Metslaa, and K.E. Cox. 1999. "Motivational and Cognitive Predictors of Text Comprehension and Reading Amount." *Scientific Studies of Reading*, 3 (3): 231–256.

Hartley. J. 2008. "You Should Read this Book!" *Educational Leadership*, 65: 73–75.

Hill, M. 1998. "Reaching Struggling Readers." In *Into Focus: Understanding and Creating Middle School Readers*, edited by K. Beers and B. Samuels. Norwood, MA: Christopher-Gordon.

Hosseini, K. 2007. *A Thousand Splendid Suns.* New York: Riverhead Books, a member of Penguin Group.

Institute of Education Sciences. 2004. *Identifying and Implementing Educational Practices Supported by Rigorous Evidence: A User Friendly Guide.* Washington, DC: U.S. Department of Education.

Irvin, J.L. 2001. *Reading strategies for the social studies classroom.* Austin, TX: Holt, Rinehart, and Winston.

Jensen, E. P. "A Fresh Look at Brain-Based Education." *Phi Delta Kappan* 89: 408–417.

Juel, C. 1988. "Learning to Read and Write: a Longitudinal Study of 54 Children from First Through Fourth Grades." *Journal of Educational Psychology* 80: 437–447.

Kaye, E.L. 2008. "Second Gracers' Reading Behaviors: A Study of Variety, Complexity, and Change." *Literacy Teaching and Learning* 10 (2): 51–75.

Langer, E.J. 1989. *Mindfulness.* Cambridge, MA: Da Capo Press.

Langer, E. J. 2005. *On Becoming an Artist: Reinventing Yourself through Mindful Creativity.* New York: Ballantine Books.

Langer, E. J. 1997. *The Power of Mindful Learning.* Cambridge, MA: Da Capo Press.

Lee, J., W. Grigg, and P. Donahue 2007. *The Nation's Report Card: Reading 2007* (NCES 2007: 496). National Center for Education Statistics, Institute of Education Sciences, U.S. Department of Education, Washington, D.C.

Lyons, C. 2003. *Teaching Struggling Readers: How to Use Brain-based Research to Maximize Learning.* Portsmouth, NH: Heinemann.

Lyons, C.A., G.S. Pinnell, and D.E. DeFord. 1993. *Partners in Learning: Teachers and Children in Reading Recovery.* New York: Teachers College Press.

McCarrier, A., I.C. Fountas, and G.S. Pinnell. 1999. *Interactive Writing: How Language and Literacy Come Together.* Portsmouth, NH.

McGee, L. M. and J.A. Schickedanz. 2007. "Repeated Interactive Read-alouds in Preschool and Kindergarten. *The Reading Teacher* 60: 742–751.

McKenzie, J. 2003. "A Lost Generation? A Million Left Behind?" http://www.NoChildLeft.com: *a Site Advocating a Sound Approach to School Improvement.*

Meier, Deborah. 2002. *The Power of Their Ideas: Lessons for America from a Small School in Harlem.* Boston: Beacon Press.

Moats, L.C. 2001. "Overcoming the Language Gap." *American Educator* 25 (5): 8–9.

Morrow, L.M. 1992. "The Impact of a Literature-based Program on Literacy Achievement, Use of Literature, Attitudes of Children from Minority Backgrounds." *Reading Research Quarterly* 27: 250–275.

Nagy, W.E., P.A. Herman, and R.C. Anderson. 1985. "Learning Words from Context." *Reading Research Quarterly* 20: 233–253.

Nagy, W.E., and J.A. Scott. 2000. "Vocabulary Processes." In *Handbook of Reading Research, vol. III*, edited by M.L. Kamil, P.B. Mosenthal, P.D. Pearson, and R. Barr. Mahwah, NJ: Lawrence Erlbaum.

National Institute of Child Health and Human Development. 2000. *Report of the National Reading Panel: Teaching Children to Read: An Evidence-based Assessment of the Scientific Research Literature on Reading and Its Implications for Reading Instruction: Reports of the Subgroups.* Washington, D.C.: U.S. Department of Health and Human Services, NIH Pub. No 00–4754.

Natriello, G., E. L. McDill, A. M. Pallas. 1990. *Schooling Disadvantaged Children: Racing against Catastrophe.* New York: Columbia University, Teacher's College Press.

Ng, S.M. 1979. "Error and Self-correction in Reading and Oral Language." Doctoral dissertation, University of Auckland Library. (Cited in Clay 2001).

Oldfather, P., and K. Dahl. 1994. "Toward a Social Constructivist Reconceptualization of Intrinsic Motivation for Literacy Learning." *Journal of Reading Behavior* 26: 139–158.

Pemberton, E.F., and R.V. Watkins. 1987. "Language Facilitation through Stories: Recasting and Modeling." *First Language* 7: 79–89.

Pikulsky, John J. 1997. *Factors Common to Successful Early Intervention Programs.* Boston: Houghton Mifflin.

Pinnell, G. S. and I. C. Fountas. 2007. *The Continuum of Literacy Learning, Grades K–2: A Guide to Teaching.* Portsmouth, NH: Heinemann.

Pinnell, G. S. and I. C. Fountas. 2007 *The Continuum of Literacy Learning, Grades 3–8: A Guide to Teaching.* Portsmouth, NH: Heinemann.

Pinnell, G.S., and I. C. Fountas. 2008. *The Continuum of Literacy Learning, K–8: Behaviors and Understandings to Notice, Teach, and Support.* Portsmouth, NH: Heinemann.

Pinnell, G. S. and I. C. Fountas. 1996. *Guided Reading: Good Teaching for All Children.* Foreword by Mary Ellen Giacobbe, Portsmouth, NY: Heinemann.

Pinnell, G. S. and I. C. Fountas(a). 2003. *Phonics Lessons with CD-ROM, Grade K: Letters, Words, and How They Work.* Portsmouth, NH: Heinemann.

Pinnell, G. S. and I. C. Fountas(b). 2003 *Phonics Lessons with CD-ROM, Grade 1: Letters, Words, and How They Work.* Portsmouth, NH: Heinemann.

Pinnell, G. S. and I. C. Fountas(c). 2003 *Phonics Lessons with CD-ROM, Grade 2: Letters, Words, and How They Work.* Portsmouth, NH: Heinemann.

Pinnell, G. S. and I. C. Fountas. 2004. *Sing a Song of Poetry, Grade 1: A Teaching Resource for Phonics, Word Study, and Fluency.* Portsmouth, NH: Heinemann.

Pinnell, G. S. and I. C. Fountas. 2003. *Sing a Song of Poetry, Grade 2: A Teaching Resource for Phonics, Word Study, and Fluency.* Portsmouth, NH: Heinemann.

Pinnell, G. S. and I. C. Fountas.2004. *Sing a Song of Poetry, K: A Teaching Resource for Phonics, Word Study, and Fluency.* Portsmouth, NH: Heinemann.

Pinnell, G. S. and I. C. Fountas. 2007 *Teaching for Comprehending and Fluency Thinking, Talking, and Writing About Reading, K–8.* Portsmouth, NH: Heinemann.

Pinnell, G. S. and I. C. Fountas. 2009. *When Readers Struggle: Teaching that Works.* Portsmouth, NH: Heinemann.

Pinnell, G.S, and I.C. Fountas. 1998. *Word Matters: Teaching Phonics and Spelling in the Reading/Writing Classroom.* Portsmouth, NH: Heinemann.

Pinnell, G. S. and I. C. Fountas(d). 2003. *Word Study Lessons with CD-ROM, Grade 3: Letters, Words, and How They Work.* Portsmouth, NH: Heinemann.

Pinnell, G.S., M.D. Fried, and R. Estice. 1990. "Reading Recovery: Learning How to Make a Difference." *The Reading Teacher* 43: 282–295.

Pinnell, G.S., C.A. Lyons, D.E. Deford, A.S. Bryk, and M. Seltzer. 1994. "Comparing Instructional Models for the Literacy Education of High Risk First Graders." *Reading Research Quarterly* 29 (1): 8–39.

Pinnell, G.S., J.J. Pikulski, K.K. Wixson, J.R. Campbell, R.B. Gough, and A.S. Beatty. 1995. *Listening to Children Read Aloud: Data from NAEP's Integrated Reading Performance Record IRPR) at grade 4.* Report No. 23-FR-04. Prepared by Educational Testing Service under contract with the National Center for Education Statistics, Office of Educational Research and Improvement, U.S. Department of Education, p. 15.

Roberts, T.A. 2008. "Home Storybook Reading in Primary or Second Language with Preschool Children: Evidence of Equal Effectiveness for Second-language Vocabulary Acquisition." *Reading Research Quarterly,* 43 (2): 103–130.

Schmidt, M.C., B.J. Askew, I.C. Fountas, C.A. Lyons, and G.S. Pinnell. 2005. *Changing Futures: The Influence of Reading Recovery in the United States.* Columbus, OH: Reading Recovery Council of North America. http://www.readingrecovery.org

Schunk, D. H., and B.J. Zimmerman. 1997. "Developing Self-efficacious Readers and Writers: The Role of Social and Self-regulatory Processes. In *Reading Engagement: Motivating Readers through Integrated Instruction* edited by J. T. Guthrie and A. Wigfield. Newark, DE: International Reading Association.

Sénéchal, M., E. Thomas, and J.A. Monker. 1995. "Individual Differences in 4-year-old Children's Acquisition of Vocabulary during Storybook Reading." *Journal of Educational Psychology* 87: 218–229.

Siegel, D.J. 2007. *The Mindful Brain: Reflection and Attunement in the Cultivation of Well-Being.* New York: W.W. Norton and Company.

Snow, C.E., M.S. Burns, and P. Griffin, editors. 1998. *Preventing Reading Difficulties in Young Children.* Committee on the Prevention of Reading Difficulties in Young Children, National Research Council. Washington, DC: National Academy Press.

Squire, L. 1996. "Your Brain: a Lifetime of Brain Fitness." Charles A. Dana Foundation, New York. Videotape (out of print). Cited in M. M. Clay in *Literacy Lessons: Designed for Individuals: Part Two, Teaching Procedures.* Portsmouth, NH: Heinemann.

Stanovich, K.E. 1986. "Matthew Effects in Reading: Some Consequences of Individual Differences in the Acquisition of Literacy." *Reading Research Quarterly* 21 (4): 360-407.

Swanson, C.B. 2008. *Cities in Crisis: A Special Analytic Report on High School Graduation.* Educational Research Center. Published by America's Promise Alliance.

Teaching Children to Read: An Evidence-Based Assessment of the Scientific Research Literature on Reading and Its Implications for Reading Instruction. 2001. Report of the National Reading Panel: Reports of the Subgroups. Washington, DC: National Institutes of Health and Human Development.

Teale, W.H. 1984. "Reading to Young Children: Its Significance for Literacy Development." In *Awaking to Literacy,* edited by H. Goelman, A.A. Oberg, and F. Smith. Portsmouth, NH: Heinemann.

Valdez-Menchaca, M.C., and G.J. Whitehurst. 1992. "Accelerating Language Development Through Picture Book Reading: A Systematic Extension to Mexican Day Care." *Developmental Psychology* 28 (6): 1106–1114.

Vygotsky, L.S. 1962. *Thought and Language.* Cambridge, MA: MIT Press.

Vygotsky, L.S. 1978. *Mind in Society: The Development of Higher Psychological Processes.* Cambridge, MA; Harvard University Press.

Walsh, D.S., G.G. Prince, and M.G. Gillingham.1998. "The Critical but Transitory Importance of Letter Naming" *Reading Research Quarterly* 23: 108–122.

Wentzel, K.R. 1996. "Social and Academic Motivation in Middle School: Concurrent and Long-term Relations to Academic Effort." *Journal of Early Adolescence* 16: 390–406.

"Why Children Succeed or Fail at Reading." 2000. *The Special Edge* 14 (1). Cited in *Educational Research Service Spectrum.* "Helping Struggling Readers at the Elementary and Secondary Levels," Arlington, VA: ERS.

INDEX

You Are 2 Steps Away from Helping Struggling Readers

Intensive and Systematic Intervention for Students at Levels A–N

Irene Fountas & Gay Su Pinnell, authors of the best-selling *Guided Reading, Guiding Readers and Writers, Teaching for Comprehending and Fluency,* and *When Readers Struggle: Teaching that Works,* present:

Fountas & Pinnell Benchmark Assessment Systems 1 & 2
Assess and Understand Students' Reading Performance

STEP 1

One-on-one, comprehensive assessment to determine independent and instructional reading levels, for placing students on the Fountas & Pinnell A–Z Text Gradient, and for connecting assessment to instruction with *The Continuum of Literacy Learning.*

For samples, visit: www.fountasandpinnell.com

Benchmark
Assessment
System

Fountas & Pinnell Leveled Literacy Intervention
Address Student Needs with 300 Systematically Designed Lessons

STEP 2

Based around carefully leveled, original books

Small group, intensive, supplementary intervention system designed to bring struggling readers and writers to grade-level competency in 12-18 weeks. Intervention can be included in a layered, RTI approach.

For samples, visit: www.fountasandpinnell.com

Leveled Literacy
Intervention

Fountas & Pinnell's
Benchmark Assessment _____ and Leveled Literacy Intervention (LLI)

Building on a lifetim_____ _____nd reflection, Fountas and Pinnell have taken their celebrated A–Z Text Gradient into a _____ as the foundation for comprehensive assessment and intervention systems that identify _____ risk and monitor the academic progress of all students.

Benchmark Assess_____ _____tem and Leveled Literacy Intervention (LLI) allow you to:

- conduct universal _____ng of students
- administer diagno_____ _____ssment t_____ _____es the problem are_____ _____easurable t_____
- collect baseline da_____ to inte_____ _____nd
- prepare a plan of _____ _____asures for monitoring _____s.

Heinemann

DEDICATED TO TEACHERS

**CALL 800.225.5800 or
FAX 877.231.6980.**